CANADA'S ENTREPRENEURS

From the Fur Trade to the 1929 Stock Market Crash

Portraits from the
Dictionary of Canadian Biography

CANADA'S ENTREPRENEURS

From the Fur Trade to the 1929 Stock Market Crash

Portraits from the Dictionary of Canadian Biography

Under the direction of John English and Réal Bélanger

Edited by
J. ANDREW ROSS
and
ANDREW D. SMITH

UNIVERSITY OF TORONTO PRESS

Toronto Buffalo London

ISBN 978-1-4426-4478-6 (cloth)
ISBN 978-1-4426-1286-0 (paper)

∞

Printed on acid-free, 100% post-consumer recycled paper with vegetable-based inks

Library and Archives Canada Cataloguing in Publication

Canada's entrepreneurs : from the fur trade to the 1929 stock market crash : portraits from the Dictionary of Canadian biography / edited by J. Andrew Ross and Andrew D. Smith under the direction of John English and Réal Bélanger.

Includes bibliographical references and index.
ISBN 978-1-4426-4478-6 (bound)   ISBN 978-1-4426-1286-0 (pbk.)

1. Businesspeople – Canada – Biography.   2. Entrepreneurship – Canada – History.   I. Ross, J. Andrew, 1971–   II. Smith, Andrew, 1976–   III. English, John, 1945–   IV. Bélanger, Réal

HC112.5.A2C35 2011   338'.04092271   C2011-906300-X

Cover: Notman and Sandham, Grand Trunk Railway Engineering Department group, composite 1877 (N-0000.73.19), McCord Museum of Canadian History, Montreal (image reversed from original).

University of Toronto Press acknowledges the financial assistance to its publishing program of the Canada Council for the Arts and the Ontario Arts Council.

 Canada Council   Conseil des Arts
for the Arts   du Canada

 ONTARIO ARTS COUNCIL
CONSEIL DES ARTS DE L'ONTARIO

University of Toronto Press acknowledges the financial support of the Government of Canada through the Canada Book Fund for its publishing activities.

Contents

Section 3: Maritime Enterprise

Section 4: The Industrial Heartland

Section 5: Railwaymen and Network Creators

Section 6: Brand Names and Big Business

Section 7: The West Booms

Preface

The Dictionary of Canadian Biography/Dictionnaire biographique du Canada is Canada's oldest and largest research and publishing project in the humanities. Established at the University of Toronto on 1 July 1959 under the general editorship of the distinguished historian George Brown, the Dictionary of Canadian Biography (DCB) represents the Canadian counterpart of Britain's Dictionary of National Biography, an intellectual monument of Victorian Britain. Reflecting Canadian values and his own academic background, Brown and the University of Toronto Press insisted that the DCB be authoritative and based upon scholarly research. They also recognized that Canada's national biographical dictionary must be bilingual, and in 1961 the Université Laval announced the partnership of the Dictionnaire biographique du Canada (DBC) with the DCB and the appointment of the eminent historian Marcel Trudel as Directeur général adjoint and Les Presses de l'Université Laval as the French-language publisher. The first volume was released five years later.

This year the DBC celebrates its 50th anniversary. Sadly, Marcel Trudel died on 11 January 2011, but this project bears witness to his imagination, the vigour of historical scholarship in Canada, and the extraordinary collaboration between two of Canada's leading universities and successive editorial teams. The DCB/DBC has published 15 volumes with almost 8,500 biographies describing the lives of those who died or were last known to be active between the years 1000 and 1930. Since 2003 all their stories have been accessible online; as well, some major biographies of individuals who died after 1930, including all deceased prime ministers of the 20th century, have been added. The public response to the website has been overwhelmingly positive. The support of the federal Department of Canadian Heritage has allowed the DCB/DBC to reach far beyond its traditional audiences of academic and genealogical researchers to enter classrooms at all levels and assist students of Canada throughout the world. It is generally recognized as the most authoritative of all national biographies because of the thorough research expected of the authors and the scrupulous care of the editors. In writing their biographies, authors consult public and private archival collections, newspapers and journals, directories, birth and death records, and a wide array of other primary sources. The project's editors endeavour to verify all facts and ensure the consistency and clarity of every text.

When Andrew Ross and Andrew Smith approached the DCB/DBC about the possibility of publishing a collection of the biographies of Canadian entrepreneurs, we were immediately receptive. Their suggestion was particularly appropriate: our project began with the bequest of James Nicholson, a Toronto entrepreneur who identified a market for birdseed and made a small fortune that established the DCB's initial endowment. We have benefited from the generosity of other Canadian entrepreneurs who have, from time to time, supported our project. More generally, the DCB/DBC recognized from the beginning the essential contribution of business in the development of Canada, and we have given businesspeople a prominent place beside politicians, cultural figures, and spiritual leaders. It has not always been easy because business history was not, until recently, a popular field among academic historians. Nevertheless, we persisted and created, in the words of National Post reporter Peter Shawn Taylor, a publication that "plays a unique role in providing access to information on our country's past business leaders" (9 Feb. 2010).

The range of the biographies in this book reflects the diversity of the stories in the DCB/DBC. While acknowledging the contributions of dominant business leaders such as Isaac Buchanan, Sir Hugh Allan, Louis-Adélard Senécal, and Sir Rodolphe Forget, we recognize the entrepreneurial character of the fur trader Muquinna, the photographer William Notman, the merchant Chang Toy, and the businesswoman Marie-Anne Barbel (Fornel).

In its choice of subjects, the DCB/DBC has heeded the importance in moving beyond the political, military, and religious leaders who dominated our earliest volumes. Later volumes take a broader approach that includes the rise of social history and profits from the availability of new resources that permit a deeper understanding of our past. There are now more biographies of women, scientists, sports figures, artists, labourers, and entrepreneurs in our volumes. The official records that chart the lives of institutional leaders do not always exist for these groups, but our contributors have taken advantage of new archival resources to write about their lives.

We would like to thank Andrew Ross and Andrew Smith for the seed that has germinated into this book. We deeply appreciate the co-operation of the authors of the biographies whose work made this exceptional contribution to Canadian business history possible. We are happy to acknowledge the ongoing support of the University of Toronto and the Université Laval. And, as always, we are pleased to recognize the work of our staff and freelancers in Toronto and Quebec City.

The DCB/DBC was the product of a gift from James Nicholson, a successful entrepreneur. George Brown and Marcel Trudel first explored and then developed the possibilities of Canadian biography. This book is a notable addition to the enterprise they began.

Réal Bélanger
Directeur général adjoint
Dictionnaire biographique
    du Canada
Université Laval

John English
General Editor
Dictionary of
Canadian Biography
University of Toronto

Notes on the Biographies

Like most of the biographies that appear in *Canada's prime ministers, Macdonald to Trudeau: portraits from the Dictionary of Canadian biography*, the 61 biographies collected in this book were published between the 1966 release of the first volume of the *Dictionary of Canadian biography/Dictionnaire biographique du Canada* (*DCB/DBC*), which covers the years 1000–1700, and the 15th volume (1921–30), which came out in 2005. Some minor changes have been made to the biographies. Over the five decades since the first volume appeared the editorial teams in Toronto and Quebec City, authors, and, on occasion, readers have discovered typographical and spelling mistakes and errors of fact. These have been corrected, and those features that facilitate cross-referencing, such as asterisks and small capitals intended to direct the reader to related biographies in the series, have been deleted. In the main, however, minor differences in style and presentation have been allowed to stand. Changes have been kept to a minimum to avoid creating versions very different from the originals, but authors were encouraged to make minor revisions to update their biographies in light of subsequent research. (Not all wished, or were able, to do so.) Readers interested in knowing more about the editorial style of the DCB/DBC with regard to names of persons, places, and institutions, terminology, and so on should consult the "Editorial Notes" at the beginning of the printed volumes.

The 62 scholars who prepared these biographies, ranging from graduate students to senior scholars, from inside academia and outside, used a variety of sources, including archival manuscripts of individuals and institutions, newspapers and journals, the debates of legislative bodies, numerous commercial documents, and printed sources. In the volumes, in the CD-ROM version of volumes I to XIV (released in 2000), and in the web-based version (ongoing since 2003 at *www.biographi.ca*), each biography is followed by an exhaustive bibliography indicating the wealth of material examined by the authors. For this book, the authors and editors have provided instead a few, select sources in which interested readers may broaden their knowledge about the subjects. Some of these items are the most pertinent of the titles listed in the original bibliographies; some are new works published since the articles first appeared; and some provide historical context for the activities of the subjects.

We hope that readers will be encouraged by what they find in this volume to learn more about the contributions of Canada's entrepreneurs to this country's history.

J. ANDREW ROSS & ANDREW D. SMITH

Acknowledgements

In undertaking this book, published both in English and in French by the University of Toronto Press and Les Presses de l'Université Laval respectively, we were helped immeasurably by several important groups of people. The first is the scholars who researched and wrote the original biographies, many of whom represent the finest in Canadian history writing of the second half of the 20th century. We are particularly grateful to those authors who were able to take the time to consider revisions and provide updated bibliographies. The second group is the editorial staff of the Dictionary of Canadian Biography/ Dictionnaire biographique du Canada (DCB/DBC), both at the University of Toronto and the Université Laval, whose vast experience and skill showed through at every turn in the process. As with all the authors who have worked with the DCB/DBC over the years, we owe a great debt of gratitude to those who edited, translated, checked, and documented the biographies, and prepared them for publication. Special recognition is due to the third group, the archivists in Ottawa, Montreal, Toronto, and Sudbury who helped with the images. We are also grateful to the reviewers who debated our selections and themes and thereby helped us make a better book. Finally, and not least, we would like to thank the two directors of the DCB/DBC, John English and Réal Bélanger, who encouraged the entrepreneurial spirit of two young historians.

J. Andrew Ross & Andrew D. Smith

Introduction

"Entrepreneurship" is a popular term in modern society, used by businesses hoping to encourage innovation among their employees, politicians aiming to raise national productivity, and academic researchers trying to understand why economic growth occurs. One of its more famous proponents was the Austrian-American economist Joseph Alois Schumpeter (1883–1950), who saw the concept as a crucial element of capitalist progress. Memorably, he called entrepreneurs "wild spirits" and "fiery souls" engaged in a process of "creative destruction" that resulted in totally new industries and a transformation of everyday life.[1]

For Schumpeter and his intellectual descendants, the history of modern capitalism was a story of transformation and the entrepreneurs who drove it, but historians also recognize that there are many other ingredients in the complex recipe for modern economic growth – institutional development, secure property rights, and sound financial systems, to mention only a few. Historians have maintained that entrepreneurship has had particular resonance for the Canadian experience. In his survey of the country's business history, Michael Bliss argued that this narrative gained its distinctiveness from "the attempt by enterprising spirits to create wealth in the sprawling, thinly populated northern half of the North American continent."[2] Canada's emergence as a major economy is testament, at least in part, to their success, but perhaps humbled by finding themselves in the shadow of the world's greatest power, Canadians have asked difficult questions about whether their entrepreneurs took advantage of all the opportunities afforded them. Has our abundance of natural resources stifled the incentive to innovate? Has Canadian business been too dependent on government support, or was this involvement necessary for the challenges of industrializing a vast land? Have individuals in some

---

1 T. K. McCraw, *Prophet of innovation: Joseph Schumpeter and creative destruction* (Cambridge, Mass., 2007), 71–75.
2 Michael Bliss, *Northern enterprise: five centuries of Canadian business* (Toronto, 1987), 8.

regions of the country simply lacked the enterprising spirit displayed by others, or were they hindered by external circumstances? Is Canadian entrepreneurship a story of success or of relative failure, especially when it is compared to that of our southern neighbour?

Seeking answers to questions such as these has motivated some of Canada's greatest historians and political economists to produce persuasive overarching narratives. Harold Adams Innis, Arthur Reginald Marsden Lower, Donald Grant Creighton, Hugh George Jeffrey Aitken, William Archibald Mackintosh, Norman Scott Brien Gras, and others achieved worldwide reputations with concepts of history that tied together geography, natural resources, international capital and trade networks, and business organization. Particularly influential were the members of the Innis school, who argued that the exploitation of a succession of "staples" – fish, fur, wheat, wood, pulp and paper, oil, and minerals – determined Canada's economic path and may have hampered diversification and industrialization. Gras launched the field of business history (and the case-study method) at the Harvard Business School and set out a framework of stages in the evolution of capitalism that could be applied to all societies. He aimed to show how institutions and cultural values, as well as economic factors and state intervention, have stimulated or retarded individual enterprise.[3]

Later historians have used, qualified, modified, or even rejected these master narratives as they delved deeper into the operations and social contexts of specific Canadian industries, firms, and individuals. One of the most useful of such explorations has been the collective effort of contributors to the *Dictionary of Canadian biography*, which one historian in the 1980s called "the most useful introduction to the study of the business system yet published."[4] In the quarter century since that comment was written, new *DCB* volumes have continued to provide insights into the lives of those who created and ran Canadian businesses.

In this collection, we have selected just 61 of the more than 2,100 subjects in the *Dictionary of Canadian biography* that fall into the "business" category, from nearly 8,500 entries overall, which, to date, focus mostly

---

3 B. E. C. Boothman, "A theme worthy of epic treatment: N. S. B. Gras and the emergence of American business history," *Journal of Macromarketing*, 21 (June 2001): 61–73.
4 Tom Traves, "Bibliographical essay," in *Essays in Canadian business history*, ed. Tom Traves (Toronto, 1984), 170–77.

although not exclusively on those Canadians who died before 1930. The period in which our entrepreneurs flourished thus ends with the stock market crash of 1929. The book contains figures whose names will be familiar to many readers, together with less famous people who stand in for thousands of others with no less significant roles in the history of Canadian business. The compilers debated widely between themselves and with the reviewers over which individuals to include. In some modern eyes, those assembled here might seem a homogeneous group, but they are quite diverse in terms of language, country of origin, religion, and social origins. The entrepreneurs we have selected include native-born Canadians as well as immigrants from France, the British Isles, the United States, and other countries. German, Chinese, and Jewish exemplars represent both their communities and the transnational ethnic networks that were important in Canadian business. Only six of the biographies are of women, but through their stories readers will see that female entrepreneurs have always been active in Canada, even at times when legal and cultural norms militated against them. We have included Métis and First Nations entrepreneurs, who represent the diverse but largely unrecorded commercial activity of aboriginal people as they faced the challenges and opportunities thrown up by European intrusion.

Although this book contains just a sample of those who energized economic life in the northern part of the continent over four centuries, we hope that some major themes will emerge. One is the significance of the international context; the geographic entity that became the nation state of Canada was, and is, a country of trade, and it has attracted capital, people, and goods from all over the world. Another motif is the ever-present role of competition, regulated or not, which drove businesses towards success or failure. The importance of adapting to change – social, cultural, economic, political, and technological – whether rapid or gradual, is also evident; enterprises were never carried on in a vacuum. The business environment in the past seldom resembled the one we know today, and the entrepreneur's role changed along with the circumstances. The regional context in which he or she operated was also paramount. It is important to note as well that, while organizational and financial growth could lead to large entities with delegated management, most businesses, at least in their early years, were small in scale and managed by owners, not employees. Later in the period covered in this volume techniques of organization and production became more important. Finally, the role of government in Canadian entrepreneurial activity is conspicuous – as facilitator, hindrance, or occasionally leader. (If there were a 62nd biography, it would be that of the state.) These underlying themes show that entrepreneurial spirit alone was not sufficient to drive Canadian business, and that opportunity was always constrained to some extent.

The book is organized by chronology, theme, and region. It begins in the 17th century, in an age of global expansion that dated from the European "discovery" of the New World nearly two centuries earlier, when hitherto unimagined opportunities for trade began to open up. Europeans had refined the needed tools during their own commercial revolutions, and there emerged "an entrepreneurial mood, the desire to accumulate, the willingness to risk capital in new business ventures, [and] the drive to compete and triumph over others."[5] This initiative was led by wholesale merchants, who were most interested in acquiring the precious metals, exotic spices, and other resources of distant lands, but the risks of transoceanic travel made state involvement a necessity. In North America it was less an age of individual enterprise than of state-directed commerce, justified under mercantilist policies that equated national power with economic self-sufficiency and saw colonies as suppliers of raw materials to the mother country.

A major instrument was the monopoly granted by the crown to enterprises such as the Compagnie de la Nouvelle-France (also called the Compagnie des Cent-Associés), chartered in 1627, and the Hudson's Bay Company, established in 1670. The HBC was given exclusive rights to the fur and other resources of the Hudson Bay watershed, an area of more than a million square miles known as Rupert's Land. One of the earliest theorists to take up the concept of entrepreneurship was Richard Cantillon (d. 1734), an Irish-born Parisian banker whose career included a stint promoting one of France's first colonial ventures, the Mississippi Company. Cantillon influenced the great Scottish philosopher Adam Smith (d. 1790), who, in *An inquiry into the nature and causes of the wealth of nations* (1776), presented a new way of thinking about the economy that emphasized the benefits for society as a whole that derived from compe-

---

5 G. D. Taylor and P. A. Baskerville, *A concise history of business in Canada* (Toronto, 1994), 8.

tition and the individual's freedom to trade in his own interest, not just the state's.

Eventually, Smith's arguments were used to dismantle mercantilism, but in the meantime the men and women featured in the first section of this book ("Doing Business in the New World") had not only to adapt to new markets and fresh challenges – hurdles to communication, a dearth of capital, and rapid technological change – but also to respond to state ambivalence towards individual enterprise. They also faced great personal, physical, and financial risks, in an era when wooden sailing vessels frequently sank and North America was often the scene of barbaric wars. Nonetheless, European merchants and coureurs de bois travelled the continent to engage with native traders such as Muquinna, form long-distance networks, and do business in a hostile environment. And while some, such as François Havy and Charles Robin, took their wealth back to Europe, many more, among them Charles Aubert de La Chesnaye, stayed, married, and contributed to colonial society.

When New France came under British rule following the Treaty of Paris in 1763, the dream of a "commercial empire of the St Lawrence," as Creighton called it, did not end; instead, the Montreal-based fur trade passed into the hands of English-speaking merchants. The conquest's impact on French-Canadian society has been the subject of intense debate. Some historians have argued that it resulted in an exodus of merchants to France and that this "social decapitation" reduced French Canadians to second-class citizens, relegated to paddling the canoes that carried English-speaking fur traders and their cargoes. Others have contended that the economy necessarily became dependent on those who had access to British credit, supplies, and markets, such as Aaron Hart and George Allsopp in this volume. A similar pattern was evident in Upper Canada (Ontario), where Scots such as Robert Hamilton provided commercial leadership. Readers will note that, in the section entitled "The Commercial Empire of the St Lawrence after 1763," the business careers of Pierre Foretier, François Baby, and Louise de Ramezay extended through the conquest, and later biographies (such as those of Georges-Élie Amyot, Sir Rodolphe Forget, Louis-Adélard Senécal, and Alphonse Desjardins) remind us that risk taking continued among French-Canadian entrepreneurs. Nonetheless, it is true that business in Lower Canada (Quebec) was dominated by a small, well-connected anglophone minority composed of men such as James McGill, John Molson, Sir Hugh Allan, William Price, and Sir Edward Seaborne Clouston.[6]

As well as surviving the transition from French to British rule, the commercial empire of the St Lawrence saw the decline of the fur trade in the Great Lakes region. In the 1770s Scottish, English, and French merchants in Montreal (including McGill) formed the North West Company and began to compete directly for furs with the Hudson's Bay Company, which maintained its monopoly over much of the continent. While the HBC, governed from London through agents in Rupert's Land, could still function well, the flexibility and drive of Nor'Westers such as John McLoughlin, who were both owners and managers, brought initial success, until the two firms were forced to merge in 1821.

Merchants also adjusted to the transformation of Upper Canada, which was flooded by white settlers. Many were loyalists fleeing the American revolution, and more were so-called late loyalists. Trade shifted to the commodities produced by farmers and lumberjacks. The major challenge was obtaining sufficient capital; the buying and selling of wheat and lumber depended on predicting markets up to a year or more into the future, and bankruptcy and failure were inevitable without dependable credit relationships based on trust. Between 1817 and 1825 and again in the 1830s, merchants formed their own banks to concentrate capital, and while many of these failed, others survived to become the ancestors of Canada's modern financial institutions.

More adaptation was required after Great Britain began its retreat from mercantilism and scrapped tariff advantages for Canadian wheat and lumber producers in the 1840s. The result was a period of economic pain and political turmoil in British North America. Indeed, the burning of the parliament buildings in Montreal by a tory mob in 1849 can be seen as an indirect outcome of the British empire's shift to a regime of free trade: the fire demonstrated the anger of merchants who felt betrayed by the mother country.[7] The impact that the end of assured access to British markets had on Canadian business is evident in the careers of John Redpath and William Price, and the policy change also had major

6 For an overview of the issues in the debate, see Taylor and Baskerville, *A concise history of business in Canada*, 75–82.

7 Donald Creighton, *John A. Macdonald: the young politician* (Toronto, 1952), 139–40.

implications for enterprises in the eastern colonies, such as those of Enos Collins, Benjamin Bowring, and Sir Samuel Cunard, whose stories are presented in the section entitled "Maritime Enterprise."

The mid 1800s launched a period of profound economic and social change that would result in a fully diversified commercial and industrial sector by the end of the century. Together with population growth, the reduced shipping costs and increased efficiencies brought about by the railways (though many benefits were often exaggerated by self-interested railway promoters) led to expanded urban markets and, with them, industrialization. Montreal was at the centre of this development; its commercial outlets, labour supply, and transportation advantages spurred a remarkable growth in manufacturing enterprises, large and small. The city sprouted flour, cotton, sugar, rolling mills and sawmills, boot and shoe works, tanneries, and shipyards, built by men such as Price, Redpath, Louis-Adélard Senécal, and Georges-Élie Amyot. In Upper Canada Hart Almerrin Massey, James Miller Williams, Theodor August Heintzman, and many others exploited burgeoning markets for products as diverse as farm implements, petroleum, and pianos. These men are profiled in the section "The Industrial Heartland."

The 19th century also witnessed profound political change as the British North American colonies took on more responsibility for their own governance. Confederation, which united the Canadas, Nova Scotia, and New Brunswick in 1867, created both a nation and a common market and spurred demand for a transcontinental railway that would forge links with the west. It should come as no surprise that entrepreneurs in a credit-based trading society were closely involved in making their needs known in the areas of commercial and corporate law and trade policy. Merchants such as Isaac Buchanan had taken up the cause of tariff protection in the 1850s, and Sir Byron Edmund Walker and other bankers would defend the National Policy that Sir John A. Macdonald's government introduced two decades later. But the greatest appeal of the policy was to the many manufacturers eager for advantage over their American competitors. Retailers such as Timothy Eaton, whose interests were much closer to those of Canadian consumers, resented the premium that such protective practices imposed on imported goods.

Many entrepreneurs involved themselves in politics, either directly as elected members of legislative bodies or as financial supporters of parties or candidates – often as both. From a modern perspective, the activities of men such as Allan, whose financing schemes contributed to the fall of the Macdonald government, seem like examples of what we would now call "crony capitalism," in which success in business depends on one's skill in cultivating close relationships with government officials, rather than on purely commercial talents.[8] But in 19th-century Canada it was not unusual for politicians to maintain active business interests, and so-called conflicts of interest were not seen as necessarily inimical to the common good. The windfall profits enjoyed by the men who built the railways with generous government subsidies might seem unjustified to us today, but Macdonald's vision of a transcontinental link could not have been realized without the managerial and organizational skills of Allan, Sir William Cornelius Van Horne, and John Rudolphus Booth (in the section "Railwaymen and Network Creators"), not to mention the men who ran the banks that helped to finance them (Walker, Clouston, and George Albertus Cox). Together with politicians, these visionaries extended the east–west transportation system of the old Great Lakes–St Lawrence waterway to the Pacific and expanded the borders of the new dominion. In the next generation the relationship between business and the state grew even tighter with the creation of crown corporations such as the Hydro-Electric Power Commission of Ontario under Sir Adam Beck in 1906 and an even larger federal body, Canadian National Railways, in 1919. This public enterprise advanced development that was beyond the means of the private sector, as well as addressing divergent regional interests, while at the same time taking advantage of the benefits of the entrepreneurial system.

By the first decade of the 20th century the products of a fully developed urban, industrial economy were being distributed across the nation, making household names of firms run by Eaton, William Notman, John Kinder Labatt, Heintzman, Peter Charles Larkin (of the Salada Tea Company), and Gilbert White Ganong; many such companies were promoted by the advertising agency Anson McKim had established in 1889. The section devoted to "Brand Names and Big Business" also contains stories of big-business creation and integration. Sir John Morison Gibson led

---

8 A. O. Krueger, "Why crony capitalism is bad for economic growth," in *Crony capitalism and economic growth in Latin America: theory and evidence*, ed. Stephen Haber (Stanford, Calif., 2002), 1–24.

the establishment of hydroelectric and related intercity streetcar systems in Ontario. Gordon Morton McGregor backed a small automaker named Henry Ford and gained the right to manufacture and sell his cars in Canada and the British empire outside the United Kingdom. Wilmot Deloui Matthews was at the centre of some of the biggest mergers and consolidations in Canadian business history, as was John Fitzwilliam Stairs (who is featured in the section "Maritime Enterprise"), who established Royal Securities Corporation, a type of company new to Canada that financed Canadian manufacturing and also extended funds to overseas projects. Not least, men such as Cox and Clouston used banks and insurance and trust companies to expand the financial means available to Canadian business, tapping both domestic and foreign sources.

Much of this business was developing in the west by the end of the 19th century. The last section in the book features entrepreneurs in banking (William Forbes Alloway), mining (Robert Dunsmuir and Ellen Cashman), transportation (Francis Jones Barnard), ranching (François-Xavier Letendre, dit Batoche, and William Edward Cochrane), retailing (Chang Toy), photography (Rosetta Ernestine Watson (Carr)), and saloon-keeping (Fanny Bendixen) in the western provinces and territories. Whether their ventures were large or small, these men and women helped to build economies and advance the frontiers of Canadian business.

We hope that this collection will serve several purposes. First, it is intended to interest a wide variety of readers, including entrepreneurs, in biographies they will find both enjoyable and instructive. Secondly, it is meant to encourage educators to incorporate entrepreneurial and business history into Canadian studies at all levels (readers looking for more material are encouraged to consult the sources given in "Further reading" lists throughout the volume). Lastly, this book aims to showcase the fine work of the contributors and editorial staff of the *Dictionary of Canadian biography*, one of the most valuable and accessible repositories of Canada's past. Readers are urged to explore further in the *Dictionary's* published volumes (15 to date), the CD-ROM version, or the website at *www.biographi.ca* to learn more about the enterprising figures who have animated Canadian business.

J. ANDREW ROSS & ANDREW D. SMITH

Further reading

Dictionary of Canadian Biography online (*www.biographi.ca*).

The Canadian Business Hall of Fame (*www.cbhof.ca*).

G. D. Taylor and P. A. Baskerville, *A concise history of business in Canada* (Toronto, 1994).

Michael Bliss, *Northern enterprise: five centuries of Canadian business* (Toronto, 1987).

G. D. Taylor, *The rise of Canadian business* (Don Mills [Toronto], Ont., 2009).

Joe Martin, *Relentless change: a casebook for the study of Canadian business history* (Toronto, 2010).

Kenneth Norrie *et al.*, *A history of the Canadian economy* (4th ed., Toronto, 2008).

Section 1

Doing Business in the New World

JOHN GUY,

colonizer, explorer, governor of the first English colony in
Newfoundland; d. *c.* March 1629.

From the beginning of the 17th century John Guy was prominent in
the civic and commercial life of Bristol. In 1603 he was elected to the
Common Council on which he served until 1629; he was also a member
of the Bristol Society of Merchant Venturers. In 1606, when sheriff of
the city, he and the mayor, Thomas James (the father of Capt. Thomas
James), became the principal Bristol subscribers to the North Virginia
Company. Four years later he was appointed governor of the colony to be
established in Newfoundland by the London and Bristol company.

It is possible that Guy was the originator of this movement to colo-
nize Newfoundland. In 1608 he had visited the island and the following
year, according to Purchas, he wrote a tract – of which no copy is known
– advocating the settlement of Newfoundland. Early in 1610 a petition
for a grant of incorporation was submitted to the Privy Council by John
Slany, treasurer of the company, and John Guy, as representatives of the
two groups of subscribers from London and Bristol. By its charter, scaled
in May 1610, the company was granted the whole island, with particular emphasis on the area of the Avalon peninsula. Before leaving, Guy
received detailed instructions as to the employment of his men and the
requirements of a good site. Elaborate provision was also made for the
government of the colony: Guy had supreme authority and was to govern
without assistance; if he died without naming a successor, his brother
Philip, who was also a subscriber to the company, was to be governor. In
the event of Philip's death, William Chatchmaid was to succeed.

On 5 July 1610, John and Philip Guy and the other colonists,
including William Colston and probably Thomas Rowley, sailed from
Bristol, reaching Newfoundland in August. The actual choice of site
was entrusted to John and, on arrival, he decided on Cuper's Cove (now
Cupids) rather than on Colliers Cove, also in Conception Bay. Much
of our knowledge of the settlement's early history comes from Guy's
letters home, which reveal his preoccupation with making the colony

self-supporting. From the outset the planters' industry was remarkable and a tribute to Guy's leadership, which always seems to have been well accepted by his men. The first winter was mild: of the 39 settlers, only 4 died. Their time was occupied in building and fortifying their habitation, in exploring and farming.

Guy returned to England in the late summer of 1611; he was at this time treasurer of the Merchant Venturers. Before leaving, he issued orders for the regulation of the fishery, to reform the disorderly practices of the visiting fishermen and placed his brother, Philip, and William Colston in charge of the colony. Early in 1612 he returned to the island, bringing more colonists.

That summer was a difficult time for Guy because of the raids of the pirate, Peter Easton. The fishermen ignored Guy's advice to attack the pirate and so suffered heavily. Guy himself was with Easton for 14 days and seems to have won immunity for the colony; there was only one incident when a colonist was shot in error. However, Easton's visit forced Guy to abandon the company's plan to establish a settlement at Renewse that year. He withdrew his men and concentrated on strengthening Cuper's Cove.

Also hindered was the journey of exploration to Trinity Bay, which Guy had intended that summer. Not until October did he set out with 18 men, including Bartholomew Pearson, and 2 boats. He explored Trinity Bay with some care, looking vainly for a passage to Placentia Bay, but his main purpose was to establish contact with the Beothuk Indians, which he did at Bull Arm. George Whittington, one of the colonists, was chosen to go ashore first to convince the Indians that they came in friendship. Guy's journal of the expedition gives a charming account of the encounter, the exchange of gifts, and the shared meal. Some furs were obtained and, after an eventful journey, Guy regained Cuper's Cove late in November. That winter was the most severe yet experienced; 22 of the 62 settlers suffered from scurvy, though only 8 died. In April 1613 Guy suddenly left for England and the expedition which he had intended to lead that summer was abandoned.

It was expected that Guy would return in the autumn of 1613, but in September he was still in Bristol. Probably he did go to Newfoundland early in 1614 but stayed only for the summer, since in December 1614 he was again in Bristol. At this time his relations with the company became strained and Guy complained bitterly of their treatment of himself and the other colonists: he had not received the land promised him nor had the men received their wages. A letter (held at the University of Nottingham in England as of the beginning of the 21st century) which he wrote in 1614 strongly suggests that his dispute with the company had gone to law; however his land must have been allotted to him by 1626, when he bequeathed it to his sons. In 1616 John Slany accused Guy of having deceived the company over the island's mineral resources. About this time John Mason was appointed governor of the colony.

Probably Guy never returned to Newfoundland but he had left the colony firmly established with over 60 inhabitants, both men and women. Cargoes of fish and merchantable timber which would help towards the cost of the enterprise had been sent home; new areas of a little-known country had been explored; a fur trade with the Indians had been begun. By comparison with the careers of the first governors of other such ventures, Guy's had been most successful.

He took up life in Bristol with renewed vigour; in 1618 he served as mayor and, the following year, became an alderman. From December 1620 until 1622, he represented Bristol in the House of Commons and was particularly prominent in the long debates on the bill for the greater liberty of fishing voyages to North America. Guy consistently opposed the bill as jeopardizing the freedom of the Newfoundland planters in the fishery. In September 1621 he represented Bristol in the government inquiry into the decline of trade. He was master of the Merchant Venturers in 1622 and in 1624 he was returned to Parliament for a further year when he again supported the Newfoundland planters in the renewed debate on the fishery.

In February 1626 Guy made a will bequeathing extensive property to his seven children and his wife, Anne; his Seaforest estate in Newfoundland he divided among three of his sons. He attended his last meeting of the Common Council in June 1628, and in May 1629, probate was granted to his wife. A monument was later erected to his memory in St Stephen's Church, Bristol.

GILLIAN T. CELL

Further reading

A. F. Williams, *John Guy of Bristol and Newfoundland: his life, times and legacy,* ed. W. G. Hancock and C. W. Sanger (St John's, 2010).

Newfoundland discovered: English attempts at colonisation, 1610–1630, ed. G. T. Cell (London, 1982).

P. E. Pope, *Fish into wine: the Newfoundland plantation in the seventeenth century* (Chapel Hill, N.C., 2004).

William Gilbert, "'Divers places': the Beothuk Indians and John Guy's voyage into Trinity Bay," *Newfoundland Studies* (St John's), 6 (1990): 147–67.

Brenda Parmenter, *The colony of Cupids and John Guy: selected materials in the Newfoundland and Labrador collection, St. John's Public Libraries* (St John's, 2010).

The westward enterprise: English activities in Ireland, the Atlantic, and America, 1480–1650, ed. K. R. Andrews *et al.* (Detroit, 1979).

CHARLES AUBERT DE LA CHESNAYE,

merchant, fur-trader, seigneur, financier, entrepreneur, member of the Conseil Souverain of New France, ennobled by Louis XIV on 24 March 1693, New France's leading businessman of the 17th century; b. in Amiens, 12 Feb. 1632; d. in Quebec, 20 Sept. 1702.

He was the son of Jacques Aubert and Marie Goupy (or Goupil). In La Chesnaye's marriage contracts and his letters of nobility, the occupation of his father is given either as "comptroller" or "intendant of the fortifications of the town and citadel of Amiens"; but in the birth certificate of his sister Anne in 1629, the father is referred to simply as Jacques Aubert "painter holding shop in Paris." Possibly the latter became intendant at a subsequent date, for the family does appear to have been well-connected socially. Acting as Anne's godparents were a son and daughter of the Duc de Chaulnes, the military governor of Picardy. Charles's godfather was Charles Parmentier, the Duc's *maître d'hôtel*. Mention is also made, in a notarial deed of 1695, of a second son, Louis, who was residing in Antwerp and acting as the business agent of the princes of Uzel and Brussels.

How and when La Chesnaye acquired his fortune is not known, but the possibility of a family inheritance would appear to be ruled out. In his last will written in August 1702, he described his parents simply as "worthy people" and himself as "quite poor" when he arrived in Canada in 1655 as the agent of a group of Rouen merchants. This position must have been an important factor in his early career. In 1660, these Rouen merchants and Toussaint Guénet, a French financier, concluded an important treaty with René Robinau de Bécancour, who represented the colony. It gave the Guénet syndicate exclusive control of the Canadian import trade for an annual fee of 10,000 *livres* and the right to collect the 25 per cent and 10 per cent taxes on beaver pelts and moosehides for an additional amount of 50,000 *livres*. The habitants considered these terms excessively generous and they managed to have the treaty rescinded by the royal council in March 1662. For two years, however, La Chesnaye had helped to manage an important enterprise and it may well have been during this period that he launched his own business career.

Shortly after the cancellation of the treaty, La Chesnaye negotiated his first major business transaction. In October 1663 the Conseil Souverain held a public auction to find a leaseholder for the Tadoussac fur trade monopoly and the taxes on beaver pelts and moosehides. Several bidders appeared on the first day, but the field was soon narrowed down to two men: La Chesnaye and Claude Charron de La Barre. Competition now became keen. Each man outbid the other in turn and the price offered for the lease rose gradually from 38,000 to 46,000 *livres* which Charron offered on the morning of the fourth day. That afternoon the customary three candles were lit to signify that the auction was about to close; but before the third flame had flickered out La Chesnaye had managed to snatch victory from his rival with a final bid of 46,500 *livres*. The lease was to run for three years and 15,000 *livres* were payable in advance at the start of each year.

La Chesnaye had other important business interests besides the beaver trade. He owned a large store in Quebec in which he kept a stock of merchandise valued at approximately 50,000 *livres*. In November 1664, he and several other merchants were accused by the syndics representing the habitants of having sold their merchandise at prices higher than those set by the council the preceding June. In reply to this charge, La Chesnaye admitted that the price he had demanded for shoes had exceeded the prescribed rates, but he claimed that he had thought that the tariff applied only to itinerant merchants and not to those who had their residence in the colony. He also pointed out that the habitants paid for their purchases in beaver pelts, whose value had remained constant in Canada but had declined sharply in France. To have followed the tariff under those circumstances would have resulted in heavy financial losses. The council was not impressed by these arguments and imposed fines on the guilty merchants. Only in 1670 did it set a new price scale for the pelts, following renewed complaints by La Chesnaye and his colleagues about the harmful effect the high value of beaver was having on their affairs.

Soon after his arrival in the colony La Chesnaye began to acquire land. In 1659 he purchased for 1,000 *livres* 70 acres on Coteau Sainte-Geneviève, one of the colony's most favoured sites for agriculture by virtue of its proximity to Quebec, and a lot on Rue du Sault-au-Matelot in Lower Town where he built a spacious home in the 1660s. He became co-seigneur of Beaupré in 1662 when he bought the share of Olivier Letardif in the company founded in 1638 to develop the large domain extending from the Montmorency River to Cap Tourmente. Bishop François de Laval, who had arrived in Canada in 1659, was also interested in obtaining this attractive seigneury, which was almost fully settled, and La Chesnaye was instrumental in helping him achieve his goal. Between 1662 and 1664, acting as the procurator of the seigneury, La Chesnaye sold his own share and those of several other members of the company to the bishop. He did not, however, sever all his connections with Beaupré. In 1668 he obtained from the new seigneur a subfief with a frontage of approximately 10 *arpents* on the St Lawrence River in the parish of Ange-Gardien and purchased another, somewhat larger, from Jean-Baptiste Legardeur de Repentigny in Château-Richer.

The fur trade, the sale of merchandise, and agriculture were thus the three basic ventures on which La Chesnaye built his career. Except for the fur trade, however, economic conditions in the colony limited rather than favoured business opportunities. Agricultural expansion was severely hindered by the small population, the Iroquois wars, the absence of external markets, and the fur trade's superior economic appeal. Until the 1690s, when card money became well established, the colony lacked a currency. This factor, joined to the impoverished condition of the habitants, obliged the colonial merchants to sell on credit and they frequently experienced great difficulty in the recovery of debts. La Chesnaye, in brief, enjoyed none of the opportunities of the business class after 1713, which was favoured by a long period of peace, a population that was relatively large, a market at Louisbourg for agricultural products, and the creation by means of state assistance of fairly important industries such as the shipyards and the Saint-Maurice ironworks.

In May 1664, as part of the crown's vast programme of colonial reorganization, Canada became the property of the newly established Compagnie des Indes Occidentales. The company was granted a 40-year monopoly of the commerce of Canada including the Tadoussac fur trade and the taxes on beaver pelts and moosehides. Shortly afterwards, Jean Talon began his famous campaign to restrict these company rights. He claimed that the monopoly discouraged the spirit of enterprise among the settlers, hindered the growth of trade, and, generally speaking, was an obstacle to the progress of the colony. His solution was to make the trade free or place it in the hands of a new company composed of himself and the principal Canadian settlers.

La Chesnaye had been named agent of the Compagnie des Indes Occidentales in 1666 and he sharply criticized Talon's proposition. In a memoir submitted to the court in 1667 he argued that no company could replace the Compagnie des Indes Occidentales unless it had at its disposal an initial capital fund of 1,300,000 *livres*. He calculated that this amount, which could not possibly be raised in the colony, would be required to buy up the company's unsold pelts and its stock of merchandise, and to attend to the colony's immediate needs. As for freedom of trade, La Chesnaye did not consider it a practical solution for he did not believe that a sufficient number of merchants would be interested in trading with Canada to satisfy its needs. La Chesnaye may have communicated his views orally to Jean-Baptiste Colbert during a trip to France in 1665, for the minister used arguments very similar to his to turn down Talon's recommendations in 1666. The will of the intendant, however, finally prevailed. During a visit to France in 1669 he obtained the abolition of the Compagnie des Indes Occidentales's monopoly.

In taking his stand La Chesnaye had no doubt been thinking of the interests of his employer, but other considerations also appear to have been involved. As a strongly established and well connected business-man, he obviously did not believe that the colony could flourish without the protection of powerful financial interests. Having witnessed the sorry performance of the Compagnie des Habitants in the 1650s, it is not surprising that he should have found Talon's recommendations distasteful for they would once again deliver the colony into the hands of petty, dishonest businessmen. In this affair, furthermore, La Chesnaye believed that the intendant had been trying to serve his own interests rather than those of the colony. In a memoir written many years later, he stated that Talon had campaigned against the Compagnie des Indes Occidentales's monopoly because he expected that its cancellation would enable him to increase his private trade in articles he imported into the colony free of freight and insurance charges.

This friction between La Chesnaye and Talon fortunately did not prevent them from cooperating on some important projects. In 1670, La Chesnaye went into lumbering, a sector of the Canadian economy which the intendant was hoping to develop. Two years later, Talon granted to him, Charles Bazire, and Pierre Denys de La Ronde the seigneury of Percé, to be used as a base for a fishing industry. La Chesnaye and La Ronde formed a company in which the former invested 13,874 *livres* and the latter 8,324 *livres*. Thus around La Chesnaye's main interests, which consisted of the fur trade, the Quebec store, and agriculture, there emerged a network of secondary activities such as lumbering, fishing, a brickyard after 1679, and for a short time mining.

In 1672, La Chesnaye sizably enlarged the scope of his operations when he leased from the Compagnie des Indes Occidentales, for 47,000 *livres* annually, the financial rights which it still exercised in Canada. These consisted basically of the proceeds from the taxes on beaver pelts and moosehides which had yielded a profit of 70,000 *livres* in 1670. The acquisition of these important revenues probably explains his decision to take up residence in La Rochelle, whose seaport was the nerve centre of commerce between Canada and France. There, he would be able to look after the marketing of his pelts and would also be close to the high circles of French finance. To collect the taxes in Canada and to manage his other affairs, he appointed his associate Charles Bazire.

From 1672 until his return to Canada in 1678, La Chesnaye figured prominently in La Rochelle's bustling commercial life. He soon won the confidence of the city's other merchants who twice elected him to the *cour consulaire*, which rendered judgments in mercantile cases. Alone or with his partners Jean Grignon, Jean Gitton, and Étienne Joulin, he owned several vessels ranging in size from 60 to 300 tons which plied the sea between La Rochelle, Quebec, Percé, the West Indies, Amsterdam, and Hamburg with cargoes of fur, fish, and assorted merchandise. Thus La Chesnaye used his years in France to expand his business and to make commercial contacts in several countries of Europe.

In 1674, Louis XIV abolished the Compagnie des Indes Occidentales. The next year he ceded to a syndicate of French financiers, acting under the name of Jean Oudiette and known as the Compagnie de la Ferme, several important commercial privileges in Canada and some of the other French colonies for 350,000 *livres* annually. The Compagnie de la Ferme's Canadian rights consisted of the Tadoussac fur trade, the proceeds of the tax on beaver pelts and moosehides, and on the wines and spirits entering the colony, and the exclusive right to market Canadian beaver in France. It was obliged, however, to purchase all the beaver pelts brought to its stores at four *livres* ten *sols* per pound weight. Three days after the conclusion of this treaty, Oudiette leased his Canadian rights to La Chesnaye for 119,000 *livres* annually, with 20,000 *livres* payable in advance. By means of this transaction, La Chesnaye gained complete control of the Canadian beaver trade, but he soon found that he lacked the resources to support such an enormous enterprise. As a result of the expansionist policy pursued by Governor Louis de Buade, Comte de Frontenac et de Palluau, far more pelts were being produced in Canada than the French market could absorb; but La Chesnaye could make no adjustment to meet these conditions for he was obliged by the terms of the Oudiette treaty to purchase all the beaver brought to him. By 1677 he was practically crushed by an enormous debt of 1,000,000 *livres*. Fortunately he was rescued by a group of powerful financiers, including Louis Carrel and Hugues Mathé, receivers general of finance for the generalities of Paris and Champagne, who brought fresh capital to the venture. The transactions that followed are far from clear, but it would appear that the new group gained control of over 80 per cent of the Canadian farm. La Chesnaye retained the balance but sold most of it for 43,000 *livres* in 1680.

The death of Charles Bazire on 15 Dec. 1677 obliged La Chesnaye to return to Canada to settle the claims made by the heirs of the deceased on some of the assets of the partnership. The matter was complicated, for the association between the two men had not been formalized by any deed, and several transactions of concern to the partnership had been entered into by Bazire in his own name. Finally, in settlement of their claims, La Chesnaye offered the heirs either one-third of all the assets he had held in common with Bazire – in the form of seigneuries, merchandise, *rentes*, and loans – or 130,000 *livres*, payable in cash, merchandise, and title deeds to some of the accounts receivable. The heirs preferred the second, perhaps as the less complicated of the two alternatives, and relinquished all claims on the remaining assets of the partnership.

This was not the end of the affair, however. Following the death of Bazire the French shareholders in the Compagnie de la Ferme had also sent an agent, Josias Boisseau, to Canada to examine the state of their affairs. Shortly after his arrival in the colony, he and La Chesnaye became involved in a violent quarrel. According to the agent, discord had broken out because he had tried to prevent La Chesnaye from defrauding his associates of large sums of money. The intendant, Jacques Duchesneau de La Doussinière et d'Ambault, and the author of an anonymous memoir of 1681, however, presented a vastly different picture of the affair. They claimed that Boisseau, who had allied himself with Frontenac, had defied with impunity both the intendant's and La Chesnaye's efforts to regulate his conduct and had built a fortune of 50,000 *livres* at the expense of the company. This version gains considerable support from a dispatch addressed to Bishop Laval by the Abbé Jean Dudouyt, the bishop's representative in Paris, in which the latter wrote that Boisseau would be hard put to account for his actions, which had caused the company heavy losses, if Frontenac were not there to protect him. Boisseau was dismissed from office in 1681 by order of the court.

These problems were not the only ones to occupy La Chesnaye's attention in the late 1670s. When he returned to the colony he found it split into two rival groups by Frontenac and René-Robert Cavelier de La

Salle's attempt to monopolize the western fur trade. La Chesnaye allied himself with the merchants who were opposed to this design, which would ruin them beyond repair if it should succeed, and became one of their leaders. It was he who was primarily responsible for grouping them in 1682 into a company – the Compagnie du Nord – which turned their attention towards Hudson Bay. Because of the prominent position he occupied in their ranks, La Chesnaye was soon bitterly attacked by members of the rival camp. In an anonymous memoir of 1680, he and his principal allies, Jacques Le Ber, Charles Le Moyne de Longueuil et de Châteauguay, and Philippe Gaultier de Comporté, were accused of trading openly with the Indians within the colonial boundaries, of smuggling furs to the English, and of sending numerous canoes into the west in defiance of the royal ordinances. These accusations probably contained considerable truth but the court appears never to have paid much attention to them. This may have been the work of Duchesneau who energetically defended La Chesnaye in his dispatches; but perhaps the government simply realized that it would be both unwise and unjust to antagonize a man who was playing a role of vital importance in the colony's economic life.

In 1680, the syndicate of financiers which had relieved La Chesnaye of the Canadian farm judged that the operation had become unprofitable and surrendered the lease to Jean Oudiette. It next had to decide how to dispose of its remaining assets in Canada, consisting of merchandise, furs, and sums of money owed to it by a large number of French and Indians. The syndicate could have pressed for the recovery of these debts, but this would have taken time and probably necessitated numerous lawsuits. Rather than follow such a course of action, it preferred to transfer the title to all its debts and assets to La Chesnaye for the sum of 410,000 *livres*, payable in four equal annual instalments. This transaction – worth nearly $1,000,000 in present-day currency [i.e., late 1960s] – is a turning-point in his career. Although the value of the debts is not given, it must have been considerably higher than the purchase price because of the risks involved in their recovery. La Chesnaye thus appears to have staked the better part of his fortune on a speculative venture which could result either in a sizable profit or a ruinous loss.

As security for payment, he mortgaged all his own assets and properties. The notarial inventory in which these are listed is an important document, for it provides a comprehensive picture of the state of his fortune in 1681. Its total value was then 476,000 *livres* made up of five principal categories: accounts receivable, 175,000 *livres; contrats de rente*, 100,000 *livres;* merchandise, 50,000 *livres;* his house on Rue du Sault-au-Matelot, 60,000 *livres;* farms and seigneuries, 66,000 *livres.* Several hundred notarial deeds in which a broad range of business transactions are recorded shed a great deal of light on the manner and spirit in which La Chesnaye administered this fortune. The image that emerges from these documents is not that of a selfish merchant uniquely interested in increasing his wealth, but that of a man who was intensely concerned with the development of the colony. Unlike the itinerant merchant, who took the profits from his Canadian trade back to France with him, La Chesnaye invested his gains in the colony and loaned them to the settlers. Unfortunately, these practices were largely responsible for his eventual ruin, which probably explains why so few people followed his example.

La Chesnaye dealt with people from all classes of society. He sold merchandise on credit for amounts ranging from a few *livres* to several thousand. Because of the disappearance of his account books, the profits he realized on these transactions are not known, but the price he charged for shoes in the 1660s suggests that he drove a hard bargain. He also made many cash loans to seigneurs and habitants, usually to enable them to improve their properties. On 1 Oct. 1666, he loaned 10,600 *livres* to Bishop Laval to permit him to meet a payment on the seigneury of Beaupré. On 25 Feb. 1679, he loaned 3,000 *livres* to Charles Cadieu de Courville, a habitant of Beauport, and 4,135 *livres* to Joseph Giffard, the seigneur, to enable them to repair existing buildings and put up new ones. These loans were made in return for *contrats de rente*, which were much like modern savings bonds. They yielded an annual interest rate of 5 to 5½ per cent, but bore no maturity date. As long as interest payments were made there was apparently no way to compel the debtor to repay the principal. At first sight this type of investment would appear ill suited to the needs of a businessman since it froze large amounts of capital. But in the context of the depressed long-term economic cycle that prevailed in the French world from 1630 to 1730 approximately, an investment that yielded 5 per cent interest was probably considered good.

La Chesnaye also had a large amount of money invested in land. He acquired his first acres in 1659 and continued to increase his holdings thereafter until he became the most important landowner of his day. His purpose in acquiring farms and seigneuries was not speculation nor merely the social prestige connected with the ownership of land. He was essentially an agricultural entrepreneur who wanted to base part of his business on the sale of wheat, peas, and other staple crops. By 1685, he had apparently achieved a measure of success, for he then settled part of a debt with a shipment of wheat worth 23,000 *livres*. That same year he and two other merchants undertook to supply the colony with an emergency stock of flour to be used in case of famine.

His seigneuries can be divided into two categories. There were those like Repentigny, Rivière-du-Loup, and Kamouraska that he acquired when they were little more than wilderness tracts, and whose development proved to be costly indeed. He spent 35,000 and 33,000 *livres* on Rivière-du-Loup and Repentigny respectively, but their commercial value was only 18,000 and 16,000 *livres* in 1680. Uncleared seigneuries were apparently worthless, for Kamouraska, which remained undeveloped until the 1690s, is not listed in the inventory of 1681. Then, there were the holdings in the vicinity of Quebec that were highly productive and very valuable. The arriere-fief of Charlesville in the seigneury of Beaupré, granted to La Chesnaye and Charles Bazire by Bishop Laval in 1677, had 16 tenants and was worth 6,000 *livres*. A fully equipped 70-acre farm in the Coteau Sainte-Geneviève was valued at 20,000 *livres* in 1680, and another in the same area was sold for 9,000 *livres* in 1679. Most of these estates, it should be pointed out, were not under La Chesnaye's direct management but, like Repentigny, were leased for cash, or, like Charlesville, were farmed out on a sharecropping agreement.

While he was negotiating his great transaction with the Compagnie de la Ferme, La Chesnaye was also laying the foundations of the Canadian-based Hudson Bay company that became known as the Compagnie du Nord. The French government approved of the formation of this trading organization which might succeed in diverting large quantities of prime beaver pelts from the British Hudson's Bay Company. In 1679 the French director of trade, Francesco Bellinzani, arranged a meeting between La Chesnaye and Pierre-Esprit Radisson, who were both in Paris at the time. The two men consulted together on the means of forming the company and it was finally agreed that Radisson would lead the first commercial expedition to the bay in return for 25 per cent of the profits. In Canada the new governor, Joseph-Antoine Le Febvre de La Barre, who had replaced Frontenac in 1682, encouraged other merchants to join the enterprise and some 193,000 *livres* were eventually invested in it. La Chesnaye was by far the most important shareholder with an investment of 90,000 *livres*.

The arrival of La Barre as governor had enabled La Chesnaye to expand his operations in yet another direction. As long as Frontenac had been in office the Great Lakes and Mississippi Valley regions had been controlled by La Salle and closed to the other merchants of the colony. La Barre, however, who was hostile to La Salle, deprived him of his posts and placed La Chesnaye and his group in possession of Fort Frontenac. A party of malcontents, led by the intendant, Jacques de Meulles, construed this gesture as proof of the existence of a partnership between the governor and La Chesnaye, and painted a dark picture of its effects on the colony. They claimed that the governor and his partner had over 30 canoes in the west under the command of Daniel Greysolon Dulhut and that a large portion of their fur was being diverted to the English. De Meulles even stated that it was to defend these commercial interests that La Barre, acting on the advice of La Chesnaye, had decided to wage war on the Iroquois. This contention was taken up 30 years later by Gédéon de Catalogne. In his *Recueil* he claimed that La Barre, in order to eliminate all competition from the west, had authorized the Iroquois to plunder the traders who could not produce his personal permit. The governor had opted for war after the Indians had overstepped these limits and attacked canoes belonging to La Chesnaye.

How true were these accusations? Independent evidence shows that those relating to La Chesnaye's western trading operations were well founded. In 1685, the furs and merchandise which he had in the west were valued at 100,000 *livres*. His implication in the contraband trade with the English seems established beyond question by the trading permit issued to him by the New York government in 1684. Some of his letters of the mid 1680s establish his connection with the Greysolon brothers, Daniel Greysolon Dulhut and Claude Greysolon de La Tourette. The statements of de Meulles and Catalogne about the origins of the war, however, are not acceptable. For it appears incredible that La Chesnaye would have wantonly exposed to destruction at the hands of the Iroquois a colony which he had worked so hard to develop and in which he had enormous sums invested. If he did advise La Barre to make war on the Five Nations it must have been because he was convinced that a display of force was necessary to overawe these Indians who had recently invaded the territory of the Illinois and seemed on the verge of waging a general war on Canada.

The year 1682 seems to be the watershed in La Chesnaye's career. The years preceding that date had been marked by several major business transactions and the expansion of his affairs. Afterwards, although the downward trend cannot be graphed with precision, decline gradually set in. Two factors – the Iroquois war and the fire which ravaged the Lower Town of Quebec in August 1682 – appear to have been principally responsible for this turn in his fortunes. The heavy material losses suffered by the colony during its war with the Five Nations no doubt made it difficult for La Chesnaye to recover from the habitants the debts which he had purchased from the Compagnie de la Ferme. As for the fire, it destroyed 55 buildings including several warehouses. La Chesnaye's properties were spared, but he loaned large sums of money to his stricken fellow-citizens to enable them to rebuild their homes. He thus depleted his cash reserves at a time when he still owed 213,000 *livres* to the Compagnie de la Ferme, which was pressing him relentlessly for a settlement. He finally discharged his debt in 1685 by transferring to his creditors the 100,000 *livres* of fur and merchandise which he had in the west, a shipment of wheat worth 23,000 *livres*, and his share of 90,000 *livres* in the Compagnie du Nord. Up to that time La Chesnaye's connection with the Hudson Bay trade had not been a profitable one. The Compagnie du Nord, plagued by misfortune and Radisson's treachery, had suffered losses of 273,426 *livres*.

For the balance of the 1680s, however, there was no noticeable change in the tempo of La Chesnaye's activities. He rejoined the Compagnie du Nord in which he had a share of 22,268 *livres* in 1691. He continued to sell large quantities of merchandise on credit or the instalment plan and to make cash loans to finance serious projects. On 8 Oct. 1683, he sold 12,000 *livres* of merchandise to René Gaultier de Varennes, payable in furs, field crops, and cash over a 12-year period. Some three months later, in return for a *rente* of 650 *livres*, he loaned 13,000 *livres* to Étienne Landron and Jean Joly to enable them to build a bakery. He also continued to increase his seigneurial holdings. Some of his important acquisitions between 1683 and 1688 were Madawaska, on the Saint John River, granted by La Barre and de Meulles; Yamaska, on the south shore of the St Lawrence near Trois-Rivières, donated by Michel Leneuf de La Vallière (the elder); Saint-Jean-Port-Joli, below Quebec, acquired from Noël Langlois in settlement of a debt of 1,160 *livres*; Le Bic, also below Quebec, from Charles Denys de Vitré in settlement of another debt of 2,050 *livres*. In 1689, La Chesnaye and a few other merchants were granted the concession of Blanc-Sablon including a part of the coast of Labrador and of Newfoundland by Jacques-René de Brisay de Denonville, Marquis de Denonville, and Jean Bochart de Champigny, Sieur de Noroy et de Verneuil, for the cod and whale fisheries.

Denis Riverin, who had sublet the Tadoussac trade from 1682 to 1685, complained that his affairs were gravely prejudiced by La Chesnaye's extensive lower St Lawrence holdings. He stated that Indians who usually dealt at Tadoussac were now trading across the St Lawrence at Rivière-du-Loup and Le Bic where La Chesnaye had posted his agents. These furs were then sent down the Saint John River, which passed through Madawaska, to Port-Royal (Annapolis Royal, N.S.), where La Chesnaye owned a trading counter. From there they could be shipped to France duty-free since the taxes of 25 per cent and 10 per cent levied on Canadian furs did not extend to Acadia. In 1684 the court issued an ordinance forbidding the settlers of the lower St Lawrence to trade with the Indians, but it modified its decision the following year. The settlers were then authorized to engage in the Indian trade but ordered not to trespass on the Tadoussac domain.

The documentation available on La Chesnaye for the 1690s suggests rather than tells of increasing financial difficulties. His relationship with his partner, Jean Gobin, is most revealing in this respect. In 1690, La Chesnaye, his son François, and Gobin formed a private company. Nothing is known of the nature of this operation but it obviously did not flourish. In 1699, the two Auberts withdrew, leaving two vessels and merchandise worth 102,000 *livres* in the possession of Gobin, on condition that he pay off the firm's debts within two years. Notarial documents also record the existence of large personal debts. La Chesnaye owed Gobin 83,264 *livres* as a result of three transactions made in 1692 and 1694. He also owed 51,681 *livres* to European correspondents and Canadian creditors, for which he signed eight separate obligations before the notary Louis Chambalon on 18 April 1695. It may have been to settle some of these debts that he began to dispose of his seigneuries. Île Dupas and Chicot were sold for 1,500 *livres*, in 1690; Charlesville and Yamaska for 6,250 and 3,333 *livres* respectively, in 1694; Repentigny for 15,000 *livres*, in 1700.

In spite of these financial difficulties, La Chesnaye remained active throughout the 1690s. In 1691, he became a member of a fishing company formed by Champigny and ten years later undertook to supply the government with 60 masts annually for a period of ten years. He also devoted much attention to the development of his seigneuries below Quebec. Twenty-seven settlers and their families took up residence in Kamouraska between 1694 and 1700 and the value of the seigneury rose to 12,000 *livres* by the latter date. It was also during those final years of his life that his prestige in the colony reached its peak. In 1693, Louis XIV granted him letters of nobility as a reward for the many years he had devoted to the development of the Canadian economy. Two years later, he succeeded the deceased Charles Legardeur de Tilly as councillor in the Sovereign Council of New France. The office should in fact have reverted to one of Tilly's sons, Pierre-Noël Legardeur de Tilly, but the latter ceded it to La Chesnaye in settlement of a debt of 6,500 *livres* which he was incapable of paying. With this office in the colonial magistrature and his letters of nobility, La Chesnaye's social metamorphosis was complete. The *bourgeois* had become a *gentilhomme*.

Ennoblement, however, was not followed by a loss of interest in mercantile pursuits. Until the end of his life, La Chesnaye remained the undisputed leader of the Canadian business community. In 1700, he became the leading shareholder of the Compagnie de la Colonie, which leased the beaver trade from the Compagnie de la Ferme. His investment in this corporation amounted to 25,000 *livres* divided into 500 shares, of which 120 had been transferred from the books of the Compagnie du Nord, which the Compagnie de la Colonie had absorbed, and 380 purchased on credit. In 1700, he went to France with Mathieu-François Martin de Lino to negotiate better terms with the Paris bankers, Pasquier, Bourlet, and Goy, who acted as the company's correspondents. Their mission was successful, for the bankers increased the amount of their loan and reduced the interest rate from 10 to 8 per cent. La Chesnaye was back in Canada in 1701 and he died the following year on 20 September.

On 26 August he had prepared his last will. This document must be read with circumspection. It may be viewed as an expression of the thoughts that preoccupied him as death drew near, or as an attempt to place his life in the best possible light. In it he stated that he had never felt much attachment to worldly goods but had simply worked for the progress of the colony "courageously and earnestly." He asked forgiveness for the many wrongs and injustices, both great and small, which he had probably committed during a long career devoted to business, but added that he could recall no specific offensive action "against any of his fellow men." He requested the celebration of a daily mass in perpetuity for the repose of his soul and those of his Canadian friends with whom he had possibly entered into business intrigues, a simple funeral service, and burial in the Cimetière des Pauvres of the Hôtel-Dieu de Québec, a name that bore no relationship to the social status of those buried there, many of whom were colonial notables. The name may have been chosen simply as a reminder of death, the great equalizer.

La Chesnaye had been married three times to daughters of prominent Canadian families. On 6 Feb. 1664, he married Catherine-Gertrude, 15-year-old daughter of Guillaume Couillard de Lespinay and Guillemette Hébert, a daughter of Louis Hébert. She died that same year, shortly after giving birth to a son. His second wife, Marie-Louise Juchereau de La Ferté, was the daughter of Jean Juchereau de La Ferté and Marie Giffard. Their marriage was celebrated on 10 Jan. 1668, and she died in La Rochelle on 7 March 1678, at the age of 26. On 11 Aug. 1680, La Chesnaye took his third wife, Marie-Angélique, 19-year-old daughter of Pierre Denys de La Ronde and Catherine Leneuf. She died in Quebec on 8 Nov. 1713. Eleven of the 18 children born of these marriages lived to adulthood. Two of the six daughters became nuns at the Quebec Hôtel-Dieu and the four others married officers of the sword and the robe in Canada and Île Royale. Of the five sons only one, François, the seigneur of Maur and of Mille-Vaches, appears to have shown any great aptitude for business. Two of his brothers, Charles and Louis, entered the army: the former in France, where he was killed between 1690 and 1693; the latter in Canada, where he joined the colonial regular troops. Pierre, known as the Sieur de Gaspé, appears to have spent his life on his seigneuries and to have devoted himself to agriculture. He was the great-grandfather of Philippe-Joseph Aubert de Gaspé, the author of *Les Anciens Canadiens*. Few details are known of the career of Louis, Sieur Duforillon, seigneur and merchant, who died in France probably in 1720.

Settling the estate proved to be a matter of extreme complexity and the question finally had to be referred to the Conseil Supérieur in 1708. La Chesnaye's fortune, according to Claude de Ramezay, his brother-in-law, had once amounted to 800,000 *livres*. His assets at his death consisted of his Quebec house, his seigneuries, 43,000 *livres* of merchandise, and approximately 282,000 *livres* of *rentes* and accounts receivable, of which 200,000 *livres* had to be written off as bad debt. Liabilities totalled 420,000 *livres*. In 1700, to simplify the settlement of the estate, La Chesnaye had donated 24,500 *livres* in *rentes* and landed property to each of his three sons from his second marriage. This amount was increased to 30,000 *livres* in 1708 and it then became the turn of the creditors to salvage what they could from the balance of the estate. The sale of La Chesnaye's last seigneuries in 1709 helped to settle some of the debts, but most of the claims made against the estate, which was in any case devolved by 1760, appear never to have been paid.

In its essentials, the career of Charles Aubert de La Chesnaye closely resembles that of the pious and austere bourgeois of 17th-century France. Some historians have pointed out that the deeply Catholic society of the *ancien régime* never fully approved of the bourgeois way of life that was based on profit and illegitimate gain. The bourgeois, in an effort to dissipate these misgivings and win acceptance, used part of their money to make bequests and donations to churches and religious communities. The case of La Chesnaye seems to corroborate this thesis. He was a member of the Congregation of the Virgin Mary and a generous benefactor of religious communities and charitable institutions. He was opposed to the sale of brandy to the Indians. Following the great fire which ravaged Quebec in 1682 he made generous loans to help fellow Canadians rebuild their homes.

In his private life La Chesnaye seems to have practised the austerity that was encouraged by the church in New France. The most useful document on this aspect of his personality is the inventory of his belongings that was made following his death. It shows that his house, despite its impressive proportions, was functionally furnished – in one room hung curtains made from old tablecloths – and that his wardrobe was simple. He usually seems to have dressed in a pair of red or grey flannel trousers, a jacket and jerkin made of serge, and an old beaver hat. His only concessions to luxury were a wig and five shirts trimmed with lace. The inventory also tells us something of his taste in reading. All but three of the 35 books he owned dealt with religious themes. Among the latter were the works of Saint François de Sales, an important figure of the French religious revival of the early 17th century.

La Chesnaye, however, was not satisfied with his bourgeois status. From an early date, like many wealthy and ambitious members of the French third estate, he was strongly attracted to the nobility. Born plain Charles Aubert, he soon added de La Chesnaye to his name. This quest for noble status might also help to explain his eagerness to acquire seigneuries. It is doubtful that he was thinking only of economic return when he spent large sums to develop land, for the same amount invested in the fur trade and the fisheries would have enabled him to net a higher profit. He may also have been thinking of the social prestige which the ownership of fine estates alone could confer.

The religious side of La Chesnaye's personality and his efforts to enter the ranks of the nobility should not be allowed to obscure the fact that the driving force in his career had been the spirit of gain and a love of risk. Often systematically, at times recklessly, he reinvested his capital, occasionally in large amounts, in productive or speculative ventures in order to realize still greater profits. His house on Rue du Sault-au-Matelot became the seat of an economic empire that extended in all directions and controlled the material resources of New France as well as the lives of a great number of habitants who had mortgaged their properties in return for cash loans. With money, in other words, came power, the quest for which cannot be discounted as a factor in La Chesnaye's career.

YVES F. ZOLTVANY

Further reading

Louis Beaudet, *Québec: ses monuments anciens et modernes* ... (Québec, 1973).

E. H. Borins, "La Compagnie du Nord, 1682–1700" (MA thesis, McGill Univ., Montreal, 1968).

J. F. Bosher, *Business and religion in the age of New France, 1600–1760: twenty-two studies* (Toronto, 1994).

Canadian Centenary Series (19v., Toronto, 1955–88), 3 (W. J. Eccles, *Canada under Louis XIV, 1663–1701*, 1964).

Guy Frégault, "La Compagnie de la Colonie," *Revue de l'université d'Ottawa*, 30 (1960): 5–29, 127–49.

J. S. Pritchard, *In search of empire: the French in the Americas, 1670–1730* (Cambridge, Eng., and New York, 2004).

FRANÇOIS HAZEUR,

prominent Quebec merchant and entrepreneur, seigneur, member of the Compagnie du Nord and the Compagnie de la Colonie, councillor in the Conseil Supérieur; b. in France, *c.* 1638; d. in Quebec, 28 June 1708.

The son of François Hazeur, a bourgeois of Brouage, and Marie Proust, he immigrated to Canada in the late 1660s with two brothers, Jean-François, Sieur de Petit-Marais, and Léonard, Sieur Des Ormeaux, and two sisters, Madeleine and Marie-Anne. They were joined by their mother and younger sister, Jeanne-Louise, following the death of their father about 1672. Jean-François and Léonard went into commerce. Of the three sisters, Jeanne-Louise and Madeleine became nuns at the Hôtel-Dieu of Quebec, and Marie-Anne married Jean Sébille, a Quebec merchant.

François took up residence in Quebec where, on 21 Nov. 1672, he married Anne Soumande, daughter of the merchant Pierre Soumande and Simone Côté. His business relations included the La Rochelle merchants Jean Gitton and Jean Grignon, Philippe Gaultier de Comporté, and his father-in-law. It may have been with their support that he opened a store in Quebec, which soon became a flourishing enterprise, and that he began to engage in the fur trade. By the early 1680s, Hazeur had become a prominent member of the Canadian business community. He was particularly active in the fur trade, equipping numerous canoes for the west and purchasing fur-trading licences (*congés*) from the original grantees. When the Compagnie du Nord was formed in 1682 for the purpose of exploiting the Hudson Bay trade, Hazeur lost no time in joining its ranks. His investment of 17,521 *livres* in 1691 was the fourth in importance, after those of the Compagnie de la Ferme, Charles Aubert de La Chesnaye, and Jacques Le Ber.

In 1688 and 1689, Hazeur began to diversify his economic activities. He formed a partnership with Soumande and Grignon which acquired control of the seigneury of Malbaie, a thickly wooded area containing many types of timber suitable for naval construction. Under the management of the three partners, the seigneury soon became the chief Canadian centre of the lumber industry. Two sawmills were built on the site, sheds and buildings put up, roads opened, and 25 to 30 workers employed in the enterprise. In 1689 Hazeur reported that the seigneury could produce annually 30,000 feet of plank, 2,000 feet of sheathing, and up to 100 masts.

Unfortunately the enterprise did not prosper, although two carpenters sent from France in 1687 had pronounced the wood to be of good quality. In 1692, Hazeur stated that he and his partners had spent 85,000 *livres* to date and recovered only a small part of their investment. Many factors had caused this state of affairs. In the spring of 1690 flooding had severely damaged the installations, and further destruction had been wrought in the fall of that year by the English expedition which was on its way to attack Quebec. The greatest handicap of all, however, appears to have been a lack of adequate transportation facilities, which prevented the partners from making sizable shipments to France. As a result, wood which had been cut for three years was still in storage and wasting away for want of a market. To correct the situation, Hazeur asked the king to place one or two of his large flutes (ships) at the partners' disposal every year; failure to do this, he warned, would probably compel them to abandon the venture.

By the late 1690s, Hazeur's interests had shifted from lumbering to other areas of the economy. On 20 Sept. 1697, he and Denis Riverin were granted the seigneury of Anse-de-l'Étang, in the lower St Lawrence, where they planned to exploit a slate quarry. Neither man, however, took an active interest in the development of this seigneury; they had become too involved in other projects. On 16 Feb. 1701, Hazeur had formed a partnership with Charles Denys de Vitré and Pierre Peire to engage in the porpoise fisheries in the section of the St Lawrence facing Rivière Ouelle and Kamouraska. The crown granted them a five-year monopoly as well as an annual gratuity of 550 *livres*. Following the death of Vitré on 9 Jan. 1703, the two surviving partners received additional support in the form of fishing equipment and in 1705 their monopoly was renewed for 15 years. This enterprise, however, met with the same ill fortune as Hazeur's venture into lumbering. By 1704, he and Peire had incurred expenses of 50,000 *livres*, and two years later their debts had risen to 60,000 *livres*. In 1707, they were in serious difficulty. Production was down to 40 barrels of oil and the minister informed Hazeur that the product was defective and overpriced.

From 1705, Hazeur also had fishing interests in Newfoundland. In that year he was granted the seigneury of Portachoix on the northwestern shore of the island and he entered into a partnership with a habitant named Pierre Constantin who agreed to settle there to hunt and fish. How this enterprise fared financially is not known but it appears never to have been more than a minor operation.

Hazeur had also retained important interests in the fur trade. On 22 Oct. 1693, he formed an association with La Chesnaye, Charles Macard, Jean Le Picard, François Viennay-Pachot and Jean Gobin, which acquired the lease of the Tadoussac trade from a Paris bourgeois named Jean-François Chalmette. In 1700, the ownership of the Tadoussac domain passed to the newly formed Compagnie de la Colonie of which Hazeur had become a shareholder. Soon afterwards, the company leased it to Hazeur and Riverin for a period of eight years at 12,700 *livres* per year. Hazeur made a substantial effort to restore the trade of this region which had been stagnating for many years before. Unfortunately, economic conditions in the early 18th century did not lend themselves to such an operation. The beaver trade was severely depressed, and the hazards facing navigation as a result of the outbreak of the War of the Spanish Succession were causing a sizable increase in the price of trade goods. By 1708, Hazeur had lost between 40,000 and 50,000 *livres* in the Tadoussac trade and his sons claimed that this was the principal cause of his financial ruin.

The only enterprise which apparently showed a steady profit during all these years and which probably was the source of capital for most of Hazeur's other undertakings was his Quebec store. His customers, like those of La Chesnaye, came from every walk of life and were scattered over the whole colony. In May and June 1695, 13 recognizances, representing a total sum of 20,202 *livres*, to cover important credit transactions were passed before the Montreal notary Bénigne Basset alone. In February 1708, it had become necessary for Hazeur to appoint a manager, Pierre Normandin, to look after his affairs in Montreal, Trois-Rivières, Batiscan, and Champlain.

Meantime, Hazeur had become a respected and prominent member of Canadian society. His house on the Place Royale in Lower Town was reportedly the finest in Quebec. He was much esteemed by the religious orders for his frequent acts of generosity and also by Governor Louis de Buade, Comte de Frontenac et de Palluau, who, on his deathbed, named him and Charles de Monseignat co-executors of his last will and testament. In 1703, Hazeur was appointed to the Conseil Supérieur in place of the deceased La Chesnaye and he acquitted himself very well of his new duties. According to Jacques Raudot, Hazeur had worked hard to familiarize himself with the functions of his office and he soon became the equal of the more experienced councillors.

Hazeur died insolvent on 28 June 1708, "missed by everyone because of his merit, his virtue, and his uprightness," according to Philippe de Rigaud de Vaudreuil and Raudot. He was survived by his second wife, Élisabeth Barbe, the daughter of Sylvain Barbe, a bailiff of the Châtelet de Paris, and Jeanne Girardin, whom he had married in Quebec on 16 Jan. 1696, four years after the death of his first wife, and by five of 13 children, all of them born of his first marriage. These included Jean-François, lawyer in the *parlement* of Paris, Joseph-Thierry, priest of the parish of Saint-François on Île d'Orléans and subsequently a member of the chapter of Quebec, and Pierre, who became known as Canon Hazeur de L'Orme. He was appointed parish priest of Champlain in 1707 and, like his brother before him, became a member of the chapter of Quebec in 1722. Marie-Anne-Ursule, the sole surviving daughter, married the king's surgeon Michel Sarrazin.

For over 30 years François Hazeur had been one of New France's most important and enterprising businessmen and he might have amassed considerable wealth had it not been for his disastrous ventures into lumbering, fishing, and the Tadoussac trade. His failure in these areas should not be imputed primarily to any personal shortcomings but to the unfavourable economic conditions of the period.

YVES F. ZOLTVANY

Further reading

J. F. Bosher, *Business and religion in the age of New France, 1600–1760: twenty-two studies* (Toronto, 1994).

P.-G. R[oy], "Notes sur François Hazeur," *Bulletin des recherches historiques* (Lévis, Qué.), 32 (1926): 705–11.

E. H. Borins, "La Compagnie du Nord, 1682–1700" (MA thesis, McGill Univ., Montreal, 1968).

CHARLOTTE-FRANÇOISE JUCHEREAU DE SAINT-DENIS, known as Comtesse de Saint-Laurent (Viennay-Pachot; Dauphin de La Forest),

daughter of Nicolas Juchereau de Saint-Denis and Marie-Thérèse Giffard; baptized 4 Feb. 1660 at Quebec; d. 28 Dec. 1732 at Quebec and buried on 30 December.

On 27 Feb. 1702 Charlotte-Françoise, acting with the king's approval, purchased for the sum of 41,333 *livres* in French currency the Île d'Orléans, which had been sold by Bishop François de Laval in 1675 to François Berthelot, king's secretary. When he had been ennobled, Berthelot had managed to have the island raised to the countship of Saint-Laurent. When she had acquired possession of the island, Charlotte-Françoise Juchereau took the title of countess, which she retained after her marriage with François Dauphin de La Forest. She arranged for her eldest son, born a Pachot by her first marriage, to bear the title also. Having been unable to meet her obligations to Berthelot, however, she had to engage in long legal proceedings, both in Canada and in France, to which she made several trips, and she proved to be a stubborn litigant. Her long struggle in the courts lasted from 1704 to 1713. Having exhausted legal means without success, she abandoned her proceedings only when the king ordered her explicitly to do so, and to return to Canada. The case, which was finally decided in Berthelot's favour, seems to have contributed to the dismissal of François-Madeleine-Fortuné Ruette d'Auteuil de Monceaux, the countess's brother-in-law, who had taken up her defence against Jacques Raudot.

A large number of notarial acts drawn up between 1698 and 1704 show that Charlotte-Françoise Juchereau was an energetic and enterprising businesswoman. Having obtained separate maintenance from La Forest in 1702, with his authorization in due form to act on his behalf, she continued to carry out transactions of all kinds (sales, purchases, loans, borrowings, ship charters, building contracts) in her own name and through straw men; the sums involved were at times considerable. Meanwhile she kept a careful watch over her children's interests. Nevertheless, she was sometimes in financial straits: in 1704, to honour a debt she owed Pierre Le Moyne d'Iberville et d'Ardillières, she had to sell all her personal goods located on her properties on Île d'Orléans; in 1705 she sold to René Lepage, the seigneur of Rimouski, her fief on the Métis River, which she had inherited from her first husband.

On 17 Dec. 1680, she had married at Beauport François Viennay-Pachot, a seigneur and businessman left a widower by the death of Jeanne Avamy; Charlotte-Françoise bore him 16 children. On 11 Nov. 1702 she was married again, this time to Captain Dauphin de La Forest.

Charlotte-Françoise earned for herself an unflattering reputation: Jérôme Phélypeaux, Comte de Pontchartrain et de Maurepas, considered her a "dangerous woman," whereas Raudot called her a "haughty and capricious" merchant who thought that as a countess she could do anything she wished. "People might perhaps have forgiven her vanity and her usurping of the title of countess," he added, "if she had at least paid her bills."

ANTONIO DROLET

Further reading

Benoît Grenier, *Seigneurs campagnards de la Nouvelle France: présence seigneuriale et sociabilité rurale dans la vallée du Saint-Laurent à l'époque préindustrielle* (Rennes, France, 2007).

Jan Noel, "'Nagging wife' revisited: women and the fur trade in New France," *French Colonial History* (East Lansing, Mich.), 7 (2006): 45–60; "New France: les femmes favorisées," *Atlantis* (Halifax), 6 (Spring 1980–81), no.2: 80–98.

Angel Kwolek-Folland, *Incorporating women: a history of women and business in the United States* (New York, 1998).

FRANÇOIS HAVY,

merchant and entrepreneur; baptized 5 March 1703 at Beuzevillette near Bolbec, France; d. at Bordeaux on 12 Dec. 1766.

François Havy, a Huguenot, first came to Canada in 1730 as supercargo aboard the *Louis Dauphin*, a ship owned by the newly formed Robert Dugard et Cie of Rouen, France. From Quebec, the *Louis Dauphin* carried a cargo of Canadian produce and forest products to Martinique and then sailed to its home port of Le Havre with a cargo of sugar. The following year, the ship again visited Quebec, returning directly to Le Havre. These two trial voyages convinced Dugard et Cie that the Canada trade was sufficiently profitable to merit long-term investment. Thus when Havy returned to Quebec for the third time in 1732, he came as a permanent factor to establish a warehouse and office. He and his assistant and cousin, Jean Lefebvre, found quarters on Rue Saint-Pierre in the merchant district of Lower Town. In 1735 they rented part of the house of Louis Fornel on the adjacent market square and from there conducted their business for more than 20 years.

François Havy and Jean Lefebvre formed a partnership in 1734 in which Havy was the senior. It is difficult to separate their activities. As

Lefebvre wrote to a business correspondent, "When our Sieur Havy or myself write you, our letters are in common. Our signatures show that there is no difference of opinion between us." Havy and Lefebvre conducted some business for their own account as permitted by the custom of the time, but they were still the employees of Dugard et Cie, which paid them salary, board, and lodging. Their position in the merchant community depended primarily upon the volume of trade they managed for the company. The trial cargoes had been small; but from 1732 to 1743 annual sales at Quebec totalled around 200,000 *livres*, except for 1740 and 1741 when receipts rose to well over 300,000 *livres*. Comparison of these figures with the rough estimates of the annual value of French imports sold in Canada prepared by the intendant reveals the relative importance of the trade Havy managed. From 1733 on it usually accounted for an eighth or a tenth of the colony's import trade, climbing to a sixth in 1738, a seventh in 1740, and a fifth in 1741. Not surprisingly, François Havy was one of the acknowledged "principal traders" of Quebec City, who in 1740 numbered only 17.

From the time of establishing the Quebec factory, Havy handled 13 company cargoes. The merchants' busy season was framed by the arrival and departure of ships from France, the West Indies, and Louisbourg, Île Royale (Cape Breton Island). Arrivals began in July and continued steadily through October. No matter how late the ships arrived, with rare exception they departed in November. When the ships dropped anchor before Quebec, they delivered their cargoes to small lightering craft. Bales, cases, and barrels for Havy's and Lefebvre's warehouse were left on the beach to be picked up by carters. Havy and Lefebvre supervised this trans-shipment, ascertained the condition of the merchandise, and declared imports of Brazil tobacco, wine, and spirits.

When the harbour was filled with ships unloading, Havy and the other merchants alerted their Montreal correspondents. The inland merchants soon arrived; money and merchandise began to change hands; and in a classic manner prices would find their level in response to the market. Rapidly, Havy and Lefebvre's warehouse began to fill with return cargo, the most important item being fur. The practical necessity of the Canadian trader's selling his furs in bales to one buyer, rather than hawking individual skins, and his need to arrange terms of credit for his purchases made it desirable that he be able to satisfy all his needs at one warehouse. Like the modern department store, Havy and Lefebvre and their competitors therefore each offered a wide assortment of merchandise. Those who could not provide this facility had to accept a smaller profit on their sales.

Bills of exchange were another important export. A large number of these were given to Canadian traders in exchange for beaver pelts by the Compagnie des Indes, which held a monopoly on their export. These bills thus represented purchasing power gained in return for a commodity export. Other bills of exchange drawn on the French government and received in exchange for Canadian paper money were employed because Canada could not provide sufficient exports to balance its foreign trade. As their continued use was a measure of Canadian economic underdevelopment, it is significant that in the 1730s and 1740s the proportion of Havy and Lefebvre's return cargoes constituted by bills of exchange declined from between 37 and 44 per cent in the years 1730–32 to 4 to 13 per cent in 1741–43. As the Canadian economy reacted favourably to a long era of peace, the quantity and range of export items were increasing.

Receiving and sending cargoes imposed a considerable burden on the Quebec factors. Goods were distributed and collected. Crew rolls were registered with the admiralty and permits and passports obtained for outgoing ships. The enormous bulk of invoices, bills of lading, accounts, and letters were prepared in triplicate. When the last ships had left, thousands of entries in daybooks had to be transferred meticulously to the ledger and then condensed into current accounts to be sent to all business correspondents. Final disposal of the cargo and the time-consuming paperwork meant that accounts were not closed until the following summer. But by the middle of November the feverish activity was over. "I wish it was never autumn at Quebec," an exhausted François Havy complained to a friend, "and I would be in better health."

Havy and Lefebvre also traded with Louisbourg, where Dugard et Cie maintained permanent relations with Léon Fautoux, a commission agent. The soldiers and fishermen of Louisbourg depended to a considerable extent upon Canadian provisions, and most company ships stopped at the fortified harbour on their return voyages from Quebec to France. Canadian cargoes of wood and grain were also suitable for the West Indian market when increased in value by dried cod available at Louisbourg. The sugar island trade remained marginal, however, as

Canada could surrender its major export of fur only in exchange for French manufactures to supply the fur trade and could neither absorb a large quantity of Caribbean produce nor provide a sufficiently large and dependable supply of provisions and forest products in return. Thus of the 68 voyages to Canada and the West Indies undertaken by the ships of Dugard et Cie between 1730 and 1755, only ten were triangular.

Company activities in Canada under Havy's direction also included shipbuilding. Between 1736 and 1745 Havy and Lefebvre launched six ships for the company having a combined value of almost 300,000 *livres*. The *Alcion* was begun in 1734, the year after a revised system of royal bounties for Canadian-built ships was established. Although bounties could not fully offset the high cost of labour in an underpopulated country, the Rouen company persevered because ships were yet another export, a means of repatriating profits made in Canada. Thus Intendant Gilles Hocquart was correct in interpreting Havy's building of so many ships as "certain proof that he found profit in the first." Havy and Lefebvre also built many smaller ships for their exploitation of sealing concessions on the north shore of the St Lawrence and Labrador, enterprises apparently undertaken on their own account.

From 1737 to 1748 they held a lease on a post at Mingan, the value of the rent being deducted annually from debts owed them by the post's owner, Charles Jolliet d'Anticosti. In 1737 they also began exploiting a post at Chateau Bay on the Strait of Belle Isle for a one-third share along with Louis Fornel and the post's concessionaire, Louis Bazil. Havy and Lefebvre appear to have maintained an interest in Chateau Bay until 1754, when the post's ship and sealing equipment, described as belonging to them, were sold at public auction at Quebec. In 1740 Havy and Lefebvre also sublet a two-thirds interest in the concession of Grand Saint-Modet. The original lease ended in 1747, but they apparently sent a ship to the post in 1758, their last known sealing venture.

In 1745 war between France and Great Britain reached the Gulf of St Lawrence. In July Abel Olivier, captain of a Dugard et Cie schooner, sent word to Quebec that Louisbourg had fallen to the Anglo-Americans. The Quebec merchants were cut off from the gulf and their sealing stations; buildings, equipment, and barrels of oil were a total loss. Although Louis Bazil had made no financial contribution to the post at Chateau Bay, Havy and Lefebvre and Fornel had invested over 100,000 *livres*. The enterprise had returned less than two-thirds of this investment.

After 1748 the sealing industry quickly recuperated, unlike the trade with Dugard et Cie. Because of the near famine in Canada resulting from a succession of crop failures, and the derangement of the fur trade and of ocean traffic by the war, Robert Dugard sent a much smaller cargo to Canada in 1744. The following year he sent nothing, English control of the Atlantic being complete. Havy decided to launch the *Astrée*, which had lain on the stocks for several years because of poor economic conditions, and to send it to Le Havre laden with seal oil and furs for which there was no other transportation.

Sales plummeted to about 100,000 *livres* in 1744 and 1745 and then to 19,000 in 1746 and 32,000 in 1747. After 1744 the company sent none of its own ships to Quebec although small amounts of cargo were sent aboard those of La Rochelle. Tempest and war combined to destroy most of the company fleet. In 1743, for instance, the *Alcion* and the *Louis Dauphin* sank in storms while returning from the West Indies, and by 1747 five more ships were lost or captured. The company was on its knees, and in October 1747 Havy and Lefebvre received word that it would cease all its trade with Canada. Since 1730 Havy had handled incoming and outgoing cargoes for his Rouen employers valued at almost 6,000,000 *livres*.

Havy and Lefebvre still had their interest in the Labrador sealing industry. Their associate Louis Fornel had died on 30 May 1745, but they maintained a close business relationship with his widow, Marie-Anne Barbel. Before the war intervened, Fornel had explored the Labrador coast beyond Chateau Bay and had discovered and laid claim to an excellent site for sealing and trade, the Baie des Esquimaux (probably Hamilton Inlet), which he named Baie Saint-Louis. With access to the coast again free, Widow Fornel claimed the concession of the post for herself and her associates, Havy and Lefebvre. On 20 Sept. 1749 they were given the concession for 12 years. At the same time, under the name Veuve Fornel et Cie, they also received a six-year lease on the scattered trading posts east of Quebec and north of the St Lawrence known collectively as the King's Posts. In 1755 they relinquished the lease, fearing war losses. They were the last lessees under the old régime.

Havy's interest in the import-export trade also remained. With other Quebec City merchants, he and Lefebvre owned a few small ships which they sent to Martinique. As general commission agents, they handled cargoes for Garisson of Bordeaux and Gardère of Bayonne. In 1750 the

Astrée stopped at Quebec on its way to Martinique, leaving some cargo in their care. For a few years in the 1750s they owned a ship named the *Parfaite Union* in company with Robert Dugard and a fourth associate, probably Jean-François Jacquelin of Quebec.

François Havy, as a Huguenot, was free neither to marry in the colony nor to bring a family to it; though prosperous he could not think of remaining in Canada permanently. The occasion of his final departure was yet another war. Havy and Lefebvre apparently decided that under hazardous but potentially profitable war-time conditions, one of them should return to France to supervise their export of merchandise to Canada and to prepare for eventual transfer of their business from the colony. In January 1756 Havy arrived at La Rochelle, having "escaped the clutches of the English." The following year he visited Rouen to accelerate the closing of his accounts with Dugard et Cie and then returned to La Rochelle, where in 1758 he declared himself resolved to stay. But trade there was at a standstill, the English once again having control of the sea route to Canada.

It was probably in 1758 that Havy married for the first time. His wife was of the François family of Bordeaux, said to be "a family both Rich and highly Respectable." In January 1759 their first child was born. But domestic happiness came too late for François Havy. The British conquest of Quebec in September 1759 destroyed the business he had built up over 30 years. Considerable assets in sealing stations and mortgages on houses in Quebec were lost. A fortune in Canadian paper money and bills of exchange was rendered almost worthless by governmental repudiation. Not without cause did he think, "The life of man is short and still it is naught but sorrow and labour."

For the last six months of 1760 Havy suffered from a severe illness. When he had sufficiently recovered, he was told of the accidental death of Jean Lefebvre some months before. He had lost his fortune, his associate and oldest friend, and his health. He was involved in more than a dozen bankruptcies. The heirs of his dead partner and other creditors were hounding him. In 1762 or 1763 the Havys moved to Bordeaux, probably to be near Mme Havy's family. In the autumn of 1766 François Havy died at Bordeaux.

The connection between the old firm of Havy and Lefebvre and Canada did not end with the conquest. In their later years at Quebec, Havy and

Lefebvre had been joined by another, younger, cousin, François Lévesque. It was Lévesque who settled their affairs at Quebec, and he remained in Canada to establish his own commerce under the British flag.

In 1763 the commission of the Châtelet acquitted François Havy of any malversation in his furnishings to the king in Canada. He had been an honest merchant. Backed by Rouen businessmen of expansive ideas, he and his partner were at the forefront of the Canadian economic advance. Could a Protestant have lived his life in New France, perhaps Havy would have been absorbed into the Canadian community, bringing with him mercantile knowledge and attitudes rare in the colony and precious in the aftermath of conquest.

François Havy's career in Canada and his relation to the colony might best be summarized by two sentences drawn from his own correspondence. "There is no metropolitan trader who worked as hard as I," he once wrote to Robert Dugard. Again, in one of his last letters to a Canadian, he expressed the privation he felt at his separation from New France: "I have always loved your Country and its people."

DALE MIQUELON

Further reading

Les Huguenots et l'Atlantique, sous la dir. de Mickaël Augeron *et al.* (1v. to date, Paris, 2009–).

J. F. Bosher, *Business and religion in the age of New France, 1600–1760: twenty-two studies* (Toronto, 1994).

J. E. Igartua, "The merchants and *négociants* of Montreal, 1750–1775: a study in socio-economic history" (PHD thesis, Mich. State Univ., East Lansing, 1974).

Dale Miquelon, *Dugard of Rouen: French trade to Canada and the West Indies, 1729–1770* (Montreal, 1978).

J. S. Pritchard, *In search of empire: the French in the Americas, 1670–1730* (Cambridge, Eng., and New York, 2004).

MARIE-ANNE BARBEL (Fornel),

merchant and entrepreneur; b. 26 Aug. 1704 at Quebec,
daughter of Jacques Barbel and Marie-Anne Le Picard;
m. 31 Dec. 1723 Louis Fornel; seven of their 14 children
survived infancy; d. 16 Nov. 1793 at Quebec.

Marie-Anne Barbel's father had risen swiftly from garrison sergeant of Quebec to office-holder, but he ended his life overwhelmed by debts. Jacques Barbel was an upstart, something not rare in the colony, and at the time of Marie-Anne's marriage his career was in the ascendant. The Fornel family, into which she married, was more stable; in the marriage contract signed by the governor and the intendant, both her prospective husband and his father are designated merchants and bourgeois of Quebec. Her future brother-in-law, Joachim Fornel, was soon to be named a canon of the Quebec cathedral chapter.

The life of Marie-Anne Barbel is of historical interest in part because of what it reveals of the role of women in the merchant class. Her business knowledge and her continuation in trade after her husband's death were typical. Although the business role of a wife under the custom of Paris is difficult to trace, Louis Fornel's delegation to Marie-Anne on 15 May 1743 of full power of attorney over his affairs during his absence on the Labrador coast demonstrates that she was informed of his activities and considered capable of business decisions. Nevertheless, in the period of her marriage, the bearing and raising of children and the managing of her household would have been the focus of her life. This emphasis changed in 1745 when her husband died.

The couple's "community of property" was not dissolved after Louis Fornel's death, his rights devolving instead upon his heirs. Mme Fornel administered this property, carrying on the family business and extending it in size and in new directions. She continued to enjoy friendship and close business relations with François Havy and Jean Lefebvre, two Huguenot merchants who had been her husband's partners in several enterprises, including the Labrador sealing industry. She was unable to continue exploitation of their sealing station at Chateau Bay, which after the War of the Austrian Succession was granted to Jean-François Gaultier, but she had more success with Baie des Esquimaux (Hamilton Inlet), a site Fornel had discovered in 1743 and renamed Baie Saint-Louis. At the time of his death he had been petitioning for a monopoly of its trade. Intendant Gilles Hocquart planned instead to unite it with the Tadoussac trading posts (sometimes called the king's posts), so that it would not adversely affect their business; however, his successor, François Bigot, granted the Baie Saint-Louis monopoly to Mme Fornel on 20 Sept. 1749. He noted that she would be developing it in company with Havy and Lefebvre, her share being only one-third. Bigot may have made the grant as part of a general strategy of thwarting his predecessor's clients, in this case the farmer of the Tadoussac trading posts, François-Étienne Cugnet, for Cugnet's lease on them was not renewed. Instead they too were leased to Mme Fornel in 1749. "Widow Fornel has a company," Bigot explained to the minister of Marine, "and nothing whatever will be lacking at the post of Tadoussac and ... the king will be well paid each year." Circumstantial evidence suggests that Havy and Lefebvre were her active partners in this venture as well, although they remained in the background, perhaps because Governor Jacques-Pierre de Taffanel de La Jonquière, Marquis de La Jonquiere, abhorred Protestants.

As her husband had done before her, Mme Fornel invested part of her profits in the relative security of real estate. The most original venture of her career was the establishment of a pottery to meet the demand arising from wartime shortages. As Havy and Lefebvre explained in a letter of 1746, "no earthenware is coming from France and it appears that as long as the war lasts it will be the same, but the country has a resource in Mademoiselle Fornel who has established its manufacture. She has a very good craftsman and her earth proves good." The pottery, finished with lead and copper glazes, was immediately successful and was even taken for the French product. The shop remained in operation until at least 1752. In that year François Jacquet signed a three-year contract with her which is revealing of the conditions of labour at the time: he was to be paid on a piece-work basis, she would provide stove wood and lighting, and, curiously, each was to hire a man and provide his food and wages. Jacquet worked in the "Briqueterie," a dilapidated building in the Lower Town.

The war of the conquest hastened Marie-Anne Fornel's withdrawal from trade. Her north shore and Labrador posts were liabilities in war-time. She made no effort to renew the lease on the Tadoussac trading posts which expired in 1755, and it is doubtful whether she was still operating at Baie Saint-Louis when her monopoly expired in 1761. Her numerous buildings in Quebec's Lower Town were destroyed in the bombardment of the city in 1759, and nothing more is heard of the pottery. In 1764 she and the Fornel heirs agreed to settle accounts with the Havy and Lefebvre heirs by paying them the sum of 12,000 *livres*, the last payment being made in 1769. An inventory of the Fornels' community property made the following year indicates a history of solid bourgeois comfort, but also considerable indebtedness resulting from wartime reversals. Between 1765 and 1771 Mme Fornel laboured to pay her debts, rebuild many of her houses, and consolidate her assets. In 1777 the Fornel property was divided among the heirs, and Mme Fornel entered into the last phase of her life, that of retirement, which lasted until her death in 1793.

DALE MIQUELON

Further reading

Lilianne Plamondon, "A businesswoman in New France: Marie-Anne Barbel, the widow Fornel," in *Rethinking Canada: the promise of women's history*, ed. Veronica Strong-Boag and A. C. Feldman (Toronto, 1986), 45–58.

Jan Noel, "N'être plus la déléguée de personne: une réévaluation du rôle des femmes dans le commerce en Nouvelle-France," *Revue d'histoire de l'Amérique française* (Montréal), 63 (2009–10): 209–41; "New France: les femmes favorisées," *Atlantis* (Halifax) 6 (1980–81), no.2: 80–98.

K. A. Young, *Kin, commerce, community: merchants in the port of Quebec, 1717–1745* (New York, 1995).

Benoît Grenier, *Seigneurs campagnards de la Nouvelle France: présence seigneuriale et sociabilité rurale dans la vallée du Saint-Laurent à l'époque préindustrielle* (Rennes, France, 2007).

JOSEPH-MICHEL CADET,

merchant butcher, businessman, and purveyor general to the French forces in Canada; b. 24 Dec. 1719 at Quebec, son of François-Joseph Cadet (Caddé), a merchant butcher, and Marie-Joseph Daveine (Davesne, Davenne); his paternal grandfather was a merchant butcher of Quebec and his great-grandfather was also one in Niort, France; d. 31 Jan. 1781 in Paris, France.

When Joseph-Michel Cadet was only four years old his widowed mother on 29 Nov. 1724 married Pierre-Joseph Bernard, a son of one of the secretaries of the minister of the Marine, Jean-Frederic Phélypeaux, Comte de Maurepas, and himself a scrivener in the Marine department, and a few years later she followed her husband to Rochefort, leaving Cadet, aged 12, to fend for himself, or so he later declared. At first he stayed with his maternal grandfather, Gabriel Daveine, with whom he afterwards recalled studying mathematics. He evidently had little formal education, for his letters are composed of more colloquial expressions and phonetic spelling than was usual for merchants and their clerks at the time, and in September 1732, before he was 13, he joined the crew of a merchant ship for a voyage to Île Saint-Jean (Prince Edward Island) and then went to work buying cattle for Augustin Cadet, his father's half-brother, a Quebec butcher.

Cadet's family relationships are worth recording to show the milieu in which he got his start as a Quebec businessman. His uncle, Michel-François Cadet, Augustin's brother, kept a shop at Quebec dealing in imported French fabrics at one time, but he was also a butcher like the rest of the family. Cadet's father's sister, Marie-Anne Cadet, married a master locksmith, Pierre Amiot, in 1714 and their son, Cadet's first cousin, Jean-Baptiste Amiot, became a successful importing merchant acting as the colonial agent of several French shipping merchants during the 1740s and 1750s. Another first cousin, Louise Cadet, Augustin's daughter, in 1755 married a Huguenot merchant, Joseph Rouffio, member of a business family of Montauban. The two uncles, Pierre Amiot and Augustin Cadet, were among the seven witnesses at Cadet's marriage on 10 Sept. 1742 to Angélique Fortier, daughter of Michel, a Montreal businessman. Another witness was a certain "Monsieur Duburon," probably Jean-Joseph Feré Duburon, an officer in the colonial regulars, whose daughter, Louise-Élisabeth, in 1738 married Denis Goguet, a La Rochelle merchant living at Quebec. After Goguet returned to La Rochelle, Cadet was one of the many Canadians who did business with him and in 1763 Goguet held over 323,000 *livres* in bills belonging to Cadet. Whether Cadet benefited by his mother's marriage to a scrivener in the Marine who died at Rochefort about 1737 as provost marshal, or by his sister Marie-Joseph's marriage (8 Sept. 1749) to a surgeon, Jean-Raymond Vignau, is not clear. His other relationships are enough to explain how he became a successful merchant butcher.

These relationships do not, however, account for Cadet's astonishing career as the last purveyor general to the French forces in Canada and a rich and powerful businessman. That career can only be explained by his ability to seize opportunities afforded by the two mid century wars which brought more and more French troops to Canada. Throughout the history of France, and indeed of most countries, vast fortunes have been made supplying the armed forces in wartime. The Bourbon governments contracted out the supplying business to syndicates of businessmen whose histories have not yet been written, and the general context of Cadet's career is not well understood. It is helpful to remember, however, that while he was making a business of army victualling in Canada many other men of a similar type were victualling other forces in the French empire. For example, under the name of Nicolas Perny, a front man, 13 French businessmen formed a company of purveyors general to the ministry of Marine and Colonies for six years beginning on 1 Jan. 1757. Among them were figures such as Pierre Escourre of Bordeaux, son of a mayor of Tournon, who also invested in slaving ventures to Angola, in the company supplying French army hospitals and other similar enterprises, and who married the daughter of a purveyor general to the navy at Martinique, Laurens-Alexandre Dahon. Other such men contracted to supply the navy with timber, cannon, anchors, and clothing. All had their fingers in many pies. This is the context in which Cadet's career must be studied for it makes little sense in the national history of Canada. In France there were hundreds of similar businessmen who failed in some cases, grew rich in others, or had ups and downs but managed, like Cadet, to marry their daughters into families of the minor nobility. Françoise Cadet married François Esprit de Vantelon, son of a king's councillor in the fiscal subdivision of Châtellerault, mayor and captain general of Châtellerault; Angélique Cadet married Jérôme Rossay, seigneur of Les Pallus, officer of the Regent of France, Philippe, Duc d'Orléans, municipal magistrate and militia captain of Châtellerault; one of Cadet's sons called himself by the sonorous name of Joseph Cadet Deschamps, seigneur of Mondon. How did their father, a mere colonial butcher, make all this possible?

According to what Cadet declared in 1761 during his interrogations in the Bastille, he had worked during the late 1730s for the official purveyor of meat to the crown at Quebec, Romain Dolbec, and had soon become an equal partner. In 1745, during the War of the Austrian Succession, he was asked by the intendant, Gilles Hocquart, to provide all the meat required by the crown and continued to do so until 1756. This activity was very profitable. Meanwhile he carried on with his own butchering business for a few years, but also ventured into other commodities, milling flour and selling it to ships' captains, buying ships' cargoes and re-selling them, and dealing in fish, fur, and general shipping. During the early 1750s he contracted with Michel Mahiet, Antoine Morin, Louis Michaud, and others to go out and gather the fish and fur at posts on the fief of Les Monts-Louis to which he had acquired the rights. He began to buy boats and even ships. In 1752, for instance, he and a partner, Nicolas Massot, sent a ship of about 140 tons, the *Joseph de Québec*, under Captain Maurice Simonin, to Martinique with a cargo of fish, timber, and oil to be sold and exchanged for a cargo of sugar for the port of Bordeaux. At Bordeaux the ship was fitted out for the journey to Louisbourg, Île Royale (Cape Breton Island), and Quebec in summer 1753 by Pierre Desclaux using a bottomry loan of 11,000 *livres* from David Gradis et Fils at 12 per cent interest. As Cadet acknowledged and as the busy files of his principal notary, Jean-Claude Panet, show, the War of the Austrian Succession gave Cadet profits and opportunities enough to become a general entrepreneur in the expansive post-war period. He imported large quantities of wine, brandy, and general merchandise from France, particularly in association with Barthélemy Martin and Jean-Baptiste-Tropez Martin and, in 1759, with Pierre Delannes and Jean-Jacques Gautier and a controller of the Marine, Jean de Villers.

The most successful businessmen in the French empire, then as always, were those who could do business with the government and obtain such official influence, offices, titles, privileges, honours, and mates for their children as money could buy. As early as 1754 Cadet wrote to the minister of Marine and Colonies offering to sign a contract as purveyor general to the crown in Canada; that is, to provision the royal stores at Quebec, Trois-Rivières, Montreal, and the outposts. He got no reply. Then, some time during the summer in 1755, he mentioned the proposal to an army officer with many business interests, Michel-Jean-Hugues Péan, adjutant at Quebec, who aroused the interest and support of the intendant, François Bigot. In October Bigot wrote to Versailles about Cadet's proposal and in July 1756 received the minister's permission to sign a contract for nine years beginning on 1 Jan. 1757. Cadet thus assumed responsibility for Canadian supplies that had hitherto been provided partly by smaller colonial contractors and partly by the French company of purveyors general working under the name of Claude Fort, whose contract expired on 31 Dec. 1756. Forty-two articles were drawn up in an official contract which Cadet and the intendant signed on 26 Oct. 1756.

Under the terms of this contract, Cadet was to give each soldier in the field a daily ration of two pounds of bread, a quarter of a pound of dried peas, and either a pound of beef or half a pound of bacon; and failing these rations he was to give cash instead. Soldiers in the town garrisons were to have one and one-half pounds of bread and a quarter of a pound each of dried peas and bacon. In winter, when fighting was usually suspended, Cadet normally paid the equivalent of these rations to the householders on whom the soldiers were quartered, and the rates were to be fixed by the intendant. This official contract concealed some secret contracts by which various officials and others were associated with the supply business. In the same month, October 1756, Cadet signed an agreement *sous seing privé* (binding but not recorded in notarial minutes) giving Péan a three-fifths share in the business, including one-fifth each for Intendant Bigot, Governor Pierre de Rigaud de Vaudreuil de Cavagnial, Marquis de Vaudreuil, and himself, or so Péan said, and he urged Cadet to keep this arrangement secret. About the same time, Cadet conceded another fifth share to be divided equally among three assistants: Jean Corpron, who kept the books at Quebec, and François Maurin and Louis Pennisseaut, who together managed a store at Montreal for supplying foodstuffs there and at the forts and posts beyond. This left Cadet with only one-fifth of the profits, but he recovered another fifth in spring 1759 when the aforementioned assistants withdrew from the association. Besides, he did not now lack opportunities for profitable contracts on the side. During 1757 and 1758 he was invited to supply Acadia and did so in association with Bigot's secretary, Joseph Brassard Deschenaux, and an army captain, Charles Deschamps de Boishébert.

Joseph-Michel Cadet was now enmeshed in one of those dubious mixtures of private and public enterprise so characteristic of Bourbon France, and how it ramified may be seen in glimpses of the lives of his associates. From 1 July 1755 to 11 June 1756, Pennisseaut and Péan were in a joint-stock trading company with the receiver general of finances for La Rochelle, Gratien Drouilhet, and the government store-keeper at Quebec, Pierre Claverie. Claverie, through his mother, Jeanne La Barthe, was first cousin to the government storekeeper at Montreal, Jean-Pierre La Barthe, who on 30 Oct. 1759 formed a business com-pany with Pennisseaut and Pennisseaut's relatives, Jacques-Joseph and Jean-Baptiste Lemoine Despins of Montreal. François Maurin had mean-while been in business with his brother-in-law, Pierre Landrière La-mouline, a chief scrivener for the Marine at Montreal, and we know, too, that Maurin was a cousin of several Huguenot merchants at Quebec, including Pierre Glemet and Jean-Mathieu and François Mounier, most of whom came from his own birth-place, Jarnac, on the Charente. Some of these, like Cadet himself, made large sums of money in the supply business during the Seven Years' War.

Cadet distinguished himself from the rest, however, by his heroic efforts to supply the colony with his own fleet of merchant ships not only in 1757 and 1758 but also in 1759 when most French shipping on the Atlantic had been stopped by the British navy and privateers. A full list of Cadet's ships would be difficult to establish because his shipping agents, especially Pierre Desclaux at Bordeaux and François Gazan and Joseph Aliés at La Rochelle, dispatched many consignments of goods to him in other men's ships. At one time or another during the three critical years, however, he bought more than two dozen ships in France and Canada, most of them late in 1758 when it was clear that no cargo space was to be had at any price for sending goods to Quebec the next spring. Many of the ships' officers and seamen were Canadian, a forgotten group in Quebec history: men such as Captain Jean Carbonnel of the *Venus* (200 tons), Captain Michel Voyer of the *Amitié* (130 tons), and Captain Joseph Massot, Second Officer André de Lange, and most of the 17-man crew of the *Magdeleine* (92 tons), a schooner which Cadet bought for 4,000 *livres* in May 1756 and lost to the enemy in April 1757. Perhaps half of Cadet's ships were wrecked or captured, but many others arrived safely at Quebec, notably a fleet of almost 20 ships under Jacques Kanon in May 1759. As Governor Vaudreuil wrote to Versailles on 7 Nov. 1759, "It is because of the help he [Cadet] had brought from France that the colony was saved for the king." We need not pretend that Cadet was entirely disinterested in order to appreciate the vigour, scale, daring, and success of his campaign to feed the starving colony.

The French government never acknowledged Cadet's achievements for at least three reasons, none of them worthy of a great nation. First, Cadet was more successful than the French navy in maintaining the transatlantic links on which so much depended. The French fleet was defeated again and again and soon abandoned normal patrolling of the imperial sea routes and even the French coasts in favour of the perennial project for invading England with a fleet of troop ships which, in this case, was destroyed at the Baie de Quiberon by Admiral Edward Hawke on 20 Nov. 1759. The ships would have been better employed in convoying merchant and troop ships, but the French authorities seemed incapable of organizing a convoy as efficient as Cadet's. Even the repatriation of the French officials and refugees after 1759 was largely done by British vessels. Mortified by its own failures, the French government was not in a frame of mind to recognize Cadet's successes. Secondly, once Quebec had been lost in September 1759 it was easy to ignore or to disparage Cadet's efforts to supply the colony and politically necessary to find scapegoats who could be blamed for the losses and failures. Cadet and other officials were natural scapegoats for the loss of Canada just as Jean Laborde was for the loss of Louisbourg and Thomas-Arthur Lally, Comte de Lally, and Joseph-François Dupleix were for the loss of French India, because they had made handsome profits in the ill-fated colonies. Here is a third reason why Cadet's achievements were not properly appreciated: he had garnered a fortune reckoned at several millions. The money was in property and bills of exchange and treasury notes deposited with Denis Goguet at La Rochelle; Barthélemy and Jean-Baptiste-Tropez Martin at Marseilles; Lanogenu and the firm of Veuve Courrejolles at Bayonne; and Pierre Desclaux, Jean-André Lamaletie, and Jean Dupuy Fils et Cie at Bordeaux; and when Cadet could do nothing more in Canada he went to France to settle his many debts and make the most of his fortune. Taken off at Quebec on a British ship, the *Adventure*, on 18 Oct. 1760, he landed at Brest on 26 November, reached Bordeaux 12 days later, where his family had been living since 1759, and arrived in Paris on 21 Jan. 1761; he was arrested four days later and imprisoned in the Bastille with most of his official colleagues from Canada.

Historians who take the ensuing trial at its face value have no difficulty in pronouncing Joseph-Michel Cadet, as the Châtelet criminal court did on 10 Dec. 1763, a monstrous criminal fortunate to get off with banishment from Paris for nine years and what amounted to a fine of six million *livres*. To make a national hero of Cadet would be uphill work as there are signs that in 1759 he was in close contact with the enemy for some dark purpose. He was never tried for that, however, and various facts and circumstances show that his case was not so simple as the Châtelet made it seem. Not all observers in Canada thought him a criminal. "I believe him to be the least guilty of all," wrote a prominent merchant, Francois Havy, on hearing of Cadet's arrest, "for he was only a tool that others made use of and he will perhaps be the only victim." The crown itself seemed to betray doubts when on 5 March 1764 it lifted Cadet's banishment and decided to release him from the Bastille and to reduce his fine by half. Whatever the significance of those decisions, French criminal justice was notoriously unfair to the accused and otherwise deficient, as many enlightened observers pointed out in that age, and it was not for nothing that the revolutionary governments abolished the Châtelet and made the taking of the Bastille on 14 July 1789 a symbol of victory over a tyrannical and backward régime. More to the point, the prosecuting ministers and magistrates made Cadet's crimes seem worse than they were by blaming him not only for selling food to the crown at high prices but also for the high prices themselves.

Cadet was faced with a typical 18th-century misunderstanding of the market mechanism which he in his commonsense way seemed to grasp clearly. He said that he "could not conceal that expenditures for the king in Canada were immense, [but] that the cause for this could only be attributed to the scarcity of goods," and goods were scarce because too few ships reached Quebec. This in turn was because "the dangers that ships and vessels faced in their freighting from France to Canada were not imaginary." In this matter the evidence seems to be on Cadet's side. Shipping insurance premiums rose from less than five per cent of the value insured in 1755 to 50 per cent or more in 1758; in 1759 insurance was often unobtainable. Freight rates to Quebec paid in France rose from 190 *livres* a ton in 1756 to from 240 to 280 *livres* in 1757; but for guaranteed delivery at Quebec in 1758 and 1759 freight rates were anything from 400 to 1,000 *livres* a ton when cargo space could be rented at all. The crown, in its infinite wisdom, took the view, on the advice of the Commission Fontanieu set up in 1758 to reduce naval debts, that anything charged above the 1756 rate of 190 *livres* was inadmissible profiteering and summarily reduced the claims of shipping merchants to that figure. The crown adopted the same principle when it explained the high wartime prices in Canada as the result of a conspiracy for which Cadet was partly to blame, and yet it now seems plain that whatever Cadet may have done, wartime conditions alone were enough to explain why food prices rose. The trial of Cadet and his associates led the general public to believe that they were particularly self-seeking, corrupt, and unscrupulous, whereas a little investigation shows that they were only doing what many other Bourbon officials did, especially in the colonies, but they had the misfortune to find unusually profitable circumstances in a colony that was subsequently lost to an enemy in wartime. The Bourbon monarchy was accustomed to reducing its short-term debts periodically by means of a *chambre de justice* which tried any-one suspected of profiteering at government expense, and the infamous *affaire du Canada* was carried out in that tradition.

Cadet's case went on for many years while various crown agencies set up to recover the money those involved in the *affaire du Canada* were condemned to pay slowly discovered that six million *livres* was too much to ask for. A commission established by a ruling of the Conseil d'État, 31 Dec. 1763, decided a year later that Cadet's debts amounted to the staggering figure of about seventeen million *livres*, of which about nine million was owing to the crown, but by 27 Nov. 1767 they had reduced the latter to 3,898,036 *livres*, which he duly paid by 20 Aug. 1768, although this was a higher figure than the royal controller for the recovery of crown assets, Pierre-François Boucher, arrived at. In the course of the investigation Cadet was imprisoned and interrogated once more from 17 February to 25 March 1766. At his death he was still compiling accounts which he hoped to render to the crown to justify himself. He had no intention, however, of paying out any more than he had to and at his death had still not satisfied his private creditors, who had formed a union in the manner of the age and elected directors who included Tourton et Baur, the well-known Paris bankers, Jean-Baptiste-Tropez Martin, a merchant formerly of Quebec but originally from Marseilles, and Arnoult, a former Paris notary. Cadet had, however, settled some of his debts, having paid 61,583 *livres* to his main Bordeaux agent, Pierre Desclaux, on 11 Jan. 1768; 52,856 *livres* to his old personal assistant, Étienne Cebet, on 23 April 1767; and so on as recorded in the files of his principal Paris notary, Maître Delage.

During the 1760s Cadet also sold off the property he owned in Canada, including a lot on the Rue Saint-Pierre, Quebec, measuring 120 feet by 90 feet (whereon had once stood a house built by a Mme Cugnet), which he sold for 22,500 *livres* to William Grant, who visited him in Paris for this purpose; three other houses in Quebec, one ruined and one that was still standing on the old Rue Saint-Paul until the early 1970s; two pieces of land on the Rivière Saint-Charles about a league from Quebec; and his seigneury, Les Monts-Louis, on the St Lawrence River about 90 leagues below Quebec. Most of this property was sold for him either by his Quebec notary, Panet, or by his old friend and assistant, Antoine-Pierre Houdin, then at Quebec.

During the last 15 years of his life, Cadet used his remaining assets and his credit to build up what we might now call a trust and real-estate business in France. He bought, sold, and managed large properties. For example, in January 1767 he bought the seigneury of Barbelinière in the parish of Thuré (dept of Vienne) through an intermediary who hid Cadet's identity, and several other estates "consisting of ancient castles partly demolished, share-croppers' houses, farms, water-mills, forests, arable lands, meadows, vineyards, thatched cottages, feudal dues … in Poitou, Maine and Touraine." Like many other dealers and speculators in France, he lived partly in Paris or its suburbs where his business was done – and where he eventually died in the Hôtel Sainte-Avoye, in the parish of Saint-Nicolas-des-Champs – and partly on one of his estates near Blois in the valley of the Loire.

No lovelier part of the world is to be found than this, the land of French princely châteaux and of the *Très riches heures du duc de Berry*, but Cadet and his wife, two middle-aged Canadians in exile, missed the remembered things of home. On 5 May 1766, Cadet wrote to Houdin in Quebec to send him two birch-bark canoes, a Canadian carriage and harness, some ploughs and some axes, and "an honest habitant youth from the Côte de Beaupré or the Île d'Orléans; a good farmer and enterprising at this work." Cadet offered a nine-year contract at 200 *livres* a year. "This man is to work my land," he wrote. "I will have great satisfaction in seeing people from my native land there. But remember I want a bachelor and a first-rate farmer." So Cadet lived on comfortably, though never very wealthy, until he died on 31 Jan. 1781; his wife died on 1 Oct. 1791. His partners in the supply business at Quebec had dispersed soon after being released from the Bastille in the early 1760s, Corpron to Nantes where he established himself as a shipping merchant, Maurin to Bordeaux where in 1770 he was described as a resident of the city living in the Place Saint-Domingue. Pennisseaut we have not been able to trace.

Joseph-Michel Cadet's career was spectacular, but he was by no means alone in rising from humble origins to the splendours of a country estate. Jacques Imbert, the Marine treasurers' agent at Quebec, whom Cadet must have known well, was born on 15 Nov. 1710 to a Montargis merchant tanner, later turned corporal in the mounted constabulary, who had married a surgeon's daughter, and after many years in Canada, where he married a Canadian girl, Imbert died a country gentleman at his château near Auxerre, having married off his only daughter, Catherine-Agathe (born at Quebec) to a royal magistrate there. The lives of Jacques-Michel Bréard, controller of the Marine at Quebec, and various merchants such as Denis Goguet, Michel Rodrigue, and Jean-Mathieu Mounier were marked by similar success. "It is a popular conviction," wrote another biographer of Cadet, Adam Shortt, half a century ago, "that private profit and public benefit cannot possibly coincide." Shortt, reflecting on Cadet's career, did not share that conviction and why should we? After all, if France had not lost Canada, Joseph-Michel Cadet might have been acclaimed as a hero and a public benefactor!

J. F. BOSHER

Further reading

J. F. Bosher, *The Canada merchants, 1713–1763* (Oxford, Eng., and New York, 1987); "'Chambres de justice' in the French monarchy," in *French government and society, 1500–1850: essays in memory of Alfred Cobban*, ed. J. F. Bosher (London, 1973), 19–40; *Business and religion in the age of New France, 1600–1760: twenty-two studies* (Toronto, 1994); "The French government's motives in the affaire du Canada, 1761–1763," *English Historical Review* (Harlow, Eng.) 96 (1981): 59–78.

André Côté, *Joseph-Michel Cadet, 1719–1781: négociant et munitionnaire du roi en Nouvelle-France* (Sillery [Québec], 1998).

CHARLES ROBIN,

businessman, judge, and JP; baptized 30 Oct. 1743 in St Brelade, Jersey, son of Philippe Robin and Anne Dauvergne, shopkeepers; d. unmarried 10 June 1824 in St Aubin, Jersey.

Although Charles Robin and his elder brothers, Philip and John, were orphaned when Charles was about 11, they all managed to acquire a good education. Philip married the daughter of the seigneur of Noirmont and subsequently filled important civil offices on Jersey. John and Charles, however, turned to the North American fisheries, in which their uncles had been occupied for many years. By 1763 John was a ship's captain engaged in the Newfoundland cod fisheries. Charles was never master of a ship, but he became well versed in nautical matters. In 1765 the three brothers joined James Pipon de Noirmont, Philip's brother-in-law, and Thomas Pipon de La Moye, John's future brother-in-law, to form Robin, Pipon and Company. That year the firm sent a brig to reconnoitre the fisheries of Cape Breton Island, and in 1766 Charles investigated the former French fisheries on Baie des Chaleurs. Having found abundant fish and excellent beaches for dry-curing on the Gaspé shore, he returned the following year to fish and to trade for timber and furs with the Acadians and Indians around Paspébiac (Que.).

Since the conquest Baie des Chaleurs had become a site of fierce competition among Nova Scotians and New Englanders, and also Quebec merchants, such as Jacques Terroux and William Smith, agent for the firm of Moore and Finlay; the losses suffered had been high. In 1768 Robin returned to Baie des Chaleurs with two vessels, only to have them seized and sold with their cargoes by customs officials who had been informed by some of Robin's competitors that he had not complied with a seldom enforced act obliging Channel Islanders to clear their vessels from England. The outcry provoked by Robin, Pipon and Company led to repeal of the act the following year, but the young firm received only about £250 compensation for its staggering loss of £2,700 sterling.

Robin had a dogged faith in the trade from Baie des Chaleurs even though, one after another, his competitors abandoned it. The limitless supply of cod easily found a market in Catholic Europe; by the 1770s he was shipping several thousand quintals (112 pounds each) of dried cod to Portugal and Spain, as well as small amounts of salmon, furs, cod oil, and wood to England and Quebec. In exchange for these products he imported goods for sale to fishermen and salt for curing. About 1770 a separate firm, Robin and Company, was formed to exploit the Cape Breton fisheries, and John was put in charge; Charles, however, had an interest in it. By that year he was resident agent for Robin, Pipon at Paspébiac, where he set up his headquarters and built flakes for curing. Another establishment was subsequently built at Percé. Initially, Charles got most of his fish in trade with local fishermen (mostly Acadian), but in 1774 he and John brought more than 100 exiled Acadians to settle on Baie des Chaleurs and Cape Breton Island. They also brought over Jersey workers to remedy a chronic shortage of manpower, the principal problem faced by fishing merchants operating in the region.

The patient building up of the Robin enterprise was almost completely undone early in the American revolution. In 1776 John Paul Jones destroyed most of John's operation on Cape Breton. Two years later American privateers came to Paspébiac, captured one of Charles's ships, which they loaded with fish and furs, and plundered and burned his stores; Robin was captured momentarily but escaped into the woods. He returned to Jersey and served for the duration of the revolutionary war as an officer in the militia, which in 1781 helped to repel an attempted invasion by the French. Charles estimated the Robins' direct losses from the revolution at £6,000, exclusive of those resulting from their inability to trade.

Robin returned to Baie des Chaleurs in 1783 as a partner in a new firm, Charles Robin and Company. He held about one-eighth of the shares in the business, most of the remainder being owned by members of the Robin and Pipon families. He also held a one-quarter interest in the Philip Robin Company, which took over the assets of Robin and Company on Cape Breton Island; they were placed under a hired manager since John Robin remained in Jersey. Charles immediately rebuilt the stores, wharfs, and living quarters at Paspébiac.

Although the capital resources at Robin's disposal were perhaps no greater than those of the dozen new energetic competitors he faced, after the war he ultimately won a near monopoly of trade in the region through a combination of experience, cunning, good contacts, hard work, and careful planning. From experience Robin knew the locations of the best fishing grounds and drying beaches. He had also acquired a perceptive understanding of the Acadian fishermen and, as a Jerseyman, he spoke and wrote their language. As well, in travels in his early years he had made useful contacts with important international fish buyers.

Robin's cunning use of a truck system of credit provided the company with long-term stability in exports. Cash was seldom used; rather, Robin credited the year's catch against the equipment, merchandise, provisions, and salt that he had advanced to the fishermen. Once hooked by credit, the fishermen found it virtually impossible to escape their indebtedness, and Robin was ensured of a dependable labour force. The system also allowed Robin to obtain dried cod at a price no higher than the amount the fishermen needed to live on.

Also important in ensuring Robin's success after 1783 were his contacts. Philip handled the European end of the business reliably and kept him supplied. With Francis Janvrin, a Jersey-based operator on Baie de Gaspé and a minority shareholder in Charles Robin and Company, he forged an agreement of non-competition for fish and of mutual service in the carrying of supplies and mail. Aware of the value of political influence, Robin obtained the support of local officials, particularly in efforts to acquire and retain the beaches and woodlots necessary to a large-scale fishing operation. In 1784 he persuaded the lieutenant governor of the Gaspé, Nicholas Cox, not to grant land immediately around Paspébiac to some 400 loyalists, and the following year he gained title to some of it for his firm. In the winter of 1787 Robin walked to Quebec to advise the provincial government on the cod fisheries; with the support of Cox, then deeply in debt to Robin's company, the government passed an ordinance in 1788 that benefited the firm in several ways, particularly by making it impossible for others to acquire large beach properties. Cox's successor, Francis Le Maistre, was a Jerseyman and friend of the Robin family, but poor health prevented his being of material assistance. The seat for Gaspé in the Lower Canadian House of Assembly was held by Edward O'Hara, a man sympathetic to Charles Robin and Company and for whom Robin campaigned actively. Robin himself held a number of posts of considerable importance locally: he was a judge of the Court of Common Pleas around 1788–92, justice of the peace from 1788, and a member of the land board for the district of Gaspé from 1789. The last position gave him a say in the examination of requests for land grants and the issuing of location tickets. Although Robin's influence resulted in the opening of a seasonal customs office at New Carlisle, near Paspébiac, he was unable to obtain bounties on exports or exemption from duties on imported goods, benefits enjoyed by the fishing industry in other colonies. Still, he was content to be protected by his allies from adverse government action; neglect of the district of Gaspé by the government at Quebec enabled him to build a monopoly unhindered.

Robin worked hard to exploit his opportunities. With the exception of his business trip to Quebec in 1787, he resided uninterruptedly on Baie des Chaleurs from 1783 to 1802. He lived a frugal, orderly existence, never married, and had few interests beyond his business. He was the principal policymaker in Charles Robin and Company and the general manager of its day-to-day operations. This authority to make on-the-spot decisions allowed him to exploit the Gaspé fisheries more successfully than his competitors, most of whom were based in London or Quebec. In 1793, for example, he was in a position to seize the opportunity of purchasing the seigneury of Grande-Rivière, which had a good beach close to rich fishing grounds; it became Robin's third major post after nearby Paspébiac and Percé.

Planning, at which Robin excelled, was conservative. Risky ventures were avoided and high profits were not considered imperative; it was deemed more important to maintain a slow, steady growth in exports and a reputation among European importers for reliable delivery of good quality fish. Increasingly Robin specialized in dry-cured cod, forgoing diversification into timber, furs, mackerel, or salt-cured cod. No innovator of techniques of production or marketing, he laboured to make conventional methods function efficiently. He sought, however, to build a self-sufficient, vertically integrated business. Most fish was obtained in trade from local fishermen but some was caught by the company's own employees; their catch was cured on company beaches by men brought in every summer from the Quebec area. Company ships also took the fish to market and brought in most supplies. In the 1790s Robin established a shipyard at Paspébiac; in addition to the shallops and small coastal schooners that were built, every two years the yard turned out a vessel of about 200 tons especially designed to carry fish to Europe. As a result of integration and the truck system of credit, Robin gained a near monopoly of dried codfish exported from the north shore of Baie des Chaleurs. His success may be attributed in part to his caution; in the organization of his fishing operations and his relations with the fishermen, Robin to a large extent carried over, with refinements to increase profits, practices employed by Jersey concerns before him and by French traders in the Gaspé prior to the conquest.

The combination of these many factors also enabled Robin to ride out the French revolutionary war, which finished off his remaining competitors. In May 1794, however, the French navy captured three of his ships en route for Paspébiac with supplies and merchandise. That autumn another, carrying 4,900 quintals of dried fish, was taken off Spain. The war brought a shortage of shipping (which the Paspébiac shipyard alleviated for him) and impaired his ability to get cargoes to market in the season of greatest demand. Eventually the war closed Robin's most important outlets, Spain and Portugal, but he was able to forge temporary ones in New England and Lower Canada. Indeed Robin was able to maintain his exports at pre-war levels, seldom shipping less than 13,000 quintals a year.

Robin retired to Jersey in 1802, when it was thought that the war had been ended by the Treaty of Amiens. By then Charles Robin and Company owned five ships, a large establishment at Paspébiac – including the shipyard, a small farm, wharfs, stages, storehouses, and lodgings for about 100 employees – a subsidiary post at Percé, and the seigneury of Grande-Rivière; the size of the company's profits is not known. Robin's chief investment in the firm had been his life rather than his money.

As a manager he had received a modest annual salary of £150, and in 1800 he estimated the value of his shares to be about £2,250; he did not leave a large estate on his death in 1824. His goal in life had been the continuance of the firm that bore his name, and to that end he had trained his nephew Philip Robin since 1783 and tutored another, James Robin, for a number of years. Philip took over as manager of operations on Baie des Chaleurs in 1803 and James as director in Jersey about 1808. Charles had trained them well, and his goal was attained: the firm dominated the economy of Baie des Chaleurs for another century.

DAVID LEE

Further reading

D. [S.] Lee, *The Robins in Gaspé, 1766 to 1825* (Markham, Ont., 1984).

Mario Mimeault, "La continuité de l'emprise des compagnies de pêche françaises et jersiaises sur les pêcheurs au XVIIIe siècle: le cas de la compagnie Robin," *Social History* (Ottawa), 18 (1985): 59–74.

R. E. Ommer, *From outpost to outport: a structural analysis of the Jersey-Gaspé cod fishery, 1767–1886* (Montreal and Kingston, Ont., 1991).

Jules Bélanger *et al.*, *Histoire de la Gaspésie* (Montréal, 1981).

MUQUINNA (Macuina, Maquilla, Maquinna),

Nootka chief on the west coast of what is now Vancouver Island, B.C.; the name, written muk^wina in proper native orthography, means "possessor of pebbles"; he apparently was active as early as 1778 and possibly died in 1795.

Muquinna was the name of a series of ranking chiefs of the Moachat group of Nootka Indians. This group had its most important summer village at Yuquot, at the mouth of Nootka Sound, and its winter village at Tahsis. Although it is not absolutely certain, there is evidence that the subject of this biography assumed leadership on the death of his father, Anapā, in 1778 and that he died in 1795, to be succeeded by another chief with the same name. Muquinna's leadership among the Nootka Indians coincided with the early years of contact with Europeans on the northwest coast and with the development of a maritime fur trade. This same period was one of rivalry between Britain and Spain on the coast in which the Indians became involved. In fact, most of what we know about Muquinna is related in or must be inferred from the journals of European explorers and fur-traders.

Although the Spanish navigator Juan Josef Pérez Hernández was in the Nootka Sound area in 1774, the first extended contact between Nootka Indians and Europeans came in 1778 when Captain James Cook spent nearly a month at Ship Cove (Resolution Cove) refitting his ships. It is quite possible that the Indian leader, not named by Cook, who held many discussions and arranged transactions with him was Muquinna. Friendly trading relations were established with the people of Yuquot, and a variety of items changed hands, including sea otter pelts, which Cook's crews later traded at great profit in Canton (People's Republic of China). The publication of the journals of Cook's third voyage revealed the profits to be made in a maritime fur trade with China. From its beginning Nootka Sound was a popular port of call for traders, and it soon became an important centre of the trade. Muquinna emerges as the dominant Indian leader at the sound.

The first expedition to the northwest coast after Cook's was that of James Hanna in 1785. In August Muquinna led an unsuccessful attack on his ship; a later Spanish account records him as saying it was provoked by a practical joke Hanna played on him. Initially most of the trading ships that called at Nootka Sound were British, but in the following years American vessels, mainly out of Boston, increasingly dominated. Muquinna traded with the British captain John Meares in 1788 and allowed him to erect a small building on some land at Yuquot, an action that was later to embroil his people in international politics. Meares describes Muquinna as "of a middle size, but extremely well made, and possessing a countenance that was formed to interest all who saw him."

The developing intensity of the maritime fur trade placed Muquinna in a strategic position. Astute Indian leaders like him could exercise a great deal of control over the trade and mould it to serve their own ends. Those who had the good fortune to be in the right place at the right time, and were sagacious enough to use their situation, became extremely wealthy as a result.

On the one side, Muquinna was able to take advantage of the popularity of Nootka Sound to manipulate competition between traders which forced prices upwards. On the other side, he was able to regulate the activities of other Indians in the area. From the time of Cook's visit it was apparent the people of Yuquot were attempting to control contacts between Europeans and other Indian groups, a pattern consolidated under Muquinna's leadership as he endeavoured to ensure that all furs traded at Nootka passed through his hands, or, at least, through those of his people. By 1792 he controlled a trading network with the Kwakiutl group at the mouth of the Nimpkish River (on the east coast of Vancouver Island); his agents used the well-established trade routes to cross the island and purchase furs which were then sold to crews visiting Nootka. Like the European captains, Muquinna knew a good deal about price differentials, and the trader John Box Hoskins reports that his profits as a broker were considerable.

Meanwhile, however, international rivalries had begun to create problems for Muquinna and his people. Spain, dismayed by the number of British vessels now off the Pacific coast to which she had long laid claim, had sent a frigate north in 1789. Muquinna had seen it arrive in May at Nootka under the command of Esteban José Martínez, who claimed the sound for Charles III. When Martínez arrested the trader James Colnett for infringing on Spanish sovereignty, the threat to a profitable trade was felt by the Indians. On 13 July Muquinna's brother, Callicum, paddled out to berate the Spanish, only to be shot dead by a seaman. Muquinna thereupon moved to Opitsat, the village of Wikinanish, Callicum's father-in-law, in Clayoquot Sound. Indian rivalries, however, required him to watch events at Yuquot closely, and when a rival visited Martínez on 1 August, Muquinna also came for a visit. He was at Yuquot again on 1 September and promised Martínez, then departing, to take care of the buildings in the small post he had established.

Much more was seen of the Spaniards in 1790. Madrid having decided to reoccupy Nootka Sound, a force under Francisco de Eliza y

Reventa arrived at Yuquot in April and began to build a small settlement. The Nootka Indians, suspicious of the Spaniards, tended to avoid the cove, and their fears were not allayed by Eliza's plunder of a local village for planks. In June Muquinna encountered an exploring mission under Manuel Quimper at Opitsat and was reassured enough that in October he helped search for survivors of a shipwreck. But Colnett arrived at Yuquot in January 1791 and before he departed on 2 March tried to win Muquinna to the British cause; Muquinna asked "to see a larger ship." He had to keep on good terms with the Spaniards, for Eliza, having heard about ritual cannibalism, had threatened to destroy his village if the act were repeated. Muquinna remained at Tahsis, and when Alejandro Malaspina visited there in August, he ratified the cession to the Spanish of land at Yuquot made in 1790.

Spain and Britain were on the brink of war in 1790 following Martínez's seizure of Colnett in 1789 and Meares's claim to own by purchase the land now occupied by the Spanish at Yuquot. The quarrel was eventually settled by the diplomatic action of the Nootka Conventions. When in 1792 Juan Francisco de la Bodega y Quadra arrived at Yuquot to arrange application of the terms, Muquinna struck up a close relationship with him and was his frequent dinner guest. Bodega became convinced, partly by Muquinna's testimony, that Meares's claim to all Yuquot was unfounded, and when George Vancouver arrived in August to repossess Meares's land, Muquinna found himself fêted by both sides during the negotiations. He proved adept in the art of diplomacy, entertaining the foreign emissaries at Tahsis. When Bodega left Nootka Sound in September, Yuquot was still in Spanish hands, and only in March 1795, after further negotiations between Spain and Britain, did the Europeans abandon the sound. Muquinna's people soon tore down the buildings and reasserted their dominance over the area they had earlier abandoned; in September a visitor, Charles Bishop, reported an Indian village stood at Yuquot. Muquinna was said to be "very ill of an ague," and a few weeks later Bishop was told by Wikinanish at Clayoquot Sound that he had died.

Muquinna was a Nootka chief in the traditional sense but also a leader whose role was changing with the impact of the Europeans. He had almost certainly attained his position of leadership at the time of Cook's visit by traditional Indian usages and validated it by potlatching as had his predecessors. But since the measure of a leader's influence and prestige was largely the wealth that passed through his hands, his position was enhanced by the profits he acquired through the control of trade with foreign visitors and exploitation of existing trading relationships with other Indian groups. Thus he probably became more powerful through the fur trade than he might otherwise have done, and this new power of Muquinna and his people was expressed in their relations with other groups in the Nootka Sound area. Nevertheless it is possible that his position was exaggerated in the journals of European visitors simply because Nootka was so important to them at this time; perhaps Muquinna's neighbour and intermittent ally, Wikinanish, the Clayoquot leader, was more powerful. Neither, however, was the kind of ruler ship captains tended to suppose: they led by influence rather than by authority and by prestige rather than power. There is no doubt, however, that Muquinna was one of the most important Indian leaders in the area during the early contact period, and his role in this phase of northwest coast history is as significant as that of any of the Europeans who sailed into Nootka Sound.

ROBIN FISHER

Further reading

Robin Fisher, *Contact and conflict: Indian-European relations in British Columbia, 1774–1890* (Vancouver, 1977).

J. R. Gibson, *Otter skins, Boston ships, and China goods: the maritime fur trade of the northwest coast, 1785–1841* (Seattle, Wash., 1992).

B. M. Gough, *Fortune's a river: the collision of empires in northwest America* (Madeira Park, B.C., 2007).

Alexandra Harmon, *Rich Indians: native people and the problem of wealth in American history* (Chapel Hill, N.C., 2010).

Section 2

The Commercial Empire of the St Lawrence after 1763

LOUISE DE RAMEZAY,

seigneur; b. 6 July 1705 at Montreal, daughter of Claude de
Ramezay, governor of Montreal, and Marie-Charlotte Denys de
La Ronde; d. 22 Oct. 1776 at Chambly (Que.).

Louise de Ramezay received her schooling at the Ursuline convent in
Quebec. Having remained single like her sister Marie-Charlotte de
Ramezay, *dite* de Saint-Claude de la Croix, she was led when she was
about 30 to take an interest in the administration of part of her family's properties. In particular she was concerned with the sawmill that
her father had built early in the century on the banks of the Rivière des
Hurons, in the seigneury of Chambly not far from his own seigneury
of Monnoir. Shortly after his death in 1724, his widow had gone into
partnership with Clément de Sabrevois de Bleury to run the sawmill.
From 1732 until 1737, however, a protracted lawsuit, which Louise
de Ramezay followed closely, set the two former partners against each
other. Mlle de Ramezay probably acquired at that period the knowledge
necessary for running the mill, as well as the other enterprises of which
she later became the owner.

For more than three decades beginning in 1739, Louise de Ramezay faithfully saw to it that the sawmill on the Rivière des Hurons was
not idle, for every year the operation had to pay 112 *livres* in rent to
the seigneurs of Chambly and 600 *livres* to her sisters and her brother
Jean-Baptiste-Nicolas-Roch, who were also heirs to their father's estate.
The mill was well situated to saw the wood from the upper Richelieu
and Lake Champlain and thus to supply timbers, planks, and sheathing to the shipyards at Quebec. Louise de Ramezay did not always run
the enterprise in person. At certain periods she supervised production
closely, collaborating with the foreman and going to Quebec to sell the
lumber; at others, having leased the sawmill and even the right to grant
land and collect the rents in the seigneury of Monnoir, she was primarily
concerned with getting her share of the revenue. When she entrusted the
mill to a foreman, she preferred him to know how to keep the accounts;
to one who was illiterate, she gave permission in his contract "to take an

hour every day to learn to read and write, and to have himself taught by one of the men hired at the mill who would take the same time to teach him." Such a clause was quite uncommon, but it gave her the hope that the foreman would eventually keep the accounts well.

Contracts for taking charge of the sawmill were made in succession at about five-year intervals until 1765, proof of success and of virtually uninterrupted operation. During her years of management, however, Louise de Ramezay had to deal with a number of problems. On the two occasions when she farmed out the sawmill she had difficulty getting the conditions of the lease carried out. First, in 1756, a lumber merchant from Chambly, François Bouthier, owed her more than 12,000 *livres* for two years of rent and goods advanced much earlier. In 1765 she again tried the experiment with Louis Boucher de Niverville de Montisambert, but at the end of a few years, as accounts were not yet settled, legal action was initiated. She no doubt was afraid at one point of finding herself dragged into a prolonged lawsuit, as her mother had been 40 years earlier. She soon agreed with Montisambert that to avoid the delays and expense of a court case it was better to have the dispute settled by the parish priest of Chambly, Médard Petrimoulx. In August 1771 the priest decided in her favour and concluded that Montisambert had to pay her 3,284 *livres*.

Louise de Ramezay was also interested in two other sawmills; these are known, however, only through documents that show her as intending to put mills into operation, in particular deeds of partnership and building transactions. In 1745 she entered into partnership with Marie-Anne Legras, the wife of Jean-Baptiste-François Hertel de Rouville, and the two entrepreneurs had a sawmill and a flour-mill built "on the seigneury of Rouville, on the stream called Notre-Dame de Bonsecours, on a piece of land belonging to the ... Sieur de Rouville." These two mills doubtless turned a satisfactory profit, since the partnership lasted 16 years; it was not dissolved until 1761, six years before the anticipated date. The second sawmill was to be located much farther south, in the seigneury of La Livaudière, west of Lake Champlain. This seigneury, which had initially been granted to Jacques-Hugues Péan de Livaudière, had been withdrawn in 1741 and returned to the king's domain. When the seigneury had belonged to him, however, Péan had granted land to a habitant from Saint-Antoine-sur-Richelieu, Jean Chartier, with the authorization "to take sawn timber on the whole of the aforementioned seigneury where the lands had not been given in grants." Moreover, a stream that crossed Chartier's land and flowed into Lake Champlain by way of the Chazy River (probably the Great Chazy River, N.Y.) could supply the power needed for running a mill. It was probably this set of favourable circumstances that prompted Louise de Ramezay to go into partnership with Chartier in August 1746 and to have a sawmill built at once on his land, near the Chazy River. Moreover, in 1749 she obtained a grant from the colonial authorities of a domain on Lake Champlain, the seigneury of Ramezay-La-Gesse, which extended on both sides of the Rivière aux Sables (probably the Ausable River, N.Y.). Although a sawmill does not seem to have been built there, the interest of this property obviously lay in its abundant timber reserves.

Louise de Ramezay did not confine her activities to the lumber industry. In 1749 she bought from Charles Plessy, *dit* Bélair, the tannery that had belonged to his father Jean-Louis and was located in Coteau-Saint-Louis on Montreal Island. In 1753 she went into partnership with a master tanner, Pierre Robereau, *dit* Duplessis, to whom she entrusted the operation of the tannery. Until she was 60, she appears to have lived mainly in Montreal, often going to Chambly and Quebec.

It is not possible with the available documentation to evaluate precisely the extent of Louise de Ramezay's economic activity. In the transactions related to the lumber or leather industries, however, she always seemed able to advance the money necessary for construction work, for fitting-out or repairs, for the foremen's and workmen's wages, for the purchase of land, equipment, and goods, or for repayment of debts contracted by a partner or employee. These are additional signs of the efficiency and success of her enterprises. She owed this success in part to her own administrative abilities, but probably even more to her social position: the descendant of a great family, the daughter of a governor, the "very noble young lady," as the documents of the period call her, enjoyed privileges that were by no means negligible. Besides an upbringing that had prepared her for the realities of her situation, her relations within the colonial aristocracy certainly on more than one occasion brought her useful advice, information, recommendations, and even a few favours in connection with the lumber industry, the exploitation of timber limits, the purchase of domains, or her own financial resources. For example, after her mother's death in 1742 she was the beneficiary of an annual and comfortable pension of 1,000 *livres*, because the authorities in France had decided to extend the pension paid to Mme de Ramezay as the widow of a former governor of Montreal. In addition, in 1746 Bishop Pierre-Herman Dosquet gave her half of the seigneury of Bourchemin, an enclave within the seigneury of Ramezay, which she demanded in the name of her family's claims on that domain: the bishop on this occasion wrote to her: "I am delighted to have this small opportunity to give proof of my attachment to your family." Thus Louise de Ramezay owned, in her own right, half of the seigneury of Bourchemin as well as the seigneury of Ramezay-La-Gesse; in addition, in 1724, along with her brothers and sisters she had inherited from her father the seigneuries of Ramezay, Monnoir, and Sorel. When all is said and done, her economic activities could rest on the kind of substantial landed fortune of which there were but few examples in the colony in the mid 18th century.

With the conquest and the establishment of the southern border of Canada, Louise de Ramezay lost her seigneury of Ramezay-La-Gesse, and also, if indeed it still belonged to her, the mill near the Chazy River. At the same period she parted with other properties. In 1761 she sold her rights to the seigneury of Sorel to her sister Louise-Geneviève, the widow of Henri-Louis Deschamps de Boishébert, for 3,580 *livres*. Three years later this property was sold to a Quebec merchant, John Taylor Bondfield, as was the seigneury of Ramezay on the Yamaska River, in which Louise had kept her share. In 1774, two years before her death, she also sold her half of Bourchemin. Monnoir apparently remained in the family until the end of the century; towards the end of her life she made grants of a considerable number of lots there at the request of habitants in the Richelieu valley.

Louise de Ramezay, unmarried and a member of the aristocracy, administered the properties for which she was responsible conscientiously and with remarkable constancy, at the same time drawing the greatest possible advantage from the privileges of her class.

HÉLÈNE PARÉ

Further reading

Réal Fortin, *Louise de Ramezay et son moulin à scie: mythe et réalité* (Québec, 2009).

Gabrielle Brochard, "Louise de Ramezay (1705–1776): parcours d'une femme d'entreprise au Canada" (mémoire de MA, univ. Michel de Montaigne Bordeaux 3, Pessac, France, 2008).

Benoît Grenier, *Seigneurs campagnards de la Nouvelle France: présence seigneuriale et sociabilité rurale dans la vallée du Saint-Laurent à l'époque préindustrielle* (Rennes, France, 2007).

O.-M.-H. Lapalice, *Histoire de la seigneurie Massue et de la paroisse de Saint-Aimé* (n.p., 1930).

É.-Z. Massicotte, "Une femme d'affaires du Régime français," *Bulletin des recherches historiques* (Lévis, Qué.) 37 (1931): 530.

Jan Noel, "New France: les femmes favorisées," *Atlantis* (Halifax) 6 (1980–81), no.2: 80–98.

AARON HART,

businessman; b. *c.* 1724, perhaps in Bavaria (Federal Republic of Germany), but more likely in England; d. 28 Dec. 1800 at Trois-Rivières (Que.).

Nothing is known of Aaron Hart's origins. Family tradition long kept up the legend of a regiment named the Hart New York Rangers which was supposed to have joined Jeffery Amherst's troops at the time of the conquest of Canada. Some Jewish historians have made of Aaron Hart an officer serving with the British forces and on Amherst's general staff. More realistically, the scholarly J. R. Marcus alleges that he was a purveyor, a sutler who is believed to have followed the troops. At that time the commissariats of European armies did in fact welcome many Jews. A masonic certificate dated 10 June 1760 at New York is the earliest document known to refer to Aaron Hart; having made up his mind to follow Amherst and Frederick Haldimand's troops northwards, Hart had probably considered it wise to provide himself with a sort of letter of introduction. Military documents, however, never mention his presence, and the next known reference to him is a receipt dated 28 March 1761 which indicates that he and Eleazar Levy had supplied merchandise to Samuel Jacobs. On 21 Oct. 1761 Jacobs wrote to Hart, and thereafter a regular correspondence confirms Aaron Hart's presence in Trois-Rivières.

In May 1762 Haldimand took over the administration of Trois-Rivières while the governor, Ralph Burton, was absent. He became patron to Hart, who was already purveyor to the troops quartered there. On 4 July 1762 a fire broke out in the town; according to Haldimand, "the merchant Hart, an English Jew who has suffered the most, may have lost [£]400 or 500." Three days later notary Paul Dielle drew up a lease between Théodore Panneton the younger and Aaron Hart. On 23 Aug. 1763 the authorities opened a post office at Trois-Rivières "in the house of Mr. Hart, merchant" that was to remain there for seven years. In the summer of 1764 Haldimand, now officially governor, wrote to Thomas Gage that "the group of British merchants in Trois-Rivières" was "composed of a Jew and of a sergeant and an Irish soldier on half pay." Hart soon became interested in the fur trade. He engaged the best-known voyageurs in the region, among them Joseph Chevalier, Louis Pillard the younger, and Joseph Blondin. His initiatives paid off and he continued to expand this lucrative undertaking.

On 7 Feb. 1764 Aaron Hart acquired his first land, buying 48 acres from the Fafard de La Framboise estate for the attractive price of £350 in cash. Seven months later he purchased a large section of the seigneury of Bécancour. In May 1765 part of the Bruyères fief came into his possession; within six months he had paid off the £500 Simon Darouet demanded for it. His enthusiasm for acquiring new properties never diminished. Hart foresaw the extraordinary possibilities present in this country, newly conquered by the British. Believing in its progress, its development, he thought of establishing a solid dynasty in Canada and he methodically laid the foundations. In 1767, convinced of the promise of his new country, he went to London to take a wife. On 2 Feb. 1768 he married Dorothy (Dorothea, Dorothée) Judah and through his marriage found himself at the centre of a large family connection. One of Aaron's brothers, Moses, had already joined him in his ventures; another, Henry, had settled at Albany, New York, and a third, Lemon, was launching the London Red Heart Rum distillery in London. At least two of Dorothy Judah's brothers, Uriah and Samuel, had gone to Canada ahead of her. Their correspondence indicates that "Mama Judah" lived in New York around 1795. The same letters give information about the close links which joined the couple to the large interrelated circle of Jews in New York, principal members being the Gomezes, Meyers, Levys, Cohens, and Manuels.

Upon his return from London in the spring of 1768 Aaron rejoined his brother Moses, who had kept a successful watch over his business affairs. Aaron dreamt of a large family and never missed a piece of land for sale or a landowner short of funds. He made loans easily and was willing to bide his time, letting the debt increase; then he would ask for security, suggest a mortgage. The old seigneurs, defeated in 1760, became his steadiest clients, and he showed some sympathy for them. He became, as it were, the accomplice of Joseph Boucher de Niverville, Charles-Antoine Godefroy de Tonnancour, Jean-Baptiste Poulin de Courval Cressé, and Jean Drouet de Richerville. Through generous and discreet loans he made the post-conquest period almost attractive for them. Time enough later to brandish his claims in front of the heirs, who, caught unawares, would scarcely know where to turn. The future belonged to the new settlers, English, Scottish, or Jewish. Aaron Hart grasped the true meaning of the events that had opened the valley of the St Lawrence to him and his people. The fact that only a small number of English-speaking persons had settled in the province prompted the British to rely on Jewish merchants. The latter regarded themselves as British and attached their names to the numerous petitions drawn up by His Majesty's old subjects. They established themselves throughout the new British colony: Eleazar Levy, Elias Salomon, Levy Simons, Hyam Myers, Abraham Franks, and some others at Quebec; Moses Hart, Aaron's brother, in Sorel; Uriah Judah in Verchères; Pines Heineman in Saint-Antoine-de-Padoue, Rivière-du-Loup (Louiseville); Emmanuel Manuel in Sainte-Anne-d'Yamachiche (Yamachiche); Joseph Judah and Barnett Lyons in Berthier-en-Haut (Berthierville); Samuel Jacobs in Saint-Denis, on the Richelieu; Chapman Abraham, Gershom, Simon, and Isaac Levy, Benjamin Lyons, Ezekiel and Levy Solomons, David Lazarus, John and David Salisbury Franks, Samuel and Isaac Judah, Andrew Hays, and many others in Montreal. This list, compiled mainly from the business papers of Aaron Hart and Samuel Jacobs, is in no way complete. Most of these Jews had arrived in the province of Quebec at the time of the conquest or shortly thereafter. Some had first engaged in fur-trading in the Great Lakes region, and then had come to Quebec and Montreal around 1763; others had come directly with the troops. For instance, Samuel Jacobs was at Fort Cumberland (near Sackville, N.B.) in 1758 and then followed in the wake of the 43rd Foot and James Wolfe's troops, reaching Quebec in the autumn of 1759.

Samuel Jacobs could in fact easily rival Aaron Hart for recognition as the first Canadian Jew. Both engaged in business on a large scale and left evidence of their activity that could supply valuable material for a whole generation of historians. For his Jewish compatriots, however, Aaron Hart's good fortune lay in having made a Jewish marriage and having been able to bring up his children, or at least his sons, in Jewish traditions. Since he lived to a respectable age, he also had the opportunity of initiating them into business himself. From 1792 he associated them closely with his enterprises. While the eldest, Moses, went off to try his luck at Nicolet, and then at Sorel, Aaron gave his shop on Rue du Platon over to the firm of Aaron Hart and Son and entrusted specific responsibilities to Ezekiel. When Moses returned he converted the company and also took advantage of the occasion to bring young Benjamin in. Carrying out a plan conceived earlier, Aaron and his sons opened a brewery across from the Ursuline convent, near the St Lawrence. By assigning large landed properties to his sons, especially the two eldest, he quite simply forced them to establish themselves at Trois-Rivières, the chosen birthplace for the Hart dynasty.

In the spring of 1800 Aaron fell ill. He fought against his illness until mid December, and then he resolved to dictate his will, "bearing in mind that there is nothing so certain as death and so uncertain as the moment of its coming." His eldest son, Moses, was to inherit the seigneury of Sainte-Marguerite and the marquisate of Le Sablé, Ezekiel the seigneury of Bécancour, Benjamin the main store, and Alexander (Asher) two plots in town. To his four daughters, Catherine, Charlotte, Elizabeth, and Sarah, he left the sum of £1,000 each, but he attached all sorts of conditions linked in particular to their marriages and their prospective offspring. Clauses of the will invariably restore assets to those who bear the Hart name. The inventory of his property carefully drawn up by notaries Joseph Badeaux and Étienne Ranvoyzé reveals not only the merchant's fortune, but also his practices and dodges. He had several bags containing large reserve funds in Spanish piastres. As for moneys owing, their entry covered 11 pages in the notaries' ledger. Not a single parish within a radius of 50 miles could boast of not having at least one inhabitant who was in debt to Hart. Of these innumerable debts, only one left unpleasant memories. In 1775, at the time of the American invasion, the Trois-Rivières merchant had supplied both sides; the Americans had paid him in paper money that had still not been honoured a quarter of a century later. For the rest, the heirs had excellent prospects. At the time of the abolition of the seigneurial system, the lists prepared by a descendant of the Judahs around 1857 revealed that the Hart clan owned entirely or in part four fiefs (Boucher, Vieux-Pont, Hertel, and Dutort) and seven seigneuries (Godefroy, Roquetaillade, Sainte-Marguerite, Bruyères, Bécancour, Bélair, and Courval). The total of the *cens et rentes* and the *lods et ventes* amounted at that time to $86,293.05.

Although in large measure supplanted, the people of Trois-Rivières had not had their final word: in 1807 they elected Ezekiel Hart to the assembly. Without quite realizing it, Ezekiel to some extent was becoming one of them. Three or four generations later the Harts would experience more fully the true meaning of the deep-rooted and tenacious resistance of the "long-time Canadians." Gradually Aaron Hart's descendants would blend into the French-speaking and Catholic population of Trois-Rivières which had somehow managed to live through the drama of 1760. Some joined the ranks of the Anglo-Protestants for a time; yet hundreds of Aaron Hart's descendants, who were firmly attached to their properties, refused to lose everything by leaving a region which resolutely remained French and Catholic. They chose to remain there, though threatened with slow but inexorable assimilation by the local majority. Today some of them jealously guard the secret of their origins and of their relative prosperity; many others are completely ignorant of them. Aaron Hart could not foresee this curious historical reversion in which those defeated in 1760 would gradually become vehicles of assimilation. The Harts of the Trois-Rivières region would have the same experience as the Burnses, Johnsons, and Ryans: mingling with the "long-time Canadians" they too would become the progenitors of the Québécois of today.

DENIS VAUGEOIS

Further reading

Denis Vaugeois, *The first Jews in North America: the extraordinary story of the Hart family of Quebec, 1760–1860*, trans. Käthe Roth (Montreal, 2011); *Les Juifs et la Nouvelle-France* (Trois-Rivières, Qué., 1968).

G. [J. J.] Tulchinsky, *Canada's Jews: a people's journey* (Toronto, 2008), 7–27.

Allan Greer, *Peasant, lord, and merchant: rural society in three Quebec parishes, 1740–1840* (Toronto, 1985), 140–45.

JOSHUA MAUGER
(baptized Josué but he signed Joshua),
sea-captain, businessman, and politician; baptized 25 April 1725 in the parish of St John, Jersey, eldest son of Josué Mauger and Sarah Le Couteur; believed married to Elizabeth Mauger, his cousin; only known child, Sarah, baptized 8 April 1754 in Halifax, Nova Scotia; d. 18 Oct. 1788 at Warborne, near Lymington, Hampshire, England.

Joshua Mauger's career before he went to Halifax in 1749 is obscure. In 1743, at the age of 18, he was master of the *Grand Duke*, quarantined at an unknown British port in December after a voyage from Naples and Leghorn. He later served for some time as master of the *Duke of Cumberland* transport until its discharge at London in March 1747. Mauger then established a base of operations at Louisbourg, Cape Breton Island. By the time the British evacuated the fortress in 1749 he had become victualler to the Royal Navy there, an appointment which suggests that he already had influential friends in London. He moved to Halifax that year and, aside from a trip to England in 1749–50, seems to have remained there until 1760.

Mauger soon came into conflict with the Nova Scotian authorities over certain of his dealings with Louisbourg. The evidence which is

available suggests that Halifax citizens who had been resident in Louisbourg were permitted to remove their possessions or the proceeds from
their sale for a year or so after Louisbourg officially reverted to French
control. In the autumn of 1749 Mauger received "Sundry Merchandise
& Stores" which he had left there. It appears, however, that Mauger used
recovery of his Louisbourg possessions as a means of avoiding the trade
restrictions imposed by Governor Edward Cornwallis, who was anxious
to discourage contact with the French. In 1750 Mauger obtained permission to land ten hogsheads of wine from Louisbourg, but he must
have imported a much larger quantity since in July and August Cornwallis ordered him to send back over 22 hogsheads. The governor
claimed that efforts were being made to make Halifax "a repository for
goods from Louisbourg and this chiefly supported and carried on by Mr.
Mauger." In November 1751 he ordered the seizure of a sloop believed
to have landed contraband from Louisbourg and, suspecting Mauger of
having received some of the goods, authorized a search of his warehouse. Mauger argued that the Vice-Admiralty Court had no jurisdiction
on land and refused to permit the search, but on the governor's orders
James Monk Sr broke open the warehouse and seized a quantity of rum.
In Mauger's defence Isaac Deschamps testified that the rum was part of
100 casks imported with the governor's permission in November 1750.
Mauger explained that at the evacuation of Louisbourg he had had to
dispose of large quantities of goods and had provided some of them
to French residents there on credit. Sebastian Zouberbuhler, acting on
Mauger's behalf, had been unable to obtain acceptable bills of exchange
or cash for the goods and had therefore accepted rum and molasses,
which he had sent to Halifax. The Vice-Admiralty Court accepted the
explanation and ordered Mauger's rum returned.

Cornwallis, obviously dissatisfied, suggested to the Board of Trade
that Mauger be dismissed as victualler to the navy. He was convinced
that unless the authorities were firm Nova Scotia would become "a rendezvous for smugglers and people who keep a constant correspondence
to Louisbourgh." Admitting that the trade was "so very detrimental," the
board noted, however, that it was not forbidden by any valid treaty or
law and was therefore not illegal. The lords of the Admiralty were willing to terminate Mauger's contract if Cornwallis thought it necessary,
but others apparently requested its continuation. Mauger seems to have

retained his position until his departure for England, and he continued to receive goods from Louisbourg at least until 1754.

Perhaps the most serious challenge to government authorities in which Mauger was involved began in December 1752 as a result of the dissatisfaction of a number of Halifax residents with their justices of the peace. When Ephraim Cook, a prominent merchant and shipowner from England, lost his commissions as JP and judge of the Inferior Court of Common Pleas and was subsequently indicted for issuing a warrant without authority, his lawyer, David Lloyd, charged the justices with partiality in the performance of their duties. Mauger, quick to support a fellow merchant, joined with 13 other Halifax citizens calling themselves "the principal Inhabitants of this Town" to support Lloyd's protest. Early in March 1753 the Council cleared the justices of the charge, but by the end of the month Governor Peregrine Thomas Hopson had appointed four new justices "to prevent any suspicion of Partiality in the Bench for the future."

During his 11 years in Nova Scotia Mauger developed wide economic interests, some of which, like his trade with Louisbourg, led to conflicts with local authorities. In the summer of 1751 he applied to Cornwallis for permission to establish a distillery in a "great store" behind his home. Refused permission on the grounds that the establishment would constitute a fire hazard, Mauger built outside the town, "with much hard labour and at great Expence having been obliged to remove almost a Mountain." Erection of the works was apparently underway by August 1751. In July the government had placed a 3d. a gallon duty on rum and other spirits, except for the products of Britain and the British West Indies, specifically to encourage the establishment of a distillery and undoubtedly with Mauger's interests in mind. By the autumn of 1752 Mauger was shipping large quantities of rum to outposts such as Fort Lawrence (near Amherst) and Fort Edward (Windsor); in 1766 the annual output of his distillery was 50,000 gallons. When William Steele applied in 1754 for permission to erect a distillery inside the town, Mauger warned that if it were situated near any of his properties he would be obliged to protest "in a public manner" because of the hazard, and the Council unanimously rejected Steele's proposal. It is not known, however, if Mauger objected when John Fillis established his distillery in 1752, or if Fillis built within the town. The two men came to enjoy a virtual monopoly of the provincial rum trade, and Fillis and Mauger's agent, John Butler, acted in concert in the early 1760s to persuade the House of Assembly to increase the protective duty. Because Nova Scotia was seriously in debt and the duties on spirits were the one reliable means of replenishing the local treasury, their adjustment in the interests of maximum revenue became the prime object of those wishing to improve the credit of the province, and they were to involve Mauger and his friends in renewed conflicts with colonial governors in the 1760s and 1770s.

William Steele probably would have found it difficult to build on land in Halifax not near any of Mauger's. Between 1740 and 1760 Mauger took part in some 52 property transactions there. He received some land in the form of direct grants from the government and acquired other properties from bankrupt merchants or from tradesmen who were indebted to him. Outside the town he owned land in Lunenburg, Annapolis Royal, and Windsor, and more extensive properties in Cumberland County, along the Saint John River, and on St John's (Prince Edward) Island. These included a 20,000-acre tract in Cumberland County, which Mauger acquired from Alexander McNutt in a legal action in 1769, and an estate of similar size on St John's Island, which he was granted in 1767 and which he disposed of in 1775. Mauger seems to have played a considerable role in the economic development of Lunenburg, where he was involved in shipbuilding and the lumber trade. In 1754 Lieutenant Governor Charles Lawrence advised that the inhabitants of the town be discouraged from seeking work in Halifax because "Their lots at Lunenburg and the Employment Mr. Mauger finds them is as much full as they can accomplish."

Mauger's extensive property holdings were overshadowed in importance by his trading activities. The largest shipowner in Halifax in the years 1749–60, he owned, wholly or in part, 27 vessels, some bought in New England, others acquired by public auction after the Halifax Vice-Admiralty Court had condemned them for illegal trade, and still others purchased as prize vessels. Mauger shipped fish and lumber to the West Indies and obtained rum, molasses, and sugar in exchange. The timber in some cases undoubtedly came from his sawmills near Lunenburg, and the fish may have come from a fishing establishment he is said to have maintained at Halifax. His ships were used to carry rum from his distillery to a store he owned at Annapolis Royal and to Minas and Chignecto, where he may also have had stores. From England, Ireland, and New England he imported a wide assortment of items, ranging from beer and raisins to glass beads, lead shot, and grindstones. He seems also to have dealt in slaves. The Seven Years' War provided him with a new outlet for his energies; he invested in privateers, as well as in the purchase of prize vessels, and acted as agent for the officers and crews of British navy vessels which captured French ships off Cape Breton.

Not all of Mauger's shipping ventures were profitable. In 1750 the French destroyed one of his vessels in the inner reaches of the Bay of Fundy. Three years later he arranged a sham sale of a schooner to Matthew Vincent of Louisbourg in order to facilitate a trading venture to Martinique only to have the mate abscond with the vessel. Each of the privateers he owned jointly with John Hale, the *Wasp* and the *Musquetto*, made one recorded capture, but neither proved profitable. The vessel taken by the *Wasp* was worth only about £342 with its cargo. The second prize was ordered released by the Vice-Admiralty Court because it was Dutch; subsequently its crew accused their captors of having tortured them, and the court, presided over by John Collier, ordered the captain and crew or their agents to pay damages to the injured parties as well as the costs of the month-long trial.

As victualler to the navy Mauger drew large amounts of provisions from both Britain and New England, especially during the war years. Mauger's British suppliers are not known, but his American source was a Connecticut partnership headed by Jonathan Trumbull, one of the colony's largest provisions dealers by the 1750s and later its governor. Mauger used his acquaintanceship with the clergyman Aaron Cleveland to make contact with Trumbull and employed John Butler to arrange the first shipment of goods in the fall of 1752. For Trumbull and his partners the trade was invaluable because for some years it provided them with virtually the only bills of exchange they could obtain. For Mauger, however, it was less than satisfactory. The provisions he received did not always meet his demanding standards, and in 1754 he began to turn to Ireland as a source of beef, pork, and butter. He complained to Trumbull that he had lost more than £100 sterling on meat sent from Connecticut. At least one lot of beef had proven inedible in spite of his having had it repacked, newly salted, and pickled on arrival. When wartime inflation made Irish goods less expensive than Connecticut provisions, Mauger ceased buying from Trumbull.

Mauger departed for England in 1760, apparently in the summer, but he maintained a lively interest in Nova Scotia. The key to his continued involvement in provincial affairs lies, of course, in the immense fortune he had built up there, a fortune he was able to protect and advance even at a distance of 2,500 miles. Exactly why he was so successful in this endeavour is not entirely clear. Contemporaries believed that by the 1770s a Mauger "party" had developed in Halifax, but it is not always easy to identify the members of this group or to determine how they were attached to Mauger. Some, like Fillis, had similar economic interests; others, like Butler, were employed by him; and still others, like Michael Francklin, became indebted to him. Perhaps more important than particular links, however, was the fact that in defending his own interests Mauger was defending a colonial financial structure from which many members of the Halifax mercantile élite benefited. He had, therefore, a base of support in Halifax, which, combined with his knowledge of Nova Scotia and his substantial investment in the provincial debt, must have given him a certain authority in England. These factors alone, however, do not explain his considerable influence with successive governments. His election to parliament for Poole in 1768, a seat he held with only a brief interruption until 1780, undoubtedly added to his prestige, but he does not appear to have been a major political figure. Nevertheless, as Sir Lewis Bernstein Namier points out, "he seems to have been listened to, even when in Parliament he sided with the Opposition." In short, his relations with the home authorities remain something of a mystery.

In April 1762 the Nova Scotia House of Assembly chose Mauger as the colony's agent in London. In that capacity he conducted a bitter campaign against Jonathan Belcher, the chief justice and lieutenant governor. On several occasions in 1762 and 1763 he appeared before the Board of Trade to demand Belcher's removal from administrative office for such offences as his refusal to permit continuation of the fur monopoly, of which Benjamin Gerrish was the principal beneficiary, and his unwillingness to extend the debtors' act, which protected settlers who had left debts behind them in other colonies and in which many members of the Halifax mercantile community had a vested interest. He complained to the board of Belcher's "Impudent Conduct" and charged that the lieutenant governor was "so unacquainted and unskilled in the Art of Government, and has behaved in such improper manner, as to have occasioned a General Dislike to him ... and Disgust to his Measures." More important for Mauger's interest was the fact that in 1762 Belcher for some time refused assent to two bills which would have modified the duties on spirits in such a way as to favour local distillers. Perhaps another reason for his attack was his inability to secure payment of bills of exchange he had supplied the government of Nova Scotia during Belcher's administration. In March 1763 Belcher was replaced by Montagu Wilmot. On Wilmot's death three years later, Michael Francklin was appointed lieutenant governor. Whether Mauger had anything to do with this appointment is not clear, but Francklin was one of his protégés and, along with Butler and Isaac Deschamps, had been entrusted with guarding Mauger's interests after his departure for England. He eventually fell heavily in debt to Mauger as well, and it would seem that his ten-year tenure of the lieutenant governorship could only have been advantageous for his patron.

Although by December 1763 Mauger had ceased to act as Nova Scotia's agent in London, he remained the colony's unofficial spokesman, with more apparent influence than a succession of governors. In that year he had been influential in securing to New Englanders along the Saint John River lands on which they had settled but to which British army officers had a prior claim; their settlement, Maugerville, was named in his honour. He also became involved in the appeals of individuals in Nova Scotia against government decisions which affected them adversely. The Nova Scotia issue which concerned him most, however, was distilling. In 1767 the House of Assembly, with a view to increasing the colony's revenue and with the support of Governor Lord William Campbell, passed a law reducing the impost on imported spirits and raising the excise duty. Since Butler, Fillis, and Francklin had been unable to block the bill, they turned to Mauger for assistance. Along with Brook Watson and other London merchants interested in Nova Scotia, Mauger petitioned the Board of Trade against the duties, which would, it was claimed, "tend to Distress the Trade and Fishery" of the province. Campbell argued that Mauger and Fillis had unjustly enjoyed a monopoly of Nova Scotia's rum trade "to the detriment of all the Merchants traders & Almost every other person in the province" and that the new duties would benefit the colony as a whole by permitting a reduction in the debt. The power of the merchants' lobby was such, however, that the board rejected Campbell's mercantilist arguments as "contrary to all true policy," and the old rates of duty were restored. The fact that Mauger and his friends held a substantial proportion of the provincial treasury notes – as they did not hesitate to point out to the board – no doubt weighed strongly in their favour. Since Campbell continued to make a nuisance of himself, Mauger and Butler began a campaign to have him removed. Although it was reasons of health that brought about the governor's transfer to South Carolina in 1773, Mauger's friends gave him credit for the removal.

The conflict over the duties on spirits clearly reveals what John Bartlet Brebner has described as "the whole apparatus of influence and dependence" that ensured "Nova Scotian subservience to London." Campbell's successor, Francis Legge, reported in 1775 that Mauger's influence was so extensive that the governor of Nova Scotia could not without complaint "introduce any measure for the public good" that was opposed to the interest of Mauger's supporters. By 1775 other voices had been raised against Mauger's "plan of Dominion" and against the "notorious" power of his agent, John Butler, but the opposition was not strong. Legge's desire to reform the customs and excise duties would have been enough in itself to attract Mauger's enmity, but his attack on the whole structure of privilege in Nova Scotia ensured his fate. Utilizing the protests sent to him by Legge's enemies in the colony, Mauger conducted a deft campaign against the governor in London. Legge was recalled in 1776, and Mauger's friends boasted that he was the third governor they had removed.

With his interests secure Mauger seems to have been content during the American revolution to reap the benefits of his investments. Indeed, those investments constituted one of the major ties linking Nova Scotia to Britain in the war years. Only in 1779 did he begin to disengage himself from Nova Scotian affairs. That year he gave his able lieutenant, John Butler, power of attorney to sell a considerable number of his holdings there. Three years later Butler's nephew, John Butler Dight Butler, was authorized to sell all his remaining property, except for two 20,000-acre tracts on the Bay of Fundy, one of them apparently the property acquired from Alexander McNutt, and his distillery and related lands in

Halifax. Finally, in 1784, Mauger sold his distillery as well. Although it is impossible to be certain, Mauger may have been experiencing financial problems in the late 1770s. The list of bankrupts in the *Gentleman's Magazine* for 1777 mentions a J. Mauger, broker, but it cannot be confirmed that this man was Joshua.

Little is known of Mauger's personal or business affairs in England. At his death he was a director of the French Hospital and an elder brother of Trinity House, both concerns that reflect his origins and background. He left most of his estate to the children of his nieces. His wife and daughter are not mentioned in his will and had presumably predeceased him.

DONALD F. CHARD

Further reading

J. B. Brebner, *The neutral Yankees of Nova Scotia, a marginal colony during the revolutionary years* (New York, 1937).

G. G. Plank, *An unsettled conquest: the British campaign against the peoples of Acadia* (Philadelphia, 2001).

Yves Frenette, *The Anglo-Normans in eastern Canada*, trans. Carole Dolan (Ottawa, 1996).

FRANÇOIS BABY,

businessman, militia officer, office holder, politician, seigneur, and landowner; b. 4 Oct. 1733 in Montreal (Que.), tenth child of Raymond Baby and Thérèse Le Compte Dupré; d. 6 Oct. 1820 at Quebec, Lower Canada.

François Baby's father was a fur trader who had been sufficiently successful before his death, four years after François's birth, to enable the boy to be educated at the Jesuit college at Quebec. His mother's family being deeply involved in the fur trade, and his eldest brother, Jacques Baby, *dit* Dupéront, being engaged in it by 1753, François too became active in what had become a family profession; another brother, Louis, was also a fur trader. By 1757 François was in partnership with Jacques and the youngest brother, Antoine, under the name of Baby Frères. While his brothers worked the fur-trade regions, François resided at Montreal, receiving and forwarding imported trade goods, exporting furs, and handling accounts with correspondents in Paris, Bordeaux, and in La Rochelle, where they included François Havy, partner of Jean Lefebvre.

During the Seven Years' War François shared to some extent in his brothers' military glories. He may have been at the battle of the Monongahela (near Pittsburgh, Pa) in 1755 under Daniel-Hyacinthe Marie Liénard de Beaujeu, and he undoubtedly served under François de Lévis at the siege of Quebec in the spring of 1760. He thus merited with Jacques, Louis, and Antoine the applause of Governor Pierre de Rigaud de Vaudreuil de Cavagnial, Marquis de Vaudreuil, who certified in July "that the sieurs Baby brothers, merchants of Montreal, have on all occasions given the greatest proofs of their zeal and disinterest in the service of the king [and] that they have distinguished themselves by their bravery and their talents, in almost all the actions that they have undertaken against the English...."

The war did not prevent the Babys from continuing in business or keeping an eye to their future interests. In February 1760, well before the capture of Montreal by the British, Simon Jauge of Bordeaux advised François by way of England, no doubt in response to queries from him, that he might make contact in London with the firm of Thomas, Thomas and Son, Jauge's correspondent there. Taken prisoner to England in September, François likely did call on the London firm before obtaining a passport to go to France. He settled in La Rochelle, probably with the intention of remaining in France if Canada was not recovered, since, like Jacques, he had refused to swear allegiance to the king of Great Britain. The Babys, nevertheless, were selling their furs on the London market and importing English trade goods by 1762. From France, François endeavoured to ensure the supply of trade goods to his brothers and maintained contacts with British and French trading houses. When it became clear that the conquered colony would remain a British possession, he liquidated most of the family's French assets and oversaw

the transfer of commercial relations to London in order to be of consequence in the reconstituted trade. Through his French correspondents he
was put in touch with a number of London firms, including Joseph and
Henry Guinaud, which soon became his principal supplier.

Baby returned to Montreal late in 1763 and once again acted as
intermediary for Antoine and Jacques, who were based at Detroit (Mich.).
However, he soon established his own wholesale business at Quebec,
importing British spirits and manufactures; by 1765 he had taken up
residence there. Although he travelled often to Montreal to conduct his
brothers' business, a permanent agent was needed in the city, and the merchant Pierre Guy was chosen. Perhaps while in London, Baby had, along
with Joseph and Henry Guinaud, entered into partnership with Michel
Chartier de Lotbinière, Marquis de Lotbinière, who needed financing for
a scheme to buy seigneuries. But by 1766, seeing no return on his investment, Baby put an end to the association. In the same year he altered
his relations with his principal London supplier – known from 1765 as
Guinaud and Hankey – and established a mutual account, whereby it
shared in the profits or the losses on its merchandise sold by Baby in the
colony; as well, Baby received a commission on sales and another for handling all the London firm's cargoes to and from Quebec. In 1767 Baby's
indebtedness to Guinaud and Hankey was £1,270 17s. 7d., a comment
on his credit worthiness in London; that year he received merchandise
valued at £2,825 4s. 6d. on behalf of the mutual account.

Like most merchants in the highly unstable commercial context of
the 1760s, Baby sought security through diversification. He added to his
items of commerce such products as planks, peas, oats, apples, silverware,
cottons, helmet plumes, and maidenhair ferns, valued for their medicinal
properties. He also speculated in wheat and furs. In 1769 he was the third
largest investor in the fur trade, but by the early 1770s Robert Hankey
was complaining that the poor quality of Baby's furs, obtained largely
from Jacques in the Detroit area, resulted in serious marketing problems
in London. In addition to these activities Baby operated at least one
schooner and possibly other vessels on the St Lawrence and its tributaries, ensuring delivery of purchases to his warehouses and sales to his customers, and carrying on a cargo trade for other merchants when possible.

In 1773 grave problems in London and France required Baby's
return to Europe. No longer satisfied with Hankey (Henry Guinaud

had become bankrupt in 1769), Baby transferred his accounts with that merchant to Thomas Pecholier, also of London, while maintaining long-standing relations with Thomas, Thomas and Son. Once again he crossed to France. He had wound up most of his family's affairs there before leaving in 1763, but not until this trip was he able to close the books on his and his brothers' holdings in paper money from the French régime as well as on certain other monetary transactions. The family, including François, had lost heavily in these matters; for example, on one occasion in the late 1760s bills of exchange drawn on Bordeaux for 11,666 *livres* netted François only 6,056 *livres* after discount. But, despite his losses, and unlike many other Canadian merchants, he had survived the difficult transition to the new economic order in the colony. Indeed, he had done quite well; in 1772 he purchased better quarters, a stone house on Rue Sous-le-Fort, at a cost of about £350.

In the course of surviving economically Baby had acquired strongly conservative political views and the social and economic credentials to become a spokesman for the Canadian bourgeoisie. His social prominence as early as 1766 is indicated by the invitation he received to sign an address of welcome that was to be offered to Lieutenant Governor Guy Carleton; his acceptance signalled his complete reconciliation to the British presence. Consequently, in 1773, with the British government labouring over a new constitution for the province, Baby was charged by the Canadian merchants and seigneurs with presenting a petition in London defining their position to the British authorities. It requested the preservation of traditional laws, privileges, and customs, the restoration of the boundaries of New France in order to include in the province Labrador and the fur trade of the west, and the distribution of patronage without distinction between British and Canadian subjects. Baby's defence of the petition was apparently of great value to Carleton, whose views corresponded closely to those of the seigneurs; the former attorney general of Quebec, Francis Maseres, who opposed the petition in large measure, affirmed in 1774 that it "has been made the foundation of the Quebec Act." Baby arrived back at Quebec in May 1774 and was rewarded for his efforts with a public letter of thanks from the defenders of the act. Probably he expected more and was disappointed at having been passed over in the appointments to the Legislative Council, formed in 1775 by virtue of the Quebec Act, in favour of others who, he wrote bitterly to Pierre Guy, "thought and worked more for their own interests than for the public good." He added, "I am very much afraid that the time is not far off when Canadians will be unable to console themselves for having asked for the new form of government."

Baby took up the threads of his business once again and began looking to new ventures. In June 1775 he commissioned construction of a new schooner at Bécancour, paying in advance the entire cost price of about £280. He engaged in sealing and fur trading at the post of Saint-Augustin (Que.) in partnership with François-Joseph Cugnet, Gabriel-Elzéar Taschereau, and Nicolas-Joseph de Lafontaine de Belcour. They invested £1,400 in the first year's operations, choosing to market their products in London through Thomas, Thomas and Son. With this new enterprise, Baby transferred his interest from the old northwest to the Labrador coast.

Operations had only begun, however, when the American invasion of the colony brought Baby's business to a temporary standstill. On 5 Aug. 1775 he was commissioned a captain in the Quebec militia, which he helped to organize, and in 1776 he was made commissary of military transport. Following the retreat of the Americans, Carleton appointed Baby, Taschereau, and Jenkin Williams to inquire into disloyalty among the Canadians east of Trois-Rivières during the invasion. Given the circumstances, the commissioners were required to display realism, restraint, diplomacy, and sensitivity. On 22 May they set out on a tour of parishes that would last seven weeks. Beginning around Quebec and the Île d'Orléans, they proceeded upriver along the north shore as far as Trois-Rivières, and then descended the south shore to Kamouraska. In each parish they collected information from the priest, mustered the militia, replaced officers who had collaborated with the Americans, publicly burned American commissions, and harangued the assembly on their duty of loyalty. They withdrew commissions from officers in 37 of some 50 parishes and fully absolved the local captain in only two. However, apart from the withdrawal of commissions, the only punishment recorded was the confiscation of weapons from those held to be lacking in sympathy to the government; it was a markedly mild and intelligent response. Apparently about this time Baby was appointed adjutant general of militia, and in 1778 he was promoted lieutenant-colonel.

Baby's conduct during the invasion also won for him the coveted appointment to the Legislative Council and he was sworn in as a member on 30 June 1778. Moreover, Governor Frederick Haldimand also took him into his unconstitutional privy council, composed of those councillors on whom he could depend for support. In late 1778 or early 1779 he appointed him a justice of the peace for the District of Quebec. Although an exaggeration, it became common opinion that he was, in the words of a woman from Boucherville, "all-powerful in the service of His Excellency the General Haldimand." Baby was one of a select few to establish a personal friendship with the usually reserved governor, and in 1780 and 1781, when Haldimand wished to buy land anonymously for a country estate at Montmorency Falls, he confided the task to Baby. Personally affable, courteous, and dignified, and now possessed of money, military rank, and political power, Baby indulged fully in the glittering social life of the upper class. In 1778 Georges-Hippolyte Le Comte Dupré, known as Saint-Georges Dupré, wrote to him, "I imagine you are like a butterfly, flying from belle to belle. I would have been charmed to have taken part in all your celebrated festivities." By 1786 the attentions of the now 52-year-old social butterfly had alighted on 15-year-old Marie-Anne Tarieu de Lanaudière, daughter of the seigneur Charles-François Tarieu de La Naudière, and they were married on 27 February. The couple would have 12 children, of whom 6 would survive Baby.

Baby's entrance into the governing class gradually reduced his commercial activities to secondary importance. In 1779 the Saint-Augustin operations suffered severe depredations at the hands of American corsairs; the same year Baby cut his connections with Thomas, Thomas and Son. However, his experience with the Labrador trade and his relations with Haldimand made him an ideal partner for the merchants George and Alexander Davison, who wanted to wrest from Thomas Dunn, William Grant, and Peter Stuart the lease of the king's posts, and with it obtain a virtual monopoly of the fur trade and fisheries along the north shore of the lower St Lawrence. The Dunn group's lease expired in 1777 but, thanks in part to Lieutenant Governor Henry Hamilton, they were able to retain the posts until 1786. Haldimand's influence carried, however; Hamilton was dismissed for his action, and on 21 June 1786 Baby and his partners signed a new lease to take effect on 1 October. Baby nominally held a one-third share in the enterprise, but in fact he no longer had a merchant's interest in the project. He had probably joined the Davisons mainly because of the political influence he could bring to bear; on 9 September, as the new lessees took over the posts, he sold his share for a pension of £150 per annum for the duration of the lease and reimbursement of his expenses for obtaining it. Thenceforth, with the exception of a small investment of £750 in the fur trade in 1787 and the posting as late as 1790 of an occasional bond for outfits sent by Jacques and Jacques's son James, François was no longer engaged in commerce.

Politically, as well as socially and economically, Baby had drifted away from the Canadian merchants, the leadership of whom had fallen to his friend and former agent, Pierre Guy. In council, Baby was a loyal supporter of Haldimand, who shared few of the merchants' concerns. In early 1780, for example, in opposition to merchants on council such as Dunn, Grant, and George Allsopp, Baby voted in favour of Haldimand's proposal to fix the price of wheat. He became one of the most active and intelligent Canadian members of the French party, led by Adam Mabane, which sought the preservation of the Quebec Act virtually in its entirety. In 1782 Mabane went so far as to promote Baby as successor to Hector Theophilus Cramahé in the position of lieutenant governor, but Haldimand proposed Hamilton. Although Canadian and British merchants continued to have diverging opinions on some points, they gradually eliminated their more important differences and worked out a number of joint political demands requiring fundamental reform, if not a complete rejection, of the Quebec Act. Baby fought their demands, including that for an elected assembly, which the Canadian merchants adopted publicly after Haldimand's departure in November 1784.

As adjutant general of the militia Baby was responsible for the application of the first militia law, passed in 1777. The ordinance established a hierarchy of officers consisting of a commander-in-chief, and an adjutant general, colonels and subordinate officers at Quebec, Montreal, and Trois-Rivières, and captains and subordinate officers in the parishes. As well as assisting the regular army in the defence of the colony, the militia was required to provide it with transport and other services, collectively known as the corvée, not all of which were subject to remuneration. The vagueness of the ordinance left much latitude for arbitrary actions and despotism on the part of the army and the militia officers; Baby was the channel through which the resulting wave of complaints poured into Carleton's, and later Haldimand's, office. But Carleton and the seigneurs, who formed the backbone of the French party, had been extremely embarrassed by the failure of the habitants to fight the Americans. They (and Baby shared their view) systematically opposed reforms suggested mainly by Hugh Finlay, Henry Caldwell, and Allsopp to reduce arbitrariness, on the grounds that the militia had to be taught to submit to constituted authority. Not until 1787, with the French party much weakened following Haldimand's return to Britain, were changes finally introduced in a general militia law and in another more clearly defining the corvée. In 1788 Baby was lieutenant-colonel in the Canadian militia at Quebec.

By May of that year, through an inheritance from the estate of his father-in-law, Baby had become one of several co-proprietors of the seigneuries of Saint-Vallier and Saint-Pierre-les-Becquets. In January 1790 his revenues from these seigneuries were estimated at only £40, but Baby expanded his holdings in them shortly after. In June he purchased a farm in Saint-Vallier for about £300, and two years later he paid another co-seigneur Pierre-Ignace Aubert de Gaspé about £125 for his one-eighth share in Saint-Pierre-les-Becquets. Yet, when appointed by Dorchester in 1790 to a committee of council charged with reporting on seigneurial tenure, Baby and another seigneur, Charles-Louis Tarieu de Lanaudière, were among those who urged its abolition. Thus, while Baby was no longer a merchant, neither was he, in his own mind, a full-fledged seigneur.

Baby was above all an office holder, and like many office holders he conducted some property transactions, although on a relatively small scale. Being wealthy and a devout Roman Catholic, he preferred to lend money through the purchase of life annuities, a form of lending acceptable to the church. He paid the borrower a certain sum in return for an annuity yielding six per cent per annum of that sum (the legal rate of interest at the time) for as long as the borrower kept the capital; the latter could buy the annuity back at any time. Between 1789 and 1806 Baby purchased at least 22 annuities for a total of 147,134 *livres*, or approximately £6,130. He had an excellent and wide-spread reputation for fairness among the élite of the colony; the largest annuities were purchased from seigneurs, merchants, and priests from Saint-Jean-Port-Joli to Montreal.

In 1792 Baby cut perhaps his last remaining link with the merchant community when he sold his house on Rue Sous-le-Fort and moved to Upper Town, at first on Rue du Parloir, then by 1795 on Rue Buade. In 1791 he was appointed to the Executive Council and in 1792 to the

Legislative Council, both bodies having been created by the Constitutional Act of 1791. In 1794, 1802–3, and 1806–7 he was speaker of the Legislative Council. He was given the opportunity to act as administrator of Lower Canada in the governor's absence, but he declined on the grounds that he could not comply with the Test Act. He did receive two lesser appointments, however, those of commissioner to administer the Jesuit estates (1800) and commissioner for the relief of persons owing *lods et ventes* (1801).

During the 1790s and early 1800s Baby was prominent in the movement to promote loyalty in the city at a time when sympathy for revolutionary France, then at war with Britain, ran high. In June 1794 he was a member of the directing committee of the Association, formed that year to support British rule in the colony, and he signed its public declaration of loyalty to the constitution and government; in January he had signed an address to Prince Edward Augustus on his departure from Quebec. By 1795 he was colonel of a newly formed battalion of Canadian militia at Quebec. In June 1799 he and Jean-Antoine Panet were the only two Canadians among 13 leading citizens who launched a voluntary subscription campaign to support Britain's war effort.

Baby reaped a number of rewards for his public expressions of loyalty and his years of service to the British colonial administration. In 1792 he applied for land on the south shore of the St Lawrence, and it was recommended that he be granted 1,200 acres; however, an application for Templeton Township in October 1793 was dismissed. In 1802, on the recommendation of Lieutenant Governor Sir Robert Shore Milnes, he was granted a life pension of £150 per annum. Six years later his salary as adjutant general was raised from £91 to £320 sterling. Moreover, as an executive councillor he was entitled to 12,000 acres of land: in 1809 he received 7,340 acres in Sherrington Township, and the remainder was granted in Tingwick Township in 1818. The following year he also received 1,800 acres in Chester Township for his militia service during the American invasion and occupation of 1775–76.

By 1810 age and ill health had begun to impair Baby's abilities. With war in the air, in October 1811 he accepted the invitation of the commander-in-chief, Sir George Prevost, to resign as adjutant general in return for the sinecure of chief road commissioner, which carried a salary of £150. He was replaced as adjutant general by François Vassal de Montviel. In 1812 Baby also resigned as commissary of militia transport. He remained attached to the militia, however, as colonel of the Cap Santé battalion.

Baby had also ceased to play an active role in the affairs of state. Although he supported Prevost in his conflict with the English party, his support was probably passive, both because of his age and of his political ties with members of that party. He remained relatively active in business, however. By 1811 he had apparently acquired a number of life annuities sold by habitants of the *faubourg* Saint-Roch to the estate of the merchant William Grant. Between 1814 and 1820 Baby purchased life annuities costing a total of £4,643. In addition, he came to the rescue of his son François by paying a debt owed by François of £700.

Baby remained to the end a highly sociable man, and his home was renowned as a rendezvous of the Quebec élite. He and his wife conducted themselves socially in a manner that the church found exemplary given their rank; at the numerous gatherings she hosted, Marie-Anne invariably dressed with a modesty that contrasted with the stylish finery of her female guests. Bishop Joseph-Octave Plessis, ordinarily critical of the worldliness of the colony's governing class, found that Baby's piety commanded his respect and friendship. At Baby's death, the directors of the Séminaire de Québec, wishing to express their gratitude for his active support of the institution, had him buried in their chapel, the *fabrique* of Notre-Dame Cathedral having closed its church to burials the year before.

To many Canadians of his time, Baby had been anglicized. He seems to have counted among his closest friends three of the most prominent members of the English party, Jonathan Sewell, Herman Witsius Ryland, and William Smith, all of whom signed his burial record. Politically, he was much more comfortable with the authoritarianism of his British colleagues of the Executive and Legislative councils than with the democratically inclined politics of the Canadian party in the House of Assembly. But if some thought he had sold his birthright to preserve his economic well-being, others felt that he had genuinely sought to serve Canadian interests as a leading member of the governing clique for almost half a century.

JOHN CLARKE

Further reading

D. [B.] Miquelon, "The Baby family in the trade of Canada, 1750–1820" (MA thesis, Carleton Univ., Ottawa, [1966]).

Québec during the American invasion, 1775–1776: the journal of François Baby, Gabriel Taschereau, and Jenkin Williams, ed. M. P. Gabriel, trans. S. P. Vergereau-Dewey (East Lansing, Mich., 2005).

Michel Brunet, "The British conquest and the decline of the French-Canadian bourgeoisie," in *Society and conquest: the debate on the bourgeoisie and social change in French Canada, 1700–1850*, ed. Dale Miquelon (Vancouver, 1977), 143–61.

P.-B. Casgrain, "L'honorable François Baby," *Bulletin des recherches historiques* (Lévis, Québec), 12 (1906): 41–46.

Pierre Tousignant, "La genèse et l'avènement de la constitution de 1791" (thèse de PHD, Univ. de Montréal, 1971): 167–69, 227.

GEORGE ALLSOPP,

businessman, office holder, politician, and seigneur; b. *c.* 1733 in England; d. 14 April 1805 in Cap-Santé, Lower Canada.

George Allsopp served in the British Quartermaster General's Department during the 1758 expedition against Louisbourg, Île Royale (Cape Breton Island), and in 1759 as secretary to Lieutenant-Colonel Guy Carleton, quartermaster general at Quebec. Following this service Allsopp entered the trade between Britain and Quebec, one of the earliest British merchants after the conquest to realize the commercial potential of Canada. In 1761 he came from Bristol to be junior partner, first at Montreal and then at Quebec, in the mercantile supply firm of Jenkins, Trye and Company. Since specialization often meant failure in the unstable colonial economy, Allsopp formed additional partnerships and diversified business interests, participating in the wheat, fur, and timber trades, the Gulf of St Lawrence fisheries, the manufacture of potash and spirits, and the production of iron at the Saint-Maurice ironworks. "A person of the most extensive Correspondence of [any]one in this Province without exception," Allsopp began about 1767 his lengthy association with the powerful London house of Olive, Watson and Rashleigh. That firm soon became his principal financial support and commercial supplier, while Allsopp became the central agent in its consolidation of significant commercial interests in Quebec.

Allsopp's trading activities were complicated after 1761 by his conflict with James Murray, military governor of Quebec, who had a strong aversion to the exploitative activities of the British merchants. They responded to the governor's attitudes by vilifying his numerous interventions to regulate economic activity. Personally provoked by Murray's interference with his trade and misrepresentation of him to imperial authorities in a manner capable of damaging his commercial reputation, Allsopp soon became the governor's most vehement critic.

Similar antagonism to the military prevailed elsewhere in North America following the Seven Years' War, but in Quebec the merchants also deplored Murray's attempt to gain Canadian support by attenuating the anglicizing policy of the Royal Proclamation of 1763 and his instructions, both of which were designed to assimilate the province into the British empire. The merchants supported the proclamation's exclusion of Roman Catholics from public office yet still expected the colony to be endowed with the full range of political and judicial institutions characteristic of British colonies. Allsopp and other merchants were consequently angered when, after the introduction of the long-awaited civil government in August 1764, Murray refused to institute an elected assembly, preferring to govern with an appointed council only. Tension mounted in September following Murray's ordinance establishing civil and criminal courts. The merchants felt that the resulting judicial system offered too many concessions to French civil law. They were increasingly concerned as well about the continued absence of a definite statement of property law, and precise regulations to govern complex commercial dealings. The most opinionated of the British community responded to Murray's policy in October 1764 when the first grand jury of Quebec, with James Johnston as foreman, delivered its ill-judged presentment, part of which Allsopp had drafted. The presentment criticized the judicial system and implicitly condemned Murray's entire administration by demanding temporary recognition of the grand jury as the only representative body in the colony, with a right to review public accounts. An appended clause, later attributed to Allsopp, opposed Roman Catholic participation on juries. The irascible merchant may also have inspired the presentment's recommendation that a garrison order compelling civilians and some soldiers to carry lanterns outside after dark be amended. In March and twice in October 1764, Allsopp had been arrested for violating this order. Each encounter was marked by violence, Allsopp's vociferous denunciations of the military, and, in October, his rapid prosecution of the soldiers involved.

Allsopp vigorously campaigned for Murray's recall. In 1765 and 1766 he, the London merchant Anthony Merry, Joseph Howard, and Edward Chinn protested Murray's restrictions of trade at the government-controlled king's posts. The resulting controversy exposed the inconsistencies of official policy, which vacillated between monopoly operation and free trade. In the midst of this debate Allsopp was appointed deputy provincial secretary and assistant clerk both of the Council of Quebec and of provincial enrolments on 15 Jan. 1766. Purchased from the absentee office holder, Henry Ellis, these largely clerical positions provided Allsopp with the security needed in a fluctuating commercial career. The appointments reached Allsopp in April, but Murray refused to install him because of his factious behaviour. The governor, however, returned to England in June, a recall for which Allsopp claimed much of the credit. Following the arrival of Guy Carleton as lieutenant governor and a thorough investigation of Allsopp's behaviour, the suspension was lifted in April 1768. The British community had been divided in its support of Allsopp's grievance over his exclusion from office. Several merchants, especially in Montreal, questioned his impartiality and disliked the militancy with which he had opposed Murray's administration. Others, such as Chief Justice William Hey, resented the close relationship between Brook Watson and Carleton and scornfully termed Allsopp a "fallen angel." Yet by 1768 Allsopp, financier, estate executor, and local property owner as well as merchant, had become a conspicuous member of the mercantile community in the Quebec district. On 22 Dec. 1768 he married Anna Marie, the only daughter of another early merchant, John Taylor Bondfield. The Allsopps were to have ten children of whom seven, six boys and a girl, would survive infancy.

Between 1768 and 1773 Allsopp attended to both his prospering business interests and his lucrative but demanding official duties, which included the annual and often controversial issuance of tavern and fur-trade licences. Although hindered by assistants either incompetent or less scrupulous than himself, Allsopp sought to exercise his functions impartially and efficiently, conscious of his own commercial reputation and Carleton's increasing scrutiny of official fee structures in the province. The positions brought Allsopp an annual salary of £200 from the British Treasury; he paid Henry Ellis £400 and pocketed the fees. Allsopp also served from 25 Oct. 1769 until 24 Oct. 1772 as deputy commissary general, charged with allocating provisions to garrisons throughout the province, a post in which his commercial knowledge proved invaluable. His own activities as a wholesale merchant were dependent on the credit accorded him by Watson and Rashleigh, for whom he was also, as early as 1769, the agent responsible for collecting the accounts of various retailers. Foremost among these was Samuel Jacobs, a merchant and grain dealer in Saint-Denis on the Rivière Richelieu. In 1766 Allsopp and Jacobs combined with John Welles under the name of Jacobs, Welles and Company to exploit a potash works in Lower Town Quebec at the former king's forges, which they leased from the crown. The enterprise was soon plagued by technical and managerial problems and failed in 1772, although without serious loss to Allsopp.

Like other British merchants, Allsopp was gradually specializing in the grain trade, revived following the war, and after 1766 he began to acquire increasing amounts of wheat from Jacobs. In September 1773 Allsopp and his brother-in-law John Bondfield purchased the adjoining seigneuries of Auteuil and Jacques-Cartier about 30 miles upstream from Quebec; the property included the seigneurial gristmill on the Rivière Jacques-Cartier. Two years later Bondfield relinquished to Allsopp his share in the seigneuries. Following the acquisition of the gristmill, Allsopp began making flour, and his grain purchases resulted in a steadily increasing debt to Jacobs and other suppliers.

From 1768 to 1773 Allsopp's trade and milling operations, official duties, and cordial relations with Carleton diverted him from public debate over colonial government. During this same period, however, it was becoming increasingly clear that the merchants' political views were vastly different from those of Carleton, who as commander-in-chief was preoccupied with provincial security and Canadian loyalty under veiled threats of French retaliation and growing restiveness in the American colonies. The Quebec Act of 1774, which Carleton had largely inspired, profoundly disappointed the merchants by providing for exclusive use of French civil law and by eliminating trial by jury in civil suits. The act also dashed all hope of an assembly and provided for an appointed legislative council which the merchants felt was too small to be representative, too susceptible to Roman Catholic influence, and too dependent on the governor. Allsopp's own ill-concealed disappointment over the absence of provisions for an assembly and English commercial law stirred up opposition to him among government supporters. He was nevertheless appointed to the Legislative Council and was sworn in on 17 Aug. 1775.

During the American siege of Quebec Allsopp held the important post, between 25 Jan. 1775 and 24 Aug. 1776, of commissary general for the Quebec garrison. His misgivings about the Quebec Act, however, were being misinterpreted by Carleton and others as disloyalty, particularly since a number of Allsopp's former business associates, including Joseph Howard, Thomas Walker, Pierre Du Calvet, John Welles, Christophe Pélissier, and John and Acklam Bondfield, supported the American cause. Suspicions of Allsopp's loyalty may have been partially responsible for his removal in 1777 as deputy provincial secretary and assistant clerk of provincial enrolments; the provincial secretary and clerk, George Pownall, had been in the colony since his appointment to those offices in 1775, but Allsopp had continued to act as deputy until 1777. Allsopp's quarrelsome nature, blatant commercial bias, perceived disregard for provincial security, and desire for more English law contributed to his radical reputation, and in 1778 he was publicly assaulted as a "rebel."

Embittered by his dismissal from all his official posts by 1778, Allsopp, in spite of the pressures, was until 1791 the most consistent and militant opponent of the provincial administration. The peak of his opposition came in March 1780. Influenced by the views of the absent chief justice, Peter Livius, and his own commercial preoccupation, the contentious merchant erupted during the near-violent session of the Legislative Council that year in a bitter but sophisticated indictment of the judicial and administrative systems sanctioned by Governor Frederick Haldimand. He condemned the elimination of jury trials and habeas corpus, the unauthorized privy council introduced by Carleton and continued by Haldimand, the absence of a clearly defined legal code to regulate commercial transactions and suits, and the inadequacies of the court system established under the Quebec Act. To combat the "seditious spirit" displayed by Allsopp and to counter growing support within council for reform, Haldimand suspended him in January 1783.

Although heavily engaged in politics, Allsopp did not neglect his wheat and flour trades or his agency for Watson and Rashleigh. In 1781 he had contracted with the seigneur James Cuthbert to buy all his available wheat for 14 years. Three years previously Allsopp had begun building a large, expensive, stone grist-mill near the mouth of the Rivière Jacques-Cartier. By 1783 this project had contributed substantially to his indebtedness, already worsened by wartime trade restrictions and strained financial relations with Watson and Rashleigh. Business matters involving his agency for the London company took Allsopp to New York that year. In 1784 he went to England to negotiate a financial settlement with the firm, promote trade for his mills, and contest his exclusion from council.

In London Allsopp was drawn almost instinctively to the lobby for the repeal of the Quebec Act. He laid his arguments before various politicians, including Thomas Powys, member of parliament for Northamptonshire, Evan Nepean, an under-secretary in the Shelburne ministry, and John Baker Holroyd, 1st Earl of Sheffield, a recognized authority on commerce and agriculture and an opponent of William Pitt's proposed relaxation of the navigation laws. The merchant's case for administrative and judicial reform, and the reconsideration of his suspension, nevertheless fell prey to the indecisive preoccupation of the Pitt ministry with constitutional change in Quebec. In business matters he was more successful, but only after much negotiation and self-assertion. Before he returned to Quebec in the fall of 1785 he had arranged, partially through a mortgage on his new mill, to repay a debt of more than £8,660 to Watson and Rashleigh and had made agreements to supply flour and biscuit to merchants involved in the Newfoundland and Gulf of St Lawrence fisheries.

During Allsopp's absence from Quebec, reform had become a popular issue through the initiative of Lieutenant Governor Henry Hamilton and others. Allied with Deputy Postmaster General Hugh Finlay, Chief Justice William Smith, and Quebec City merchant William Grant, Allsopp supported measures debated between 1785 and 1787 for judicial reform, notably those favourable to commercial activity. In 1787, during a formal investigation into the administration of justice, Allsopp sharply condemned the inconsistency of decisions in commercial cases rendered by the Court of Common Pleas. Since 1777 this court had been handling all civil cases, and Allsopp, because of its inconsistency, had made every effort to avoid it. He argued that the variability in its decisions resulted from the lack of a definite legal code for the judgement of commercial transactions. Instead there was the confusing use of legal elements from the outdated French mercantile code and even from the laws of New France and of the colony of New York. Between 1787 and 1791 he continued to play a leading role in the efforts by British and Canadian committees to convince Governor Carleton, now 1st Baron Dorchester, and the British parliament of the necessity for a representative assembly and English commercial law.

Agitation within the province over constitutional change was marked by a bewildering variety of opinion. Many merchants learned with dismay of the government's intention, stated in the Constitutional Act of 1791, to divide the colony, thus separating them politically from the loyalists in what became Upper Canada. Nor did the new act completely repeal the Quebec Act or provide for a commercial code. Encouraged, however, by the provisions for an assembly balanced by a legislative council, and less concerned with the political and commercial implications, Allsopp enthusiastically claimed partial responsibility for having "produced a most excellent Constitution for Canada, preferable in several respects to that enjoyed by the other Colonies." He contested the election of 1792 for Upper Town Quebec but was defeated by his former reform associate William Grant. Allsopp was further disappointed when Dorchester's recommendation for his appointment to the first legislative and executive councils under the act was rejected by William Wyndham Grenville, the Home secretary.

In business throughout the period from 1786 to 1791 Allsopp concentrated almost exclusively on wheat buying, milling, and marketing, and the shipment of flour and biscuit from Jacques-Cartier and his Lower Town Quebec warehouses and wharf. He undertook much custom grinding in addition to the production of his own flour and biscuit. His principal markets were Montreal provisioners, the Gulf of St Lawrence fisheries, the West Indies, government supply contractors, and local con-

sumers in Quebec. By 1788 Allsopp's milling complex, capable of producing 65,000 *minots* or 22 per cent of the colony's annual production,
ranked first in the province. Fully aware of the intricate mechanics of the
grain trade, he repeatedly advocated the exportation of flour rather than
bulky wheat. Although Quebec merchants such as Allsopp were hampered by the negative effects of the Canadian climate and current agrarian practices on the quality of wheat and flour produced, they hoped to
find compensation in the severance, following the American revolution,
of supplies to the empire from American sources. In 1789, after a British
act of the previous year had failed to establish reciprocal trade between
Quebec and the British West Indies, Allsopp led a delegation of millers,
bakers, coopers, and merchants in the presentation to Dorchester of a
proposed amendment to make the act operative. Supported by the Legislative Council, the proposals were referred to Britain but lost in more
pressing constitutional debates.

By 1790 Allsopp's seigneurial revenues of £600 per annum made
him the eighth most important individual seigneur in the colony. His
commercial stability was seriously threatened in 1793, however, when
fire destroyed his main grist-mill near the mouth of the Jacques-Cartier.
Allsopp was forced to renegotiate his financial obligations to Brook
Watson, whose rigid control of Allsopp's financial base spurred the merchant's contempt. In 1795 a settlement was concluded. Between that
year and 1798 operations were largely restored at the stone mill; from
1795 as well Allsopp leased the nearby Portneuf baronial mill. The
Jacques-Cartier seigneurial mill, which in June 1796 had also burned
down, was reactivated, and a third grist-mill was added to the complex.

Although Allsopp still entered into other smaller but profitable
transactions, he now viewed the processing and sale of flour as the "only
eligible trade." He supplied flour to his bakeries at Jacques-Cartier and in
Lower Town Quebec for the local market; he also sold flour and biscuit
to the exporters Lester and Morrogh and to Monro and Bell, suppliers to
the government contractor Alexander Davison. Allsopp was able to rely
increasingly on the advice and assistance at Jacques-Cartier of his eldest
son, George Waters Allsopp, but his plan to expand his trade through
the placement of his other sons in foreign market centres did not materialize. By the time of his death, John, Robert, and William had participated in the family trade at Quebec; Carleton became a merchant abroad
and James entered the British army. Allsopp's wife and daughter spent

much of each year throughout the 1790s at Cap-Santé near the mills, while Allsopp reluctantly resided for lengthy periods at Quebec where his business was conducted.

At Quebec Allsopp pursued various other interests ranging from the Quebec Fire and Agriculture societies to large-scale land speculation in the Eastern Townships. Complications in the controversial land-granting system prevented the family from exploiting much of Allsopp's granted land until after his death, particularly in Farnham and Maddington townships. On the basis of his knowledge of commercial law and past experience as a Court of Appeals judge (a duty of legislative councillors), Allsopp petitioned for a judgeship in 1794. This position was denied, but on 12 June 1799 he was appointed a justice of the peace for Quebec.

Governed by bitter memories of his political humiliation, Allsopp had apparently avoided any involvement in provincial politics after 1792. He nevertheless retained his faith in the British constitution, the theoretical foundation of his earlier reform campaign. In response to the French revolution he praised the constitution's balance of monarchy, aristocracy, and democracy as the most effective means of controlling an elected body. According to available evidence, Allsopp refrained from any assessment of Lower Canadian politics during the 1790s and his response to the emerging political contest between Canadian and ministerial groups for legislative control is uncertain. During the 1796 election campaign of his son George Waters, however, he did express concern over the vigour of Canadian opposition.

The longevity and extent of Allsopp's business activities establish him as a principal commercial figure in Quebec between 1760 and the 1790s. Through partnerships and diverse wholesale trading interests he quickly prospered, and as the principal agent in Canada for Brook Watson he figured significantly in that powerful merchant's penetration into virtually all aspects of the Quebec trade. Secured by this association and the apparent availability of long-term credit, Allsopp specialized increasingly in the wheat trade but gradually declined in prominence as a wholesaler. Following the construction of the Jacques-Cartier grist-mill, the turning-point of his career, Allsopp emerged as a major industrialist and, by 1788, the province's largest flour producer. Intense competition from other producers and wheat exporters, the demands of full-time management, and heavy financial obligations to Watson eventually forced him to forsake plans for retirement to England. He remained active as a business-man and magistrate until at least 1804. On 26 March 1805 the death in Quebec of his wife, who was long a stabilizing influence upon him, came as a severe blow, and he died in Cap-Santé less than three weeks later following a series of crippling strokes. The business was continued by George Waters Allsopp, but in 1808 the grist-mills were offered for lease.

DAVID ROBERTS

Further reading

Michael Bliss, *Northern enterprise: five centuries of Canadian business* (Toronto, 1987), 108–28.

H. [M.] Neatby, *Quebec: the revolutionary age, 1760–1791* (Toronto, 1966).

PIERRE FORETIER,

businessman, landowner, seigneur, office holder, and militia officer; b. 12 Jan. 1738 in Montreal (Que.), son of Jacques Foretier and Marie-Anne Caron; d. there 3 Dec. 1815.

Pierre Foretier came from a family of tradesmen. His grandfather Étienne Foretier was a baker in Montreal; his father, a shoemaker, had obtained master's papers in 1721 in Paris, where he apparently worked at his trade for some years before returning to New France. After 1735 Jacques Foretier lived in Montreal, where he extended his activity to the operation of a small tannery in the *faubourg* Saint-Laurent. In 1743 he went into partnership with a merchant-tanner, Jean-François Barsalou, for the joint use of their tanning mills. Jacques Foretier died in 1747, and his wife kept the tannery going for some years; she died in 1754.

Orphaned at 16, Pierre Foretier was placed in the care of the children of his mother's first and second marriages, with whom he lived until he himself married. He seems to have resided at first with his half-brother, Jacques Paré, probably in the seigneury of Châteauguay, and then with his half-sister, who was married to Bazile Desfonds, a shoemaker in the *faubourg* Saint-Laurent who had once been apprenticed to his father. On 16 Jan. 1764, in Montreal, Foretier married Thérèse, daughter of the merchant Jean-Baptiste Legrand. Their five daughters were to marry men prominent in Lower Canada, among them Denis-Benjamin Viger, Louis-Charles Foucher, and notary Thomas Barron. Four years after his wife died in 1784, Foretier married Catherine Hubert, widow of the merchant Thomas Baron; she too predeceased him, and there were no children from this marriage.

Pierre Foretier's business career began in 1761, the date of the earliest references to his trading and land transactions. From 1762 he appears as a trader or merchant, probably dealing in dry goods and various articles for the fur trade. Around the same time he set up one or several stores. In 1775–76 he was running his father-in-law's store on Rue Saint-Paul, and he owned another on Rue Notre-Dame. Ten years later he was selling fine cloth, crockery, cutlery, clothing, shoes, combs, books, and a variety of small articles in a store connected to his house on Rue Notre-Dame, which apparently was the only one then belonging to him; his business was worth 14,324 *livres*. Subsequently he abandoned this sort of trade, which he had carried on by himself, but there is no indication as to when he closed his store.

His partnerships with other merchants had a very different purpose. Late in 1764 or early in 1765 Foretier had joined with Joseph Périnault to enter the fur trade. The two formed a partnership in April 1765 with Henry Boone, a Montreal merchant, and a Mr Price, Boone's partner at Quebec, to engage in the fur trade and to run a canoe loaded with merchandise to Michilimackinac (Mackinaw City, Mich.). The total capital invested amounted to at least 11,657 *livres*, 5,285 being put up by Foretier and Périnault; they were to receive a third of the profits. Price and Boone attended to selling the furs, Périnault stayed at Michilimackinac, and Foretier served as supplier for the expedition. This agreement was not renewed. Foretier and Périnault probably maintained an interest in the fur trade in 1766 and 1767, but there is no record of their activity. Their partnership seems to have come to an end around 1767. In 1769 Foretier on his own sent a canoe with merchandise worth £150 to Lake

Ontario, and four years later he invested more than £800 to send two canoes and seventeen *engagés* to Michilimackinac. He accompanied this final expedition and stayed in the *pays d'en haut* in 1773.

The following year Foretier took a new partner, Jean Orillat. The company was active in the fur business, particularly in 1777 and 1778, when it invested £9,930, and then an additional £2,625, in the trade. Foretier and Orillat fitted out their own canoes, but they also advanced merchandise and funds to other traders. In addition the company sought to diversify its activities; from 1776 and apparently until 1782, it furnished the government of the colony with powder. In 1776 Foretier and Orillat obtained a contract for supplying the British government with articles for presents to the Indians. The contract amounted to £14,000, and they received a five per cent commission. Because Orillat had been taken prisoner by the Americans during the invasion of 1775–76, the authorities made James Stanley Goddard responsible for looking after Indian presents. Although the partnership between Foretier and Orillat was disrupted by the war, it continued until Orillat's death in 1779; the company's accounts were not officially settled until 1783. Foretier, who had been the largest Canadian investor in the fur trade in 1774 and 1777 and had placed substantial sums in it in 1778, got out of it after Orillat's death, although in 1782 he went security for Joseph Sanguinet's expedition to Michilimackinac (Mackinac Island, Mich.). Foretier's career took a different direction, and the transformation is probably attributable in part to changes occurring in the fur trade and to the increasing difficulties faced by Canadian merchants. But another factor influenced the thrust of Foretier's commercial activity: from 1780 his real estate holdings were becoming more and more profitable.

Foretier's earliest property investments dated from 1761, when he began to purchase land in the *faubourg* Saint-Laurent, at the level of what is now Sherbrooke Street. He first bought two small parcels in the sub-fief of La Gauchetière, and then in 1762 acquired 30 acres at Côte à Baron, to which he added 6 more in 1764. Foretier embarked on his first development project in the *faubourg* Saint-Pierre, subdividing his land and selling the lots. But this initial venture failed; the *faubourg* Saint-Pierre was too isolated and too far from the town to attract many buyers.

Foretier made his principal purchases in 1765. With his partner at that time, Joseph Périnault, he bought two parcels of land from Marie-

Anne-Noële Denys de Vitré – her three-quarters of the sub-fief of Closse (a property located partly in the *faubourg* Saint-Laurent) and her three-quarters of the seigneury of Île-Bizard – as well as 54 secured annuities (23 on Closse). Périnault made his share over to Foretier in 1767, and two years later Foretier purchased the remaining quarters of the two properties, which belonged to Mathieu-Théodore Denys de Vitré. In 1769, then, Foretier owned all the sub-fief of Closse, an immense area 2 *arpents* wide and over 45 *arpents* in depth. Later, particularly after 1780, he purchased a number of adjacent lots, either in the sub-fief of La Gauchetière or at the northern tip of Closse.

Foretier's purchase of the Closse sub-fief was part of a long-term strategy, since it offered little prospect of quick subdivision; its development would extend over nearly half a century. Foretier's main concern at the time of purchase seems to have been to reduce the cost of his investment to the bare minimum. Thus he reached an agreement with the Sulpicians, who were the seigneurs of Montreal Island, that his sub-fief would be added to their domain and then granted back to him in simple roture (for an annual rent); in this way he avoided paying the heavy cost of the *quint*, a tax amounting to a fifth of the price. A first deed of merger concerning three-quarters of the sub-fief was concluded in 1765, and a second one concerning the last quarter in 1778. Around 1790, however, the Closse sub-fief was being developed. Foretier realized how much income he had forgone in making over the *cens et rentes* and *lods et ventes* to the Sulpicians. Pleading that the Sulpicians had "taken" his sub-fief from him, he launched a suit to regain possession of his seigneurial rights, which he won in 1796. He was able consequently to add revenues as seigneur to the profits from subdividing and the secured annuities.

Particularly in the years 1797–1806, Foretier also developed a large number of lots he had acquired between 1781 and 1784 in the southwest of the *faubourg* Saint-Laurent. Once again, as with his other properties, he bought, subdivided, and sold lots, usually by means of secured annuities. This last block of land, which was close to the old town, may have been his most lucrative property investment.

Foretier owned about a quarter of the *faubourg* Saint-Laurent, the equivalent of the area within the town's fortifications. To make these purchases he had invested 83,000 *livres* over a period of 50 years; the land that he subdivided brought him 186,000 *livres*, which made his total profit 103,000 *livres*. To this sum was added the income from the secured annuities and his seigneurial rights, as well as from the sale of produce and the rental of meadows and wood and pasture lands.

Foretier's real estate operations were not limited to the urban setting; his strategy for developing Île-Bizard was, however, very different from the one he used in the *faubourg* Saint-Laurent. He sought first to consolidate his hold on the seigneury by buying back the five sub-fiefs already granted on it; he could not control the pace of development unless he had sole authority to grant land. The process took several years, for the last sub-fief was not rejoined to the domain until 1788. It is interesting to note that the grants he made reflected the timing of his acquisition of urban properties, the periods of greatest activity being 1765–74, 1785–89, and 1795–1805. The number of land grants rose from 83 in 1781–82 to 107 in 1813; the population of Île-Bizard grew to 508 in the same period and included not only farmers but a number of tradesmen. Foretier took a close interest in the running of his seigneury. He erected a communal mill in 1772–73 and rebuilt it after a fire in 1790. He paid close attention to the situation of his censitaires and kept meticulous accounts. At the end of his life his grandson, Hugues Heney, was running the seigneury and accounted to him for the smallest details of his management. The seigneury of Île-Bizard certainly contributed heavily to Foretier's fortune. In 1781–82, for example, the communal mill brought him 1,800 *livres*, the *cens et rentes* 1,087 *livres*.

From his youth Foretier had been interested in commerce, the fur trade, and landed property, all activities requiring considerable initial capital. Astonishingly enough, he apparently lacked both the capital and the contacts that would explain his rise in the business world. No signs of a large family fortune can be found: his parents' estates were modest indeed. Some attribute his success to money from his first wife, but Thérèse Legrand brought him no dowry. Jean-Baptiste Legrand, a fairly well-to-do merchant, probably gave Foretier the benefit of his experience and his financial help, but there is no record of a substantial loan or gift to his son-in-law to enable him to launch his career. Certain elements of Foretier's success consequently remain obscure. On the other hand, his real estate ventures demonstrate his ability to make good deals and to purchase sites on terms that did not necessitate the initial outlay of large sums. Thus Foretier's earliest acquisitions were all made through secured annuities, with the capital not being paid off until much later. Even his biggest purchases, Closse and Île-Bizard, were not acquired with cash but rather by a life annuity of 3,000 *livres*, which Foretier had to carry with Périnault from 1765 to 1767 and then by himself until 1789. The other large disbursements at the start of his career were in 1769 (1,100 *livres*) and 1770 (3,000 *livres*). It was not until the period 1780–92 that Foretier made other purchases with cash or repaid secured annuities. He also frequently transferred both bonds and secured annuities to minimize the transactions that had to be settled in ready money. It is highly probable that in commerce and the fur trade Foretier had had recourse to similar methods to turn a profit on his initial capital, which may have been relatively modest.

Foretier also played an important role in the public life of Lower Canada. Along with other Canadian and British merchants he took part in the reform movement before 1791, and he was one of the members of a committee of Canadians from the Montreal district working for this cause. He was also among those asked to stand as candidates in the first elections for the House of Assembly of Lower Canada in 1792. He ran for Montreal West, where he was defeated. In 1796 he was again a candidate but decided to withdraw before the elections. Appointed a justice of the peace in 1779, he retained that office until his death; as one of the most prestigious JPs of the District of Montreal he was responsible for swearing in provincial officials. He sat on many committees and commissions: he was a member of the commission appointed to investigate aliens arriving in the province (1776), of a committee appointed by the Montreal merchants to study the problem of damaged goods (1779), and of the commission to superintend the House of Correction at Montreal (1803–7); he was also "commissioner with authority to carry out church repairs" (1794–1814).

During the occupation of Montreal by American troops in 1775–76 Foretier showed himself an active loyalist. He had letters delivered to Guy Carleton in Quebec and lent support to a small force of Canadians and Indians being formed at Vaudreuil, providing them with munitions and supplies. He made this contribution to the British cause despite the presence in his home of an American colonel with his aides-de-camp and servants, and despite the close watch kept on him. When hostilities ceased, Foretier continued to show support for the government. He was an active member of the Canadian militia of Montreal, serving in succession as major of the 2nd Battalion (1789–1800) and then as its lieutenant colonel (1801–3), and as colonel of the 3rd Battalion (1804–15).

Foretier also took a close interest in matters of religion. In 1783 he went to London to seek permission from the government to recruit Catholic priests as teachers for the Collège Saint-Raphaël in Montreal. Two years later he was elected churchwarden in the parish of Notre-Dame, an office he held until at least 1787. He may also have been interested in various charities, since he bequeathed large sums to the parish of Notre-Dame, the Hôtel-Dieu, and the Hôpital Général. These legacies amounted to 36,000 *livres*, about a quarter of a fortune estimated at 140,000 *livres* in addition to the value of his lots and buildings.

Foretier's way of life and the considerable fortune he had accumulated bear witness to his success in the business world and public life. He occupied an imposing residence on Rue Notre-Dame that had belonged to his father-in-law, Jean-Baptiste Legrand. In addition to the furniture and numerous and sometimes luxurious fixtures, he had a huge library and a collection of silverware. He also owned a seigneurial manor at Île-Bizard. The inventories made after his first wife's death in 1785 and his own death in 1816 make it possible to examine the evolution of his fortune. In 1785 Foretier was still engaged in both commercial and real estate activities; his links with the fur trade had just been broken. The situation is clearly revealed by the assets of the joint estate, which were estimated at 344,493 *livres*: these included, among other items, the inventory of the store (14,394 *livres*), secured annuities (116,548 *livres*), debts in connection with the landed and seigneurial property (20,901 *livres*), debts of a commercial type due in the form of notes, bonds, and accounts receivable (126,970 *livres*), and even debts owing to the firm of Foretier and Orillat (34,179 *livres*). The last two categories, however, included a large number of doubtful debts that swelled the assets. The liabilities of the joint estate amounted to only 109,915 *livres*, making its net worth 234,578 *livres*, plus 31 lots and buildings. Thirty years later Foretier's wealth was based essentially on his real estate. Of assets valued at 140,142 *livres*, the secured annuities (119,327 *livres*) represented the most important element, followed by the property and seigneurial debts (11,139 *livres*). His liabilities were only a fraction of what they were in

1785 and arose primarily from small current expenses; his properties were free of debt. Foretier had therefore accumulated a fortune estimated at 140,011 *livres*, as well as 34 lots and buildings of unknown value.

When Foretier died, he left a will and numerous codicils designed to prevent his huge fortune and numerous properties from being split up. He stipulated that his estate not be subdivided and tried to exclude certain members of his family, in particular his son-in-law Denis-Benjamin Viger, from any part in managing it and from the income it brought in. Foretier's heirs refused to accept the restrictions imposed on them by the will; they contested the deceased's right to dispose of the assets which their mother, Thérèse Legrand (who had died in 1784), had bequeathed to them and of which he had enjoyed only the usufruct. They agreed, therefore, to disregard the terms of the will and to share the estate equally. Foretier, however, had named his neighbour and friend, Toussaint Pothier, as his executor, and Pothier saw to it that Foretier's wishes were respected. Pothier launched a suit which, after extensive legal proceedings, gave rise on 20 Feb. 1827 to a decision by the Court of King's Bench for the District of Montreal in his favour. On appeal, the provincial Court of Appeals at Quebec on 30 April 1830 set aside the judgement, ruling that the terms of Foretier's will were invalid in the case of Thérèse Legrand's estate and applied solely to the assets in Foretier's estate. The decision made it necessary to evaluate and divide the assets of the two estates and led to another series of lawsuits which dragged on until 29 March 1841, when Foretier's own assets and those bequeathed by Thérèse Legrand were finally separated. It was not until 23 July 1842, however, that the assets from the Legrand estate were divided among the various heirs. Thus for more than 25 years the improvement of the sub-fief of Closse and the other properties in the *faubourg* Saint-Laurent was halted, and in his own way Foretier continued to influence property development in Montreal.

Pierre Foretier was a notable figure in the early years of the British régime. His career spanned more than half a century and encompassed a crucial period in the economic and social development of Lower Canada. His participation in business was not confined to one sector: he was both a retailer and a wholesale merchant, a supplier and financial backer in the fur trade, a lender and speculator, a seigneur and the largest Montreal property owner of his generation. Through the breadth and diversity of his activities he defies simplistic definition. His role in the political and social life of his era also illustrates the complexity of the Lower Canadian merchants' reactions to the transformation their society experienced in the decades after the conquest.

JOANNE BURGESS

Further reading

J. E. Igartua, "The merchants and *négociants* of Montreal, 1750–1775: a study in socio-economic history" (PHD thesis, Mich. State Univ., East Lansing, 1974).

É.-Z. Massicotte, "Le bourgeois Pierre Fortier," *Bulletin des recherches historiques* (Lévis, Québec), 47 (1941): 176–79.

H. [M.] Neatby, *Quebec: the revolutionary age, 1760–1791* (Toronto, 1966).

Carolyn Podruchny, *Making the voyageur world: travelers and traders in the North American fur trade* (Toronto, 2006).

Fernand Ouellet, *Lower Canada, 1791–1841: social change and nationalism*, trans. Patricia Claxton (Toronto, 1980).

Claude Pronovost, *La bourgeoisie marchande en milieu rural, 1720–1840* (Sainte-Foy [Québec], 1998).

Richard White, *The middle ground: Indians, empires, and republics in the Great Lakes region, 1650–1815* (Cambridge, Eng., 1991).

JAMES McGILL,

merchant, office holder, politician, landowner, militia officer, and
philanthropist; b. 6 Oct. 1744 in Glasgow, Scotland, second child
and eldest son of James McGill and Margaret Gibson;
d. 19 Dec. 1813 in Montreal, Lower Canada.

The McGill family, probably originating in Ayrshire, had been resident in Glasgow for two generations when James was born. They were metal workers and, from 1715, members of the hammermen's guild and burgesses of the city. Their fortune rose with Glasgow's when, following the Union of 1707, the English colonies were opened to Scottish commerce. In 1756, on James's matriculation into the University of Glasgow, his father was described as "mercator." The McGills had risen from tradesmen to traders.

When and in what circumstances James McGill emigrated is not known. In 1766 he was in Montreal en route to the *pays d'en haut* as "the deputy" of the Quebec City merchant William Grant. McGill probably wintered on Baie des Puants (Green Bay, Lake Michigan), for in June and July 1767 he was at Michilimackinac (Mackinaw City, Mich.) supervising the dispatch of canoes. He was at Montreal in 1770, but in 1771–72 he was in the field near Fond-du-Lac (Wis.). Like other traders working the southern hinterland of the Great Lakes, McGill conducted simultaneously a number of enterprises with different partners. As early as 1767 he began trading on his own account, obtaining licences for two canoes and cargoes valued at £400. He also posted bonds totalling £2,400 for four traders, one of whom was Charles-Jean-Baptiste Chaboillez, a veteran in the southwest trade. By 1769 McGill had begun his long association with Isaac Todd; about 1770 he also joined with his brother John McGill. John Askin of Michilimackinac, and later of Detroit (Mich.), was McGill's agent, or "forwarder," rather than a partner.

In "constant residence" at Montreal from 1775, McGill adapted his family's urban tradition to Canada. His suppliers were Brickwood, Pattle and Company of London, whose goods he distributed among traders operating in the Indian country. As a minor member of the Anglo-

American merchant community, McGill may have felt it expedient to adopt its political views; once in 1770 and twice in 1774 he signed petitions praying for "a general assembly." Possibly the omission of his name from a memorial against the Quebec Act suggests an improving status that enabled him to act independently. The occupation of Montreal by the troops of the Continental Congress from November 1775 to May 1776 made him conspicuous; he had been one of the group that had negotiated the city's surrender. He had no truck with rebels, however, and his house became a loyalist rendezvous. His steadfastness cost him 14 puncheons of rum when his cellars were ransacked. "Unhappy people" was his characterization of the despoilers; "many of our Mont^{rl} Rebels," he added, "[have run] off with the others."

On 2 Dec. 1776 McGill's marriage with the widow Charlotte Trottier Desrivières, *née* Guillimin, was solemnized by the Reverend David Chabrand Delisle, Montreal's first regularly appointed Anglican pastor. McGill acquired a family, the two surviving sons of Charlotte's first marriage. The elder, François, would become McGill's partner and principal heir. The younger, Thomas-Hippolyte, would be provided with a commission in the Royal Americans (60th Foot) and his son, James McGill Desrivières, would be the object of much solicitude at the end of McGill's life. McGill was fond of children, and he appears to have been drawn especially to the one that bore his name. The years 1775–76 were decisive in McGill's career; marriage brought him into Mrs McGill's wide family circle and his commercial position was thus stabilized. His political position was unexceptionable. Shortly after his marriage McGill secured the highly desirable Bécancour house between Rue Notre-Dame and Rue Saint-Paul near the Château Ramezay. It had been the property of Thomas Walker, one of the chiefs of "our Mont^{rl} Rebels."

In 1776 McGill received his first public appointment, as justice of the peace. It was renewed periodically, and he was thus brought into the administration of Montreal, a function of the justices until 1833. In all, McGill held ten appointments, of which four were of significance: he served in 1788 and 1789 as a member of a commission of inquiry into Jeffrey Amherst, 1st Baron Amherst's claims to the Jesuit estates (educational endowments being considered by many as an alternative use for proceeds from these lands); participated in 1798 with Thomas Blackwood in the French royalist colony at Windham, Upper Canada;

supervised from 1802 the demolition of the old walls of Montreal and the elaboration of plans (entirely abortive) for urban renewal and beautification; and from 1800 oversaw the Lachine turnpike, the first modern road west of the city.

McGill's business also prospered. In 1775, in association with Todd, Benjamin and Joseph Frobisher, and Maurice-Régis Blondeau, he sent 12 canoes to Grand Portage (near Grand Portage, Minn.), a shipment that "appears to mark the beginning of large-scale trade to the Northwest ... and of the Northwest Company," according to the historian Harold Adams Innis. Three years later McGill himself was at Grand Portage, probably the farthest point west he reached. With the adoption of the 16-share organization in 1779, McGill and Todd were among the largest shareholders in the NWC. Yet shortly afterwards the McGill group dropped out. Nevertheless, McGill himself continued to post bonds for traders going to the northwest. Todd and McGill retired to "the Ohio Country," the arc lying south of the Great Lakes. McGill noted about 1785 that this region supplied £100,000 of the total of £180,000 to be derived from the trade in all the territory between "the mouth of the Ohio ... [and] Lake Arabaska [Athabasca]."

The warehouses on Rue Saint-Paul were the centre of the McGill empire. Furs from Detroit and Michilimackinac were exported to Great Britain. Some went by devious ways to New York and John Jacob Astor. The suppliers of furs, the Indians, were carefully cultivated, silver jewellery being bought for them in Montreal. Imported from the West Indies were tobacco, sugar, molasses, and rum; from Britain, metalware, textiles, and powder and shot. Transportation presented problems; the continuation after 1783 of a ban on private shipping on the Great Lakes, begun as a war measure in 1777, provoked McGill to protest. Rudimentary banking was carried on: notes were discounted, foreign currency exchanged, and the pensions of loyalists and French *émigrés* safeguarded. McGill's good personal relations with Governor Guy Carleton, 1st Baron Dorchester, were exploited to corner "the flower" supply market of the Great Lakes military posts.

In 1783 the Treaty of Paris, which ceded the Ohio country to the United States, caused McGill and his associates great vexation. In London, Todd, along with other merchants, protested. McGill himself blew hot and cold. In 1785 he threatened to keep his goods at Montreal if "there was the slightest possibility" of a British withdrawal from the ceded territory. At the same time he boasted, "I am clearly of opinion that it must be a very long time before they [the Americans] can even venture on the smallest part of our trade."

In the threatened area, Detroit was of prime importance. Its geographical advantages were patent and, from 1780 or 1781, it was the home of John Askin, one of McGill's oldest associates. Askin's waning success in the fur trade, along with his vast speculation in land, put him heavily in debt to the McGill partners. In brief, they accepted land in lieu of their trade claims and found themselves in legal difficulties after 1796 when Detroit was transferred to the United States. In compensation McGill acquired land on the Canadian side of the Detroit River, along Lake St Clair, and elsewhere in Essex and Kent counties, Upper Canada.

The Detroit land deals, effected between 1797 and 1805, signalled McGill's entry into systematic land speculation. Earlier acquisitions had been made haphazardly: a farm at L'Assomption, Lower Canada, a water lot at William Henry (Sorel), Montreal properties, a distillery, and probably Burnside, his summer home at the foot of Mount Royal. From 1801 land was secured methodically; that year he acquired 10,000 acres in Hunterstown Township and 32,400 acres in Stanbridge Township, and it was probably in this period that land was secured in Upper Canada near Kingston and York (Toronto).

McGill's public career approached its apex in the late 1780s. In 1787 he was described as "Militia Mad," the euphoria being produced by the attainment of his majority; in 1810 he would become the colonel commandant of the 1st Battalion of Montreal's militia. He began to figure in petitions deploring "the anarchy and confusion" in the administration of civil law. In 1794 he denounced the disturbances in Montreal that attended the embodying of the militia. Two years earlier he had been returned for the riding of Montreal West to the House of Assembly established by the Constitutional Act. His candidacy for the speakership, the highest honour in the assembly, was a tribute to his competence in French and English. In 1792 as well he was appointed to the Executive Council. McGill did not stand for re-election to the assembly in 1796, but he was returned for Montreal West in 1800, and then for Montreal East in 1804.

Around the turn of the century new men entered McGill's business circle: François Desrivières probably in 1792 and Thomas Blackwood eight years later. The newcomers may have prompted new ventures. From 1792 to about 1794 Todd, McGill and Company was a co-partner in the reorganized NWC. In 1796 McGill began to export squared timber. He and Todd were among the planners of a bank in 1807, and McGill himself was active in the Lachine turnpike project. Nor were the old trades neglected. In 1808 McGill joined in the protest against United States interference with the fur traders' shipping at Niagara (near Youngstown), N.Y.

McGill's business career epitomized much of the economic development of Lower Canada in the late 18th century. His stake in the fur trade reached its peak in 1782 when he made the largest investment in the colony, some £26,000. By 1790 his investment had fallen to £10,000, the fourth most important that year. Thomas Douglas, 5th Earl of Selkirk, noted in 1803 that McGill had retired from the fur trade but remained in "the ordinary Colonial trade." The property on Rue Saint-Paul was sold five years later, and in 1810 the affairs of James and Andrew McGill and Company, which had succeeded Todd, McGill and Company in 1797, were wound up. New interests – "the ordinary Colonial trade," the manipulation of land, and other activities – had replaced the fur trade. By such means, in a changing economic environment, did James McGill and his fellow merchants assure the metropolitan supremacy of Montreal.

Perhaps warned by deaths in his family circle, of his brothers John and Andrew in 1797 and 1805 and of his sister Isobel, probably in 1808, McGill made his will in January 1811. The major assets were real estate in Lower and Upper Canada and investments in the United Kingdom, the latter not specified as to character or amount. There were also extensive mortgage holdings. The chief beneficiaries were Mrs McGill, her son François, and James McGill Desrivières. Old friends were remembered (even the tiresome Askin), the Montreal poor, the Hôtel-Dieu, the Sisters of Charity of the Hôpital Général (Grey Nuns), the Hôpital Général of Quebec, and two Glasgow charities. Alexander Henry grumbled that McGill's fortune went "to strangers ... [and] his wife's children, Mrs McGill is left comfortable, but young Desrivières will have £60,000."

McGill also left £10,000 and the Burnside estate of some 46 acres towards the endowment of a college or a university, specifying that the college or one of the colleges of the university should bear the name McGill. The Royal Institution for the Advancement of Learning, the agency of the provincial government responsible for schools, was required to open the college or university on the Burnside site before the bequest became operative. It was not till 1821 that a charter was obtained and not till 1829 that teaching began in what is now McGill University. McGill was not a theorist about education; his concern was with "endowments etc," in the Reverend John Strachan's phrase. Strachan certainly encouraged the benefaction. He had joined the McGill circle in 1808 when he married Ann Wood, Andrew McGill's widow. The actual form of the bequest was doubtless drawn from McGill's own experience of some 25 years before as a commissioner in the inquiry into the Jesuit estates.

The last 18 months of McGill's life were clouded by the War of 1812. In February 1812 he warned Governor Sir George Prevost of the approaching crisis, probably on the authority of Astor, and on 24 June he communicated the actual declaration. McGill saw no active service but, since he was senior militia officer in Montreal, with the rank of colonel, his staff duties were heavy. He was greatly concerned with the disturbances that attended some of the early militia levies. His civil responsibilities also increased: in 1813 he became temporary president of the Executive Council. He was recommended for membership in the Legislative Council, but death intervened before the appointment became effective.

McGill's death was sudden; "he had no Idea of going off half an Hour [before] he died" on 19 Dec. 1813. Two days later he was buried in the Protestant cemetery (Dufferin Square), but in 1875 the body was reinterred on the university campus. Contemporaries "reckoned [him] the richest man in Montr[l] & ... [one who could] command more cash than anyone"; they savoured "the elevated stations" he attained and admired "the sonorous voice" as he rendered voyageurs' songs at the convivial gatherings of the Beaver Club. Portraiture presents a less awesome figure. A miniature of about 1790 shows McGill in his prime. The painting by Louis Dulongpré of only some 15 years later shows the onset of ill health.

James McGill was an 18th-century man. His economics were those of the pre-Adam Smith world. His partnerships, the most complex form of business organization that he knew, were with relatives or close friends. He shared the Enlightenment's tolerance of confessional divergences; born into the Church of Scotland, he died an Anglican, and half-way through life married a Roman Catholic. He contributed to the support of both the Presbyterian and the Anglican churches at Montreal. In 1805 he became a member of the building committee of Christ Church, which was still in the process of erection when McGill died in 1813. His support of Roman Catholic causes has been noted in connection with his will. McGill felt a strong attachment to place. He left Montreal only on business – there were no sentimental journeys to Scotland. To Montreal his chief benefaction was a university, for which, with characteristic practicality, he gave land and the nucleus of an endowment.

J. I. Cooper

Further reading

J. I. Cooper, *James McGill of Montreal: citizen of the Atlantic world*, ed. James Woycke (Ottawa, 2003).

J. E. Igartua, "The merchants and *négociants* of Montreal, 1750–1775: a study in socio-economic history" (PHD thesis, Mich. State Univ., East Lansing, 1974).

H. [M.] Neatby, *Quebec: the revolutionary age, 1760–1791* (Toronto, 1966).

Carolyn Podruchny, *Making the voyageur world: travelers and traders in the North American fur trade* (Toronto, 2006).

Fernand Ouellet, *Lower Canada, 1791–1840: social change and nationalism*, trans. Patricia Claxton (Toronto, 1980).

Claude Pronovost, *La bourgeoisie marchande en milieu rural, 1720–1840* (Sainte-Foy [Québec], 1998).

ROBERT HAMILTON,

businessman, politician, judge, and office holder; b. 14 Sept. 1753
in Bolton, Scotland, son of John Hamilton and Jean Wight;
m. first 1785 Catherine Askin, widow of Samuel Robertson,
and they had five sons; m. secondly *c.* 1797 Mary Herkimer,
widow of Neil McLean, and they had three sons and a daughter;
d. 8 March 1809 in Queenston, Upper Canada.

The power and influence of Robert Hamilton derived largely from his association with the fur trade and the supply of the British army. Like many middle class Scots of the late 18th century he came to British North America through connections in the fur trade. In March 1778 he signed a three-year contract with the Ellice brothers in London, England. They were Lowland Scots long prominent in the southwest fur trade (below and to the west of lakes Huron and Superior) and were major provisioners of the British forces during the American Revolutionary War. By July 1779 Hamilton was in the province of Quebec where he served an apprenticeship as a clerk at Montreal and at Carleton Island (N.Y.) while building up a small trade at the upper posts on his own account. In May 1780 he left the Ellices to form a partnership with the New York loyalist Richard Cartwright at Fort Niagara (near Youngstown, N.Y.). There they built a solid trade with the British army and its quasi-military adjunct, the Indian Department. British officers were impressed by the respectability, the patriotism, and the dependability of the firm.

Hamilton and Cartwright were supplied and, in part, financed probably by the Montreal firm of Todd and McGill, one of the oldest and most prosperous houses in the southwest fur trade. Isaac Todd and James McGill arranged a co-partnership between their Niagara associates and John Askin, their most successful client at Detroit (Mich.). Hamilton's contacts with the military and new associations within the southwest fur trade laid the basis for the remarkable enterprises he built in early Upper Canada. Indeed, the Laurentian mercantile networks provisioning and supplying the military and the fur trade were the most highly developed organizations in the geographically fragmented and institutionally weak province before the War of 1812. Association with them brought a few privileged merchants the only substantial affluence and power the young colony had to offer.

In 1782 Hamilton and Cartwright opened a branch of their firm at Oswego (N.Y.) but, with the winding down of the war, they moved it to Carleton Island in 1783. The decade after the war was not a propitious time for Niagara merchants: of the 18 firms receiving goods there in 1783, only four were still functioning in 1789. The rest had been driven under by the post-war depression, the drying up of military demand, and the unpromising market offered by the pioneer loyalist community. Hamilton, however, operating in continuing partnership with Cartwright until 1790, not only survived this period but prospered by concentrating his efforts on forwarding and receiving for the fur trade rather than on local merchandising. The advantages of this decision were solid: the fur trade required little investment and yielded a steady profit not directly dependent on the price of goods or the state of the local market.

Some time in 1784 or 1785 Hamilton established himself at Niagara, and shortly thereafter began building a residence and shop at what was to become Queenston (Ont.). Cartwright established himself at Cataraqui (Kingston, Ont.). By the late 1780s, according to one observer, they became agents for the shipping of all private goods on Lake Ontario. This thriving trade required extensive transportation facilities beyond the means of small up-country merchants such as Hamilton. Fortunately, capital was provided and construction undertaken both by leading Montreal merchants and by the British military. It was the good luck of Hamilton that his suppliers, Todd and McGill, were the first to build a major private vessel on the lake after the war. He then became the Niagara agent for the 120-ton *Lady Dorchester*, built in 1788, as well as for Todd and McGill's second ship, the 137-ton *Governor Simcoe*, built in 1794. Their monopoly of private shipping ended that same year but the enterprise continued to be profitable thereafter. The transportation infrastructure – storehouses, wharfs, and portages – was built by the military, and initially Hamilton was able to use army facilities for his own carrying business. The profits he realized from the carrying trade while the local economy remained depressed and primitive provided a solid base for expansion of his enterprises and his subsequent rise to prominence.

The Niagara area was the major trans-shipment point on the route to the west. The main portage was located on the east (American) side of the Niagara River until the end of the revolution. Then the Montreal fur traders successfully lobbied for the right to portage their goods on the west bank and subsequently awarded their business to Hamilton and another local merchant, George Forsyth, who was also closely connected to the fur trade. In 1791, with the major Montreal trading companies providing support and financial sureties, Hamilton, Forsyth, John Burch, and Archibald Cunningham won the lucrative contract for the portaging of all military goods. Since the army had already built transportation facilities, Hamilton's overhead was low and, more important, his profits were high.

In addition to his partnership with Cartwright, his contacts with the army, and his associations within the fur trade, Hamilton developed a network of family alliances to secure his interests. In 1785 he married the daughter of his partner, John Askin, thus cementing an alliance that would serve both families for more than a generation. The marriage brought him other contacts at Detroit, most notably the powerful William Robertson. That same year Hamilton began to establish his own Scots relations in the Niagara peninsula. Over the next seven years, he sent home for four of his cousins: Thomas Clark and the Dicksons, Robert, Thomas, and William. Each served an apprenticeship in his enterprises before being placed in businesses that were, in fact, adjuncts of Hamilton's own and were, as well, closely linked to the fur trade and military supply. Hamilton and his cousins remained closely allied during his lifetime. Their circle expanded to include even Old World acquaintances, such as Robert Nichol, and the second generation of the Dickson–Clark families in a complex net of business agreements, partnerships, coordinated land speculations, and mutual lobbying for office and patronage.

The supply of the army and fur trade was the mainstay of Hamilton's businesses. The victualling part of it was almost exclusively for the army because the fur trade tended to purchase its provisions closer to its western centres of operation. With the aid of Todd and McGill and the assent of the military, Hamilton became in 1786 the agent for the supply of flour to the Niagara garrison, which was the only significant market for local produce until shipment began down Lake Ontario to Lower Canada in 1800. Distance and fluctuating supply kept local prices high and the market proved capacious: until 1798, the military purchased all the produce the Niagara peninsula could offer. Because of the comparatively large garrison and Niagara's strategic location as the major supply centre for western posts, by 1800 the army was buying 61 per cent of its total victualling requirements for the colony at Niagara. Hamilton claimed the lion's share of the Niagara market, providing annually between 35 and 100 per cent of local military purchases by value. His virtual monopoly was a consequence of the military's desire to buy in bulk, of the momentum generated by his early establishment in business, and, in no small part, of the preference and special privileges the military awarded him because of his reputation.

Portaging also retained its importance in the regional economy. By the late 1780s, the only period for which statistics are available, an average of 30 per cent of all trade goods by value were moving west by the lakes route over the Niagara portage; 40 per cent of all furs returned east by the same route. The southwest remained the major destination of these goods: 80 per cent of private supplies passing over the portage in 1790 were for Detroit or Michilimackinac (Mackinac Island, Mich.) rather than the far west. The volume of this traffic was substantially augmented by military items, in the main, provisions for the upper posts. Hamilton was fortunate; he continued until his death to receive an unbroken string of lucrative portaging contracts from the military. Total profits on the portage in 1798, for instance, were in the range of £2,500 New York currency, a substantial sum for the three up-country merchants then involved.

Hamilton's provisioning and carrying operations were notable in providing him with a sizeable amount of disposable capital; at this early period all his customers paid him in specie, an important advantage for a merchant in a society where currency was always scarce. All indications point to the likelihood that he invested this money in local enterprises, particularly retailing and land speculation. Whereas the shops of most merchants were small, localized concerns, Hamilton's Queenston store, where he sold large quantities of common goods and a wide selection of luxury items, was the equivalent of a modern regional retailing centre. It drew customers from the length and breadth of the peninsula, and by 1803 he had for some time employed an agent annually to collect his 500 to 600 accounts over as many as 22 townships. He also owned and operated a horse-powered grist-mill, a tannery yard, and a distillery. At his death in 1809, 1,200 individuals owed him the astounding sum of £68,721 New York currency.

Hamilton undoubtedly was the chief land speculator in early Upper Canada. The total known amount of land in which he held an interest by purchase, grant, or mortgage was 130,170 acres. If contiguous, his lands would have stretched one township deep from the Niagara River almost to Burlington Bay (Hamilton Harbour). About 50 per cent of them were located in his own county of Lincoln, with a second major concentration in the counties of Oxford and Norfolk. He had acquired his land rapidly, purchasing close to 43 per cent of his holdings in the peninsula (other than those obtained by grant or mortgage) between 1791 and 1799. Although he invested heavily in land, much of it undoubtedly came to him as payment for outstanding debts. Only 11 per cent of his total holdings came as direct grants from the crown.

Hamilton considered land a commercial speculation. He did not believe in the social desirability or economic potential of establishing great landed estates for himself or his heirs. Rather he saw economic development depending upon yeoman farmers, preferably of American origin, who would clear and work one or two lots; to such individuals he planned to sell his lands. In the main, Hamilton showed little concern for either the quality or the saleability of his acquisitions. A large portion was interior and isolated, with poorly drained soils, land that would not come under cultivation rapidly. With the financial resources at his disposal, he was confident that his family could hold large parcels of land, even poor land, long enough for it to become marketable. This was long-term speculation; during his lifetime, he disposed of only 13 per cent of his total holdings.

From an early period, the political power of Hamilton's economic patrons assured him office. When the government in distant Quebec made its initial appointments for the upper country, it sought recommendations from those who knew the region best – officers of the British military and Indian Department and prominent members of the Montreal fur-trading community. Hamilton's patrons in these circles, particularly Sir John Johnson, assured his appointment in 1786 as one of the original justices of the peace at Niagara, in 1788 as a member of the land board of the Nassau District and as a judge of the district Court of Common Pleas, and finally, in 1792, as a member of the Legislative

Council of Upper Canada. Hamilton proved assiduous in attending to his official duties. Although he seldom exploited his offices directly for personal gain, he was able to use them to affect general matters related to his commercial activities.

The political and social goals of Robert Hamilton were pragmatic and limited; he showed little interest in institutional or social development. In the council, he was rarely concerned with any issue not directly touching himself or his mercantile connections. Despite the restricted nature of his politics, he was nevertheless embroiled in political controversy throughout much of his career. He was at the centre of a commercial élite extending to Kingston and Detroit that dominated affairs along the Great Lakes. His economic power gave him an unparalleled influence over regional society and that power and influence were, not unnaturally, resented; indeed, they became a major issue of the early politics of the peninsula.

The sharpest challenge to Hamilton's ascendancy came during the administration of Lieutenant Governor John Graves Simcoe. The most immediate concerns of contemporaries were economic: the transfer of land, the satisfaction of claims for debt, and the control of the market of greatest significance to the province, army provisioning. It is a measure of Hamilton's prominence that he, with Cartwright, was the focus of debate on these issues and for a time the Simcoe administration was marked by a clash between the regionally based major merchants attempting to defend their privileges and the newly established provincial executive trying to centralize power in its own hands. Simcoe's initial disdain for merchants, shared by many of his 18th-century military colleagues, contributed to the animosity between the two groups. The political élite, often unaware of or naïve about local conditions, was spurred to action by regional grievances against mercantile domination.

The first significant dispute between the two groups emerged from province-wide agitation over the control of army provisioning. Todd, in conjunction with Robertson, had lobbied successfully for a contract giving preference to their foremost Upper Canadian clients, Cartwright, Hamilton, Askin, and David Robertson, William's brother. The resulting monopoly generated much controversy and Simcoe manœuvred to secure cancellation of the contract in 1794. Although successful, his action had little impact on the pattern of supply because the government took no additional measures to loosen the economic grip of the major merchants.

A second bone of contention was the supposed influence of merchants such as Hamilton in the local courts and land boards. Simcoe attempted to address this complaint by altering the structure of the courts and by abolishing the boards. Because of the merchants' entrenched social power, however, these moves were only partially successful.

Transfer of land was the third, and potentially most contentious, issue. Before 1796 land holding was based on certificates that gave possession, but not necessarily ownership and the right to alienate. Land speculators, Hamilton chief among them, who had acquired a good deal of land by purchasing certificates, feared the government might not uphold their legality. In this matter, Simcoe proved sympathetic; however, a final solution was not reached until 1797 with the establishment of the first Heir and Devisee Commission, whose commissioners, including Hamilton, were allowed great latitude in recognizing the legality of land transfers.

Towards the end of his administration Simcoe increasingly acknowledged the legitimate and, indeed, the necessary influence of merchants on the economy and even on the politics of the colony. One signal of this change was his appointment in 1796 of Hamilton as lieutenant of the county of Lincoln, the most important office in the region. After Simcoe's administration Hamilton's interest in legislative politics declined sharply. The major conflict had been between officials and entrepreneurs over their respective powers and prerogatives. Now that those battles had been fought and the relationship between the political and economic élites had been defined to his satisfaction, Hamilton, from being a frequent opponent of government, became a staunch, if generally quiescent, supporter of it.

Hamilton exercised immediate personal control over patronage within his own area from the establishment of the Nassau District in 1788 until his death. When he became lieutenant of the county of Lincoln he had the right to appoint or recommend justices of the peace and to nominate militia officers. Moreover, he had great power over the selection for offices in the whole area west of York (Toronto). By his use of a potent combination of political and economic influence, he was able to place his sons, his cousins, and the whole second generation of the Askin family in official as well as commercial posts. Hamilton was not part of any local compact of office holders nor did he stand in a

client–patron relationship to a provincial "family compact." His power over patronage rested largely on his own local influence. So far as
it did depend upon the provincial political structure, it rested squarely
upon his personal connection with the lieutenant governors. His most
profitable association in this regard was with Peter Hunter. Of the 13
appointments outside his own district that Hamilton influenced, 8 were
made during Hunter's administration. Indeed, the reformer Robert
Thorpe complained of the "scotch pedlars" who "had insinuated themselves into favour with General Hunter … there is a chain of them linked
from Halifax to Quebec, Montreal, Kingston, York, Niagara & so onto
Detroit…." Thorpe labelled these Scots a "Shopkeeper Aristocracy." As
he implied, Hunter was connected to many of the merchants by their
Scottish origins. He had served as an officer in British North America in the immediate post-revolutionary period when links between the
military and the Laurentian traders were especially strong. He had been
commandant at Fort Niagara in 1788 and, from 1789 to 1791, he had
served at Montreal. During this period he became acquainted with a
number of merchants and maintained these relationships up to his return
to the province in 1799 as lieutenant governor.

In his later years Hamilton's immediate concerns were to protect and
nurture the patronage and influence obtained from the provincial government, for himself and his connections, and to defend his interests in
the regional politics of the peninsula. He was, however, less successful
in the politics of his own area than in provincial politics and patronage.
Indeed, the privileges Hamilton and the merchants associated with him
derived from outside contacts fuelled popular resentment. Hostility to
monopoly which had first broken out in 1791 reached its peak in 1799
and 1800. A proposal by Hamilton, Clark, and George Forsyth to make
extensive improvements to the Niagara portage, to be financed by higher
charges, caused a local furore and resulted in a massive petitioning campaign. This hostility to the merchants carried over into the election of
1800, when loyalist officers such as Ralfe Clench and office holders such
as Isaac Swayze campaigned successfully against the merchants' candidates and excluded them from seats in the peninsula. Hamilton, however, in conjunction with his cousins and other connections such as John
Warren and Thomas Welch, was able to secure the election of Surveyor
General David William Smith in the riding of Norfolk, Oxford and Mid-

dlesex. The division between the major merchants and the coalition of officers, office holders, and petty merchants diminished after 1806 with the rise of a parliamentary opposition, usually associated with Thorpe, William Weekes, and Joseph Willcocks. The perceived radicalism of this group drove the merchants and their former opponents together in common cause against their radical foes.

In his private affairs, Hamilton adopted to the full the lifestyle of a gentleman. In 1791, when others in the peninsula might be considering the construction of their first permanent homes, Hamilton began to build an impressive Georgian mansion. Perched on the escarpment, high above the Niagara River at Queenston, the house with its two-storey greystone façade, side wings, and covered galleries, rose incongruously above its modest wooden neighbours and the pioneer clearings. Hamilton entertained lavishly at his home and his guests included Prince Edward Augustus, who, in 1792, stopped there for refreshment during his visit to the falls at Niagara. Elizabeth Posthuma Simcoe, wife of the lieutenant governor, was a constant companion of Mrs Hamilton. Surrounding his home, Hamilton kept a fairly extensive farm, a practice that reinforced his public image as a man of the landed gentry. He and his children showed a marked respect for books and learning. To indicate his own status and to prepare his offspring for their future social roles, Hamilton was assiduous in their education; all received their higher education in Scotland.

His respectability was based upon more than possession of the trappings of gentility. Hamilton closely associated himself with those institutions that provided concrete opportunities for benefitting the community, such as the Niagara Agricultural Society. He was a founding member and its second president, succeeding Simcoe. The society kept a small library that it eventually donated to the Niagara Library, another institution of which he was a founding member. He was also a provincial deputy grandmaster in the Masonic Lodge of Upper Canada.

Robert Hamilton died on 8 March 1809 after a prolonged illness. His passing was accorded the respect owed by his community to its most prominent citizen. "His funeral, as you may imagine, was attended by a vast concourse," wrote a former tutor of the Hamilton children, "and since the first settlement of the country nothing of this kind has occurred to occasion so much real sorrow." Hamilton's enterprises survived him only for the remarkably brief span of three years. The pillars of his commercial edifice, provisioning and portaging, had been cracking in the last decade of his life. After 1800 army provisioning had become progressively less significant in the local economy with the opening of an export market in Lower Canada. This development stimulated major competition to Hamilton's firm from men such as James Crooks and Richard Hatt and slowly lowered its effectiveness. Again, after 1800, portaging became less profitable with the decline of fur-trading activity, most notably in the southwest. Military shipping also declined as agricultural output in the vicinity of the army posts became sufficient to supply garrisons' needs. Finally, the establishment of a powerful and well-financed portaging rival on the American side of the Niagara River exacerbated Hamilton's situation.

His heavy investment in land and extensive use of credit in his retail operation made it difficult for Hamilton to offset his declining profits in portaging and provisioning. This situation was complicated after his death by the ineptitude of his heirs, the coming of the War of 1812, and a complex will that virtually froze the assets of his estate until 1823. Although some of his sons such as Alexander, George, and John rose in time to be successful entrepreneurs, office holders, and public figures in the higher echelons of Upper Canadian society, none succeeded to the social and political predominance that his enterprises had made Robert Hamilton's prerogative.

BRUCE G. WILSON

Further reading

B. G. Wilson, *The enterprises of Robert Hamilton: a study of wealth and influence in early Upper Canada, 1776–1812* (Ottawa, 1983).

G. M. Craig, *Upper Canada: the formative years, 1784–1841* (Toronto, 1963).

Alan Taylor, *The civil war of 1812: American citizens, British subjects, Irish rebels, & Indian allies* (New York, 2010).

JOHN MOLSON
(John Molson Sr),

businessman, landowner, militia officer, and politician;
b. 28 Dec. 1763 in Moulton, Lincolnshire, England, son of
John Molson and Mary Elsdale; m. 7 April 1801 Sarah Insley
Vaughan in Montreal, and they had three children; d. 11 Jan. 1836
in Boucherville, Lower Canada.

Having lost his father by the time he was six and his mother when
he was eight, John Molson was put under the guardianship of his
maternal grandfather, Samuel Elsdale. Early in July 1782, at the age
of 18, he emigrated to Montreal, and immediately became involved in
various commercial endeavours with family friends who had arrived at
the same time as he. He went into the meat business with the two James
Pells, father and son, who were both butchers, and then he joined in a
brewing enterprise which Thomas Loid (Loyd) set up that year at the
foot of the Courant Sainte-Marie in the *faubourg* Quebec.

Coming as he did from the English gentry, Molson naturally wanted
to own a farm. During his first year in the colony he bought 160 hec-
tares of land in Caldwell's Manor, south of Montreal. He parted with it
in the spring of 1786, when he began to run the brewery. He had sued
Loid for repayment of a debt in the summer of 1784, and as Loid had
formally admitted the justice of the case, the buildings had been seized
and put up for auction. At an initial sale on 22 October there had been
no offers, but at the second, held on 5 Jan. 1785, eight days after Molson had attained his majority, he was the only bidder. He put James Pell
Sr in charge of the brewery and on 2 June sailed for England from New
York. He could now settle his business affairs himself.

In England, Molson bought some equipment for the brewery.
Returning to Montreal on 31 May 1786, he took over management of
the operation. He oversaw the enlargement of the plant and began to
buy grain for the coming season of malting and brewing. His first purchase, on 28 July, was an exciting event for him, as the entry in the little notebook he kept for his expenditures shows: "28th, Bo^t 8 bush^s of

Barley to Malt first this Season, Commencement on the Grand Stage of the World." Rarely does the spirit of enterprise find such clear expression but, as a letter from Molson to his business agent in England indicated, it also spurred the Lower Canadians: "People here are more of an enterprising spirit than at home, as it is in a great measure owing to that restlessness that induces them to quit their native shore."

During the next 20 years Molson dedicated himself to his business. He invested in it all the funds at his disposal in order to enlarge his facilities and production. It is estimated that he received about £10,000 sterling from a succession of inherited properties, including the family home, Snake Hall, which was sold on 11 June 1789. Molson had turned away from the import-export business in 1788 because the risks were too great and the profits too slow; he also foresaw that the large-scale fur trade would run into increasing difficulties. He therefore did not seek to diversify his activities during this period. In 1806 he considered opening a brewery in York (Toronto) and was warmly encouraged to do so by his correspondent D'Arcy Boulton, who also hailed from Moulton, but nothing came of the idea.

Molson preferred to reinvest continually in his Montreal establishment and for that purpose went occasionally to England, as in 1795 and 1797, to buy equipment. The young immigrant had decided to put his money into a sector which was at the forefront of technological innovation in that country during the late 18th century. The influx of loyalists fleeing the American revolution and the arrival of British immigrants seeking a better quality of life allowed him to extend his market beyond that of francophones. He encouraged barley farmers by supplying them with seed, which was regarded as a loan to be paid back in kind at the rate of two bushels for one.

After his return from England in 1786, Molson had begun living with Sarah Insley Vaughan, who was four years older than he. They remained together and had three children: John, born in 1787, Thomas, born in 1791, and William, born in 1793. They were married on 7 April 1801 at Christ Church in Montreal; according to the declaration they made in the marriage contract drawn up that day by notary Jonathan Abraham Gray, they wanted to acknowledge their mutual affection and, taking advantage of Lower Canada's civil law, legitimize their three children. Sarah signed the contract and the church register with a cross.

Not much is known about how well the young entrepreneur fitted into Montreal business circles, then dominated by the big fur merchants, most of them Scottish. From June to December 1791 and from June 1795 to June 1796 he is known to have held the masonic office of worshipful master of St Paul's Lodge, which indicates that he had a connection with a social group who recognized him. Molson had been married in the Church of England because at the time it was the only Protestant denomination legally permitted to keep registers of births, marriages, and deaths. But as early as 1792 he had contributed financially to the building of the Scotch Presbyterian Church, later known as St Gabriel Street Church, and he remained an active member until at least 1815. In this way, he associated with the community of important Scottish merchants in Montreal.

During the first decade of the 19th century, conditions arising from the Napoleonic Wars were transforming the economy of the St Lawrence valley and giving it new life: the fur trade economy was gradually replaced by the lumber economy, at a time when agriculture was expanding, particularly in Upper Canada. Steam, the new source of energy, led to technological innovations, and after a great deal of experimenting and testing, ships could be propelled with it, for a time at least, on inland water-ways. In 1807 Robert Fulton began to sail the *Clermont* on the Hudson; in 1808 some businessmen from Burlington, Vt, commissioned brothers John and James Winans of that town to build a steamboat for the run along Lake Champlain and the Rivière Richelieu to Dorchester (Saint-Jean-sur-Richelieu); in June 1809 the *Vermont* went into service.

By a notarized contract on 5 June, Molson became the third member and financial backer of a partnership founded by John Jackson, "mechanic," and John Bruce, "shipbuilder," who were building a steamboat to carry passengers between Montreal and Quebec. The most surprising technical aspect of this undertaking was the construction of the engine at George Platt's foundry in Montreal. On 1 Nov. 1809 the *Accommodation* left Montreal at two o'clock in the afternoon; it reached Quebec 66 hours later, on Saturday, 4 November, at eight in the morning, after 30 hours at anchor in the shallows of Lac Saint-Pierre; the return trip to Montreal up the St Lawrence took seven days. The vessel had regular sailings from June to October 1810, the engine having been made more powerful during the winter. The partnership ended with Molson buying the shares of Bruce and Jackson, who said they could no longer take the substantial losses being incurred. In the meantime, on 7 Sept. 1810, Fulton had proposed to Molson the joining of their two enterprises; the terms of the proposal did not seem sufficiently advantageous to Molson, who took no action. Late in October he left Montreal for England to order a steam-engine for the next ship, the *Swiftsure*, from the firm of Boulton and Watt. The vessel was under construction in Hart Logan's shipyard on Rue Monarque in Montreal from August 1811 and it was launched on 20 Aug. 1812.

To diversify his interests Molson had again chosen a sector in which the most recent technological advances had occurred. The brewery had been expanding since 1786, bringing him ever-increasing profits, and hence he was able to assume the losses experienced with the *Accommodation*. He did try to obtain a measure of protection by asking the House of Assembly on 6 Feb. 1811 for a monopoly of steam navigation on the St Lawrence between Montreal and Quebec. His request was put forward by Joseph Papineau and Denis-Benjamin Viger and granted by the assembly, but was rejected by the Legislative Council. With the outbreak of the War of 1812, however, circumstances would prove extraordinarily favourable to shipping on the St Lawrence. Molson offered his ship to the army for the duration of hostilities, but met with a refusal. The military none the less had to use it occasionally on a commercial basis for transporting troops and their supplies. Molson took part in the war as a lieutenant in the 5th Battalion of Select Embodied Militia. Promoted captain on 25 March 1813, he resigned his commission on 25 November.

Early in 1814 another steam-engine was ordered in England. The *Malsham*, which was built in Logan's shipyard as well, was launched in September and went into service immediately. The *Lady Sherbrooke* was added in 1816 and the *New Swiftsure* in 1817. With the end of the war between France and Britain and the economic depression beginning in 1815, British immigrants began to arrive at Quebec in growing numbers and to seek transportation up the St Lawrence, towards the Great Lakes, and on the Richelieu and the Ottawa. In 1815 Molson purchased a wharf with all its facilities at Près-de-Ville in Quebec from Robert Christie and Monique-Olivier Doucet; in 1819 he also bought a house at 16 Rue Saint-Pierre. On 16 Feb. 1816 he had obtained from the Executive Council a 50-year lease on a waterfront lot at Montreal with a renewal option, and he proceeded to put up a wharf. It was located in front of a property he had purchased from Sir John Johnson on 16 Dec. 1815, on which stood a private residence at the corner of Rue Saint-Paul and Rue Bonsecours; in 1816 Molson added two wings to the building and turned it into the Mansion House Hotel. A wharf at William Henry (Sorel) apparently fitted into this network as did the sizeable commercial activity to obtain on contract the wood for steam, which was to be delivered to the various wharfs up and down the St Lawrence where the ships called. By about 1809, Molson had introduced his sons, John, Thomas, and William, to the manufacturing aspects of his enterprises. On 1 Dec. 1816 he formed the first of a long series of partnerships with them under the name John Molson and Sons. Having transferred greater responsibilities in his enterprises to his sons, Molson could become active in politics. In March 1816 he was elected to the House of Assembly for Montreal East. Politics were closely interwoven with the fundamental interests of the merchants in Lower Canada. Molson did not attend the 1817 session; he was probably not even in the colony. The 1818 session having begun on 7 January, he presented himself on 2 February to be sworn in and take his seat. In the 1819 session, which was prorogued on 24 April, he participated from the opening till about 20 March.

Molson was an active member of the assembly. All the important issues attracted his attention: trade, public finances, banks and currency, inland shipping, education and health, municipal by-laws, fire protection, regulations for public houses and inns, the House of Industry (of which he was a trustee in 1819, according to Thomas Doige's directory), and the Montreal Library. Two questions concerned him more directly, the Lachine Canal and the Montreal General Hospital. From 1815 to 1819 he took part in the debate over the construction of the canal, speaking out for a private undertaking and a route that favoured his shipping interests. In January 1819, with the support of the merchants, he presented a petition to the assembly for the establishment of a public hospital in Montreal. The petition was not accepted by the house because of a procedural error that was declared on 18 March; Molson was still in attendance on 19 and 20 March, but did not appear again.

Two elections were held in 1820: the first in March, which Molson lost, and a second in July, rendered necessary by the death of George III (as was the rule in that era), which he did not contest. The Montreal

General Hospital was founded that same year as a private institution, and the four Molsons contributed to the subscription launched to buy a lot on Dorchester Street and put up the building.

Even when not in the assembly, Molson continued to follow events closely. In 1822 the presentation to the House of Commons in London of a plan for the union of Upper and Lower Canada caused a political stir in the colony. In Montreal some eminent businessmen, Molson among them, formed a committee in support of the bill which held a public meeting and collected 1,452 signatures.

The description that Hector Berthelot gave of Molson in the Montreal newspaper *La Patrie* in 1885 has often been repeated; on the basis of old people's recollections going back as far as 1820, he portrayed Molson in blue tuque, wooden shoes, and homespun. His final paragraph, however, has not always been noted: "After he closed his brewery at night, he took off his rustic garb, donned black evening dress and a white waistcoat, and sported a pince-nez on a long ribbon. When he was dressed grandly, Mr Molson behaved like a steamboat owner." But probably also not kept in mind is Édouard-Zotique Massicotte's caution in his introduction to the 1916 edition of Berthelot's articles that during his lifetime the writer was considered less a historian than a humorist.

At the time Molson was transferring managerial responsibilities in the shipping firm to his eldest son, some financial groups in Montreal (in particular the brothers John and Thomas Torrance and Horatio Gates) and at Quebec (John Goudie, Noah Freer, and James McDouall, among others) were beginning to compete fiercely on the St Lawrence, launching various steamboats. The competition led to over-investment, and then to consolidation of the firms. On 27 April 1822 the St Lawrence Steamboat Company was created, with assets including six ships, three belonging to the Molsons; its management was handed over to John Molson and Sons, which held 26 of the 44 shares. Rivalry with the Torrances continued for some time, but it was finally resolved by cartel agreements on services, prices, and even co-ownership of certain ships.

Meanwhile the Mansion House Hotel had burned down on 16 March 1821; rebuilt in 1824, the year in which Molson acceded to the rank of worshipful sword bearer in the Provincial Grand Lodge of Lower Canada, it was renamed the Masonic Hall Hotel. Molson became provincial grand master for the district of Montreal and William Henry in 1826. At the end of December 1833, finding himself in opposition to his council on a matter of principle, he resigned. Upon the death of John Richardson in 1831, the chairmanship of the Montreal General Hospital fell to Molson. When the cornerstone of the part to be named the Richardson Wing was laid, Molson officiated as provincial grand master in a ceremony at which masonic honours were rendered.

In the early 1820s, as the shipping assets had been removed from John Molson and Sons and placed in the St Lawrence Steamboat Company, the family firm had to be reorganized. In addition, Thomas Molson had decided to settle in Kingston, Upper Canada, and his departure entailed another large withdrawal of assets from the firm. An agreement establishing a new John Molson and Sons was made in 1824, to take effect retroactively from 1 Dec. 1823, the date on which the accounts of the former company had been stopped. William Molson took over management of the brewery from Thomas.

In 1825 Molson Sr gave up his residence in the *faubourg* Québec of Montreal and moved to Belmont Hall, a magnificent house at the corner of Sherbrooke and Saint-Laurent. For some time he had owned Île Saint-Jean and Île Sainte-Marguerite, which form part of the Îles de Boucherville. It was to these islands that his ships returned in the autumn for their winter berths and on them Molson established an estate to which he could withdraw now and then. There he kept a sheep-breeding establishment large enough that the sales of meat to butchers and wool to wholesale merchants appeared in the company accounts. On 10 March 1825 the Theatre Royal company was formed. The principal shareholder, Molson received 44 shares worth £25 each in return for a property he transferred to it on Rue Saint-Paul.

Although during his term as an assemblyman Molson had taken an interest in the founding of the Bank of Montreal, he had made no financial commitments. He had offered to put up the bank building on one of his properties, but the board of directors had unanimously turned down his proposal and had decided on 10 Oct. 1817 that the bank would buy a lot and erect a building itself. John Molson Jr was elected to the board of directors in 1824. In the crisis that split the board in 1826 and put Richardson's group in the minority, Frederick William Ermatinger gave up his place so that Molson Sr could become president. A short time later John Jr resigned to enable Ermatinger to regain his seat. During the elder Molson's term of office, which lasted until 1830, the bank had to deal with the liquidation of major fur-trading houses that declared bankruptcy, in particular Maitland, Garden, and Auldjo and the firms linked with the brothers William and Simon McGillivray. It was Simon who had recommended that Molson be named to succeed William as provincial grand master for the district of Montreal and William Henry, notifying him by a letter sent from London in 1826.

In 1828 John Molson and Sons had its responsibilities narrowed; as the agent of the St Lawrence Steamboat Company it was concerned only with shipping. A new partnership was formed under the name of John and William Molson, bringing together the two Johns and William. John Jr withdrew in April 1829, however, and the association was dissolved; on 30 June a new John and William Molson was founded, which included only Molson Sr and William. On 1 May John Jr had set up Molson, Davies and Company with the brothers George and George Crew Davies; as for William, he went into partnership on 1 May 1830 with his brother-in-law John Thompson Badgley to create Molson and Badgley. Molson Sr acted as financial backer and stood surety for both undertakings. In the mid 1820s, with a workshop attached to the brewery on Rue Sainte-Marie as a basis, Molson had established St Mary's Foundry, handing it over to William's management. In 1831, on the eve of the opening of navigation on the Rideau Canal, Molson Sr joined with Peter McGill, Horatio Gates, and others in forming the Ottawa and Rideau Forwarding Company.

Once more in the early 1830s an important new field for investment was being opened up by technological innovation: the railway. On 14 Nov. 1831, after an earlier petition had been rejected, a group of 74 Montreal businessmen, including Molson, asked the assembly for incorporation as the Company of Proprietors of the Champlain and St Lawrence Railroad; they planned to build the very first railway in either Upper or Lower Canada, from La Prairie to Dorchester. Molson Sr bought 180 shares in the company, thus becoming the largest shareholder, but he was not named to its initial board of directors, which was formed on 12 Jan. 1835.

It was clear that by now Molson was interested only in investing: "I have retired from any active part in business for some years past," he wrote to the London bankers Thomas Wilson and Company in 1830. He had run in the 1827 elections in Montreal East but had been defeated. However, Matthew Whitworth-Aylmer, 5th Baron Aylmer, called him to the Legislative Council in January 1832, along with Peter McGill. The previous year, upon the death of the man generally considered the dean of the Montreal business community, John Richardson, George Moffatt had been appointed. The three men focused to such an extent on the same questions and causes that one can truly speak of the Molson–McGill–Moffatt trio. Together they sat on most of the committees for public investment, taxation, and monetary, banking, and financial matters. Their shared opinions and interests were patent in the dissent they voiced in February 1833 on the question of sharing with Upper Canada the customs duties collected at Quebec. They took the opportunity to ask that the counties of Montreal and Vaudreuil be detached from the lower province and annexed to the upper one. Like McGill and Moffatt, Molson belonged to the Constitutional Association of Montreal, even though he was less active in it than his eldest son. During his four years as a legislative councillor, he was even more assiduous than he had been as an assemblyman 15 years before; on 23 Dec. 1835, less than three weeks before his death, he was still taking part in council.

Towards the end of his life, he became interested in the organization of a Unitarian congregation in Montreal, which among its supporters had a great many merchants of New England origin. In 1832 he was one of a group that purchased a lot for which a chapel was planned, but the initiative was set aside for a while when the pastor died.

In 1833 William Molson added a large distillery to the brewery. The following year Thomas left Kingston to rejoin his brother in Montreal. Through a new partnership contract with their father, signed on 21 Feb. 1835 but retroactive to 30 June 1834, they formed John Molson and Company; once more John Jr did not join the firm.

Molson had lost his wife on 18 March 1829, and in his seventy-second year he was stricken with an illness that swiftly brought about his own death, on 11 Jan. 1836, at his estate on Île Sainte-Marguerite. The newspapers carried quite detailed eulogies, but *La Minerve* mentioned one of his qualities in a somewhat veiled fashion: "Mr Molson belonged to that small number of Europeans who, coming to settle in Canada, reject all national distinctions; just as he had started his fortune with those born in this land, so he always had a large number of Canadians in his employ, whose loyalty must have helped to ensure his considerable profits." The funeral took place at Christ Church in Montreal on 14 January, and he was buried in the old cemetery of the *faubourg* Saint-Laurent. Later his remains were transported with his wife's to Mount Royal Cemetery, to rest in the impressive mausoleum that their sons put up in 1860. The day after his funeral the board of the Bank of Montreal decided that the directors would go into mourning for 30 days.

Minutes before his death Molson had dictated his last wishes to notary Henry Griffin, in the presence of Dr Robert Nelson and Frederick Gundlack. He required his sons to do what they had been incapable of doing during his lifetime: work together in the same enterprises. Each of them, as both residuary legatee and executor of the will, was part owner of the others' businesses or benefited from the income that these brought in, and each was accountable to his brothers. As the will included some ambiguous parts on which even the notary and the two witnesses could not agree, the brothers instituted legal proceedings against one another, with John on one side and Thomas and William together on the other. At the end of five years they wearied of these disputes and by a strange twist asked the two people whom their father had named in his will to be executors along with them, Peter McGill and George Moffatt (who had both withdrawn), to serve as arbitrators and set the conditions for the division of the assets and income, defining reciprocal rights and obligations. Not until 1843, seven years after their father's death, did the three brothers truly come to respect his last wishes.

A portrait of John Molson is in the family's possession. In a will made on 30 Jan. 1830 he had stipulated: "It is my will that my portrait painted in oil shall be the property of such of my sons and their heirs as shall own the said brewery after my decease." Perhaps he was seeking to tell posterity which of his numerous enterprises he considered to be the most important; it was the one that had marked his "Commencement on the Grand Stage of the World."

ALFRED DUBUC

Further reading

B. K. Sandwell, *The Molson family* (Montreal, 1933).

Merrill Denison, *The barley and the stream: the Molson story; a footnote to Canadian history* (Toronto, 1955).

S. E. Woods, *The Molson saga* (Garden City, N.Y., 1983).

Douglas Hunter, *Molson: the birth of a business empire* (Toronto, 2001).

Karen Molson, *The Molsons: their lives & times, 1780–2000* (Willowdale, Ont., 2001).

JOHN McLOUGHLIN
(baptized Jean-Baptiste),
physician, fur trader, and merchant; b. 19 Oct. 1784
near Rivière-du-Loup, Que., son of John McLoughlin, a farmer,
and Angélique Fraser, daughter of Malcolm Fraser; d. 3 Sept. 1857
in Oregon City (Oreg.).

John McLoughlin's first choice of a career was influenced by his mother's brother Dr Simon Fraser. McLoughlin decided at an early age to study medicine; he was only 14 when he began an apprenticeship with Dr James Fisher of Quebec, and was not yet 19 in May 1803 when he was granted a licence to practise in Lower Canada. But on 26 April of that year he had signed an agreement with McTavish, Frobisher and Company, partners in the North West Company, to serve as physician and apprentice clerk for five years. The sudden switch to the fur trade appears to have been motivated by an incident involving an army officer that made it prudent for McLoughlin to leave the province. His NWC agreement was negotiated by Dr Fraser, whose brother Alexander was a partner in the concern. McLoughlin contended later that it was Simon McTavish's virtual promise of exceptional prospects that induced him to accept a five-year engagement at the low stipend of £20 per year.

McLoughlin was sent first to the NWC depot at Kaministiquia (Thunder Bay, Ont.), where, contrary to his expectations, the departure of the medical officer, Henry Munro, made it necessary for him to act in that capacity. But he was soon spending winters at trading posts, since there was little need for professional services until the annual meeting.

In 1806 he was at Rainy Lake and in 1807 he built a post at Sturgeon Lake in the Nipigon department where his winter companion was Daniel Williams Harmon. McLoughlin's towering physique impressed the Indians and he proved to be a shrewd and effective trader, although he was probably of only average ability as a physician.

McLoughlin would have left the NWC in 1808, when his apprenticeship expired, if it had not been for the financial needs of his brother David, who was studying medicine in Edinburgh. McTavish had promised Dr Fraser that McLoughlin would be paid £100 a year if he were required to practise medicine, but McLoughlin was told that the promise was personal and had died with McTavish in 1804. After hard bargaining McLoughlin secured a three-year agreement for £200 a year from William McGillivray, McTavish's nephew and successor as head of the Montreal firm, renamed McTavish, McGillivrays and Company, and in 1811 he was able to make the promise of a partnership in 1814 a condition of the contract's renewal.

McLoughlin's whereabouts from 1808 to 1811 remain obscure. His first posting as a wintering partner, in 1814, was to the Lac la Pluie district, where he had been stationed since 1811, but in 1815 he moved to Fort William (formerly Kaministiquia). He was becoming concerned about the violence that marked the intense and costly rivalry between the NWC and the Hudson's Bay Company, and he was one of an NWC party which arrived "judiciously late" at the Red River settlement (Man.) in June 1816, thereby avoiding any active part in the attack on the colony that resulted in the massacre at Seven Oaks (Winnipeg). Nevertheless, McLoughlin was one of the partners arrested by Thomas Douglas, 5th Earl of Selkirk, in mid August when he arrived with a military force and occupied Fort William. McLoughlin was not clear of the ensuing legal entanglements until he was found not guilty at a trial at York (Toronto) in October 1818.

Both before and after the trial McLoughlin continued to be stationed at Fort William. It was an excellent listening post and from what he saw and heard he became convinced that unless changes were made in management the battle with the HBC would result in the bankruptcy of the NWC. At the annual meeting of 1819 he was able to defeat William McGillivray's efforts to have the existing agreement between the wintering partners and the Montreal agents, McTavish, McGillivrays and Company, extended or renewed, and by the autumn he was prepared to come to terms with the HBC. Through Samuel Gale, Selkirk's lawyer, he inquired anonymously in London whether the wintering partners "could obtain from the Hudson's Bay Company their outfits and supplies of goods & sanction to trade" if they agreed to send their furs to the HBC. The ascendancy McLoughlin had gained over the partners is evidenced by Gale's comment to Jean, Countess of Selkirk, that "the wintering partner" who posed the question possessed "influence to withdraw almost every useful member of the North West Association."

Shortly before the annual meeting of 1820 McLoughlin had an unexpected visitor. In 1817 Governor Sir John Coape Sherbrooke had issued a proclamation calling upon both the HBC and the NWC to keep the peace, but violence had continued. Early in 1820 Henry Bathurst, 3rd Earl Bathurst, the colonial secretary, instructed the HBC to require its servants to obey the proclamation. He also sent a similar message to the NWC to be delivered by the HBC. Both orders were carried to Lower Canada by George Simpson, newly appointed governor-in-chief locum tenens of the HBC, and, with typical bravado, instead of handing Bathurst's communication to the NWC agents in Montreal, he decided to deliver it himself at Fort William. There on 28 May he and McLoughlin met for the first time. McGillivray complained later about the cordiality of McLoughlin's welcome, and in view of the critical importance of Simpson's influence on McLoughlin's later career, this first friendly encounter was of some significance.

At the annual meeting that followed, the wintering partners again refused to renew the agreement, and 18 of them authorized McLoughlin and Angus Bethune to proceed to London and negotiate with the HBC on their behalf. But Simon McGillivray, representing the Montreal agents, also arrived in London for talks with the HBC. McLoughlin, apart from his presence, which evidenced the division in the ranks of the NWC, played no part of consequence in the negotiations that resulted in the coalition of the two companies in March 1821. He had been taken ill in London, and he spent the winter of 1821–22 in Europe, much of it under the care of his brother David in Paris. Back in North America, he attended the meeting of the Council of the Northern Department at Norway House (Man.) in July 1822. Simpson had previously intimated that McLoughlin's experience at Rainy Lake made him the officer best qualified to manage the Rainy Lake district and he was duly appointed its chief factor in 1822 and again in 1823.

The coalition had presented many problems to Simpson, now governor of the HBC's Northern Department, one being the policy that should be pursued in the Columbia district, a huge area west of the Rockies centring on the valleys of the Columbia River and its tributaries, in which the NWC had been active since 1813. Returns had been disappointing and in 1824 Simpson visited the Columbia district with a view to gauging its future. He had already decided that a change of command was essential; Chief Factor John Dugald Cameron was transferred to Rainy Lake and McLoughlin was assigned to Fort George (Astoria, Oreg.), the district depot. With the departure in the spring of 1825 of Chief Factor Alexander Kennedy, who was in charge of Fort George, McLoughlin would be the only chief factor in the entire district. He was probably chosen for the important post because the Columbia was vulnerable to American competition, and he had been successful in holding competing traders at check in the border district of Rainy Lake. Simpson overtook him en route and they arrived together at Fort George on 8 Nov. 1824.

McLoughlin assumed his new position at a difficult time, for in Simpson's view "mismanagement and extravagance" had been "the order of the day" in the Columbia. "Everything," he wrote, "appears to me … on too extended a scale *except the Trade.*" The remedies Simpson proposed included drastic reductions in personnel and the substitution of home-grown produce for the costly provisions that had been imported from Europe. To complicate matters, the agreement between Great Britain and the United States concerning joint occupation of the area was due to expire in 1828, and it remained to be seen whether it would be extended. The HBC had already concluded that the Columbia River was the farthest south boundary that the American government was likely to accept, and recognized that it might well insist upon the 49th parallel. Throughout his years in the Columbia, McLoughlin would have to reckon with the possibility that the district might at any time be riven in two by a boundary settlement.

Important changes had already been made by the end of the five months Simpson spent in the area. A new post, Fort Vancouver (Vancouver, Wash.), which would become the district's headquarters, had been built 100 miles upstream on the north and, it was hoped, British side of the Columbia, in a country suitable for agriculture. James McMillan had been sent to explore the lower reaches of the Fraser River (B.C.) with a view to finding a possible site for a new district depot north of the 49th parallel. The activities of the Snake River expeditions, which trapped far and wide south of the Columbia and its tributaries, were to be intensified, since the area was, in Simpson's words, "a rich preserve of Beaver and which for political reasons we should endeavour to destroy as fast as possible." Finally, McLoughlin took note of Simpson's remark that, to the company's shame, it was still "nearly totally ignorant" of the Pacific coast and the trading possibilities it probably presented.

Policy differences with Simpson were to play a determining role in McLoughlin's later career, but there was no sign of friction in 1825. Simpson had been impressed by McLoughlin and, in view of the remoteness of the Columbia and the many changes he was expecting, he departed from the usual HBC policy and instructed McLoughlin in 1825 to assume "a certain discretionary or controlling power" over "appointments, Outfits," and other important arrangements for all the posts and operations in the Columbia. McLoughlin thus became in effect, if not yet in name, superintendent of the district, a status he was to retain for nearly 20 years.

Simpson had developed a lively personal interest in the Columbia, which he was convinced could become a valuable property, both in itself and as a buffer area that would discourage American traders from penetrating to the district of New Caledonia to the north. He paid a second visit to the coast in 1828 and found that under McLoughlin's management a very marked improvement had taken place in the Columbia's affairs. Personnel had been reduced, the new farms at Fort Vancouver would soon make the district free of dependence on imported provisions, a flour-mill and a small sawmill were in operation, and salmon was being salted in some quantity. In 1827 the 70-ton schooner *Cadboro* had arrived. Although too small to make much of an impression in the coastal trade, it had enabled McLoughlin to establish Fort Langley (B.C.) on the lower Fraser and to send trial shipments of deals and spars to Monterey (Calif.) and Honolulu. McLoughlin's managerial capacity had perhaps been best shown in his reorganization of the Snake River trapping expeditions. The parties, formerly consisting mostly of freemen and Iroquois, had been reduced in size and made to include a much higher proportion of company servants. The cost of supplies advanced to the trappers on credit had been lowered and prices paid for furs had been increased, measures that discouraged desertion and the sale of furs to American traders encountered in the wilds. Routes to be followed were left to the discretion of the commander, who from 1824 to 1830 was the redoubtable Peter Skene Ogden.

Two points of major importance had been settled by the time Simpson reached Fort Vancouver. Some months before, the joint occupation agreement between Great Britain and the United States had been extended indefinitely, and plans for the district could therefore be made on a long-term basis. Secondly, Simpson had come to the coast by way of the Fraser River, had found it useless as a travel route, and had therefore abandoned the idea of developing Fort Langley to replace Fort Vancouver as the district depot. McLoughlin, always firmly attached to Fort Vancouver, welcomed the decision and in 1829 rebuilt the fort on a larger scale on a more convenient site nearer the river.

Simpson had nothing but praise for McLoughlin's efforts. "Your whole administration," he wrote in March 1829 at the end of his visit, "is marked by its close adherence to the spirit of the Govr & Committees wishes and intentions, and is conspicious for a talent in planning and for an activity & perseverance in execution which reflect the highest credit on your judgement and habits of business."

Plans for the development of the coastal trade received much attention during Simpson's five-month stay. Although McLoughlin had been unable to participate in it effectively, he had learned a good deal about its nature. The famed sea otter, for long the only skin of much interest to traders, had become scarce. As a result, "anything and everything was included that might aid to make a paying voyage." Beaver and other land skins were collected, and most of them, brought to the coast by inter-tribal trading, originated in the interior, in what the HBC looked upon as part of its fur preserve. The ships frequenting the coast were American, and they usually depended on a supplementary activity, furnishing supplies and provisions to the Russians in Alaska, to make their voyage profitable.

Simpson and McLoughlin soon had two countermeasures in mind: the establishment of trading posts on the coast that would intercept the furs coming from the interior, and an effort to persuade the Russians to purchase their supplies from the HBC instead of from the American ships. The coastal trade would require ships, men, and supplies, and in March, shortly before Simpson left for the east, McLoughlin's hopes of having them available in 1829 were dashed when the supply ship *William and Ann* was wrecked on the Columbia bar, with the loss of its crew and cargo. The same day an American trading ship entered the river and it or its consort competed with the HBC for the next two years, forcing McLoughlin to pay higher prices for furs at the very time he was ill supplied with trade goods.

It was 1831 before he was able to see to the construction of the projected chain of coastal trading posts. The first, Fort Nass (B.C.), built by Ogden on the Nass River, was soon renamed Fort Simpson and in 1834 it was moved to Port Simpson, a better site on the coast. Fort McLoughlin (near Bella Bella), established by Chief Factor Duncan Finlayson, his second in command, followed in 1833 and in the same year Fort Nisqually (near Tacoma, Wash.), intended to be a farming centre and depot for coastal shipping, was built by Chief Trader Archibald McDonald. McLoughlin intended to build a post some distance up the Stikine River, the mouth of which was in Russian territory. But a preliminary survey in 1833 betrayed this intention, and neither the Russians nor the Indians wished to see their trade in furs disrupted. When Ogden arrived in the *Dryad* to build the post, he found that the Russians had blocked the river by establishing a fort of their own and by stationing a well-armed brig in its mouth. The importance of what later became known as the "*Dryad* incident" arises from a statement McLoughlin sent to London that estimated costs and losses arising from the affair at no less than £22,150 – a claim that was to play an important part in later negotiations with the Russians.

McLoughlin's experience with ships and sea captains was almost uniformly unfortunate. Shipbuilding at Fort Vancouver was not a success. The supply ships from London, arriving in the spring, were to engage in the coastal trade before sailing for London in the autumn, but wrecks, late arrivals, and drunken and uncooperative captains played havoc with the plan. From these circumstances sprang McLoughlin's strong prejudice against ships as opposed to trading posts. Ships, he contended, were expensive to maintain and required crews with special skills, whereas someone was always available who was capable of building a trading post and taking charge of it. He made his views clear in 1834 when the brig *Nereide* arrived, the intention being that she should remain on the coast and her captain, Joseph Millar Langtry, should become head of a marine department. In McLoughlin's view neither the ship nor the department was necessary, and he sent the *Nereide* and its captain back to England. In 1827, in what he doubtless later came to regard as a misguided moment, he had suggested that a steamboat, able to move about regardless of winds and currents, might be useful on the coast, but by the time the *Beaver* arrived in 1836, he looked upon it as an unnecessary and costly extravagance.

McLoughlin soon had to reckon with a marked increase in American interest in trade and settlement in the Columbia region. Late in 1832 Nathaniel Jarvis Wyeth arrived at Fort Vancouver, having travelled overland from Boston. He proposed to collect furs and cure salmon to send to market in ships that would bring him supplies both to meet his own needs and for sale to American trappers in the Rockies. Nothing came of this immediately, since Wyeth's first ship was wrecked. He spent the winter at Fort Vancouver, where McLoughlin gave him a friendly welcome. On his way eastward in the spring he sent a letter to the governor and the London committee of the HBC proposing a cooperative agreement. The committee refused, but in 1834, having established a post on the Snake on his way west, Wyeth was back at Fort Vancouver. There he renewed his proposal for a measure of cooperation, and McLoughlin finally agreed, to the displeasure of his superiors. His reasons for doing so were twofold: he was fearful that Wyeth would establish a supply line of his own if he refused, and he was confident that Wyeth's enterprise would fail.

The episode reveals a good deal about McLoughlin's character and trading strategy. He lacked the ruthless streak that was part of Simpson's make-up, and saw no reason why a trading rival should necessarily be regarded as a personal enemy. Nor did he always subscribe to Simpson's doctrine that opposition must be pressed relentlessly to the last skin. It was usually cheaper and equally effective to oppose a competitor only to the point at which his enterprise became unprofitable. This happened to Wyeth's venture: he sold out to the HBC in 1837.

When Wyeth first appeared McLoughlin suspected that in addition to furs and salmon he was also concerned with plans to bring American settlers to the attractive valley of the Willamette River (Oreg.), which flowed into the Columbia from the south, close to Fort Vancouver. The suspicion was unfounded, but when Wyeth reappeared in 1834 he was accompanied by the Reverend Jason Lee, the first of the Methodist missionaries who were to cause McLoughlin much trouble. Unlike the missionaries of other denominations, the Methodists took a marked interest in this world's goods, and when Lee returned to New England on a visit in 1838 he became a vigorous advocate of immigration to the Oregon country. McLoughlin was not surprised; he had long been convinced that it was only a matter of time before the area would become part of the United States. Further evidence had come late in 1836 when William A. Slacum arrived, ostensibly to view the country and visit friends. McLoughlin suspected rightly that he was an American agent. He had indeed been sent by the secretary of state to spy out the land, and his glowing report on the Columbia stimulated interest in settlement there.

McLoughlin, firmly wedded to the Columbia, had declined hitherto to leave it on furlough, but in 1838 the governor and committee of the HBC called him to London, since a review of the district's affairs was clearly essential. He left Fort Vancouver on 22 March 1838 and returned on 17 October of the following year. The meetings were friendly and successful. Early in February 1839 the HBC concluded an agreement with the Russian American Company which gave the HBC a lease of the Alaskan panhandle. In return, the HBC agreed to supply the Russians with certain furs and commodities, including agricultural products. To provide the latter, the Puget's Sound Agricultural Company was to be organized. McLoughlin's authority was to extend to the company, and in view of these new developments he received a formal appointment "to the principal superintendence or management" of the Columbia district and was granted an additional £500 a year, over and above the sum due to him as chief factor.

James Douglas, a recently promoted chief factor who had been in the Columbia since 1830, was sent in 1840 to conclude arrangements with the Russians at Sitka (Alaska), which included the take-over of Fort Stikine and the building of Fort Taku. But McLoughlin's cherished plans for his chain of coastal posts were to be rudely upset when Simpson, bound on a journey around the world, arrived at Fort Vancouver on 28 Aug. 1841. A week later he left in the *Beaver* to visit Sitka and the northern posts, and when he returned he informed McLoughlin that a complete reorganization of the coastal trade was called for; the agreement with the Russians had changed the entire trading picture of the region. All the northern posts except Fort Simpson, which would act as a northern supply depot, were to be closed, and Simpson was confident that the *Beaver* would "answer every necessary & useful purpose, in watching and collecting the trade of the whole of that line of Coast." McLoughlin was outraged, and contended that this decision had been made behind his back and without consultation, but Simpson was adamant. He and McLoughlin met subsequently at Honolulu, where an HBC agency had been opened in 1833, and the coastal trade was again discussed. McLoughlin had come armed with accounts that he felt proved the superiority of forts over ships (and especially over the *Beaver*), but Simpson held to his decision and instructed McLoughlin to begin by closing forts Taku and McLoughlin in 1843.

A further instruction that was not to McLoughlin's liking followed. For several reasons – the boundary question, again a very live issue, the dangers of the Columbia bar, upon which two supply ships had been lost, and the proximity of Fort Vancouver to the Willamette valley, where American immigrants were settling in some numbers – Simpson had decided that a new district depot farther north was essential. McLoughlin was therefore instructed to find a suitable site on the southern end of Vancouver Island, a decision that resulted in the founding of Fort Victoria (Victoria) in 1843.

From Honolulu, Simpson went to Sitka, but before sailing for Siberia he paid a second visit to Fort Stikine. He arrived on 27 April 1842, to find that McLoughlin's son John, who had been in command of the post, had been murdered by his men the previous week.

Simpson jumped to conclusions, in some measure understandable in view of his knowledge of young McLoughlin's past history. After making good progress in studying medicine in Paris, McLoughlin Jr had committed some unpardonable offence that forced him to leave France. Later he had become involved in the filibustering expedition led by the self-styled general James Dickson which set out for Red River. A few stragglers, including McLoughlin, arrived there in December 1836. Simpson then intervened and offered him a clerkship. In June 1837 McLoughlin was assigned to the Columbia. There he seems to have done well. After serving at Fort Vancouver he was sent to Fort Stikine in 1840, and, owing to staff transfers, was left in sole charge of the fort in 1841. Simpson evidently assumed that young McLoughlin had simply reverted to type. He accepted the charges of terror, violence, cruelty, drunkenness, dissipation, and neglect of duty made by the men, took depositions to support them, and notified McLoughlin of the murder in a letter the wording of which was little less than brutal. He left Charles Dodd temporarily in charge and continued his journey. Later he went so far as to remark to the governor and the London committee of the HBC that the murder had been committed "under circumstances that in my humble opinion, would in an English Court of Justice be pronounced justifiable homicide." Grief stricken and enraged, McLoughlin began a relentless effort to assemble evidence to refute Simpson's allegations, knowing much better than Simpson the turbulent character of the men who had been assigned to Stikine, "the worst characters among our men on the Coast." He succeeded, but he became obsessed with the matter and dealt with it at wearisome length in letter after letter to the governor and committee. He also criticized several men under his command, including Donald Manson and John Work, for their lack of initiative in helping him bring the murderers to justice. Although McLoughlin substantially proved his case, Simpson was indispensable to the HBC and McLoughlin was warned that he must make up his quarrel with him or face transfer or retirement. He failed to do so, and by the spring of 1844 London had decided that "nothing" would then do "but McLoughlin's removal."

There were, of course, other factors involved. The general management of the district was being questioned; the profits were alleged to be only a fraction of those tabulated in McLoughlin's accounts. Differences over the merits of trading posts remained unresolved. McLoughlin's treatment of the American immigrants who were flowing into the Willamette valley was much criticized. He was a humanitarian at heart; he received the immigrants kindly and provided the needy with seeds, implements, and supplies, often on credit. By the spring of 1844 several hundred settlers had received advances totalling £6,600, a sum that alarmed the governor and the London committee. Both they and Simpson failed to realize that, apart from other considerations, McLoughlin's policy was realistic, for settlers were not likely to starve quietly with the well-filled warehouses of Fort Vancouver near by.

The falls on the Willamette River were the cause of further difficulties. McLoughlin had long considered them "the most important place in this country." He and Simpson had visited them in 1828 and in later years he sought to establish claims to properties adjacent to them, both on his own behalf and, on instructions from Simpson, on behalf of the HBC, thus clashing with the Reverend Alvan F. Waller, an aggressive Methodist missionary assigned to the nearby Willamette mission. Under American law which all realized would probably apply soon, foreign corporations could not pre-empt land and Waller believed that the interests of the HBC, and probably McLoughlin's as well, could be encroached upon with impunity. In 1842 McLoughlin had the properties at the falls surveyed and subdivided and laid out the town of Oregon City and in 1844 he was able to arrive at a settlement with the mission, when it was being closed. But disturbing developments had taken place in the interval. In 1843 a provisional government for Oregon had been organized, and in July it had adopted a law regarding land claims, a clause of which was aimed directly at McLoughlin and the HBC. McLoughlin concluded that the only way in which he could hope to protect the company's claims was to purchase them himself, and in March 1845 he sent Simpson bills to the value of £4,173 in payment. It is still a moot point whether McLoughlin intended this to be more than a pro forma transaction, but Simpson accepted the bills and they were charged to McLoughlin's personal account.

Simpson was well aware that this purchase would force McLoughlin's retirement, since he would have to move to Oregon City to take personal charge of the mills and properties there, but other steps to procure his retirement had already been taken. In November 1844 Archibald Barclay, secretary of the HBC, had written to inform McLoughlin that the governor and committee felt that the advantages they had anticipated from the Columbia being placed in the charge of one person had not been realized, and that his post of general superintendent and its supplementary salary would end on 31 May 1845. In June 1845 the Council of the Northern Department set up a three-man board of management for the Columbia, to consist of McLoughlin, Ogden, and Douglas.

It was assumed correctly that McLoughlin would react by going on furlough (Work was then added to the board of management). Humiliated and bitter, McLoughlin moved to Oregon City in January 1846, and on 26 March notified the HBC that he would not be returning to active duty. The company was not vindictive; the financial terms of his retirement were generous. After the year of furlough he was granted leave of absence for two years, and formal retirement was thus delayed until

1 June 1849. Thereafter he received his full share as a chief factor for another year, and a half share for five years. The bad debts incurred by immigrants were never charged to his account.

In spite of his friendliness with American settlers, McLoughlin was so closely identified with the HBC that he continued to be a victim of their violent prejudice against the company, even after he left its service. In 1846 the British government had accepted the 49th parallel as the boundary and two years later the Oregon Territory was created. McLoughlin applied as promptly as possible for American citizenship, granted finally in 1851, but this action did not safeguard his properties. In 1850 Samuel R. Thurston, Oregon's first delegate to Congress, sponsored the Oregon Land Donation Law, a clause of which reserved McLoughlin's holdings for educational purposes. McLoughlin was never dispossessed, but it was not until 1862, five years after his death, that the state legislature conveyed the bulk of his properties to his legatees upon payment of a nominal sum.

McLoughlin spent the last years of his life at Oregon City, where he was active as a merchant and mill owner, and engaged in an export trade in lumber and other commodities. He was for a short time mayor of the city. His youngest son, David, recalled in 1892 that, owing to his great shock of white hair, the Indians called him "Pee-kin – the White Headed Eagle of the Whites." Over the years the major role he had played for two decades in the early history of the northwest was recognized and he has long been known as the father of Oregon. His home in Oregon City is now the McLoughlin House Museum, a national historic site, and he was one of the two pioneers chosen to represent Oregon in the National Hall of Statuary in the Capitol, Washington, D.C.

About 1810 McLoughlin had contracted a marriage according to the custom of the country with Marguerite Waddens, daughter of Jean-Étienne Waddens, and previously the country wife of Alexander MacKay, who was lost in the *Tonquin* massacre of 1811. They had two sons and two daughters, all born before McLoughlin went to the Columbia. They were formally married on 19 Nov. 1842 at Fort Vancouver by the Roman Catholic missionary François-Norbert Blanchet. Mrs McLoughlin died in 1860 at the age of 85. McLoughlin also had another son born some time before 1810.

In his famous "Character book," written in 1832 before any differences had arisen between them, Simpson described McLoughlin as "a man of strict honour and integrity but a great stickler for rights and priviledges" and commented upon his "ungovernable Violent temper and turbulent disposition." He added that McLoughlin "would be a Radical in any Country – under any Government and under any circumstances," an interesting remark in view of the sympathy McLoughlin showed a few years later for the rebels of 1837. William Stewart Wallace has suggested that their contrasting stature was a contributing cause of the friction between McLoughlin and Simpson: "McLoughlin probably had for Simpson the almost instinctive dislike of the big man for the small man who is set over him." The remoteness of the Columbia was also a factor; it took almost a year to receive a reply from London, and many months even to hear from Norway House (Man.). As the man on the spot, McLoughlin often felt that he knew best, and at times he had to take action before he could receive advice or direction. But the deep differences that developed in 1841–42 over the coastal trade and his son's murder ultimately made him an impossible subordinate. In retrospect McLoughlin realized that those winter months had been the turning-point. In his last letter to Sir John Henry Pelly, governor of the HBC, written on 12 July 1846, he made the bitter comment: "Sir George Simpsons Visit here in 1841 has cost me Dear."

W. Kaye Lamb

Further reading

R. S. Mackie, *Trading beyond the mountains: the British fur trade on the Pacific, 1793–1843* (Vancouver, 1997).

R. G. Montgomery, *The white-headed eagle: John McLoughlin, builder of an empire* (New York, 1935).

James Raffan, *Emperor of the north: Sir George Simpson and the remarkable story of the Hudson's Bay Company* (Toronto, 2007).

S. A. Royle, *Company, crown and colony: the Hudson's Bay Company and territorial endeavour in western Canada* (London, 2011).

Gaspé, Que., about 1871

The fishery was Canada's oldest export industry and was brought into being with the help of businesspeople like John Guy and Charles Robin. This painting by Philip John Ouless of a fishing outport hints at the technological changes that transformed Canada's maritime economy in the 19th century, as it shows both sailing ships and a steamship. The buildings of the Robin and John Le Boutilier trading companies are visible in the background. Each company had a large warehouse and other buildings, such as offices, a smithy, and a boarding house for the apprentices.

Norway House – inside the fort, Man., 1878
The fur trade was one of earliest European business enterprises in Canada, and the
networks of transportation, communication, and trade created by companies such as
the Hudson's Bay Company and its rivals provided the foundation for development
of the northern half of the North American continent. In this photo, First Nations fur
traders wait patiently for the HBC store to open, just as they might have a half century
before when Norway House was the site of the HBC council meetings attended by
John McLoughlin.

Market day, Jacques Cartier Square, Montreal, Que., about 1900
This lively photograph is a reminder that the vast majority of Canadian entrepreneurs have operated small enterprises serving local markets.

Part of sealing fleet laid up in Victoria harbour, Oct. 1891
As the activities of Benjamin Bowring attest, sealing has a long tradition in
Newfoundland, but it was also a major industry on the west coast. In the late 1880s
attempts by the United States to restrict the access of Canadian sealers to the Bering
Sea caused major diplomatic headaches for Sir John A. Macdonald's government. In
the foreground are rafts of lumber to be broken up and loaded onto ships.

Montreal harbour from Custom House, about 1872
In the 1870s steamships like those of Sir Samuel Cunard had captured most of
the transatlantic passenger trade, but sailing vessels were still cost-competitive for
shipping cargo (note how most of the vessels have sails). The quayside railway siding
facilitated the exchange of goods between the port and inland cities. In the early 1870s
dissatisfaction with the Grand Trunk Railway prompted shipping magnate Hugh Allan
to try the railway business himself.

A young Canadian worker, 1877
This photoengraving by Eugene Haberer depicts James McDonald from Collingwood, Ont., in the workshop where he was employed as a machinist and engineer. He is a reminder that entrepreneurs required the skills of many employees – from unskilled labourers to technical experts – to help their businesses prosper.

Assorting the ore, Huntington Copper Mining Company's works, Bolton, Que., 1867
Economic necessity often forced women to engage in activities considered unladylike
by the middle classes. Women in business might be subject to the same criticism, but
the second half of the 19th century saw an increasing number of female entrepreneurs.

Specimen of mining scenery, B.C., 1865
This photo of a gold-mining operation was taken in the Cariboo district, an area served by Francis Jones Barnard's Cariboo Express. The next year Fanny Bendixen established her saloon in Barkerville, a town in the district. North American gold rushes typically began with an influx of many lightly capitalized prospectors who worked their claims individually or in partnerships.

Charles Labelle's store, 1894 – house and sign painter and decorator, Sudbury
This painting and decorating business in Sudbury, Ont., was owned by a francophone entrepreneur in a predominantly English-speaking city. Like many settlements on the resource frontier, Sudbury boomed after the start of nickel mining in the 1880s, which created demand for products and services like Labelle's.

Finished roll of newsprint, Spanish River Pulp & Paper Co., Sault Ste Marie, Ont., about 1925
Newsprint was one of the important new staples of the early 20th century; despite Canada's diversifying economy, entrepreneurial opportunity was still available in resource industries.

Section 3

Maritime Enterprise

ENOS COLLINS,

seaman, merchant, financier, and legislator; b. at Liverpool, N.S.,
5 Sept. 1774, first son of Hallet Collins and Rhoda Peek;
d. at Halifax, N.S., 18 Nov. 1871.

Hallet Collins was a merchant, trader, and justice of the peace in Liverpool, N.S. He married three times, and was the father of 26 children; when he died in 1831 he left an estate of £13,000. His second child, Enos Collins, received little formal education, but went to sea at an early age probably as a cabin boy on one of his father's trading or fishing vessels. Before he was 20, he was captain of the schooner *Adamant*, sailing to Bermuda; in 1799 he served as first lieutenant on the famed privateer *Charles Mary Wentworth*. An ambitious young man, Enos Collins soon obtained part-ownership in a number of vessels trading out of Liverpool. During the Peninsular War he made a large profit by sending three supply vessels to break the Spanish blockade and replenish the British army at Cadiz.

Soon Enos Collins's ambitions outgrew the opportunities offered even by the thriving seaport of Liverpool, and he moved to Halifax where, by 1811, he was established as a merchant and shipper. During the War of 1812 he was an astute partner (with Joseph Allison) in a firm which bought captured American vessels from the prize courts and sold their cargoes at a profit. Probably the firm prospered too by illegally including New England in the war trade between Nova Scotia and the West Indies. Collins was part-owner of three privateers, including the *Liverpool Packet*, the most dreaded Nova Scotian vessel to ply New England waters during the war.

In the decade after the war Collins participated in numerous business enterprises. He was successful in currency speculation, backed many trading ventures, carried on his mercantile activities, and entered the lumbering and whaling businesses. Like most of his contemporaries, he invested in the United States; it was rumoured that his American investments equalled his holdings in Nova Scotia. By 1822 Collins's ambitions seem once more to have outgrown his surroundings. Sir Colin Campbell wrote to the colonial secretary, Charles Grant, 1st Baron Glenelg, in 1838, "Sixteen years ago he [Collins] was about to remove from the Province for ever but was induced to remain by an offer made to him … of a seat in the council."

Collins's move into the principal governing body of the colony, the Council of Twelve, indicated the extent of his success. In 1825 he reinforced his position as a member of the ruling élite by marrying Margaret, eldest daughter of Brenton Halliburton. In keeping with his social and economic position Enos Collins built a fine estate, Gorsebrook, where he and his wife entertained the governor and other leaders of the community. Collins and his wife had nine children, of whom one son and three daughters lived beyond childhood.

In 1825, after several unsuccessful attempts to gain a banking charter from the government, Enos Collins and a group of merchant associates – Henry H. Cogswell, William Pryor, James Tobin, Samuel Cunard, John Clark, Joseph Allison, and Martin Gay Black – formed a partnership and founded the Halifax Banking Company. The banking venture was the natural outgrowth of successful mercantile activity which provided each partner with the necessary capital to finance the new enterprise. Although Cogswell was president of the company, Collins was the dominant partner; the bank's transactions were conducted in the building which housed Collins's firm and the venture soon became known locally as "Collins' Bank."

One of the least attractive events of Enos Collins's career concerns the "Brandy Dispute" of 1830. In 1826 the assembly had imposed a tax of 1s. 4d. on foreign brandy in addition to the 1s. imposed by the imperial government. The customs collector decided that a duty of 2s. was sufficient, but he failed to inform the assembly of his decision. In 1830 E. Collins and Company petitioned the assembly demanding a refund on their duty, arguing that the customs collector had given them an unfair rate of exchange on the doubloons with which they paid the tax. Their petition provided the assembly with the information that the full tax was not being collected. The assembly immediately passed a bill restoring the full tax, but the council, controlled by Enos Collins and his associates, refused to accept the bill. For some time no tax was collected on imported spirits, and Collins, taking full advantage of the situation, proceeded to sell his stocks of brandy without paying a penny into the treasury. His behaviour provoked an angry reaction in the assembly and from the local press. Unfortunately for Collins and the other importers, George IV died, causing an election in Nova Scotia. The "Brandy Election" of 1830, fought on the issue of the tax, resulted in the return of an assembly which quickly reimposed the duty; the council accepted their decision. Not only did this dispute tarnish Collins's name, but it also provided an issue around which criticism of the Council of Twelve could be concentrated.

During the 1830s Collins continued to expand his business activities and to participate in governing the colony. In 1832, despite Collins's objections, the council granted a charter to the Bank of Nova Scotia and destroyed the monopoly of the Halifax Banking Company. Soon the two banks were involved in a currency battle which weakened the financial stability of the colony and gave Reformers another point of departure for attacks upon the ruling oligarchy. The decade witnessed growing discontent with the rule of the Council of Twelve, until, in 1837, the British government decided that reorganization was necessary. The new Executive Council of Nova Scotia did not originally include Enos Collins, but, at Governor Colin Campbell's insistence, Collins became a member on 8 May 1838. He continued in the position until 6 Oct. 1840, when a second reorganization necessitated his resignation. During the turbulent 1840s and 1850s Collins refrained from active politics, but he was a financial backer of the Conservatives.

Enos Collins spent the last 30 years of his life in partial retirement keeping a close eye on his investments but withdrawn mainly to the privacy of Gorsebrook. The battle against confederation provided the last fighting ground for the old man. Breaking a lifetime allegiance with the Conservatives, Collins threw his whole-hearted financial support behind Joseph Howe, Mather Byles Almon, and other members of the anti-confederation league. The vehemence with which Collins opposed the scheme is best expressed by Howe: "Enos Collins who is now ninety years of age ... declares that, if he was twenty years younger, he would take a rifle and resist it."

Enos Collins was an astute, hard-headed, and even progressive businessman. With an estate estimated at $6,000,000, he was rumoured to be the richest man in British North America. He belonged to the Church of England and supported it financially. Like his contemporaries, Collins recognized that the ruling class was responsible for the less fortunate and less successful members of society. He was a member of the Poor Man's Friend Society and gave generously to the blind and to other philanthropic ventures which were common in 19th-century Halifax.

Collins's life, however, does not represent a complete success story. He strove to become a member of the ruling oligarchy in a period when the changing times were giving political and social power to a much broader segment of the community. Long before Collins died, the way of life which he wanted and had achieved through his material success was disappearing. His stand against confederation was the last losing battle of a man who failed to recognize the vast changes occurring in British North America between 1840 and 1870.

DIANE MURRAY BARKER AND D. A. SUTHERLAND

Further reading

"Letters and papers of Hon. Enos Collins," ed. C. B. Fergusson, Public Archives of Nova Scotia, *Bulletin* (Halifax), 13 (1959).

Dan Conlin, "A private war in the Caribbean: Nova Scotia privateering, 1793–1805," *The Northern Mariner* (St John's), 6 (October 1996), no.4: 29–46.

J. M. Beck, *Joseph Howe* (2v., Kingston, Ont., and Montreal, 1982–83).

Brian Cuthbertson, *Johnny Bluenose at the polls* (Halifax, 1994).

BENJAMIN BOWRING,

watchmaker and businessman; baptized 17 May 1778 in Exeter, England, one of three children of Nathaniel Bowring and Susannah White; m. 9 Oct. 1803 Charlotte Price in Wellington, Somerset, and they had five sons and one daughter; d. 1 June 1846 in Liverpool, England.

Benjamin Bowring came from a family that had been involved for over two centuries in the woollen industry in Exeter. After receiving his early education at the Unitarian chapel academy in his mother's native Moretonhampstead, he apprenticed to watchmaker Charles Price, whose daughter he later married. Three days before his marriage, he opened his own watch-making shop in Exeter, and he built it into a prosperous business. A Nonconformist, Bowring was a strong supporter of the abolition of the slave trade and generally took an active role in Exeter's social life.

Looking for new opportunities for his trade, in 1811 Bowring visited Newfoundland, which at the time was experiencing substantial growth in both its population and its fishery. No doubt his knowledge of the colony came from the long-standing connection of West Country merchants with the island's fishery. During the Napoleonic Wars, St John's was a booming frontier port whose population had increased from just over 3,200 in 1794 to approximately 10,000 in 1815.

Having made several trips to St John's between 1811 and 1815, Bowring became one of the port's permanent residents in 1815; the following spring his wife and family joined him. His early years in Newfoundland were marked by a depression in the fishery and by temporary set-backs when his watch-making shop was destroyed several times by fire during the period 1816–19. While he pursued his craft, his wife opened a small dry-goods store attached to the shop. Her business venture proved successful and Bowring decided to abandon watch-making to concentrate on what was a growing retail trade. He was able to establish himself firmly in the uncertain St John's economy of the 1820s because of his family's business connections in England through which he bought the necessary dry goods and manufactured products. During a poor fishery many merchants would fail, but Bowring was willing to take risks and this adventurous spirit was a decided asset to him. In 1823 he was secure and bold enough to purchase two schooners to transport goods from England and return with Newfoundland cod and seal products. The following year Bowring changed the name of his firm to Benjamin Bowring and Son when his eldest son, William, became a partner.

In addition to serving on the executives of several educational and charitable societies in St John's in the early 1820s, Bowring was a strong advocate for the establishment of a municipal government to implement, among other measures, fire safety and building regulations. He and his fellow merchants believed that the existing system of government, whereby Newfoundland was administered by an imperially appointed governor, was inadequate to deal with the increasing political problems of both capital and colony. In 1826 an incorporation scheme for St John's, of which Bowring was a prominent promoter, failed because of differences within the business community as to what form of taxation the proposed municipality should adopt. Following this failure, Bowring and other community leaders renewed their efforts to secure a colonial legislature for Newfoundland, which was finally instituted in 1832. However, his enthusiasm for the new legislature quickly waned after 1833 when politicians divided along religious lines and disputed issues of patronage. Nevertheless, Bowring was pleased that one of the first acts of the House of Assembly in early 1833 was to provide for a compulsory fire brigade in St John's.

This new attempt at fire protection proved no help when Bowring's premises and much of the south side of Water Street were burnt on 7 July. The loss postponed for a year his decision to turn over the Newfoundland business to his son, Charles Tricks (William had drowned in 1828). It was Benjamin's intention to build up a strong English side to the firm by providing the goods St John's needed and marketing Newfoundland fishery products in England and Europe. As he still had sufficient capital to re-establish business in St John's, he decided to do so. Once the premises were nearly completed in mid 1834, he gave control of the firm to Charles and with the rest of his family returned to England. In 1835 he set up a trading company, known as Benjamin Bowring, in Liverpool. Bowring remained in regular contact with his son, offering advice and examining the accounts of Benjamin Bowring and Son. Under Charles's direction the company underwent substantial expansion during the 1830s and it entered the front ranks of the Water Street mercantile establishments. Crucial to its growth was the decision after 1834 to have the firm become directly involved in the lucrative seal fishery by providing its own vessels and building a storage vat at St John's for the oil. The increased volume in business was a boost to the Liverpool company, whose financial and business transactions were closely tied to those of the Newfoundland enterprise. In 1839 the name of the latter firm was changed to Bowring Brothers when Charles's brother Henry Price became his partner. Two years later they were joined by their brother Edward.

The association of Henry and Edward with the management of

Bowring Brothers enabled Benjamin to turn over control of the Liverpool operation in 1841 to Charles, who none the less retained supervision of the Newfoundland company. Under Charles the Liverpool firm, renamed C. T. Bowring and Company, became a major international shipping and insurance business, while Bowring Brothers became one of the leading firms in the cod and seal fisheries and in the provision of foodstuffs and manufactured goods to Newfoundlanders (its expansion was continued under Charles's son Charles R.). Benjamin Bowring's legacy is in the establishment of both businesses which, the St John's *Newfoundland Patriot* wryly noted in 1839, were passed on to the "whole 'tribe of Benjamin.'"

MELVIN BAKER

Further reading

Shannon Ryan, *Fish out of water: the Newfoundland saltfish trade, 1814–1914* (St John's, 1986); *The ice hunters: a history of Newfoundland sealing to 1914* (St John's, 1994).

S. T. Cadigan, *Hope and deception in Conception Bay: merchant-settler relations in Newfoundland, 1785–1855* (Toronto, 1995).

Memorial University of Newfoundland, Maritime History Group, *The enterprising Canadians: entrepreneurs and economic development in eastern Canada, 1820–1914...*, ed. L. R. Fischer and E. W. Sager ([St John's], 1979).

Sir SAMUEL CUNARD,

merchant, shipowner, and entrepreneur; b. 21 Nov. 1787
at Halifax, N.S., second child of Abraham Cunard and Margaret
Murphy; m. 4 Feb. 1815 at Halifax Susan Duffus (1795–1828),
and they had two sons and seven daughters; d. 28 April 1865 in
London, England.

Samuel Cunard's father was a descendant of German Quakers who had immigrated to Pennsylvania in the 17th century. His mother's family had immigrated from Ireland to South Carolina in 1773 and to Nova Scotia with the loyalists a decade later. In 1783 Abraham Cunard came with the British forces to Halifax where he was employed as a foreman carpenter in the army. On 7 Oct. 1799 Edward Augustus, Duke of Kent, commander-in-chief in British North America, appointed Abraham master carpenter to the Contingent Department of the Royal Engineers at the Halifax garrison; he continued to work for the army until his retirement on 22 Oct. 1822.

Abraham Cunard did not limit his career to his official duties. During the French revolution and the Napoleonic era the British army and navy greatly expanded their facilities at Halifax, creating a need for more houses, wharves, and commercial premises. Ignoring the stipulation of his appointment that he "give up every other occupation," from the 1780s to 1812 Abraham slowly acquired property in the north suburbs near the dockyard, some of which he rented. He was careful to obtain water rights for all lots fronting the harbour in order to build wharves.

The Cunards are remembered as a thrifty family, with Samuel knitting a sock as he drove the family cow to pasture, and the boys selling vegetables from their father's garden at the town market or to neighbours. Although he probably attended the Halifax Grammar School, Samuel was largely self-educated. He always emphasized the importance of a plain English education for a business career, but his own sons Edward and William received a classical education at King's Collegiate School and King's College, Windsor, N.S.

Samuel early proved to be a shrewd trader and at the wharves bought goods which he sold in town. Although he did not follow his father's trade, he had an extensive knowledge of timber. His father's acquaintance among the military enabled Samuel to train as a clerk for the Royal Engineers; from 1811 to about 1812 he was first clerk at the engineers' lumber-yard at a salary of 7s. 6d. daily and £20 lodging money annually.

About 1812 the firm of A. Cunard and Son was founded to enter the timber and West Indian trade. It had been granted considerable excellent timber land in Cumberland County, some of which was free and some purchased, and was selling timber abroad, chiefly in Britain, and to the Halifax Dockyard. The Cunards also profited from the War of 1812. They were licensed by Governor Sir John Coape Sherbrooke to trade with the United States as early as 6 July 1812, and traded with New England. They imported goods from Britain valued at £6,272 in January 1814, and took part in the trade with Castine, Maine, after the British army captured that port.

The Cunard fortunes are reputedly based on the shrewd purchase at Halifax of an American prize (name unknown) with a valuable cargo. It is known, however, that the Cunards' schooner *Margaret*, on a voyage from Martinique to Halifax in 1814, was captured by an American privateer. Fortunately for her owners she was recaptured on 16 March and brought into Halifax, where Judge Alexander Croke of the Court of Vice-Admiralty returned the schooner to the Cunards upon payment of one-eighth appraised value for the ship and cargo of sugar, molasses, and rum.

The Cunard firm continued to be active in the West Indian trade. Customs returns in 1813 and 1814 show them importing spirits, molasses, brown sugar, and coffee from Martinique, St Lucia, Dominica, Jamaica, Guadeloupe, Trinidad, Demerara, and Surinam. A. Cunard and Son also acted as agents for various ships owned by others; these included in 1813 the *White Oak*, owned in Bermuda, and in 1814 the Liverpool schooner *Harlequin*.

Samuel Cunard was under middle height, with a well-knit frame, a mouth showing strength of character and decision, and brow and eyes indicating intelligence. As he was to write to his daughter Jane, government positions did not offer enough opportunities for an ambitious young man and "frequently lead to old age with a small pittance but little removed from poverty." A merchant, however, with patient industry generally succeeded. Throughout his life Samuel was to carry out his belief that no one succeeded without application and close attention to business, and he was long remembered for his brisk step, quick and ready movements, and his air of "push." He had the skill to choose for his staff men of high calibre who were hard and faithful workers and to inspire them to work as quickly as he did.

As an able-bodied young man during the War of 1812 Samuel volunteered for service in the 2nd battalion of the Halifax Regiment of militia and eventually became a captain. He was selected by the Halifax Court of Quarter Sessions as one of the citizens to organize a night watch to patrol the town after the disturbances in 1817. Samuel had become a member of the exclusive Sun Fire Company on 11 Feb. 1809 and was president in 1821. In this period Halifax was protected by volunteer fire companies which were as renowned for social activities such as balls and sleigh rides as for fighting fires. From 1821 to 1835 he was to serve as one of the firewards appointed by the Halifax Quarter Sessions to direct those fighting the flames and to decide on demolitions to stop the spread of fire.

By the end of hostilities between Britain and the United States in 1815, Samuel had become accustomed to conducting business in a wartime economy. Immediately after the war the Cunard firm continued to expand. That summer the Cunards purchased at a public sale for £1,325 two lots in the north suburbs of Halifax which were no longer needed by the military, in order to construct wharves and warehouses. Surveyor General Charles Morris supported their successful petition for water rights 500 ft out into the harbour in front of property they owned on Water Street because of "their well known character, for active exertion and enterprize in useful improvements and commercial pursuits."

With the withdrawal of most of the British naval and military forces, trade diminished and unemployment grew. This situation was aggravated by the arrival of large numbers of immigrants. Lieutenant Governor George Ramsay, 9th Earl of Dalhousie, selected Samuel Cunard and Michael Tobin to assist penniless immigrants arriving from Europe and Newfoundland at Halifax, and in the autumn of 1817 gave them £100, which they used largely to transport newcomers to districts in the province where they could find work or obtain board on farms for the winter in return for their labour. To help Haligonians on the verge of starvation Tobin and Cunard opened a soup kitchen which distributed 100 gallons of soup daily. In the winter of 1820 Cunard, Tobin, and John Starr administered a soup house at an expense of 50s. daily, where 320 people received one meal each day, and in 1821 the provincial legislature granted £33 to continue its operation.

Although probably hampered by lack of capital Samuel decided to diversify and expand the Cunard business. From his position with the Royal Engineers he had become acquainted with army and navy officials and the company was soon known for prompt assistance to the admirals and generals and for obtaining needed supplies; it was paid generously with money or favours. The Cunard firm contracted to carry the mail by sailing packet between Halifax and Boston and Halifax and St John's, Nfld; it also sometimes carried the Bermuda mail after the British naval dockyard was moved there in 1819. A. Cunard and Son had also tendered in 1815 to supply a 100-ton vessel for government service to protect the trade and fisheries and prevent smuggling, to sail to New York for mail in winter, to transport the lieutenant governor on official tours, and to move men or supplies to military outposts. The firm purchased a vessel for £1,500, and after inspection by naval officers it was taken into service as the sloop *Earl Bathurst*. In the summer of 1817, however, Lord Dalhousie decided that a larger vessel was required. The Cunards sold the sloop for £375 and bought the *Chebucto* in England for £2,960. This brig was hired for government service at £2,400 sterling per annum. Although Samuel estimated annual expenses of £2,325, including depreciation, complaints were made from Halifax and London to Colonial Secretary Henry Bathurst, 3rd Earl Bathurst, that Cunard had boasted about profits of £1,930 on the vessel and an additional profit because British bills of exchange had a premium of 15 per cent at a time when foreign currency was scarce. In consequence the lieutenant governor was instructed to advertise for tenders in 1822; the lowest bid was for £1,500 annually from Cunard, who explained to Sir James Kempt that the firm had no other employment for the brig and was reluctant to dismantle her. An estimate made at the time for the Colonial Office of the annual operating costs for the services requested of this type of vessel was £1,400. The Cunards ran this service for the government until 30 June 1833.

By the early 1820s Samuel had become virtual head of the Cunard firm. His parents moved to a farm at Pleasant Valley (Rawdon Gold Mines) in Hants County, and he became responsible for his younger brothers as well as his own wife and children; he also assisted his wife's family when the business of his father-in-law, William Duffus, failed. Abraham Cunard died at Rawdon on 10 Jan. 1824 and on 1 May S. Cunard and Company formally emerged. Abraham's will appointed his older sons Samuel, William, and Joseph as trustees of his property, and on 15 Dec. 1826 a settlement was made: for the sum of £1,550 Samuel and Joseph, the surviving trustees, transferred Halifax property to another brother, Edward, who had been taken into the business about 1825 to run the Halifax office after acting as master of various vessels owned by Samuel. Four days later Edward sold to Samuel one of the lots, which Samuel already occupied, and one-third of three water lots for £550, and to Joseph a one-third share for £500. The younger brothers John, Thomas, and Henry did not share in the assets of the firm.

Apparently each of the Cunard brothers acted individually rather than as a company in buying and selling wooden sailing ships. The large number of *Margarets* (after their mother) and *Susans* (after Samuel's wife) and the frequent re-registrations make determining the exact numbers difficult, but Samuel had at least 76 sailing ships registered at Halifax between 1817 and 1850, and Edward registered five more vessels built by Alexander Lyle of Dartmouth in 1840–41 which are usually attributed to Samuel's ownership. Of the 76 it is estimated that 28 were sold abroad, 21 sold in Halifax, two in Pictou, one in Newfoundland, three in the West Indies and one in Saint John, 14 unknown, and six wrecked. Of the 28 sold abroad, ten were disposed of in London, ten in Liverpool, and one each in Hull, Bristol, Aberdeen, Dundee, Banff, Belfast, Limerick, and Galway.

Except for his mail boats Samuel Cunard kept his vessels for only a few years, to be sold when he needed replacements, or saw an opportunity for profit. At first he bought former prizes, but later purchased ships constructed in Nova Scotia and Prince Edward Island. Before 1827 Samuel sold some ships locally. Beginning in that year, however, he sold a few ships abroad from Halifax each year; three vessels registered in 1826 were sold in Britain in the summer of 1827.

Even during bad winter weather in the 1820s Cunard's vessels were sailing to and from the West Indies bringing in rum, molasses, sugar, and some coffee, and carrying out dry and pickled fish, hoops and staves, mackerel, alewives, codfish, lumber, tea, and oil. Mostly he used his own ships. Besides trade with the Miramichi area and with Newfoundland, Cunard imported cargoes from London and Liverpool of dry goods, anchors, cables, coal, and even a fire engine in 1827 ordered by the Halifax Fire Insurance Company; from Philadelphia flour, meal, and fruit; from Boston naval stores, flour, tobacco, and seeds; and from New York corn, wheat, apples, nuts, and books.

During the 1820s Cunard prospered. The adjustment to peace in Nova Scotia had been aggravated by crop failures, the readmission of the Americans to the fisheries (under the British-American Convention of 1818), the lowering of imperial duties on foreign timber, and the removal of the Royal Navy's dockyard facilities to Bermuda in 1819, but provincial trade expanded after 1824. The emergence of young entrepreneurs like Cunard and Enos Collins, alert to every opportunity for increasing their capital, was assisted by the death or retirement of an older generation of merchants, such as James Fraser, James Moody, William Forsyth, and John Black, most of whom had been financed from abroad, and by the return of others to Britain with their profits as soon as the war ended. Earlier businesses were branches of British merchant houses, but now native Nova Scotians began to dominate the business scene.

Both Cunard and Collins joined in petitions in 1820 from Halifax merchants to the assembly to ask for bounties on flour to allow Nova Scotians to compete with the Americans in the West Indian trade and for a duty on flour imported from the United States. Cunard's increasing importance in business circles is shown by his election to the Chamber of Commerce of the reorganized Nova Scotia Commercial Society in 1822; he was its president in 1834.

The Cunards' brig *Prince of Waterloo* engaged in the whale fishery off Brazil from 1819 to 1821, and in 1827 Samuel Cunard, Joseph Allison, and Lawrence Hartshorne were trustees for the Halifax Whaling Company, which employed the *Pacific*. In 1834 and 1836 the Cunards' ship *Susan and Sarah* went on whaling voyages, and their 421-ton *Rose* returned to Halifax in April 1839 after a two-year voyage with 2,400 barrels of black and sperm oil to learn that there were not enough funds left to pay her the full government bounty of £2 per ton.

Cunard subscribed £1,000 for stock in the Shubenacadie Canal Company and was chosen a vice-president in 1826. Along with Collins, Martin Gay Black, and five others, he was an original partner of the Halifax Banking Company formed on 1 Sept. 1825, subscribing £5,000 of its £50,000 capital. In 1831 the partners of this company held more than one-third of the provincial funded debt totalling £21,459, Cunard's holdings being £506 as compared to £2,559 for Henry Hezekiah Cogswell and £450 for Collins. There were objections in other parts of the province to the concentration of so much wealth in the capital. Cunard withdrew from the company in 1836, becoming a resident director of the Bank of British North America. Possibly this move was influenced by the fact that the Bank of Nova Scotia, formed in 1832 as a rival of the Halifax Banking Company, was the bank used by the General Mining Association.

Samuel Cunard was one of the small shareholders in the Annapolis Iron Mining Company, incorporated by the legislature of Nova Scotia in 1825 to smelt and manufacture iron in Annapolis County; the largest shareholder was Cyrus Alger of Boston. After some success the enterprise was abandoned because the American shareholders wished to concentrate on the sale of pig iron in the United States, and the Nova Scotians on manufacturing finished products, but the company may also have been influenced by a yield lower than anticipated.

Cunard was always looking for opportunities to expand his business. On 9 Jan. 1826 he made a proposal to Lieutenant Governor Kempt to lease the Cape Breton coal mines for 30 years at £6,000 per annum and a royalty of 2s. per chaldron on coal shipments over 60,000. He stipulated that Sydney be made a free port and emphasized the value of the American market and the necessity of investing capital in the equipment at the mines and of building wharves and breakwaters. A month later Kempt observed to Robert John Wilmot-Horton at the Colonial Office that if Sydney were made a free port, the demand for coal would increase so much that the Cunards' proposed lease and royalties would not be large enough, but he admitted that "The Messrs. Cunards are Persons of Considerable Capital quite equal to carry on this Establishment & perfectly acquainted with the Country." Later that year, however, the rights to exploitation of the province's minerals were granted to the General Mining Association, and Cunard's bid failed.

Cunard was more successful in obtaining the tea agency from the East India Company. When he learned in July 1824 of the proposal to ship cargoes of tea directly from Canton to Quebec in East India Company ships, he went to London to explain to the company the transportation problems of contrary winds and ice for ships sailing from Quebec to provide the Maritime provinces with their annual tea supply. On 11 Feb. 1825 Cunard and Zealmon Wheeler of Venner, Brown, and Wheeler, Saint John, N.B., applied jointly for the contract to import tea into Halifax and Saint John on the same terms as Forsyth, Richardson, and Company of Montreal, the agents for the Canadas. It was hoped that the lower prices offered by these firms would prevent smuggling of tea from the United States. Previously most of the tea exported from London to Nova Scotia and New Brunswick had been shipped by Bainbridge and Brown, London commission merchants and ships' brokers, who purchased it at East India Company auctions in London. Bainbridge and Brown offered to sign bonds as security for Cunard and Wheeler. However, Cunard alone received the agency for the Atlantic provinces. John Bainbridge, an active member of a committee of London merchants trading in British North America which was particularly interested in the timber trade, was appointed provincial agent for the Nova Scotia legislature on 23 Feb. 1826, and remained Cunard's friend until his death.

After the first 6,517 chests of tea shipped directly to Halifax from China by the East India Company arrived, a public sale was held at Cunard's warehouse on 19 June 1826. Quarterly auctions at the stone warehouse by Cunard's wharf, with Cunard as auctioneer, became customary. He retained the agency until 1860.

In the 1830s Cunard was re-exporting equal amounts of tea to New Brunswick and Newfoundland, some packages to Jamaica, Bermuda, Demerara, and Barbados, some to Forsyth, Richardson, and Company at Montreal late in the season before navigation of the St Lawrence River was closed, and a few packages and chests each autumn to Prince Edward Island, without paying duty. In 1831 Enos Collins attempted to oust Cunard from the tea agency. Possibly Cunard was exaggerating his profits to his colleagues in the Halifax Banking Company. Between October 1825 and April 1831 he remitted approximately $95,362 in Spanish dollars and £85,754 sterling to the East India Company.

Cunard sold about two-thirds as much tea as Forsyth, Richardson and Company. Although Cunard's commission on East India funds was only 2 per cent, it was useful to have large sums of money available, even for a short period, to help finance his own operations. He may have used some of the capital for financing his part of the steamship line in 1839 by withholding payments to the East India Company, for he was prompt with his remittances until 1840. In that year and the one following the company had to request Cunard to remit the balance due; he did so soon afterward.

Although in later life Samuel Cunard declared that "he kept his politics to himself," he was a strong supporter of the Tory party. In April 1826 he was persuaded by "merchants and other respectable inhabitants" of Halifax County to offer himself as a candidate for election to the provincial assembly and issued an election card. He withdrew early from the contest, however, because he objected to the candidates and voters having to waste three weeks on an election campaign at such a busy season of the year for farmers and fishermen, and thus allowed the other candidates to be elected by acclamation.

Cunard owed his appointment to the Council of Twelve in 1830 to his position in the mercantile community; by that time his fortune was estimated at £200,000. He took his seat in the Council on 6 Nov. 1830 after the Brandy Election, and Joseph Howe expressed in the *Novascotian* the hope that "the same liberal and expansive views which have distinguished Mr. Cunard as a merchant, may be observable in his legislative character. He is wealthy and influential – he need fear no man, nor follow blindly any body of men; and we trust that he will not disappoint the hopes which many entertain of the benefit to be derived from his weight in the counsels of a branch, that, at the present moment, is really in no good odour throughout the Province." Alexander Stewart, a member of the assembly for Cumberland and a strong advocate for the Bank of Nova Scotia, objected to another appointment from the capital.

For the first three years Cunard faithfully attended both executive and legislative meetings of the Council, and was active on committees dealing with public accounts and revenue and the value of coinage. He was motivated by what he thought would be best for business. However, Cunard expected the same efficiency from public servants as from his own employees. In 1832 a committee of three councillors – Cunard, H. H. Cogswell, and Joseph Allison – investigated a complaint against

William Cleveland, county treasurer, in his capacity as clerk of the licence, for allowing too many people to sell spirits without a licence, and reported that Cleveland "is an inattentive careless Officer, and has for a long time neglected to perform the duties of his office in a vigilant and effective manner...." Cleveland was dismissed.

As the 1830s progressed the Council of Twelve came increasingly under attack by the Reformers, who objected particularly to the fact that five councillors, including Cunard, were directors of the Halifax Banking Company. Cunard also had increasing influence in British business and governmental circles. When Reformer William Young met Colonial Under-Secretary Henry Labouchere in London on 16 June 1839 he declared that "we were perfectly aware of all the influence at work against us, that of the Bishop [John Inglis], S. Cunard, Col. [John] Yorke &c."

During most of 1834 and 1835 Cunard was absent from Council meetings. He was present for most of 1836 and 1837, but not active on committees. He remained an executive councillor when the Council was divided into executive and legislative branches in 1838, but attended only a few meetings between 1838 and 1840, when he had become involved in the beginnings of his transatlantic steamship line. Thus he probably did not mind being asked to resign on 1 Oct. 1840 at the request of Lieutenant Governor Lucius Bentinck Cary, 10th Viscount Falkland, to make room for Reformers in the coalition. He was allowed to retain the title of "Honourable."

The Tory press was indignant that Cunard, "the greatest benefactor Nova Scotia ever had ... is deemed unfit to have a seat in the councils of his country...." The Reformers, however, said Cunard should not be in the Executive Council because he "is no statesman ... nor does he aim at the amelioration of the political condition of his countrymen." In 1844 the editor of the *Morning Chronicle* wrote bitterly against the address of the Halifax Tories to Sir Charles Metcalfe which expressed concern about the "mischievous effects of party and intemperate Legislation." "This is a gross libel upon the people of Nova Scotia. Who utters it? Cunard, Collins & Co. The Old Bankers of the Old Council – who were dismissed by her Majesty from power, for their ultra-Toryism, and unfitness for office ... who used the power with which they were clothed, for their own benefit and the benefit of their friends, *regardless of the wishes or interests of the people....*"

After the breakdown of the coalition of Tories and Reformers in December 1843, the Tories formed a government under James William Johnston with a bare majority over the Reformers. By-elections became crucial, including one in the spring of 1845 in Pictou, where Cunard exerted his influence for the Tories and apparently arranged with local Reformers for a Tory victory by acclamation in return for a few minor offices for the Reformers. Howe was angry because there was no hope of defeating the Tories before the next election: "Such a treaty is worthy of such a negotiator, and will long be held in remembrance as a proof of the gentleman's talents for diplomacy, and the gullibility of the men with whom he had to deal." But in the 1847 elections for responsible government Cunard assured Howe of his neutrality.

The success of the Cunard firm in its early years had been based in large part on the timber trade with Britain, which was encouraged by the tariffs placed on Baltic timber during the Napoleonic Wars. In 1821, when the British government announced its intention of reducing the Baltic duties, Cunard had been chosen by the Halifax Chamber of Commerce to deliver to the colonial secretary a petition to keep them. The expansion of the Cunard firm into the Miramichi area of New Brunswick was a natural outgrowth of its timber interests. The Cunards may have been at Chatham as early as 1820, and Samuel Cunard received a deed to Egg Island on 13 July 1821. After the Miramichi fire of 1825, Joseph and Henry Cunard used the capital of the family firm for the aggressive building of a timber empire over the south bank of the Miramichi in rivalry with Alexander Rankin. This rivalry became so important to Joseph that he ceased to worry about profits and when questioned about the prices Cunard brothers were selling at said: "We don't give a damn so long as we sell more deals than Gilmour, Rankin & Co." The business was conducted as Joseph Cunard and Company, the partners being Joseph, Samuel, Edward, and Henry (who withdrew in 1841 to farm at Woodburn). The Halifax-based firm of S. Cunard and Company provided most of the goods required by Joseph Cunard and Company, and shipped to Miramichi, Richibucto, and Bathurst most of the food products and manufactures needed by the lumbermen, the shipbuilders, and their families. It received in return shingles, staves, lumber, dry and pickled fish, salmon, and alewives, which they sold in the West Indies. S. Cunard and Company also sold tea and rum to Gilmour, Rankin, and Company and to Joseph Samuel at Miramichi.

The timber business necessitated large amounts of capital because two years elapsed between shipment of supplies to lumber camps and the receipt of cash from the sale of lumber. The situation was aggravated by the wildly fluctuating timber market in Britain. Bainbridge and Brown, writing from London to John Ward and Sons at Saint John on 20 Oct. 1826, reported poor prices for ships and timber in London and Liverpool and remarked: "We have two of Cunards Miramichi cargoes at the Clyde & two at Leith & cannot sell a stick...." However, the demand for timber rallied in the 1830s and the Cunards expanded.

Samuel tried to control his headstrong younger brother Joseph. He wrote from Halifax on 28 Nov. 1838 to protest the additional capital sunk in a grist mill, pointing out the folly of discounting at 90 days and then having to pay four or five per cent for drawing funds in Saint John. Customarily merchants met their obligations by issuing notes or bills of exchange which were circulated like cheques; Joseph Cunard and Company in Miramichi issued large numbers for the convenience of the trade as there were no banks in the district. The notes were payable in Halifax at the office of S. Cunard and Company. In 1839 nearly every remittance received from the Miramichi by Halifax merchants consisted principally of Cunard's notes; "Publicola" (Richmond Robinson, a law student with William Young) speculated in the *Acadian Recorder* on 2 Nov. 1839 that these notes in circulation amounted to £80,000. In Samuel's absence his son Edward Cunard denied that more than £10,000 had ever been in circulation, and insisted that the amount outstanding was £4,000. "Publicola" observed that this postponement of settling debts would allow the firm to pocket quietly £1,000 through interest saved, and also warned the merchants of Halifax that in a financial panic Samuel Cunard could refuse to honour the notes because they had been issued by Joseph.

In the 1830s the West Indian trade diminished in importance for Nova Scotia merchants because of increased American competition and a decline in sugar production. S. Cunard and Company was bringing in only enough rum, molasses, and sugar to supply lumbering operations in Miramichi and Prince Edward Island. The clear-sighted and enterprising head of the firm turned its warehouses into bonded warehouses for other firms, and attempted to expand its trade with Britain in such goods as flour, dry goods, cordage, and glass, as Halifax was still the leading wholesale centre of the Atlantic provinces.

By the spring of 1834 the depression in Nova Scotia had deepened. In Halifax there were 600 houses for rent, shops were glutted with produce, and cash was locked up in the banks. Cunard was astute in avoiding failure. He had already competed to secure the contract to provide wharf space in Halifax for the General Mining Association. The long-established firm of Belcher, Binney, and Company had expected to be agents for the English mining company, but, when the company's engineer, George Blackwell, had returned to England strongly recommending Cunard's wharf and warehouses, Cunard's offer was accepted in 1827. At first Richard Smith, a mining engineer from England, acted as general agent in Nova Scotia as well as superintendent of operations, but since the GMA monopoly was resented by local capitalists, in 1834 the association shrewdly appointed Cunard as their local business agent and a director of the corporation.

When Cunard became GMA agent, the company owed the Bank of Nova Scotia over £16,000. By 9 April 1835 the overdraft had risen to £25,480 and at the request of William Lawson, president of the bank, Cunard reduced it by £6,000. In the financial crisis of 1837 the board prevailed on Cunard to reduce it to £10,000. In 1839 Cunard's Halifax firm was awarded the contract to supply coal to the Halifax Dockyard, but his own ships seldom carried coal cargoes.

In December 1842 Cunard attempted to counter the popular supposition that the GMA was reaping large profits by stating that "no interest or return" had "yet been paid." Large capital expenditures had been made in expectation of almost unlimited demand for coal in the United States, but the company was meeting increasing competition from American anthracite coal. When the United States increased its tariff on foreign coal in 1842, Cunard asked the Nova Scotian government for a reduction in royalties and threatened that the GMA would lay off miners unless the government agreed; the royalties were reduced and the annual £3,000 rent was waived. Cunard's letters reveal his complete devotion to the interests of the corporation. As the GMA monopoly became steadily more unpopular over the years, Cunard became the buffer in conflicts between the British and Nova Scotian governments and in disputes between miners and owners. Yet it was acknowledged that under "his guidance and management the operations of the Company" were wisely and properly conducted. Cunard's connections with the GMA gave him a power base in Pictou County where he wielded political and business influence behind the scenes.

While in England in 1838, Cunard was approached about forming a Prince Edward Island land company by George Renny Young of Halifax, who was in London as legal counsel for a number of landowners in Prince Edward Island to present to Colonial Secretary Charles Grant, 1st Baron Glenelg, their case against any escheat of their lands. Cunard was easily persuaded to join Andrew Colvile (agent for the 6th Earl of Selkirk), Robert Stewart, and Thomas Holdsworth Brooking, Young's father-in-law, in forming a joint stock company called the Prince Edward Island Land Company with a local board comprised of Young, Samuel Cunard, and Joseph Cunard. They purchased the 60,000-acre estate of John Hill for £10,000 and the mortgage on the 102,000-acre estate of John Cambridge for £12,000 sterling, £8,400 of which was paid immediately with the backing of London bankers Prescott, Grote, and Company and of the Liverpool Union Bank. Samuel and Joseph Cunard held six-tenths of the shares, Colvile two-tenths, and Brooking and Young one-tenth each.

In August 1838 Young and Cunard went to Prince Edward Island to visit their estates and to discuss the land tax with Lieutenant Governor Sir Charles Augustus FitzRoy. They assured him that they wanted "a common line of policy between the Proprietors and their tenants calculated to restore peace and to promote the prosperity of the Island." At a meeting in Charlottetown on 20 Oct. 1838 a disagreement over the appointment of a solicitor for the land company split the board when Young insisted upon his younger brother Charles, and Samuel upon his son-in-law James Horsfield Peters. This quarrel resulted in Samuel's buying out his partners on 26 March 1839, but it left ill feeling with the Youngs.

In the early years Cunard reserved the rights to all timber fit for shipping, shipbuilding, or exportation on leases which he granted; the timber taken off paid for the land. With his land purchases in Prince Edward Island, Samuel obtained the right to collect £2,535 in arrears of rent on the Cambridge estate. Many tenants paid but some cattle and land were seized for past rents by his agent, J. H. Peters, in 1842 and 1843, and new leases issued to new tenants. On Lot 45 in Kings County about 200 people assembled on 17 March to reinstate forcibly a man named Martin Heaney into possession of a house and farm from which he had been legally ejected; 50 soldiers had to be sent from Charlottetown to restore order on the Cunard estates.

As an alert shipowner Cunard was aware of the development in steam vessels and noticed increasing numbers of such vessels at Liverpool and on the Irish Sea. In 1825, in anticipation of the proposed steamship service by the American and Colonial Steam Navigation Company of Great Britain around the British Isles and once a fortnight to Halifax and New York, negotiations were begun for a steamboat between Quebec and Halifax to connect with the mail packets from Falmouth, England. With contrary winds sailing ships sometimes took 23 days to reach Quebec from Halifax. The Lower Canadian legislature offered £1,500 in three annual instalments and the Nova Scotian house offered £250, but no capitalists were attracted until subsidies were doubled in 1830. Samuel Cunard was only one of over 200 shareholders (including his brothers Henry and Joseph) from Quebec and the Maritimes in the Quebec and Halifax Steam Navigation Company formed in 1830 and incorporated the next year. Among prominent businessmen and merchants of Lower Canada were John Forsyth, William Price, Sir John Caldwell, Noah Freer, George Black, and William Walker. Samuel was elected head of the Halifax committee of the shareholders.

The contract for building the steamship was given to John Saxton Campbell and Black. The ss *Royal William*, launched 27 April 1831 at Cape Cove, Quebec, sailed to Halifax on 24 August, calling at Miramichi (where Joseph Cunard was her agent) and Pictou. J. G. Denter, second engineer on board, later recalled that Samuel Cunard repeatedly visited the *Royal William* and inquired into every particular regarding her speed, sea qualities, and consumption of coal. Unfortunately for the owners the outbreak of a cholera epidemic at Quebec in 1832 forced the ship into quarantine at Miramichi and Halifax; it sat idle a large part of the season and suffered heavy financial losses. In the spring of 1833 the steamship which had cost £16,000 to build was sold at Quebec to the mortgagees for only £5,000. In a letter of 7 May 1833 to Sir Rupert Dennis George, Nova Scotia's provincial secretary, Cunard bitterly blamed the Quebec committee for allowing the frost to burst the pipes and injure the machinery and he stated, "I do not think … [the provincial bounty] should be paid in consequence of the Boats only making one trip during the whole Season.… They have already received £3,975 from this Province the whole of which is lost by the Management of the Quebec Committee and the object in view frustrated."

Although rapid communication was imperative for colonial merchants, the mails for America were still carried by the Falmouth packets taking 30 to 70 days to cross the Atlantic. On 7 Nov. 1838 the British Admiralty advertised for tenders to carry mails by steam from England to New York via Halifax. Two tenders were received from Britain but neither was satisfactory. The closing date had passed before Cunard heard the news in Halifax. Believing "that steamers properly built and manned might start and arrive at their destination with the punctuality of railway trains on land," he sailed to England to submit his own plan for an "ocean railway," with a letter from Nova Scotia's lieutenant governor, Sir Colin Campbell, reminding the Colonial Office that Cunard was "one of the firmest supporters of the Government" with "a good deal of influence in this community...."

Fortunately the comptroller of steam machinery and packet service and advisor to the Admiralty was Arctic explorer William Edward Parry, who remembered with pleasure his service as a young naval officer at Halifax during the War of 1812. On 11 Feb. 1839 Cunard offered to provide steamboats of not less than 300 h.p. to carry the mails from England to Halifax and back twice monthly, and also to provide a branch service in boats of not less than 150 h.p. to Boston, and one from Pictou to Quebec while the navigation was unobstructed by ice. For this he asked £55,000 sterling yearly for ten years, and he promised to have the steamers ready by 1 May 1840. The Admiralty accepted Cunard's offer.

In order to obtain steamships Cunard consulted James Cosmo Melvill, secretary of the East India Company. He recommended Robert Napier, a foundry owner and engineer in Glasgow who had provided steamships for the company. On 25 Feb. 1839 Cunard wrote to William Kidston and Sons of Glasgow (who had had a branch in Halifax) asking them to obtain estimates from Napier. The latter offered to build a vessel of 800 tons and 300 h.p. for £32,000 but agreed to lower his price to £30,000 when Cunard ordered three vessels. Napier, a leader in establishing Glasgow as a great steamship-building centre, decided before the contract was signed with Cunard on 18 March 1839 that these steamships would have to be larger for safe Atlantic voyages and offered to provide the extra work on the engines at no additional cost if Cunard would pay for the structural changes. The Nova Scotian agreed, indicating he wanted "to shew the Americans what can be done in Glasgow and that neither Bristol or London Boats can beat them."

When Cunard could not sell stock in his steamship company in Britain or America, Napier approached a fellow shareholder in the City of Glasgow Steam-Packet Company, James Donaldson, a wealthy cotton broker. Donaldson consulted George Burns of Glasgow, who controlled the Belfast trade and was interested in shipping as well as the commission business. Burns "entertained the proposal cordially," inviting Cunard to meet David MacIver, an ambitious young Scot, who was the agent for small firms in the coastal trade. After various negotiations Burns persuaded some friends to form a co-partnership on 14 May 1839 to take over Cunard's mail contract. In a few days £270,000 was subscribed for "The Glasgow Proprietors in the British and North American Royal Mail Steam Packet Company." At first Cunard subscribed £55,000 for his 110 original shares but that amount was only gradually paid up; in the final arrangements of 23 May 1840 Cunard subscribed £67,500, George Burns £5,000, his brother James £5,000, and David and Charles MacIver £4,000.

The Glasgow investors were businessmen – cotton brokers, West Indian merchants, insurance brokers, iron merchants, warehousemen, textile manufacturers, produce merchants, shipping agents, and so on. Some of them were now seeking outlets for capital because of the decline of the West Indian trade, but most were interested in steamship companies. There was no Nova Scotian capital except for Cunard's investment, the financial losses of the *Royal William* making it difficult to raise money locally.

Haligonians were delighted with Cunard's contract and immediately subscribed £8,000 to build a new hotel for the expected passengers. On 9 April 1839 the Halifax *Times* rejoiced that a "new era will commence in Provincial prosperity from the moment the first steam packet reaches Halifax – and … the time is not far distant when it will become the centre of steam navigation for the whole American continent." That spring, however, a meeting of Boston merchants requested larger steamships to run directly through to Boston, instead of a branch service from Halifax, and offered to provide a suitable pier and dock and facilities for a quick transfer to railways. Cunard agreed, and finally the Maritimes realized that Boston had become the western terminus instead of Halifax.

The first scheduled steamer, *Britannia*, arrived at Halifax at 2 A.M. on 17 July 1840 with Cunard and his daughter Ann on board, discharged passengers and mail as quickly as possible, and sailed on to dock at East

Boston at 10 P.M. two days later. There Cunard received a warm welcome and 1,800 invitations to dinner. The *Acadian Recorder* commented:
"We are quite sanguine that our Boston neighbours *calculated* right when
they so nobly encouraged Mr Cunard's splendid project. His steamships
will enable Boston to become more important than New York in a little
time...." It was the Bostonians who called the line the Cunard Steam
Ship Company or the Cunard Line of Packet Steam Ships long before
the company was legally incorporated as the Cunard Steamship Company in 1878. The regular service of the Cunarders increased foreign
trade to Boston by 100 per cent in one year. Yet the expectations of both
Halifax and Boston to become the centre of navigation for the whole
North American continent failed because geography gave Montreal and
New York access to richer hinterlands.

Although historians of Nova Scotia, Scotland, or England assume
that the partner in the enterprise from their own country deserves sole
credit for the success of the steamship line, available evidence indicates
that all important actions were undertaken after consultation among the
major partners, although Burns superintended shipbuilding activities
and financing, Cunard had special responsibility for negotiations with
the British government over contracts, and the MacIvers managed the
operations of the fleet at Liverpool. A letter from David MacIver in Liverpool in 1841 chided Cunard for his low spirits over difficulties about
the application to the British government for a second contract and the
low profits. MacIver argued that this had been an experimental year and
we "are now arrived at that point where we must turn this experience to
profit."

Difficulties with his own financial affairs added to Cunard's concern over the lower-than-expected profits of the steamship contract.
Although he blamed his brother Joseph's loose business methods for
their financial crises, he himself was overextended because of his Prince
Edward Island land purchases and his borrowing to pay Robert Napier,
and because the sailing ships built by Joseph and Samuel were selling
slowly. These problems coincided with a cyclical downturn in the British
economy. When Cunard, Ingram, and Company in London (formed to
handle Cunard's interests in England) failed to accept drafts, it precipi-
tated the crisis of 1842.

On 25 Sept. 1841 Cunard had borrowed £15,000 sterling from the

British and North American Royal Mail Steam Packet Company for two
years and mortgaged his 110 original shares and all rights in the company and in five steam vessels registered in Glasgow. Profits and dividends
on shares of stock and commissions due to Cunard or his son Edward as
the company's agent in North America were to be used to pay interest
on the loan and to pay up the stock subscription. Samuel was allowed
five per cent on the gross earnings of the ships (which amounted to
about £8,000 to £10,000 annually). This sum was to be placed to his
credit until the steamship shares were fully paid up; then his creditors
would receive any profits made.

Cunard was considered to be one of the wealthiest men in Nova
Scotia when he suddenly departed London for Halifax by one of his
steamships to escape a writ of attachment for £2,000 taken out against
him by Leyland and Bullen, Liverpool bankers. Cunard's escape in
March 1842 had been assisted by Duncan Gibb, a timber merchant and
for many years Liverpool agent for Pollok, Gilmour, and Company, who
had hidden him in a cottage and then provided a boat to row him out
after the steamer had left her moorings. Cunard had arranged with most
of his creditors for three years in which to discharge his obligations.
His property was mortgaged for £47,000 and he owed about £130,000
sterling but claimed assets of £257,000.

Acting as his father's attorney in March 1842, Edward Cunard
Jr was trying to collect as much money as possible, and even sold his
father's farm in Rawdon. William Henry Pope later claimed that three
lots purchased in Prince Edward Island in 1839 for £9,600 were resold
in 1842 for £25,000. On 9 and 11 March 1842 Samuel Cunard and his
brother Edward mortgaged their warehouses, wharves, and premises on
the east side of Water Street in Halifax for £9,000 at 6 per cent interest to Samuel's good friend, Stephen Wastie Deblois, a merchant and
auctioneer at Halifax. John Duffus, Cunard's brother-in-law and a dry
goods merchant, used his influence with the directors of the Bank of
Nova Scotia and the Bank of British North America, of which Cunard
was a director, to provide assistance in preventing his bankruptcy. A special meeting was held by the directors of the Bank of Nova Scotia on
5 April 1842, and four days later a directors' by-law was suspended to
allow a £45,000 loan secured by Duffus. The president of the bank,
Mather Byles Almon, along with Duffus, Alexander Murison, James

Boyle Uniacke, and Joseph Starr, became trustees for the property of Samuel, Edward, and Joseph Cunard. In June and July 1842 the Bank of Nova Scotia reluctantly paid £4,000 sterling to enable the Cunards to liquidate the debt due to Leyland and Bullen to prevent a fiat of bankruptcy being issued against Samuel.

The trustees of Cunard's English creditors were Charles Walton, William George Prescott, and Robert Carter, all leading London businessmen. Among creditors were the Bank of Liverpool, North and South Wales Bank, and Prescott's bank in London, as well as others who had probably advanced shipbuilding supplies or were commission merchants.

Cunard was 55 years old in 1842 and might have been looking forward to some relaxation, perhaps retiring to a small estate as did many English merchants. He must have enjoyed being entertained in London, at parties given by such hostesses as Mrs Caroline Sheridan Norton, and his difficulties must have hurt his pride. He had to give up his directorship in the Bank of British North America. The English creditors allowed the Cunards living expenses but they could not leave their places of business in Nova Scotia and New Brunswick without permission from the trustees, and Edward Jr and Robert Morrow had to go to England for the firm. Ironically, in the midst of Samuel's financial crisis the citizens of Boston forwarded a large silver vase as a testimonial to the frequent, rapid, and safe steamship service between Liverpool, Halifax, and Boston.

Resolutely Samuel devoted his attention to the widespread interests of the Cunards. Shipbuilding activities were increased both in New Brunswick and at Alexander Lyle's shipyard in Dartmouth. In the fall of 1845 Cunard was one of the sponsors of a meeting to discuss the controversial proposal of an English company to construct a railway from Halifax to Quebec, but the project collapsed amidst personal and political rivalries. Samuel and Edward Sr attempted to separate their business from Joseph's and the co-partnership was advertised to be dissolved on 31 Dec. 1845. But late in 1847 Joseph Cunard's enterprise on the Miramichi collapsed and during 1848 the timber trade in New Brunswick dropped to one-third of the 1847 value. As Joseph's ships and timber remained unsold in Liverpool, he admitted that the burden of his misfortunes in business had "in a great measure fallen" on his brother Samuel. Nevertheless, profits from the steamship company steadily paid off the loan borrowed from the Nova Scotia trustees and a formal deed was signed 1 April 1846 reconveying the steamship company stock to Samuel and his son. It is estimated that they received about £20,000 a year between 1841 and 1844 from commissions for the agency in Halifax and Boston and from dividends on the stock. The Bank of Nova Scotia loan was paid off on 11 Dec. 1850.

Cunard must have been delighted to resume his visits to Britain and to take a more active part in the steamship company. Even before his brother Edward died in 1851, Samuel evolved the pattern of travelling back and forth between England, Nova Scotia, Boston, and New York. With the help and experience of Henry Boggs, a longtime Halifax employee, he let his younger son William and his nephew James Bain Morrow run the Halifax firm, which was finding the GMA agency increasingly profitable. One or two of his daughters usually accompanied him on his visits to England.

In the negotiations of 1846 for the renewal of the mail contract of the steamship company, Cunard revealed great diplomacy and tenacity. Merchants and manufacturers in England objected to the renewal and the Great Western Steam-Ship Company of Bristol appealed for an open competition. The chancellor of the exchequer, Henry Goulburn, in defending the Cunard contract, differentiated the company from its competitors and stated that "this establishment owed its origin entirely to the activity of the colonists of Nova Scotia and its neighbourhood, and he for one would be sorry to do anything against the zeal and activity of the colonists." A ten-year contract with Cunard, George Burns, and Charles MacIver, with a yearly subsidy of £145,000, provided for weekly voyages from Liverpool alternating to Boston and New York after 1 Jan. 1848. By that date both the company and the British Post Office realized the necessity of New York sailings because of competition with the Oceanic Steam Navigation Company. Edward Cunard Jr was transferred to the New York office, and in 1849 married the daughter of a New York merchant. MacIver had become sole partner of D. and C. MacIver after his brother David's death in 1845, and in the next three decades became the leading figure among Liverpool shipowners. By 1867 the Burns, Cunard, and MacIver families owned all the shares in the company.

In the 1850s the English line had intense competition from the American Collins Line, which had faster, larger, and more luxurious ships and twice as large a subsidy from the American government, and from the Inman Line which by 1857 was carrying one-third of the Atlantic passenger trade. The Cunard line met this increased competition with bigger ships, which recaptured the speed record from Collins and then lost it again. After two of Collins' steamers were shipwrecked, the Cunards stressed their reputation for safety. The competition ended when the Collins Line became bankrupt in 1858, but by the mid 1860s a score of companies were competing for passengers on the transatlantic route, and the Cunard firm had to turn to iron screwships which were more economical with coal consumption and which had more space, despite Cunard's preference for paddle-wheelers.

Cunard always seemed able to reach an understanding with the officials controlling post office contracts, for he wrote from London to his daughter Jane on 24 May 1850: "I have succeeded in making some very good arrangements about my contract have got it extended four years beyond the former period & some other advantages – they are always very good to me." The Canadian government wished arrangements to be made on the termination of the existing Cunard contract for the St Lawrence mail service to be transferred to the Allan Line (owned by Hugh Allan of Montreal), but while negotiations were still underway, the Cunard contract was renewed four years early. This 1858 contract required the Cunard line to provide at least eight vessels of 400 h.p., and weekly service from Liverpool to New York and a fortnightly service to Halifax and Boston for an annual subsidy of £173,340. The Cunard steamer stopped calling at Halifax after 1867.

The British government supported Cunard in part because of the strong recommendations from naval and military officers about the fitness of the Cunard vessels for war purposes and their more efficient convertibility into men-of-war as compared with any other vessels under contract for the packet service. With the outbreak of the Crimean War, Cunard immediately placed his ships at the service of the British government and advised the Admiralty about obtaining and adapting other steamships for war service. Eleven ships of the Cunard fleet were used to carry troops, horses, and supplies to the Crimea and two became hospital ships. On 9 March 1859 in recognition of the valuable services rendered by the steamship line, particularly during the Crimean War, Cunard was created a baronet.

Samuel had given his English residence as his permanent address for the first time on the 1858 contract, the year George Burns retired from active management in the company, but Cunard continued to maintain his home in Halifax also. Only his youngest daughter Elizabeth remained with her father; the others had married English army officers stationed at Halifax.

Cunard was still regarded by the Colonial Office as an expert on the Maritime provinces. By 1860 he had become the largest and most influential land proprietor in Prince Edward Island and was considered by the British government to be the landlords' spokesman. When the Island legislature requested a special land commission to settle disputes between landlords and tenants on the Island, Henry Pelham Fiennes Pelham Clinton, 5th Duke of Newcastle-under-Lyme, consulted Cunard about appointments to the proposed commission. Not all the proprietors agreed to be bound by the commission's award but the most important did. The commission discovered that Cunard had 971 tenants in 16 townships on 999-year leases with terms of 1s. sterling per acre; the 64,889 acres leased (out of 134,293) should have paid £3,435 annually, but the average rent collected for the previous three years had been only £2,310. Some tenants had paid in cash and some in produce. By 1860 arrears of rent amounted to £17,073. In 1859 Cunard's agent, George Wastie DeBlois, had remitted profits of about £2,000 in Island currency to Cunard in London.

The land commission proposed that the operation of the Land Purchase Act of 1853, brought in by George Coles's Liberal government, should be extended to the whole Island, the British Treasury guaranteeing the sum of £100,000, and that a system of compulsory sale by arbitration should be organized. Immediately upon publication of the commissioners' report in the Island newspapers, Cunard was writing to Newcastle on 2 Oct. 1861 as "one of the largest proprietors in the Island" to object to the proposal that the tenants be allowed to have their farms valued by arbitrators. He argued that although the maximum purchase price was to be the value of the rent for 20 years, the arbitrators might decide that a fair price was two or three years' rent. He feared that arbitration would subject the proprietor to enormous costs – perhaps half the value of the farm. Newcastle vetoed the Island assembly's attempt to implement the commissioners' proposals. Many Islanders blamed the influence of the London proprietors for the British government's refusal to provide funds to buy out the landlords and for not forcing them to compulsory sale by arbitration. Because Cunard and other landlords knew the Islanders would be disappointed by the failure of the commission, they made another offer after consultation among themselves, to be open for a five-year period from 1 May 1862, which would let tenants buy land at a price equivalent to 15 years' annual rent. The Executive Council of Prince Edward Island refused it.

All the proprietors found it difficult to collect their rents during the ensuing agitation sparked by the Tenant League. Cunard wrote to the Colonial Office on 24 Feb. 1863: "There is no tenant on the Island who cannot pay his rent, if he is industrious and sober," but pointed out that "while the agitation is kept up by designing people, rent will not be paid nor money laid up to purchase farms; time is wasted and money spent in attending political meetings." That year the Island government had appointed Edward Palmer and W. H. Pope to proceed to England to confer with the Colonial Office and the landlords. In October their request for implementation of the land commission's recommendations was forwarded by the Colonial Office to Cunard who objected to forgiving arrears of rent and to the proposed terms of sale to tenants. He pointed out that from 1841 to 1862 he had paid £8,641 for land taxes to the Island government on his own and his son's uncultivated lands, at a rate double that of cultivated land. Since the devaluation of Island currency reducing the pound sterling to 16s., Cunard claimed, the value of his rent and sales of land had been lowered by 25 per cent. He compared the 1863 rent paid by his tenants on the Island to that paid by a farm labourer in Britain "who cannot get shelter for his family for double that rate per week."

Pope declared that the Island was "Ireland on a small scale," vigorously disputed many of Cunard's contentions, and called upon the landlords to compromise. The Colonial Office listened to Cunard's demand that neither the Island legislature nor the imperial government should interfere "with our property, in any manner different from that in which private estates in England could be dealt with." Despite these years of argument, the Cunard holdings of 212,885 acres were sold to the Island government in July 1866, a year after Cunard's death, for $257,933.30; the rents had become difficult to collect, and cash was needed to pay the legacies left to his daughters.

In his will Cunard left his real and personal estate to his sons Edward and William and £20,000 to each of his six daughters. In June 1865 Henry Boggs wrote from London to M. B. Almon: "I miss our old friend Sir Samuel C – I think he has left £600,000 – this is a good large sum for him to have accumulated since *the date* that you and I remember him to have had little or nothing – so much for Steam in 20 Years...." Other sources estimated his fortune at £350,000.

Although early in life Cunard was imperious, he learned diplomacy and became a skilful and persuasive negotiator. His contemporaries admired him for the contribution to transatlantic communication by the line popularly called by his name. Without Cunard's prestige and diplomacy, the contract signed after his death in 1867 was far less favourable, paying only £80,000 annually for a weekly service from Liverpool to New York. Dividends which had been eight per cent under the old partners, dropped to two per cent or less.

In the early years of his career Cunard took a prominent part in community activities, St George's Anglican Church in Halifax, and various charitable organizations as well as mercantile affairs which extended throughout the Atlantic provinces. Although he supported the Halifax Mechanics' Institute with a handsome donation when it was organized in 1832, and was praised as "a gentleman whose purse is never closed when a good work needs encouragement," he did not take an active part in its meetings. He was one of the charter members of the Halifax Athenaeum established in December 1834. Most of his local activities were tapering off in the 1850s; he ceased to be lieutenant-colonel of the 2nd battalion of the Halifax militia in 1857, and after 19 years as president of the Halifax Steam Boat Company, he resigned in 1855. One of his first official appointments, on 9 April 1816, had been as commissioner of lighthouses on the Nova Scotia coasts. He retained his interest in lighthouses for the rest of his career, and in 1852, when he was consulted on the subject by Provincial Secretary Joseph Howe, he stated: "Altho I am occasionally absent from home I leave behind me those who are competent to do the duty and when I am here I do not spare myself and my experience may be considered worth something."

Cunard was gratefully remembered for employing his capital in shipbuilding activities in the hard times of the 1830s because this enterprise had circulated money "where there would otherwise be poverty and stagnation." He could be ruthless to a rival or an enemy, but, although legally he could have refused to assume Joseph's debts, the Halifax firm gradually made payments to the creditors year after year.

In the opinion of William James Stairs, Cunard was "the ablest man I have ever known as a merchant of Halifax" – "he made both men and things bend to his will." His competitiveness and his obsession not to waste time were important characteristics of his personality. Peter Lynch, a prominent Halifax barrister, recalled Cunard as cool, calculating, a man of keen perception whose whole mind was devoted to carrying out any project he had in hand. Nevertheless Cunard was admired at home and abroad as a successful colonial and for his contributions to the steamship trade. He was one of the first native Nova Scotians to build a business empire, but, like the successful British businessmen and officials who made their fortunes in the colonies, he retired to England where his descendants settled. True to his family motto "By perseverance" he had overcome obstacles to become an English merchant prince.

PHYLLIS R. BLAKELEY

Further reading

D. A. Butler, *The age of Cunard: a transatlantic history 1839–2003* (Annapolis, Md, 2003).

F. E. Hyde, *Cunard and the North Atlantic, 1840–1973: a history of shipping and financial management* (London and Basingstoke, 1975).

J. G. Langley, *Steam lion: a biography of Samuel Cunard* (Halifax, 2006).

Michel Mollat, *Les origines de la navigation à vapeur* (Paris, 1970).

D. B. Tyler, *Steam conquers the Atlantic* (New York, 1939).

JAMES WILLIAM CARMICHAEL,

businessman and politician; b. 16 Dec. 1819 in New Glasgow, N.S.,
elder of the two sons of James Carmichael and Christian McKenzie;
m. 5 June 1851 Maria Jane McColl (d. 1874) in Guysborough, N.S.,
and they had one son and five daughters; d. 1 May 1903 in
New Glasgow.

The son of the founder of New Glasgow, James William Carmichael
attended Pictou Academy, and then became a clerk in his father's
store and "occasionally went as supercargo" on his vessels. He gradually
took over his father's mercantile and shipping businesses in the early
1850s, and by 1854 the firm was known as J. W. Carmichael and Company. Carmichael's brother, John Robert, became a partner sometime
afterwards, but left in 1863. George Rogers McKenzie, Carmichael's
maternal uncle and a prominent New Glasgow shipbuilder and ship's
captain, had a loose business association with Carmichael and his father and constructed some of his vessels in their yard. The relationship
between McKenzie and Carmichael, who later acquired his uncle's business, was particularly close, and Carmichael honoured McKenzie by flying the initials GK on his house-flag for nearly half a century.

The first vessel registered in Carmichael's name was the 129-ton
Helen Stairs of 1851, and from 1857 to 1869 he built at least 14 more.
His ships conducted an extensive trade in supplies from Pictou County
to the lumber camps of the Miramichi River, N.B., and during the period
of operation of the Reciprocity Treaty with the United States (1854–66)
they also transported coal from the Pictou fields to American markets.
Although the building and use of wooden ships declined in the 1870s,
Carmichael remained active. By then his yards were the most important
in Pictou County, and he constructed his largest vessel, the 1,174-ton
Thiorva, in 1876.

New Glasgow's shipping industry stood out in the Maritimes
because a larger number of its vessels were owned locally and because
its peak of construction occurred in the mid 1850s, relatively early compared with the course of building in other ports. The latter development

has been attributed to the increase in outlets for investment caused by the growth of the region's land-based economy, in particular the development of the coal industry, and the consequent withdrawal of capital from shipbuilding. Carmichael was attracted by these opportunities from the beginning of his business career and through them he broadened his investment base. Involvement with the land-based economy was in fact characteristic of Nova Scotian shipowners, who were prominent in developing the towns in which they were located.

One of Carmichael's first entries into a non-mercantile field was his acquisition of an extensive lease of coal-producing areas after the abrogation of the monopoly of the General Mining Association in 1858. He attempted some development and expended $3,200, but like many in the region eventually sold the lease to an intermediary, who in turn sold it to a foreign syndicate. When Graham Fraser and George Forrest McKay, who had ironed ships in Carmichael's yard, established the Nova Scotia Steel Company Limited in 1882, Carmichael contributed $10,000, and two years later his son, James Matheson, became a director. During the late 1880s, however, the Carmichaels cautioned against the company's plans to produce iron locally, and in 1894 James Matheson resigned over a financial dispute. Carmichael was a minor shareholder in the Nova Scotia Glass Company, which he supplied with boxes for packing the glass. He likewise took part in the export trade in lumber, establishing the first steam sawmill in Pictou County in 1874, and between 1883 and 1892 he operated the New Glasgow Tannery Company in partnership with James C. McGregor. Carmichael's major involvement with industry, however, was with the Acadia Iron Foundry, founded by his brother-in-law Isaac Matheson in 1867. The firm, later I. Matheson and Company, became a prominent manufacturer of boilers.

Notwithstanding this support of local firms, Carmichael indulged in manufacturing only as a complement to his main lines of business. His agency for the Bank of Nova Scotia (1866–86) as well as his presidency of the New Glasgow Marine Insurance Association and his chairmanship of the New Glasgow Underwriters' Association were similarly tied to his principal interests.

Although deeply committed to wooden sailing-ships during the heyday of the industry, Carmichael had from an early date been interested in vessels which employed new technologies. In 1854 and 1865, for example, McKenzie and Carmichael had constructed steamers for the ferry service which connected New Glasgow and Pictou with Prince Edward Island. Carmichael stopped building wooden vessels in 1883 and, like many other Nova Scotian shipowners, began placing orders with prominent builders of iron ships on the Clyde River in Scotland. In 1885 he had constructed the *Brynhilda*, the first iron ship built for and owned by a Nova Scotian. He and I. Matheson and Company were active in lobbying the provincial government to promote the use of iron and steel steamers. The company in fact pioneered the construction of steel steamers in Nova Scotia, its largest, the 485-ton *Mulgrave*, being built in 1893 for Carmichael's firm. In 1898 James Matheson Carmichael analysed the prospects for a Nova Scotian shipbuilding industry based on steel and steam. He boldly predicted "We will have half a dozen shipyards within the next ten years" and lamented that 20 years had been lost to the industry because shipbuilders had preferred to invest in cotton factories and sugar refineries, "[from] the management of which we have perhaps not gained much glory and less profit." But the Carmichaels were ambivalent about their allegiances. While insisting that government support was necessary in order to stimulate domestic production, they rejected Canadian independence of British vessel registration, though such independence was also necessary to prevent Canadians from buying and registering ships in Britain, the older Carmichael arguing, for example, against the establishment of a Canadian Lloyd's register of shipping.

By diversifying his investments, Carmichael was able to maintain his position in Pictou County, and his worth grew steadily. In 1872 his combined assets were valued at just over $183,000; by the time of his death they had grown to nearly $583,000. The firm of J. W. Carmichael and Company continued – its iron and steel vessels would be active in international shipping until World War I – but the members of his family became *rentiers*, collecting dividends through a firm of Halifax stockbrokers. In 1962 the firm went into voluntary liquidation, and $670,000 was bequeathed to charitable organizations.

Although Carmichael and the New Glasgow mercantile community financed local industrialists and welcomed them into their families, they were less inclined to agree with their politics. The merchants were Liberals and uncompromising supporters of free trade, the industrialists Conservatives and protectionists. Carmichael himself supported the Liberals after his election to parliament for Pictou in 1867 as an opponent of confederation. Ousted in 1872 and re-elected in 1874, he was defeated in the general elections of 1878, 1882, and 1896, and in a by-election in 1881. Carmichael was undismayed by his frequent losses, which were caused in part by quarrels among the Liberals and in part by the fact that Pictou County was benefiting from the National Policy of the Conservatives. He remained a key figure in the provincial and national parties, and he was on good terms with Edward Blake, Alexander Mackenzie, and Wilfrid Laurier. In parliament he spoke in favour of free trade and Maritime rights, objecting to "Nova Scotia occupying a position of inferiority and existing by sufferance." His most controversial stand was in 1876, when he opposed a tariff on coal that the Conservatives had proposed in order to help market Nova Scotian coal in central Canada. Carmichael argued that it was impossible to organize trade between Ontario and Nova Scotia because of the difficulties of transportation and added that it was preposterous to think that Nova Scotian coal could compete with American coal merely because of the duty of 50 cents a ton. This stand cost him electoral support in a region highly dependent on the coal industry and caused him to be burned in effigy by a group of coalminers. In 1898 Carmichael was appointed to the Senate, from which he resigned a week before his death.

Carmichael was active in the community life of New Glasgow. Lieutenant-colonel of the 5th Regiment of Pictou militia, vice-president of the Pictou County Rifle Association, and a member of the council of the Nova Scotia Rifle Association, he was also a founding director of the Aberdeen Hospital and president of the New Glasgow auxiliary of the British and Foreign Bible Society. In religion he was an anti-burgher Presbyterian, and joined Primitive Church when it was founded in 1845. Carmichael took part in the negotiations which merged Knox and Primitive churches in 1874 as the United Church, and he was subsequently chairman of its board of trustees until his death. In 1875 he was one of those behind the drive for incorporation of the town, and he served as a fire warden and a trustee of public property.

In 1903 Carmichael died peacefully at his home. He left a legacy of charitable and religious work, but he had been first and foremost a businessman. His only son having predeceased him, the family was represented in the 20th century by his daughters, who made a reputation as reformers, social activists, and supporters of charities and the arts. Caroline Elizabeth, for example, became president of the National Council of Women of Canada and was awarded an honorary doctorate by Dalhousie University. She nevertheless remained faithful to her past, gave generous support to the Liberals, and, in later years, was described as a "lady in dark clothes" driven by a uniformed chauffeur.

L. ANDERS SANDBERG

Further reading

L. D. McCann, "The mercantile-industrial transition in the metals towns of Pictou County, 1857–1931," *Acadiensis* (Fredericton), 10 (1980–81), no.2: 29–64.

L. [D.] McCann and Jill Burnett, "Social mobility and the ironmasters of late nineteenth century New Glasgow," in *People and place: studies of small town life in the Maritimes*, ed. L. [D.] McCann (Fredericton and Sackville, N.B., 1987), 59–77.

Ian McKay, "The crisis of dependent development: class conflict in the Nova Scotia coalfields, 1872–1876," *Canadian Journal of Sociology* ([Edmonton]), 13 (1988): 9–48.

E. R. Sager, with G. E. Panting, *Maritime capital: the shipping industry in Atlantic Canada, 1820–1914* (Montreal, 1990).

Daniel Samson, *The spirit of industry and improvement: liberal government and rural-industrial society, Nova Scotia, 1790–1862* (Montreal and Kingston, Ont., 2008).

ROBERT TINSON HOLMAN,

businessman; b. 13 March 1833 in Saint John, N.B.,
fourth and youngest son of James Holman and Sarah Chadbourne;
m. 27 July 1864 Ellen MacEwan of Summerside, P.E.I., and they
had ten children; d. there 11 Dec. 1906.

Robert Tinson Holman's father had emigrated from his native Devon, England, to Saint John in 1819 and by the time of Robert's birth he was involved in shipping and had opened a store. Several relatives, including Robert's cousin James Henry Holman, immigrated over the next few years and provided a large family network in Saint John. While Robert was still a youth, his father suffered business reversals and he left school at age 13. He clerked in a mercantile house in Saint John and for a few months in a law office, but in 1848, in pursuit of employment, he moved to Boston, where he stayed for about two years. Several other members of the family were already there and Robert's relationship with kin in the United States was to continue throughout his life.

The eldest of James Holman's sons, Samuel Chadbourne, who also worked in Boston, came to Prince Edward Island in 1851 and set up a store in Charlottetown. Robert joined him, but Samuel's accidental death a year later led to the closing of the business. Another brother, James Ludlow, and a brother-in-law, John Andrew, were by then in business in St Eleanors, some 40 miles west of Charlottetown, and Robert joined them. Andrew saw more promise in the nearby town of Summerside, and he and Robert became partners there in John Andrew and Company in 1855. The partnership was dissolved the following year with heavy debts. At the time Holman considered moving to Hamilton, Upper Canada; instead, he appears to have received some assistance from his brother James Ludlow, and took sole responsibility for the Summerside business.

The timing of Holman's decision was fortunate, for the town would prosper in the shipbuilding boom of the 1860s. By 1864 he had constructed a large brick warehouse and in 1867 he was able to purchase a wharf and a shipbuilding site from James Colledge Pope. The main line of the Prince Edward Island Railway was run through the site in 1872 and Holman's wharf became an important transfer point for agricultural goods shipped abroad. By 1873 he had consolidated his landholdings on the waterfront and had acquired a number of water-lots from the government, making it difficult for competitors to operate anywhere in the vicinity. Holman's increased business required additional storage space and in 1875 he built a four-storey building, the biggest in the province at the time. In 1895, to accommodate both retail and wholesale operations, a large brick store was erected, which the Summerside *Pioneer* claimed to be the largest mercantile establishment in the Maritimes. Following the death of James L. Holman in 1877, Robert acquired much of his property, including the newly opened Island Park Hotel, one of the pioneer tourist resorts of the Atlantic region. The hotel business was not a success, however. A more important acquisition from the estate was an additional wharf on Summerside's waterfront.

R. T. Holman, in contrast to many other local merchants, was not involved in shipbuilding, but he acquired vessels. Of the nine he is listed as having owned between 1866 and 1896, most were relatively small; the larger ones, including the *Kewadin* and the *Pawashik*, were used in the transatlantic trade. Although the shipping side of his business *per se* was not a financial success, owning vessels allowed him to exploit other opportunities by giving him more control over his ability to participate in the markets for agricultural produce. Surviving records show that until the mid 1870s Holman's sales of merchandise and speculation in produce accepted in payment resulted in large profits. The value of merchandise sold annually increased from about $12,000 in 1860 to $196,000 in 1875. His net worth in 1876 was estimated by agents for R. G. Dun and Company to be between $50,000 and $100,000. Subsequently, in spite of steady profits on merchandise, Holman experienced several years of overall loss, the result of bad debts, reduced sales, and losses on the operation of vessels and on speculation in commodities. In 1883 he became one of the first merchants to export lobsters and for some time thereafter they show up as a profitable item in his statements.

Holman had become sufficiently secure in his business interests by 1866 to attempt a risky venture, the founding of the *Summerside Progress and Prince County Register*. It was edited by Thomas Kirwan, but it was well known that Holman was the owner and backer of the newspaper.

With regard to the issue of the day, the union of the Maritimes and Canada, it opposed confederation and endorsed instead annexation to the United States. In July 1866 the *Progress* espoused a return to "the good old days of reciprocity," which, given the financial success that Holman had experienced under the Reciprocity Treaty, before its abrogation in March, is hardly surprising. Three years later Holman hired Henry Lawson as editor and the paper adopted a more moderate stance. Holman appears to have sold it in 1876.

Unlike many merchants of the period, Holman was not involved in fraternal organizations or associations, and he does not appear to have held office at any level of government. Although he would be identified by the press in 1903 as a "lifelong liberal," his activities were evidently not within the sphere of organized federal or provincial politics. His main concerns were mercantile and his few public activities appear to have been connected with business. One of the petitioners for the incorporation of the Summerside Bank in 1865, he served as a director from 1870 to 1880. In 1896 he was a shareholder in the newly incorporated Summerside Electric Company Limited. Following the founding of the Summerside Board of Trade in 1900, he served as one of its councillors. He was drawn into the major controversy of the day – the most appropriate wintertime route for steamer service between the Island and the mainland – and in an uncharacteristic step he publicly indicated his position. Summerside, one of two ports with regular and direct service, connected with Pointe-du-Chêne and Shediac, N.B. Holman, other board members, and the editors of local newspapers were involved over a three-year period in a press war against Charlottetown, which connected with Pictou, N.S.

R. T. Holman was a merchant who stood apart from the social life of his small community, who apparently neither sought nor gained political favours, and who possessed unorthodox religious beliefs. Though Holman had been born into a Baptist family, his father had left the church in 1835 following a doctrinal disagreement with a clergyman. It is not evident how Robert's views on religion developed, but the census of 1861 listed him as a "universalist" and by the 1870s he had abandoned organized religion in favour of free thought. Not content to object passively to the predominant religious sentiment of the community, he brought speakers to Summerside to preach humanism. One example of his antipathy was his response to the province's proclamation of Thanksgiving in 1899. He protested in a half-page advertisement in the *Pioneer* that the day should be "free from cant, free from hypocracy and free from policy" and that consequently his stores would remain open.

In a memorial booklet published by the family after Holman's death in 1906, following a short illness, mention is made of his interest in "modern thought," with no reference to Christianity. The booklet contains "The declaration of the free" by Robert Green Ingersoll, a leader in the American free-thought movement in the 19th century, and "Abou Ben Adhem" by English critic James Henry Leigh Hunt. The *Charlottetown Guardian* concluded in its obituary that Holman was not "in the ordinary acceptation of the word a religious man," but it applauded his philanthropic activities.

Just prior to Holman's death, his business was incorporated as R. T. Holman Company Limited, with shares distributed among his family. Two sons, James LeRoy and Harry T., succeeded him in the management of the firm, which would continue for more than 70 years. Holman was acknowledged in obituaries to be the province's leading businessman. Newspapers spoke of his mercantile talents, but his skills in wholesale and retail merchandising, shipping, and exporting produce, as well as in identifying such new industries as the lobster trade, were not unique. What appears to have made the difference in Holman's case was his ability to combine these activities so effectively. He was aided by Summerside's rapid economic expansion and, when business contracted in the 1880s, he diversified and was able to recover from reduced sales. That he succeeded as a merchant is a testament to his individualism; even allowing for journalistic flourish, one might conclude, as did the editor of the *Guardian*, that "he was in many respects a remarkable man."

H. T. HOLMAN

Further reading

R. A. Rankin, *Down at the shore: a history of Summerside, Prince Edward Island (1752–1945)* ([Charlottetown], 1980).

Douglas Baldwin, *Prince Edward Island: an illustrated history* (Halifax, 2009).

M. G. Blackford, *A history of small business in America* (Chapel Hill, N.C., 2003).

JOHN FITZWILLIAM STAIRS,

industrialist, financier, and politician; b. 19 Jan. 1848 in Halifax, second child of William James Stairs and Susan (Susanna) Duffus Morrow; m. first 27 April 1870 Charlotte Jane Fogo in Halifax, and they had seven children; m. secondly 14 Aug. 1895 Helen Eliza Gaherty, née Bell, in Almonte, Ont., and they had one daughter; d. 26 Sept. 1904 in Toronto.

John Fitzwilliam Stairs was born into a family on the verge of prominence within Halifax's mercantile élite. His grandfather William Machin Stairs was founder and principal of a hardware and ship chandlery firm, and his father was a partner. After the death of his eldest son in 1860, W. J. Stairs focused his hopes and ambitions on John Fitzwilliam. Young Stairs was educated at the Reverend James Woods's school and Dalhousie College, attending the latter as an "occasional student" from 1865 to 1867. On reaching his majority in 1869 he became a partner in the family firm of William Stairs, Son and Morrow and was appointed manager of the Dartmouth Rope Works, an ambitious venture which his father had established that year to supply cordage to the department of the firm selling ship chandlery, ships' outfits, and fishery goods.

The rope-works was a self-contained industrial community. In addition to an oakum factory, it had housing for employees, a building which served as a school on weekdays and a church on Sundays, and the longest structure in the province, a 1,200-foot rope-walk, at one end of which stood the manager's residence, which still survives. The works flourished under Stairs's paternalistic direction, and by the mid 1870s it was described as "the most extensive and complete" manufacturing complex of its kind in the country. It not only supplied the local market and carried on a thriving export trade with Britain and Europe, but it also led the continent in the production of binder twine. After the erection in 1883 of a factory purpose-built for manufacturing binder twine, the latter gradually replaced cordage as the most marketable product, and the works came to have a virtual monopoly on twine in Canada. Credit for turning the rope-works into the most successful one in the country belongs to Stairs, whose skills as an industrial manager it showed perfectly. In 1890 Stairs became president of the Consumers' Cordage Company Limited, a Montreal-based combine which brought together the seven largest rope-manufacturing firms in Canada; the management of the Dartmouth Rope Works devolved on his brother George, a fellow director of Consumers'. Ownership of the works by the Stairs family firm ended in 1892 when it was purchased by Consumers'.

The success of the works was responsible for the development of the north end of Dartmouth, and it also launched Stairs's political career. In 1877 he became alderman for Dartmouth's Ward 3, which comprehended the north end. He served two one-year terms and in the election of 1879 lost by two votes to the incumbent warden. A Conservative like his father and an enthusiastic advocate of the system of protective tariffs introduced by the National Policy, particularly because of the potential benefits of that policy to his company, Stairs entered the Nova Scotia House of Assembly in a by-election for Halifax County in November 1879. Within a month he had been appointed minister without portfolio in the cabinet of Simon Hugh Holmes. When the ministry dissolved in May 1882 after Holmes's resignation, Stairs declined to serve under the new premier, Attorney General John Sparrow David Thompson. As a close associate of Holmes, he chose to follow him into retirement. Perhaps, too, he had seen the writing on the wall, since the government was defeated in the election of that year. In 1883 Stairs stood unopposed for warden of Dartmouth. He was elected to a second one-year term in 1884 but did not offer in 1885.

The rope-works provided Stairs with capital to invest in other manufacturing industries. His first, and in the event his most far-reaching, involvement was in steel making. In 1882 the Nova Scotia Steel Company Limited was formed at New Glasgow by Graham Fraser and George Forrest McKay to make steel and steel products. Stairs owned nearly four per cent of the stock, and a similar portion was subscribed by William Stairs, Son and Morrow. As a director of the company and its successors for 22 years, Stairs was the driving force behind the acquisitions, expansions, mergers, and recapitalizations which culminated in 1901 in the organization of the Nova Scotia Steel and Coal Company Limited. His involvement also represented, in the words of historian T. W. Acheson, "one of the few examples of inter-community industrial activity in this period" in the Maritimes.

Stairs's entry into federal politics in 1883 had been engineered by Sir Charles Tupper, the leader of the federal Conservatives in Nova Scotia, who held Stairs's father in the highest esteem. The appointment of Matthew Henry Richey as lieutenant governor of Nova Scotia created a vacancy in the House of Commons for Halifax, and Stairs received the Conservative nomination. Because the Conservatives had taken both Halifax seats at the general election the previous year, the Liberals did not bother to field a candidate and Stairs was returned by acclamation. As a protégé of Tupper, Stairs rapidly became intimate and influential with Sir John A. Macdonald. He urged the prime minister in 1885 to invite Thompson to join the cabinet after he himself had apparently declined a position. Although Stairs spoke infrequently in parliament and did not distinguish himself in debate, he was an excellent committee man.

Stairs's shortcomings as a constituency politician were revealed when he faced the electorate for the first time in the general election of 1887. Relatively unknown by the voters, he conducted a poor campaign, and he was hampered by the manifesto of the Conservatives, based on the National Policy, which made no attempt to address the needs of the farmers and fishermen in the riding. The result was that he lost to the Liberal Alfred Gilpin Jones, a relation by marriage.

At the general election of 1891 the return of Tupper from Britain, where he had been Canadian high commissioner, guaranteed that Stairs would reoffer in Halifax. Rural electors, fearful of the Liberal platform of unrestricted reciprocity, forgot their resentment that the National Policy chiefly benefited the industrial urban classes and helped Stairs to defeat Jones by 927 votes. Stairs and his colleague, Thomas Edward Kenny, were, however, charged by Jones and his running mate, Edward Farrell, with bribery and other illegal acts, and although they were cleared of personal involvement the election was declared void. Kenny and Stairs were victorious in the by-election of February 1892, but their majorities were reduced by more than half.

The fact that Halifax began to develop as a centre for industrial finance during Stairs's second term as an MP was not a coincidence, since he aggressively exploited his position to serve his business career. He had worked behind the scenes to overcome parliamentary opposition to the formation of Consumers' Cordage, and in 1893 he procured a federal act of incorporation for the Eastern Trust Company, of which he was president and his father the principal shareholder. An example of a new kind of financial intermediary in Canada, Eastern Trust was organized with the support of the Union Bank of Halifax as a quasi-industrial development bank. Not surprisingly, it helped recapitalize Nova Scotia Steel, for which it also acted as a trustee for bond holders and a registrar of bonds. In addition, Stairs introduced bills of incorporation for new manufacturing companies in the Maritimes and for regional mergers, and he used his influence to help impose or substantially increase tariffs protective of Maritime manufacturing companies, especially those in which he was involved. He was less successful in obtaining preferential freight rates on the Intercolonial Railway that would enable manufacturers in the Maritimes to compete in central Canadian markets.

Stairs did not reoffer in the general election of 1896. His reasons for standing down in favour of Robert Laird Borden are obscure. The received account is that he was intending to move to Montreal because of business interests, but his sojourn there was brief and he resumed his provincial political career the following year. If the intention was that Borden would be a locum tenens for one term, by its end Stairs had become too involved in provincial politics to resume his career in Ottawa and in 1901 Borden would be chosen leader of the federal Conservatives.

After the defeat of the federal Conservatives in 1896, Tupper went to Nova Scotia to reorganize the provincial party and prepare it for a general election; when in October a Liberal-Conservative Union on the British model was established, Stairs became president and de facto leader of the party. The 1897 election was a disaster for the Conservatives: they returned only three candidates, Stairs finishing fifth of six in Halifax County. He had been savaged by the Liberal *Morning Chronicle* of Halifax, which claimed that he supported protective tariffs because of personal interest, and his reputation as a monopolist and corporate wheeler-dealer undoubtedly also hurt his electoral chances.

Stairs gamely continued as leader, but in the general election of 1901 the Conservatives were reduced to two MHAS. He had stood in Colchester County, where he finished last of four, although the race was very close. Preoccupied with improving his chances of winning, Stairs had not bothered to issue an election manifesto and had left the management of the campaign largely to Charles Hazlitt Cahan, a former Conservative house leader and close business associate. Despite his second consecutive defeat, he did not step down as leader, and in March 1904 he became president of the newly formed Liberal-Conservative Association of Nova Scotia. Ever the optimist, Stairs told the press that he had never seen the party in better shape in Nova Scotia. He did not live to witness the annihilation of the Conservatives in the federal election of November.

It is doubtful whether greater efforts by Stairs after 1896 would have improved the fortunes of the Conservatives, since the province was enjoying good economic times, the Liberals had given "a highly creditable government performance," and the former Liberal premier William Stevens Fielding was federal minister of finance. Notwithstanding his lack of success, however, Stairs was well thought of in the party. He was unique among Nova Scotia Conservatives of the late 19th century in voluntarily renouncing a successful career in Ottawa in order to enter the uncertain realm of provincial politics. His failure to revive the provincial party was more than balanced by his aid in giving birth to the careers in federal politics of Thompson and Borden.

If by the late 1890s Stairs was politically a spent force, his business career was flourishing as never before. A director of the Nova Scotia Sugar Refinery Limited of Halifax since 1886, he arranged a merger of the refinery, the Halifax Sugar Refinery Limited of Woodside (Dartmouth), and the Moncton Sugar Refining Company on behalf of a Scottish syndicate aiming to consolidate the Maritime sugar-refining industry. The result was the launching of the Acadia Sugar Refining Company Limited in August 1893. Stairs became president of the new combine, which was registered in England because he was unable to have it incorporated in Nova Scotia. It is likely that Eastern Trust was founded in order to ensure the successful flotation of Acadia, since the latter's assets were mortgaged to Eastern Trust to underwrite the bond issue.

In 1895 Stairs became vice-president of the Nova Scotia Steel Company Limited, formed by the amalgamation of the Nova Scotia Steel and Forge Company Limited, successor to the Nova Scotia Steel Company, and the New Glasgow Iron, Coal and Railway Company, whose successful flotation in 1891 he had helped achieve. The amalgamation was in line with his belief that the firm could expand its share of the market by combining all aspects of production and marketing within one asset base and exploiting fragmentation among its competitors. In 1897 Stairs replaced Graham Fraser as president of Nova Scotia Steel, and he became president of its successor, Nova Scotia Steel and Coal, when it was created in 1901. His innovative techniques, including manipulation of the stock market in order to raise investment capital, helped Nova Scotia Steel and Coal show the largest operations in the history of Nova Scotia steel making during the fiscal year of 1903–4, the last full year of his presidency.

Other regional manufacturing concerns in which Stairs was interested were the Robb Engineering Company Limited of Amherst, N.S., of which he became a director, and the Alexander Gibson Railway and Manufacturing Company of Marysville (Fredericton), which he attempted to reorganize in 1902 and of which he also became a director. Stairs did not invest in either company, and it is possible that he got involved because the other directors believed that his name on their letterhead would attract potential investors.

During the last three years of his life Stairs entered competitively into banking, an area new to him. No eastern Canadian financier recognized more clearly that "having [Maritime banks] absorbed by [central Canadian] institutions creates a likelihood of our interests being sacrificed" to those of central Canada, and that the only way to maintain local control of Maritime banks was to amalgamate them in a single institution capable of resisting absorption by central Canadian interests. He did not, however, pretend that such a pan-Maritime bank could compete on an equal footing with banks in central Canada; his chief goals were to reduce the unhealthy competition caused by the large number of Maritime banks and ensure that regional corporate mergers were financed by a single regional investment bank.

Using as a base the Union Bank of Halifax, of which the Stairs family and their family business were the largest shareholders and Nova Scotia Steel the largest depositor, Stairs developed and began to implement a bold plan to create a pan-Maritime bank by merging smaller banks with the Union. His first acquisition was the Commercial Bank of

Windsor, which the Union Bank purchased in 1902. The sale was negotiated by the young, self-styled promoter William Maxwell Aitken. The
precise circumstances of the meeting of the two men are unknown, but
it appears that Aitken introduced himself out of the blue and asked Stairs
for a job and that Stairs was sufficiently impressed to offer him one.
Aitken was soon ensconced as executive assistant to Stairs, who began to
treat him like an adopted son.

The Commercial Bank transaction earned Aitken $10,000, which
he invested in a new company, Royal Securities Corporation Limited, the
first agency east of Montreal for retailing stocks and bonds. Royal Securities, of which Stairs became president and Aitken secretary and general
manager, opened for business in the spring of 1903. Operating in an area
where, unlike banking, little or no competition existed, Royal Securities
soon developed into an investment bank which helped finance the local
manufacturing industry and specialized in Central American and West
Indian public utilities. Among the earliest and most successful of the latter was the Trinidad Electric Company. This company had commenced
operations in 1901 with Stairs as president, and its success had been
partly responsible for Stairs's decision to establish Royal Securities.

Stairs's next objective was the People's Bank of Halifax. In April
1903 he and "his most intimate friend," Robert Edward Harris, a Halifax
corporate lawyer, bought 18 per cent of the stock of the bank, becoming
the largest shareholders. In response to the initiative, the bank's capital
stock rose from $700,000 to $1,000,000. But the increase was artificial:
the directors (chief of whom was the president, John James Stewart) and
the general manager had concealed a fraud which would have caused the
bank to fail because they were anxious to obtain the increase in stock
and the prestige conferred on the bank by Stairs becoming a shareholder.
If Aitken, George Stairs, and Royal Securities had not assumed Stairs's
liability soon after his death, his relatively modest personal estate of some
$238,000 would have been exhausted when the fraud was discovered.

Although Stairs denied that he was attempting to acquire control of
the People's Bank when he purchased the stock, he intended to merge it
in the national bank he was organizing. In June 1903 he headed a Halifax syndicate which petitioned parliament for an act of incorporation for
the Alliance Bank of Canada. The legislation was passed on 24 October.
Capitalized at $5,000,000, the new bank reportedly made "substantial

progress toward organization." Difficulties over financing, however, prevented the Alliance from applying to the Treasury Board for a certificate authorizing it to commence business within the statutory one-year period of grace, and Stairs and the provisional directors petitioned parliament for an act which would allow them an extension of nine months.

Such an act was passed on 10 Aug. 1904. Ten days or so later, Stairs and Aitken went to Toronto, ostensibly to arrange underwriting for the new bond issue by Nova Scotia Steel and Coal, but in reality to borrow money in order to finance the acquisition of the People's Bank by the Union Bank and to start up the Alliance. Stairs caught a cold which turned into pneumonia, and he was taken to hospital on 9 September. Although he was expected to recover, 17 days later he died of heart disease, complicated by kidney failure and pneumonia. The Alliance Bank expired with him, as did any hope of Halifax remaining the eastern Canadian centre of high finance.

Stairs's death came as a surprise to everyone, but he had been unwell for some time, suffering from lumbago and general decline, and colleagues had commented on how poorly he looked. The last photographs of him reveal a man frail and prematurely aged, and even he had accepted the necessity of a long vacation. His body was conveyed to Halifax, where he was given an imposing funeral.

Stairs had been scarcely less prominent in church and community affairs than in the business world. A pillar of Fort Massey Presbyterian Church in Halifax, where he was superintendent of the Sunday school from 1888 to 1894 and again from 1896, and of which he was elected an elder in 1903, he was president of the Nova Scotia Sunday School Association at the time of his death. He had been appointed a member of the board of governors of Dalhousie in 1893, and he was elected chairman in 1899. Stairs was an enthusiastic advocate of advanced technical education, which he believed would arrest the migration of talent to Ontario, and the School of Mines was inaugurated at Dalhousie in 1902 almost entirely because of his efforts. After his death the idea of a chair in his name at Dalhousie was suggested. Although the chair did not materialize, a memorial stained-glass window was placed in Fort Massey Church by his widow and children in 1909.

The most conspicuously successful promoter of mergers and financial intermediary in turn-of-the-century Nova Scotia, Stairs was also a major figure in the transition from industrial to finance capitalism, as evidenced by his creation of Royal Securities, an institution of a type then unknown in Canada. As the leading corporate financier in the Maritimes, he was innovative and aggressively competitive but also courageous, far-seeing, and optimistic, believing that Maritime manufacturing industries could compete successfully with central Canadian firms if they had equal access to markets through rail links and winter ports. Adept at marshalling and manipulating capital, he did not hesitate to raise money in Montreal, Toronto, and overseas. And although Stairs was a businessman first and a politician second, by becoming an important regional politician he was better able than pure businessmen to influence a potentially hostile economic environment.

Stairs was twice married. His first wife died of diphtheria in 1886, and in 1895 he married a 32-year-old widow, Mrs Helen Eliza Gaherty, to whom he had almost certainly been introduced through his fellow MP Bennett Rosamond. Stairs appears to have named the only child of his second marriage after Rosamond's mother. He was survived by six of his eight children and his wife, who died in 1963 in her hundredth year.

BARRY CAHILL

Further reading

T. W. Acheson, "The National Policy and the industrialization of the Maritimes, 1880–1910," *Acadiensis* (Fredericton), 1 (1971–72), no.2: 1–28.

J. M. Gibbons, "National dreamers, the National Policy and the sugar trade" (MA thesis, St Mary's Univ., Halifax, 1994).

J. D. Frost, *Merchant princes: Halifax's first family of finance, ships and steel* (Toronto, 2003).

G. P. Marchildon, "John F. Stairs, Max Aitken and the Scotia group: finance capitalism and industrial decline in the Maritimes, 1890–1914," in *Farm, factory and fortune: new studies in the economic history of the Maritime provinces*, ed. Kris Inwood (Fredericton, 1993), 197–218.

GILBERT WHITE GANONG,

teacher, entrepreneur, politician, and lieutenant governor of New Brunswick; b. 22 May 1851 in Springfield, Kings County, N.B., son of Francis Daniel Ganong and Deborah Ruth Kierstead; m. 18 Oct. 1876 Maria Famicha Robinson in St Stephen (St Stephen-Milltown), N.B.; they had no children; d. there 31 Oct. 1917.

A devout Baptist all his life, Gilbert Ganong traced his family back to Jean Guenon, a Huguenot exile from La Rochelle, France, who immigrated to what is now New York City in 1657. Ganong's paternal great-grandfather, Thomas, came to New Brunswick in 1783 with other loyalists. Ganong, the second youngest of six children, was raised in comfort in Springfield, where his father was a merchant and a farmer. Like many of his contemporaries, he obtained his teacher's licence to support greater ambitions. In 1873, after four years of teaching, he had saved over $400 for medical school, but his elder brother James Harvey persuaded him to join him in establishing a grocery business instead. "G. W. Ganong, Commission Merchant, Etc" opened in May 1873 in St Stephen, a small town in Charlotte County, New Brunswick, across the St Croix River from Calais, Maine.

Over the next three years, the brothers recruited another brother and sister to join them, renamed the firm "Ganong Brothers," and added a bakery and confectionery factory to their business. Having survived a major fire in 1877, they were well placed to take advantage of the protectionist tariff introduced by the federal Conservatives after their return to power in 1878. In 1879 the brothers opened a soap factory, and in 1885, to facilitate expansion of both businesses, they dissolved their partnership. The St Croix Soap Manufacturing Company went to James; Gilbert retained the other enterprises under the firm name of Ganong Brothers.

The following year Gilbert built a new, three-storey confectionery factory on St Stephen's main street. Financed in part with an $8,000 mortgage to the trustees of a Saint John estate, the new factory employed 100. The town of St Stephen supported the development with a ten-year exemption from all rates; this concession was renewed periodically, and similar concessions granted for subsequent factory improvements. In 1888 and again in 1903 the factory was rebuilt on the same site after being destroyed by fire.

Census figures from 1891 reveal that Ganong Brothers was a significant national as well as regional manufacturer, producing close to seven per cent of the nation's confectionery, with five per cent of the industry's employees. The firm sold its products across Canada, in Newfoundland, and in Bermuda. In 1892 Ganong incorporated the business as a New Brunswick company, called Ganong Brothers Limited; in 1916 the provincial company was wound up, but the business continued as a federal company with the same name. G. W. Ganong was the principal shareholder and president. A small number of relatives and long-term employees comprised the remaining group of shareholders and the board of directors.

In 1894 the firm gave up its bakery to specialize in confectionery manufacturing. Over the next two decades it established a subsidiary to produce packaging materials, and opened a second confectionery company, this one in Saint John. Company tradition holds that Ganong Brothers "invented" the five-cent chocolate nut bar when the factory superintendent wanted a handy snack to put in his pocket when he went fishing. Ganong took pride in using the latest equipment, and in recruiting highly skilled male candy makers from New England to supervise the manufacturing process. As in the confectionery industry generally, female workers packed the finished candy, and company minutes frequently record discussions of how to attract more girls to St Stephen. Recruiting efforts included trips to Britain, and the opening in 1906 of Elm Hall, a boarding-house for female employees. Applicants for rooms had to provide a letter of reference from their minister.

Ganong was a staunch Conservative, and represented Charlotte County in parliament from 1896 to 1908. In his election card for his first campaign in May 1896, he committed himself to supporting the general trade policy of the Liberal-Conservative party and to working for all legislation that would advance the temperance movement. His victory over Arthur Hill Gillmor, by 472 votes, came from the towns and inland areas. A member of the opposition for his three terms in parliament, Ganong spoke on matters affecting his business; he supported the Alien Labour Bill of 1897, even though it might have restricted his ability to hire workers who lived across the river in Calais, opposed the attempt to establish labelling standards which would enable consumers to distinguish between pure maple sugar and products which combined maple with other sugars, and denounced the Liberal government's failure to introduce prohibition despite the majority in favour in the plebiscite of 1898. Ganong also argued for his constituents, repeatedly asking for harbour improvements and better communications for coastal and island communities. In these appeals he resorted to the nativism that shaped much public discourse of this period, chiding the government for "frittering away the public money on Doukhobors, Galicians and Finns."

As a reward for political service, including financial support for the local Conservative newspaper, and leadership in raising money and volunteers for World War I, Ganong succeeded Josiah Wood as lieutenant governor of New Brunswick in 1917, but died three months later. The firm survived; Arthur Deinstadt Ganong, the new president, was a nephew, who had joined the firm when his uncle was first elected to parliament. G. W. Ganong's success in business had made him wealthy; although he invested in mortgages and other companies, the single largest asset in his estate was his shares in Ganong Brothers. Most of these he left to his widow. On her death on 30 Nov. 1934 her estate was valued at over $1 million.

MARGARET E. MCCALLUM

Further reading

David Folster, *The chocolate Ganongs of St. Stephen, New Brunswick* (Fredericton, 1990).

M. E. McCallum, "Family, factory and community: a social history of Ganong Bros., confectionery manufacturers, St. Stephen, New Brunswick, 1873–1946" (PHD thesis, Univ. of Toronto, 1987).

Section 4

The Industrial Heartland

WILLIAM PRICE,

lumber merchant and manufacturer of planks (deals);
b. 17 Sept. 1789 at Hornsey, near London, England, third son of
Richard Price and Mary Evans; d. 14 March 1867 at Quebec.

William Price's parents, originally from Wales, moved to Middlesex at the end of the 18th century. The family probably belonged to the upper middle class, and although its financial situation was precarious after Richard Price's death around 1804, William's mother, with eight children to provide for, was able to count on friends important in business and government. After a few years at Hammersmith College in London, William began to study law under a cousin, a lawyer of the Inner Temple, but had to give up this career. At age 14 he became an employee of Christopher Idle, a prominent London businessman. Six years later, on 10 May 1810, he landed at Quebec as a clerk in a branch of the Idle firm, at a wage of £135 a year. Much of the correspondence between Price and his family and friends during these early years has been preserved. These letters show that he was well educated in spite of his interrupted studies, and that family feelings remained strong despite distance. William's eldest brother David, who traded with Portugal and Latin America, assumed the role of father, and followed his younger brother's career closely, lavishing advice on him and arousing his ambition: "If you get nothing but your salary by going to Quebec," he wrote, "you are doing little better than stand still." And, in another letter: "I trust it may please Heaven to strengthen us; that we may finally succeed and stand in due season on an independent footing." This solidarity did not weaken with time: in 1817 William lent his savings to his brother Samuel who was on the verge of bankruptcy, and in 1843, when William himself was in difficulty, David went to Canada to give him moral and financial support.

Information on Idle's business in North America is imprecise. It may be this firm that, at the beginning of the Napoleonic Wars, obtained a monopoly on orders of Canadian lumber for the Admiralty. Price devoted most of his time to filling such orders, travelling through the forests of Vermont, the Ottawa valley, and Upper Canada to select timber for masts. Planks cut in Lower Canada's sawmills completed the cargoes of square timber. The firm also imported wines and other goods, but the Quebec store does not seem to have had an important place in this trade.

Price's first biographers note his services during the War of 1812. A major in the militia, he is thought to have raised a cavalry corps, organized an artillery battery at Quebec, and acted as a courier for Governor George Prevost. In any case, he was in Halifax by March 1813, where he negotiated for his employer the purchase of five ships intended for the Royal Navy.

In 1815 Price took over management of the Quebec office from William Oviatt, who returned to England. In the years of recession that followed, he concerned himself with supplying food to the Maritime provinces and undertook some business on his own account in the West Indian market, but without conspicuous success. The Idle firm, badly managed in England, was close to ruin, and Price was looking for financial backers and a form of partnership to enable him to take advantage of the experience he had acquired during his first ten years in Canada. He finally decided on the proposal made by Parker and Yeoman, timber brokers in London. The agreement concluded on 1 May 1820 created three distinct business firms, one in London, the William Price Company in Quebec, and the partnership of Peter McGill and Kenneth Dowie in Montreal. Following a new arrangement in 1823, Parker and Yeoman was succeeded by a company formed by James Dowie and Nathaniel Gould, in London, which from then on financed the entire undertaking, chartered ships, and disposed of colonial produce. After Kenneth Dowie left for Liverpool, Peter McGill continued to trade corn on his own in Upper Canada. At Quebec, the William Price Company specialized in the export of timber. Each of the four partners, Price, McGill, J. Dowie, and Gould, received a quarter of the shares and profits in each of the three firms, although the capital invested was not equal. Price, whose sole contribution was a sawmill of little value not far from Quebec, was chosen because of his reputation as an experienced businessman and his technical knowledge. As he was to do the major part of the work at the port of loading, he levied a commission of 5 per cent on his operations, which was added to his share of the profits.

Until 1843 Price always acted in the name of the company. He drew bills of exchange on Gould and Dowie for advances to local contractors, the preparation of cargoes, and the purchase of operation of sawmills. Canadian banks accepted only short term bills, which the London partners had to honour as they became due, even if about 18 months had to be allowed between the first outlay and the payment for delivery of lumber in England. At the least contraction of the market, the accounts of the Canadian partners were liable to be overdrawn.

At the time Price concluded these arrangements, the commercial climate was still unsettled. In the British House of Commons, the Liberals were violently attacking the exorbitant preferences granted Canadian timber during the war as being no longer justified. But in 1821 a commission of inquiry recommended only a minor readjustment, and, reinforced by these tariff advantages on the British market, the colonial timber trade soon entered a new period of expansion. The company's business followed the rhythm of general growth. After a quiet beginning, its volume of exports soared. It was exporting about 50 cargoes of lumber a year around 1827, then the average rose rapidly to 75, and from 1833 on nearly 100 ships left each year for England from Quebec and the ports of the lower St Lawrence. This represented a turnover of £70,000, and more.

Price was both an exporter of square timber and manufacturer of planks or deals. Bit by bit manufacturing outstripped strictly commercial operations, but the latter, as his first source of capital, was the foundation of his remarkable success. Like other Quebec lumbermen in this period, he bought from various contractors the pine and oak cribs that came down each spring from the Ottawa valley, Upper Canada, and the seigneuries upstream from Quebec. He often granted advances to his customers to help them set up a lumbercamp and dispatch lumber to Quebec, keeping their production for himself at a price fixed at the beginning of the winter. The loads were completed by staves and barrel hoops, as well as planks bought from local sawmills. The company had offices and a warehouse on Rue Saint-Pierre at Quebec, two roadsteads on the south shore, with wharves, breakwaters, and workshops, and a sawmill at Hadlow Cove. In the New Liverpool roadstead, at Lévis, the principal port of loading, there were some 60 employees during the shipping season.

A large part of the exports made by Price, perhaps the most important part, was intended for the shipyards of the Admiralty. Six or seven tender-ers, representing large firms which had invested in the Canadian trade, wrangled over orders for masts and construction timber which would go as high as £150,000 or £200,000. Between 1830 and 1850 the firm of Brockelbank and Holt usually won out, and entrusted Price with the completion of the deal. These contracts, which extended over several years, were important for stability, because they reduced the impact of the commercial crises that jeopardized so many other colonial enterprises.

Most of the ships transporting timber to England were hired by Gould and Dowie, but the company also possessed a few barks and brigs, two three-masters, and several schooners for coastal trade. Between 1820 and 1850 some 40 vessels, built at Quebec and Montreal and in the shipyards of the upper St Lawrence, were registered in the name of Price and his partners. After 1850 Price apparently no longer equipped ships for transatlantic voyages, but he kept a fleet of schooners to serve his establishments, as well as steamships to tow sailing vessels in the Saguenay, and later on to link this region with Quebec.

Price deserves a special place in Canadian economic history primari-ly as a contractor. The profits realized in trade were gradually reinvested in sawmills and lumbering. Before 1830 the company bought almost all its planks from various small firms in Lower Canada. Price encouraged the owners to increase their production, financed them, and subsequent-ly acquired the mortgaged sawmills. Thus, before 1838, the sawmills of Batiscan, Saint-Vallier, Bic, Rimouski, Métis (Métis-sur-Mer), La Malbaie, those of Anse-à-l'Eau and Moulin-Baude near Tadoussac, and those of Bytown (Ottawa) and Crosby in Upper Canada, were entered on the company's books. Often co-ownership was involved and usually Price was the owner in fact long before he held legal title.

He was already an important contractor downstream from Quebec when he established himself in the Saguenay region, a vast untapped expanse which the crown leased to the Hudson's Bay Company. Through one of his men, Alexis Tremblay, dit Picoté, Price encouraged and financially supported a group of people from La Malbaie, who went to settle as squatters along the Saguenay. Between 1838 and 1842 this community, called the "Vingt-et-un," built nine sawmills at the mouths of the principal tributaries of the Saguenay. By 1840 Price was having planks for England loaded there, and two years later repurchased all the sawmills outright. Large numbers of settlers soon arrived and, as Price had foreseen, the government had to yield to the pressure for colonization. In 1843 the lands were put up for auction.

With astonishing rapidity, Price bought all the sawmill sites in the valley and fjord, and along the north St Lawrence shore on both sides of Tadoussac. To take on timber, ships came as far as Grande-Baie, the most important manufacturing centre before 1850. As early as 1842 Price was associated with the enterprises of Peter McLeod, which were located at the mouths of the Chicoutimi, Moulin à Baude, and Shipshaw rivers. A Montagnais on his mother's side, Peter McLeod could claim his natural rights and install sawmills in the upper Saguenay, a territory the HBC was attempting to retain. Similarly, by concluding agreements with other contractors such as William Charles Pentland, Félix Têtu and Frédéric Boucher, and Édouard Slevin and James Gibb, Price managed to extend his monopoly from Tadoussac to Bersimis. He also controlled the north shore from La Malbaie to Rivière-Noir. At the same time, he consolidated his positions on the south shore of the St Lawrence by going into partnership with Pierre-Thomas Casgrain and Nazaire Têtu at Trois-Pistoles and John Caldwell at L'Isle Verte, and thus established himself in some ten villages between Montmagny and Cap-Chat. His partners were generally not in a position to export planks to England. So long as there were no other important outlets, Price's connections in England enabled him to monopolize the whole market without difficulty, and to wait for the right moment to redeem the other shares, a process he had completed by about 1860.

To supply the mills, Price acquired substantial reserves of timber. On the south shore, he bought the township of Armagh and part of the Rimouski and Métis seigneuries, some 240 square miles, but still only a tiny fraction of the area being exploited. According to the policy in force from 1826 on, contractors exploited the forests of the province as agents of the public domain in return for the annual payment of felling dues. Price, a skilful and discreet man, was able to get round the officers of the crown, oust competitors, foresee the needs of his enterprise long before they arose, and thus put his hands on about 7,700 square miles of forest, in addition to timber limits in the Ottawa valley of an extent hard to determine. These immense reserves were concentrated on each side of the Saguenay and to the northeast of Lac Saint-Jean.

The turning point in Price's affairs came in 1843, just after he had worked his way into the Saguenay region. Until then his partners had supported all his ventures, but suddenly relations became strained. The preference granted to Canadian timber was reduced and finally abolished, at a time when the English market was shrinking dangerously. The situation was aggravated by the near bankruptcy of McGill. Gould and Dowie ordered the liquidation of the company, limited the working capital until the final winding up, and insisted on full remittances at the end of each fiscal year. They criticized Price for his 5 per cent commission, blamed him for having tied up some £130,000 in sawmills, and ordered him to get rid of them forthwith. But in the middle of a slump, there obviously were no takers. The 1846 fire at Grande-Baie was a culminating stroke. So long as the William Price company had been borne along on the economic boom, the man had remained hidden behind a laconic business correspondence and uncontroversial balance-sheets. But when disaster struck, he made himself heard, and it was then possible to perceive what was behind his success. "If you fail or retreat or show your star to be on the wane, powerful enemies start up against you," he scribbled on a memo pad. An obstinate man, he rejected all advice. He would not close his sawmills, he would not go to England to wait out the crisis quietly. Instead he appealed to his brother David, who advanced him £6,000 and came to Canada to help him clear up his accounts. For four years he fought unceasingly to get from banks and former partners the means to preserve his credit and the forest empire he was building for his sons.

He already had three sons working with him. Rather than abandon the fight, he declared in a letter to McGill that he was ready to sell Wolfesfield, send his family to the country, and go to live with his sons in the company's offices. Wolfesfield, which he kept despite everything, was a magnificent property on the Plains of Abraham, acquired by Price at the time of his marriage in 1825 to Jane Stewart, one of the daughters of Charles Grey Stewart, a customs inspector at Quebec. The couple was to have 14 children. The father initiated the elder sons at an early age into his business, beginning with the technical side. When still young, they worked in the sawmills in the Saguenay and the lower reaches of the river. Price sent them to England as apprentices, and made them travel on the Continent and in Scandinavia to complete their training.

The old company continued to function while settling its accounts and narrowly escaped bankruptcy; at the same time Price used his credit with the government and the public to acquire new properties and timber limits in his own or his sons' names. Business recovered, and in 1849 annual production of planks in all the mills downstream from Quebec reached £90,000; about half of this came from Price's own sawmills. He quickly redeemed his partners' shares, and in 1853 the old company's timber represented no more than 10 per cent of exports. The founding of the company of William Price and Son in 1855 was the realization of an ambition that had sustained him throughout his career.

He had no other ambition. He had been invited to be a member of the Legislative Council several times, but had refused. Politics were of no concern unless they served his interests directly, and for this end unofficial approaches were often most effective. As a young man he had many a good laugh over the debates that split the assembly of Lower Canada, and only a crisis as grave as the one that began in 1834 penetrated his indifference. He was a member of the subcommittee of the Constitutional Association formed at Quebec that year, but this brief entry into public life had no sequel. His contemporaries often said that in 57 years in Canada he scarcely ever took the trouble to vote. The fate of his business was linked more closely to imperial policy. Price and his partners followed attentively the "subversive" campaigns of the "Manchester school" that threatened their privileges, and they witnessed with dismay the collapse of the preferential system, but he was not among those who went so far as to advocate annexation. Moreover, his enterprises survived competition, and because of their geographical location long continued to be turned towards the British market.

At the end of his life, Price represented the Tory of the old school, for whom the motto was still "Ships, colonies, and commerce." He had been one of the founding members of the Quebec Board of Trade, and was a member of the Baron Club, and of the Literary and Historical Society of Quebec, but his work scarcely permitted him to mingle with the British officers and businessmen in exile at Quebec. He readily derided those who conducted their affairs from the seclusion of their offices. Price was a man of the lumbercamps and log-runs. "I have," he wrote to Dowie, "to find intelligent explorers and judge their reports, have roads planned and made, rivers cleared, lakes dammed, engage superintendents, contractors, engage men for them, buy their homes, cattle, hay, oats; engage schooners, ... buy provisions.... I have to negotiate with the Commissioners of crown lands. It takes local influence, tact, vigilance...."

As long as his strength permitted, Price spent most of his time at his businesses, making the trip to the Saguenay two or three times in winter by roads unsuitable for vehicles and sleeping in makeshift shelters. In 1861 the region already had about 12,000 settlers. It was a closed world which, except for the new agricultural enclaves to the south of Lac Saint-Jean, was entirely dependent on Price. Work in the sawmills and road-steads in summer alternated with tree felling in the forest in winter. An improved sweating system totally cut these people off from the outside world, and bound them hand and foot to their master's pleasure. One had to push farther and farther inland to find pine and spruce of a good size. The settlers sowed seeds in the tree-stripped and burnt-out areas of the Baie des Hahas (Baie des Ha! Ha!), and Chicoutimi became the new centre of activities. Price ruled the region; charitable when his men were docile, he was ruthless towards those who disputed his dominion. "Everywhere the nobility and generosity of the Master are proclaimed," wrote Bishop Charles-François Baillargeon in a letter to him, on his return from a tour of the parishes and missions. Prominent citizens went further. According to Denis-Benjamin Papineau, in *Le Canadien*: "This gentleman is without question the foster-father of this young settlement; his stores full of supplies and clothing of all kinds are open to everybody. It is eminently right that his humanity, his fairness and that of his agents, should win the confidence and hard work with which these poor people, in their zeal and gratitude, repay him." There were, it is true, a few discordant voices in this chorus of praise. Rumour had it that Price had schemed underhandedly to get possession of McLeod's holdings, and in 1849 a few daring settlers even signed a petition to the governor, denouncing Price's monopoly of the land, saw and grist mills, and waterways blocked by booms. In the memorandum that he sent to James Bruce, 8th Earl of Elgin and 12th Earl of Kincardine, refuting these accusations, Price quoted testimonies of gratitude such as the following: "Grandfather Price, I came here with my wife, my eight children, and barely enough to eat. Now I am all right, thanks to you."

Towards the end of his life, Price developed a fascination for agronomy. On every official visit to the Saguenay, there was an obligatory stop at one of his model farms. In other areas he could rely on well-chosen and well-trained managers, and on his sons, who were a credit to him. After he had been the representative in the assembly for the new county of Saguenay for a long time, David Edward was elected a legislative councillor in 1864. William Evan lived more modestly in the Saguenay, and became well liked. Edward George took care of the company's interests in England. Henry Ferrier, the only one to marry, left to carry on trade in Chile, while young Evan John continued his studies.

At the end of his career the government had presented Price with a timber slide a mile long, which brought the logs from Lac Saint-Jean over the Petite Décharge into the sawmills. Thanks to this shoot, the firm still loaded 500,000 planks each year for England, while a variety of products – boards, railway ties, fence posts, battens, and shingles – was taken by schooner to Canadian and American markets. Did the old man know that the forests were being depleted, and that his sons lacked innovative ability? When he died at Wolfesfield in 1867, his long-established industry was no longer growing, but it had not begun to decline. The people of the Saguenay erected a statue to him on the heights of Chicoutimi. The country was changing rapidly, and was escaping the Prices. One by one the sawmills ceased to turn, but the family kept its forests and lands. Thirty years later a grandson, the second William Price, came to the Saguenay to create the paper industry, reviving the fortune of the Prices and the economy of the region.

LOUISE DECHÊNE

Further reading

Gérard Bouchard, *Quelques arpents d'Amérique: population, économie, famille au Saguenay, 1838–1971* ([Montréal], 1996).

Louise Dechêne, "William Price, 1810–1850" (mémoire de MA, univ. Laval, Québec, 1964).

D. [S.] Lee, *Lumber kings and shantymen: logging, lumber and timber in the Ottawa valley* (Toronto, 2006).

A. R. M. Lower, *Great Britain's woodyard: British America and the timber trade, 1763–1867* (Montreal and London, 1973).

Christian Pouyez *et al.*, *Les Saguenayens: introduction à l'histoire des populations du Saguenay, XVIᵉ–XXᵉ siècles* (Sillery [Québec], 1983).

JOHN REDPATH,

contractor and industrialist; b. 1796 at Earlston, Berwickshire, Scotland; d. 5 March 1869 at Montreal, Que.

Of John Redpath's life in Scotland before he left at the age of 20, we know only that he trained as a stone mason. In the early 1820s he emerged as a major building contractor in Montreal, supplying the stone for the new Notre-Dame Church and the Lachine Canal in partnership with Thomas McKay. The canal was one of the most important public works of the early 19th century in Lower Canada and in building its locks Redpath gained a sound reputation. In 1827 and 1828 McKay and Redpath were engaged in building the locks at Jones Falls on the Rideau Canal, "the most extensive engineering undertaking at any one location along the Canal." Redpath then seems to have returned to Montreal, although until 1831 he apparently retained an interest in a partnership with major contractors on the canal including McKay, Thomas Phillips, and Andrew White.

It is not clear what business Redpath pursued after he returned to Montreal. He was already well-to-do and moved rapidly to the highest level of the Montreal business community. In 1833 he was elected to the board of directors of the Bank of Montreal, the city's leading financial institution; until his death he was a director, after 1860 a vice-president, and a large shareholder. But like most of his wealthy colleagues Redpath put money into several enterprises of Montreal's burgeoning economy of the 1840s, 50s and 60s. An investor in the Montreal Fire Assurance Company and the Montreal Telegraph Company, and a director of both, he also invested substantial sums in Canadian mining ventures – some in the Eastern Townships – including the Belvedere Mining and Smelting,

Bear Creek Coal, Rockland Slate, Melbourne Slate, and Capel Copper companies. In addition, he owned shares in a copper smelter, a large share of the Montreal Investment Association, and much of the most desirable mountainside property in Montreal, and he had investments in shipping, the Montreal Towboat Company and the Richelieu Company. He was also a promoter of the Canada Marine Insurance Company, the Metropolitan Fire Insurance Company, and the Canada Peat Fuel Company.

Despite these many financial interests and substantial wealth, Redpath would not have stood out among many equals in Montreal had it not been for his decision in 1854 to begin construction of the first sugar refinery in the Province of Canada. His was one of the largest establishments among more than 20 new plants in the recently opened industrial belt along the Lachine Canal. Redpath had started several years earlier to purchase land along the canal from the Sulpicians, the provincial government having not long before authorized the use of the canal's water for industrial purposes. His seven-storey factory, whose towering smokestack became one of the city's landmarks, represented an immense investment for Redpath, the sole owner. He put £40,000 into land, buildings, and machinery, and disposed of a like amount in working capital. Within a year, he had more than 100 employees and was producing 3,000 barrels of refined sugar per month for the Canadian market. His plant depended entirely on supplies of cane sugar imported from the West Indies, much of it in his own ships, the *Helen Drummond* and *Grace Redpath*, named after his daughters. By 1862 he was importing about 7,000 tons of raw sugar annually. Under the protection of favourable tariffs conveniently established by the Canadian government in 1855 – the year Redpath's factory opened – the business prospered. By the mid 1860s another sugar refinery had been established in Montreal to compete with Redpath's. In 1858 Redpath had brought his eldest son, Peter, and in 1862 his son-in-law, George Alexander Drummond, a young Scottish engineer, into the firm. He made plans to retire gradually as more of his sons came of age, perhaps to enjoy his new country house, Terrace Bank, built on one of his Mount Royal properties overlooking the city where his substantial fortune had been founded.

Redpath had served a brief and undistinguished term as a member of Montreal's city council from 1840 to 1843, but he had provided the province with other useful services. During the late 1830s he was a member of the Lachine Canal commission. In 1839 he was appointed to the newly created provincial Board of Works, resigning on 24 April 1840, and in 1845 he served on the commission of inquiry into the management of the Board of Works along with William Cayley, Frédéric-Auguste Quesnel, George Sherwood, and Moses Judah Hayes.

Redpath was president in 1849 of the Montreal Annexation Association, which enjoyed broad, yet brief support from many of the city's prominent businessmen. Requests for assistance from other annexationists, including Hugh Bowlby Willson, editor of Toronto's *Independent*, were forwarded to Redpath. There is a strong possibility that as an aspiring industrialist, who would have been concerned about markets for manufactured goods, Redpath was in part responsible for the emphasis in the association's manifesto on the supposed advantages for Canadian manufacturers in union with the United States. His concern was perhaps reflected in his announcement to the annexationists in October 1849 that thousands of skilled Canadian artisans were moving to the United States. With the rapid decline of annexationism in Montreal in 1850, Redpath turned his interest in public welfare onto surer paths.

He had always been a charitable man in the best Christian tradition. He supported established institutions such as the Montreal General Hospital, the Montreal Presbyterian College, and the mechanics' institute, all of which he served as a director, but he also, at the head of a small group, sought government assistance to fight Montreal's white slavery traffic and, working through the local Magdalene Asylum, to redeem "unfortunate females, many of whom are poor immigrants who have been decoyed into the abodes of infamy and shame which abound in this city." He also secured support for an insane asylum from the government, and helped establish the Protestant House of Industry and Refuge. A devout Free Church Presbyterian, Redpath was a founder of the Presbyterian Foreign Missions, the Labrador Mission, the Sabbath Observance Society, and the French Canadian Missionary Society; to the latter he left a substantial legacy.

Redpath had ten children by his first wife, Janet McPhee (Macphee), whom he married in 1818. Following her death in 1834 he married Jane Drummond, and they had seven children. Only two of his sons, Peter and John James, appear to have joined the refinery. One of Redpath's daughters married John Dougall, editor of the *Montreal Witness*, another Henry Taylor Bovey, a well-known McGill University professor, and another George Alexander Drummond, who became the principal figure in the refinery and a prominent Montreal businessman.

GERALD J. J. TULCHINSKY

Further reading

Douglas McCalla, "Sojourners in the snow? The Scots in business in nineteenth-century Canada," in *A kingdom of the mind: how the Scots helped make Canada*, ed. P. E. Rider and Heather McNabb (Montreal and Kingston, Ont., 2006), 76–96.

Gerald [J. J.] Tulchinsky, "Studies of businessmen in the development of transportation and industry in Montreal, 1837–1853" (PHD thesis, Univ. of Toronto, 1971), 425–29.

C. D. Allin and G. M. Jones, *Annexation, preferential trade and reciprocity: an outline of the Canadian annexation movement of 1849–50, with special reference to the questions of preferential trade and reciprocity* (Toronto and London, [1912]), 136.

JOHN KINDER LABATT,

farmer and brewer; b. 1803 at Mountmellick (County Laoighis, Republic of Ireland), eldest of the seven children of Valentine Knightley Chetwode Labat (Labatt), whose Huguenot ancestors came from the Bordeaux region of France, and his wife Jane; d. 26 Oct. 1866 at London, Canada West.

L ittle is known of the early life of John Kinder Labatt. In August 1833 he married Eliza Kell, a relative of the great Norwich banker,

Daniel Gurney, at Twickenham, Middlesex County, England. They were to have five sons and nine daughters. John and his wife immigrated to Upper Canada and in January 1834 purchased a 200-acre tract from the Canada Company in Westminster Township, just south of the town of London. In 1843 he acquired 200 acres adjacent to his lot from Colonel Thomas Talbot for £50. He prospered in farming, sent his sons to the Caradoc Academy, the best boarding school in the region, and in 1844 played a leading role in the construction of Christ Church (Church of England) at Glanworth.

In 1846–47, possibly because of temporary difficulties with his English investments which were being handled by his father-in-law, Labatt visited Great Britain and considered remaining there, but the high cost of living sent him back to Canada. He sold his farm and invested £2,000 in the brewery operated by his friend Samuel Eccles, located, as it still is, on the south branch of the Thames at the foot of Talbot St. This was the oldest brewery in London, having been established by John Balkwill in 1827–28, then acquired by William Balkwill and Thomas W. Shepherd before it was sold to Eccles in 1847. Labatt and Eccles, as the firm was called, was soon producing three brands, XXX, XX, and X; Labatt prospered sufficiently to be able to buy Eccles's interest when the latter retired in 1854. Labatt then changed the name to the London Brewery, and advertised himself as a brewer, maltster, and dealer in barley, malt, and hops. His third son, John, joined him in 1864, while his two elder sons, Ephraim and Robert, went to work with brewer George Weatherall Smith in Prescott, Ont. Robert bought the business there in 1868 after Ephraim's death the previous year.

Labatt was also active in the affairs of London. He was a member of the town council for St David's Ward in 1850–51 and of the council of the Board of Trade in 1863. Interested in transportation ventures, he was one of the principals of the Proof Line Road Joint Stock Company, which extended communications north of London after 1849, and an incorporator of the London and Port Stanley Railway in 1853. He also helped establish the London Permanent Building and Savings Society and the Western Permanent Building Society, which were absorbed by the Huron and Erie Savings and Loan Society in 1865 and 1866 respectively. He was a parishioner of St Paul's Cathedral (Church of England) and was prominent in aiding the needy of London in the great depression of the late 1850s.

When John K. Labatt died in 1866 his estate was valued at $16,000. The firm was purchased by his son John under the terms of the will and the presidency of the company remained with John, then with John's sons John S. and Hugh F., until 1956. The corporation became a public company in 1945 and was controlled by the family trust until 1964, by which time it was one of Canada's largest breweries.

FREDERICK H. ARMSTRONG

Further reading

Ian Coutts, *Brew north: how Canadians made beer & beer made Canada* (Vancouver, 2010).

Labatt Brewing Company Limited, *Good things brewing – for 150 years* (Toronto, [1997?]).

Nicholas Pashley, *Cheers! an intemperate history of beer in Canada* (Toronto, 2009).

G. C. Phillips, *On tap: the odyssey of beer and brewing in Victorian London-Middlesex* (Sarnia, Ont., 2000).

ISAAC BUCHANAN,

merchant, politician, and pamphleteer; b. 21 July 1810 at Glasgow, Scotland, fourth son of Peter Buchanan and Margaret Buchanan; m. 27 Jan. 1843 Agnes Jarvie at Glasgow, and they had 11 children; d. 1 Oct. 1883 at Hamilton, Ont.

Isaac Buchanan's father was a successful manufacturer who later became a merchant in Glasgow. During the Napoleonic Wars Peter acquired Auchmar, an historic 1,378-acre estate in Buchanan parish, Stirlingshire, possession of which entitled him to add "of Auchmar" to his name. He was an elder of the Church of Scotland, and his Glasgow home was often visited by leading lay and clerical figures in the evangelical wing of the Kirk. The family valued education, and Isaac, after attending the Glasgow Grammar School, began preparing for university and a profession. Then, instead, in October 1825, he began an apprenticeship with the Glasgow firm of William Guild and Company, West Indian merchants. Buchanan always said this decision was entirely his own, and entirely impromptu; his father, however, had recently lost heavily in the depressed Caribbean trade, and the set-back to the family's fortunes may well have prompted the change in plans.

William Guild had branches in Jamaica and Honduras, but he decided that Montreal might be a better place to launch his own son, William Jr, in business. In March 1830 he and his son formed William Guild Jr and Company of Montreal, dry goods importers; Buchanan, whose energy and enthusiasm had greatly impressed the elder Guild, was made junior partner, to receive one-quarter of the profits. Buchanan left home for the first time early in April, travelling to Montreal via Liverpool and New York. To compete with established firms, the new business sought out merchants arriving in Montreal for the first time, most of them from Upper Canada. Because these merchants lacked capital, sales to them could be made only on 12 months' credit. This use of credit alarmed the elder Guild, who feared his capital would be locked up in Canada; accordingly, Buchanan suggested that the firm be relocated farther from their competition and closer to their customers in order to try to secure cash business. In December 1831 Buchanan moved to York (Toronto) and in 1832 opened William Guild Jr and Company, possibly the first and certainly the largest exclusively wholesale firm in the town. But again sales could be made only on a long-term credit basis.

Despite periods of loneliness and depression, Buchanan was confident of Upper Canada's future. He speculated in land, bought some steamboat shares, and then, with his only surviving brother, Peter, agreed to buy the Guilds' share in the York business. In 1834, using their two-thirds share of their parents' estate, about £12,000 sterling (much of it realized from the sale of the Auchmar estate in 1830), the brothers opened Peter Buchanan and Company in Glasgow, to handle finances and purchases, and Isaac Buchanan and Company in Toronto, to manage sales and credit. The two brothers jointly owned each company. An important ally was Robert William Harris, dry goods manager of the Guild firm in Toronto, who in 1835 became a partner in Isaac Buchanan and Company.

Isaac Buchanan quickly became a figure of some note in Toronto. He helped found in 1835 the city's board of trade, of which he was president from 1835 to 1837, the St Andrew's Society in 1836, of which he was also president, and the Toronto Club, the city's first men's club; and he was chairman of the trustees of the Presbyterian St Andrew's Church. He found himself resented by the city's Tory oligarchy, which he in turn regarded as extremely provincial. He was particularly aggrieved by the inferior position of his church, the Church of Scotland, in Upper Canada, and in 1835 published a newspaper extra to demand that it be given a share of the revenues from the clergy reserves. Like most of his later pamphlets and open letters, this was important more as a symptom of local problems than as a contribution to their solution; Buchanan seldom had strikingly original ideas to present, and his strident rhetoric did little to persuade the unconvinced.

On the outbreak of rebellion in Upper Canada in early December 1837, Buchanan accepted a commission in the local militia and served in Toronto and then on the Niagara frontier. He saw his chief problem as being the troops he commanded, all Irishmen, "incarnate devils," but, he pledged, "if I do get to close Quarters with these infernal Rebels and Yankees I am prepared to sell my Life as dearly as I can." In February 1838, back in Toronto, he published a warning that "the selfish principles of the high church party" would soon provoke another rebellion unless changes were made to provide equal distribution of funds from the clergy reserves. That month, however, he left for Britain, to place the 1838 orders for Isaac Buchanan and Company and to take charge of the Glasgow office for 18 months; meanwhile Peter came to Upper Canada.

In 1839, inspired by high profits for 1838 at Toronto and by low prices in Britain, Isaac Buchanan decided to increase Peter Buchanan and Company's shipments vastly, borrowing heavily to finance this venture from their Glasgow bank and a number of mercantile firms in Glasgow and in England. To sell these goods, Peter Buchanan and Harris had to expand the firm's clientele rapidly. But now the business, with its heavy accounts outstanding in the western part of Upper Canada, could, Isaac Buchanan feared, be outflanked by a strong firm based in

Hamilton, and rumour had it that several Montreal firms were planning such branches. To anticipate them he went to Hamilton in the spring of 1840, rented a very large warehouse nearing completion, and with John Young, Hamilton's leading merchant, founded a new business known as Buchanan, Harris and Company. To help attract customers to so small a centre a grocery department was opened and to buy its supplies an office was needed in Montreal. Using the firm's western connection, the man hired to manage this Montreal office, James Law, soon built it into a highly successful operation, known from 1845 as Isaac Buchanan and Company (the Toronto firm of this name having ceased to exist); it had a warehouse on the Lachine Canal and to its substantial grocery trade were added iron, hardware, and grain. Buchanan's decisions to expand were taken largely without consulting his brother, but backed by rapid Upper Canadian expansion and his partners' business abilities, they succeeded handsomely. By the end of 1843, Peter and Isaac's original capital had increased fivefold. But Isaac found little pleasure in business routines, which offered an unsatisfactory outlet for his "superabundant vitality."

In 1841, under the auspices of a new governor general, Charles Edward Poulett Thomson, 1st Baron Sydenham, Upper and Lower Canada were united in one province. Although when he was in Glasgow Buchanan had protested the appointment of Thomson because of the governor's links to the Baltic trade, he soon agreed entirely with him on the union and the clergy reserves, and on the importance of pursuing policies for economic development that would transcend older colonial issues. Hence Buchanan readily accepted nomination in the governor's interest in the election of 1841 to represent Toronto, citadel of the compact Tories, and he contributed £1,000 to help his cause. In a bitter campaign, which Buchanan's speeches did nothing to calm, Buchanan and John Henry Dunn won a narrow victory, receiving strong support from many Toronto merchants.

At the first session of the post-union assembly, Buchanan claimed to "have been very *instrumental* in all thats going on." Most notably, he helped to block Sydenham's proposed provincial bank of issue, which would, he feared, shrink the money supply in Canada West and, by destroying many businesses (though not his own), reduce commerce there to total dependence on Montreal merchants. But it was not his nature to seek or to understand compromises and alliances, and he found the role of private member ultimately uncongenial. Thus he returned to Glasgow while his brother again came to Canada; after missing the 1842 session, he resigned his seat early in 1843, convinced that his basic aims, the union and "responsible government," had now been safely achieved.

Buchanan was not an original or a leading theoretician on constitutional matters, and his opinions here were typical of many moderates. In essence he thought the term "responsible government" implied that the oligarchical rule of the 1820s and 1830s had ended and that a majority in the Legislative Assembly would now dictate the complexion of the government. But the term need not imply the full application of the principles of cabinet government as Robert Baldwin understood them. Specifically Buchanan considered that the governor had a central responsibility to work to preserve the British connection and to prevent the spread of American ideas in Canada; the governor was entitled to act independently to fulfil this responsibility. To Buchanan and many like him, such as William Henry Draper, Baldwin was a dangerously doctrinaire extremist who, while personally above reproach, was surrounded by potentially subversive influences; Baldwin's ideas were seen as leading inevitably to a breaking of the imperial tie.

While in Glasgow, Buchanan courted and married Agnes Jarvie, the daughter of a Glasgow merchant, who was half his age. Throughout their life together she was a vital and loyal support to him. In mid 1843 they returned to Canada, planning that Isaac would earn enough for them to retire eventually to Scotland. In keeping with this more conservative objective, he agreed to his brother's plan to close the Toronto store at the end of 1844 and to consolidate the Upper Canadian business at Hamilton, the more successful branch; another department, hardware, was now added. Thus, Buchanan, Harris and Company became full-fledged general wholesale merchants, with the intention of monopolizing the trade of those customers whom they chose to support with credit.

Despite his resignation as MLA, Buchanan never really left politics; while in Britain, for example, he advocated legislation along the lines of the Canada Corn Act of 1843, for the passage of which he always claimed some credit. Back in Toronto, he strongly criticized the Reform ministers, led by Louis-Hippolyte La Fontaine and Baldwin, for resigning from the Executive Council in late 1843. Their actions, he said, were too narrowly partisan and indeed, because more than a few of their followers were republicans, threatened the British connection. Principally in the columns of Hugh Scobie's Toronto newspaper, the *British Colonist*, he engaged in an increasingly acrimonious correspondence with several Reform leaders, including James Hervey Price, James Lesslie, and Francis Hincks; it was published in February 1844 under the title *First series of five letters, against the Baldwin faction*. During the election of 1844 he campaigned widely in Canada West in support of Governor Sir Charles Theophilus Metcalfe.

Buchanan was in Glasgow as the disruption of the Church of Scotland built up in the early 1840s, and, following events closely, he unhesitatingly took the evangelical side. On his return to Canada West, he became "one of the key lay figures" in the establishment of the Free Church of Scotland. He was chairman of its Sustentation Fund board; neutralized Scobie's newspaper, the voice of moderate Presbyterianism, by using subsidies; and contributed a total of at least £650 to the foundation of churches bearing Knox's name in Toronto, Hamilton, and eight to ten other locations in Canada West. Within the Free Kirk, he took a moderate stand, opposing both clerical control of church property or the press and complete congregational control (which he regarded as an American principle), and he advocated that the Free Kirk obtain a fair share when funds from the clergy reserves were distributed.

Late in 1844, the Buchanans and their newborn son, Peter, moved to Hamilton. At once Isaac took steps to found the Hamilton Board of Trade and in April 1845 he was elected its first president. Yet by summer he was once more on the move, journeying to New York in response to the first Drawback Law of the United States, which remitted duties on foreign goods being re-exported to Canada. There in August he opened an office, similar in purpose to the earlier Montreal one, to buy and sell on the firm's behalf in the New York market.

Buchanan was still in New York when repeal of the Corn Laws was announced early in 1846; immediately he took ship for England, to lobby and to write widely to newspapers and politicians both there and in Canada. Repeal, he predicted, would, in a "fiery ordeal," lead to Canada's annexation to the United States. His partners, his brother especially, doubted the acuteness of the danger and the wisdom of his alarmist talk, and there is no evidence that his views were heeded. Nevertheless, determined to continue his crusade, he quit the business in 1848, sold his Hamilton house, and returned to Scotland where he lived first in Edinburgh and then in Greenock. A pamphlet, which appeared in 1850 as an extra edition of the *Greenock Advertiser*, is representative of his views. Entitled *Moral consequences of Sir R. Peel's unprincipled and fatal course*, it argued that free trade would not only cost Britain her colonies but also, without monetary reform, sharply increase imports over exports, thereby drastically increasing unemployment in Britain. The same year, with the issue of free trade in mind, Buchanan organized an essay contest for working men on "their own interests," offering prizes totalling £200 for the best essays.

Britain's prosperity in the 1850s belied Buchanan's predictions, while in Canada West the business he had left also prospered remarkably. His crusading activities having been costly, Isaac decided in 1850 to return to business, probably in Liverpool. Peter, doubting his ability to succeed alone, persuaded him instead to rejoin the old business at Hamilton. Discussion of Isaac's return set in motion major changes in the business, beginning in 1851 with the opening of a new branch at Liverpool, known as Buchanan, Harris and Company, and another at London, Canada West, in partnership with Adam Hope, and known as Adam Hope and Company. With his wife and five children, Buchanan moved back to Hamilton in late 1851. His readmission to the partnership, however, led to arguments that culminated at the end of 1853 in the establishment by Young and Law of a separate business, competing directly with that of the Buchanans and Harris. To defend their position, the Buchanans further expanded their trade as the Upper Canadian boom of the mid 1850s rushed to its peak. By the end of 1856, their firms' total assets, principally outstanding accounts in Canada West, exceeded $3,000,000; liabilities were just over half this figure. Isaac Buchanan's share of the firm's capital, though much smaller than his brother's or Harris's, exceeded $200,000; he was rich, and his business was among Canada's largest.

Signalling his intention to live permanently in Hamilton, Buchanan built between 1852 and 1854 a large and attractive house, called "Auchmar," on an 86-acre estate and farm that he named "Clairmont Park," situated on the mountain outside the city. He sought to improve the local schools (though his sons received much of their schooling at a private academy in Galt and his older daughters were sent to Edinburgh for their later education) and he was a leader in the "Hamilton Educational Movement," which in 1855 secured a charter for a college in the city; lack of funds prevented further progress on the project. He also gave the land and £25 for the new MacNab Street Presbyterian Church. Indeed, although he made enemies by a somewhat high-handed manner, his generosity was legendary, and few local causes can have gone entirely unpatronized by him.

To Buchanan, his most important cause was Hamilton's Great Western Railway. He was a director of it in 1853–54 and, for longer periods, of some of its subsidiary lines. But his real power in the Great Western was informal, the result of his relationship with his brother and with Harris who were more central figures in the company. In 1854 it became plain that the member for Hamilton, Sir Allan Napier MacNab, was abandoning the Great Western for its rival, the Grand Trunk. Ignoring a written pledge to his brother to eschew active politics, Buchanan ran for election. His aim, he said, was only to compel MacNab to change his views on the railway and on the clergy reserves, which Buchanan now felt should be secularized because it was impossible to divide the funds equitably among the churches. MacNab, easily evading these issues, won re-election convincingly.

In 1856 Buchanan sought to persuade the Great Western to take control of the "Southern route," the most direct route between Michigan and Buffalo, N.Y. Charters for the Amherstburg and St Thomas Railway and the Woodstock and Lake Erie Rail-way and Harbour Company had been granted by parliament in 1855 and 1847 respectively and together they covered this route. The former charter had not been acted upon by its promoters and the latter project was stalled for lack of funds, but in the summer of 1856 Buchanan learned that Samuel Zimmerman, the great contractor, was moving to take full control of both charters. He was convinced that Zimmerman, with Grand Trunk backing, would build the line, and capture the valuable American through trade, thereby destroying the Great Western and with it Hamilton's commercial independence. With John Smyth Radcliff, vice-president of the Great Western, Buchanan set out to battle Zimmerman, ignoring the unfavourable state of capital markets, the resistance of shareholders in the Great Western to new expenditure, and the opposition of Charles John Brydges, the powerful managing director of the Great Western, and also without consulting Peter Buchanan and Harris, who were in England. First, without immediate expenditure, Buchanan secured control of one of two competing boards of the Amherstburg and St Thomas. He then paid £25,000 to one or more of the directors of the Woodstock and Lake Erie to induce them to resign from its board in favour of his nominees and gave a bond to that company's bank, guaranteeing to pay its debts. Radcliff issued drafts to reimburse Buchanan, but these the Great Western's board in London, England, refused to accept. Attempting, unsuccessfully, as it turned out, to have the board reverse this decision, Buchanan rushed to England. There he also faced his brother and Harris, who were appalled that he had committed himself to pay more than $1,000,000; in order to protect their credit they demanded his resignation from the business. Nominally no longer a partner, Isaac remained active in the business, when time permitted, because Harris was too ill to manage at Hamilton alone.

Two committees of the provincial assembly explored aspects of the tangled Southern railway issue in 1857. To both, Buchanan told his story candidly, for he had, he said, acted from the highest of motives, and had not sought personal profit. Remarkably, although he was sharply criticized for bribery, Buchanan's reputation for honesty, affluence, and even business competence apparently survived almost unscathed. Nevertheless his experience before these committees convinced him that he needed to be in the assembly to protect his Southern interests. Stressing the need to build the Southern line under the auspices of Hamilton businessmen and politicians, he again ran for Hamilton in 1857, and, aided by the usual large outlay of funds, won handily. Once in the assembly he helped to secure passage in 1858 and revision in 1859 of the charter for a company called the Niagara and Detroit Rivers Railway Company. This consolidated the Amherstburg and St Thomas and the Woodstock and Lake Erie railways, and its provisions defined the legal relationships in such a way that Buchanan was cleared from further liabilities. Ultimately, Buchanan's 1856 venture into the Southern cost him over $200,000, but the wounds to his honour and self-esteem haunted him more in the years to come, and in an effort to vindicate his judgement and to secure some return from his outlay he later sank still more money into the Southern project when William Alexander Thomson took it up.

Yet he really had little to do with the ultimate creation of the Canada Southern Railway, which was finally built after 1870. The episode is revealing of Buchanan's overestimation of his power and his lack of perspective on the feverish railway politics of the 1850s.

In 1857 the great boom of the 1850s ended in a sharp crash. In response, Buchanan early in 1858 led in the formation of the Association for the Promotion of Canadian Industry, an organization of manufacturers and merchants in Canada West who pressed for tariff protection. Tariffs did rise in 1858 and 1859, but despite Buchanan's later claim to have been the father of Canada's protective tariff, the government's need for revenue, not this association, was probably the major cause of the decision to raise them; nor are the links between this increase and the later National Policy tariff strong enough to support his claim.

The collapse of 1857 left the city of Hamilton effectively bankrupt as a result of its heavy borrowing for railways and waterworks. With others from the city, Buchanan sought to negotiate a refinancing with the creditors (most of them in Britain) and then to see it through the assembly. In 1864 he at last secured passage of a law that reorganized the city's debts and allowed it to resume payments. Throughout this period Buchanan continued to patronize Hamilton organizations. Closest to his heart were the Hamilton Board of Trade, for which, as its current president, he secured a charter of incorporation in 1864, and the 13th (Hamilton) Battalion of Infantry (later the Royal Hamilton Light Infantry), of which he was founder in 1862 and lieutenant-colonel for about two years.

Buchanan's career in the legislature was genuinely independent: no party, he said, was sufficiently patriotic. Yet his intense opposition to "political economy" pushed him towards the Conservatives, and for three months in the spring of 1864 he became president of the council in the short-lived government of Sir Étienne-Paschal Taché and John A. Macdonald. Buchanan is, however, remembered more for his economic writings in these years, notably *The relations of the industry of Canada, with the mother country and the United States* (1864), edited by Henry James Morgan whose *Sketches of celebrated Canadians* Buchanan had recently subsidized. Like most of his works, *Relations* was largely compiled from his speeches, previously published letters, and extracts from favourite authorities such as Henry Charles Carey, an American economist, and John Barnard

Byles, a British jurist. Still regretting the victory of Manchester-style liberalism in Britain, he spared no opportunity to criticize those in Canada, particularly George Brown, who held similar views. In arguments that were distinguished more for repetition and forceful language than for political insight, analytic rigour, thoroughness, or subtlety, he dwelt on the need for reform of the tariff and the currency.

A protective tariff, he argued, would limit imports of goods that could be manufactured locally, put the many unemployed to work, encourage immigration, and keep in circulation in the province money that would otherwise have flowed abroad. Unlike Canadian protectionists of later periods, he strongly advocated a Canadian–American *zollverein*, that would extend reciprocity to manufactured goods and erect a common Canadian–American tariff against outside goods. Revealing his continuing concern with imperial issues, he argued that a *zollverein* would help to decentralize the manufactures of the empire, for both British working poor and British capitalists and their capital would then come to Canada to secure full access to the American market. The increased urban population in Canada which would have to be fed would free agriculture in Canada West from dependence on a single crop and hence from soil exhaustion. Thus, protection was in the interest of all producers, including the farmer and the working man; convinced that the latter would agree, he had long advocated universal manhood suffrage. Representation by population in the union parliament he opposed, however, because the present tariff was being sustained with the help of votes from Canada East.

On the currency question, Buchanan called for the issue of irredeemable paper currency, "*emblematic* money instead of money *containing in itself intrinsic value....*" This would free Canada from the "*sudden expansions and contractions*" that foreign trade and purely monetary factors induced. "Our error lies in this, that the circulation is based upon and in proportion to GOLD, the rich man's property, instead of upon LABOUR, the poor man's property – that this basis is therefore a thing that can be sent away instead of a thing that cannot be sent out of the country...." In this case, he said, the desired object could be achieved simply by eliminating the "*vicious interference of* [monetary] *legislation, militating against the laws of nature.*"

Buchanan's ideas derived from wider bodies of protectionist and currency thought. Though in some ways internally inconsistent, as his opponents often noted, they were informed, finally, by a conservative outlook on society, and he was better at criticizing than at proposing convincing alternatives. Although it is doubtful if his writings were widely read or attracted many consistent supporters, they do have a place in the limited literature of social criticism in mid-Victorian Canada.

Buchanan's publishing and politics cost him much time and money (indeed his expenditures from 1860 to 1864 averaged the enormous sum of $25,000 annually) and the Buchanan enterprises, which he had formally rejoined in 1858, had also been severely struck by the crash of 1857. Only months before his death in 1860, Peter Buchanan had drastically reorganized their business to enable it to recover from its problems if given careful management. But, although he was aware of the situation, Isaac gave little time to his business, and his decisions, when he could be brought to make them, were often harmful to it. Thus the main Hamilton and Glasgow business, despite large annual sales, ran increasingly deeper into debt. Only a narrow escape from failure in 1864 induced Buchanan to resign from the assembly on 17 Jan. 1865 and to turn all his energy to saving the business. Most important, he persuaded the very capable Adam Hope to move to Hamilton in 1865, but it was now too late. In the fall of 1867, Buchanan, Hope and Company and Peter Buchanan and Company failed.

By offering his creditors more than did his two erstwhile partners, Hope and Robert Wemyss (the Glasgow manager since Peter's death), Buchanan secured control of the business estate. Although he reopened an importing business in 1868 at Hamilton, under the name Buchanan and Company, the firm dealt only in dry goods because Buchanan now lacked the capital to do a general business. He did not reduce expenditures sufficiently for the smaller scale of his business, and Hamilton had become less and less an ideal location for a dry goods importer. In 1871 he could not pay the last two instalments due to his old creditors. Endeavouring to protect a position in the business for one son, he transferred control of the Hamilton firm to John I. Mackenzie in 1872. Two years later he was ousted from the Montreal firm by the other partners there, Robert Leckie and F. B. Matthews, as they sought, ultimately unsuccessfully, to avoid bankruptcy themselves. The New York and Glasgow offices expired for lack of business. A variety of highly speculative ventures failed to yield profits, and businesses into which Buchanan put his four older sons, who had received modest bequests from their uncle, likewise lost money.

By 1876 Buchanan had sold the mountain estate, given such assets as remained to him to his creditors, and was living in rented quarters in Hamilton. Though he still wrote and held some honorific local positions, he was now entirely dependent for income on a testimonial organized by friends at his urging. He applied to the Liberal government of Alexander Mackenzie for a postmastership, but, not surprisingly, was refused. The creditors, some of whom were aggrieved by Buchanan's recurrent promises since 1860 that his financial situation would soon improve, would not give him his final discharge from his second bankruptcy until 1878. Early in 1879 the Macdonald government appointed him an official arbitrator for disputed property expropriations in connection with public works, and this appointment enabled him to live his last years in modest but once more secure circumstances. Although the careers of his three oldest boys did not prove successful, his fourth son, James, after an early bankruptcy in Hamilton in the 1870s, went on to earn a fortune in Pennsylvania. In 1900 he bought back the old family home in Hamilton, and some of his sisters lived there for almost 30 years thereafter.

Isaac Buchanan is remembered chiefly for his writings and his role as a grandee in Hamilton, but also for his careers in politics, railways, the church, and early Toronto business. He was a leader within Upper Canada's Scottish community particularly before 1846, and though the focus of his concerns shifted thereafter, his values and activities continued to reflect his links to Scotland and to indicate the importance of the Scots in Upper Canadian life. Yet he was probably most important as a businessman, for here he had his greatest success and earned the wealth that underlay his other roles. Although his very range of activities made him scarcely a "typical" entrepreneur, his confidence in the future of Upper Canada, his willingness to take risks, and the success he gained thereby exemplify the intertwined processes of Scottish expansion overseas and Upper Canadian business development in the provincial economy's formative years. If in the end his business failed, that too was far from an unusual outcome.

DOUGLAS MCCALLA

Further reading

Douglas McCalla, *The Upper Canada trade, 1834–1872: a study of the Buchanans' business* (Toronto, 1979); "Sojourners in the snow? The Scots in business in nineteenth-century Canada," in *A kingdom of the mind: how the Scots helped make Canada*, ed. P. E. Rider and Heather McNabb (Montreal and Kingston, Ont., 2006), 76–96; "Seeing pioneers as modern: rural Upper Canadians go shopping," in *Temps, espace et modernités: mélanges offerts à Serge Courville et Normand Séguin*, sous la dir. de Brigitte Caulier et Yvan Rousseau (Québec, 2009), 139–50; "Des pays d'en haut au Haut-Canada: la formation d'une économie de colonisation," *Histoire, Économie et Société* (Paris), 4 (décembre 2008): 87–107.

Letters of Adam Hope, 1834–1845, ed. Adam Crerar (Toronto, 2007).

J. C. Weaver, *Hamilton: an illustrated history* (Toronto, 1982).

James Belich, *Replenishing the earth: the settler revolution and the rise of the Anglo-world, 1783–1939* (Oxford, Eng., and New York, 2009).

THEODOR AUGUST HEINTZMAN
(at birth his name was given as Theodore August Heintzmann),

piano manufacturer and inventor; b. 19 May 1817 in Berlin; m. there 1844 Matilda Louisa Grunow (Grunno, Grennew), and they had six sons and five daughters; d. 25 July 1899 in Toronto Junction (Toronto).

Before World War I the Heintzman trade mark on pianos was probably better known throughout the British empire than the name of either Sir Wilfrid Laurier or Sir Robert Laird Borden. Unfortunately, the background of Theodor August Heintzman, the founder of Heintzman and Company, is not as well known. Several unofficial biographies, encyclopedia entries, and company testimonials exist, but few touch upon the years before his arrival in Toronto in 1860. Those which do are often obscure and contradictory in detail, for he did not leave any personal papers among the company records. Biographical sketches that Heintzman did approve of, and that apparently were later accepted by his family, indicate that his early years were spent in the common or grammar schools of Berlin. Heintzman's father owned a cabinet factory that also manufactured piano-actions, keys, and boards, a trade which undoubtedly influenced Theodor in his future profession. At one point young Heintzman apprenticed as a cabinet-maker (possibly with his father) and later he learned key-making under Bacholtz. In 1831 he and his brother, Charles, were apprenticed to William Grenew (perhaps an uncle but conceivably Theodor's future father-in-law), a piano manufacturer in Berlin who specialized in the tradition of producing the entire high-quality instrument from materials refined by a single craftsman. It is not entirely clear whether Heintzman spent all his years in Berlin as a piano-maker; various biographies mention him as an instrument-maker, as an optician, and even as a machinist credited with producing the draft for the first locomotive built there. After his marriage in 1844, Heintzman worked for his wife's uncle as a piano- and instrument-maker. The military and political unrest in Berlin during the 1840s persuaded her family to emigrate to New York in 1849. The younger couple followed a year later with their children.

Upon arriving in New York, the Heintzmans moved into an apartment in Greenwich Village and Theodor easily found employment with the piano-makers Lighte and Newton. Several sketches have fostered the myth that Heintzman and Heinrich Engelhardt Steinweg, the founder of the Steinway piano firm, worked at the same bench for the above company. They arrived in the same year in North America but historical records demonstrate little more relation between these founders of the continent's major piano firms. In the year of the Heintzmans' arrival, two of their children died. Perhaps to escape from these sad memories, the family moved in 1852 to Buffalo, where Theodor worked for the Keogh Piano Company. A year later he entered into a partnership, Drew, Anowsky, and Heintzman. It seems to have backed the Western Piano Company, of which Heintzman was a part-owner. (A square piano built by this firm about 1854 was still in the possession of the Heintzman family in 1980.) Heintzman was able to pull out of the company with several thousand dollars before it went bankrupt during the financial panic of 1857.

There exists little doubt that the Heintzmans emigrated to Toronto in 1860. There does, however, appear to be a great deal of confusion as to how and when Heintzman entered the piano business in this city. The most plausible explanation, one supported by a measure of historical evidence, is that a Toronto piano manufacturer, John Morgan Thomas, met Heintzman in Buffalo and persuaded him to work in his plant, perhaps as foreman. (The later report by an agent of R. G. Dun and Company that Heintzman "faild in conn[ection] with J. Thomas" suggests a closer business arrangement.) Since Heintzman was an exceptionally skilled piano craftsman in comparison to the piece-work assemblers in most North American factories, it is not unreasonable to believe the popular story that he assembled his first Canadian piano single-handed in his kitchen during the first year he spent in Toronto. Whatever its origin, the first piano Heintzman made in Canada sold immediately, the superior detail of the cabinet and the brilliant tone setting it apart from other North American models. Heintzman used the profit from this sale to build several other pianos over the next few years, though he had yet to establish a formal company. The "Heintzman Tradition" of Toronto was nevertheless founded on the high-quality pianos produced entirely by Heintzman in the early 1860s.

In 1864 Heintzman's daughter Anna Matilda Louisa married Karl (Charles) Bender, a well-established tobacconist and a fellow member of the German Evangelical Lutheran Church on Bond Street. Bender helped finance Heintzman's business venture, Heintzman and Company, which was located on Duke (Adelaide) Street in 1866. In 1868 the small concern was able to expand to a shop on King Street West, where it soon employed 12 hands who produced 60 pianos a year. Increasing demand for the old-world craftsmanship of Heintzman pianos resulted in the company's moving about 1873 to larger premises a few doors away, where there would be space for a factory, an office, and a salesroom. Heintzman devoted his attention exclusively to the technical side of the business. He was able to improve upon the interior quality of his pianos by an invention for which he received the Canadian patent. This was the agraffe bridge, a transverse metal bridge that extends across the cast-iron frame of the piano to keep the strings from slipping and, at the same time, improves the clarity in the treble and produces a brilliant, high tone. Sébastien Érard of Paris had produced such a bridge in 1809, but Heintzman perfected it, obtaining Canadian patents in the process in 1873, 1882, 1884, and 1896. The foundations of the Heintzman piano dynasty in Canada had been laid in under 20 years.

In 1875 Bender retired from Heintzman and Company and two years later he died. The growing firm suffered little from the loss of its major financial backer. Nor did it notice the sudden departure of one of its chief craftsmen, Heintzman's cousin, Johann Gerhard Heintzman, who left in 1877 after a minor dispute to set up a rival piano shop on Queen Street (it was to be absorbed by the older company when Gerhard died in 1926). By the mid 1870s T. A. Heintzman's work was ready to be exported overseas and to garner awards. In 1876 Heintzman pianos won a prize at the centennial exhibition in Philadelphia and three years later they were exhibited for the first time at Toronto's Industrial Exhibition. By the time of Heintzman's death in 1899, his pianos had won at least 11 awards and diplomas in the United States and throughout the British empire, including the prestigious William Prince of Wales Medal in London in 1886.

During the 1880s the Heintzman company was producing an average of more than 500 pianos every year, an output that was based on Heintzman's reputation for high-quality work, his ongoing technical improvements, and tariff protection under the federal government's National Policy. In Heintzman's opinion the growth of the dominion would produce an upward demand for his pianos and consequently he took steps to acquire larger premises. In 1882 the Canadian Pacific Railway bought 46 acres just west of Toronto, an area later named Toronto Junction. In 1888 Heintzman moved his factory there, to a site on what became Heintzman Avenue. The property on King Street was retained as a warehouse and a show-room. That same year he became a naturalized Canadian citizen and the Heintzman and Company name was legally registered. By 1890 the firm was to be counted as one of Toronto's largest manufacturing concerns, employing more than 200 craftsmen and producing 1,000 pianos a year.

In 1890 Heintzman moved into a magnificent Victorian villa, the Birches, on Annette Street, a few feet away from his new factory. His home soon became a residential showpiece and a frequent meeting-place for the German Reform Club, of which he was a member. Heintzman was also a freemason and a major benefactor of First Lutheran Church when it rebuilt its wooden structure on Bond Street. Though he witnessed the continued growth of his company during the last years of his life, personal loss and poor health were taking their toll on the ageing craftsman. On 22 Jan. 1890, three days before the Birches was completed, his wife had suddenly died. Heintzman's health began deteriorating soon afterwards. In 1897 a lavish and well-publicized 80th-birthday party was held for him at the Birches, attended by most of his employees, many local officials and dignitaries, and members of the German Reform Club. Reports of the festivities noted Heintzman's good health, but in reality he was on his final journey. Increasing frailty (attributed by some to cystitis) was evident soon after his birthday. In December of that year his son Charles Theodore, who had managed the Toronto Junction factory, died.

During the 1890s control of the company fell increasingly into the hands of Heintzman's son George Charles, born the year the Heintzmans settled in Toronto. While all sources confirm that it was the elder Heintzman's superior craftsmanship that established the Heintzman tradition in Canada, there is little doubt that George was the aggressive salesman behind the company's national and international success. It was he who foresaw the potential for expansion during the early years of the National Policy and insisted upon opening the huge factory in Toronto Junction. When the Toronto market appeared to be temporarily saturated with Heintzman pianos, he passed out advertising handbills to farmers in northern Ontario, taking cattle and horses in payment for pianos (many of these animals, however, died in the Heintzman warehouses before they could be sold). When the first transcontinental train to Vancouver arrived in 1887, George was on it with a carload of pianos for sale. (Some may have found their way west earlier: apparently a Heintzman piano was played in the Regina barracks of the North-West Mounted Police during the North-West rebellion in 1885.) As well, it was George who insisted on exhibiting pianos at the Colonial and Indian Exhibition in London in 1886. Not only did the company win the Prince of Wales Medal, but George sold the 30-odd pianos he had brought with him, laying the basis for a worldwide export business. In 1888 he was able to have a Heintzman piano played at the Royal

Albert Hall before Queen Victoria, who was overheard to remark, "I didn't realize such beautiful instruments could be made in the colonies." George was the natural choice to continue the company's affairs during the 1890s, although a co-partnership agreement signed in 1894 legally split the operation between the elder Heintzman, George, Charles, and two other sons, Herman and William Francis.

In January 1899 Theodor August Heintzman underwent an operation at St Michael's Hospital but his health continued to deteriorate. In July he was still able to visit his factory but a chill, caught one evening while sitting on his porch, was enough to cause him to lapse into a coma. He died on 25 July in his home and was buried beside his wife in Mount Pleasant Cemetery. He was survived by three sons and three daughters. Heintzman and Company passed into the hands of his sons Herman and George. Under the terms of his father's will, George also received the Birches and its contents "for his faithful devotion to the interests … of Heintzman & Co." He would serve as its president until his own death in 1944.

GAYLE M. COMEAU

Further reading

J. A. Ross, "'Ye olde firme' Heintzman & Company, Ltd., 1885–1930: a case study in Canadian piano manufacturing" (MA thesis, Univ. of Western Ontario, London, 1994); "Retailing a household name: Heintzman & Co. pianos, 1887–1930," in *The territories of business*, under the dir. of Claude Bellavance and Pierre Lanthier (Sainte-Foy [Québec], 2004), 203–16.

Wayne Kelly, *Downright upright: a history of the Canadian piano industry* (Toronto, 1991).

JAMES MILLER WILLIAMS,

carriage maker, manufacturer, entrepreneur, and politician;
b. 14 Sept. 1818 at Camden, N.J.; m. in 1842 M. C. Jackson of
London, Canada West, and they had three sons and a daughter;
d. 25 Nov. 1890 in Hamilton, Ont.

James Miller Williams apprenticed as a carriage maker in his birthplace before immigrating with his family to London, Upper Canada, in 1840. There he plied his trade, and within two years entered into partnership with Marcus Holmes to manufacture carriages. He soon bought out his partner and ran the business alone until he moved to Hamilton. By 1851 he was operating the Hamilton Coach and Carriage Factory which employed 70 men and produced ten vehicles per week, many of them for public transit. The increasing number of fare-paying passengers on both urban and interurban lines was shifting the carriage industry away from concentration on vehicles for individual use. Williams also contracted to manufacture cars for the Great Western Railway. Some time before 1857 he and his partner, H. G. Cooper, established the firm of Williams and Cooper, carriage manufacturers. Cooper bought him out in 1859.

In the 1850s Williams became interested in petroleum. Few at the time knew much about petroleum, although James Young in Scotland and Abraham Gesner in Nova Scotia sparked some interest in it. Questions of supply and demand and of uses, as well as technical problems of recovery, refining, and transportation, were still unanswered, and it was not certain whether petroleum could become the foundation for a viable industry. For many years the existence of petroleum in southwestern Ontario had been known, and the Geological Survey of Canada had drawn attention to the deposits, but commercial possibilities had not been explored. However, about 1850 two brothers from Woodstock, Henry and Charles Nelson Tripp, became interested in the possibilities of producing asphalt from the "gum beds" of Enniskillen Township in Lambton County. They acquired land on Black Creek, began producing asphalt, and in 1854 incorporated the International Mining and Manufacturing Company. The following year their asphalt received an honourable mention at the universal exhibition in Paris. However, the Tripps were unsuccessful financially and the company passed to Williams. By 1857 J. M. Williams and Company was refining petroleum, albeit crudely, at Oil Springs, Lambton County, and by 1860 Williams had set up a refinery in Hamilton; the next year he and his associates, working as the Canadian Oil Company, had reportedly invested over $42,000 in the venture.

Much fruitless debate has taken place over whether Williams was the first man in North America to drill successfully for oil. A claim has been made for Edwin Laurentine Drake of Pennsylvania. Williams was working finds before Drake, but because he left no record of his work, and his early ventures were of little interest to contemporary journalists, there is no way of knowing whether his early wells were drilled or dug and cribbed. The significant fact is that he was the first entrepreneur with sufficient capital, business acumen, technical understanding, and tenacity to tackle the petroleum of Lambton County. Spurred by the sudden growth in the use of petroleum-based lubricants and illuminants, he succeeded in his enterprise, thereby demonstrating the viability of an Ontario petroleum industry.

Like many of his contemporaries, Williams was an entrepreneur of diverse interests. His investment in oil through such companies as J. M. Williams and Company and the Canadian Oil Company was only part of his career. He gradually passed control of the oil interests to his son, Charles Joseph Williams, and in 1879 sold the Canadian Oil Company to him. His success in oil led him into the financial and investment field. He was actively involved in the Hamilton Provident and Loan Society, the Mutual Life Association of Canada, the Victoria Mutual Fire Insurance Company of Canada, the Bank of Hamilton (founded in 1872), the Hamilton and Lake Erie Railway, the Hamilton and North Western Railway, and the Wellington, Grey and Bruce Railway. By 1871 Williams had established J. M. Williams and Company, manufacturers of wholesale tin ware, a firm he sold to his son in 1876.

Financially successful and secure, Williams turned to politics. First elected an alderman in Hamilton, he was returned to the Ontario legislature as the Liberal member for Hamilton in 1867, 1871, and 1875. Upon his retirement from politics in 1879, he was appointed registrar of Wentworth County, a position he held until his death in November 1890.

NORMAN R. BALL AND EDWARD PHELPS

Further reading

Christina Burr, *Canada's Victorian oil town: the transformation of Petrolia from a resource town into a Victorian community* (Montreal, 2006).

Gary May, *Hard oiler! The story of early Canadians' quest for oil at home and abroad* (Toronto, 2008).

Ed Gould, *Oil: the history of Canada's oil & gas industry* (Saanichton, B.C., 1976).

HART ALMERRIN MASSEY,

businessman, office holder, JP, and philanthropist; b. 29 April 1823 in Haldimand Township, Upper Canada, eldest son of Daniel Massey and Lucina Bradley; m. 10 June 1847 Eliza Ann Phelps in Gloversville, N.Y., and they had five sons, one of whom died in infancy, and a daughter; d. 20 Feb. 1896 in Toronto.

Born on his father's farm in Northumberland County, Hart Almerrin Massey was educated locally and at Watertown, N.Y., where he had relatives; between 1842 and 1846 he attended three sessions at Victoria College, Cobourg. An experienced teamster and farmer, he was given title to the homestead in January 1847, the year Daniel Massey opened a foundry near Newcastle. Five months later Hart married a young American girl whose Methodist Episcopal upbringing complemented his own devout Methodism (he had undergone conversion at age 15). They settled in Haldimand, where Massey came to notice as a school trustee, magistrate, and member of the local reform association.

In 1851 he moved to Newcastle, becoming superintendent of his father's works, and two years later, on 17 January, they formed a partnership, H. A. Massey and Company. By the late 1840s mechanization of agriculture had spread from the northeastern United States into Upper Canada, where the production of implements would be nurtured by protective tariffs, and patent legislation. Between 1851 and 1861 Hart, following rapid American technological developments with calculated interest, returned from trips to New York state with a series of production rights – for a mower, a reaper, a combined reaper and mower, and then a self-raking reaper – that were to enhance the reputation of the Massey foundry. At the provincial agricultural exhibition in October 1855 its implements garnered prizes. In February 1856, nine months before Daniel's death, the partnership was dissolved. Hart became sole proprietor of the business with Daniel's strong financial backing in the form of interest-free notes totalling £3,475. Under Hart's aggressive direction, the foundry flourished.

Having established an excellent credit rating, Massey enlarged the Newcastle works in 1857. An advertisement in the *Newcastle Recorder* listed a broad range of products, including steam-engines, lathes, stoves, tinware, and a combined mower and reaper "with Massey's improvements." It characteristically boasted that the firm could "compete with any establishment of a similar kind in Canada or the United States." Hart apparently did worry, however, about the dumping of implements in the province by American manufacturers during the economic recession of 1857 and he shared that concern at a meeting in Toronto for the promotion of Canadian industry. As a result of the tariff increases of 1857–58, American competitors were virtually excluded.

In 1861 some 31 factories (mostly foundries) in Upper Canada were producing agricultural implements worth more than $454,000 annually. Contributing factors were the ready adoption of mechanical harvesting devices by farmers (beginning apparently in Northumberland and Durham counties), a scarcity of farm labour, increases in wheat production, completion of railways, and further reduction of American competition because of the Civil War. Massey recognized the potential, but his firm's output of implements was valued in the 1861 census at only $2,000 and, as in most other factories, those implements still constituted a small segment of Massey's output. Greater annual production of implements was recorded for Massey's major competitors: Luther Demock Sawyer and P. T. Sawyer of Hamilton, Alanson Harris of Beamsville, Joseph Hall of Oshawa, Peter Patterson of Vaughan Township, William Henry Verity of Francistown (Exeter), and Ebenezer Frost and Alexander Wood of Smiths Falls. But only Hall had invested more in his works than Massey and only a few reported any concentrated production of mowers and reapers. In this line Massey would climb.

During the 1850s and early 1860s Massey consolidated his standing as an excellent business manager, developing sound networks of supply and distribution and the means for expansion. In 1861, a key year, he obtained the rights to produce a mower and a self-raking reaper invented by Walter Abbott Wood of New York. He immediately put these acclaimed machines into production and boldly presented them to the province's farming community. Having grasped early the need for advertising, Massey took steps during the winter of 1861–62 to publish his first profusely illustrated catalogue, using American graphics. It showed the medal awarded for his threshing machines in 1860 by the Board of Arts and Manufactures of Lower Canada. The prominent reference to successful field trials and prizes, much coveted by Massey for mass publicity, became a standard feature of his sales literature. In March 1864 fire destroyed the Newcastle works, forcing Massey to assume a $13,500 loss, but the plant was soon rebuilt to meet a stream of orders for implements. Other products were dropped. In 1867 his combined reaper and mower, sent by the Board of Agriculture of Upper Canada to the international exposition in France, won a medal, with Massey present to commence promotion. His first European orders followed. That year he brought into the business his 19-year-old son Charles Albert, a graduate of the British American Commercial College in Toronto who shared his father's entrepreneurial flair.

Rising also was Massey's prominence in Newcastle. For the local Methodist congregation he helped erect a new church and served as Sunday school superintendent. He continued to act as a magistrate, and in 1861 was appointed coroner of the United Counties of Northumberland and Durham. A freemason, he joined Durham Lodge No.66 in 1866, becoming a master mason 11 years later. He also became head of the Newcastle Woollen Manufacturing Company.

Such was Massey's commercial success that in September 1870 he took steps (effective in January) to have his company incorporated as a joint-stock firm, the Massey Manufacturing Company, with a capital of $50,000. Hart was president and Charles vice-president and superintendent, clearly his father's successor. In September 1871 Charles was left in charge when the Masseys, apparently because of Hart's ill health, moved to Cleveland, Ohio. Chester Daniel, the sickly second son, engrossed in Methodist activity, saw in the move "God's guiding hand to bring Father under better influences ... and for the spiritual general good of our whole family." Massey meant to enjoy his semi-retirement: in 1874 he built a "princely mansion" on Euclid Avenue at the edge of the city. Shocked, Chester soon accepted it: "Father said he wouldn't live on any other street."

The Masseys remained in Cleveland until 1882. Hart took well to life there and in 1876 became an American citizen. Politically, his reform interests may have become Democratic leanings, but that is uncertain, for the family admired Republican presidents Ulysses S. Grant and Rutherford Birchard Hayes. He travelled a great deal, touring the southern states a number of times, once in 1873 with the Reverend William Morley Punshon. Soon after the move, Hart, his daughter, Lillian Frances, and Chester had entered Ohio's Methodist community; Hart was particularly active in the erection of churches, sabbath school affairs, camp meetings, and conferences. As president of the trustees of First Methodist Episcopal Church, he sanctioned a typically Methodist set of "General Rules," drafted by Chester. Those prohibiting "laying up treasure upon earth" and borrowing money or "taking up goods" without the "probability of paying" give point to the family's evolving philosophy of philanthropy and its reconciliation of wealth and faith.

During these years Massey became imbued with the evangelicalism of the Methodist Episcopal Church. He early embraced the principles of the Chautauqua Assembly, established at Chautauqua Lake, N.Y., in 1874 by Lewis Miller, another manufacturer of agricultural implements, and Methodist Episcopal clergyman John Heyl Vincent, whose stepsister would marry Chester. Organized as a popular religious-educational movement in a camp setting, the assembly also became for many rich Methodists a summer resort. Massey, a trustee, had a tent and in 1880 he erected a "fine cottage of the Swiss style of architecture."

Not surprisingly, Massey was drawn into business in Cleveland, with mediocre results. He was president of the Empire Coal Company (1873–74) and the Cleveland Coal Company (1876–77), and he invested in residential real estate. His combined undertakings left him, when he returned to Ontario, with little more than worked-out mines, problems of realty management, and an unshakeable reputation for "being *little and mean,"* as one Cleveland lawyer later put it. Still, he had no reason to worry. As a result of Charles's bullish management and relentless publicity (notably with catalogues and *Massey's Pictorial,* a tabloid begun in 1875), the Newcastle works had continued to prosper. In 1874 the tariff on implements had been raised to 17.5 per cent and in 1879, under the Conservative government's National Policy, it would go to 25 per cent. In 1876 Charles could assure a parliamentary committee that the tariff level was satisfactory. During the current depression the business, an agent for R. G. Dun and Company reported, was "going on in a very careful way & not pushing trade." In 1878 it introduced the Massey harvester, "the first machine of wholly Canadian design." Instant success created unprecedented demand, which, with the bounty from the tariff increase, enabled a major expansion and relocation.

Hart appears to have begun foresightedly accumulating land in Toronto as early as 1872. Negotiations initiated by Charles in September 1878 to acquire much of the Ordnance reserve block on King Street, near railway lines, were easily concluded the following spring. His father came to Toronto to superintend the construction of works. Production resumed that fall. In Cleveland or Toronto, Hart participated in or advised on developments between 1879 and 1884 that significantly affected the company. In the fall of 1879 the Ontario Agricultural Implement Manufacturers' Association was formed, a means by which the Masseys and other producers, notably A. Harris, Son and Company of Brantford, could control prices and output. The refinement of self-knotting devices for binding grain had an enormous impact. In 1879 the Masseys purchased their first model for a self-binder from Aultman, Miller and Company of Ohio. Their acquisition of the Toronto Reaper and Mower Company in September 1881, and of its patent rights, led them in 1882–83 into the purchase of further American prototypes, field trials, and the production of a lucrative line of binders. Purchase of manufacturing and sales rights for at least one American machine was arranged by Hart Massey and Lewis Miller at Chautauqua in August 1882.

Because of their binders, both the Massey and the Harris firms achieved extraordinary sales during the 1880s. In the summer of 1881, to capitalize on Manitoba's promise as a major grain producer, the Masseys opened a branch in Winnipeg managed by Thomas James McBride. In Toronto their newly organized department for popular advertising used lithographic illustration to promote the Massey brand name by such means as idyllic depictions of the "model Canadian farmer who patronizes the Massey Mfg. Co." In 1881–82 the Massey works was enlarged and in January 1882 Chester came to Toronto to begin *Massey's Illustrated*, an advertising handout that would become a periodical directed at rural subscribers.

Anticipating direct involvement with the growing firm, Hart moved to Toronto in the summer of 1882, purchasing a property on Jarvis Street later named Euclid Hall. That fall he was struck by an illness falsely diagnosed as terminal stomach cancer. "We passed through *great sorrow*," Chester confessed in his diary. In December the family joined the cathedral of Methodism in Canada, Metropolitan Church. By early January Massey was able "to devote his whole attention" to the complex business Charles had shaped so efficiently. Politically he had found it commercially expedient to adopt both the Conservative party and its protectionist policy.

The three Masseys were a potent combination in Canadian manufacturing, a team that participated vigorously in the cut-throat competition of the implement industry. An increase in the tariff to 35 per cent in 1883 served not only to solidify the position of delighted Canadian manufacturers but to intensify the so-called binder war between the Massey and Harris firms. In June and July 1883, the Massey company sent some 19 flag-decked box-cars of machines to Manitoba via the United States, "the largest solid freight train from any single manufacturing firm" to leave Canada, one newspaper claimed. In bitter contrast, Charles's sudden death from typhoid on 12 Feb. 1884 hit his father hard, leaving him with the deep persuasion that the family should never be forgotten by the public and the realization that the company was his responsibility again. A hall was opened at the works in December in memory of Charles for workers' concerts, readings, meetings, and later a sabbath school. Publication by Massey of a memorial sketch of Charles and a collection of sermons and condolences illustrates his propensity to aggrandize his family in the public eye. Still, through the mid 1880s Massey received sympathetic treatment in newspapers throughout the dominion.

From the time he resumed control, at 61, Massey dominated his firm in a paternal, calmly aggressive fashion, taking advice only from a few valued employees and company officials, among them his sons. He planned methodically to tighten his control of the company and ensure its growth. In 1884, against the wishes of other shareholders, and again in 1885, he increased the company's capital stock, a necessary step, he explained, in order to be able to build warehouses in Montreal and Winnipeg, carry a large inventory of binder twine (indispensable for mechanized harvesting), and accommodate the slow collection of debts from farmers on machinery. The firm could thus "avoid borrowing," something he rarely did. Privately he manoeuvred without sentiment to acquire company assets, wresting a large portion of stock from a company officer and some even from Charles Massey's estate. In March 1887, when stock was again increased, Chester recorded that Massey had succeeded in purchasing "*all* the stock ... held by parties outside our family."

The Canadian binder market was now largely controlled by Massey and Harris: in 1884 Massey sold 2,500 in Ontario, Harris 1,700, and Patterson 500. In 1885, professing great confidence in the northwest despite the North-West rebellion, Massey sent another much-publicized freight train to Manitoba, with 240 "Famous Toronto Light Binders." A *Globe* advertisement proclaimed: "Riel! Poundmaker! Big Bear! Clear the Track, Implements of Peace to Supplant those of War." Western farmers, however, would become synonymous for Massey with difficulty in collecting; in July he was one of a delegation to Sir John A. Macdonald from the boards of trade of Toronto, Montreal, Winnipeg, and Hamilton urging disallowance of the Manitoba act exempting property under certain values from seizure. In 1886 a Massey agency was set up in Montreal and by May 1887 the Maritimes and British Columbia also had agencies. In Ontario, Massey's membership in the Binder Manufacturer's Association scarcely hid his part in efforts to control the market in binder twine. Working through a tractable minister of customs, Mackenzie Bowell, Massey laboured to secure reduced duties on imported sheet steel, elimination of duties on some parts, and especially, when the firm began selling abroad, an increase in drawbacks (the refund of duties on parts or materials used in machines made for export).

The depth of Massey's control of his company was sounded in 1886. His Toronto works, employing some 700 workers, was easily the city's largest factory. He had never experienced organized industrial unrest. By quietly rewarding long-time service, encouraging technological innovation by employees, or doffing his black suit-coat to appear in group photographs, Massey had cultivated close association with his men. Indeed, his genuine and sometimes progressive interest in them and his notions of popular education – the sort he knew from Cleveland and Chautauqua – can be seen in the creation of a reading-room (and with it the Workman's Library Association), a band, a mutual benefit society, and, in 1885, an in-house workingman's newspaper, the *Trip Hammer*. Nevertheless, in 1883 complaints over wage reductions had emerged through Maple Leaf Assembly 2622 of the Knights of Labor. In February 1886 some 400 workers peacefully struck over wages and Massey's dismissal of five members of the local. Here he was supporting the plant superintendent, William F. Johnston, whose long service and technical contribution to the firm's patents had earned him a solid place. The Knights' leader, Daniel John O'Donoghue, described Massey as a "brute ... devoid of soul." Massey was unnerved by the Knights' "unwarranted interference." A hastily distributed circular brought him promises of support from implement producers throughout the province. However, faced by solidarity among the workers, the intervention of Mayor William Holmes Howland, and the decision on day three by the highly skilled tool-room to join the strike, an embarrassed Massey conceded on day five. Saving face where he could, he took steps to repair labour relations (he opposed the "eight-hour" movement that spring on the grounds that workers would not be able to make ends meet) and to restore the operating efficiency that was vital to his plans for the company in 1886.

In his report to stockholders in April 1886, Massey lamented the "labour question" and also the "continued financial embarrassment of the country," especially pronounced on the prairies where agriculture was proving to be uneconomic. For him, the solution to the company's problems, including the war with the Harris firm, lay in expansion, not further into western Canada – "that Lone Land" he called it – but into foreign trade. With its large capacity the firm could "make nearly twice the number of machines that our Canadian trade would demand." This capacity, combined with demands for labour-saving implements from other grain-growing countries and the continuation of drawbacks, enabled Massey to counter Canada's shorter seasons and greater transportation costs and its emerging agrarian backlash against the high costs of tariff-protected machinery by entering overseas markets, one of the first North American producers to do so.

By March 1887 Massey had selected his second cousin Frederick Isaiah Massey, vice-president of the Iowa Iron Works and head of a firm of commission merchants in Chicago, as manager for Britain and Europe. He himself had prepared the ground, by attending the Colonial and Indian Exhibition in London in August 1886 to measure the competitive strength of his "Toronto Light Binder." This and other machines won medals and pre-arranged sales produced useful testimonials, from among others former governor general John George Edward Henry Douglas Sutherland Campbell, Marquess of Lorne, and later from Henry Charles Keith Petty-Fitzmaurice, 5th Marquess of Lansdowne. In early 1887 Massey took steps to open a branch in Argentina. That year 24 binders were sent to Australia on speculation; by May 1888 Walter Edward Hart Massey, who had joined the firm after Charles's death, was chastising his father for delays in shipping machines to London and Australia, where field trials in 1889 confirmed their superiority – or so the Masseys claimed – over those of the McCormick Harvesting Machine Company in the United States and others.

The response in Canada to Massey's international success was highly favourable. The press viewed it in terms of national well-being, a point he too never failed to make. Moreover, returning from the London exhibition, he had a euphoric welcome from his workers, whom he credited for the company's success at the "Colonial" and to whom he promised fair treatment. "This is a very great change in the last 8 months," the *Canadian Labor Reformer* observed.

Much of Massey's prominence in the 1880s was based unarguably on his entrepreneurial ability and on the managerial core he developed after Charles's death. His interests in international expansion and drawbacks suggest a totally pragmatic grasp of the National Policy and the limits of the Canadian market. At the same time he made every effort to exploit the protected industrial environment in which the firm operated and was ever mindful of its political origin. In September 1887 Sir John A. Macdonald, who was being pressed on protection, exhorted Massey to buy into a "first class newspaper" in order to voice his opposition to commercial union with the United States and unrestricted reciprocity. Four months later, in a mood of "crisis," the prime minister invited Massey and other supporters to meet with him to consider "energetic steps" for maintenance of the National Policy. However, a discerning interview with

Massey on the tariff, in the *Toronto Daily Mail* of 13 Feb. 1888, reveals he had grievances despite protection: high duties on imported steel and iron (the cost advantages of British supplies had long disappeared and Massey now bought in Ohio and Pennsylvania), the need for more rolling mills in Canada, political favouritism towards Nova Scotia's budding steel industry, from which he also bought, and his professed difficulties in getting rebates on exported machinery. Claiming smugly, and with some political ambiguity, that he could compete effectively against American producers in an open market of commercial union, Massey meanwhile pushed for the removal of duties on imported materials. Such elimination, he told the *Mail*, bluntly linking his business and national prosperity, was vital in "fostering" the foreign market needed by Canadian manufacturers. In 1888–89 he continued to negotiate with Bowell over the removal of duties on parts, and in March 1888 he met with finance minister Sir Charles Tupper to discuss both the reduction of duties on iron and the "enormous taxation on agricultural implements."

In Toronto Hart had been moving to increase operating efficiencies. A printing department was started in 1886 under Walter, then the company's creative secretary-treasurer. The Masseys' flair for advertising and mass appeal is evident in their use of cartoons, colour, and grass-roots humour: the product lines for 1887 were labelled "Bee-Line Machines" and on delivery days in rural Ontario, farmers were given the hard sell at receptions featuring "crushed drive wheels on toast," "crank shaft pie," and other mechanical delights. However, in 1888–89, he failed in an attempt to gain control of and move the Hamilton Iron Forging Company, a supplier and Ontario's only large producer of primary shapes. In Toronto, his offer to the city to build a malleable-iron works in exchange for ten taxless years produced controversy in council as the strategy of granting such bonuses to industry became suspect.

There were other difficulties. Massey's personal parsimony – the petty side of his business *persona* – was becoming as well known as his King Street factory. In 1887 the cost of treating his sick daughter while she was travelling on a Canadian Pacific Railway train in the west prompted a complaint to general manager William Cornelius Van Horne. Accusations of "gall and nerve" drifted in. His support for such local Conservatives as Frederick Charles Denison and for the National Policy apparently failed to give Massey real standing in Ottawa (he and Macdonald were certainly incompatible personally). His recommendations in 1888 for municipal reform in Toronto – significant in terms of his later philanthropy – were ignored, in part because of his use of American models and also because his genuine interest in reducing pauperism through tax relief for the "labouring man," subsidized lectures, and more parks and libraries was thought impractical. If Massey was dissatisfied, the *Evening Telegram* retorted, he should seek public office. Clearly, any goals he envisioned as he began turning his thoughts to social welfare would have to be accomplished privately. In 1888, to give shape to his dream of a major music hall in Toronto, he asked Sidney Rose Badgley, a Canadian architect in Cleveland, for the plans for that city's hall.

A bitter controversy over the federation of Victoria College with the University of Toronto and its move from Cobourg reveals two basic components of Massey's last years: his philanthropy and the attendant censure of his activities. In the fall of 1888 he offered $250,000 to maintain Victoria as an independent college at Cobourg. But a series of vicious articles in the *Toronto World* in December, by editor William Findlay Maclean, alleged Massey had reneged on a prior pledge of financial support for federation. Maclean claimed further, during the much-publicized libel suit filed by Massey, that the pledge had been made to such prominent Methodist leaders and federationists as Edward Hartley Dewart and John Potts in exchange for their support in the Masseys' "squeeze-out" of company stockholders years before. Also dragged out in the *World* was a suit against Massey by his Cleveland church over a subscription he had refused to honour. Obviously, wrote Maclean in stinging but legally clever ridicule, Massey had "worked the hay fork racket" on the college's senate by swindling and embarrassing the federationists. In January 1889 a plea of justification was allowed in the courts for a trial in the next assizes.

Though sensitive to such criticism, especially when it appeared to attack his cherished agrarian background, Massey could rarely be distracted for long from his determination to dominate implement production in Canada. Carefully staged by W. F. Johnston, superintendent of the Toronto works and probably Massey's best operator, field trials in July 1889 at the Paris exposition produced awards, which Massey tried to build on through a vainglorious but unsuccessful effort to secure a Legion of Honour from France and recognition of his achievements there by the Canadian government. That year, however, he did receive important confirmation by a committee of the Privy Council of the high level of drawbacks that he wanted to claim. In the spring of 1890 Massey took over the Hamilton Agricultural Works of L. D. Sawyer and Company, forming Sawyer and Massey Company and thus adding a subsidiary strong in threshing machinery. Also that year he bought out the Sarnia Agricultural Works. In one of his few major miscalculations perhaps, Massey balked at a chance to acquire controlling interest in the Hamilton Iron Forging Company.

A Methodist in business, Massey invariably found time for religion and philanthropic endeavour. He subscribed to Metropolitan Church's Home Missionary Society (organized in 1888 for evangelistic, mission-school, and charitable work) and to other such groups in Toronto. In May 1889 he was a delegate of the Sabbath School Association of Ontario to the international Sunday school convention in London, England. Early in 1889 John Miles Wilkinson, an audacious downtown Methodist minister, won Massey's confidence with grandiose plans for a "People's Tabernacle." Daring to probe the aloof Massey, Wilkinson spurred him on in June: "I hope Mr. Massey you have not given up your intention of erecting a building that will immortalise the donor & will bring incalculable good to the present & to future generations." The project would be given shape that winter by the illness of Frederick Victor, Hart's beloved youngest son and a student at the Massachusetts Institute of Technology in Boston. In January he was brought home in W. C. Van Horne's private railway car; his death in April, like that of Charles, struck hard at Massey.

The year 1890 brought other strains. In February J. H. Hillerman, a Cleveland insurance agent and defendant in a case brought by the 66-year-old Massey, complained with much truth to Chester: "Your father seems to have a chronic notion that anyone who in any way refers to his business methods is persecuting him." In March the libel trial involving the *World* opened, only to find for Maclean. By June, however, amid increasingly negative press over the alleged libel and the federation issue, Massey had left for London on a bold corporate initiative.

Locked in costly competition with the Harris firm, Massey and his sons had resolved at the end of 1889 to "sell their business to an English company." As a first step, their British subsidiary had been formally registered and capitalized in December. An apprehensive F. I. Massey viewed the proposed sale as a "radical ... change in business." In May 1890 the Massey board agreed to sell the parent company "for re-capitalization under British charter" and empowered Hart to carry out negotiations. These got bogged down when a British accounting firm was unable to verify the annual profit levels claimed by Massey, whose testy refusal to pay its expenses negated his awkward efforts to revive the bid. Returning to Toronto, he was forced to beat down a moulders' strike between October 1890 and July 1891 at his Hamilton and Toronto works. Of greater significance, the Harris firm's revolutionary open-ended binder, capable of cutting grain of any length, had been put into production for the British market, giving it a clear lead in technology and potential foreign sales.

This lead, the sheer cost of continued competition, the loss of family on both sides, and undoubtedly Massey's British bubble, encouraged Massey and Alanson Harris to consider merging. Though historians credit Massey with taking the initiative – he excelled in the blunt business of buy-outs and forced merger – his papers are mute on this subject. Other sources, however, including the board minutes of the two companies, reveal much. Blithely ignoring weak anti-combines legislation, the Massey and Harris groups moved quickly. By late January 1891 negotiations were under way for a combination of the Massey and Harris firms and the Consumers' Cordage Company of Montreal; in February the Harris board, abandoning its own interest in selling out to an "English syndicate," accepted the Masseys' proposal (conveyed through T. J. McBride of Winnipeg) for a merger that excluded Consumers' Cordage; on 6 May the Massey-Harris Company was established; on 22 July it was formally incorporated. No new capital entered the firm and controlling ownership remained with the two families. The technical excellence of the Brantford firm was reflected in the placement of James Kerr Osborne as vice-president and Lyman Melvin Jones as general manager, but Massey held the presidency and with it the largest block of shares and personal control of patents, production methods, and facilities. Between 1891 and 1895 he orchestrated amalgamations with Massey-Harris that further eliminated competition and strengthened its position in specialized lines, including ploughs, steam tractors, and threshing machines. The only major Ontario works not taken in was the factory of Frost and Wood in Smiths Falls, according to the *Monetary Times* in

November 1891. Massey-Harris was seen as a monopoly, but because the merger had been concluded during a lingering depression, it had to face the financial consequences of several years of aggressive over-selling on credit. Moreover, in the year before the merger, the two firms had accounted for only about half of the domestic sales of large implements in Canada – small manufacturers and to a lesser extent American producers still held a share of the market – and in the decade following Massey-Harris would never capture more than 60 per cent. Between 1892 and 1895 the value of its domestic sales dropped, though there were compensations in export sales.

Massey recognized the difficulties, but old age, illness, and his diversion of interest to philanthropic endeavour would undermine his ability to deal effectively with increasingly complex problems of corporate business. In Manitoba, where Massey and Harris had sold much on credit, there was a massive load of indebtedness. Western farmers in reaction pointed to the grip of the CPR, the grain monopoly, and the protective tariff policy and its industrial offspring. Massey could look to T. J. McBride in Winnipeg for practical advice on collections, but he could never totally comprehend agrarian discontent: "People are using every means possible to vent their spite on the Massey-Harris Co. on account of its consolidation. Why they should do this when they are actually getting their machines at a lower price than they did before, seems strange to us. No doubt it rises very largely from the Patrons of Industry." Rural newspapers throughout Ontario turned against Massey as his manufacturing and philanthropic interests were confronted by new and vocal strains of radical agrarian and social criticism. In Ottawa opinions of him had changed drastically.

In 1893 he confidently lobbied for the Senate seat left vacant by the death of Methodist businessman John Macdonald. Massey felt entitled for reasons besides his support of the Conservative government "since 1878." Naïvely he emphasized his ability to "control and influence more votes than any other businessman," the need for a strong Methodist voice in government, his contribution to the welfare of Canadian farmers, and his "advancement of Canada's industrial enterprise." As if industrial achievement merited political reward, he proudly told Prime Minister Sir John Sparrow David Thompson: "My long experience has enabled me to systematise and put into successful operation one of the largest manufacturing industries in the world." Indeed he had, but neither Thompson nor his finance minister, George Eulas Foster, tolerated the ageing millionaire the way Macdonald had, and it was left to Mackenzie Bowell to tell Massey bluntly that the seat had been promised to James Cox Aikins.

Ottawa had changed its position too on tariffs. Foster and Thompson were both mindful of western agitation for the elimination of tariffs on implements. In 1893–94, with exceptional vigour, Massey fought Foster's much lauded reduction of tariffs on implements, formally announced in March 1894. Yet in 1893 he had welcomed the Democrats' push in the United States to reduce tariffs as an inducement to expand southward. Newspapers picked him up: "How can he contend that he can compete with the American manufacturers in their country but not in his own?" asked the *Globe* in November. In truth, discerning limited growth in the Canadian market, Massey had masterfully crafted plans for the international trade of Massey-Harris. In 1894 he secured, through Bowell, an unprecedented 99 per cent drawback on materials put into machines for export and, from his own board, a mandate to establish, by August 1895, an American plant. It would facilitate production for export by having access to electricity (if near Niagara Falls), cheaper rates on iron, and better transit to the east coast.

In 1894 Massey began to falter in his direction of Massey-Harris because of his poor health and engrossing devotion to philanthropic work. By the end of 1895 his health had worsened, the result he was told of "heart disease" or "disease of mucous membrane of the colon." At times he could attend to business, getting drawbacks "in proper shape" and lobbying on the tariff, but he became caught in a pathetic round of medical consultations and restorative trips. Walter Massey later noted that from 1894 his father, then 71, spent little time on the details of business. Much of the management shifted to him, but with tension. He was irked by the elder Massey's involvement in petty law suits in 1895, one resulting from his repeated attempt to form a British syndicate to take over Massey-Harris (an intriguing case that also sheds light on differences in business outlooks in North America and Britain). Both Walter and F. I. Massey in London seriously questioned the commercial wisdom of Hart's move into the production of bicycles, then a popular rage, but they indulged him in a harmless fascination with the prospect of building automobiles. Finally, in a letter in July 1895, after scolding his ailing father for tinkering with the steam launch at the family's Muskoka camp, Walter unloaded his frustration over Hart's procrastination on the move into the United States. "This whole matter rests with yourself.... Mr. McBride would be available from Winnipeg at any time to take hold of the U.S. business and is only too willing to go."

If Massey's competence in business had become impaired, his philanthropic vision became clearer despite close public scrutiny. During his years in the United States he had been drawn to the evolving gospel of wealth – a component of evangelical Protestantism (including Wesleyan doctrine) that held diligence in business to be a Christian duty and wealth to be a trust from God. For Massey, this belief had been reinforced at Chautauqua and through exposure to such popular evangelical revivalists as Dwight Lyman Moody of Chicago. In Toronto during the 1880s, with the Methodist church adapting to a wealthy laity and systematic benevolence growing as a means of grace, Massey received strong clerical and lay encouragement in his sober drive to fill his self-claimed role as a "steward" of God. Other Methodist businessmen, for example John Macdonald, set strong examples. A fervent temperance advocate, Massey continued to support the inner-city mission work of Metropolitan Church. In February 1893, identifying himself in a letter to John Carling as one of its "foremost workers," he announced his final goal: "I am preparing for the distribution of my means to the best advantage in the interests of Canada, and am desirous of doing what I can during the remainder of my days towards the advancement of these interests, and the giving of my time largely for the benefit of the public."

Between 1891 and his death in 1896 Massey zealously supported or began an impressive array of mission and charitable initiatives, among them the Methodist Social Union of Toronto (1892), the Children's Aid Society, the Salvation Army's Rescue Home in Parkdale, the Methodist camp at the family's Muskoka resort (1891), a sanatorium project with William James Gage, and industrial training in Toronto's schools. Popular evangelists such as D. L. Moody (whom many Methodists shunned) and the team of Hugh Thomas Crossley and John Edwin Hunter received Massey's enthusiastic support. His donation of $40,000 in 1892 to endow a theological chair at Victoria College (he had eventually accepted relocation and federation) signalled the philanthropic thrust of his last years. In late 1892 he advertised for suggestions on how he could use his wealth "for the greatest good." Patiently he sifted the responses, favouring Methodist institutions. He received in return the recognition he publicly and privately desired. In May 1895 Albert Carman, general superintendent of the Methodist Church, closed his thanks to Massey for support of Albert College, Belleville, with "Praying you be guided and strengthened in all these grand designs, and that you find satisfaction on earth and reward and glory in heaven."

Massey's philanthropic involvement and the public response to it are best illustrated by two well-known projects, both built under his authoritarian control. The mission hall grew out of an urban mission begun in the mid 1880s by members of Metropolitan Church (notably Mary T. Sheffield), the need of the Central Lodging House Association of Toronto for larger quarters, and Massey's well-funded evangelical drive. By December 1892 he had made the project his own, securing sketches from noted Toronto architect Edward James Lennox for a "Mission Hall & Men's home" and gathering information on self-help programs from such institutions as the Industrial Association of Detroit and the Department of Charities and Corrections in Cleveland. Within months it had become identified as a memorial to Fred Victor. His typical insistence upon total involvement led to disputes with both Lennox and the builders. The mission opened in October 1894 to minister to the urban poor and to house homeless men, and was operated by the Toronto City Missionary Society, basically a management board set up by Massey. As a result of his financing and attention to detail, the mission (by contemporary standards) was an exceptional facility, with programs in five departments: evangelical (including deaconesses), industrial, educational, mercy and help, and physical activity. It and the Presbyterians' St Andrew's Institute, established in 1890 by Daniel James Macdonnell, were ambitious church innovations, reflecting pioneering efforts in England, Scotland, and the United States in the 1880s. The Massey mission, in the opinion of Margaret Prang, was a "new approach to old social sins in an urban setting" but it was "essentially conservative and rested on no fundamental criticism." The only cure for idleness was still Jesus Christ. Massey rejected outright the radical social reforms espoused by American economist Henry George and others. Within months of opening, the Fred Victor Mission was attracting more men than it could accommodate, many from the "most degraded class in our community," Massey was told. But he focused on its cleanliness and the objectionable appearance of men "lounging around on the street in front of the doors." Ironically, he was the major early benefactor of Wesley College, Winnipeg, a vigorous source of the nascent Social Gospel that would draw inspiration from the conditions of the very farmers who had turned on him.

Similar patterns were evident with the music hall. Though never members of the city's social élite, Massey and his family had long participated in its musical life, again a reflection of their Chautauqua experience. Massey bought organs for Methodist chapels, both Charles and Fred had had musical interests, and music figured in the workers' programs at the Massey factory. As a vice-president of the reorganized Toronto Philharmonic Society in 1891, Massey knew its leader, Frederick Herbert Torrington, organist and choirmaster at Metropolitan Church. Torrington's achievements plus his own turn to philanthropy spurred Massey to build the grand hall that he had been contemplating as yet another memorial to Charles. Designed by S. R. Badgley and built under the supervision of Toronto architect George Martell Miller in 1893–94, Massey Music Hall opened on 14 June 1894 with a performance of the *Messiah*. An ailing Massey attended against his doctor's order. Again his almost fanatical involvement produced disputes, with the builders and with Torrington, even though ownership and management had been turned over on 5 June to a board of trustees comprised of John Jacob Withrow and Chester and Walter Massey. In October, apparently during a disagreement about fees, Torrington threatened to file suit over Hart's insinuation that he and others were attempting to "crush" him. Claiming misinterpretation and reacting perhaps to other pressures, Massey threw his generosity in building the hall in the maestro's face. Despite Massey's refined interest in architecture, the *Canadian Architect and Builder* attacked the exterior of the hall for being "about as aesthetical as the average grain elevator." Still, it had outstanding acoustical properties and immediately became a major centre for musical and public functions; in the fall of 1894 a series of "evangelical meetings" were held there by D. L. Moody, whose waning appeal had forced Massey to defend the event.

Attitudes toward Massey became harshly polarized before his death. His wealth attracted an extraordinary volume of virulent anti-capitalist sniping, especially from the militant Patrons of Industry, who articulat-

ed agrarian discontent in Ontario and the west. In 1892 the Patrons'
Canada Farmers' Sun ridiculed the motives behind Massey's liberality and
singled out his music hall: "Canada never knew the dead Massey, and it
wants no public monuments erected in his name." Two years later, Patron
John Miller, speaking before the Trades and Labor Council of Toronto,
condemned combines and Massey's use of money squeezed from farmers and his own workers for "buildings such as that 'Bummers' Roost'
at the corner of Jarvis Street." Massey served as a lightning-rod too for
the reformist impulse in religious and social debate. His "ostentatious
acts of public charity," which many believed threatened to destroy true
Christianity, were lampooned by such publications as *Grip*. New social
definitions of Christianity emerged to challenge, on intellectual grounds,
"economic inequities" and religious opiates such as that propounded by
Moody, which appealed to wealthy evangelicals like Massey.

Massey resolutely followed the coverage in the press. The careful
segregation of negative commentary in the scrapbooks kept by the family and the barely submerged bitterness of Massey's sons testify to its
feelings. Occasionally Massey entered the debate. To his reaction over
a piece in the Ottawa *Daily Free Press* about the music hall, the journal
retorted as others had: "Massey seems to regard the remarks ... as reflec-
tions upon his business methods, his personal honor and his reputation
as a manufacturer, but he is mistaken." Most of the coverage of Massey
was laudatory however – philanthropy could still produce rewards on
earth – and of course farmers continued to buy Massey-Harris machines.
Typical of institutional response to Massey's support was a report in the
Sunbeam, journal of the Ontario Ladies' College, the Methodist school in
Whitby where a feeble Massey spoke in mid 1895: "In listening to Mr.
Massey one is powerfully impressed by his earnest and devoted manner.... He is simply the steward in whose hands God had entrusted the
means of assisting in good work, and [one] hopes that his mind may
rightly direct him in such matters." At the same time, relishing his rare
public appearances, at the Toronto Industrial Exhibition on "Pioneer's
Day," at the Victoria Industrial School in Mimico (Toronto), and in other
sympathetic forums, Massey took an old man's delight in his log-cabin
origins. These easily found a place in the growing number of formulaic
sketches of Massey, such as that in Benjamin Fish Austin's *Prohibition
leaders of America* ([St Thomas, Ont.], 1895).

Massey never left his house after January 1896 and he died on the evening of 20 February. At Massey Music Hall Haydn's *Creation* was being performed under the auspices of the Trades and Labor Council; at the end the conductor announced Massey's passing, whereupon the dead march from Handel's *Saul* was reverently performed. The death brought forth an outpouring of obituaries and testimonials to his personal and industrial stature, ranging from hostile commentary to equally distorted eulogies by James Allen, pastor of Metropolitan Church. Undisputed was Massey's key role in building the largest agricultural implements manufactory in the British empire, in which business he was quietly succeeded as president by his son Walter. The *Toronto Evening Star*, which could not have known of Massey's private acts of charity, provided one of the fairer contemporary assessments of this "austere man": "He expected and exacted a similar punctiliousness from those with whom he did business. By many this was misconstrued into harshness. His charity, splendid as it was, was not such as to make him popular. It moved always on public lines. Even in his generosity, Mr. Massey was a business man.... His wealth served to relieve collectively, the individual being lost sight of in the aggregate.... Mr. Massey's charity, working with such stately aloofness, did not provoke that intense love and enthusiasm excited by individual acts of mercy.... But his was not the impulsive charity that springs from an exuberant disposition. He gave because he thought it was his duty, not because he loved much."

Massey's grandson Charles Vincent recalled Massey as a "tall gaunt frock-coated figure, his features softened by a white beard, driving to church in an over-full landau behind a pair of well-chosen coach-horses with an old coloured coachman in antique garb on the box, while on the back seat he sat in supreme enjoyment with his adored grandchildren tumbling about his knees, a patriarchal figure of the old school." Not all the grandchildren received that affection and, as Vincent privately confessed to his own sons, Massey had been "bred in a narrow faith" and consequently had "blind spots" in his character. Yet, as historian Merrill Denison has observed, given the breadth of Massey's achievements and the range of reaction to him over time, any narrowly focused image "fails completely to capture any of the interesting conflicts of a rich and complex personality."

The *Star* correctly forecast that "Massey's reputation as a public benefactor lies in the hands of his executors." By his death, he had given away more than $300,000 – on the music hall, on the mission, and on Methodist institutions (mostly colleges) from New Westminster to Sackville. Under his estate (worth almost $2,200,000, most of it in business assets, including some $150,000 in overdue "farmers' paper"), generous but not extravagant provision was made for the family. In the Chautauqua spirit of educational pursuit, major gifts were again made to Methodist colleges (Victoria College, Mount Allison College, and the newly founded American University in Washington). The residue, well in excess of $1 million, was to be distributed by his executors in accordance with that spirit. The lengthy and difficult task was carried out by the reclusive Chester, his sister Lillian, and, later, Chester's son Vincent; it continues in the Massey Foundation.

DAVID ROBERTS

Further reading

Merrill Denison, *Harvest triumphant: the story of Massey-Harris, a footnote to Canadian history* (Toronto, 1948).

Mollie Gillen, *The Masseys: founding family* (Toronto, 1965).

E. P. Neufeld, *A global corporation: a history of the international development of Massey-Ferguson Limited* (Toronto, 1969).

WILLIAM NOTMAN,

photographer and businessman; b. 8 March 1826 in Paisley, Scotland, first child of William Notman and Janet Sloan; d. 25 Nov. 1891 in Montreal.

William Notman was born into an educated, industrious, and ambitious family, which, at a time of general upward mobility in the Scottish rural classes, had risen in two generations from the ranks of farmers, miners, and millworkers to the level of the urban commercial and professional bourgeoisie. His grandfather had been a dairy farmer; in 1840 his father, a designer and manufacturer of Paisley shawls, moved from the large town of Paisley to Glasgow and worked as a commission agent before establishing a wholesale woollen cloth business. Able to obtain a good education, William studied art with a view to making it his career, but he was persuaded instead to enter the family business, which, it was felt, would offer him more security. He worked first as a travelling salesman and then became a junior partner about 1851. On 15 June 1853 he married Alice Merry Woodwark in the Anglican church at King's Stanley, England. They settled in Glasgow, soon had a daughter, and looked forward to a comfortable future. By the mid 1850s, however, Scotland was in the grip of a depression, and William Notman and Company slid into bankruptcy. Aspects of the failure did not reflect well on Notman, and he found it expedient to emigrate to Lower Canada.

Shortly after arriving in Montreal, Notman found employment with Ogilvy and Lewis, a wholesale dry goods firm, and in November 1856 his wife and child joined him. With the onset of the winter slack season, he obtained leave of absence to start a photographic business. He had grown up during the period of the discovery and development of the earliest photographic techniques (Nicéphore Niepce had produced the first permanent photographic image in the year of Notman's birth), and he had practised photography as an amateur in Scotland. By late December 1856 his business was in operation; shortly after, he was obliged to hire assistants. Within three years his parents, a sister, and his three brothers had joined him in Montreal.

Notman's first important commission was from the Grand Trunk Railway in 1858 to photograph construction of its Victoria Bridge at Montreal, considered an engineering marvel. Over the next two years Notman produced photographs and stereographs of all phases of its construction, and their quality, along with the importance of the bridge, earned him an international reputation. When the Prince of Wales visited Montreal in August 1860, Notman, at the request of the Canadian government, prepared its gift of a portfolio of photographs in two gilt-trimmed, leather-bound covers, enclosed in a silver-mounted bird's-eye maple box. According to family tradition, Queen Victoria was so pleased with it that she proclaimed Notman "Photographer to the Queen." Notman first used this designation in an advertisement in the Montreal *Pilot* of 14 Dec. 1860 – and displayed a duplicate of the maple box to demonstrate to visitors the elaborateness of the gift.

Notman's business sense was, indeed, a fundamental ingredient in his formula for success. Portrait work was the bread and butter of his trade, and the competitiveness of his prices as well as the variety of poses and services he offered drew customers from all economic stations. Middle- and lower-class French Canadians tended to prefer French Canadian studios, however, even though many of Notman's photographers were francophones. The cream of Notman's business was provided by services of a luxurious nature; as early as 1857, for example, he offered life-sized enlargements of portraits, coloured in oil or water-colours and displayed in ornate gold frames. His growing reputation as a portraitist eventually attracted almost all the notables of Canada, French- and English-speaking, to his studio, and visitors from overseas and the United States sought him out. Among his subjects were Sir John A. Macdonald and Louis-Joseph Papineau, bishops Francis Fulford and Ignace Bourget, Prince Arthur and Sir Donald Alexander Smith, Henry Wadsworth Longfellow and Harriet Elizabeth Beecher Stowe, Sitting Bull (Ta-tanka I-yotank) and Buffalo Bill (William Frederick Cody).

In addition to individual portraits, Notman produced group portraits of athletic clubs, social gatherings, and prominent families. Set in an appropriate background, these portraits were composite photographs put together under Notman's direction by a staff of photographers and painters. The composites were produced by photographing each person in the studio, cutting the figures out of the prints, and then pasting them on a painted background. Copies were made for sale in various standard sizes. Because even the tiniest figures in the group came out as high quality portraits, Notman could confidently expect to make at least one sale to every person in the picture, and many photographs depicting major sports or social events were bought by the general public as souvenirs. The immense size of some of the scenes and the great number of people who appeared in them – often as many as 300 – combined to attract wide attention.

Notman also became well known for his photographs of Canadian scenes and life. From the beginning he and his photographers compiled a large stock of negatives loosely catalogued as "views." His relentless pursuit of images to add to the files eventually led him or his photographers to cross the new country from coast to coast, training their cameras on the land and the activities it generated, including lumbering, mining, hunting, and farming; on the rivers and seas and the vessels that fished or plied them; on the cities, growing in the east or mushrooming in the west, and the industry, trade, and business that supported them; on the resorts and hotels in the major holiday centres; on the construction of the Canadian Pacific Railway, which, with other railways, bound all these environments into a whole; and on the people who made up the country from prairie Indians to Montreal magnates. In Montreal he photographed pedlars, newsboys, woodcutters, and other humble members of the Montreal street fraternity. These photographs were produced in the studio using props and painted backgrounds so as to make them appear to have been taken outdoors. The same techniques were applied in the creation of series on caribou and moose hunting featuring Colonel James Rhodes and his Indian guides.

The great variety of "views" that Notman offered in an age when amateur photography was severely limited, and the moderate prices he charged, ensured that his photographs would be attractive to anyone wishing to record visits or illustrate to others the merits of their locality. As well, he ensured availability in various forms, including albums and stereographs, and in many locations, such as his studio, stationery and book stores, all major Canadian hotels, the transcontinental trains, and every large railway station in the country.

Notman's success was due only in part, however, to his initiative, resourcefulness, and aggressiveness as a businessman. His artistic talent gave him a product of superior quality to sell, and his readiness to experiment and introduce new techniques and ideas kept him in the forefront of a highly competitive field. In 1860 and 1869, for example, he photographed solar eclipses for Professor Charles Smallwood of the McGill Observatory, the photographs of 1869 serving to illustrate an article by Smallwood in the *Canadian Naturalist* (Montreal). In the winter of 1864–65 he adopted the magnesium flare as an artificial source of illumination, a technique that had been introduced in England only shortly before. He also led in the introduction of cabinet-sized photographs in North America.

Notman owed some of his success to the quality of the painters he hired, for their work was often an integral part of the final product. He was employing William Raphael on commission before 1860, but, dissatisfied with Raphael's work, he engaged John Arthur Fraser that year to head a new art department, created to colour photographs, retouch negatives, and paint studio backgrounds. To assist Fraser, 18-year-old Henry Sandham was hired, and the art department eventually attained impressive proportions.

His personal and professional interest in art led Notman to establish relations with Montreal's most prominent painters. Several of them, Fraser, Sandham, Otto Reinhold Jacobi, Charles Jones Way, and Robert Stuart Duncanson, along with Cornelius Krieghoff, were represented in Notman's first book, *Photographic selections*. Published in 1863 "to foster the increasingly growing taste for works of art in Canada," it was composed of 44 photographs of paintings, most by old masters, and two views from nature. Two years later Notman published a second volume, containing 11 photographs from nature and a greater number of photographic reproductions of contemporary Canadian paintings. Meanwhile, in 1864 he had published *North American scenery...*, composed entirely of photographic reproductions of landscapes by Way. And while Notman was reproducing works of the painters, at least two painters, Jacobi and Krieghoff, were using Notman photographs as the basis for some of their works.

Notman also fostered the development of painters and other artists in his city through his support of the Art Association of Montreal, established in January 1860. Not only was Notman a charter member but the formative meeting was held in his studio. He lent canvases from his growing private collection to be shown at the association's conversaziones and provided photographs as prizes. Anxious that a permanent gallery be obtained for the association, he offered as a gift to it a life-sized painted photograph of Bishop Fulford if, within five years, a building was acquired in which to display it. Meanwhile his studio was, as it had been in the past, the centre of the Montreal art community and a gathering point for visiting artists. In his huge reception room Notman held numerous exhibitions of painting and sculpture; the best known artists of the day, including Napoléon Bourassa and Robert Harris, frequented it. There in 1867 the Society of Canadian Artists was formed, three Notman painters (Fraser, his brother William Lewis Fraser, and Sandham) being among the charter members. Not until 1878, however, was a permanent art gallery, specially designed for the purpose, constructed; Notman had chaired the building committee. From 1878 to 1882 he also acted as a councillor to the Art Association of Montreal.

In addition to the books on works of art, Notman published the highly popular *Portraits of British Americans, with biographical sketches*, produced from 1865 to 1868 in collaboration with John Fennings Taylor. In 1866, discerning a heightened interest in sports as a leisure activity, Notman published three portfolios of photographs entitled *Cariboo hunting, Moose hunting*, and *Sports pastimes and pursuits in Canada*. Although he did not publish books after 1868, photographs from his studio illustrated other publications such as Henry George Vennor's *Our birds of prey ...* (1876). In 1869 a half-tone reproduction of a Notman photograph of Prince Arthur in George-Édouard Desbarats's *Canadian Illustrated News* constituted the first commercial use of this technique. It demonstrated once again Notman's place in the forefront of photography.

By the mid 1860s Notman had 35 employees in his Montreal studio, including photographers and painters, their apprentices and assistants, bookkeepers and clerks, receptionists and secretaries, dressing-room attendants, and printing, dark-room, and finishing personnel. Before the end of the decade his work was in such demand that he decided to expand. In the spring of 1868 he opened a branch studio in Ottawa, the capital of the new confederation, under the management of young William James Topley, who had been apprenticed to him for three years. Later that year a Toronto studio was launched under the name of Notman and Fraser, John Arthur Fraser having been taken into partnership and given management of the studio to avoid his leaving the fold. Fraser maintained the Notman tradition of artistic excellence, employing for a time the budding painters Horatio Walker, Homer Ransford Watson, and Frederick Arthur Verner, among others; in 1880, however, he left Notman to embark on a successful career in painting. Notman studios were opened as well in Halifax in 1870 and in Saint John, N.B., two years later, and during the 1880s he operated at least 20 studios, seven of which were in Canada. Seasonal studios at Yale College and Harvard University catered to the student trade.

Notman had been making inroads into the American market since 1869 when he had received the contract to photograph the staff and students of Vassar College. He was a regular contributor to the influential *Philadelphia Photographer*, edited by Edward Wilson, an admirer of his work, who often featured Notman's art, innovative methods, and Montreal studio. In 1876 Notman astutely joined Wilson in forming the Centennial Photographic Company to obtain the monopoly on photographs taken at the Philadelphia Centennial International Exhibition that year; the company, which employed Fraser as art superintendent, had a staff of 100 housed in a large building on the grounds. Notman also participated in the exhibition through a display of his studios' photographs; they won a gold medal from the British judges. Notman photographs had already earned medals at exhibitions in Montreal in 1860, London in 1862, and Paris five years later, and would earn others in Australia in 1877, Paris again the following year, and London in 1886.

Meanwhile, in Montreal the studio had continued to grow until in 1874 it employed a staff of 55. During the mid 1870s it alone produced some 14,000 negatives a year. In 1877, in order not to lose Sandham, Notman made him a partner in the Montreal firm, which was renamed Notman and Sandham. By 1882, however, the painter had left to pursue a career in the United States. A decline in business, possibly a delayed consequence of difficult economic conditions in the 1870s, was reflected at the end of that decade and in the early 1880s in a decrease in staff, which reached a low of 25 in 1886 before climbing back to 38 by 1892.

In addition to making and selling photographs Notman gave instruction to beginning photographers. How extensive his courses were is unknown, but his influence as a teacher becomes clear when it is realized that all the managers and photographers in his divers studios served their apprenticeship under him. During his 35-year career as many as 40 photographers were on the Montreal payroll alone, and a large number of these later successfully operated their own studios.

The management of Notman's enterprise would have overwhelmed the average man. Supervising a numerous staff, nurturing budding artistic talents, keeping abreast of technological and artistic developments, planning transcontinental trips, devising new ventures, signing contracts, and still keeping his own photographic talents finely tuned must have taxed the ingenuity, strength, and humour even of this dynamic man. Yet Notman carried on other activities and contributed particularly to the development of his adopted community. He was active in real estate and held part-ownership of some 295 lots in Longueuil; most were auctioned off in June 1873. He was part of the syndicate that built the luxurious Windsor Hotel, opened in February 1878. For many years he was a member of the Longueuil Yacht Club, of which he was president in the 1870s. An ardent yachtsman, he furthered interest in the sport by offering the "Notman Cup" as a prize at local meets. He also promoted rowing by bringing in outstanding crews to provide high-calibre competition. Originally members of Zion (Congregational) Church, Notman and his family joined St Martin's (Anglican) Church in Montreal in 1868 and attended St Mark's Church, Longueuil, when they resided there during the 1870s; Notman served as minister's warden at St Mark's for several years and was a financial pillar. He was a governor of the Montreal General Hospital in the 1880s at least and a member of the Young Men's Christian Association.

The Notmans had seven children, and all three boys worked in their father's business, where they had trained as photographers. One, William McFarlane, became a junior partner in William Notman and Son in 1882 following Sandham's departure. Notman's brothers as well as some of his nieces and nephews were all on staff at one time or another. William himself continued to be active as a photographer until his death, from pneumonia, on 25 Nov. 1891. He had always paid close attention to his firm and he invariably refused to rest, even after a cold, which ultimately proved fatal, had begun to progress rapidly. A contemporary described him shortly after his death as a man "singularly modest and unobtrusive," thoughtful and deliberate, "well informed of the events of the day, and quick to note their trend," decided and "even tenacious" in his opinions. Two sons carried on the firm, William McFarlane from 1891 until his death in 1913 and Charles Frederick from 1894 until 1935, when he sold the business to Associated Screen News.

Notman's personal authorship of photographs produced by his studio is rarely documented, but whenever it is the same style is evident, characterized by simplicity and economy, tending to starkness in some cases and even to abstraction in others. Notman had the ability to extract the essence of his subject through his choice of viewpoint, light, and line, and he was able simultaneously to describe it accurately and to provoke in the viewer an emotional response to it. As a portraitist, Notman, because of his attraction to the monumentality of form and his mastery of line, light, and composition, imbued his most prominent subjects with heroic – not to say mythic – qualities in tune with the nationalistic fervour that embraced the new country of Canada. On the other hand, because Notman photographs also accented realism and authenticity of dress or equipment, they constitute a valuable social record.

The production of Notman's studios, however, is of historical value for reasons more fundamental than authenticity of detail. Notman had an insatiable appetite for learning, recording, and expressing. His photographs document almost the entire range of activities in late Victorian Canada, and he gathered together the most talented photographers and painters available in order to do so more effectively than he could have done alone. Furthermore, he gave his photographers and painters a freedom within broad limits that enabled them to express their reaction to what they saw in such a manner that their production reflects their own style while bearing his distinctive mark. Since many went on to become prominent, Notman was instrumental not only in recording and expressing the essence of his era but also in forming others who could do so effectively through their art.

Notman took all of Canada as a subject worthy of his cameras. Through the establishment of relatively autonomous regional studios, he was largely able to avoid imposing on the rest of Canada the view from Montreal. Nevertheless, his personal vision was centred on that city, which was, in truth, the heart of the country. Even Vancouver, the "end of the track," was linked directly to it through the builders of the CPR, and almost every place in between was tied to it at least indirectly. Notman's Montreal reflected the transitional nature of a land and a people poised at the watershed between the 19th and 20th centuries, ready, as Sir Wilfrid Laurier fondly believed, to assume the mantle of a great power. Notman expressed imperial Montreal through his portraits of its great men – whose reputations were international – and photographs of imposing buildings. He depicted the local city through his portraits of average Victorian Montrealers, often conducting their ordinary business. In the harbour he caught squat, steam-driven vessels being loaded beside majestic, wooden sailing ships. And beyond the city his photographers captured labourers dwarfed by the Rockies in scenes symbolic of the immense task that Canada – led by Montreal – had given itself, that of harnessing to an industrial and trading economy the potential in natural resources of half a continent.

STANLEY G. TRIGGS

Further reading

Roger Hall *et al.*, *The world of William Notman: the nineteenth century through a master lens* (Toronto, 1993).

Portrait of a period: a collection of Notman photographs, 1856–1915, intro. E. A. Collard, ed. J. R. Harper and S. G. Triggs (Montreal, 1967).

S. G. Triggs, *The composite photographs of William Notman* (exhibition catalogue, McCord Museum of Canadian History, Montreal, 1994); *William Notman: the stamp of a studio* (Toronto, 1985); *William Notman's studio: the Canadian picture* (exhibition catalogue, McCord Museum of Canadian History, 1992).

D. [R.] Reid, *"Our own country Canada": being an account of the national aspirations of the principal landscape artists in Montreal and Toronto, 1860–1890* (Ottawa, 1979).

S. [G.] Triggs *et al.*, *Victoria bridge: the vital link* (exhibition catalogue, McCord Museum of Canadian History, 1992).

LOUIS-ADÉLARD SENÉCAL
(often written Sénécal, but he signed Senécal),

merchant, shipowner, entrepreneur, and politician; b. 10 July 1829 at Varennes, Lower Canada, son of Ambroise Sénécal, a farmer and grain merchant, and Marie-Anne Brodeur; m. 15 Jan. 1850 at Verchères, Delphine, daughter of Lieutenant-Colonel Joseph Dansereau, a merchant; d. 11 Oct. 1887 in Montreal.

The Sénécal family came from Rouen, France. Adrien, a tailor by trade, immigrated to New France in 1673. Settling first at Trois-Rivières, he moved a few years later to Boucherville where his descendants turned to farming, and increased rapidly in number. Little is known of Louis-Adélard's early years, although his father is believed to have moved the family to Verchères soon after his son's birth. It is thought that he went to the local parish school, that he spent about two years in Vermont, during which he attended the common school in Burlington for some months, and that he returned to Verchères at the end of the 1840s. His marriage contract reveals a businessman's prudence: the couple agreed to community of property but each retained certain objects and rights acquired before the marriage. One clause provided that the wife could "on giving up community [of property] take back what she had brought to it," and another stipulated that the husband was to keep a legacy from his mother, amounting to £6,500 (sterling), which he "had employed for the purchase of trade goods and other chattels."

For Senécal, the years following his marriage were formative. On 13 May 1850, with Michel Senécal of Saint-Marc, he set up a general store at Verchères under the name of L. A. et M. Senécal. The contract provided that each partner would invest £100 in the firm's capital stock. Michel was to manage the store and keep the books, to be closed annually on 1 May; he was to receive a salary. The partnership was to run for three years, and provided that the parties "could not withdraw from the said company for any reason whatsoever." At the end of each year losses or profits were to be shared equally. It is to be noted that in this contract the role of Louis-Adélard was not specified, and it was Michel who took on the day-to-day management of the undertaking, leaving his partner the time to attend to other business. On 12 July 1851, L. A. et M. Senécal was prematurely dissolved by mutual agreement: Michel bought the business with all the buildings, stock, and accounts, in return for a number of promissory notes issued in favour of Louis-Adélard.

In the autumn of 1851 Ambroise Sénécal joined forces with his son, appointing Louis-Adélard special procurator and sole business agent for a grain business. Louis-Adélard was authorized to buy grain for his father, set the price, and collect arrears of payment. Responsible for storage and delivery as well as for the bookkeeping, he agreed not to trade in grain on his own account. His father advanced the working capital and paid him a commission, while retaining access to the account books at any time and his right of veto in important decisions.

At the beginning of 1852 Louis-Adélard Senécal was forced to announce his bankruptcy, as a result of losses incurred in earlier commercial transactions. On 15 January he came to an agreement with the 24 creditors, who for the most part were Montreal suppliers of earthenware, paint, hardware, and other articles. His debts amounted to £1,864, and he agreed to pay eight shillings on the pound, in five quarterly instalments without interest. Among his creditors were the Richelieu Company, of which he would one day be president, and Adolphe Roy, who later became one of his principal financial backers. Ostensibly at least, Senécal was ruined – a painful situation which allowed his family to display its solidarity. At the time of the agreement of January 1852 his father mortgaged three properties to reassure Louis-Adélard's creditors, and his wife gave up her rights to a lot which he sold on 25 June for £4,000. Back on his feet again, Senécal kept his eyes open for a profitable venture and on 2 March 1853, in partnership with his father and father-in-law, he bought the steamship *George Frederick* for $4,700 from Edwin C. French of Cornwall, Canada West. They renamed it *Verchères* and Louis-Adélard, who had somehow learned the art of navigation, became its captain. On 9 April, before all the ice had gone from the river, the *Verchères* made a memorable maiden voyage from Ogdensburg, N.Y., to Montreal and, with the establishment of regular service between Verchères and Montreal a few months later, "le capitaine Senécal" (as he was later dubbed by the people of the region) would unknowingly become a local legend.

In the mid 1850s shipping was a promising field of endeavour. Neither roads nor railways were as yet serious competitors. In the Richelieu region there were signs of a new vitality and settlers were filling in the back sections of the seigneuries, between the Yamaska and Saint-François rivers. With the progress of industrialization in the United States from the 1840s and the Reciprocity Treaty in 1854, a promising axis for trade between Montreal and New York was opening via the Richelieu River, an axis strengthened in the 1860s by the American Civil War. No doubt Senécal did not immediately see all these possibilities, but he became aware of them as time passed. Even more important, shipping brought him into contact with the Montreal business community as well as with local figures, thus opening horizons to challenge his imagination and daring. According to an article in *La Minerve* of Montreal in 1887, Senécal established links between William Henry (Sorel), Canada East, and Montreal with the *Verchères* soon after it commenced service in 1853, between Sainte-Anne-de-Sorel and Montreal with the *Yamaska* at the beginning of 1858, between the Saint-François River and William Henry with the *Cygne,* and between Quebec and Montreal with the *Ottawa* in 1860 – the last endeavour to compete with the Riche-lieu Company. This simplified outline, emphasizing Senécal's personal accomplishments during these years, disguises a much more complex, collective activity. It seems that Senécal was always a co-owner of the vessels, and his role in the different companies that were involved varied considerably. The case of the *Verchères* is revealing. On 4 Aug. 1854 he joined with his father-in-law and his brother Adolphe (who had inher-ited his father's share of the original company) to form a new company, Senécal, Dansereau et Compagnie to use the *Verchères* on the St Law-rence. Ownership of the company was divided into three equal parts, and its assets would consist of the *Verchères* as well as any other barges or boats the partners might acquire. The partners undertook to give priori-ty to the venture and not to carry on any independent shipping business. All three could, as individuals, enter into transactions on behalf of the company and had unrestricted access to the account books. The part-nership agreement was renewed periodically, with changed terms and a succession of partners: on 25 April 1855 Joseph Dansereau acquired Adolphe Senécal's share; on 9 Feb. 1857 Louis-Adélard sold a third of his stock to Pierre-Édouard Malhiot; and on 28 July the firm became Dansereau et Compagnie. More important, from 1855 the terms were altered to allow the partners to work alone or in other shipping compa-nies, a change probably made at the request of Louis-Adélard, who was seeking to diversify his investment portfolio.

Senécal's entrepreneurial spirit showed in his readiness to seize eve-ry opportunity for profitable shipping transactions. On 30 Nov. 1855 he acquired a share in the People's Line. On 28 Jan. 1858 he went into partnership with other businessmen in the Yamaska Navigation Com-pany, capitalized at $12,200; he expected thereby to be able to engage in transportation on the Yamaska and Saint-François rivers, as well as on the St Lawrence between Saint-Hugues and Montreal. It was Sené-cal who built the *Yamaska* for this company – in less than two and a half months, according to his obituary – as well as the *Cygne*. In 1859 he went into partnership with Sévère Dumoulin and Édouard-Louis Pacaud to form the Compagnie de Navigation de Trois-Rivières. In the same year, he joined his brother Adolphe, as Senécal et Senécal, to buy grain on commission in the parishes along the St Lawrence, and transport it to Victor Hudon's mills in Montreal. The following year he managed an office at Sorel for the Yamaska Navigation Company. He continued to diversify his activities and on 5 Feb. 1862 undertook to build five barges at a cost of $7,500 for H. Robertson and Company of Montreal. In April 1869, with Pierreville merchant Henri Vassal, Montreal merchant Louis Tourville, Adolphe Roy, and others, he set up a dredging enterprise, the St Francis and Yamaska Rivers Improvement and Deepening Company, with a capital reserve of $100,000.

The increased demand for labour, grain, hay, and manufactured products engendered by the American Civil War stimulated intense economic activity in the region of Montreal and the Richelieu River in the early 1860s and provided speculators with numerous opportunities. Senécal, who had been in business for some ten years, was in a position to take full advantage of these circumstances. Hundreds of notarial documents relative to land purchases, the transport of goods, shipbuilding, and lumber production attest to his feverish and wide-ranging activity. In effect, trade between Montreal and New York State via the Richelieu region formed the backbone for all his projects during this period. He is reputed to have had an interest in a fleet of some 11 steamships and 89 barges, used to transport lumber and grain between Montreal, Sorel, and Whitehall, N.Y. These barges (some 100 to 125 feet long and 20 to 23 feet wide, with holds 4 to 7 feet deep) cost about $1,500 each and could carry 6,000 to 10,000 bushels of wheat. Shipping became the springboard for an extension of Senécal's business, and the region between the Yamaska and Saint-François rivers, which in addition to a number of seigneuries included the townships of Wickham, Grantham, and Upton, constituted the territorial base for his economic interests.

During this period Senécal plunged boldly into land speculation. In 1860 he bought from Jonathan Saxton Campbell Würtele, a merchant and seigneur of Rivière-David, about $1,500 in copyholders' arrears. This contract apparently enabled him to acquire certain lots belonging to copyholders unable to pay their debts. Senécal was to use this method many times. Even more important was the purchase, in February 1866, of all the properties of Charles James Irwin Grant, Baron de Longueuil, in the township of Upton, with the capital and arrears on the rents, a sizeable acquisition, including 300 claimable debts totalling £10,287. On the purchase price of $24,000, he was to pay $12,000 down, $7,000 on receipt of the titles, and $5,000 in the next 18 months. Isaac

Coote, Grant's agent, entered the service of the purchaser and took charge of managing the estate. In March 1866 Senécal increased his holding by buying the entire estate of the late Ignace Gill, including a magnificent property bordering on the Odanak Indian Reserve, a piece of land on Île Ronde, and some lots in Durham and Upton townships. On 6 April he delegated Henri Vassal to settle the debts and liabilities of the estate. Then on 15 Feb. 1867 he completed his holdings by acquiring for $3,000 a number of lots owned by Grant in the townships of Hereford and Barford as well as in New Hampshire. But he was not solely interested in purchasing large blocks of land; the minute-books of local notaries record numerous transactions in his name concerning the purchase or sale of small lots. For example, apparently through the good offices of a municipal secretary, he bought several small parcels in the parish of Saint-David, sold by the corporation of Yamaska County for tax arrears, including a group of nine lots acquired on 7 Jan. 1867 for $149.43.

This property speculation did not prevent Senécal from expanding his network of businesses. On 15 Dec. 1862 he went into partnership with Carlos Darius Meigs, a skilled workman of Saint-Guillaume, under the name of Senécal et Meigs. At first the firm confined itself to operating a sawmill on the David River. Senécal provided the working capital and had sole right to the profits. Meigs managed the mill, was responsible for maintaining the equipment, and guaranteed to process annually 30,000 pine logs into planks, laths, and shingles; he received a monthly salary of $100, as well as a commission on the sawn lumber. Subsequently the company expanded into buying and selling barges, speculating in land, and dealing in mortgages: it usually lent at between 8 and 20 per cent interest. On 12 Oct. 1866 Senécal, acting in both his own name and that of the company, appointed Edward Campbell Wurtele, a merchant of Saint-David, general and special agent to manage the affairs of the firm and to direct the commercial operations he himself had undertaken until then.

Relieved of various responsibilities, Senécal took advantage of the heavy demand for timber of all kinds to invest in other mills; he developed a plan to build a modern mill with a large productive capacity at Pierreville, and hence sought to tighten his hold on vast areas of forest. He next endeavoured to reconcile his interests in lumber manufacture and in landed property; thus he had land cleared to supply his sawmills, then sold the land to settlers, who undertook as partial payment to clear another lot for him, and so the cycle began again.

In the spring of 1866, therefore, Senécal undertook to set up the Pierreville Steam Mills Company. He went into partnership with Henri Vassal, Valentine Cooke (a merchant of Drummondville), Louis Tourville and Joseph-Guillaume Tranchemontagne (both merchants of Montreal), and also with his associate Meigs. The partnership agreement of 12 May provided for an authorized capital of $24,000, divided into shares of $1,000. The board of directors, consisting of a president (Senécal) and a secretary (Vassal), was to deal with current matters, and an annual meeting of the shareholders would determine the distribution of dividends, elect the directors, and examine the account books. On 15 Aug. 1866 the Legislative Assembly ratified this agreement, despite a petition signed by about 100 opponents who claimed the proposed company was likely to monopolize the processing of timber in the region. Work began in the autumn, at a tongue of land on the Île du Fort, in the lower part of the Tardif channel, a body of water 50 to 100 feet wide that provided a natural passage for the wood to the mill. Meigs obtained the $26,500 contract for the construction of the establishment, to consist of two buildings: a sawmill 75 by 55 feet, equipped to produce 50,000 to 60,000 feet of planks daily, with a circular saw, five frames holding 89 vertical saws, and modern devices for making laths and shingles; and a flour-mill 65 by 46 feet housing, in addition to the millstones, machinery for carding and fulling cloth. A complex assembly of boilers and steam-engines drove the machinery. The company facilities included breakwaters, a bridge linking the Île du Fort to the north shore of the channel, and a loading dock. Meigs was given the responsibility of running the establishment and maintaining the equipment for two years, in return for a commission based on production. The mill began operations in December 1866 and immediately became an important centre of local development: it even became fashionable to take a trip from Sorel to visit it. *La Gazette de Sorel* of 21 Aug. 1869 noted that the establishment – which then included three mills, a carding-mill apparently having been added – employed more than 120 men and produced 83,000 feet of lumber daily, and that since the spring 59 vessels had left Pierreville, mostly bound for the United States; furthermore, the company is

reported to have bought from the government a 37,000-acre timber limit in the townships of Simpson, Grantham, and Wendover. Senécal was
closely involved in the management of the company. His principal concerns were keeping the mill supplied with logs, selling and distributing
planks, and maintaining the firm's working capital. Since the company's
cash reserve was small, it was often short of funds and Senécal resorted
to discounting notes receivable to obtain liquid assets. Much later, his
partners publicly accused him of having used the company to obtain
funds for himself, either by personally collecting the discount on notes
endorsed by the company, or by demanding excessive advances for logs
which were not always delivered. In this way he eventually incurred a
$40,000 debt to the company.

Senécal needed liquidity because of the growing multiplicity of his
business operations. On 28 Jan. 1867 he and Vassal formed Vassal et
Compagnie, to trade (from 14 Jan. 1867 to 1 May 1870) in "dry [and
perishable] goods, grain, and any other items." The partners invested
the same amount and all profits and losses were shared equally. On 25
March 1867 Senécal formed a partnership for a period of five years with
Edward Campbell Wurtele, under the name of Wurtele et Senécal, to
trade in lumber and grain with the United States, using 15 barges valued at $15,000. Here again, the partners had equal shares in the firm's
capital, divided profits and losses equally, and were each authorized to
make transactions binding on the company, which had its headquarters
at Sorel.

By the autumn of 1867 Senécal was therefore the central figure in
a vast commercial network. He was 38, and his contemporaries estimated (though without proof) that his annual volume of business reached
$3,000,000. After living in Verchères during the 1850s, and then at
Saint-David or Saint-Guillaume during the 1860s, he settled his family
in Montreal. But his roots were in the Sorel region and he liked to identify himself as a Pierreville merchant. His father and father-in-law having died, he seems to have remained close to only one of his brothers,
Ambroise, with whom he carried on business. He had two daughters:
Delphine, who married Charles-Ignace Gill on 1 Jan. 1870, and Octa-
vie, later the wife of William Blumhart. His two sons-in-law became
both the sons he did not have and his business partners. For the present,
Senécal was powerful and his fame had already spread far and wide.

Auguste Achintre in his *Manuel électoral* describes him as "tall, thin, bony, with a long neck, long legs, a bare forehead, prominent cheekbones, a keen eye, [a man] of few words"; always on the move, "he does not walk, he runs: if he sometimes stops, it is in a vehicle, to gain time, to decipher twenty telegrams and to reply to them." The key to his success lay in an irrepressible imagination which allowed him to marshal scattered resources around projects swiftly conceived and swiftly executed, extraordinary physical endurance, boldness and sang-froid in both the conception and realization of projects, rather flexible business ethics, and ever-alert curiosity. These qualities enabled him to bring together in aid of any given project Montreal capitalists to whom he paid high rates of interest, regional agents whose participation he secured through commissions or profits, and cheap local manpower. He knew all the tricks to get working capital: discounting bills of exchange, overdrawing his account, mortgaging property, manipulating the funds of the businesses he managed, ignoring dates of payment, charging exorbitant interest, quick speculation, and so forth. But Senécal was a conductor with a weakness: he played without a score – he had no overall accounting system for his transactions – and without rehearsal; he liked to conceive and execute pieces but did not like to develop them in detail.

It is not surprising that Senécal decided in the autumn of 1867 to have a go at politics; the double mandate enabled him to run in both the provincial riding of Yamaska and the federal constituency of Drummond and Arthabaska. For this powerful man, politics was another way of doing business, one more trump card. This opportunistic attitude did not prevent him, in this period, from having a few political ideas. He was at first linked with the Rouges, as a result of a previous relationship with Jean-Baptiste-Éric Dorion, whose newspaper *Le Défricheur* (L'Avenir) he had financed; this paper, at Senécal's request, had then passed into the hands of Wilfrid Laurier. Senécal stood in 1867 as a Liberal candidate; he sat in the Quebec Legislative Assembly until 1871 and in the House of Commons until 1872. He was a discreet member, more active and talkative in committees where he drew on his business experience than in the house where he expressed himself with difficulty. Plagued with financial problems, he was often absent from parliamentary sessions.

On 20 Nov. 1867 Senécal went bankrupt in his own name and in the name of Senécal et Meigs, and deposited "all his assets and personal effects, property, books, letters and documents" with the official assignee, Tancrède Sauvageau. The bankruptcy brought about the dissolution of the Wurtele et Senécal partnership, Senécal giving up his rights in the company. A provisional statement of the creditors – for, as Sauvageau noted, "M. Senécal in drawing up the said statement had recourse to his memory rather than to his account books, having not kept regular accounts" – evaluated the bankruptcy at about $410,000, without considering debts to at least 14 other creditors. The real reasons for this bankruptcy remain obscure. Contemporaries felt that the business crisis precipitated by the closing of the American market following the end of the Reciprocity Treaty in 1866 caught Senécal short: he had fixed assets and inventories but no liquid assets to meet his many obligations. He proposed a composition with his creditors by which he would reimburse fully the preferred creditors' debts, amounting to $17,480, and pay 50 cents on the dollar, in semi-annual payments of $30,000, for the rest. He also agreed to the nomination by the creditors of three trustees to administer his property, with management expenses up to $2,500 annually to be charged to the estate. In return, he requested that Meigs and Vassal be discharged from liability for the notes they had endorsed. These terms were accepted by the 51 creditors at meetings held on 7 Dec. 1867 and 22 Jan. 1868, and on the latter date the property was officially transferred from Tancrède Sauvageau to the trustees. An important clause in the deed of transfer, however, declared that Senécal was to be employed at an undisclosed salary to administer and realize the estate under the supervision of the trustees, and to proceed with the business he had previously conducted. Senécal therefore was again in charge of his property, but under the vigilant eye of three trustees. With Meigs and Vassal, he continued his operations in the Pierreville Steam Mills Company, which had not been directly affected by this bankruptcy.

Senécal was not at the end of his troubles. On 20 June 1868 the Pierreville mills burned down: he rebuilt them in 47 days, equipping them with 146 vertical saws. In August fire razed his factory "for the extraction of liquid from hemlock bark" at Saint-Guillaume. On 14 Jan. 1870 fire again devastated the mills at Pierreville, but he got them back in operation, reportedly in 30 days. These were indeed difficult years and when he signed the marriage contract of his daughter Delphine, on 31 Dec. 1869, he was only able to provide her with $6,000 to be paid in six instalments, or, in the event he had no cash, in land and real property. No doubt unable to meet the repayment obligations of his 1867 composition with his creditors, Senécal was again declared insolvent at the beginning of 1870 and control of his property reverted to the official assignee, Sauvageau. According to a statement of his creditors, his debts totalled $407,559.79, and involved major Montreal firms: Adolphe Roy et Compagnie ($71,939), the Merchants' Bank of Canada ($66,899), E. Hudon, Fils et Compagnie ($61,310), Louis Gauthier ($31,060), the Banque du Peuple ($30,055), Louis Tourville ($17,008), Thomas Wilson ($16,773), and P. Larose ($16,509). The Pierreville Steam Mills Company made a claim of $15,079. The creditors held an emergency meeting. There were differences of opinion and, it can be surmised, much activity behind the scenes. On 11 Feb. 1870 Vassal offered to buy the assets of the bankrupt estate, paying the creditors eight cents on each dollar owing, with notes falling due over a period of several months. The notes, curiously enough, were endorsed by Adolphe Roy and Thomas Wilson. The creditors accepted Vassal's offer on 18 February and he immediately became the owner of Senécal's property. Nevertheless he was not free to sell the assets without Sauvageau's consent until the notes given as a guarantee had been paid. In this transaction, Vassal seems to have been in collusion with his partner and, four days later, "all the movables and intangible assets which have been sold and assigned to the said Henri Vassal" returned to Senécal for the sum of $35,000, which Vassal declared he had received. On 26 September Senécal also recovered from Vassal some 60 lots in Saint-Bonaventure and some 50 in Saint-Guillaume for $45,222, apparently paid in cash. He mortgaged these properties in December to borrow $44,000 from Adolphe Roy and Thomas Wilson, the Montreal financial backers who continued to give him credit and honour his notes, "in order to sustain his business and help him in his speculations." In October Senécal and Vassal had made an agreement terminating their commercial operations and settling the share due to each; considering the small proportion of assets allotted to Vassal, it is clear that in all these undertakings he was little more than Senécal's agent. At the end of 1870, therefore, Senécal was by no means ruined as a result of his bankruptcy: still alert and on the look-out, he was waiting for better times.

Railway construction, which in the 1870s became a large-scale endeavour in Quebec, provided Senécal with a field of activity that came to occupy almost all his time, as shipping and lumbering had done in the 1850s and 1860s. He did not, however, abandon his still considerable interests in the Sorel region, but increasingly relied on such agents as his brother Ambroise (appointed on 16 March 1870), Charles-Ignace Gill (9 Jan. 1871), Pierre-Nérée Dorion (3 March 1871), and Louis Caya (25 Nov. 1873). At the beginning of the 1870s Senécal worked principally on building the Richelieu, Drummond and Arthabaska Counties Railway, of which he progressively obtained control. In the autumn of 1871 he completed the 48-mile section connecting Sorel and L'Avenir via Drummondville. Opened in 1872, this line rapidly became unusable when the wooden rails did not stand up to the rigours of the Quebec climate. On 12 November Senécal therefore sold the line to the South-Eastern Counties Junction Railway Company for $100,000. Three years later, this company gave him the contract to rebuild the Sorel–Drummondville section with steel rails and extend it south to Acton (Acton-Vale). The construction of this track, which was completed in 1876, proved truly epic and put Senécal's talent, energy, and enthusiasm to the test. Working in difficult circumstances and beset with obstacles, he was at the mercy of governments for financing, local interests for the route, businessmen for working capital, and inexperienced workmen and rudimentary equipment for construction. In order to succeed, he needed allies in the various levels of government and straw men in the head offices of the companies he directed. For this purpose he intervened in elections, and to help candidates of his choice maintained good relations with papers such as *Le Pays* (Montreal). But by 1871 Georges-Isidore Barthe, the mayor of Sorel, had denounced the advent of the "reign of shady speculation," the practice of purchasing "electors retail" and reselling them "wholesale later," and the existence of a local network of politicians in Senécal's pay: Charles-Ignace Gill (member for Yamaska in the Quebec Legislative Assembly, 1871–74), Joseph-Nestor Duguay (member for Yamaska in the House of Commons, 1872–74), Jean-Baptiste Guèvremont and a man named Marchessault, both active in municipal politics. With the aid of his newspaper *La Gazette de Sorel*, Barthe also stood up for the taxpayers' interests against Senécal's plan to get the municipalities to increase their railway subsidies and to pay them before the completion of work. The mayor was not anxious to finance an individual who provided no guarantee, manipulated head offices, determined the location of stations to suit his friends, and claimed $80,000 when he was owed barely $27,000. These two implacable enemies engaged in a fight to the finish. In 1872 Senécal forced Barthe to resign as mayor over an issue involving a conflict of interest. In the federal election in Richelieu that year, he helped ensure the victory of Michel Mathieu, which entailed the defeat of the ex-mayor. Nevertheless, Barthe was re-elected mayor at Sorel in January 1873.

In the field of railway construction, Senécal used the procedures that had served him so well in the past. He obtained the necessary lumber from his own mills on the Yamaska River, in Kingsey Township, and elsewhere. Straw men collected the grants and were responsible for the expenditures, the exact amount of which is unknown. He also had well-known financial backers, including Valentine Cooke (manager of the South-Eastern Counties Junction Railway Company), Adolphe Roy (now the president of the Pierreville Steam Mills Company), and Louis-Hercule Lafleur (a Montreal merchant). To get money quickly, he used his favourite technique – land speculation. In the autumn of 1873 alone, he bought 1,775 acres of land in the district of Arthabaska, 1,300 acres in the township of Wickham, and 800 in the township of Kingsey, not to mention the 6,450 acres he acquired for the Pierreville Steam Mills Company. His insatiable need for liquid assets led him to make things difficult for his friends. Around 1873 he is thought to have swindled Adolphe Roy out of $17,000 by issuing notes without funds to cover them, and in 1878 he apparently conspired to put the Pierreville Steam Mills Company into bankruptcy.

His need of money may also explain why in 1874 he abandoned the provincial Liberal party, which had been relegated to the opposition. He had long known that political power and capital on a grand scale went hand in hand and that charters and grants were obtained if "one is on the right side." An anecdote illustrates the kind of motivation behind his political activity: having invited his principal organizer in Yamaska County, Antoine Laferté, to desert to the Conservative camp, he apparently said to him: "Toine, I have decided to change parties and to wear blue, ... with the Bleus I am going to make a lot more money ... and we are going to get rich." While he was associated with the Liberal party, Senécal had dreamed of a coalition of Bleus and Rouges in provincial politics, in order to facilitate his relations with the government. But

Henri-Gustave Joly, the leader of the Quebec Liberals, opposed such a coalition in December 1874 and, as a crowning ingratitude, the Liberal party, once in power in Ottawa, refused to appoint Senécal a senator. Consequently, he began to cast sidelong glances at the Bleus. He made the acquaintance of Joseph-Adolphe Chapleau and Arthur Dansereau of the Conservative leadership, and in the federal by-election in Drummond and Arthabaska in 1877 took a stand against Laurier, whose defeat he ensured. Ironically, thanks to Luc Letellier de Saint-Just's *coup d'état*, the Liberals came to power in Quebec in 1878 just when important decisions were about to be taken concerning the Quebec, Montreal, Ottawa and Occidental Railway. This railway, launched and owned by the government, was to go along the north shore of the St Lawrence. The ambitious Senécal, who scented a killing in this venture, as well as in railway politics as a whole, wanted to be in on the spoils. Far from meeting his expectations, the new government, on the initiative of the premier, Joly, even refused to pay him $15,000 as reimbursement for work already completed. Senécal therefore used every possible means to get the lieutenant governor, Letellier de Saint-Just, relieved of his post and the Joly government defeated in the Legislative Assembly. Despite financial difficulties which forced him to mortgage his insurance policies, he was instrumental in the ousting of the Liberals from power in 1879. Upon becoming premier, Chapleau was therefore in no position to ignore him, especially since Senécal expected some expression of gratitude.

The Conservatives' assumption of office marked the beginning of a form of secret government in which the dominant figures were Dansereau, the party's publicity man, and Senécal, its treasurer. In office until 1882, the Conservative party was none the less torn by disputes: the ideological factions of moderate "Chapleautistes" and ultramontane "Castors" competed for intellectual dominance while rival financial factions – in particular the Canadian Pacific Railway Company, the Grand Trunk Railway of Canada, Sir Hugh Allan and the Montreal Ocean Steamship Company, and the Bank of Montreal – each sought to get their hands on issues of government bonds, railway grants, and the ownership of the Quebec, Montreal, Ottawa and Occidental Railway. On 1 March 1880 Chapleau appointed Senécal superintendent of the last-named company; Senécal brought in his son-in-law William Blumhart as secretary and general supplier. Senécal's salary was to equal 2.5 per cent of the net profits from the operation of the railway. He was given an official mandate to manage in the best interests of Quebec a company that was a heavy burden for the government, and an unofficial mandate to exploit the railway as an instrument of power for the "Chapleautistes." He himself added a third mandate: to take care of his own interests. The challenge was worthy of the man. He carried out his responsibilities by completing the Quebec, Montreal, Ottawa and Occidental through the construction of branch lines feeding the main line, and then transforming the railway into an instrument for patronage and a major source of revenue for the party. This was indeed a dark period in the political history of Quebec, when the man responsible for a public company was also the chief treasurer of a political party, and Senécal earned a severe rebuke from Laurier in an article entitled "La Caverne des 40 voleurs" in L'Électeur of 20 April 1881. In this article Laurier labelled Senécal a swindler, claiming that he had stolen from many of his former associates and ruined them, and he accused him of seeking to do the same with the people of Quebec. This virulent attack provoked Senécal into suing Laurier for "a false, scandalous and defamatory libel." The trial opened in Montreal on 5 Oct. 1881 and Laurier's counsel presented a survey of Senécal's business career, going back as far as 1858 when he was found guilty of receiving $50 under false pretences – a decision later reversed by a higher court. Accusation followed accusation and during the whole of October the trial was the centre of attention across the province. When it finished on 2 November the jurors were irremediably split and the case closed without a verdict. None the less, the expression "Sénécaleux" from then on became synonymous in the public mind with cheat, thief, and pilferer of the public purse.

As superintendent of the Quebec, Montreal, Ottawa and Occidental, Senécal reconstructed on a grand scale the scenarios that had become his trademark. Thus he bought the St Lawrence and Industry Village Rail-road, repaired it with materials belonging to the Quebec, Montreal, Ottawa and Occidental, and then sold it at a high price to the government. His greatest success was the liquidation of the Quebec, Montreal, Ottawa and Occidental in 1882. In February, he managed to sell the western section (Montreal–Ottawa) and its branch lines to the CPR for $4,000,000, realizing a personal profit generally estimated at $100,000. During the negotiation of the sale of the eastern section (Montreal–

Quebec), Senécal was involved as the unnamed principal behind the North Shore Railway financial syndicate, one of the two groups interested in the purchase. This syndicate included Thomas McGreevy, Joseph-Aldric Ouimet, and Alphonse Desjardins. Senécal's participation was revealed at the beginning of March, soon after the provincial cabinet had accepted the North Shore Railway offer of $4,000,000, and, despite a heated debate over Senécal's activity as a government employee, the Legislative Assembly approved the transaction, which was officially sanctioned on 27 May. In December Senécal resold this section to the Grand Trunk. He thus made an immediate profit on the sale, receiving both cash and shares in the Grand Trunk as payment, and then later realized a second profit when the shares rose in value with the Grand Trunk's sale of the same section to the CPR in 1885.

This crucial episode in railway development may in the end have been to Quebec's advantage, but definitely proved beneficial for Senécal. Certainly he made many enemies who attacked him from all sides – for example, the Liberals in *L'Électeur* and the Ultramontanes in a pamphlet entitled *Le Pays, le Parti et le Grand Homme*, which was published at Montreal in 1882. Yet, on the other hand, he became one of the most influential men in Quebec at the beginning of the 1880s. In 1880 he had been practically insolvent, to judge from the 78 notices of protest served on him by creditors, but by 1882 he was on his feet again financially. Managing a government undertaking had also opened new horizons. In 1881 and 1882 he went to France, as superintendent of the Quebec, Montreal, Ottawa and Occidental Railway, to negotiate the issue of a public loan, and he made contact with some of the important international financiers. After Chapleau left for the federal scene in 1882, Senécal decided to carve a place for himself in the vast network of international capital. He was rich enough to afford newspapers that lavished praise on him, and he benefited from his relations with the high financial circles of Montreal, where he was feared for his low cunning and admired for his boldness and energy. Furthermore, he had some important leverage: he was president of the Richelieu and Ontario Navigation Company (1882–87), the North Shore Railway Company (1883–86), and the Montreal City Passenger Railway Company (1883–84). In 1883 he was given the cross of commander in the French Legion of Honour, which earned him a demonstration of friendship and testimony of admiration from the highest-ranking Montreal political and financial figures, both English and French. The celebration was no mere public event. In a sense it became an historic moment, establishing for succeeding generations the image of a mythical Senécal who, in the words of Jean-Baptiste Rolland, "personifies the commercial and industrial genius of the country," and who, according to Chapleau, was the living symbol of the economic awakening of French-speaking Canadians. Quoting the motto which had inspired him all his life – "where there's a will, there's a way" – Senécal affirmed his resolve to continue his labours on a national scale.

The issuing of public bonds in Paris and the establishment in Quebec of the Crédit Foncier Franco-Canadien in 1881 had aroused an infatuation for "*vieille* France" in political and financial circles. It was fashionable to trade with France, which might become an important partner in the economic recovery of French Canadians and the development of Quebec's resources. Rumour had it that Senécal had returned from France and England in 1882 full of fresh ideas. In fact he was nursing three large projects that involved millions of dollars and brought him the adulation of some Montreal financiers: a company to install a transatlantic cable from Halifax to the coast of England, thereby decreasing the cost of telegraphic communications; a shipping link between Rouen and Quebec, financed by capital from Rouen, Montreal, and governmental sources; and a colonization company, drawing on international capital, to develop Quebec's natural resources. These were ventures worthy of an American "tycoon." The third project, the General Colonization and Industrial Enterprise Company, was beyond a doubt the most ambitious ever conceived by Senécal. The company, with a capital of 6 to 10 million dollars, was to be based on the acquisition of the properties comprising the estate of the late George Benson Hall, which included the famous mills at Montmorency (now part of Beauport), with their extensive timber limits in the Gatineau, Saint-Maurice, and Beauce regions, as well as the Radnor ironworks near Trois-Rivières and several townships, or parts thereof, in southern Quebec.

With Sir Charles Tupper (the Canadian high commissioner in London) and other associates, Senécal concentrated particularly on this last project during 1883. On 29 January Hall's heirs signed a promise of sale to Senécal. The following month Senécal asked the Quebec Legislative

Assembly to grant a charter to the company, which included 27 prominent financiers from various regions of Quebec, and five foreign investors: R. H. Kimball, a New York banker; J. Belloni, owner of collieries
in the United States; René Manraize, a Paris merchant; Émile Bonemant,
a French agronomist; and Bradley Barlow, a Vermont senator. At the
end of February, fearing that lobbying by the ultramontane members
might block the grant of the powers demanded by the company, Senécal bought from Sherbrooke businessman Charles King the charter of
the Eastern Townships Land and Improvement Company, which conferred extensive powers and enabled him to conduct his operations more
freely. On 7 June he acquired the Hall properties in his own name for
$1,600,000: $250,000 was paid in cash and four payments, ending on
2 July 1884, were scheduled for the remainder. Although the stakes were
high, Senécal realized a substantial profit when he resold these properties two months later to the General Colonization Company (which he
had meanwhile incorporated) for "$2,500,000, with $1,000,000 immediately, in paid-up company stock, and the balance of a million and a
half, also in paid-up stock, as soon as he has supplied the company with
a full discharge of any mortgage on the said property."

Still in search of investors, Senécal went to Europe in the autumn of
1883. He had numerous discussions with Poursin-Escande (the Canadian government agent in Paris), Hector Fabre (the Quebec representative
there), Sir Charles Tupper, and one Fichet (a millionaire from Le Havre,
France). Negotiations dragged on and, worse still, an article in the *Mail*
of Toronto and the *Morning Chronicle* of Quebec attacking Senécal's cred-
ibility put investors on their guard. Back in Canada in December, Senécal
launched a libel action for $200,000 (raised to $250,000 in November 1884) against the first newspaper and another against the second.
It seems, on the evidence of a handwritten note in Senécal's papers, that
in January 1884 "the insurers in Edinburgh reportedly received unfavourable information from Montreal and changed their minds." Was
this to be the end of a splendid dream? On 29 Jan. 1884 the board of
directors of the General Colonization Company – on which sat Senécal, John McDougall Jr, Charles Rudolph Hosmer, Louis-Joseph Forget,
Télesphore-Eusèbe Normand, Jean-Baptiste-Amédée Mongenais, Paul-
Étienne Grandbois, and Jean-Baptiste Renaud – for want of capital revoked
the purchase of the Hall properties concluded with Senécal the preceding

year. Through his attorney, Alexandre Louthood, Senécal followed suit with Hall's heirs, thus losing his first payment to them of $250,000 and the interest on a payment of $210,000 which he owed. But despite his disappointments he did not give up, and on 15 February negotiated the purchase of the Radnor ironworks from Hall's heirs for $150,000. On 3 June this contract was renewed until 1 September on other terms but finally expired when the first instalment of $25,000 was not met.

Senécal's three national ventures collapsed for reasons still unknown. In fact, both the transatlantic cable project and the proposed Rouen–Quebec shipping company met the same fate as the General Colonization Company: despite some support in both French and English political circles, Senécal was unable to attract the capital necessary for projects of this magnitude. For 18 months they had claimed much of his time and energy, but had not prevented him from investing in a great many undertakings, such as the Coleraine Mining Company on 11 Oct. 1882, the Magog Textile and Print Company ($10,000) on 2 May 1883, and the Compagnie d'Imprimerie of *La Minerve* the following year. At the time of his death he held securities in the Anglo-Canadian Asbestos Company ($12,738), the Beet Sugar Company of the Province of Quebec ($1,000), the Sovereign Fire Insurance Company of Canada ($1,000), the Canadian Electric Light Company ($40,000), the Grand Trunk Railway of Canada ($500), the Household Fire Extinguisher Company ($2,000), the Megantic Mining Company ($10,000), the Richelieu Paper Manufacturing Company ($5,000), and the Royal Electric Company ($2,000). Various speculations accompanied these investments. On 19 Nov. 1885 he even attempted to return to railway construction, going into partnership with Philippe-Elisée Panneton and Marie-Louise-Alphonsine Giroux, the wife of Télesphore-Eusèbe Normand of Trois-Rivières, in order to build the Saint Lawrence, Lower Laurentian and Saguenay Railway, which would link Saint-Jean-des-Piles to the Quebec and Lake Saint John Railway. Two years later only a 22½-mile section had been built.

Senécal's great interest henceforth was the Richelieu and Ontario Navigation Company. On 13 Feb. 1882 he had been elected president, ousting Hugh Allan, who since 1875 had managed the company with an iron hand and made it one of Canada's largest shipping firms. In 1882 the company, operating between Quebec City and the Great

Lakes, had a paid-up capital of about $1,500,000 and 22 ships. None the less, its earning capacity was decreasing, net profits having dropped from $90,722 in 1880 to $32,682 in 1881. The shareholders' dissatisfaction had served the purpose of Senécal, who aspired to the presidency to realize an ambitious project: to amalgamate the eastern section of the Quebec, Montreal, Ottawa and Occidental Railway with the Richelieu and Ontario Navigation Company to secure a monopoly of transportation on the St Lawrence. He had acquired 559 shares in the company – playing the stock exchange on margin, wrote *La Minerve*, pilfering from the public treasury, said his enemies – had found allies among the groups opposed to Allan, and had succeeded in getting himself elected director and then president.

Senécal's immediate objective was to make the company show a profit. The new board of directors took an inventory of assets, examined the various departments, analysed the books, revised the charges, and signed agreements with rival companies. Thus on 11 March 1882 the Quebec, Montreal, Ottawa and Occidental, of which Senécal was still general superintendent, undertook to pay $2,000 annually to the Richelieu and Ontario Navigation Company, provided the latter agreed to cancel its services to Maskinongé, Louiseville, and Yamachiche. On 16 November a similar agreement, involving a one-week suspension of services to Quebec, was concluded, in return for a payment of $1,000, with the North Shore Railway financial syndicate, which now owned the eastern section of the Quebec, Montreal, Ottawa and Occidental. It was at a meeting on 21 November that Senécal really showed his hand: he persuaded the directors to allow the North Shore Railway syndicate, of which he was also president, to lease the Richelieu and Ontario Navigation Company for 99 years at the rate of $80,000 annually. When the syndicate agreed in December to sell the eastern section of the Quebec, Montreal, Ottawa and Occidental to the Grand Trunk, Senécal abandoned his attempt to unite these two great companies and to monopolize maritime and rail transportation in the St Lawrence region.

The administrative reforms instituted by Senécal in the operations of the Richelieu and Ontario Navigation Company did, however, begin to bear fruit. To the great satisfaction of the shareholders, profits rose to $85,806 in 1882 and the board of directors succeeded in reducing the operating costs by $24,000. During 1883 the company continued its cost-cutting policy, reducing staff and salaries wherever possible. Sorel became the sole "depot of the fleet," where the ships were laid up in winter and repaired. Moreover, efforts were made to eliminate rivals, or at least to reduce their number. By managing to place three of its directors, including Senécal, in the head office of the rival Lake St Francis Railway and Navigation Company, the Richelieu and Ontario extended its control.

Absorbed by his great international projects, Senécal was often absent during 1883, missing 26 of the 54 meetings of the board of directors of the Richelieu and Ontario. Subsequently he attended with greater regularity and used his energy to thwart its numerous competitors. In February 1885, in order to consolidate the firm's position in the western section of its territory, he signed an agreement with the Rome, Waterton and Ogdensburg Railway Company, whose terminus was at Cape Vincent, N.Y. By its terms, the Richelieu and Ontario was to provide a marine link between this terminus and Montreal, Toronto, and even Niagara Falls, Ont., on an agreed timetable and rates. It thus effectively excluded its competitors from a large part of the traffic in goods originating in New York State.

In 1886 the Richelieu and Ontario became interested in the Longueuil Navigation Company and the Laprairie Navigation Company among others, and on 5 February the directors authorized Senécal to increase their company's capital by $200,000 in order to acquire these two transportation companies. During the same year the Saguenay River circuit, operated by the St Lawrence Steam Navigation Company, was made over to the Richelieu and Ontario for nearly $200,000, with the guarantee that no other link would be set up by the former in the same sector or in any other sector served by the purchaser.

Thus, thanks to Senécal's aggressive policy, the prestige, profitability, and ascendancy of the Richelieu and Ontario Navigation Company increased greatly. His activity with this company also brought him personal advantages. Through the support of a number of members appointed to the board by virtue of shares which he had assigned to them, Senécal had made sure he had control of the company. It is not altogether clear how he proposed to utilize this power, but the inventory of his assets at his death shows that he had begun to use the company's funds for his own purposes and owed it $17,115.

Senécal was, however, beginning to feel the wear and tear of the

years and in the autumn of 1886 he was forced to stay away from the
board meetings on his doctor's orders. His friend Chapleau insisted on his
being appointed to the Senate, an honour which he had been denied in
1883. Sir John A. Macdonald allowed himself to be persuaded this time
and on 25 Jan. 1887 invited Senécal to take the place of Louis-Rodrigue
Masson. It was the last token of appreciation offered to him by the Conservative party he had served so well. Stricken with paralysis at the beginning of October, Senécal passed away on 11 Oct. 1887 at his mansion on
Rue Dubord in Montreal. His estate was left in extreme confusion. The
notaries valued his assets at approximately $514,280, not counting his
share in the Saint Lawrence, Lower Laurentian and Saguenay Railway;
his liabilities, amounting to $700,000, included a gift of $50,000 to
each of his two daughters. The inventory also mentions other assets of
$800,000 from legal actions still in process, such as his $250,000 suit
against the *Mail* and another of $100,000 against Laurier.

To follow Senécal's career is to describe in detail the fluctuations in
the state of Quebec's economy during the second half of the 19th century. In 1850, when he was about 20, he had already begun to speculate
in grain and lumber, and then to trade in them; by the end of his life he
had become the most important French Canadian capitalist of his time.
In the mid 19th century, trade in merchandise was an important source
of profit, a situation he was able to exploit to the full. From the outset he
applied himself rigorously (even in a scandalous and dishonest fashion,
his critics alleged) to the accumulation of capital, in order steadily to
enlarge his participation in a given economic sector or to launch into
other promising fields. With capital amassed as a local merchant, Senécal
broke into shipping, thanks in particular to the purchase of boats, shipbuilding, the rental of barges, and dredging. Continuing to expand his
interests, he turned to lumber manufacture and trade, as well as to land
speculation, in the end becoming an important landowner.

Despite his three bankruptcies, a consequence of too rapid an economic ascent, Senécal displayed cleverness and foresight, temporarily
slowing down his activity and then, at the beginning of the 1870s,
venturing into railway construction, an expanding field of considerable
promise. At that time, by coordinating his economic and political efforts,
he made an important place for himself in this sector of activity. His
administrative participation in the Quebec, Montreal, Ottawa and Occi-

dental, as well as in the North Shore Railway Company, placed him at the nerve centre of Quebec's railway system, a position from which he was well able to derive personal profit. The projected monopoly in shipping through the Richelieu and Ontario Navigation Company, at the beginning of the 1880s, shows the extent to which he had succeeded in asserting himself. Moreover, it was in this period that he decided to try his luck in business on the international scene. The project of the General Colonization Company alone involved him in a $3,000,000 transaction, but it collapsed for want of investors, causing Senécal enormous losses. Having returned to the national scene, the "capitaine de Pierreville" devoted his attention to the Richelieu and Ontario Navigation Company during the last years of his life.

In a period marked by the extensive growth of trusts in the United States and of large companies like the CPR in Canada, Senécal throughout his career remained an individual capitalist and conducted his affairs in a distinctively personal manner. Disdaining any integrated system of accounting, resorting to innumerable agents, sometimes acting against his own partners, and using for his personal investments the funds of companies for which he was responsible, he managed to conceal his operations from his contemporaries, but nevertheless was unable to gain the confidence of large investors and bankers who were indispensable to the success and continuance of his projects. Because of his complex personality and the aggressive way in which he conducted his affairs, he acquired a controversial and contradictory public image; he was seen on the one hand as a political, monopolistic, and pilfering "boss," and on the other as a patriot incarnating the economic ascent of French Canadians.

Despite the disorganized state of his affairs at his death, Senécal had succeeded in following the changing economic currents of his day better than any of his French Canadian contemporaries. The diversity and significance of the economic activity in which he engaged placed him in the front ranks of Canadian capitalists in the 19th century. Yet, although he was a leading entrepreneur who put a great deal of money to work, Senécal lacked the perspicacity to enable the painstaking bringing to fruition of projects which might have remained important national institutions in the economic development of Quebec.

HÉLÈNE FILTEAU, JEAN HAMELIN, AND JOHN KEYES

Further reading

B. [J.] Young, *Promoters and politicians: the north-shore railways in the history of Quebec, 1854–85* (Toronto, 1978).

Gaétan Gervais, "L'expansion du réseau ferroviaire québécois (1875–1895)" (thèse de PHD, univ. d'Ottawa, 1978).

Alain Gamelin, "La Compagnie des moulins à vapeur de Pierreville, 1866–1906" (mémoire de MA, [univ. du Québec, Trois-Rivières], 1980).

Charles Gill, *Notes historiques sur l'origine de la famille Gill de Saint-François du Lac et Saint-Thomas de Pierreville, et histoire de ma propre famille* (Montréal, 1887).

P.-A. Linteau *et al.*, *Histoire du Québec contemporain* (2v., Montréal, 1979–86), 1 (*De la confédération à la crise (1867–1929)*, 1979).

Joseph Schull, *Laurier: the first Canadian* ([Montreal], 1965).

G. J. J. Tulchinsky, "Une entreprise maritime canadienne-française: la Compagnie du Richelieu, 1845–1854," *Revue d'histoire de l'Amérique française* (Montréal), 26 (1972–73): 559–82.

Section 5

Railwaymen and Network Creators

Sir HUGH ALLAN,

shipping magnate, railway promoter, financier, and capitalist;
b. 29 Sept. 1810 at Saltcoats (Strathclyde), Scotland, second of five
sons of Alexander Allan and Jean Crawford; m. 13 Sept. 1844
Matilda Caroline Smith, and they had nine daughters and four sons;
d. 9 Dec. 1882 at Edinburgh, Scotland, and was buried
27 December in Montreal, Que.

Hugh Allan was born into an Ayrshire family with large shipping interests. From the early 1800s his father and older brother, James, operated vessels on the North Atlantic between Glasgow and the St Lawrence. After a parish-school education in Saltcoats, Hugh at age 13 began working in the family's Greenock counting-house of Allan, Kerr and Company. He immigrated to Montreal in 1826 and clerked with grain merchant William Kerr until 1830, when he embarked on a "grand tour" that included Upper Canada, New York, a return to his native Scotland, and his first visit to London. In April 1831 Hugh returned to Canada and after meeting James Millar, a fellow Ayrshireman who may have acted as Alexander Allan's Montreal agent, became commission agent in Millar's general merchandising firm of Millar, Parlane and Company, one of Montreal's leading importers. Participating in several areas of the firm's operations (including shipping, shipbuilding, and purchasing grain from local merchants), Allan advanced rapidly in the company and, as was so often the case in the Montreal merchant community, the primary catalysts in his success were family connections, social bonds, and access to capital. In 1835 the company was reconstituted as Millar, Edmonstone and Company; Hugh was named a partner and with his father's assistance quickly helped expand the firm's shipping operations. The next year the company acquired the 214-ton barque *Thistle*, the first vessel in what was to become one of the largest merchant fleets on the North Atlantic. Several other vessels, built by Montreal master shipwright E. D. Merritt, were added over the next two years, including the *Alliance*, a 434-ton steamer for the Montreal–Quebec City run, which probably also towed the firm's sailing ships through the difficult Sainte-

Marie current to the Montreal harbour. A large portion of the capital required for this expansion was supplied by mortgages held on these ships by Allan's father and brothers in Scotland.

Most of the early ships, such as the *Gypsy, Blonde,* and *Brunette,* were ocean-going but Allan, recognizing the advantages of uniting river and ocean transportation, began building small schooners for use on the St Lawrence: with this dual capacity and the general improvement in the St Lawrence valley economy the company's business expanded rapidly. By the mid 1840s the firm controlled 5 to 12 per cent of the total ocean-going trade of Montreal, bringing trade items such as pig-iron and soap from Glasgow and carrying Canadian wheat to British markets. The addition of the *Albion, Caledonia, Montreal, Amy Anne, Toronto, Canada,* and *Favourite* to the fleet for both river and overseas traffic gave Edmonstone, Allan and Company (as the firm was renamed in 1839) the largest shipping capacity of any Montreal-based firm. In 1848 it had a capital of £30–40,000 and two years later was described by a credit-rating service as an "old safe & [respectable] House." Its business increased by 25 per cent in 1851 and it maintained a network of agents as far west as Brantford and London in Canada West into the 1850s. By 1859 Edmonstone, Allan and Company, "one of the Wealthiest concerns in the Province," was known for its responsible management, its links to trading houses in London, Liverpool, and Glasgow, and the spreading of its owners' influence into allied shipping, railway, and banking concerns: it was "as good as a Bank," and run by "active, pushing" men. The firm continued as one segment of the intricate shipping interests of the Allan family and in April 1863 became H. and A. Allan.

Even by the early 1850s Allan's shipping ambitions had been outstripping those of William Edmonstone, his older partner. As president of the Montreal Board of Trade (1851–54), Allan advocated the establishment of a government-subsidized, regular steamship line between Montreal and British ports. Such an enterprise, he argued, would not only provide regular mail service but would also benefit Canada by increasing the number of immigrants and by protecting her exports and imports which many contemporaries believed were threatened by the American Drawback Laws of 1845–46. The deepening of the St Lawrence ship channel through Lac Saint-Pierre to 16 feet in 1853 made possible the inauguration of this service. But, though Allan took the initiative as official head of the Montreal business community and personally as an entrepreneur, there was keen competition. Samuel Cunard expressed interest, as did a consortium formed in 1852 (including Thomas Ryan, Luther Hamilton Holton, and James Blackwood Greenshields of Montreal along with the Liverpool firm of McKean, McLarty and Lamont). At the same time, expecting to secure the contract, Allan raised capital from his family (including his younger brother Andrew) and Canadian investors such as George Burns Symes, William Edmonstone, Sir George Simpson, William Dow, John Gordon McKenzie, Robert Anderson, and John Watkins, and formed a rival syndicate. Despite its Canadian investors, the syndicate was an international enterprise based on careful family management on both sides of the Atlantic: Andrew had immigrated to Montreal in 1839 to join Hugh while two other brothers, James and Bryce, handled business in Greenock and Liverpool. Despite Allan's lobbying and his powerful position in the Montreal commercial élite, the rival consortium, incorporated as the Canadian Steam Navigation Company in 1853, was awarded the first government subsidy of £24,000 for the Montreal–Liverpool run, which began that year. The shortcomings of this firm were obvious almost immediately, however, and Allan decided to utilize new technology (steam, screw propellors, and iron hulls) in his continuing attempt to capture the contract. Instead of building ships in Canada as Edmonstone, Allan and Company had done in the 1840s, Allan's syndicate commissioned two fast and powerful steamers, the *Canadian* and the *Indian*, from Clyde shipbuilders late in 1853. On 18 Dec. 1854 the syndicate was incorporated as the Montreal Ocean Steamship Company and in 1856, with the help of Conservative politicians such as John Rose, George-Étienne Cartier, and Lewis Thomas Drummond, it finally secured the contract, and the £24,000 subsidy, to provide regular fortnightly steamship service between Montreal and Liverpool during the summer season and between Portland, Maine, and Liverpool from November to May. By 1859 service was on a weekly basis and Allan reported his capital investment in the company at £3,500,000.

Since much of his profit depended on improved navigation facilities, direct subsidies, and troop-carrying, as well as mail and other government contracts, Allan was assiduous in pampering Canadian and British officials. For example, a former troop-carrier, the *Sarmatian*, was refit-

ted to carry John George Edward Henry Douglas Sutherland Campbell, Marquess of Lorne, and his wife, Princess Louise Caroline Alberta,
Duchess of Saxony, to Canada in 1878. With 25 servants and a special
piano, the royal party of 14 was lodged in staterooms decorated with
blue silk, the royal arms, and self-adjusting mahogany beds in which
seasickness was "rendered impossible, the bed adjusting itself to every
motion of the vessel, so that its pitch and roll cannot be felt."

Royalty was of course only the cream of Allan's business; his ships
also carried immigrants, troops, the mail, wheat, and general cargo. Like
most shippers to Britain, Allan profited from that country's wars in Africa and the Crimea. In 1862 the British secretary for war, Sir George
Cornewall Lewis, brought suit against Allan for "exorbitant" and "enormous" charges in conveying military baggage at rates at least five times
those of other carriers. Allan responded in a "rough" and "overbearing"
manner, seizing the baggage until the case was settled. The transport of
immigrants was a company specialty. In the 1850s for a fare of £3 10s.
passengers travelled in steerage and provided their own food, although
like most companies Allan's carried "a good supply of biscuits." By the
1870s the Montreal Ocean Steamship Company (popularly known as
the Allan Line) had a government contract for the conveyance of "assisted passengers." The firm's promotional literature noted that indigent
passengers would receive free Grand Trunk rail passes from the government and assured immigrants that "Canada is a cheap place to live in"
where even the poorest could have "the confident hope" of becoming
a landowner. The captains guaranteed a "religious, sober but cheerful
atmosphere" on their ships, and female steerage passengers were provided with stewardesses and assured of the strict separation of the sexes.
Less reassuring were the company's six-shilling "steerage passenger kit,"
which included "a patent life-preserving pillow," and the fact that death
regularly occurred among passengers.

As Allan's transatlantic trade in immigrants, manufactured goods,
and natural resources expanded he was forced to look to North American railways: an ambitious steamship-fleet owner preferred not to leave
major supply routes to the vagaries of competition. Although by the early 1870s Allan had become Canada's most flamboyant railway entrepreneur, he had moved slowly into railways. He had stock in the Champlain
and St Lawrence Railroad in 1851 and lost heavily in Detroit and Mil-

waukee Railway stock, but he was not an important promoter until the significance of the Grand Trunk Railway's monopoly became apparent.

In 1859, when the Victoria Bridge opened in Montreal for through traffic from Canada West to Portland, Allan and the Grand Trunk made a ten-year traffic arrangement. His steamers were soon dependent upon Grand Trunk deliveries: 1,304 of 1,885 freight-car loads shipped by Allan from Portland in 1873 came from the American Midwest via the Grand Trunk. Allan was frustrated by this dependence. He wanted the Grand Trunk to triple its winter deliveries to Portland to 35,000 tons and to coordinate freight arrivals with the departures of his steamers. He also felt threatened by the railway's arrangements with competing New York and Boston shippers and by rumours that it planned to establish its own steamship line. Worried about access to his western hinterland, Allan in 1873 expressed "a desire to protect ourselves."

Coinciding with Allan's disenchantment with the Grand Trunk was the Canadian government's commitment to build a railway to British Columbia. By 1870 his lieutenants had appeared on railway boards with charters to build west. Constructing its line west from Ottawa, the Canada Central Railway had Allan's lawyer, John Joseph Caldwell Abbott, as its vice-president in 1870. Another of Allan's agents, Louis Beaubien, was the major promoter of the Montreal Northern Colonization Railway of which Allan became president in 1871; purportedly a local railway to transport firewood from the Laurentians to Montreal the road had a flexible charter permitting connections to the Canada Central Railway. Capitalizing on the French Canadian colonization movement and support from priests such as François-Xavier-Antoine Labelle, Allan's railway benefited from generous laws and financial guarantees from the provincial government, municipal subsidies from most communities along the route, and a $1,000,000 subscription from the city of Montreal. For a short period three of Allan's associates (John Hamilton, Abbott, and Beaubien) were directors of the North Shore Railway which was to join Quebec City with Montreal. Allan also owned half the stock in the proposed Ontario and Quebec Railway which would link Toronto and Peterborough to the Ottawa valley line. These railways would funnel trade to the port of Montreal and could be integrated into a major trunk system to the Pacific. He was also on the incorporating boards of two railways in the Maritimes: the Eastern Railway (1870) and the

Northern and Western Railway (1871–72). His experience with government contracts, his connections with prominent Conservatives such as Sir John A. Macdonald, and his reputation as a leading employer and model citizen in Montreal made Hugh Allan, probably Canada's most important capitalist by the 1870s, a logical contender for the Pacific contract.

It was the minister of finance, Francis Hincks, who in August 1871 told Allan that Northern Pacific Railroad backers in the United States led by George William McMullen and Charles Mather Smith were also interested in the Pacific contract. In December Allan signed an agreement with the Americans and began enticing prominent Canadians to support the syndicate he was forming. As usual, his approach was through the pocketbook. He predicted that Charles John Brydges of the Grand Trunk would join for $200,000 worth of stock and David Lewis Macpherson for $250,000. Neither, however, did join and Macpherson, hostile to American involvement, soon established a rival, Toronto-based syndicate. In June 1872 Macpherson's group was incorporated as the Inter-oceanic Railway Company of Canada and Allan's as the Canada Pacific Railway Company.

With a federal election called for the summer of that year Allan had more luck with the politicians. After trying unsuccessfully to unite the Ontario syndicate with Allan's group, Macdonald left Montreal matters in the hands of Cartier and Hincks. Although anti-American and employed as the lawyer for the Grand Trunk, Cartier, in failing health, was forced to accept Allan's terms. Using the influence of his clerical friends, stressing French Canadian nationalism, and alluding to the economic impact of his Montreal Northern Colonization Railway which would have its terminus in Cartier's riding (Montreal East), Allan brought Macdonald's Quebec lieutenant into line. Thomas White, editor of the Montreal *Gazette*, met with Cartier for a three-hour discussion of railway policy, and two city aldermen and four city councillors called on him at home. Five prominent Montrealers including Joseph-Adolphe Chapleau, a rising young Conservative, and Charles-André Leblanc, an old school friend, visited Cartier in Ottawa and urged him to award the Pacific contract to Allan. By 1 July 1872 Allan felt he had won over 27 of Cartier's 45 French Canadian MPs. On 30 July the politician signed an agreement drawn up by Allan and Abbott which acceded to the former's wishes concerning the railway. Nevertheless, despite massive last-minute contributions from Allan, Cartier was defeated in Montreal East.

Although the Conservatives were returned to power, Allan's plans to build the Pacific railway came apart in the months after the election. Macdonald finally forced him to make a clean break with his American backers but the Americans, incensed at being dropped, threatened the prime minister with a public disclosure of their involvement, not only in the railway but also in the Conservative election campaign. Allan was apparently able to mollify them before he embarked for England late in February 1873 in an attempt to raise capital. The crisis seemed over. However, his lack of success with the powerful London financial houses was soon overshadowed by the disaster which was now taking shape at home. The vague yet persistent rumours of scandal that had permeated Montreal for months were about to take concrete form in Ottawa. On 2 April Lucius Seth Huntington rose in the House of Commons to charge that Allan, financed partially by Americans, had purchased control of the western railway by contributing huge sums to the Conservatives. The Pacific Scandal had broken. Allan's damning correspondence with his American backers as well as his financial manipulation of the Conservatives eventually became public knowledge and led to the collapse of the Macdonald government on 5 November. Allan himself had returned from England to testify before the royal commission on the Pacific railway.

The scandal and the subsequent trimming of the project by the government of Alexander Mackenzie ended Allan's involvement in the western road but his interest in other railways continued. Still active as president of the now bankrupt Montreal Northern Colonization Railway, he engineered its takeover by the Quebec government in 1875. He was active in the St Lawrence International Bridge Company and his bank, the Merchants' Bank of Canada, continued to lend money to railways such as the Kingston and Pembroke, the Grand Junction, and the Cobourg, Peterborough and Marmora Railway and Mining Company. Just before his death he participated in three different syndicates, each organized to buy the Quebec, Montreal, Ottawa and Occidental Railway from the Quebec government.

Allan had used some of the same tactics in trying to gain a monopoly of the shipping trade on the St Lawrence. Although himself a shareholder in the Richelieu Company, formed a generation earlier by Montreal and Richelieu valley professional men and merchants, Allan challenged it by establishing the Canadian Navigation Company to operate on the upper St Lawrence and in 1869 by buying two steamers which he threatened to use on the Quebec City–Saguenay run. In return for his promise to divert the steamers elsewhere the Richelieu Company offered him an annual "indemnity" of $4,000 for five years and free wharfage for his vessels at their Quebec City docks. He soon pressured the company on another route by selling a Canadian Navigation Company steamer to the Union Navigation Company (apparently also an Allan operation) for use in competition with the Richelieu Company on the profitable Montreal–Quebec City run: in 1874, after the Richelieu Company had rejected amalgamation with him, Allan sold the Union Navigation Company two more steamers. A year later the Richelieu Company, with its revenues plummeting, was forced to accept amalgamation with the Canadian Navigation Company to form the Richelieu and Ontario Navigation Company. Both Hugh and Andrew Allan were directors of the new company and Hugh was president for six years.

He continued his efforts to minimize competition in the St Lawrence valley. Lengthy negotiations and a sham bankruptcy by the Chambly and Montreal Navigation Company led to its purchase by the Richelieu and Ontario Navigation Company. The St Lawrence Steam Navigation Company, owned by the powerful Molson family, was a more formidable competitor and Allan settled for traffic arrangements with it. In 1879 his friends in the Conservative party, Macdonald and Charles Tupper, arranged for the lowering of government tolls and the removal of boulders near the Richelieu and Ontario's Saint-Lambert docks. Despite mergers, consolidation, and government favours, business was not good and by 1878 the company's dividends had fallen to 2.5 per cent. There had been grumblings in 1876 about Allan's actions as company president, the wide distribution of free passes, the misuse of company funds, and the Allan family's growing monopoly of trade on the St Lawrence. Louis-Adélard Senécal, a well-known Quebec City entrepreneur, received growing support for his plan to incorporate the Richelieu and Ontario Navigation Company and the Quebec, Montreal, Ottawa and Occidental Railway into a new, integrated transportation system in the lower St Lawrence valley. Senécal and his companies quietly bought up

Richelieu and Ontario shares and just a few months before Allan's death succeeded in ousting him from the board.

Hugh Allan displayed an early and persistent interest in banking and credit institutions. While still in his thirties he became a director of the Bank of Montreal and remained on the board for ten years (1847–57). In 1856, in addition to 204 shares in the Bank of Montreal, he had shares worth £8,000 in the Commercial Bank of Canada, £1,000 in the Bank of Upper Canada, and £2,020 in the City Bank of Montreal. He was a director of the Montreal Credit Company (1871), held 100 shares in the Maritime Bank of the Dominion of Canada (1873), and was president of the Provincial Permanent Building Society (1871) which became the Provincial Loan Company in 1875. His most important banking endeavour began when, as a source of capital and to service his financial needs, he established the Merchants' Bank of Canada. Run as a family business, it was chartered in 1861 but did not open until 1864. Allan was routinely elected president until 1877 and then was re-elected president in 1882. Andrew Allan, who was on the board from 1861 to 1883, succeeded his brother as president in 1882 and their brother-in-law, Jackson Rae, was the bank's first cashier. In 1868 Hugh, the bank's largest shareholder, held 2,658 of its 12,176 shares while Andrew had 875 shares. By the late 1870s, however, there were other large shareholders in the bank, such as Robert Anderson whose 5,042 shares held in 1878 exceeded the combined holdings of the Allans.

In its first years the Merchants' Bank was dominated by Hugh Allan, who faithfully attended board meetings to approve bank policy, appointments, and major loans. He handled problems in England and when in Montreal often went to the head office on Saturdays to count the money and supervise the burning of mutilated bills. This was not an idle exercise. In 1868 he discovered a shortfall of $500 in bank funds: seven employees were dismissed and criminal charges were laid against the accountant and head teller. In 1873 the board, which routinely rubber-stamped Allan's decisions before 1877, wired him concerning the bank's biggest liability, the bonds of the Detroit and Milwaukee Railway: "Board approves: do best you can." And two years later it said: "Scheme set forth in [your letter] or any settlement approved by you will be satisfactory."

The Merchants' quickly established a reputation as one of Canada's most aggressive banks. Allan reported immediate and growing profits that averaged 10 per cent of the bank's paid-up capital: $30,502 in the first year of operation, $100,671 in 1867, and $726,120 in 1871. In 1868 the Merchants' took over Kingston's floundering Commercial Bank of Canada. According to Allan, who had been a Commercial Bank shareholder and handled the negotiations, it had liabilities of $1,170,960 and assets of $2,666,680, much of the latter being in stocks and bonds of doubtful value. Allan's offer of one Merchants' share for three Commercial shares was accepted; the takeover gave the Merchants' Bank 17 branches in the important Ontario hinterland and expansion in Ontario was rapid. In Quebec, however, the bank was hesitant to move beyond Montreal; in 1871 it had only two branches in Quebec outside Montreal, but there were 22 Ontario branches, 16 in towns of less than 5,000 inhabitants. By the mid 1870s the bank had opened a branch in London, England, had nine employees in New York, and had built a fine head office of Ohio stone on Montreal's Place d'Armes.

Allan's association with the Merchants' Bank brought benefits beyond special borrowing privileges, profits on shares, and his annual presidential salary ($4,000 in 1874). The bank was part of an expanding, interlocking commercial and industrial empire in which one sector generated business for another. It could be as simple as a $5,000 bill to the bank from Allan's shipping company for transporting Quebec bonds to the bank's London office. His Citizens' Insurance Company of Canada insured the bank's employees and invested $36,000 in its stock. His Montreal Telegraph Company rented space in the bank's Ottawa building, and the Montreal Elevating Company, of which he was a director, was voted overdraft privileges of $3,000 by the Merchants' board. In 1875 a contractor for one of Allan's railways defaulted and brought the Banque Jacques-Cartier to its knees, but the Merchants' helped prop it up with a time extension. Often the benefits to Allan were more direct. In April 1872 he was given 165 shares held by the bank in the Ontario Woollen Company and one month later the board authorized a credit line of $20,000 to the company. In 1876 he borrowed $300,000 from the bank (using his bank stock as collateral) to aid his Vale Coal, Iron and Manufacturing Company. Another of his companies, the Montreal Cotton Company, was given a $50,000 bank advance "on their own paper."

In 1877 the Merchants', by then Canada's second largest bank, nearly collapsed and it became clear that the handsome profits announced annually by Allan had been achieved by carrying losses forward. The bank was further weakened by sloppy inspection procedures and loans administration, over-expansion into small Ontario towns, and heavy losses on the New York gold market and on two major investments. From the Commercial Bank it had inherited Detroit and Milwaukee Railway bonds with a face value of $1,735,350. These bonds matured in 1875 but the bank was unable to redeem them for even 20 per cent of their face value. The bank made another questionable investment in May 1876 when Allan told the board that the bank had bought at par £4,185,333 of a Quebec government bond issue necessitated by the bankruptcy of Allan's Montreal Northern Colonization Railway and its sister project, the North Shore Railway. Faced with the reluctance of British financiers to invest in Canadian securities outside the public sector and the collapse of the province's two most important railway projects, the government had little choice but to raise construction money itself. Although Allan assured a worried bank stockholder that the loan to the province was "mutually advantageous," the bank's London manager reported that it would be "impossible" to place the Quebec bonds on the London market, even at 95 per cent of their face value.

In February 1877 Allan resigned as president because of what he called "absurd rumours" and "senseless" clamour raised by "a few interested Brokers, and by personal enemies of mine." The new president, John Hamilton, moved quickly to save the bank. The Bank of Montreal and the Bank of British North America lent the Merchants' $1,500,000 on the guarantee of the directors' promissory notes, and a new general manager, George Hague, was hired from the Bank of Toronto. He wrote off $113,143 for losses in the Montreal office, $222,611 on branch losses, a $198,704 loss in the New York office, $633,000 in bad debts, $305,196 on the Detroit and Milwaukee bonds, $553,000 on losses in other securities, and $223,991 "from unanticipated difficulties in placing the [Quebec government] loan on the London Stock Exchange." Allan exhibited remarkable resilience by regaining the presidency of the bank in 1882.

His dealings with the Merchants' Bank show how he constructed a complex commercial and industrial empire by constantly expanding his interests. The telegraph was a natural adjunct to his steamship and rail communication. Allan was associated with the Canada Atlantic Cable Company, was president of the Montreal Telegraph Company (1852), and was a director of two American companies, the Troy Telegraph Company and the Western Union Telegraph Company. He was also an early participant in the development of the Canadian telephone industry; in 1878, using lines installed by the Montreal Telegraph Company, he made one of the first Canadian long-distance telephone calls, from Montreal to Princess Louise in Ottawa. Of more importance were the lengthy negotiations of the newly established Bell Telephone Company with Allan, resulting in its purchase of the Montreal Telegraph Company's "telephone plant" for $75,000. Allan was active in other transportation sectors that were directly related to his shipping interests: warehousing, elevator, station, bridge, and tunnel companies. President in 1870 of the Montreal Warehousing Company (established in 1865 to erect sheds and warehouses), which held its board meetings in the offices of the Montreal Ocean Steamship Company, he was also a director of the Montreal Railway Terminus Company (1861), the Canadian Railway Station Company (1871), and the St Lawrence International Bridge Company (1875). As his dealings with the Grand Trunk illustrate, Allan knew the importance of the American Midwest. With prominent Americans James Frederick Joy and Henry Porter Baldwin of Detroit and Nathaniel Thayer of Boston, as well as important Canadian investors such as George Stephen and William McMaster, Allan was on the incorporating board of the Detroit River Tunnel Company in 1870. Five years later, with four Montreal merchants (including his brother Andrew), he chartered the St Lawrence and Chicago Forwarding Company.

Allan also participated in at least five insurance companies. As well as an important source of capital, these companies provided fire and marine-loss protection for his interests. His entry into injury and life insurance for his workers allowed him to recoup a percentage of wages and may have been a reaction to the development of provident societies and other working-class protective organizations. He was associated with three marine insurance companies: he was a founding director of the Marine Mutual Assurance Company of Montreal in 1851, of the Canada Marine Insurance Company in 1868, and 14 years later (with Andrew) of the St Lawrence Marine Insurance Company of Canada. His most important insurance operation, however, was incorporated in 1864 as the Citizens' Insurance and Investment Company (after 1876 as the Citizens' Insurance Company of Canada). Hugh Allan was its first president and Andrew was a perennial member of the board. Citizens' bonded the employees at the Merchants' Bank and provided fire insurance for Hugh's companies. His stevedores on the Montreal docks had one per cent of their pay deducted for compulsory accident insurance with the company, which covered only "on-the-job" injuries and did not apply to sickness. Permanently injured employees received $5 a week, and in the event of death $500 was paid to the family. In 1872 Allan was listed as a director of the Canada Life Assurance Company and was named in the charter of the Manitoba Insurance Company. That same year Andrew was a director of the Confederation Life Association.

Manufacturing in Montreal took off in the period from 1861 to 1881 and Allan was active in organizing capital for dozens of companies in cotton and wool textiles, shoemaking, iron and steel, tobacco, and paper. The vehicle for the increasing concentration of capital was the developing business institution, marked by the separation of management and ownership and by the advent of the stock market. In textile production as in many other instances, Allan had the capital to get in on the ground floor, and he was able to benefit after 1878 from the National Policy. Canadian textile production had risen dramatically between 1861 and 1871, and grew even more sharply after 1878 when the tariff on woollen goods was doubled and the tax on imported cotton increased from 17.5 to 30 per cent. With tariff protection the value of Canadian cotton production tripled in four years to $1,753,500 in 1884. Allan was president of the Cornwall Woollen Manufacturing Company and owned 165 shares in the Ontario Woollen Company. George Stephen – fellow Scot, president of the Bank of Montreal, and the city's leading wholesale merchant – had interested Allan in cotton textiles and the two financiers capitalized on the willingness of Cornwall, Ont., to subsidize textile production. Allan became president of a Cornwall firm, the Canada Cotton Manufacturing Company, in 1872, and was an incorporator of the Stormont Cotton Manufacturing Company Limited eight years later. He had also helped found the Montreal Cotton Company in Valleyfield, Que., in 1874. With dividends of 11 per cent in 1880, 20 per cent in 1881, and 14 per cent in 1882, Montreal Cotton stock sold at a premium of up to 60 per cent in 1881–82.

Profits were high but working conditions in the cotton mills were notorious. Allan, never noted as a model employer, was more concerned with profit than with the welfare of his employees, and his cotton mills were the subject of complaints concerning wages, drinking water, child labour, and industrial accidents. Weavers in the Canada Cotton and Stormont Cotton mills were paid $5 a week in 1888 and a dyer in Cornwall was paid $1.25 a day. In the Montreal mill ten-year-old children worked barefoot through the winter.

Allan took an early interest in the production of iron, steel, and rolling-stock. Impressed by the efforts of Toronto and Hamilton manufacturers to satisfy the Grand Trunk's needs, he and Stephen exhorted Montreal merchants in 1870 to show "enterprise and energy" by investing in the Canada Rolling Stock Company. Allan was also a director of the Canadian Railway Equipment Company (1872) and the Ontario Car Company (1882), and with Peter Redpath and Stephen he owned the Montreal Rolling Mills. Specializing in nails, tacks, and pipe, this company, one of the four largest ironworks in Quebec, declared a 7 per cent dividend in 1878.

The interruption of American tobacco imports during the Civil War had given a boost to tobacco manufacturing in Montreal, and Allan served as president of the Adams Tobacco Company (1882). Pulp and paper was another growth industry, doubling its production twice between 1861 and 1881. Allan was a director of the Canada Paper Company, one of the first industrial companies to be listed on the Montreal Stock Exchange. A cheap labour base, access to capital, and improved transportation systems contributed to the rapid growth of shoemaking in Montreal in the decade 1861–71, the value of production rising from one to nine million dollars. Hides came from the west, tanning was done in Quebec City, and the finished leather was sent to Montreal. Allan was president (1882) of the Canadian Rubber Company of Montreal, one of the oldest shoe and boot makers in Montreal.

Allan was also active in exploiting natural resources such as land, fish, and mining. His interest in western land speculation may have developed from his Pacific railway project and the western operations of the Merchants' Bank. President of the Montreal and Western Land Company, he visited western Canada just a few months before his death in 1882. In that year he was also president of the North-West Cattle

Company and the Canada and Newfoundland Sealing and Fishing Company. An active mining speculator, he was an original shareholder in the Montreal Mining Company founded in 1847. By 1855 the company was plagued with stock manipulation, haphazard bookkeeping, unwarranted dividends, and a debt of £19,340 to the Commercial Bank. In addition, that year the company was implicated in a scandal involving the transfer of 200 shares of stock to John Ross, former attorney general of Canada West and president of the Grand Trunk Railway. Arranged by Cartier, Ross's quick profit of £1,000 was apparently necessary to facilitate the location of a county court-house at the site of a company mine in the Bruce Peninsula. Allan was furious at the deal which had not been entered on the company's books. He denied being the mysterious purchaser of the stock Ross obtained and, after leading an investigation which found "extreme irregularity," he resigned as president. Also associated with the Mulgrave Gold Mining Company, Allan was a director of the Vermont and Canada Marble Company and president of the Thunder Bay Silver Mining Company (1882).

Coal, the primary energy source for steamships, railways, and manufacturing industries, was Allan's most important mining interest. His investment in Nova Scotia's Pictou mines rose rapidly in the 1860s and he was the only Canadian director in 1865 on the founding board of the New York–based Acadian Coal Company. In 1873 he was involved in the establishment of the Vale Coal, Iron and Manufacturing Company. President of the company until his death, he placed the head office in Montreal and used $300,000 of his Merchants' Bank stock as collateral to construct the company's railway, wharf, surface plant, and miners' houses: his son Hugh Montagu Allan later inherited the company presidency. The National Policy again benefited Allan. Its tax of 50 cents a ton on imported coal allowed the Vale Coal Company to retain large Montreal coal consumers such as the North American Glass Company and the New City Gas Company of Montreal (later the Montreal Gas Company).

Allan, in addition to land held by his companies, owned a substantial amount of property himself. By 1872 his holdings included Ravenscrag (his 609,260-square-foot estate on Mount Royal) and the 79,260-square-foot site of his former home on Rue Sainte-Catherine on which stood a dozen stores and a music hall. Aside from his summer estate, Belmere, on Lac Memphrémagog in the Eastern Townships,

Allan, never a gentleman farmer like his brother Andrew, owned at least four properties on the outskirts of Montreal, each in an area of potential urban expansion. He held a 13,637-square-foot site in Hochelaga (now part of Montreal), a village on the eastern limits of the city, where one of his companies, the Montreal Northern Colonization Railway, proposed to locate its terminus and yards, and 30 acres on Côte Sainte-Catherine (now part of Outremont) on the northern extremity of the city. Near the Lachine Canal he held 79 acres himself plus 8 acres owned jointly with Robert James Reekie, with whom he also shared 26 acres in Saint-Henri (now part of Montreal), another potential area for manufacturing expansion. Besides his two residential sites Allan owned three properties within the city of Montreal, including an 11,637-square-foot site in the west-end ward of Saint-Antoine. He held two properties in the business core, a 9,553-square-foot property in the Place d'Armes banking district (probably the site of the Merchants' Bank) and a 26,850-square-foot site on McGill Street where his shipping company had its head office.

Although he was astute in obtaining what he wanted from governments, Allan's political influence was largely behind the scenes. Indeed, he apparently did not consider the act of voting to be of great importance, noting in 1873 that he had voted in only one parliamentary election. He had, however, volunteered for military service in the rebellions of 1837–38, reaching the rank of captain, and in 1849 he was a prominent anti-annexationist. A lifelong Conservative, he directed some $400,000 to the party's federal campaign in 1872 while pursuing the Pacific contract; his lawyer noted that Conservative policies were so favourable to Allan's interests that a contribution three times as large would have been justified. Campaign contributions were only one means of manipulating politicians: George-Étienne Cartier's constituents needed jobs in Allan's proposed railway shops, Francis Hincks's son wanted a position in the bank, and politicians sailed on Allan's ships and danced at his parties.

Controlling Canada's second largest bank increased his political power. The Merchants' Bank made loans to the provinces of Manitoba and Quebec, and to the city of Winnipeg. Favoured politicians were named by head office as solicitors for local branches and ex-finance minister John Rose became the bank's London solicitor. Future prime minister J. J. C. Abbott had a $1,000 annual retainer as the bank's Montreal lawyer in 1866. Sir Charles Tupper and Sir John A. Macdonald became special solicitors for the Winnipeg branch in 1883.

Even more dramatic evidence of the link between the state, politics, and business is provided by politicians who were among the Merchants' debtors. Although John Hillyard Cameron's large debt was the subject of board discussions in February 1870, Macdonald was probably the bank's most prominent debtor and it seems clear that the prime minister granted favours to his creditors. Macdonald and Allan had apparently not corresponded before 1868 when the Merchants' Bank inherited the former's debt of almost $80,000 to the Commercial Bank. Soon after, Allan jogged Macdonald's memory: "when quite convenient I will be glad to receive your proposals for settlement." Before settling his debts Macdonald did his best to cater to Allan. He helped him get favourable provincial legislation from Quebec, informed him of cabinet discussions on lighthouses, and accepted his choice as emigration agent, assuring him that the new agent would be as "friendly as possible" to his steamship operations. In November 1869 Macdonald asked the bank to accept the property held as collateral and his life insurance policies as payment. When the bank accepted these terms he wrote to Allan thanking him for his "kindness" and added that Francis Hincks was at work on banking policy. In February Macdonald apologized for not giving Allan's Montreal Telegraph Company a monopoly on government business; according to Macdonald it was "impolitic" to raise the matter. Despite the Pacific Scandal, the two men remained in touch. Allan wrote to Macdonald in 1878 asking for tariffs on rubber goods, shoes, hose, sewing machines, cottons, woollen goods, coal, and wrought iron.

Allan took a direct approach to what he described as "influencing" newspapers. He expedited European news via his telegraph and steamers to friendly newspapers, and his bank made loans to important publishers such as Georges-Isidore Barthe of Sorel and John Lovell of Montreal. The latter received a loan to publish the *Canada directory*, apparently on the condition that he handle the printing for Allan's telegraph and steamship interests. The Montreal *Gazette* was under Allan's influence for years. Although he sold his share of the paper to Richard and Thomas White in 1870, the new owners remained in debt to him and had a $20,000 "accommodation" at the Merchants' Bank, which also loaned money to their timber operations in Pembroke, Ont. Given this financial link, the *Gazette* usually paid careful tribute to Allan's activities and ideology as it did on 28 July 1871: "We mentioned yesterday a rumour to the effect that Mr. Hugh Allan had been honoured by the Queen in having had conferred upon him a Baronetcy.... That his eminent services in connection with ocean steam navigation have been thus recognized is matter for sincere congratulation among all classes of the people in Canada. No Knight in the Queen's galaxy of Knighthood, has more worthily won his spurs. And it is a subject of honest pride to Canadians that one who has done so much to develop the great interests of the St Lawrence route, has not only reaped the pecuniary rewards which enterprise and indomitable pluck, such as he has shown, richly deserve, but has also been honoured with well merited distinction by his Sovereign." The material basis of the *Gazette's* legitimizing function could hardly have been made more direct than when Allan traded part of the Whites' debt for editorial support. During the 1872 campaign for a $1,000,000 subsidy for his Montreal Northern Colonization Railway, Allan deducted $5,000 from their loan. "Immediately after," his lawyer commented, "we noticed that the advocacy of the *Gazette* was all that could be desired."

Allan also took the direct approach in dealing with Quebec politicians such as Hector-Louis Langevin and Cartier. He subsidized their campaigns, arranged for them to rub shoulders with the British élite, named their friends as company lawyers, and advertised in their newspapers. In return he received charters, favourable legislation, and the repeal of laws he disliked. His interference was blunt and the results usually swift. "Allan has telegraphed wishing the St. Lawrence navigation act repealed," Langevin wired Macdonald. "The Quebec government have promised me it shall be done."

Although a member of a Scottish shipping dynasty Allan never let ethnicity dominate over business sense. Dozens of Scots such as William Dow, George Burns Symes, and John Redpath shared boardrooms with him, but others such as David Lewis Macpherson and John Young never hesitated to sabotage his projects. The latter was perhaps Allan's most persistent opponent. They were members of two competing bourgeois groups in Montreal and their political and economic quarrels spanned a 25-year period. Young, as commissioner of public works, played a major role in blocking Allan's application to provide steamship service between Montreal and Liverpool in the early 1850s. A vociferous Liberal by the late 1860s, Young enraged Allan by attacking public subsidies to his railways and by advocating free trade with the United States. Allan, a manufacturer and protectionist, complained to the prime minister about Young's "annexationist" ideas. In 1873, however, he repaid old debts when the Merchants' Bank refused a $6,000 loan to the bankrupt Young. Nor did he show special leniency to other errant Scottish friends. Isaac Buchanan, a prominent Hamilton wholesaler, railway entrepreneur, and politician, owed Allan's bank $55,000 in 1872. Over a four-year period Buchanan tried, apparently without success, to ease the terms: his wife reminded Allan of their common heritage and Buchanan made courtesy calls to Allan's home and sent condolences on the death of his brother. As his interests spread across the continent Allan chose partners who brought him capital, local or ethnic prestige, political influence, or technical expertise.

Allan was cynical and astute in exploiting the Roman Catholic clergy and French Canadian bourgeoisie. While still a youth he had spent two winters in the villages of Sainte-Rose (now part of Laval) and Sainte-Thérèse where he learned to speak French, and as a young commission agent he had bought grain from French Canadian merchants along the Richelieu River. Publicly he was a model of tolerance: "I assure you, to whatever nationality you may belong, you will have full justice in everything I have to do with; I know nothing of nationality; I am desirous of getting the best man in the best places and of giving everybody fairplay." With the means and the power to placate, manipulate, or, if necessary, discipline his allies in the local French Canadian élite, he also knew which pockets to line and which priests to pamper, his aim being, he explained to an American colleague, to show French Canadians where "their true interest lay." When in 1871 he bought the controlling interest in and became president of the Montreal Northern Colonization Railway, an enterprise with important nationalist overtones, he went "to the country through which the road would pass, and called on many of the inhabitants. I visited the priests, and made friends of them, and I employed agents to go amongst the principal people and talk it up. I then began to hold public meetings, and attended to them myself, making frequent speeches in French...."

Allan cultivated leading French Canadian clergymen. In 1870 he authorized a special stop of a company steamer for Louis-François Laflèche, the new bishop of Trois-Rivières, permitting him to disembark in his own diocese on his return from Rome. Prominent Catholic laymen such as Louis Beaubien were named to his boardrooms; Joseph-Édouard Lefebvre de Bellefeuille, a leading Ultramontane and friend of Bishop Ignace Bourget, was secretary in several of his companies. François-Xavier-Antoine Labelle, the amiable curé of Saint-Jérôme who was Allan's favourite cleric, was described by one Quebec editor as "Sir Hugh's right arm." At a dinner held in his honour in February 1872 Allan interrupted toasts to pay tribute to Labelle. In November he invited Labelle to a Ravenscrag ball "for although I do not expect you would dance, and more especially the fast dances, you might like to see it. I expect to have about 500 people at it. Will you come?"

Like many of their English-speaking counterparts, French Canadian opinion-makers showed great respect for Allan. Bishop Bourget freed Labelle from his parish duties so that he could participate in the campaign to raise municipal subsidies for one of Allan's railways. In 1871 the bishop's newspaper, Le Nouveau Monde, praised the Montreal Northern Colonization Railway as "une œuvre nationale" and endorsed Allan's efforts to deepen the St Lawrence shipping channel and to build a new bridge over the river. Le National, founded in 1872 by Montreal Liberals, also supported his Pacific railway scheme and the $1,000,000 municipal subsidy which he sought from the city. Le Journal de Québec described him as "le chevalier de Ravenscrag" and La Minerve felt that his presence on a railway board gave "a moral guarantee."

But Allan was never free from criticism. The working conditions in his factories, his manipulation of government subsidies and policies, and his attempts to establish monopolies and purchase politicians all prompted objections from various elements in society. The most severe attacks, both from his contemporaries and from historians, concern his conduct during the negotiations for the Pacific contract. He was not, however, more corrupt than fellow Canadian businessmen or old political friends such as Cartier or Macdonald. Political payoffs, hidden backers, the use of foreign capital, the manipulation of contracts, and the diverting of public funds for private use were norms of the business morality of the day. The chevalier of Ravenscrag was resented more for his successes than for his methods, and his most powerful opposition generally came not from offended Canadian nationalists but from rivals in Montreal and Toronto. Many of the comments of his detractors, especially those concerning his close ties with French Canadians, were often repeated. "The contest [for the Pacific contract] has been, really, between Ontario and Quebec," a bitter D. L. Macpherson had written to Macdonald in 1872. "Quebec has secured the prize – thanks to *French domination*."

Allan's accumulation of wealth, climaxing in an estate estimated at between six and ten million dollars, enabled him, his family, and his heirs to live in privileged circumstances. The Allans hosted governors general and royalty, had 11 "live-in" domestics in their Montreal residence, and owned a private steam yacht, *Lady of the Lake*, for summer use on Lake Memphrémagog. In 1860 Allan had bought the Simon McTavish estate on the slopes of Mount Royal and over the next three years built Ravenscrag, the mansion which in the opinion of one editorialist surpassed "in size and cost any dwelling-house in Canada, and looks more like one of the castles of the British nobility than anything we have seen here." Designed in Italian Renaissance style by the architectural firm of Hopkins and Wiley, the mansion's 34 rooms included a billiard room, a conservatory, a library, and a ballroom that could accommodate several hundred guests. From the 75-foot tower there was a fine view of the city, the port, and the distant Green Mountains of Vermont.

Little is known of Allan's personality or private life. Apparently a handsome man, he appears in photographs as a short, somewhat stocky individual with a full beard and moustache that offset his mid life baldness. He was a member of the Tandem Club and the Montreal Citizens' Association (1868), an honorary member of the North British Society of Halifax (1871), and president of the St Andrew's Society (1848–50). A curler, presumably of some ability since he was named skip in 1852, he served as president of the Montreal Curling Club in 1846–47 and 1874–75. Described by his minister as a man of "little sentiment" who believed that "religion consisted mainly in a man doing his duty," Allan was accorded accolades and individual honours from the clergy, the military, and the crown: a Montreal-area priest described him as "a new Hercules," he was named a lieutenant in the Montreal 3rd Battalion (1847), and he was knighted by Queen Victoria's own hand in England in 1871.

His philanthropic activities seem restricted for one of his wealth and rank although it is not clear if this was typical of his Montreal peers.

A lifelong Presbyterian, he attended St Gabriel Street Church and later St Andrew's Church. He served as the Presbyterian representative on the board which divided the clergy reserves, and was chairman of the church's temporalities board in the 1870s. He made minor donations, usually through his wife, to the Montreal Ladies' Benevolent Society and the Protestant Orphan Asylum, but his major philanthropic activity was the Montreal Sailors' Institute, of which his brother was president (1872) and of which the Allans were the primary patrons. Hugh did become a lifetime governor of the Montreal Protestant House of Industry and Refuge after making a $500 contribution in 1863, and he was a member of the first board of the Protestant Hospital for the Insane (1881).

In 1882, the year after his wife's death, Allan died of a heart attack while visiting his son-in-law in Edinburgh. The body of the "deceased knight" was returned to Montreal, placed in a highly polished oak coffin with silver handles, and laid out in Ravenscrag. The funeral, held on 27 Dec. 1882, caused the closing of the stock exchange for the afternoon. The hearse, preceded by a squad of city police and a detachment of firemen, was followed by his family; political, commercial, and industrial luminaries; "employees from the manager down to the workers on the wharves"; and some 2,000 citizens. After the service in St Andrew's, Allan was buried beside his wife in the family mausoleum in Mount Royal Cemetery.

It was symbolic that he should die in the land of his birth and be buried with honour in his country of adoption. A member of an important Scots shipping family, he had been trained by his father's colonial associates and, as a young man, promoted to partnership in a prominent Montreal merchant house. His operations were characterized by internationalism: he did business in London, Liverpool, Glasgow, New York, and Chicago; he transferred the ships he purchased from Canada to Scotland; and his Merchants' Bank had some of its most profitable activities in New York. At the same time, able in many instances to exploit both French and English Canadian nationalism, he remained a staunch anti-annexationist. Combining capital, international ties, and a willingness to invest in new forms of transportation, he had built Canada's most important steamship company. He increased his company's power by carefully attending to the protection of markets, soliciting favourable legislation, obtaining subsidies, and limiting competition.

From his shipping base Allan expanded vigorously into the industrial economy which developed after 1860, exploiting Montreal's growing metropolitan strength and widening markets brought by the transportation revolution. With improved technology, the increasingly bureaucratic nature of business, and the revised political structures of confederation, he became one of Canada's first monopoly capitalists. Despite some false starts and without the rationalization of later industrial organization, Allan developed an integrated financial, transportation, and manufacturing empire. His ships carried immigrants, his factories hired them and made the material for their clothes, his land companies sold them land, and his financial agencies insured them and lent them money.

Capital was the key. Perhaps the most knowledgeable Canadian entrepreneur in the use of subsidies and public capital, he could tap both long- and short-term funds from his contacts in commercial banks, savings banks, insurance companies, and mortgage cooperatives. Rather than being just a model Canadian entrepreneur who profited in systematic fashion from the economic opportunities offered by Canada, Allan emphasized the importance of capital – and not management or technical skills – as the central factor in permitting the exploitation of emerging economic sectors in mid 19th-century Canada.

BRIAN YOUNG IN COLLABORATION WITH GERALD J. J. TULCHINSKY

Further reading

T. E. Appleton, *Ravenscrag: the Allan Royal Mail Line* (Toronto, 1974).

H. G. J. Aitken, *The Welland Canal Company: a study in Canadian enterprise* (Cambridge, Mass., 1954).

Pierre Berton, *The national dream: the great railway, 1871–1881* (Toronto and Montreal, 1970).

K. H. O'Rourke and J. G. Williamson, *Globalization and history: the evolution of a nineteenth-century Atlantic economy* (Cambridge, Mass., 1999).

F. C. Bowen, *A century of Atlantic travel, 1830–1930* (Boston, 1930).

JOHN RUDOLPHUS BOOTH,

industrialist; b. 5 April 1827 near Waterloo, Lower Canada,
son of John Booth and Eleanor Rooney (Rowley); m. 7 Jan. 1853
Rosalinda Cooke (d. 1886) in Kingsey township, Lower Canada,
and they had five daughters and three sons;
d. 8 Dec. 1925 in Ottawa.

The second eldest of the five children of an Ulsterman and his wife, John R. Booth was born in the Eastern Townships. Historian William E. Greening reports that as a child he "spent his spare time building miniature mills and bridges along the tiny rivulet that flowed through his father's farm." Whatever his early interests, it was with a modest elementary education that he left home as a youth. He contemplated joining the California gold rush before finding employment with the Central Vermont Railroad, chiefly as a carpenter on bridge projects. He also had some involvement in the construction of a paper mill in Sherbrooke, Lower Canada, and a sawmill near Hull. Upon completion of the latter, its owner, Andrew Leamy, engaged him to manage the operation for a year. He then ran a shingle mill in premises in Hull rented from Alonzo Wright, but within months it was destroyed by fire.

Around 1854 Booth and his wife had moved across the river to Ottawa, where J. R., as he became known, furthered his understanding of the lumber trade and water-power. Having leased Philip Thompson's large sawmill on Chaudière Island, between Hull and Ottawa, which was selected in 1857 as Canada's capital, he tendered successfully in 1859 for a contract to supply lumber and timber for the new Parliament Buildings. In harvesting timber for this project, he is credited with introducing horses to replace oxen in skidding logs to water. (The acreage he acquired southwest of Ottawa for pasturing his horses would later become the Dominion Experimental Farm.)

The financial success of the contract, and of a short-lived partnership with American lumberman Albert W. Soper, allowed Booth in 1864 to purchase the Thompson mill and the adjoining mill-lots of Lyman Perkins. More significant, his reputation for reliable performance facilitated his access to additional capital. In 1867, with the backing of the Bank of British North America and on the advice of his cousin Robert R. Booth of Pembroke, he bought the valuable pineries on the Madawaska River previously owned by John Egan. Following this acquisition, which he later described as the basis of his fortune, he joined the effort to construct works to facilitate timber drives, as a founder of the Upper Ottawa Improvement Company, formed in 1868 to build dams, slides, and piers; in 1888 he would become the founding president of the Madawaska Improvement Company Limited. In addition to steadily expanding his milling and driving operations, he had established docks and a lumber storage and distribution centre in 1868 at Rouses Point, N.Y., a planing mill and box factory in 1875 in Burlington, Vt, and a sales office in 1877 in Boston. With these facilities he was said to be "the only Canadian lumberman at the time who manufactured his own lumber in his own American mill."

During the economic downturn of 1874–76 Booth had continued to accumulate timber limits at low prices, thus eliminating his dependence on other suppliers. Eventually covering 640,000 acres, his limits extended throughout the Ottawa watershed, encompassing parts of the Madawaska, Bonnechere, Petawawa, Mattawa, and Montreal rivers in Ontario and the Coulonge, Black (Noire), Dumoine, and Kipawa rivers in Quebec. Montreal lumber merchant and biographer George Arthur Grier has claimed that Booth, an incessant traveller throughout his domain, "knew the forest as a sailor knows the sea, and his success was largely due to the fact that he never overestimated its potentialities." Between 1872 and 1892 his manufacture of lumber increased from approximately 30 million board feet to 140 million, an expansion that made his operations the largest in the world. Booth's output of 115 million feet in 1896 was more than double that of any other major Ottawa valley firm, including McLachlin Brothers of Arnprior and Bronsons and Weston of Ottawa; by 1900 all of the coastal mills in British Columbia were producing only 100 million feet annually.

As a natural extension of milling, Booth's operations had grown to include a far-reaching transportation network. His involvement with forming and financing the Canada Atlantic Railway in 1879 had drawn him into construction when the original proponents were unable to complete the project. He embraced this new phase of his career with enthusiasm. Railways offered his lumber business three major advantages: reduced labour costs on timber drives, freedom from the seasonal constraints on shipping, and speed. In 1882 Booth completed the 136-mile linkage of the CAR between Ottawa and Coteau-Landing on the St Lawrence, from which point the line eventually secured access to the Central Vermont; initially, the crossing had to be done by barge, but in 1890 this interruption was eliminated by the opening of a railway bridge across the river. To link the pinelands of Georgian Bay, his own upper limits, and the Ottawa River, Booth had started in 1884–86 with a small railway connecting lakes Nipissing and Nosbonsing. Next, the Ottawa, Arnprior and Renfrew and Ottawa and Parry Sound railways were chartered in 1888 and amalgamated in 1891 as the Ottawa, Arnprior and Parry Sound Railway, which was built in 1892–96. During construction, in 1893 Booth successfully disputed the rights to a strategically important pass near Wilno, which the rival Canadian Pacific had also claimed, and he sought to influence the southern boundary of the newly created Algonquin Park to avoid conflict with his line. (In the end, it ran through the park and Booth secured limits there.) Apart from the advantage the OAPS offered Booth in the lumber trade, for others the route cut 800 miles off the journey from Chicago to Montreal, with mile-a-minute service along the Ottawa–Montreal segment. To secure even more traffic, especially grain, Booth established elevators at Depot Harbour near Parry Sound, as well as at Duluth, Milwaukee, and Coteau-Landing. He eventually added a small fleet of ships to what was recognized as the largest privately owned railway in the world. The OAPS was merged in 1899 into the Canada Atlantic, and in 1904 Booth sold it for $14 million to the Grand Trunk, which he served as a director until it became part of the Canadian National system.

The empire of J. R. Booth was constantly susceptible to devastation by fire, in the bush, on his railways, and at the Chaudière. His mills were severely damaged in 1893 and again in 1894, when, not surprisingly, he needed 20 British, 5 American, and 3 Canadian firms to underwrite his insurance. In 1895 his Burlington facility was gutted. The disastrous fire of 1900 that cut through Hull and Ottawa caused Booth losses estimated at between one and one and a half million dollars. A major fire in 1903 consumed 10 million feet of lumber, 8 railway cars, and numerous buildings and nearby homes. On the occasion of a conflagration at his mill in September 1913, the second in a week, his son and superintendent, Charles Jackson, discounted the likelihood of arson: the fire, he told the *Ottawa Evening Journal,* appeared "to be just one of those things which visit such plants periodically." The risk had become such a concern to Ottawa's residents and city council, however, that there was considerable resistance in 1917 to J. R. Booth's use of a river-lot at the end of Bronson Avenue for storage. It was the government's need for the property to house a new heating plant for the Parliament Buildings that pushed Booth's mountains of lumber out of Ottawa.

With vast timber resources at his disposal, Booth's concepts of conservation were largely defined in terms of controlling bush fires, which he usually blamed on settlers and prospectors. At the same time his mills attracted attention as concern mounted over the effect of sawdust, trimmings, and other waste on navigation and fisheries. Following the passage of federal legislation in 1873 that prohibited dumping in water, Booth was convicted and fined. Despite a vigorous legal campaign begun against him and other owners in 1885 by Antoine Ratté, an Ottawa wharfinger and boatbuilder whose business suffered from mill refuse, Booth declined to alter his practices until early in the 20th century. He complied, it appears, only because a fire that destroyed much of his plant provided an opportunity to introduce new procedures to eliminate dumping directly into the water.

Beginning in the 1850s, the periodic public examinations of the crown's water rights and works at the Chaudière, including Albert and Victoria islands, had become matters of consequence to the industrial complexes concentrated there. Crown reviews led to legal adjustments to Booth's ownership in 1889 and 1901. His interests stood to be affected too by Quebec's grant to private hands of 31 acres of river-bed, which figured prominently in the complex legal preparations begun in 1900 by Æmilius Irving and others for a reference to the Supreme Court of Canada over jurisdiction and the exact location of the Ontario–Quebec boundary. In February 1903 a perplexed *Ottawa Citizen* asked "Who owns the river?" The matter was no clearer in 1905 when Ezra Butler Eddy of Hull took Booth to court over water diversion.

As the traditional lumber trade approached its zenith – the final raft of squared timber would be taken down the Ottawa by Booth's men in 1908 – Booth embarked upon a number of new ventures. Following a fire at McKay Milling at the Chaudière, he purchased the site for pulp production, a sector pioneered by Eddy. Constructed in 1905, the new plant let him make more effective use of the large quantities of softwood he had previously been forced to sell. Also in 1905, his winning bid for the 1,700-square-mile concession of the Montreal River Pulp Company allowed him the convenience of cutting both pulpwood and pine in the same limits. With 26 grinders, the ground-wood section of Booth's mill was capable of a daily production of 182 tons; four digesters provided 30 more of sulphite pulp. Upon encountering difficulties in disposing of his pulp, Booth entered the papermaking business with a mill that put out some 150 tons of newsprint daily. Other new undertakings were purely speculative. In association with Michael John O'Brien, for instance, Booth used the Dominion Nickel-Copper Company to consolidate mineral properties in the Sudbury area. These holdings, which the principals never intended to develop, would be sold in 1915 to the British America Nickel Corporation, a syndicate organized by Frederick Stark Pearson. Booth's ventureship was also evident in his board positions, including directorships in Foster-Cobalt Mining (1907) and Canada Cement (1909).

By all accounts Booth, a short man with a white beard and unfading physical vitality, was a picturesque figure, though his rough language, disdain for publicity, and plain dress put him, according to Sandra Gwyn, "decidedly beyond the pale" in Ottawa society. Still, his commercial stature commanded attention. Even late in life, he was renowned for his memory, his detailed knowledge of plant operations, and his direct participation in virtually every aspect of his firm, an involvement that periodically led to injury. There are any number of stories about visitors who eventually located him in his lumber yards or at building sites. One typical legend credits him with identifying a new horse on the day of its arrival at his mill, despite the fact that about 500 horses worked in his yards and woods. Not until 1921, during a trade slump and when Booth was 93, did he convert his operation from a sole proprietorship to John R. Booth Limited.

His managerial style was captured by Charles Christopher Jenkins in *Maclean's* (Toronto) in 1922: "So far as one can learn, John R. Booth has never encouraged initiative or originality in those he has hired as executives, a failing which seemingly has not debarred him from becom-

ing one of the wealthiest and mightiest masters of industry in Canada."
More recently, archivist Neil Forsyth has portrayed Booth as "autocratic
in the extreme; employees did what they were told or departed." In testimony to the royal commission on the relations of labour and capital in
1889, Booth frankly professed no knowledge of regulations under the
Ontario Factories' Act. Writer Doris French has characterized his association with labour as "old-fashioned and feudal"; no model employer,
J. R. knew that his workforce was transient, seasonal, and traditionally
resistant to organization. He was a leading figure in opposing a general strike that affected his Burlington mill. In 1891 Booth and eight
other owners were hit with a massive, prolonged strike by Chaudière
millworkers over subsistence wages and 11- or 12-hour days, an action
eventually led by the Knights of Labor. The call-up of police and the
militia probably had Booth's approval if not his active encouragement.
In a strike in 1918 unionized paper-mill workers in Ottawa demanded increased wages from Booth or a public investigation, but he flatly
refused any concession; they struck again in 1921.

There were, of course, paternalistic exceptions in Booth's treatment
of labour. During a strike at the Grand Trunk that shut down his mills
in July 1910 and put 2,000 men out of work, he paid his employees
full wages for their lost time. In the somewhat misleading words of the
Citizen, "By one of the most generous acts in a long career of charitable
deeds and looking after the best interests of his many employees, Mr.
Booth had again shown the men that he was one of them." He has also
been credited with introducing the eight-hour day to the forest industries of the Ottawa valley in 1911 on his own initiative.

Although there is some indication that Prime Minister Sir Charles
Tupper may have attempted to recruit him as a Conservative candidate
in May 1896, Booth was by no means prominent politically. He usually devoted such time as he cared to allocate to public affairs to matters
directly related to his industrial concerns. As a papermaker, for example,
he joined ranks with Charles Christopher (Carl) Riordon, E. B. Eddy,
and others to campaign for prohibitions on the export of unmanufac-
tured pulpwood to the United States, and he successfully lobbied for
cutting rights to birch in Algonquin Park. Only in opposition to Sir Wilfrid Laurier's advocacy of reciprocity in the federal contest of 1911 did
he appear to take an active role in the electoral process.

In Ottawa, Booth, a Presbyterian, quietly made substantial financial contributions to community projects, including the Young Men's Christian Association building and St Luke's Hospital, which he helped found in 1897 and endowed in 1914 with a new wing. Described as "a believer in and a generous patron of clean, manly sport," he was a member of the Ottawa Amateur Athletic Club and the Ottawa Rowing Club. In 1903 he was named honorary president of the Canadian Reading Camps Association, which distributed literature to and promoted night schools in lumber and mining camps. At the time of World War I, he made the largest donation to purchase equipment for the No. 1 Automobile Machine-Gun Brigade.

By the time he was in his nineties, Booth had achieved a reputation of legendary proportions tinged with the romance of the northern woods, even though by 1919 his production was being eclipsed by W. C. Edwards and Company Limited and others. On 27 March 1920, in a rare public appearance and to a "rousing ovation," Booth dropped the puck for a Stanley Cup match between the Ottawa Senators and the Seattle Metropolitans. Within the timber industry he received plaudits as honorary president of the Canadian Lumbermen's Association. Booth's achievements inspired C. C. Jenkins to describe him in 1922 as one of those "men who have transformed the dreamy melody of the living waters into a roaring chant of commercial conquest." In the words of Michael Grattan O'Leary in the *Ottawa Evening Journal* in 1925, the Booth to remember was "not the great magnate whose wealth is the envy of many and the wonder of more; but the great pioneer, the man whose genius and imagination tamed the wilderness ... and, above all, did more than any man of his time to build up this Ottawa Valley." On the occasion of his death in December 1925, following two months of confinement at his Ottawa residence, Prime Minister William Lyon Mackenzie King generously referred to him as "one of the fathers of Canada." Buried beside his wife in Beechwood Cemetery in Ottawa, Booth was survived by his sons Jackson and John Frederick and his daughter Helen Gertrude Fleck.

Booth's fortune was a subject of much speculative commentary during the latter years of his life, with estimates ranging up to $100 million. At the time of the marriage in 1924 of his granddaughter Lois Frances Booth to Prince Erik Christian Frederik Alexander of Denmark, it was rumoured that Booth contributed half of her $4-million dowry. J. R. issued a formal denial. At his death his estate was officially valued at almost $7.7 million; the property was later re-evaluated upwards. Although succession duties exceeding $4 million were paid in 1927, Ontario Premier Mitchell Frederick Hepburn subsequently claimed more and invoked the legislature to overcome the legal obstacles. The heirs eventually paid another $3 million.

Contemporaries often referred to J. R. Booth as a lumber king, the equivalent perhaps of today's media moguls. Booth understood the regional economy of the Ottawa valley and its relationship to international trade as well as or better than any of his peers. Through hard work, resolute determination, and longevity he contributed greatly to the private economy of the government town that Ottawa had become.

JAMIE BENIDICKSON

Further reading

J. R. Trinnell, *J. R. Booth: the life and times of an Ottawa lumberking* (Ottawa, 1998).

Neil Forsyth, "J. R. Booth: career of a lumber baron," *Archivist* (Ottawa), 14 (1987), no.5: 10–11.

Peter Gillis, "Rivers of sawdust: the battle over industrial pollution in Canada, 1865–1903," *Journal of Canadian Studies* (Peterborough, Ont.), 21 (1986–87): 84–103.

J. W. Hughson and C. C. J. Bond, *Hurling down the pine: the story of the Wright, Gilmour and Hughson families, timber and lumber manufacturers for the Hull and Ottawa region and on the Gatineau River, 1800–1920* (2nd ed., Old Chelsea, Que., 1965).

A. R. M. Lower, *Great Britain's woodyard: British America and the timber trade, 1763–1867* (Montreal and London, 1973).

H. V. Nelles, *The politics of development: forests, mines & hydro-electric power in Ontario, 1849–1941* (Toronto, 1974).

Sir ROBERT GILLESPIE REID,

railway contractor; b. 12 Oct. 1842 in Coupar Angus, Scotland,
son of William Robertson Reid and Catherine Gillespie;
m. 17 Aug. 1865 Harriet Duff in Auckland, New Zealand,
and they had three sons and one daughter; d. 3 June 1908
in Montreal.

Robert Reid's father owned a linen mill at Coupar Angus. After leaving school Robert was apprenticed to an uncle, a stonemason at nearby Leys of Hallyburton. He worked as a mason in the area of his home town for a few years, and then emigrated to Australia to prospect for gold in 1865, meeting his future wife during the passage. The gold-rush had passed its peak by this time and Reid found that prospecting was not so lucrative as he had hoped. A partnership to work a claim did not pan out and he turned to practising his trade, finding his skills in demand on public works in New South Wales. Eventually he began working on the construction of stone viaducts in the Blue Mountains there, thus initiating his involvement with railway construction.

Reid returned to Coupar Angus in 1869, presumably to take on some role in the family business, his father having died in 1867. In 1871 he emigrated once again – without his young family – to North America. In all likelihood he was looking for opportunities in railway construction and, although he travelled first to New York, he soon concluded that there was greater promise in Canada, perhaps on the understanding that construction of a transcontinental railway was imminent. He went on to Ottawa, where according to family tradition his first job involved stone work on an extension to the Parliament Buildings. In 1872 he was working on masonry abutments for the Grand Trunk Railway's International Bridge between Fort Erie, Ont., and Buffalo, N.Y., completed in 1873. He brought out his family from Scotland in that year and took up residence in Galt (Cambridge), Ont., where he formed a partnership with the contractor James Isbester. For the next few years, as the "outside man" of Isbester and Reid, he worked on subcontracts with the Grand Trunk in Canada and the United States, and then on bridges along the Ottawa River for the Quebec, Montreal, Ottawa and Occidental Railway.

In the late 1870s Reid moved to the United States, to work in construction of the American trans-continentals. He apparently established his family in California, although for the next five years he was employed chiefly in Texas. In 1880 Reid worked on bridges for the Southern Pacific, including a bridging of the Colorado River at Austin which gave him a reputation for being able to overcome difficult geographical obstacles within budget. In 1882 he subcontracted to build iron and masonry bridges for 250 miles of the International line, west of San Antonio and into Mexico, among them a bridge over the Rio Grande. The next year he finished a railway bridge over the Delaware Water Gap, N.J.–Pa. It is reported that this contract solidified his reputation as a bridge contractor of uncommon ability and especially as a man who stuck to his word. Despite having been brought into the project after work had commenced, and despite being abandoned by the original contractor when it became apparent that the contract would not cover the costs of construction, Reid completed the bridge.

His reputation now established, Reid returned to Canada late in 1883. He had retained at least some connections among Canadian railwaymen, and he may have been actively recruited by the Canadian Pacific Railway. Whatever the case, he was quickly entrusted with some of the CPR's most difficult subcontracts, building bridges along the north shore of Lake Superior. Reid's work would appear to have been exemplary, and it earned him the lasting trust of William Cornelius Van Horne, then vice-president of the CPR, and most especially of Van Horne's assistant Thomas George Shaughnessy, who became a lifelong friend. His achievements included the near-legendary Jackfish Bay section of the line, which necessitated the most difficult network of tunnels and bridges east of the Rockies.

Reid's work commanded respect both for his abilities and for his propriety in financial matters and led to a contract, reputedly without a tender, to work on the Lachine Bridge, near Montreal; it was completed in 1886. By this time he had taken up residence in Montreal. Then, in 1887, Reid began a contract in Ontario to complete the Sudbury branch of the CPR, an 86-mile line from Algoma Mills (Algoma) to Sault Ste Marie. This was a milestone in Reid's career: it was his first contract to construct a railway line and it was the first time he was joined by his eldest son, William Duff, who was increasingly to become the "outside man" for his father. In that year as well he and Isbester undertook to build the foundations of a bridge at Grand Narrows, Cape Breton, and a 46-mile stretch of the Intercolonial Railway between the narrows and Point Tupper, near Port Hawkesbury; both were completed in 1890. Reid contracted the "inflammatory rheumatism" that was to plague him for the rest of his life while standing in Bras d'Or Lake to oversee a critical stage in the construction of the bridge.

Although by 1890 Reid had made a substantial fortune in railway contracting, it is for his work in building the railway across Newfoundland that he is chiefly known. On 16 June that year, as the Grand Narrows Bridge was being completed, he and George Hodgson Middleton signed an agreement with the government of Sir William Vallance Whiteway to take over construction of the main line from Harbour Grace Junction (Whitbourne) to Halls Bay. Reid's involvement was welcomed in Newfoundland since he was personally wealthy and well connected (letters of recommendation had come from Van Horne and engineers Sandford Fleming and Collingwood Schreiber). Construction of the railway had been floundering for nearly a decade: the original contractor had gone into receivership after completing an 84-mile line from St John's to Harbour Grace and the government had constructed a 26-mile branch line to Placentia as a public work.

Reid and Middleton contracted to build the 261 miles from Harbour Grace Junction to Halls Bay within five years for $15,600 per mile – Reid was willing to accept Newfoundland government bonds as payment – and agreed to operate the Placentia branch without subsidy. This project was decidedly the largest that Reid had taken on and the first that he was unable to oversee at every stage. By this time, however, he had a number of trusted employees, many of them Perthshire Scots who had worked under him in Canada. His sons, particularly William (known in Newfoundland as W.D.), also increasingly involved themselves in construction. Reid became, for the first time, the "inside man," based in Montreal. He rarely visited Newfoundland except in the summers and usually wintered in California after 1890.

Although construction was progressing satisfactorily, in May 1892 Reid and Middleton broke their connection for "personal reasons" and Reid agreed to fulfil the contract. As the line neared completion the Whiteway government decided to continue it to Port aux Basques (Channel–Port aux Basques), abandoning the idea of a terminus at Halls Bay. In May 1893 Reid contracted to complete the line – to be known as the Newfoundland Northern and Western Railway – within three years on the same terms, and to operate it for ten years in return for grants of 5,000 acres of land per mile operated.

Early in 1894, 17 members of the House of Assembly were accused under the Corrupt Practices Act and the Whiteway government fell. The ensuing political uncertainty led Reid to suspend construction, since his railway bonds had become unsaleable. The political situation, coupled with several years of poor fisheries and the feeling in world financial markets that Newfoundland had overextended itself in its eagerness to have a railway built, contributed to a bank crash in December.

Reid became more active in the affairs of the colony when it appeared that the government might have to default in the aftermath of these developments. Whiteway returned to power in February 1895, and Reid encouraged a delegation to Ottawa to seek confederation with Canada and also helped bring his bankers, the Bank of Montreal, into Newfoundland to sort out the mess left by the collapse of the banks. His contacts in the Montreal financial community enabled Colonial Secretary Robert Bond to arrange a loan which avoided a default, and construction of the railway resumed in June. As the line approached Port aux Basques in 1897 Reid commissioned the construction of a steamship, the *Bruce*, to connect the Newfoundland with Canadian rail lines, thus beginning his involvement with coastal shipping.

In the spring of 1897 the Whiteway government had begun to anticipate a general election and the completion of the main line, which was sure to bring widespread unemployment. The government then contracted with Reid to build three branch lines. The act authorizing construction also empowered the government to make another contract in order to consolidate the railway system under a single operator. After Whiteway's party lost the election of October 1897, Reid began to negotiate with the new prime minister, James Spearman Winter, and his minister of finance, Alfred Bishop Morine, for an agreement to extend his operating contract beyond 1903. The railway contract of 1898 made provision for Reid to operate the main line for 50 years in return for a further grant of 5,000 acres of land per mile. He also undertook to operate the New-foundland coastal steamer service with a government subsidy and take over operation of – and eventually purchase – the government telegraph line. In return for an immediate payment of $1,000,000 and the future reversion of a portion of Reid's lands the government agreed that after 50 years the railway was to become the property of Reid's successors.

The bill concerning the contract, introduced into the legislature on 28 Feb. 1898, moved quickly and was passed on 15 March. Governor Sir Herbert Harley Murray had at first sought to withhold royal assent but was instructed to sign by British colonial secretary Joseph Chamberlain in a dispatch dated 23 March. However, Chamberlain's instructions also included a strong statement questioning the wisdom of the contract, for local publication: "Practically all the Crown Lands of any value become … the freehold property of a single individual.… Such an abdication by a Government of some of its most important functions is without parallel.… The Colony is divested for ever of any control over or power of influencing its own development." The contract became the more controversial after it was learned in November that finance minister Morine had been on retainer as Reid's solicitor during the negotiations. A significant faction of the Liberal opposition (led by Edward Patrick Morris) had voted for the contract, but Bond, now Liberal leader, was able to use the uproar over Morine's role and the opposition of the Colonial Office to unite his party against the Conservatives.

Early in 1900 Reid and Morine were in London attempting to raise £1,000,000 to develop Reid's properties when the Winter government fell. Upon returning to Newfoundland Reid applied to the new Bond government to have the 1898 contract assigned to a limited liability company, having learned that British financial backing to develop his lands would not be forthcoming as long as the "Reid empire" remained a sole proprietorship. Bond refused. After a November general election in which the Conservatives, led by Morine and financed by Reid, were trounced by Bond's Liberals, Reid agreed to renegotiate the contract. A new one was signed on 22 July 1901. The government resumed full ownership of the railway and telegraph, after paying back Reid's $1,000,000 plus interest, and submitted the question of his losses on the operation of the telegraph to arbitration. Reid also returned 1.5 million acres of land to the crown in exchange for $850,000.

By this time Reid had turned virtually all of the day-to-day management of affairs to his sons – indeed, William had negotiated the 1898 contract while his father wintered in California. In fact, it appears that the impetus for this contract had come in part from Reid's sons, who wished to get out of the railway business and make their own fortunes by exploiting the resources of the Reid lands. The founder remained president of the Reid Newfoundland Company until his death, although he felt the plan to develop its lands had been irretrievably damaged by the renegotiation of the 1898 contract.

From the signing of the 1898 contract Reid ceased to be as favourably regarded in Newfoundland. For the remainder of his life the government was in the hands of Bond, and the premier developed an increasing dislike for the Reids (most particularly William, who schemed to bring about Bond's removal). It seems likely that Reid strongly disapproved of the participation of his son and Morine in the 1904 Conservative election campaign, for he had issued a directive that railway employees were to refrain from becoming involved in politics. Although he was, for the most part, removed from Newfoundland affairs, the Liberals portrayed him as "Czar Reid" and built their popular support at his expense. His residence remained in Montreal, where he was a director of the CPR (after 1903), the Royal Trust Company, and the Bank of Montreal. In 1905 Reid offered to sell all his Newfoundland holdings to the government for $9.5 million, or just his interest in the railway and steamships for $3.5 million, because he felt that animosity towards the Reid Newfoundland Company was making its continued operation of the railway unworkable and hindering the development of its lands. Bond refused to consider the offer.

Reid did not make his customary summer visit to Newfoundland in 1906, his health having deteriorated to the point where he was unable to walk. Knighted in 1907, he made his last visit to Newfoundland that summer. He died of pneumonia at his home in Montreal on 3 June 1908. As his funeral was taking place there on 6 June, shops in St John's were closed for a half hour, and the railway and steamships ceased operation for 15 minutes.

Reid's will directed that his interest in the Reid Newfoundland Company was to be "realized and disposed of as soon as possible" and advised his heirs not to "invest any part of my estate in any new enterprise or in any speculative or Hazardous investments in Newfoundland or elsewhere." His family, however, would continue to operate the Newfoundland railway until 1923, and the Reid Newfoundland Company was to manage the Reid lands until they were purchased by the provincial government in the 1970s.

By all accounts Robert Gillespie Reid was a competent contractor, taciturn and scrupulous in an age when railway contractors were not particularly noted for such qualities. The work for which he is best known, the building of the Newfoundland railway, came after the most active stage of his career had passed. Yet, the line across Newfoundland was very much the achievement of his will and ability. In Newfoundland questionable motives and high-handed political tactics later became associated with the name Reid, but these may be in large part attributed to his sons, and particularly the mercurial William.

Robert Cuff

Further reading

S. T. Cadigan, *Newfoundland and Labrador: a history* (Toronto, 2009), 151–61.

Frank Cramm, "The construction of the Newfoundland Railway, 1875–1898" (MA thesis, Memorial Univ. of Nfld, St John's, 1961).

J. K. Hiller, *The Newfoundland Railway, 1881–1949* (St John's, 1981).

A. R. Penney, *A history of the Newfoundland Railway* (2v., St John's, 1988–90).

Sir WILLIAM CORNELIUS VAN HORNE,

railway builder and official, capitalist, and artist; b. 3 Feb. 1843
near Chelsea (Frankfort), Ill., eldest child of Cornelius Covenhoven
Van Horne, a lawyer and farmer, and Mary Minier Richards;
m. March 1867 Lucy Adaline (Adeleine) Hurd of Joliet, Ill., and
they had two sons, one of whom died in childhood, and a daughter;
d. 11 Sept. 1915 in Montreal and was buried in Joliet.

Dutch ancestors of the Van Horne family came to North America
in the 1630s; William Van Horne's mother was of German and
French-Pennsylvanian stock. The family moved to Joliet in 1851, and
when William was 11 his father died, leaving the family in poor circumstances. William took whatever odd jobs he could find. Among other
tasks, he carried messages for the local telegraph company, where he
learned the basic elements of telegraphy. His formal schooling ended
when, at 14, he was so severely punished for drawing and circulating
some unflattering caricatures of his principal that he never went back.

Van Horne obtained work in the telegraph office of the Illinois Central Railroad. He would change jobs frequently, occupying increasingly
responsible positions and learning everything he could about railway
operations; apparently he could decode telegraphic messages by simply
listening to the clicks rather than recording and reading them. While
working as a freight checker and messenger on the Michigan Central, he
was so impressed when its superintendent arrived in his private car that
he resolved to become a railway superintendent. His mischievous sense
of humour and propensity to play practical jokes, traits that would stay
with him for life, kept pace with this determination. On one of his early
railway jobs he wired a metal plate in the freight yards so that anyone
stepping on it received a mild electric shock. When the shop foreman
became a victim, Van Horne was fired.

In 1862 he became ticket agent at the Joliet office of the Chicago
and Alton Railroad. He rose rapidly in its service, becoming a divisional
superintendent. In 1872 the Chicago and Alton acquired the struggling
St Louis, Kansas City and Northern, and named Van Horne its general

superintendent; he helped make it profitable, but it was sold in 1874. Chicago and Alton officials then appointed him general manager and, in 1877, president of another moribund railway, the Southern Minnesota; under his management it too became productive. In 1878 he took on as well the superintendence of the parent company, the Chicago and Alton. From there he moved two years later to become general superintendent of the larger Chicago, Milwaukee and St Paul.

Van Horne's work brought him into close contact with James Jerome Hill, Minnesota's most aggressive railwayman. In 1880 Hill and his associates, among them George Stephen of Montreal, signed a huge contract with the Canadian government to build the Pacific railway. Two experienced American builders were appointed: Alpheus Beede Stickney as general superintendent of western construction and Thomas Lafayette Rosser as chief engineer. Construction began on 2 May 1881, but it soon became apparent to Hill, the only member of the syndicate who had practical experience building railways, that Stickney and Rosser were unable to organize work in a satisfactory manner. Not only was their progress in construction disappointing, but evidence was also mounting that both of them were engaged in private land speculations detrimental to the interests of the company. Under pressure from Hill, Stickney retired in October 1881. Hill then recommended that Van Horne be obtained to manage the construction of the Canadian Pacific Railway. "I have never met anyone," Hill had written to Stephen a week before Stickney's retirement was announced, "who is better informed in the various departments: Machinery, Cars, Operations, Train Service, Construction and general policy which with untiring energy and a good vigorous body should give us good results." Luring Van Horne from the Chicago, Milwaukee and St Paul had the added advantage of weakening one of Hill's expansion-minded American rivals. Offered one of the highest salaries paid any railway manager, Van Horne accepted; he arrived in Winnipeg on 31 December and began work as general manager on 2 January.

By 1882 parts of the line had been completed. Andrew Onderdonk, another American engineer, had signed or taken over contracts to build some of the most difficult mileage from the Pacific into British Columbia's interior. Van Horne would have responsibility for the construction of three major portions: the section from the end of track in 1881 at Flat

Creek (Oak Lake) in western Manitoba to a juncture with the rails being laid by Onderdonk; the line north of lakes Huron and Superior from Callander, Ont., to Thunder Bay; and gaps in the line between Thunder Bay and Winnipeg.

Shortly after his arrival Van Horne promised that 500 miles of track would be laid on the prairies in 1882, more than any company had ever built in a single year. He regarded speed as essential since the railway's cash and land subsidies were earned only as portions of the line were completed, inspected, and opened. The subsidies paid for trackage on the prairies, where costs were relatively low, were needed to pay for the high anticipated costs of construction in the Rocky Mountains. In addition, the company could expect to carry little through freight, hence its earnings from operations would remain low until the main line was finished. Van Horne believed that the success of the CPR depended on the rapid development of revenue-producing services which only the completed line could offer. In order to avoid serious delays if any of the contractors or subcontractors did not meet their schedules, Van Horne organized a "flying wing" of labourers who, under his control, could swing into action to carry out the work. The American firm of Langdon, Shepard and Company did not lay the promised 500 miles: they completed only 417 miles of main line, although, if branch lines, sidings, and the laying of rails on previously graded roadbeds were included, it was still possible to claim that the full mileage had been built.

Van Horne's experience with Langdon and Shepard was none the less sufficiently strained that they were granted no further contracts. Instead, the somewhat mysterious North American Railway Contracting Company, a shell formed primarily to attract investors and controlled by the CPR, was incorporated in New Jersey. It signed a contract with the railway under which unissued CPR stocks and bonds would be transferred to the new company if it raised the necessary funds and completed the main line. North American immediately hired two construction managers, James Ross for the mountain section from Calgary to the end of Onderdonk's work, and John Ross (no relation) for the section north of Superior. North American, however, failed in its financial arrangements in 1883, forcing the CPR, specifically Van Horne, to become its own contractor. The Rosses retained their positions and quickly negotiated numerous smaller contracts with aspiring Canadian builders. The construction managers at the end of steel had primary responsibility, but as general manager Van Horne, who had transferred his office and residence to Montreal in 1882, vigorously reviewed the contracts and subcontracts to ensure conformity. Changes in locations, specifications, and contractual obligations also required his constant attention.

Tall and massively built, Van Horne was a man of immense physical energy, capable of ferocious drive and Herculean effort. In a crisis he could work exceptionally long hours, sometimes walking or riding by buggy over lengthy distances of rough terrain to visit construction sites. He was, moreover, capable of decisive action. Within a month of taking office he had gathered sufficient evidence regarding Rosser's speculations that he terminated his services. Members of Rosser's engineering staff were also replaced when it was found that some of their plans and profiles, which were of potential use to speculators, had disappeared. In Ontario, where the CPR had absorbed the Canada Central Railway, its contractor, whose progress did not satisfy Van Horne, was replaced by a vigorous protégé, Harry Braithwaite Abbott. Superintendence of the western division was entrusted to the aggressive John Egan, another former Chicago, Milwaukee and St Paul associate, in spite of loud criticisms of his Fenian sympathies. Later, in the mountains, several bad sections could not be completed in time for the driving of the last spike, so Van Horne authorized the construction of temporary track around those spots but refused the compensation demanded by the unfortunate contractors. His actions earned him a reputation as a "Napoleonic master of men," but many contemporary descriptions of him, such as Robert Kirkland Kernighan's account in the *Winnipeg Daily Sun* in 1882 of the "terror" of Flat Creek who "cuffs the first official he comes to just to get his hand in" and whose arrival at the end of steel results in a "dark and bloody tragedy enacted right there," were products of fevered journalistic licence as the CPR was pushed forward.

Van Horne invested little of his own money in the CPR during construction, and his involvement in the financial crises which almost wrecked it in 1883, 1884, and 1885 was largely restricted to expressions of courage and determination when syndicate members and politicians seemed ready to admit defeat. In the early spring of 1885 he was not at the end of track in the Rockies when the company's inability to pay its contractors, and rumours of impending bankruptcy, resulted in a bitter strike. However, he did warn the syndicate repeatedly of the consequences if the pay car was not dispatched, and he sent out numerous tough messages supporting the larger contractors and the North-West Mounted Police who were trying to keep the men at work. Also that spring, when the rebellion led by Louis Riel broke out in the northwest, Van Horne was intimately involved in the arrangements for the movement of troops and supplies over the partially completed line north of Superior. These services earned the company the gratitude of the government and, of greater importance, the subsidies and guarantees needed to complete construction of the main line. On 16 May 1885 the last rail on the Superior section was laid and on 7 November the last spike was driven at Craigellachie, B.C., by Donald Alexander Smith. Van Horne's contribution did not go unrecognized: on 14 May he had been elected to the CPR's board of directors and immediately afterwards he became vice-president as well as general manager.

During construction the directors had made two important decisions, one with Van Horne's concurrence, the other because he and the government insisted on it. The first involved a change to a southerly route across the prairies and through the Rockies, using the Kicking Horse Pass (located by Albert Bowman Rogers) rather than the Yellowhead Pass, originally recommended by Sandford Fleming. This change, for which J. J. Hill bore primary responsibility, was an attempt to guard against the diversion of Canadian traffic to the Northern Pacific Railroad, then a dangerous rival both of the CPR and of the Great Northern system, which Hill and other members of the CPR syndicate were building in the American northwest. The other decision was Van Horne's insistence on the immediate completion of the difficult line north of Superior. The government had stipulated this route as a condition of its contract, but Hill and others on the syndicate wanted to delay and perhaps renegotiate. There was virtually no local traffic on this barren, 1,000-mile section across the Canadian Shield: operations could be profitable only if the section carried large volumes of traffic generated elsewhere. Until it was completed, all of the CPR's construction materials for the west and almost all of its freight had to pass over Hill's St Paul, Minneapolis and Manitoba Railroad. Uncomfortable with this dependence and with his sights set on a strong through traffic, Van Horne vigorously supported the government's determination to have the all-Canadian route finished. At the same time, he recognized the strategic value to the CPR of access to railways south of Superior, in the United States. As president of the CPR, a position he assumed on 7 Aug. 1888 after Stephen retired, he was in a strong position to act on this perception.

Protection of CPR territory was aided considerably by the monopoly provision of the company's charter. Persistent protests from the province of Manitoba forced the federal government to repeal the provision in 1888, but its loss facilitated a new initiative. Van Horne used funds obtained as compensation to complete acquisition of two lines south of the border: the Minneapolis, St Paul and Sault Ste Marie and the Duluth, South Shore and Atlantic. Thereafter, in any freight-rate war with an American railway, the CPR could temporarily avoid its expensive line north of Superior and use the southern lines to fight for traffic to and from the Canadian west and the American northwest. Hill viewed these acquisitions as outright invasion. A number of CPR shareholders still had substantial interests in his American lines and eventually they enforced an accommodation acknowledging the territoriality of both systems. Despite their strong respect for each other, tension between Van Horne and Hill, particularly over control of traffic to Duluth, Minn., would continue throughout Van Horne's presidency and allegedly contribute to his decision to resign.

During the six years Van Horne had served as general manager, his greatest achievement was unquestionably the construction of the CPR's main line and the most urgently needed feeder lines and auxiliary facilities. He maintained firm oversight and control of all major construction and operational matters, but placed trusted managers in key positions and gave them considerable autonomy. Those not enjoying his confidence were given reduced assignments or relieved of their duties.

The fate of several construction managers illustrates his methods. On the mountain section, the work of James Ross demonstrated the continuous accountability and local autonomy central to Van Horne's system. Although there were some sharp disagreements, in which Van Horne's opinion usually but not always prevailed, the two men respected and trusted each other. On the western portion of the Lake Superior section, John Ross was less successful and he never enjoyed Van Horne's complete confidence. Nor did James Worthington, construction manager of the Canada Central, which would become the eastern section of the Superior line. Worthington resigned in May 1884 after a disagreement with Van Horne and in the spring of 1885 John Ross followed suit. Their places went to Harry Abbott. When arranging troop movements during the North-West rebellion, Van Horne worked closely with Abbott, then in charge of the eastern part of the Superior section, but he personally assumed responsibility for most of the arrangements on the western part, where John Ross was still directing work. After completion of the Superior line, Abbott was reassigned, in 1886, to finish and upgrade the main line in British Columbia so that it could be opened for traffic. Other key operating managers appointed by Van Horne included William Whyte, superintendent of the Ontario division until he replaced Egan after that tough, often unpopular officer resigned, and Thomas George Shaughnessy, who had been enticed to leave Van Horne's old road, the Chicago, Milwaukee and St Paul, to become chief purchasing agent of the CPR in 1882. A ruthless auditor, Shaughnessy kept Van Horne informed of all major and potentially troublesome developments, but he also had Van Horne's complete trust to make the necessary and appropriate decisions pertaining to his area. Once the main line was built, Shaughnessy would prove invaluable in the operation of the CPR.

To build up traffic, Van Horne directed the fabrication of increasingly complex systems that integrated agricultural and timber lands, grain elevators, flour mills, port facilities and terminals, maritime fleets, express and telegraph operations, and passenger and tourist services, including large hotels. To publicize the completed CPR, Van Horne, himself an art connoisseur, did not hesitate to turn to professional artists. John Arthur Fraser and Lucius Richard O'Brien, among others, received commissions in the 1880s to execute paintings of the Rockies for promotional exhibitions, and the inspiring photographic work of Alexander Henderson would lead to the formation of a photography department within the CPR in 1892. At the same time, but without the nationalistic/frontier aura of its western drive, Van Horne and the CPR moved steadily to expand in eastern Canada, in direct competition with the established Grand Trunk Railway. In the 1880s the CPR completed a line to Windsor, Ont., with through trains to Chicago, and a series of acquisitions and construction projects was launched to take it across Quebec and Maine to the Maritimes.

By the time Van Horne became president in 1888, the company had survived its greatest financial difficulties. During his presidency it spent enormous sums to improve the main line and to build or acquire branches linking it to the northern prairies and parts of western Manitoba. In eastern Canada links to southwestern Ontario and the Atlantic had been forged. By 1890 the basic system was complete and Van Horne, always an enthusiastic supporter of commercial, industrial, agricultural, and colonization schemes that would generate revenue-producing traffic, reluctantly agreed that the company had built too far in advance of immediate requirements. The country had to be allowed to catch up before more traffic-generating branches were launched or freight rates were lowered. Consequently there was a halt in new construction and stiff resistance by the CPR to any reductions of rates until the volume of traffic increased. This resulted in growing popular resentment of the company's cautious policies, which, many believed, hampered rapid economic growth and development. The desired national expansion came after 1895, and the CPR responded. Van Horne had a leading role in 1896–97 in negotiations with the new Liberal government of Wilfrid Laurier over a subsidy for a line through the Crowsnest Pass into the rich Kootenay mining region of British Columbia, primarily to counter competition from Hill's Great Northern and the Spokane Falls and Northern Railway. These negotiations led not only to construction but also to the historic Crowsnest Pass agreement, passed by parliament in 1897 and instituted the following year, which lowered CPR freight rates over the entire prairies, thus assisting the expansion of agriculture.

Van Horne was a builder, with a grand vision of what western Canada and the CPR could become, and he received much personal recognition, including an honorary KCMG in 1894. (An American citizen, he would acquire naturalized status a year before his death.) But he apparently did not find the day-to-day operations of an established and profitable railway as challenging as construction. Still full of vigour but now forced by bronchitis to spend some time in hot climates, he resigned the presidency on 12 June 1899, at age 56; he would maintain a presence as chairman of the board until 1910 and, to no one's surprise, he became involved in other visionary development projects.

Major steam-railway construction had come to a standstill in the early 1890s in Canada, and even the most successful contractors had had to turn to related fields for work. Many found it in the electrification of street railways; Van Horne was invited to join several of these projects, in Toronto, Montreal, Winnipeg, and Saint John. Personal interest, and a concern that new Canadian urban electrification projects be integrated with CPR freight and passenger services, led to his acceptance, but he would not become dominant in any Canadian street-railway company. Many adventurous Canadian builders extended their street-railway talents to British, Caribbean, and Central and South American cities, hand in hand with such capitalist entrepreneurs as Benjamin Franklin Pearson and Frederick Stark Pearson. Van Horne was involved in projects in Birmingham, England, and in a number of South and Latin American countries, but Canadian interest in electrifying the mule-drawn tramways of Havana, Cuba, became particularly important for him after his resignation in 1899.

Cuba had been convulsed by rebellion against Spain and in 1898 the United States intervened, establishing a temporary military government. In an attempt to block undue pressure from the swarms of promoters and financial buccaneers attracted by this occupation, the American government enacted legislation that prohibited new charters but did not prevent the acquisition of existing ones. Even before the military government was ensconced, three syndicates were vying for control of Havana's tramways. Van Horne, who traced his involvement to an encounter with Cuba's minister in Washington and who knew several key American politicians, was a member of the Canadian consortium, but an American group with stronger links to Washington and the new military government prevailed. The Canadians negotiated a merger with the Americans, and Van Horne became a director of the amalgamated undertaking. His financial commitment, however, was relatively small.

In January 1900 Van Horne paid his first visit to Cuba, where he quickly recognized a much more challenging opportunity: Cuba's steam railways were in need of reorganization and there was no trunk line. His discovery that some railways had been built without charters on privately owned land such as plantations led to the conviction that he could circumvent the law on charters if he acquired land along the proposed trunk route and built pieces of a private line on each section. To make this assemblage possible, the Cuba Company was incorporated in 1900 in New Jersey, with Van Horne as president, and he and his associates together pledged $8 million. Van Horne then began to build, but not without problems. The railway had to cross municipal and provincial roads and it needed access to the business districts of towns and cities. When the necessary permissions or concessions were not forthcoming, Van Horne simply stopped construction, throwing thousands of labourers out of work, and threatened to by-pass the centres. The resulting political pressure, combined with Van Horne's cordial demeanour, invariably produced the required support. Federally owned lands and roads posed greater difficulty since the charter law did not allow the military governor to grant concessions to use or cross such property. Van Horne suggested the brilliant expedient of a revocable permit, under which the railway could build but permission could be revoked when a civilian government took power. No action would ever be likely, however, if the railway maintained good relations with the public and communities derived economic gain.

In addition to the railway, the Cuba Company (renamed the Cuba Railroad Company in 1902) invested in developments designed both to benefit the populace and to generate needed traffic. Large tracts were acquired and opened to settlement under a colonization program devised by Van Horne. In a pattern of development similar to that established for the CPR, sugar mills and plantations, hotels, harbour and wharf facilities, town-sites, and mining and lumbering operations were also acquired or built. One entirely new port, Antilla, was developed in partnership with the United Fruit Company. In Camagüey, where the Cuba Railroad Company had its headquarters and a grand station, former barracks were converted into a luxurious resort, the Hotel Camagüey. Nearby Van Horne established his own hacienda and a large experimental farm, following the example of the 7,000-acre, stock-breeding farm he had set up in East Selkirk, Man. The support given locally to the projects of the Cuba Railroad Company stood in sharp contrast to the hostility elicited by other Latin American ventures with which Van Horne was involved. The electric tramways of Havana, for example, were disliked and Van Horne tried to hide his involvement. When offered the presidency of the Havana Electric Tramway Company, he refused because he feared that it might undermine goodwill toward the Cuba Railroad Company. He nevertheless remained a shareholder and sometimes a "silent managing partner" in numerous unpopular and exploitative ventures.

Although in North America Van Horne was most devoted to the

CPR, he participated and invested in a host of other enterprises. Some companies, notably Canadian Salt, Laurentide Paper, Dominion Iron and Steel, Dominion Steel, North West Land, the Equitable Life Assurance Society of the United States, Royal Trust, and a number of western flour-milling and elevator companies, became quite profitable; other interests, including a sardine-packing plant, a powder factory, and several gold-mining ventures, were failures. Over the years Van Horne was a director of at least 40 companies and he invested in many more. These investments, along with the CPR and his Cuban interests, made him an exceptionally wealthy man and one of Canada's most prominent capitalists. Despite his weak complaints that his purse could not match the resources of some of his CPR associates, Van Horne enjoyed his luxuries, including drink and cards (he could outlast his contemporaries at both). The most visible marks of his affluence were his massive home on Rue Sherbrooke in Montreal; his Cuban estate and Covenhoven, his summer home on Ministers Island, N.B.; and his substantial collection of art. There was, indeed, a refined side to his swaggering railway persona.

A knowledgeable collector of fossils in his youth, Van Horne, after his move to Montreal, began to acquire art in a serious way, as did other CPR builders and financiers. His collection of old Dutch and Flemish masters and important French, English, Spanish, and American painters, which some critics regarded as one of the best in Canada, was assembled in an eclectic manner. He refused to buy any work, no matter how famous or inexpensive, if he did not find it satisfying. His treasures also included one of the best collections in North America of ancient Asian (particularly Japanese) porcelain and pottery. He became an expert on firing and the finish of his specimens, and he laboured for years compiling and illustrating a catalogue of these works, a sizeable portion of which he gave to the Royal Ontario Museum in Toronto. This interest, together with his efforts as president of the CPR to promote increased trade with Japan, earned him a special invitation to visit as a guest of the emperor.

William Van Horne was not only a collector but also an artist in his own right. An excellent violinist who enjoyed playing classical pieces, he is better remembered for his painting. As a child, when he saw a geological textbook that he could not afford, he copied it, illustrations and all. His skill at caricature, which had ended his formal education, found later expression in the sketches of technical and descriptive details that accompanied much of his correspondence. He seemed to have a photographic memory and cherished spontaneity, which he did not believe could be taught in art schools: he usually painted quickly, at night, in a studio in his Montreal mansion. (The artificial lighting sometimes seems to have produced distorted tones in his work.) Although he had ability, critics suggested that his paintings "do not at all adequately express his efficiency or powers, simply because they were too hasty."

Van Horne, like many of those associated with him in Canadian railways, contributed generously to hospitals, art galleries, and public parks. As well, he made more modest donations to a few military and educational causes. Also like his fellow railwaymen, Van Horne was suspicious of most forms of charity. He was willing to invest, and lose, large sums in the development of model farms which would promote better farming methods in western Canada or Cuba, but he did not usually assist the urban mission work done by men such as James Shaver Woodsworth, believing it to be demoralizing in effect and destructive of independence of character. Only the immediate relief of clear cases of distress elicited any support from him.

Van Horne also tried, generally, to avoid involvement in partisan politics, even though railways and other work brought him into frequent contact with political figures. His assessments of politicians were often critical, but he had a high regard for their craft, whether in the form of function, influence, or humbug, and he clearly understood the importance for the CPR of political affiliation. The CPR had been viewed by the Liberals as a Conservative corporation since its creation, and its strong intervention in the federal election of 1891 bolstered this belief. Subsequently, Van Horne attempted discreetly to align his company with the Liberals, and he channelled his efforts through two leading Ontario Liberals in particular, party organizer and MP James David Edgar and journalist John Stephen Willison. Some months before the election of 1896, Edgar told Willison that Van Horne "believes firmly that we are going to win, and he does not lack ability to draw a few conclusions." Almost immediately after the election, which brought Laurier to power, the Crowsnest negotiations began.

On only two important occasions did Van Horne engage in direct partisan combat. The first had come in the late stages of building the

CPR main line, when syndicate members and company officials besieged Ottawa with desperate demands for financial assistance. The second occurred in 1911 when the Laurier government negotiated a reciprocity agreement with the United States. Van Horne believed that industries which had grown up behind the protective National Policy were threatened by reciprocity, and he campaigned aggressively "to bust the damn thing." He was not, however, a doctrinaire protectionist. At other times he strongly supported free trade measures, particularly those that would reduce American tariffs against Cuban sugar.

In late 1913 Van Horne experienced his first "definite illness" in the form of an attack of rheumatism. Humiliated by this condition, he fought it, but by early 1914 he was forced to learn to use crutches. In 1915, during World War I, he was selected by Prime Minister Sir Robert Laird Borden to head a commission on resources, but Van Horne's death on 11 September intervened. A Unitarian funeral service was held at his Montreal home and a special CPR train took his body back to Joliet for burial in Oakwood Cemetery.

Sir William C. Van Horne liked big things: the largest and best locomotives, the biggest salary earned by a North American railway executive, generous (sometimes double) meals, big Cuban cigars, the massive Camagüey hotel, the huge gardens and broad roof of his beloved Covenhoven, the unusually large rooms and high ceilings of his Montreal home, the size of many of his own paintings and most cherished works of art, the grandeur of the Rocky Mountains and the CPR's hotels, his visions of world-wide systems of commercial transportation and trading, and the greatness of the British empire. This passion for bigness, complemented by a usually keen eye for detail, was matched by exceptional energy, vision, and enthusiasm which made it possible for Van Horne to achieve or obtain many of the great things he so prized. His interests were numerous and varied, but construction of the CPR was his greatest contribution to Canada. As a railwayman, he had many rivals. Others were more successful as financiers, promoters, and lobbyists, but none equalled his achievement in the building and operation of integrated systems of railway transportation and economic development, first in Canada and later in Cuba.

THEODORE D. REGEHR

Further reading

Pierre Berton, *The last spike: the great railway, 1881–1885* (Toronto and Montreal, 1971).

J. A. Eagle, *The Canadian Pacific Railway and the development of western Canada, 1896–1914* (Kingston, Ont., 1989).

W. K. Lamb, *History of the Canadian Pacific Railway* (New York and London, 1977).

Sir EDWARD SEABORNE CLOUSTON,

banker; b. 9 May 1849 in Moose Factory (Ont.), son of James Stewart Clouston, a chief trader of the HBC, and Margaret Miles, mixed-blood daughter of Robert Seaborn Miles, a chief factor of the HBC; m. 16 Nov. 1878 Annie Easton in Brockville, Ont., and they had two daughters; d. 23 Nov. 1912 in Montreal.

Educated at the High School of Montreal, Edward Clouston began work for the Hudson's Bay Company in 1864. The following year he became a junior clerk with the Bank of Montreal, an institution in which his father held stock. Shrewd, energetic, exacting, tactful, private, and taciturn, Clouston attracted responsibility. After several years in Brockville, Hamilton, and Montreal as an accountant, in 1875 he was attached to the bank's quarters in London, England, and the following year he joined its office in New York. In 1877 he was recalled to Montreal as assistant inspector.

In Montreal Clouston made the most of his experience and the support of two prominent men who would serve as vice-president and president of the bank, Donald Alexander Smith and George Alexander Drummond. Smith, a friend of Clouston's family, came to view the young man "like his son." Their antecedents in the fur trade were similar and after Smith became Canada's high commissioner in London in 1896 Clouston represented his financial and philanthropic interests in Canada. In 1879 Clouston became assistant manager of the bank's Montreal branch and two years later he was appointed its manager. He was promoted assistant general manager of the entire bank in 1887, acting general manager in 1889, associate general manager in 1890, and finally general manager in 1891. Although his first years as general manager were marked by a number of fluctuations in international finance, shareholders continued to receive their 10 per cent dividend and the bank to consolidate its pre-eminence within Canada and to expand its activities abroad. Clouston held the post of general manager, for which he would eventually receive $35,000 annually, including benefits, until his resignation in December 1911. In 1905 he became a director and vice-president; he would retain these positions until his death in 1912.

Opposed to excessive competition within the Canadian banking community, in 1890 Clouston, along with Byron Edmund Walker, Thomas Fyshe, and others, had organized the resistance of the chartered banks to the federal government's proposed amendments to the Bank Act of 1871. One proposal required chartered banks to establish a circulation redemption fund, the size of which Clouston was able to limit. Having met on three occasions before making representations to the government, the leaders of the chartered banks had become sufficiently well organized to play an unprecedented role in drafting the legislation governing their own conduct. All their charters were renewed and the government's proposed reforms, which had been backed by growing public demand, were emasculated.

The success of the banks' concerted effort led to the foundation of the Canadian Bankers' Association in December 1891. Clouston served a term as president the following year, and then sat on its executive council until he resumed the presidency in 1899, significantly on the eve of the decennial review of the Bank Act. He would retain the presidency until a week before his death. After its federal incorporation in 1900 the Canadian Bankers' Association became a closed shop, with powers to control the redemption fund and to punish members who violated the association's rules; in Clouston's words, it became "an agent of government in administering the Bank Act." According to Gregory P. Marchildon, Clouston became the "most powerful banker" in Canada. His international prestige was such that his advice would be sought by the Indian Currency Committee in 1898.

In January 1893 the Bank of Montreal, then twice the size of its closest Canadian competitor, replaced Baring Brothers and Company and Glyn, Mills, Currie and Company as the Canadian government's agent in London, England. Three years later it also became the government of Quebec's London agent. These lucrative agencies enhanced the Bank of Montreal's international standing (during Clouston's tenure it boasted of being the world's third largest bank) and enabled it to tap and to direct the flow of British capital. They also augmented the bank's influence on government policy; in fact, Clouston came to view his bank as Canada's central bank, and, as Marchildon remarks, his handsome portrait graced "the notes issued by the Bank of Montreal, the country's de facto currency." Although he plied political leaders with advice, his lectures to Prime Minister Sir Wilfrid Laurier on the need to reduce government expenditures, sell the Intercolonial Railway, and cease subsidizing other lines, especially those competing with the bank's major client, the Canadian Pacific Railway, were not successful. Clouston railed frequently and publicly against Ontario premier James Pliny Whitney's promotion of public ownership of the hydroelectricity generated at Niagara Falls.

Under Clouston's direction, the Bank of Montreal expanded, largely through the absorption of existing banks. It acquired the Exchange Bank of Yarmouth in 1903, the People's Bank of Halifax in 1905, and the People's Bank of New Brunswick in 1907, and also assumed the assets of the bankrupt Ontario Bank in 1906 and some of those of the Sovereign Bank of Canada in 1908. Moreover, the Bank of Montreal continued to finance Canadian corporate expansion at home and abroad, especially in hydroelectric power, transportation, lumbering, and metallurgy with clients such as John Rudolphus Booth, Edward Wilkes Rathbun, the Laurentide Paper Company Limited, the Dominion Iron and Steel Company Limited, and the Royal Securities Corporation Limited. In addition, the bank purchased the bonds of American and Quebec railways.

The bank also promoted Canadian corporate interests abroad. In 1895 it became banker to the government of Newfoundland and was thereby committed to financing the Reid Newfoundland Company, founded by Robert Gillespie Reid, and the Dominion Iron and Steel Company Limited's interest in iron ore from Bell Island. The bank became a partisan of the colony's union with Canada.

With access to increasing pools of British capital as well as to technical and managerial expertise Clouston supported the financial cliques from Halifax, Toronto, and Montreal which set up various hydroelectric and traction companies in Latin America and the Caribbean and promoted Canadian investment in those regions. Under his direction the Bank of Montreal helped finance the Mexican Light and Power Company (of which Clouston was a leading shareholder, director, and in 1908–9 president) and its subsidiary, the Mexican Electric Light Company, as well as the Mexico Tramways Company, the Demerara Electric Company, and the Rio de Janeiro Tramway, Light and Power Company.

The line Clouston and his colleagues drew between personal and corporate interests was an uncertain one. His position made him a useful, and often an automatic, corporate director, particularly of companies financed by his bank. Thus, he served as president, vice-president, or director of over 20 prominent firms. Nothing illustrates the potential conflict more dramatically than his involvement in the controversial attempt in 1908 to lease the floundering Mexican Light and Power Company, financed in part by the Bank of Montreal, to the Mexico Tramways Company, in which he had an interest. Normally what Drummond, the bank's president, advised, Clouston endorsed, and vice versa; this issue, however, initially divided the two men, and also the Montreal business community. Clouston subsequently rallied to Drummond's plan for defeating the proposal, but they lost control of Mexican Light to a group of Toronto, British, and American interests.

Although Clouston was reputed to have been a perceptive judge of character, his misguided confidence in the durability of the Mexican dictator, General Porfirio Díaz, and the stability of investments in the republic entailed considerable loss to the bank when Díaz was removed in the revolution of 1911. These losses, together with his handling of the Mexican Light and Power controversy, and his faith in William Maxwell Aitken's financial acumen and support for Aitken's pushing of the Western Canada Cement and Coal Company (owned by Sir Sandford Fleming) into bankruptcy during the great merger which led to the creation of the Canada Cement Company in 1909, may have cost him the presidency of the bank and hastened his retirement. By 1910 he seemed to have lost the confidence of the board of directors. Contrary to public expectations, after five months of deliberation following Drummond's death in February 1910 the board chose Richard Bladworth Angus as president rather than the younger and more qualified Clouston. In November 1911 Clouston submitted his resignation; the public explanation was ill health. In return he received a year's salary, the option of purchasing the general manager's house for $100,000, and a retainer of $15,000 as long as he remained outside the service of another bank.

In civic affairs Clouston supported the formation of the Citizens' League of Montreal and financed its campaign of 1909–10 to obtain a board of control for the city. Two years previously he had joined with other prominent businessmen to improve the city's water supply and to provide more adequate fire protection for commercial property downtown. A vice-president of the Montreal Crematorium Limited and a life governor of the Montreal Protestant House of Industry and Refuge, he was also a benefactor of the Congregation of Notre-Dame, the University Settlement of Montreal, and the Boy Scout movement.

Despite his exacting business career Clouston was a keen sportsman, a good football, lacrosse, and racquet player, a snowshoer, fancy skater, curler, swimmer, yachtsman, golfer, and motorist. He belonged to at least 10 sports clubs and associations and held some executive positions. A trustee of the Allan Cup and the Minto Cup, he donated a cup to the Montreal Horse Show and a trophy to the Royal Life Saving Society to encourage competitive swimming. As a director and vice-president of the Parks and Playgrounds Association of Montreal, Clouston, with his wife (who was vice-president of the ladies' committee), took an active part in the preservation of Mount Royal Park.

Clouston was generous in his support of health services. He served as governor (1893–1912) and president (1910–12) of the Royal Victoria Hospital and as governor of six other hospitals in the Montreal region. He was an executive member of the St John Ambulance Association and sat on the provincial council of the Red Cross Society. He was also a benefactor and president of the Montreal Association for the Blind.

Like many of Montreal's merchant princes, Clouston supported education, and was a patron of theatre, music, art, and libraries. He was a governor of the Fraser Institute and of McGill University and a member of the Champlain Society. A benefactor and councillor of the Art Association of Montreal, he possessed "many fine pictures" and donated the stained glass windows for the Royal Victoria Hospital's chapel.

A staunch imperialist, Clouston persuaded the bank to make generous and unprecedented contributions to South African War charities and in 1909 promoted the creation of an imperial press service. Described by the *Montreal Daily Star* in 1907 as a millionaire, Clouston was created a baronet in 1908 and sought and received a coat of arms from the College of Arms in England. He and Lady Clouston entertained lavishly at their Montreal residence and at Boisbriant, their 300-acre estate at Senneville, a property evaluated at $35,000 in 1898. At Boisbriant Clouston could indulge his interest in horse breeding, fruit growing, and horticulture. He was a director of the Montreal Horticultural Society and Fruit Growers' Association of the Province of Quebec.

Clouston's sudden death was announced across Canada and in the United States and Great Britain. At St Peter's Church, Eaton Square, in London, a memorial service was attended by Smith, now 1st Baron Strathcona and Mount Royal, former governors general, and numerous titled friends and associates. Although his funeral in the Church of St John the Evangelist in Montreal was private and unostentatious, it was attended by the city's corporate and political élite.

Described as the epitome of Canadian banking, Clouston was canny, powerful, and austere, although far from cautious or conservative in financial matters. A thinker and a listener, he surrounded himself with strong, loyal men resembling himself. He was hailed as a patron of arts and letters, a patriot, and a benevolent and generous employer, particularly considerate of his employees. Given his reputation as a man of few words, the Canadian Bankers' Association felt that silence was "the most fitting tribute to his memory." Clouston deserves a major biography, but until then many questions on his life and career will remain unanswered.

CARMAN MILLER

Further reading

Christopher Armstrong and H. V. Nelles, *Southern exposure: Canadian promoters in Latin America and the Caribbean, 1896–1930* (Toronto, 1988).

Merrill Denison, *Canada's first bank: a history of the Bank of Montreal* (2v., Toronto and Montreal, 1966–67).

Donna McDonald, *Lord Strathcona: a biography of Donald Alexander Smith* (Toronto and Oxford, 1996).

G. P. Marchildon, *Profits and politics: Beaverbrook and the Gilded Age of Canadian finance* (Toronto, 1996).

R. T. Naylor, *The history of Canadian business, 1867–1914*, intro. Mel Watkins (2v. in 1, Montreal, 1997).

ALPHONSE DESJARDINS
(baptized Gabriel-Alphonse),

journalist, office holder, newspaper owner, and founder of the *caisse populaire*; b. 5 Nov. 1854 in Lévis, Lower Canada, son of François Roy, *dit* Desjardins, and Clarisse Miville, *dit* Deschênes; m. 2 Sept. 1879 Dorimène Roy-Desjardins in Sorel, Que., and they had ten children, three of whom died in infancy; d. 31 Oct. 1920 in Lévis.

Alphonse Desjardins was the eighth of 15 children. His father, who had been a farmer before becoming a day labourer, occasionally handled business deals, but he was an alcoholic and could not hold a job for long. His mother had to do housework for the neighbours to make ends meet. Nevertheless, all the boys would succeed in carving out desirable careers for themselves. After finishing elementary school at the École Potvin, Desjardins attended the Collège de Lévis from 1864 to 1870, completing the four-year commercial course and the first year of the Latin one. His academic record shows that he was capable of excellent work but was inconsistent. He had to leave school in July 1870 because the classical program was too heavy a financial burden.

From 1869 Desjardins did his military service at the annual camps of the 17th (Lévis) Battalion of Infantry, in which his elder brother Louis-Georges was adjutant. Alphonse was soon promoted to sergeant-major and on 17 Oct. 1871 was sent to the Red River settlement in

Manitoba with a contingent of reinforcements that had been dispatched to repel a Fenian invasion. His military career was brief, however. On his return he found employment in 1872 with *L'Écho de Lévis* and the following year he was its Ottawa correspondent. When it ceased publication on 12 July 1876, Desjardins went to Quebec City and joined Joseph-Israël Tarte's editorial staff at *Le Canadien*, a newspaper of which Louis-Georges had recently become co-owner. In addition to short news items, press reviews, and the occasional column on local events in Lévis, he wrote a few lead stories. In 1877 and 1878 he was assigned to cover the debates in the Quebec Legislative Assembly.

Like Louis-Georges, Desjardins was active in the Conservative party. During the federal election of 1878 he served as secretary to its central committee in Lévis and participated in campaigning. His professional experience and political commitment earned him the position of recorder of debates at the Quebec Legislative Assembly from 1879 to 1889. He had to summarize the members' speeches and report their main points in a publication subsidized by the government. In this period Desjardins was involved in cultural and economic organizations. He was president of the Institut Canadien de Lévis in 1883 and a member of the council of the Chambre de Commerce de Lévis from 1880 to 1893. On 14 Dec. 1889 Desjardins learned that, to reduce public expenditures, the government of Honoré Mercier would no longer underwrite publication of the debates. In fact, since coming to power in 1887, Mercier's Liberals had been planning to remove the work from the hands of this former Conservative activist, especially since his brother was a leader in the Conservative opposition at Quebec.

Faced with finding other employment, Desjardins returned to journalism. On 9 July 1891 in Lévis he launched *L'Union canadienne*, a daily in which he supported the program of the federal Conservative party. But on 10 October, for reasons of health, he had to cease publication. To obtain other work, he called on his political friends, with the result that on 22 April 1892 the Conservative government in Ottawa appointed him French-language stenographer for the House of Commons. He would hold this position until he retired in 1917.

But Desjardins was not one to be satisfied with the challenges faced by a civil servant. Attentive listening to parliamentary debates set him thinking and asking himself questions about the country's social and economic problems. And it was in the reforms proposed by Catholics who were concerned with social issues that he sought solutions. He read (doubtless shortly after its publication in 1891) the encyclical *Rerum novarum*, which had a profound influence on him. He also kept abreast of the work of French sociologist Frédéric Le Play and other writers connected with that school of thought. A subscriber to the magazine *La Réforme sociale* (Paris), in 1899 he became a member of the Société Canadienne d'Économie Sociale de Montréal.

As for practical matters, Desjardins was especially fascinated by mutual aid societies. In 1893 he put together a massive file of "notes to be used for a study of life insurance." There were many mutualists among his acquaintances. One of his elder brothers, François-Xavier, was a publicist for the Union Saint-Joseph d'Ottawa, a mutual aid society. His fellow citizens in Lévis had set up a number of such organizations, including a branch of the Société des Artisans Canadiens-Français, which opened in 1889, and the Société de Construction Permanente de Lévis, which had been founded in 1869. From 1892 to 1895 Desjardins sat on the board of directors of the latter company, which provided mortgage loans to its members.

A bill to prevent usurious practices, introduced in the House of Commons on 6 April 1897 by Conservative Michael Joseph Francis Quinn, marked a turning-point in Desjardins's life. Quinn cited the case of a Montreal man sentenced to pay interest charges of $5,000 on an initial loan of $150. Desjardins was deeply disturbed and became more aware than ever of the gaps in the way credit was organized. Small borrowers had almost no access to ordinary banks. How could they be kept from having to turn, in their need for a loan, to moneylenders who often had no hesitation in exploiting them? This question would not go away. A little later he came across a book by the Englishman Henry William Wolff, *People's banks, a record of social and economic success* (London and New York, 1893). On 12 May 1898 he wrote to Wolff, seeking further information. Through him Desjardins obtained the names of many French, Belgian, Italian, and Swiss cooperators, who were all directors of people's banks or rural credit unions, and he got in touch with them. He spent several months carefully studying the documentation he was sent and trying to assess the merits of the diverse models of credit cooperatives. Taking into account the economic, social, and cultural differences between Canada and Europe, he opted for a new model largely based on European rules of organization.

As time went on Desjardins interested others in his work. He often discussed the project with his curé, François-Xavier Gosselin, and with priests at the Collège de Lévis, where from 1893 to 1900 he taught shorthand during the intervals between parliamentary sessions. He also solicited the advice of fellow mutualists, among whom he recruited the colleagues who helped him to draft a constitution and by-laws and to set up his savings and loan cooperative.

The Caisse Populaire de Lévis was founded on 6 Dec. 1900 at a meeting attended by about 80 people, including several leading figures in the city. It was defined as a cooperative savings and loan society with limited liability and fluctuating capital. Its structure was similar to that of Italian people's banks but it also had characteristics borrowed from German rural credit unions. Its only unique organizational rule was that of fluctuating capital, which permitted members to demand a refund of their five-dollar share at any time with due notice. The essential function of the *caisse* was to extend loans to members using their collective savings. While it provided easier access to credit, it sought also to develop habits of thrift and foresight.

On 23 Jan. 1901 the Caisse Populaire de Lévis began operations. It was a success from the start, thanks to the tireless work of Desjardins and the unwavering support of his wife, Dorimène, Father Gosselin, and the priests at the Collège de Lévis. By 30 November it had 721 members, who held nearly 2,000 shares at five dollars a share. Desjardins was jubilant and believed more strongly than ever in the ideal he had pursued since the beginning: "to create a vast network of *caisses populaires*." But before this could happen, he had to gain acceptance for the idea that the *caisse populaire* was the kind of credit cooperative best suited to the needs of the people of Quebec. Indeed, Desjardins was not the only one in the province taking an interest in the matter of people's loans. For several years promoters of agriculture had been thinking of introducing the system of German rural credit unions set up by Friedrich Wilhelm Raiffeisen, in the hope of providing a source of loans for farmers. In January 1900 the Conservative MLA for Wolfe, Jérôme-Adolphe Chicoyne, had in fact introduced a bill to this effect. After being redrafted twice, the measure was finally adopted as the Quebec Agricultural Syndicates' Act of 1902.

Not long after the passage of this law, which he would certainly have liked to block, Desjardins took the first steps towards getting the federal parliament to provide a legal framework for the operation of *caisses populaires*. He already had the support of Frederick Debartzch Monk, the leader of the Quebec wing of the federal Conservative party, Henri Bourassa, and, from the government side, Rodolphe Lemieux and Solicitor General Henry George Carroll. However, the minister of finance, William Stevens Fielding, thought *caisses populaires* came under provincial jurisdiction because, strictly speaking, they were merely local organizations and were not in the banking business. In 1904 Desjardins tried in vain to make him change his mind. He had no greater success with the prime minister, Sir Wilfrid Laurier, who gave him an interview on 24 July. Possibly he did not get a better hearing because he had been a Conservative activist. Be that as it may, he realized he would achieve nothing unless he brought strong pressure to bear on the government.

Fortunately, time was on his side. The Caisse Populaire de Lévis continued to enjoy success, from which its founder gained increasing renown. Many now regarded him as an authority in his field. An indefatigable worker who was persistent, methodical, and meticulous, he planned everything carefully, leaving nothing to chance. Through study and practice he had gained a reputation as an expert who inspired confidence. Proud and perhaps a bit vain, he knew how to present his accomplishments in the best light. He was not a gifted orator, however, and was even described as "slightly austere," "with no outward attractiveness." His strength lay in his intelligence, competence, and organizational flair.

Late in 1904 Desjardins succeeded in setting up an association to support him in his dealings with the federal government. Founded at the Université Laval on 21 December, the Action Populaire Économique had as one of its aims the passage of legislation that would develop savings and loan cooperatives in Canada. Such prominent figures as Archbishop Louis-Nazaire Bégin, Edmund James Flynn, Adélard Turgeon, Thomas Chapais, and Charles Langelier agreed to become members of it. The lobbying of the group and its members' petitions to Laurier had no effect, however. In desperation, Desjardins turned to the provincial government. In March 1905 he submitted to the attorney general, Horace Archambeault, a bill he had drafted with lawyer Eusèbe Belleau. Lomer Gouin, who became premier and attorney general shortly thereafter, seemed favourable, but there was an obstacle. The bill was just a reworded version of the 1902 Quebec Agricultural Syndicates' Act, and would logically have required repeal of that law. The government wanted time to examine the question thoroughly, and the session ended before a decision was taken.

Desjardins and his wife, Dorimène, were deeply disappointed. Since 1903 she had served as manager of the *caisse* in Lévis whenever he was in Ottawa. It now had more than $40,000 in assets, and she worried more and more about their personal responsibility in the absence of legal protection. Desjardins had also organized three other *caisses*, in Saint-Joseph-de-la-Pointe-de-Lévy, Hull, and Saint-Malo, Que., which were in the same unfortunate situation. The couple were clearly on the verge of despair. In May, Desjardins even confided to a priest at the Collège de Lévis that he was thinking of liquidating everything, but the support and encouragement of Father Gosselin and Archbishop Bégin helped them get a grip on themselves.

In 1906 everything was settled. On 28 February Gouin introduced in the assembly the proposed Quebec Syndicates' Act, which was passed unanimously on 5 March and received royal assent four days later. It was truly a victory for Desjardins. At last, he wrote, "the work can take off…, assert itself, and stop living in the shadows." This statute also made the *caisse populaire* the basic model on which savings and loan cooperatives would henceforth be organized in Quebec.

Desjardins did not abandon his goal of a federal law, however. On 23 April 1906 Monk introduced in the commons a bill drafted by Desjardins. It was sent to a select committee for study, which on 11 April 1907 recommended "that the government take charge of the measure and have it passed." The Act respecting industrial and co-operative societies was adopted unanimously by the commons on 6 March 1908. On 15 July, breaking with custom, the Senate blocked it, on the grounds that it would infringe on the powers of the provinces. Clearly many senators did not share this view, since the legislation was defeated by a single vote. Some of its opponents were under pressure from the Retail Merchants' Association of Canada, which objected to it because it would have allowed the creation of potential competitors in the form of consumers' cooperatives. Until 1914 a few MPS would try in vain to enlist the House of Commons in getting legislation on cooperation passed.

The years from 1907 to 1915 were the most active of Desjardins's career. He began promoting the establishment of other *caisses populaires* in the fall of 1907. Abbé Philibert Grondin, a young priest at the Collège de Lévis, joined him in conducting a publicity campaign in the press. From 1909 Grondin's articles appeared almost every week in *La Vérité* and occasionally in *L'Action catholique*. In 1910 he brought out *Le Catéchisme des caisses populaires*, a little booklet that by questions and answers presented all necessary information about the aims, organization, and functioning of these institutions. For his part, Desjardins busied himself answering the many requests for information, and took every opportunity to give public lectures. He also published, in pamphlet form or in newspapers and magazines, many articles in which he pointed out the merits of his *caisses populaires*. The economic and social thinking set out is clear and coherent, with a touch of satire. Desjardins observed that the common people were victims of the concentration of economic power and the many abuses of capitalism, and he stressed their isolation and lack of economic organization. By joining together to form cooperative enterprises, workers and small producers would be best able to defend their financial interests. He associated cooperation with the ideals of democratization and economic decentralization. Through the *caisses populaires*, he also hoped to foster agricultural development, stem emigration from rural areas to American towns, and thus ensure "the greatness and future prosperity of the country." By consolidating savings, the *caisses* would make it possible to form a "national capital fund" through which French Canadians could increase their influence and protect their interests as a people.

The *caisse populaire* was no ordinary financial enterprise. Desjardins defined it as a social undertaking in the sense of the church's teachings on society, an entity the parish élite ought to encourage in order to improve the material and spiritual conditions of the common people. In particular, Desjardins counted on the clergy, whom he asked to participate in the administration and, if necessary, the management, of the *caisses*. Concerned about social issues, of which *Rerum novarum* had made them more aware, they were taking an increasing interest at the turn of the century in organizations that might contribute to the material and spiritual uplifting of the working classes. They saw such institutions as a way of defusing social conflict, counteracting socialist propaganda, and protecting religious values and the church's moral authority. They also considered them necessary to stimulate agricultural progress and to slow the exodus from the land and emigration to the United States. Convinced of the benefits of people's savings and credit, a number of bishops hastened to recognize the *caisses populaires* as a Catholic social undertaking which they recommended to their clergy's attention. The Catholic social action organizations set up during the years from 1900 to 1910 included the *caisses* among the means of achieving their goals. As a result, Desjardins was invited to speak at the youth congress organized by the Association Catholique de la Jeunesse Canadienne-Française in 1908, and at the congress of the Ligues du Sacré-Cœur in 1910. He was even invited to the sacerdotal congress in Montreal in 1913, where he was the only lay speaker. That year, on the recommendation of Archbishop Bégin, Pope Pius X made Desjardins a commander of the Order of St Gregory the Great in recognition of his Christian dedication and his contribution to social action. The clergy apart, a few key figures in the nationalist movement, such as Henri Bourassa and his colleague Omer Héroux, were among the most ardent promoters of the *caisses populaires*.

Thanks to all this support, the *caisses populaires* became more and more widely known. Desjardins said he was swamped by requests from people who wanted to organize a *caisse* in their parish. From 1907 to 1915 he founded no fewer than 136. He also made an effort to supervise their operations, and to that end he corresponded regularly with many managers, both men and women. He accomplished all this in his spare time, with no financial assistance whatever. He often thought about the possibility of a government grant to the Action Populaire Économique to finance a publicity service, for which he would be responsible, but the fear of political interference kept him from making any such official request.

Desjardins's accomplishments were noted in several Canadian provinces, and in particular by the French-speaking communities in the west. However, Ontario was the only province to which he extended his activities. He founded 18 *caisses populaires* there between 1910 and 1913, in addition to helping organize a *caisse d'économie* in 1908 for federal civil servants in Ottawa.

As early as 1908 the fame of the *caisses populaires* had spread beyond the borders of Canada. Desjardins received many American visitors, and requests for information kept flooding in. He visited the United States five times between 1908 and 1912, going to New Hampshire, Massachusetts, New York City, and Rhode Island. He was welcomed by politicians and various associations to which he spoke, and in Massachusetts and New York City he helped draft bills that would lead to the creation of savings and loan cooperatives similar to the *caisses populaires*. Desjardins also took advantage of these trips to set up some ten *caisses populaires*, mostly in French-speaking communities in Massachusetts, where he spent five weeks in June and July 1911. In 1912 he was even invited to Washington by the president of the United States, William Howard Taft, to take part in a conference of American governors on agricultural credit.

In 1914 Desjardins began to feel the first symptoms of the uraemia that would frequently force him during the last six years of his life into convalescence between brief periods of remission. In 1916 he reluctantly handed over responsibility for founding *caisses* to a committee under Abbé Grondin. The following year he had to give up his duties as House of Commons stenographer. With the help of his daughter Albertine, his wife, and Grondin, he carried on as well as he could his correspondence with a number of *caisse* managers and directors, to whom he gave advice and encouragement. Knowing that his illness was terminal, he anxiously considered ways of ensuring that his work would endure. He wanted to bring the *caisses* together within a federation, as the European systems did, that would make available the technical and financial services necessary for their security and growth. This federation would be responsible for carrying out an annual inspection of its member institutions and would organize a central *caisse* to administer the surplus funds held by some local *caisses* and provide loans to those others short of money. But Desjardins felt a resistance on the part of the *caisses*. They objected to the idea of paying dues to finance the federation and were afraid of losing their autonomy. Three months before his death he proposed, without success, that they hold a meeting to study his plan. There were at that time in Quebec some 140 active *caisses* with a total membership of more than 30,000 and assets of $6,300,000.

Although it remained unfinished, the work of Alphonse Desjardins aroused admiration, and many of his contemporaries had been able to grasp its full social and economic significance. *La Vérité* saw it as "a heritage whose value cannot yet be estimated." *L'Action catholique* predicted that the *caisses* would become "the solid base of the French Canadian national fortune," and saluted their founder as "one of the great benefactors of his race."

PIERRE POULIN AND GUY BÉLANGER

Further reading

Majella St-Pierre, *Alphonse Desjardins, entrepreneur* (Montréal et Charlesbourg, Qué., 2001).

Pierre Poulin, *Histoire du mouvement Desjardins* (2v. to date, Montréal, 1990–   ), 1 (*Desjardins et la naissance des caisses populaires, 1900–1920*, 1990).

Pierre Poulin *et al.*, *Desjardins, 100 ans d'histoire* (Sainte-Foy [Québec] et Lévis, Qué., 2000).

Yves Roby, *Alphonse Desjardins et les caisses populaires, 1854–1920* (Montréal, 1964).

Ronald Rudin, *In whose interest? Quebec's caisses populaires, 1900–1945* (Montreal and Kingston, Ont., 1990).

Guy Bélanger et Claude Genest, *La caisse populaire de Lévis, 1900–2000: là où tout a commencé* (Sainte-Foy et Lévis, 2000).

Guy Bélanger, *Dorimène Desjardins: cofondatrice des caisses populaires Desjardins, 1858–1932* (Lévis, 2008).

Sir ADAM BECK,

manufacturer, horseman, politician, office holder, and philanthropist; b. 20 June 1857 in Baden, Upper Canada, son of Jacob Friedrich Beck and Charlotte Josephine Hespeler; m. 7 Sept. 1898 Lillian Ottaway in Hamilton, Ont., and they had a daughter; d. 15 Aug. 1925 in London, Ont.

The Prometheus of Canadian politics during the first quarter of the 20th century, Sir Adam Beck brought the inestimable benefit of cheap electric light and power to the citizens of Ontario through a publicly owned utility, the Hydro-Electric Power Commission of Ontario.

He had to fight continuously to build Hydro, as it came to be called, but supported by municipal allies he succeeded in creating one of the largest publicly owned integrated electric systems in the world. Brusque and overbearing, he made many enemies in the process, even amongst his friends, as he rammed his projects forward, frequently over the objections of the governments he notionally served. His ruthless determination to expand Hydro, with little regard to the cost, led eventually to a movement to rein him in. He spent his last years pinned down before three public inquiries as lawyers, accountants, and political adversaries picked over every Hydro expenditure. These public humiliations broke his spirit but failed to diminish his enormous popularity. Adam Beck more than any other public figure in Ontario reshaped the institutional life of the province by making electricity a public utility and legitimizing, through his accomplishments, public ownership as an effective instrument of policy throughout Canada.

Beck came from an enterprising immigrant family of builders and makers. In 1829 Frederick and Barbara Beck had emigrated from the Grand Duchy of Baden (Germany) to upstate New York, and then had moved to the Pennsylvania Dutch community of Doon (Kitchener) in Upper Canada, where they settled on a farm and built a sawmill. Their son Jacob, who had stayed behind to work first as a doctor's apprentice and later in the mills and locomotive works of Schenectady, joined them in 1837. A few miles from his parents, in Preston (Cambridge), he opened a foundry. When fire destroyed it, his friends rallied and he was able to rebuild bigger than before. His first wife, Caroline Logus, whom he married in January 1843, died soon after the birth of a son, Charles. In 1843 Beck had recruited a skilled iron moulder from Buffalo, John Clare (Klarr), to join him; Clare would cement the alliance by marrying his sister in September 1845. With Clare and another partner (Valentine Wahn) running the business, Beck returned to tour his homeland, where he met Charlotte Hespeler, the sister of his Preston neighbour, merchant-manufacturer Jacob Hespeler. When Charlotte came out to Canada, she and Beck were wed, in October 1845; a daughter, Louisa, was born in 1847, followed by two sons, George and William. In a move typical of his venturing spirit, Jacob suggested relocating his company closer to the projected line of the Grand Trunk Railway, but Clare refused. So in 1854 Beck dissolved the partnership and bought

190 acres on the route of the railway ten miles west of Berlin (Kitchener). There he laid out a town-site, which he named Baden, and built a foundry, a grist mill, and a large brick house. Beck's businesses flourished on the strength of iron orders from the railway, and a brickyard and machine shop were eventually added. It was in this thriving hamlet that Adam Beck was born in 1857.

Adam passed a bucolic childhood exploring the edges of the mill-pond with his brothers, poking about the sooty recesses of the foundry with the workmen, and horseback-riding with his sister. He was sent off to attend William Tassie's boarding school in Galt (Cambridge), where he showed no particular distinction; a slow and indifferent student, he preferred riding to reading. His formal education ended at Rockwood Academy, near Guelph. On his return to Baden, his father, who abhorred idleness, set him to work as a groundhog (a moulder's apprentice) in the foundry. It was said by those who knew Adam that he inherited his enterprising spirit, his determination and visionary ability, and some of his sternness from his father, and a love of public service from his mother. Adam's career as a moulder came to an end with the failure of his father's businesses in 1879. At age 63 Jacob Beck, unbowed, started afresh once again, this time as a grain merchant in Detroit. Louisa and the youngest members of the family, Jacob Fritz and Adam, accompanied their parents; one of the older boys, William, stayed in Baden to run the cigar-box manufactory he had started in 1878. Adam returned to work briefly in Toronto as a clerk in a foundry and then as an employee in a cigar factory. With $500 in borrowed money, he joined William and their cousin William Hespeler in a cigar-box factory in Galt in 1881. Hespeler eventually left the partnership, but the two Becks persisted and built a modestly successful business. In 1884, with the inducement of a five-year tax exemption and free water, they moved their works to London, Ont., to be closer to the centre of the province's cigar-making industry. William left soon afterwards to open a branch in Montreal and for a time Adam worked in partnership with his brother George; from 1 Jan. 1888 Adam was the sole proprietor of William Beck and Company, which later became the Beck Manufacturing Company Limited.

Cigar boxes would appear to be a fragile basis on which to build a fortune or a political career. The smoking of cigars, however, was a major rite of male sociability during the Victorian era. Earlier in the century cigars consumed in Canada had originated in Germany and later they came from the United States. The imposition of the National Policy tariff of 25 per cent on rolled cigars but not on tobacco leaf led to the migration of the industry to Canada. London was one of the first major centres where the leaf grown in Ohio, Pennsylvania, and Wisconsin entered the dominion, and it was there and in Montreal that the domestic cigar-making business took root. In London the industry would reach its peak around 1912, when 22 companies, employing 1,980 workers, produced more than 20 million cigars. Situated on Albert Street, the Beck factory was essentially a veneer plant. Cedar logs and specialty woods from Spain and Mexico arrived by rail, were stored in the yard for seasoning, and then were peeled into strips to make not only cigar boxes but also cheese boxes and veneer for furniture and pianos. Toiling side by side with his workers (25 in 1889, rising to 125 in 1919), Beck built a thriving business, taking orders, setting up equipment, manhandling logs, and wheeling the finished boxes to customers. (He himself was a non-smoker, an enduring fatherly influence.) Eventually the company supplied all of the main cigar makers with the boxes, labels, and bands in which their products were shipped. Until he was 40, business was Adam Beck's main preoccupation.

In the years after 1897 he emerged much more prominently in public life. He got out more, married, offered himself for public office, and turned the management of his firm over to his brother Jacob. An avid sportsman, he had played baseball as a boy; in London he played tennis and lacrosse and, with a group of bachelors, organized a toboggan club. On the advice of his doctor he took up riding again for relaxation. But nothing with Adam Beck could ever be just a recreation – he quickly became a breeder of racehorses and a competitive jumper. His social life revolved around the London Hunt Club where, in 1897, he became master of the hounds, a post he would hold until 1922. A mutual love of horses and riding brought the muscular Beck and the slim, strikingly beautiful Lillian Ottaway together at a jumping meet; she was 21 years his junior. After a whirlwind courtship they were married in 1898 at Christ's Church Anglican Cathedral in Hamilton. Lillian, who had been raised in Britain, spoke with a slight English accent, had a lovely soprano voice, rode with gusto, and carried herself regally. Her mother, Marion Elizabeth Stinson, from a wealthy Hamilton family, had married an English barrister, who died before Lillian was born. At 5 Lillian returned to Canada when her mother married a prominent Hamilton lawyer. After a honeymoon tour of Europe, Beck triumphantly brought his bride to London, Ont., where they promptly acquired the most ostentatious house in the city, Elliston, the estate of Ellis Walton Hyman, and proceeded to make it even grander, with his and hers stables, under a new name, Headley. From being a sporting, business-possessed bachelor, Beck, with his young wife on his arm, moved effortlessly into the very centre of London society. She sang in the cathedral choir, their house and grounds were the envy of the city, and they made a romantic and devoted couple at dinners and hunt club affairs. Winston Churchill stayed with them on his lecture tour of 1900–1, as did Governor General Gilbert John Murray-Kynynmound Elliot, 4th Earl of Minto, and Mary Caroline, Countess of Minto, in 1903.

As Adam Beck came out into society, he developed an interest in public life. In provincial politics London had long been a Conservative fief – William Ralph Meredith held the seat from 1872 to 1894. The Liberals captured it in a by-election when Meredith was appointed to the bench. At the next general election, in March 1898, Beck entered the lists for the Conservatives, ultimately falling 301 votes short of beating the Liberal Francis Baxter Leys. Although he perhaps should not have expected a better result, having no previous political experience or strong organization, he left the field feeling slightly wounded. Nevertheless, his political energies were channelled into the Victoria Hospital Trust, to which he was appointed by the city in 1901. Here he scandalized supporters with his aggressive approach towards patients' rights, his attacks on hospital inefficiency, and his hands-on way of managing repairs economically. It is said that Beck, realizing that he was not likely to be reappointed, ran for mayor to outflank his opposition. In any case, he offered himself and was elected in January 1902. Making few promises, preferring instead to be judged by his works, he plunged into the first of what would be three one-year terms. His administration was marked by a vigorous, reforming tone that discomfited the aldermanic coterie. He promoted civic beautification by offering a prize from his own purse for a garden competition. He persuaded the city to take over the operation of the London and Port Stanley Railway when the private operator's lease expired. He cleaned out the fire department, promoted public health, and became involved in the leadership of the Union of Canadian Municipalities, whose annual convention he brought to London in 1904. Beck thus learned the political craft at the top of local politics, as a mayor without a long apprenticeship. He entered public life as an oppositionist, a critic who used his personal popularity to drive his reluctant colleagues forward and to cleanse the municipal stables. Despite his class position as a manufacturer, in politics he developed the style of a populist champion of the ordinary citizen against the establishment. Although one might have glimpsed intimations of his future in these London years, it would have required an extremely vivid imagination to see in this maverick local politician the system-building Napoleon of provincial politics that history would know as Sir Adam Beck.

In the election of May 1902 the leader of the Conservative party, James Pliny Whitney, encouraged Beck to run again, with the offer of a cabinet post. Although the party as a whole was unsuccessful, the popular Beck beat Francis Leys by 131 votes and thus, for the next two and a half years, he would serve as both mayor and MPP of London. It was in his capacity as mayor of a southwestern Ontario industrial city that he came in contact with a group of activists from his home district of Waterloo County who had become agitated by the hydroelectric power question. Led by the manufacturer Elias Weber Bingeman Snider and the enthusiast Daniel Bechtel Detweiler, the anxious businessmen and municipal politicians of the industrial centres of the Grand River valley had begun to organize themselves to obtain Niagara power that they believed would otherwise go to Toronto and Buffalo. They had met in 1902 to study the situation, and then formed common cause with the politicians of Toronto concerned about private monopoly. At first they hoped the provincial government could be persuaded to undertake the distribution of cheap power to the municipalities. Talks with the Liberal premier, George William Ross, who refused to take on the inevitable debt, convinced them that if they wanted control over electrical distribution they would have to do the job themselves. Beck went as an observer to the first meeting of this group, the Berlin Convention of February 1903, a gathering of 67 delegates representing all of the main towns and cities in southwestern Ontario; he came away an active convert to municipal intervention. In response to this public pressure, in June the Ross government passed legislation (drafted by Snider) authorizing a commission of investigation to explore the possibilities of cooperative municipal action and a statutory framework within which the municipalities could create a permanent commission to operate a distribution system. Snider was the obvious choice as chair of this Ontario Power Commission, which more frequently went by his name. Beck along with Philip William Ellis, a Toronto jewellery manufacturer and wholesaler, and William Foster Cockshutt, a Brantford farm-implements manufacturer, were chosen by the municipal delegates to serve with Snider as commissioners. Thus, in the fall of 1903, Beck began a crash course on the power question. It was a subject ideally suited to his developing temperament, and he could readily identify with the professed goals: economic electrical light and power, equity between the different manufacturing regions, and the welfare of the common people. The vision of sensible, non-partisan, and public-spirited businessmen and municipal leaders (such as himself) appealed to Beck. He could also subscribe to the implicit attack on monopoly, social privilege, and finance capitalism. This was a moral universe in which he felt right at home.

As the Snider commission began working out the details of a municipally owned hydroelectric distribution system in 1904, Beck sensed the weakness of the voluntary, cooperative structure. It lacked the authority to order the power companies to surrender sensitive information vital to the enterprise, and the municipalities could not agree on much for long. Financing a collective municipal enterprise without provincial backing would be fraught with difficulties. The more he studied the question the more he became convinced that the province would have to play a major role, not just facilitate municipal activity. This growing conviction coincided with a major shift in the political landscape. The Liberal party was losing its hold over the electorate. Rooted in rural Ontario, it had trouble coming to grips with issues important to the rapidly growing urban constituencies. The Conservatives had crept to within three seats of upsetting the Liberals in 1902. In January 1905 Whitney's Conservatives swept to a landslide victory, capturing 69 of the 98 seats. In London, the increasingly popular Adam Beck won with a plurality of 566 votes.

The hydroelectric question had not figured prominently in the campaign. The change in government, however, catapulted Beck into a position of some influence provincially. On 8 February he was made a minister without portfolio in the new administration. After the election,

Whitney grandly promised that the water-power of Niagara "should be as free as air" and be developed for the public good. "It is the duty of the Government," Beck insisted in his populist fashion, "to see that development is not hindered by permitting a handful of people to enrich themselves out of these treasures at the expense of the general public." To that end Whitney cancelled an eleventh-hour water-power concession granted by the Ross government and on 5 July he appointed Beck to head a hydroelectric commission of inquiry. It was empowered to take an inventory of available water-power sites, gather information on existing companies in terms of their capital costs, their operating expenses, and the prices they charged, and recommend an appropriate provincial policy with respect to the generation and distribution of hydroelectricity. Beck continued to be a member of the Snider commission but clearly he had moved on to a broader conception of the power question; he now wielded a much more powerful regulatory and investigative instrument and could act with the authority of the province. Henceforth he would be the undisputed leader of the hydro movement.

The Snider commission, which reported first, in March 1906, recommended the construction of a cooperatively owned hydroelectric system linking the major municipal utilities to generating facilities at Niagara under the control of a permanent power commission financed and managed by the subscribing municipalities. In the weeks that followed, the Beck commission, in the first of its five regional reports, and more particularly the activities of Beck himself, superseded the Snider notion of a municipal cooperative. Beck's initial report, on Niagara and southwest Ontario, prepared the way instead for provincial action by pointing out the excessive rates charged by private power companies, and the inherent difficulties of government regulation. He gave an important speech in Guelph urging direct provincial intervention. He inspired a mass meeting of municipal representatives at Toronto city hall and, on 11 April, a demonstration on the lawn of the legislature demanding that the province empower a commission to generate, transmit, and sell power to the municipalities at the lowest possible cost, and regulate the prices charged by the private providers. Beck also orchestrated a deluge of petitions from the municipal councils. All of this effort was intended to soften up his colleagues in cabinet, most of whom harboured deep suspicions about public ownership in general and Beck's movement in particular. The strategy worked. The Whitney government hesitantly introduced legislation on 7 May (Act to provide for the transmission of electrical power to municipalities) which, in effect, created a three-member provincial crown corporation (though it was not called that), the Hydro-Electric Power Commission of Ontario. Operating outside the usual civil service constraints and with extensive powers of expropriation, this body would have full powers to purchase, lease, or build transmission facilities financed by provincial bonds. Local utilities could buy power from the commission only after municipal voters had approved the contract and the enabling financial by-law. Astonishingly, Beck's extraparliamentary organization cowed even the opposition: the bill passed unanimously in less than a week.

In organizational terms Beck had pushed on beyond an unwieldy municipal cooperative to a provincial crown agency. In doing so he had alienated some of his friends, especially in the way he had shoved Snider aside and unilaterally appropriated studies done by the Snider commission for his own investigation. Nonetheless he had created a broad coalition of municipal activists behind his determination to build a publicly owned, provincial system. But there were many possible forms, involving different degrees of state intervention, that the organization might take. The government remained ambivalent, guarded, and internally divided. What eventually emerged as Ontario Hydro, however, was Beck's creation over the opposition of his cabinet colleagues. On 7 June 1906 Whitney appointed Beck chairman of the new commission, as expected. Needed engineering expertise would come from Cecil Brunswick Smith. And to balance Beck's populism and rein in his enthusiasms, Whitney also persuaded a reluctant John Strathearn Hendrie of Hamilton to serve, Beck's peer as a horseman, a man of his wife's class, and a known supporter of the private power companies, among them the Hamilton Electric Light and Cataract Power Company Limited.

The private interests, especially the group promoting the only Canadian firm at Niagara, the Electrical Development Company of Ontario Limited from Toronto, having failed in their first attempts to derail Beck, now bent their minds to seeking some reasonable accommodation with the government. There were many in the cabinet, the premier included, who were sympathetic to this point of view. The Electrical Development Company was in a precarious financial position; a collapse would be a costly blot on the province. Whitney insisted that every consideration be given the company in negotiating the contract for power in early 1907 with the winning bidder, the American-based Ontario Power Company, and then with respect to the construction of the transmission line. In each case negotiations failed. The premier did not conceive of his policy as a *guerre à outrance* against the private interests. He believed in talking tough, but in the end was willing to come to terms. Unlike Beck, Whitney was a practitioner of brokerage politics. Beck, a newly formed ideologue, was not prepared to bargain away what had formed in his mind as a just alternative to private control. It was possible that neither of them knew the truth about themselves, though in time they came to a realization of their honest differences. For his part Beck had to manoeuvre against the wishes of his premier and colleagues in cabinet. From their point of view he could be unpleasant, ruthless, even unprincipled. He would change his mind without notice, withhold information, go back on deals, and alternately retreat in a sulk or play the rude bully.

Beck proved a formidable champion. The Toronto market was a key element in his grand scheme. Without access, which the city wanted, he could not deliver cheap electricity to southwestern towns, but Toronto's system was controlled by the Electrical Development Company. In the resulting contest over a proposed by-law to fund a municipal network powered by Hydro, Beck's emotional, simplistic rhetoric was a telling factor. He also profited from the ineptitude and arrogance of his corporate opponents in Electrical Development, Frederic Thomas Nicholls, Sir Henry Mill Pellatt, and William Mackenzie, whose financial reputations had already taken a beating from the royal commission on life insurance in 1906. During the winter of 1907–8 by-laws endorsing the contracts with Ontario Hydro were approved by municipal ratepayers with huge majorities in Toronto and elsewhere. Hydro policy also proved extremely popular in the election of June 1908, in which the government increased both its popular vote and its number of seats. Beck now had a dual mandate from the municipal and provincial electorates. When a desperate Mackenzie amalgamated several enterprises into one utility in 1908 and then belatedly attempted to forestall provincial ownership with a counterproposal to build the system and distribute power under government regulation, the offer came too late. The government had gone so far it could not safely turn back; a publicly owned transmission company would have to be created. Mackenzie and his colleagues had played the game badly and when they lost, after having been given every possible consideration, they turned viciously on Beck and the government. Their quixotic campaign to undermine provincial credit in British financial circles, and then to seek disallowance in Ottawa of key Hydro legislation, served only to bring Whitney and Beck closer together and solidify the political foundations of Ontario Hydro.

Using electricity generated by the Ontario Power Company, the Hydro-Electric Power Commission became an operating entity in a series of theatrical turning-on ceremonies that began in the fall of 1910 and continued into 1911 as successive towns and cities were wired into the grid. Each of these civic festivals became an opportunity for Beck to recount the triumph of public power over private greed. His hostility towards the private power companies, who were now his competitors, and his shameless self-promotion as the champion of "The People's Power," deeply troubled his colleagues. Moreover, his independent conduct raised awkward questions about the precise relationship between the management of Hydro and the government. Before the election of December 1911 Whitney floated a trial balloon, suggesting that the time had come to make Hydro a department of government, under the full control of the cabinet. Beck did not openly attack the proposal, but once he was acclaimed in his own seat and the government was re-elected, his municipal allies, acting through the Ontario Municipal Electric Association, formed in early 1912, launched an aggressive campaign on his behalf; it not only supported Beck as chairman of a quasi-independent commission, but also (in February) brought him a handsome $6,000 salary, without requiring his resignation from the legislature.

With this vote of confidence from the people and somewhat more reluctantly from the premier, Beck struggled within a competitive environment to build Hydro through dramatic price cutting and political showmanship. In his campaign to expand consumption Beck became an electrical Messiah: in speeches and publicity he extolled the power of abundant cheap light to brighten the homes of working people; cheap electricity would create more jobs in the factories of the province; hydro would lighten the drudgery of the barn and the household; and electric railways radiating out from the cities into the countryside would create more prosperous, progressive farms even as light and power made brighter, cleaner cities. With his famous travelling exhibits of the latest electrical appliances (popularly called circuses), rural tests, and local Hydro stores (where household appliances were on display), and in parade floats, newspaper and magazine advertisements, and a host of speeches, Beck presented public hydro as an elixir, but he was no snake-oil salesman. He understood the economics of the electric industry better than his competitors or his critics. Along with utilities magnate Samuel Insull of Chicago, Beck realized that the more electricity he could sell, the cheaper it would cost to acquire. It was a difficult lesson to teach. He even had to browbeat some of the more fiscally conservative municipal utilities, most notably the Toronto Hydro-Electric Power Commission, to pass the lower rates on to consumers. In the process he continued to expand his publicly owned system at the expense of his private competitors.

In Toronto and across the province, Beck acquired a more ardent following than the government itself. At home he and his family continued to rise in public esteem. London's municipal electric utility, which received its first hydro from Niagara in 1910, became a model for progressive business promotion and Beck loyalism. Personally Beck maintained an active interest in civic politics. When the water commissioners proposed a treatment facility to take more water from the tainted Thames River, he boldly promised to find enough clean fresh water in artesian wells. The city took him up on this offer, voting $10,000 for the purpose. In 1910 Beck drilled the wells, installed electrical pumps, and brought the project in on time and on budget, or rather, he absorbed the excess costs himself. In two grand gestures Beck brought light and water to the growing city in the same year.

However, it was in the field of public health that the Becks made their greatest contribution. Sometime in 1907 or 1908 the Becks' young daughter, Marion Auria, contracted tuberculosis. Her worried parents sought out the best specialists in America and in Europe. Mercifully her case responded to treatment. But the Becks became concerned for those families in their community who lacked the means to provide their children with medical care. Everyone, they believed, ought to have close access to first-class tuberculosis facilities. Accordingly, in 1909 Adam and Lillian Beck organized the London Health Association to provide a sanatorium. From local individuals and organizations they raised $10,000 (led by their own donation of $1,200), the city contributed

$5,000, and the province added $4,000. On 5 April 1910 Governor General Albert Henry George Grey, 4th Earl Grey, opened the Queen Alexandra Sanatorium in the village of Byron, west of the city. For the rest of their lives the Becks remained deeply attached to this sanatorium and made its maintenance and expansion their passion. As president from its inception to his death in 1925 and a sometimes overbearing physical presence on the weekends, Adam Beck personally oversaw all major and even many minor renovations.

A society beauty, Lillian Beck also continued to be a fiercely competitive horsewoman. The Beck stables produced a string of outstanding hunter-class horses that won Adam and Lillian international recognition. In 1907 they competed in the Olympia Horse Show in London, England, where Lillian's horse My Fellow won its class. To remain competitive, the Becks leased an estate in England in 1913 to maintain their equestrian operation at the highest international standards. From that time onward Lillian and Marion lived about half the year in England; Adam paid extended visits when his schedule permitted. In 1914 their prize-winning horses Melrose, Sir Edward, and Sir James were counted among the finest middleweight and heavyweight hunters in the world. The Becks also competed regularly at the National Horse Show in New York City where, in 1915, Lillian was named a judge over chauvinist protests, famously breaking down the barriers of this once exclusively male domain.

Adam Beck's contribution to London had been publicly recognized in an unprecedented dinner given in his honour on 25 Nov. 1913. At this glittering affair, attended by 500 in the Masonic Temple, Anglican bishop David Williams proclaimed him "incorrupt and incorruptible"; Roman Catholic bishop Michael Francis Fallon eulogized his vision, character, and charitable works; and the mayor and city council gave him a silver candelabra and tray. While the ladies looked on from the galleries, the head-table guests were served their dinners from a small electric railway. According to the *London Free Press*, this banquet was "the most remarkable and spontaneous demonstration of affection and regard ever tendered a public man in London." Visibly moved, Beck spoke briefly of his satisfaction at lightening the load of the poor, the housewife, the farmer, the merchant, and afflicted children, and pledged to carry on the fight to create a renewed citizenship based upon "service, progress and righteousness." These local honours were crowned the following year when he received a knighthood in the king's June honours list. He was now Sir Adam, the Power Knight, and Lillian formally became what she had long been in style, Lady Beck. Charging at fences on horseback, or driving the rapidly growing Hydro system forward, Sir Adam Beck was at the height of his power in 1914.

Re-elected by a large majority in the general election of 29 June 1914, Beck directed a major structural transformation of Hydro during his next term with fewer constraints than in the past. Whitney, who died in September, was replaced by a less adept premier, William Howard Hearst. Beck's nemesis, John Hendrie, resigned from the Hydro-Electric Power Commission to become lieutenant governor. Beck thus had a much freer rein, though Hearst did not include him in his cabinet. Hydro's head set about expanding his organization with a powerful lobby, the Ontario Municipal Electric Association, zealously behind him. Beck and the regional municipalities fixed upon electric radial railways as a major force for modernization and rural reconstruction. In 1913 the Hydro Electric Railway Act and amendments to the Ontario Railway Act had prepared the way legislatively. A web of light lines that connected farms, towns, and cities and delivered transportation at cost under a public authority had enormous appeal and Beck became its most ardent hot gospeller. He managed to have the abject London and Port Stanley Railway electrified as a glowing prototype. Coincidentally the baseload of the proposed railways would greatly increase electric consumption and drive Hydro to a new stage of development as a fully integrated regional monopoly that provided hydroelectric generation, transmission, and distribution services as well as high-speed transportation. This grandiose vision of electrical modernization had commensurate costs, which Beck somewhat disingenuously managed to minimize.

In 1914 Hydro and the municipalities received legislative permission, subject to ratepayer approval, to enter into the inter-city electric railway business. By stages Hydro acquired the legal authority to generate power as well as distribute it through the purchase of a utility (Big Chute) on the Severn River and the construction of regional power stations in 1914–15 at Wasdell Falls, also on the Severn, and Eugenia Falls, near Flesherton. These were sideshows, however; the centrepiece of the proposed integrated system remained Niagara. In 1914 Hydro quietly began planning for a massive hydroelectric station there, but there was precious little water left at Niagara to turn the turbines. A treaty negotiated with the United States in 1908 limited the amount that might be diverted for power purposes; the three existing private companies at Niagara had already acquired, between them, the rights to most of the Canadian quota. Beck had made the development of the hydroelectric system into the central issue on the Ontario political agenda when conflict broke out in Europe in August 1914.

The Becks threw themselves wholeheartedly into the war effort. In 1912 the military authorities had cleverly put Adam's organizing talents and his knowledge of horses together by naming him to a remount committee. At the outset of the war he took charge of acquiring horses for the Canadian army in the territory from Halifax to the Lakehead. In June 1915 he assumed this responsibility for the British army as well, an appointment that brought him an honorary colonelcy. Inevitably, allegations arose that his agency either paid too much for horses or acquired unsuitable remounts, but the claims were not substantiated upon investigation. Together Adam and Lillian Beck also made personal contributions to the war effort, donating all of their champion horses to the cause. Lieutenant-General Edwin Alfred Hervey Alderson, for example, rode Sir James, Adam's most famous horse. Lady Beck, in England for most of the war, working with the Canadian Red Cross Society, devoted herself particularly to ensuring that wounded veterans were welcomed into British country homes for their convalescence. The Queen Alexandra Sanatorium in Ontario was expanded in 1917–18 to accommodate the rehabilitation of wounded returnees. The arrangement worked well, but in the later stages of the war battle-hardened veterans began to complain about the hospital's stern regimen, much of which was attributed to Sir Adam's "Germanic" direction. In 1916, for his local and patriotic help, Beck had received an LLD from the Western University of London, which he served as a director and later as chancellor.

At first the war had relatively little impact on Beck's plans for Hydro. The municipal elections of January 1917, for example, revolved around the approval of by-laws for Hydro radials and vague authorization for the future generation of power at Niagara. Then the rapidly increasing power demands of wartime industrialization provided the overriding urgency, later in 1917, to overcome opposition to the purchase of one of the power companies at Niagara (Ontario Power) and forge ahead with the construction of a large diversion canal and a world-scale plant at Queenston, which would make much more efficient use of the available water. Shamelessly using the moral purpose of the war, Beck hemmed in his private competitors even more, setting the stage for their eventual acquisition, though the negotiations would be unduly drawn out, litigious, and embittered. However, war, inflation, railway nationalization, and the demands of automotive technology for better roads combined to damp enthusiasm for the radial railway project. Moreover, the problem for the Hydro-Electric Commission now was not finding ways of selling surplus power, but rather keeping up with galloping industrial, commercial, municipal, and domestic demand. When the war ended, Hydro's transformation into an integrated utility producing as well as transmitting its own power was much closer to realization. Its corresponding administrative growth had been grandly marked by the ornate office building begun on University Avenue in Toronto in 1914 and occupied in 1916. Sir Adam had a good war, but he emerged from it a wounded politician.

From the very beginning there had been critics of the Hydro project and Beck's management of it. Canadian private producers and British investors placed obstacles in the way during the early stages. As Hydro advanced, it attracted new critics: private power advocates from the United States, who viewed the progress of public ownership in Ontario with alarm. In 1912 a New York State committee of investigation, the Ferris committee, issued a censorious report. A year later a prominent American hydroelectric expert, Reginald Pelham Bolton, denounced the unorthodox financing of Hydro in *An expensive experiment: the Hydro-Electric Power Commission of Ontario* (New York, 1913). Between 15 July and 23 Dec. 1916 James Mavor, a professor of political economy at the University of Toronto, published a devastating critique of Hydro's lack of accountability, dictatorial methods, and tendency to subvert democracy in a series of articles in the *Financial Post* (Toronto), later reprinted as *Niagara in politics: a critical account of the Ontario Hydro-Electric Commission* (New York, 1925).

In the final analysis Beck was his own worst enemy. His authoritarian management style invited criticism. In 1916 the provincial auditor, James Clancy, threw up his hands at Hydro's accounting practices. Beck embarrassed his premier and government with surprises. He was not one to compromise, even with his friends. A scrapper and sometimes a bully, he intimidated his staff and his municipal allies, and regarded the government and the legislature with disdain. He was more popular and more powerful than the premier, and he acted as if he knew it. Hydro, in his mind, was bigger than any government and he was the personal embodiment of Hydro. Cautious people who wanted to know in advance how much projects would cost were battered into submission and put on his list of enemies; when the bills added up to two or three times the initial estimates, there were always convoluted exculpatory explanations. Dismissing his censors, Beck stormed ahead, fuming with rage at the conspiracies mounted against him and bristling with indignation at the slightest criticism. Even Beck's defenders tired of his haughty, domineering ways. A frustrated Hearst, when accused by Beck of hindering Hydro's development in the spring of 1919, rebuked Sir Adam for never taking him into his confidence, for his presumptuous attitude towards parliament, and for saddling others with responsibility for Hydro's mounting debt. Beck responded by withdrawing his support from the government and by announcing his intention to run independently in the upcoming election.

The election of October 1919 came as a devastating blow to Beck and, potentially, to his project. As an independent in London, he was defeated by his sole opponent, Dr Hugh Allan Stevenson, the Labour candidate, who benefited from disaffected Tory votes, some nastiness about Beck's ethnic background, and a vocal uprising amongst the returned soldiers in the Queen Alexandra Sanatorium. The timing could not have been worse. Beck's massive Queenston hydroelectric station lay only half completed and the radial railway scheme had stalled; however, Beck's enormous popularity, which transcended party lines, saved him. The victorious but leaderless United Farmers of Ontario initially sounded him out as a possible premier, but both sides quickly thought better of it. Although Labour strongly supported Hydro, the UFO were much more reserved, especially about Beck's radial-railway enthusiasms; they preferred improved roads. As chairman of the Hydro-Electric Power Commission, Beck had also been an MPP and, for much of the time, a minister without portfolio. The election broke that political connection with the government in power. The eventual premier, Ernest Charles Drury, had little choice but to keep Beck on as chairman, but he appointed a tough ex-soldier, Lieutenant-Colonel Dougall Carmichael, to the commission to keep him in line.

Over the next four years the new government and the tempestuous Power Knight remained locked in combat. For much of the time William Rothwell Plewman, a reporter for the *Toronto Daily Star*, acted as unofficial mediator between Hydro and the premier, who was determined that Hydro do the government's bidding and not the other way around. On 6 July 1920 the government announced a royal commission to reconsider Beck's radial program in light of the rising costs, disappointing experience in other jurisdictions, and technological change. Beck immediately orchestrated a campaign of resistance. In emergency meetings on the 8th at Toronto city hall and the Hydro building, for instance, the Hydro-Electric Radial Association registered its "strong disapproval" of the commission. Provincial treasurer Peter Smith responded for the government that it would not be stampeded. In July 1921 the commission, chaired by Robert Franklin Sutherland, produced a report that was highly critical of radials and recommended construction of only a much reduced system. Meanwhile, Beck had wasted valuable political capital in an acrimonious takeover of Sir William Mackenzie's Toronto Power Company Limited and its related electric and radial companies and in fighting the City of Toronto over an eight-track entry corridor for a mammoth radial system. Characteristically, he condemned the Sutherland report in an intemperate pamphlet and urged the municipalities not to let up in their campaign. The adverse report, a hostile provincial government, and defeats for radial by-laws (particularly in Toronto) in the municipal elections of January 1922 effectively put an end to Beck's radial dream.

Drury, concerned at the spiralling costs of the Queenston hydro-electric plant, wanted an inquiry into this project as well. At first Beck agreed. However, when his hand-picked expert, Hugh Lincoln Cooper, questioned the design, recalculated the costs upward, and insisted upon changes in the power canal to enhance capacity, Beck rejected his advice and appointed another consulting engineer. The turbines had begun to turn on the first phase of this huge project on 29 Dec. 1921, but there seemed to be no relation between the estimates Beck presented and the mounting bills; in one year the difference amounted to $20 million. Unable to explain the situation, Colonel Carmichael offered his resignation, which the premier refused. The cost of the undertaking, now much larger, had ballooned from the initial $20 million to $84 million and counting. Drury, who had to guarantee the bonds for the over-budget project and take political responsibility for it, insisted upon a commission of inquiry with a sweeping mandate to examine the overall operations of Hydro, not just Queenston. This commission, appointed in April 1922 and chaired by Liberal lawyer Walter Dymond Gregory, became in effect an adversarial audit of Beck's management that involved scores of witnesses, produced thousands of pages of testimony, and ran into the middle of 1923.

These political setbacks were, in some respects, the least of his problems. On 17 Oct. 1921 his beloved wife had died from complications following surgery for pancreatitis. Sir Adam and Lady Beck had been a deeply devoted couple despite their often long absences from one another. Living in the Alexandra apartments next to the Hydro building, they had only just begun to settle into life together in Toronto society. Moreover, she had been the one mellowing influence in his life. He was devastated by the loss. A widower, he was now also the single parent of a fiercely independent teenager. With the check upon his temper in a Hamilton grave, he became more difficult and erratic in the face of his daughter's defiance and the ascendancy of those he considered to be his political enemies. These were the years of Beck's towering, black rages.

Beck had run Hydro as a private corporation. Honest and incorruptible personally, he nevertheless paid scant attention to the niceties of accounting. He would routinely spend funds authorized for one purpose on any project he deemed in the interests of Hydro, including local by-law campaigns. For Beck the ends justified the means. Meanwhile, his vision of a provincial, publicly owned hydroelectric monopoly that served the municipal utilities and provided power at the lowest possible cost had been largely realized. In 1923 Hydro served 393 municipalities and distributed 685,000 horsepower using facilities in which over $170 million had been invested. Beck was a magnificent builder. There could be no denying his accomplishments, though, as the hearings of the Gregory commission showed, his management style, planning, political methods, and accountability to the legislature could be questioned.

The vexations suffered at the hands of the UFO government eventually drew Beck back to the bosom of the Conservative party in self-defence. In the election of June 1923 he stood as a Conservative in his old London riding. The irony of a civil servant running as a candidate in opposition to the government was not lost on Drury or the *Farmers' Sun* (Toronto), but Beck managed to get away with it. This time he won with a plurality of more than 7,000 votes – a wonderful personal vindication. George Howard Ferguson's Conservatives swept the province, and Beck returned to cabinet in July as a minister without portfolio. Ferguson brought the Gregory inquiry to an abrupt conclusion and made much of the fact that Sir Adam's general stewardship of Hydro had been supported in the commission's voluminous evidence and summary reports. Beck's probity could be stressed while quietly the government used the critical aspects of Gregory's reports to bring Hydro more fully within the framework of financial and political accountability.

Then, just when it seemed these clouds had passed over, Beck's personal integrity came under attack from an unexpected source. Hydro secretary E. Clarence Settell absconded with $30,000 in Hydro funds and left a blackmailing letter itemizing Sir Adam's alleged misdeeds. When he was apprehended in October 1924 heading for the border with his mistress, he added further charges to the indictment. Wounded by Settell's treachery, and by now a very sick man, Beck had to endure yet another inquiry as judge Colin George Snider conducted an investigation of more than 40 specific allegations having to do with the private use of automobiles, misappropriation of public money, unauthorized expenditures, conflicts of interest in tendering, and irregularities in expense records. Issued in December, Snider's report condemned Isaac Benson Lucas's management of Hydro's legal department and Frederick Arthur Gaby's conflict of interest in a dredging contract within the engineering department, but it found no evidence of serious wrongdoing by Beck. Save for a few petty mistakes in his expense accounts, the commission exonerated him. Settell went to jail for three years. Although another attempt "to get" Sir Adam, in the words of the Toronto *Globe*, had failed, the critics continued the battle of the books against Hydro. Beck thundered back with vigorous refutations in pamphlets that put his fighting spirit on full display. Returning to London one night by train, he gestured in some excitement to his travelling companion and long-time ally Edward Victor Buchanan, head of London's utilities: "Look out there! The lights in the farms. That's what I've been fighting for."

The political struggle and quarrels with his daughter over her determination to marry Strathearn Hay, whom he deemed unsuitable in part because he was related to the Hendrie family, exhausted Beck, whose health and mental outlook deteriorated. It took Howard Ferguson's intervention to persuade him to attend Marion's wedding in January 1925. Ordered to rest by his doctors, who had diagnosed his illness as pernicious anaemia, Beck went to South Carolina for a holiday in February, and then he underwent transfusion treatment at Johns Hopkins Hospital in Baltimore. There he brooded about his beloved Hydro, strategies for the hydroelectric development of the St Lawrence River, and the continuing machinations of the private power interests, and he grumbled that the premier and his colleagues in government were neglecting him. He was a broken man by his own admission.

In May, Beck quietly slipped back to his home in London, where he attempted to conduct Hydro business by telephone from his bedroom. He weakened rapidly over the summer and died on 15 Aug. 1925 in his 69th year. Beck's passing shocked the province; the seriousness of his condition had not been widely understood. The death announcement occasioned a spontaneous outpouring of grief, with eulogies pouring in from every quarter. His obituaries filled pages in the newspapers. "Canada has not produced a greater man than the late Sir Adam Beck," declared *Saturday Night* (Toronto) as it enshrined him in the national pantheon along with Sir John A. Macdonald, George Stephen, 1st Baron Mount Stephen, and Sir William Cornelius Van Horne. Ontario city halls were draped in black, the Hydro shops and offices closed in tribute, and in London business ceased for an hour. Thousands lined the streets for his funeral cortège. The ceremony at St Paul's Anglican Cathedral, attended by all the major political figures of the province, was also broadcast over the radio. As his funeral train mournfully passed from London across Beck's political heartland to Hamilton, where he was to be interred in Hamilton Cemetery under a granite cross beside his wife, farmers and their families paused from their toil and men swept their hats from their heads. The entire Toronto City Council attended his burial. It is a small irony that Beck lies in what he would have considered enemy ground, Hamilton, the last bastion of private power. But for once his wish to be beside his wife overcame his prejudices.

Sir Adam Beck's death marked the end of an unusual period in

Ontario politics, one in which the chairman of Hydro had exercised greater power and influence than the premier and commanded a broad-based, populist political following much stronger than any political party. In building Hydro, Beck almost succeeded in creating an institution that was a law unto itself and for a long time it would continue to demonstrate some of the characteristics of independence. He died a wealthy man with an estate valued at more than $627,000, although his manufacturing business had been in decline for some years. His salary from his chairmanship of Hydro over 20 years totalled $197,000. Some of his wealth may have come to him from his wife. After making numerous small bequests to relatives and charities, he left a trust fund of approximately half a million dollars to his daughter and her heirs.

Beck's memory was kept alive by the Ontario Municipal Electric Association, Hydro, and the citizens of London. In 1934 Toronto and the Hydro municipalities raised a splendid monument to him that still commands University Avenue. This brooding statue, by Emanuel Otto Hahn, and Beck's grave in Hamilton became sites of regular pilgrimages and wreath-laying ceremonies by the heirs and successors to the OMEA as they struggled to perpetuate the notion of Hydro as a municipal cooperative. Hydro publications regularly stressed the vision and legacy of Beck during the era of growth after World War I; eventually the much enlarged power stations at Queenston were renamed Beck No. 1 and Beck No. 2 in his honour. In London a new collegiate was named after him and a nearby public school was named after Lady Beck. The Women's Sanatorium Aid Society of London built a charming chapel, St Luke's in the Garden, across from the Queen Alexandra Sanatorium in memory of the Becks in 1932. The sanatorium itself became the Beck Memorial Sanatorium in 1948. In print, W. R. Plewman's vivid 1947 biography captured the greatness of Beck and the tempestuous nature of his personality. Merrill Denison's commissioned history of Hydro in 1960 established continuity between the transcendent hero figure at the beginning and the transforming, province-girdling corporation Hydro had become in the postwar era.

As the obituaries noted, Hydro itself was Beck's greatest monument. He worried on his deathbed that political partisanship would overcome it and that Hydro as an independent entity would not survive. But in his absence it continued to flourish, firmly rooted in the towns and cities, along the back concessions, and amongst the merchants, workers, farmers, and homemakers of the province. Hydroelectricity generated and delivered by a crown corporation to municipally owned utilities at the lowest cost had become an Ontario institution that would outlive changing governments and passing ideologies. That had largely been Sir Adam Beck's doing.

H. V. NELLES

Further reading

Merrill Denison, *The people's power: the history of Ontario Hydro* ([Toronto], 1960).

N. B. Freeman, *The politics of power: Ontario Hydro and its government, 1906–1995* (Toronto and Buffalo, N.Y., 1996).

K. R. Fleming, *Power at cost: Ontario Hydro and rural electrification, 1911–1958* (Montreal and Kingston, Ont., 1992).

H. V. Nelles, *The politics of development: forests, mines & hydro-electric power in Ontario, 1849–1941* (Toronto, 1974).

C. W. Humphries, *"Honest enough to be bold": the life and times of Sir James Pliny Whitney* (Toronto, 1985).

Grand Trunk Railway Engineering Department group, composite 1877
The railways were crucial for entrepreneurs to open up and connect markets, and were profitable businesses in their own right. Men like Louis-Adélard Senécal, Sir Robert Gillespie Reid, Sir Hugh Allan, and Sir William Cornelius Van Horne combined engineering, financial, and managerial skills to create great Canadian railways like the Grand Trunk and the Canadian Pacific.

LINE 45; OR OUR WALL OF CHINA.

Line 45; or our Wall of China (12 Feb. 1876)
This cartoon by Henri Julien depicts the perception of many entrepreneurs that low tariffs allowed cheap American industrial goods (represented by Uncle Sam) to be dumped into the Canadian market at the expense of Canadian industry (represented by a habitant). In 1879 the National Policy erected a tariff wall that protected some Canadian industries from foreign competition, but many Canadian businesses and consumers resented the resulting increases in prices.

Jewish butcher sign, the Ward, Toronto, about 1910
This photo was taken in the Toronto slum known as the Ward. Non-Jewish Canadians often had ambivalent feelings about Jews, admiring their entrepreneurial spirit while worrying that they might create social instability, an attitude also applied to other entrepreneurial immigrant groups like the Chinese.

William Notman Studio, 17 Bleury Street, Montreal, Que., about 1875
Combining both artistic sensibility and business sense, Notman was not only a successful businessman but also a recorder of the Canadian business elite of the late 19th century. In this location he employed over 50 people, and by the mid 1880s he had some 20 studios in Canada and the United States, making his business one of Canada's first successful international expansions in the service sector.

Anson McKim's office, Montreal, Que., 1903
Anson McKim played an important role in the Canadian advertising industry and
the advent of a mass consumption society. His clients included the Bank of Montreal,
Henry Birks and Sons, the T. Eaton Company Limited, Labatt and Company, and
Henry Morgan and Company.

Public auction at old town hall, Regina, 1906
Viva voce auctioneers once performed an important economic function in the
allocation of resources, especially in an era when business failure was common.
The building under construction at the right also reminds us that business on the
prairies grew rapidly during the boom that coincided with Sir Wilfrid Laurier's time
as prime minister.

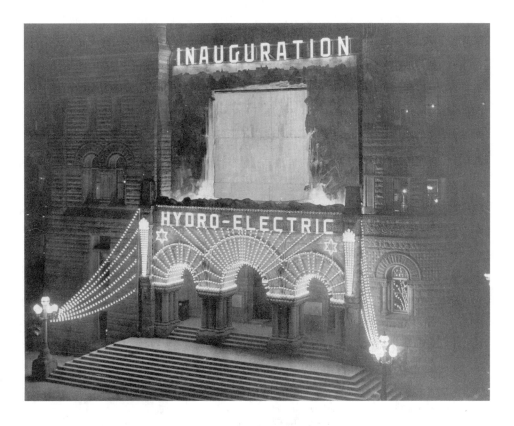

Inauguration of hydro-electric power in Toronto, City Hall, May 2, 1911
Public or private ownership of the electricity system in Ontario divided the business community, but industrialists such as Sir Adam Beck led the way in policy decisions. The decision of the provincial government to bring the industry into public ownership was driven by the desire of manufacturers for cheap electricity and illustrates the emergence of a distinctively Canadian brand of entrepreneurship by the state, the crown corporation.

Toronto Stock Exchange board, 1910 or 1912
As Canadian businesses grew, they had greater need for capital, for which domestic sources became more important. Banks were not always an option for more speculative industries, especially mineral exploration, and stock exchanges in Toronto and Montreal served an important purpose by concentrating the financial resources of individual investors and supplying the proceeds to business. Brokers like Rodolphe Forget became entrepreneurs in their own right.

American tourists in an automobile, Ottawa, Ont., 1925
The advent of mass motoring, and mass tourism, accelerated the integration of Canada into the American economy by facilitating social and economic exchange between the two countries. In the automobile industry, Gordon Morton McGregor produced cars for Canada and the imperial market outside the United Kingdom.

His Majesty's Airship R-100, over the Canadian Bank of Commerce, the tallest building in the British empire, August 1930
This photo shows Toronto's financial district as it looked at the start of the Great Depression. The 1929 stock market crash marked the beginning of a new era in Canadian capitalism, characterized by much more state intervention in the economy. It also inaugurated Toronto's eclipse of Montreal as Canada's undisputed financial capital.

Section 6

Brand Names and Big Business

TIMOTHY EATON,

merchant; b. March 1834 in Clogher, near Ballymena (Northern Ireland), fourth son of John Eaton, a tenant farmer, and Margaret Craig; m. 28 May 1862 Margaret Wilson Beattie, and they had five sons and three daughters; d. 31 Jan. 1907 in Toronto.

Descended from Scottish bondsmen taken to Ulster before 1626, Timothy Eaton, according to family research, was born two months after the decease of his father, who died on 30 Jan. 1834. He was raised on a farm outside Ballymena, one of Ulster's major linen markets and a regional centre for the export of agricultural produce. Attendance at the local National School was followed by a brief period at an academy in Ballymena, from which Timothy was withdrawn in 1847 on the master's advice. Whether his removal was solely due to lack of academic interest or the result of problems arising from the Great Famine is unclear. Thus, at the age of 13, Eaton was apprenticed to a Mr Smith, related by marriage to the Craig side of the family, who owned a general store in nearby Portglenone. Smith was strict and Eaton found some aspects of his employment onerous enough to wish the agreement terminated. Rather than lose the £100 bond posted at the commencement of his service, his mother persuaded him to continue. Her death in 1848 undoubtedly reinforced the sturdy self-reliance that had been fostered by both farm life and a Presbyterian upbringing. Upon completing his apprenticeship in 1852, he worked briefly for another Portglenone merchant, employment that allowed him to acquire the funds necessary for a move to the New World.

Emigration had increasingly been the resort of Ulster Presbyterians anxious to better conditions damaged by the British move towards free trade in place of colonial trade preferences. In 1854, following the path taken earlier by three of his sisters and his brothers Robert and James, Eaton travelled to the Georgetown area of Upper Canada, where a maternal aunt and her husband had settled in 1833. He found employment as a junior bookkeeping clerk at a small general store in Glen Williams, just outside Georgetown.

From 1853 to 1856 Upper Canada experienced a period of prosperity, the result of demands arising from the Crimean War and the construction of the Grand Trunk Railway. Motivated by the possibility of greater local development and personal success farther west, Eaton and his brothers moved in the winter of 1855–56 in order to start up business in the Huron Tract, an area still undergoing settlement. Robert established himself in St Marys, Blanshard Township's largest centre; Timothy and James opened a small general store in the nearby hamlet of Kirkton. In July 1856 James became postmaster there and received the contract for the mail service between Kirkton and St Marys. Timothy, the active partner in J. and T. Eaton, had overall responsibility for the daily business of the store and post office, while James involved himself in other business ventures. The store's merchandise, initially dry goods and groceries, was purchased on long-term credit from Adam Hope of London, then affiliated with Peter and Isaac Buchanan of Hamilton. In 1860, perhaps in an attempt to use up produce received in exchange for his wares, Timothy Eaton added baked goods to his grocery line.

The economic depression of the late 1850s severely confined trade and commerce in Canada. Wholesalers, among them the Buchanans, tried to reduce losses by requiring firm security, in the form of property mortgages or life-insurance policies, on strictly limited quantities of goods. The Eaton business seems to have weathered the depression better than most and mortgage accommodation granted by the Buchanans was rapidly repaid. With possibilities for further growth restricted by the Eatons' rural location and the establishment of another store in Kirkton, Timothy moved in the winter of 1860–61 to St Marys, where he established a bakery, but local competition shortly compelled its dissolution.

In May 1861 Eaton, again in partnership with his brother James, opened a general store in St Marys. Though he advertised his intention to sell all goods for cash, he continued to advance credit to his customers. Despite long-accepted myths, Timothy Eaton was not the first merchant to introduce cash sales to Canadian shoppers, for even before the depression this concept was gaining acceptance. Many North American urban merchants had found that selling for cash allowed them to offer cheaper prices and thereby increase their volume of sales. Widespread adoption of this practice, however, was rendered impossible in much of rural Canada by the severe shortage of specie.

During the period 1860–67, one of agricultural prosperity in western Upper Canada, the Eaton business expanded and raised its ranking with Hope and Isaac Buchanan to the top 10 per cent of their more than 250 customers. Just as Toronto wholesalers used the Grand Trunk to penetrate much of the western part of the province in search of markets, Timothy Eaton extended his own commercial horizons by establishing an early connection with John Macdonald, a leading Toronto wholesaler and a fellow Methodist. (Eaton had converted to Methodism in 1858.) However, any hopes for expansion in St Marys were restricted by limited growth in a centre served by numerous general stores, and in December 1868 the Eaton brothers' partnership was dissolved. Leaving James in possession of the store, Timothy moved with his family to Toronto, where, early in 1869, he took the route traditionally followed by retailers and established a wholesale business. Little evidence exists regarding this venture, which he set up with an investment of $5,000 at 8½ Front Street West. It seems likely, however, that its out-of-the-way location and a generally unstable business climate, including extremely stiff competition, caused its swift termination.

Rejecting the possibility of opening a grocery store because of his dislike of dealing with "Licquors," Eaton returned to a familiar retail line, dry goods. In December 1869 he paid $6,500 to James Jennings and John Brandon, fellow worshippers at Elm Street Methodist Church, for their dry-goods business in rented premises at 178 Yonge Street, known as Britannia House. All goods would be sold at fixed prices for cash only, an excellent concept for a merchant whose custom would be derived from strangers of unknown financial circumstances. Although located near Queen Street, well away from the fashionable retail district of King Street, Eaton was now established in the line that would serve as the advance guard of the retail industry in the changes it was undergoing. Furthermore, by directing his appeal to the growing ranks of working men and women who received regular cash wages, he tapped a developing market that would form his base for future growth. Increasing urbanization and industrialization, a burgeoning population, and rising living standards ultimately effected a democratization of luxury. Demand increased for goods formerly purchased only by a middle-class or wealthy clientele at retail stores such as those in Toronto of Robert Walker or William Allan Murray.

Eaton initially purchased most of his merchandise on long-term credit from John Macdonald. However, convinced that the prices charged by Toronto wholesalers were excessive, in the early 1870s he made the first of many trips to Great Britain, where he located cheaper sources of supply. Despite early difficulties, annual sales at the Eaton store rose from $25,416 in 1870 to $154,978 in 1880. Since expansion was obstructed by Robert Simpson's store, which moved to 174–76 Yonge Street in 1881, and by Knox's Church on Queen Street West, Eaton acted instead to fulfil an earlier wish, and in 1881 he opened a wholesale house at 42 Scott Street. Guided by a strong sense of what was practical and profitable, he soon realized that the wholesale industry was experiencing diminishing returns and that the retail trade offered greater opportunity for gain, from increased volume and rapid turnovers of stock rather than mark-up, as had earlier been the case. He therefore brought his wholesale business to a swift end in the summer of 1883.

In order to achieve his retail goals, Eaton had purchased property in November 1882 at 190–96 Yonge Street from Charles Page for $41,000. By demolishing the stores there, he was able to erect an imposing, three-storey building featuring many architectural innovations, such as electric lighting, large skylights that allowed light to penetrate all floors, and a fire-sprinkler system. Since he did not wish to frighten away his working-class customers, no attempt was made to imitate the luxurious décor of some American stores. The new store opened on 22 Aug. 1883, but, in an indication of his competition with Simpson, Eaton kept his old store at 178 Yonge locked and vacant for the duration of his lease, more than six months, so that Simpson could not move in and take advantage of the Eaton connection.

Eaton's store underwent almost continuous expansion from 1884 through the purchase of properties on Yonge, Queen, Albert, James, Orde, and Louisa streets and on Trinity Square. By 1907 the business covered 22 acres of prime downtown land. Operating a vastly expanded establishment demanded a larger market. Many new services were therefore introduced: waiting-rooms, restaurants, parcel checks, free bus service from train and boat stations, and shoe repair – all designed to prevent customers from patronizing other stores. The initiation in 1884 of a mail-order service using catalogues extended the concept of cash sales for fixed prices and gave Canadians across the country access to merchandise not otherwise available. As in the store, goods found unsatisfactory could be exchanged or the money was refunded. In Toronto special sales drew people to the store during seasons formerly accepted as slow, January, February, and August. Attractions such as animated exhibitions, after-hours musical programs, fashion shows, and the Santa Claus parade introduced in 1905 kept the Eaton name to the fore. As the store grew in size so too did the company's expenditure on advertising, until by 1900 the *Toronto Daily Star* was carrying a full-page advertisement each day. This was a far cry from the two-inch insertion common in the 1870s, but the stress as then was on the Eaton guarantee of quality, value, and service.

Having thus established his reputation, Eaton firmly repudiated attempts by family members to trade on the Eaton name. In 1888 his brother James, who had moved to Toronto in 1882, advertised his clothing store as a branch of Timothy's establishment. James's son John Weldon took similar liberties in 1895 when he opened a full-line department store. Timothy publicly dissociated himself from both ventures, which were established on shaky foundations, achieved only limited success, and soon failed.

To the ever-increasing variety of dry goods sold in his store Eaton added new product lines, among them sporting goods, musical instruments, drugs, groceries, and furniture. By the early 1890s his early dry-goods store had been transformed into a new entity, the department store, examples of which also developed in other major Canadian cities. The official incorporation of T. Eaton Company Limited on 21 April 1891, with a capitalization of $500,000, resulted in few changes in the firm's procedures. In line with its president's belief in financial privacy, the company continued as a family-owned institution and no financial reports were made public. Although some senior personnel were allowed to acquire an interest in the company, more than 80 per cent of the shares were held by family members at all times. In April 1905 capitalization was increased to $1,000,000.

Eaton's enormous influence on merchandising trends in the 1890s, notably through his willingness to venture into constant expansion and innovation, set him apart from all his Toronto competitors. In an attempt to secure ever better prices, he was quick to take advantage of the desire among manufacturers to procure stable markets and a reduction in their costs by selling direct to retailers. Manufacturers' agents seeking large orders regularly besieged Eaton's buying office in Toronto, as well as those opened in London (1892) and Paris (1898). Backed by the power of volume and sure financial security, the company could persuade them to meet its terms. Eaton even got some manufacturers to produce goods marked with the Eatonia brand.

The alacrity with which other retailers adopted the practice of direct buying was in large measure responsible for the decline in the wholesale sector of the dry-goods industry, and the 1890s saw the failure of several large businesses, among them those established by Adam Hope and William McMaster. Toronto wholesalers, however, successfully dissuaded some Canadian manufacturers from making direct sales. To enable him to acquire the Canadian material necessary for his growing production of a wide range of ready-to-wear clothes for men and women, Eaton was compelled in 1892 to establish a separate firm, Wilson and Company. The entrance into manufacturing in 1890, a logical extension of the production of custom-made garments by his store's millinery work-room, was but another attempt to reduce costs and prices. Eaton's establishment of the Paint, Oil and Chemical Company of Toronto Limited in 1897 and the T. Eaton Drug Company in 1906 allowed for further diversification. Additional savings were achieved through Eaton's farms at Georgetown and Islington (Toronto), which supplied dairy products for the store and feed for its delivery horses.

Growth in population and an expanding retail sector in Winnipeg convinced Eaton of the need to protect his market in western Canada, where his mail-order catalogue had become an institution. Despite his initial misgivings about managing a store so far from Toronto, the company's first branch store opened in Winnipeg in the summer of 1905. The decision proved a wise one for, although the five-storey building was located away from the city's retail centre, it achieved such success as to require immediate expansion.

In an environment where bankruptcy was common, Eaton's success was due in large measure to his close attention to costing and accounting and the early departmentalization of his store to maximize responsibility and accountability. With each department functioning independently, nothing was left to chance for the profit test simplified the process of decision-making. As the store grew in size and its operation became more complex, its future would not be jeopardized by conservative complacency and extravagant waste. Despite his published statements to the contrary, Eaton, by urging his buyers to secure the best possible terms from suppliers, continued to take advantage of the traditional long-term credit system when purchasing merchandise. Cash sales and rapid turn-overs of stock, exceeding the store average of four times a year in many departments, then ensured excellent fiscal fluidity.

Eaton's vivid memories of his early working life gave him a sympa-thetic attitude towards his employees. A pioneer in the early closing move-ment, in 1876 he began a reduction of working hours from the 12-hour day then customary. By January 1904 the store closed daily at 5:00 P.M. and beginning in 1886 employees enjoyed a half holiday on Saturdays during the summer months. Since the company's statistics clearly dem-onstrated that shorter hours would effect no appreciable decline in sales volume, Eaton could reduce overhead costs while promoting his reputa-tion as a benevolent employer. The implementation of a primitive medical plan in the 1890s further enhanced this image. Although Eaton strongly opposed trade unions, and he faced strikes on different occasions in his departments, it seems likely that the growth of these organizations during the 1880s and the expressed concern of the provincial government about working conditions also influenced company policy.

During Eaton's business career, the number of employees rose from four in 1869 to more than 7,000 in 1907. His considerable ability to manage this vast sales and administrative staff, many of whom were unskilled women entering the workforce for the first time, was the result of his willingness to delegate authority. In common with many of his contemporaries, such as John Macdonald, Eaton initially recruited mem-bers of his family in the management of the store. His eldest son, Edward Young, began his career at the age of 17 in 1888; he was joined in 1893 by his brother John Craig. However, like other employees, they were required to work their way up. Both inherited the Eaton flair for business and it was largely at Edward's urging that many technological changes were introduced into the store's operations. John was primarily respon-sible for the establishment of the Winnipeg store, having persuaded his father of the need for a western outlet. Edward's early death in 1900 compelled Timothy to remain as president until his own death in 1907, at which time John assumed the burden. Eaton also hired profession-al managers and, by encouraging their initiative, he benefited from the implementation of ideas that increased both efficiency and productivity. At their urging, for instance, notice was taken of changes introduced in large American stores.

Because of Eaton's novel sales techniques and aggressive expansion, his store, and others like it, became the focus of widespread hostility. Indeed, department stores on both sides of the Atlantic drew the wrath of many small retail merchants. In Canada complaints also emanated from the pharmaceutical industry, the Patrons of Industry, rural merchants, and wholesalers. The strong lobbying for a special tax on department stores undertaken by the Association of Retail Merchants, founded in Toronto in April 1897, and the complaints lodged before Toronto's municipal Court of Revision in 1895 and 1897 regarding evasion of existing taxes by the Eaton company, resulted in an increase in its assessment each time. These actions also drew attention to a commercial grievance, the personalty tax on stock-in-trade, which merchants had long denounced, especially since they already carried the burden of customs duties and taxes on land and buildings. The legislation that resulted from the investigation into municipal taxation by the Ontario assessment commission in 1900 abolished the personalty tax but subjected department stores to a special tax similar to one implemented in Prussia.

Buttressed by a personality of great independence, Eaton deplored the idea of government intervention in business and, given his enormous volume of imported merchandise, heartily resented the National Policy tariff introduced in 1879. He believed that success naturally accompanied industry and efficiency and in 1883 saw no reason for the government "to impose upon the working classes of Canada" merely to encourage expansion in the manufacturing industry. Though never openly identified as a Liberal supporter, he was known to be a great admirer of Sir Wilfrid Laurier. In 1899 he acted with other Toronto businessmen, among them George Albertus Cox and Walter Edward Hart Massey, to create a second Toronto paper committed to the Liberal party, by financing the takeover of the *Evening Star*. Members of the group received shares in exchange for several large payments, but little return was expected on this investment. Since Eaton was wholly occupied in the operation of his store, he seldom participated in other commercial activities, though he was elected a director of the Dominion Bank in 1899.

Eaton's social beliefs, which reflected his business philosophies, and his religious faith played a role in his philanthropy. (Compared with those of Macdonald, the Masseys, and other leading Methodist businessmen, Eaton's givings were limited in range.) He was guided by the optimistic and practical maxims of the day regarding hard work, thrift, and punctuality; he had sympathy only for those in genuine need. Ailing employees, Christian organizations overburdened with debt, among them the Salvation Army and the Young Men's Christian Association, and victims of a fire near Ottawa in 1897 all had reason to be grateful for his generosity. In 1905, at the request of Joseph Wesley Flavelle, Eaton pledged to help build a new general hospital in Toronto.

In converting to Methodism at age 24, Eaton had followed a path already taken by his brothers Robert and James. Perhaps he also felt that Methodism, with its emphasis upon the principle that God helps those who help themselves, afforded a more positive doctrine for life in Canada than did Presbyterianism, with its Calvinistic stress on predestination. For Eaton, God through the saving grace of Jesus Christ was a real presence. This belief was a sustaining force when he and Maggie suffered the loss, in infancy, of two sons and a daughter during their early years in Toronto and the tragic death of their son Edward in 1900. From 1869 Eaton was a regular worshipper at Elm Street Church. In 1887, in his capacity as an elder, he became involved with others in establishing a new church in the Bloor–Yonge area, Western Methodist (later Trinity), which he and his family formally joined two years later.

An ardent enthusiast of evangelical religion, Eaton enjoyed attending revival meetings when visiting preachers, as he wrote to James in 1874, attempted to wake "up all the old crochety & stiff dead members" in the city. His faith led him privately in 1897 to oppose the introduction of Sunday streetcars since he was convinced that this would produce a city no longer fit to be called Toronto the Good. Although he expected his buyers to abide by his own strict Sabbatarian principles when on business, no such constraints were placed on their private lives. He firmly believed that a person exposed to the proper Christian behaviour of others could be persuaded to improve. Hence he opposed the "Soup and Bread" operations of the Salvation Army in Toronto. "Persons who fall under your control in the Shelter," he lectured Commissioner Herbert Henry Booth in 1894, "are surrounded by Christian people and you get acquainted with them, obtain an influence over them, and ultimately lead them to Christ in this way; not so by distributing promiscuously to 'Dead-beats' and 'tramps' on the Street.... I like best to deal personally man to man; know your man and help him all you can." Though equally impatient with those within the Methodist community who did not share his evangelical drive, Eaton reputedly remarked that, as he grew older, he came to the conclusion that he could not judge everyone by his own standards. That may have been the case, but he continued nevertheless to try to exert his influence in those realms, spiritual and commercial, where he wielded power.

By the turn of the century Toronto's retail sector was vastly different from that which had existed earlier. The city's growth and the introduction of streetcar service on Yonge Street in 1861 had been responsible for the gradual movement of retail activity from King to Yonge. Wholly aggressive in outlook, retailers now operated in an environment of highly impersonal competitive trading. Timothy Eaton, and others like him, by taking advantage of market forces had effected an overall change in the industry. The sheer weight of manufacturing output and the pressure of population growth and consequent demand created retail needs that could not be met by traditional shopkeepers. Eaton's experience compelled him to recognize that the merchant who wished to survive had to change with the times. He himself thrived on the competition that forced the elimination of many small retailers. As just one player in such a market, he served as a vital link between the producing and consuming ends of the economy. This role is amply reflected in his company's sales volume. It rose to $53,367,000 by 1914, vastly outpacing the $14,081,451 of the Robert Simpson Company, which had continued to cater primarily to the middle class.

By the mid 1890s financial success allowed the Eatons outwardly to adopt the comfortable life-style of other wealthy Torontonians. However, they continued to maintain their former, simple ways and eschewed the social vices of cards, dancing, drinking, and smoking. Their large residence at the corner of Spadina Road and Lowther Avenue, to which they moved in 1888, allowed them to walk to Western Church, and thus to conform to the Sabbatarian principles of the head of the family, who refused to use his horse and carriage on Sunday. The summers spent at a lake-front property in the Muskoka area allowed Timothy to enjoy the company of his grandchildren. As in the past, the store and his involvement with the church absorbed by far the major portion of his life. By nature abrupt, gruff, and outspoken, although sentimental and kind where his family was concerned, he had little time for or patience with the superficial niceties of social intercourse. Consequently, the family demonstrated little interest in participating in Toronto's active social scene.

Timothy Eaton spent his last years in a wheelchair because of a series of accidents at the turn of the century. He died suddenly from pneumonia in January 1907 at the age of 72, and his passing stunned Toronto's commercial community. He left an estate worth $5,250,000, the result, it was pointed out in obituaries, of his operations in the Toronto retail trade and of "his enlightened faith in printer's ink." He had come a long way from the time when he assured John Macdonald that his assets were "a wife, five children and seven dollars."

JOY L. SANTINK

Further reading

J. L. Santink, *Timothy Eaton and the rise of his department store* (Toronto, 1990).

Rod McQueen, *The Eatons: the rise and fall of Canada's royal family* (Toronto, 1998).

Donica Belisle, *Retail nation: department stores and the making of modern Canada* (Vancouver and Toronto, 2011).

GEORGE ALBERTUS COX,

capitalist; b. 7 May 1840 in Colborne, Northumberland County, Upper Canada, son of Edward William Cox and Jane Tanner; m. first 28 May 1862 Margaret Hopkins (d. 1905) in Peterborough, Upper Canada, and they had three sons and two daughters; m. secondly 14 April 1909 Amy Gertrude Sterling in Toronto; d. there 16 Jan. 1914.

Of English parentage, George Cox was educated in the public and grammar schools of Colborne. He went to work there in 1856 as an operator for the Montreal Telegraph Company, which made him its Peterborough agent two years later. He also sold stationery, dabbled in photography, served as a travel and express agent, and in 1861 added an agency for the Canada Life Assurance Company, then based in Hamilton. Cox later said that on the day he became a Canada Life agent, he planned on becoming the company's president.

As befitted an insurance salesman, Cox became a prominent citizen. Between 1872 and 1886 he served seven one-year terms as mayor of Peterborough, but he failed narrowly to be elected as a Liberal to the Ontario legislature in 1875 and to the dominion parliament in 1887. He was a devoted Methodist, contributing generously to local churches, working to build Methodist institutions, and campaigning vigorously for temperance during the Scott Act referendum of 1885 in Peterborough.

Cox built up his eastern Ontario branch of Canada Life until it was doing almost half the company's business. As well, he was said to have a phenomenal eye for real estate. Gradually he accumulated large property holdings in the Peterborough area. In 1878 he became president of the fledgling Midland Railway, and he was instrumental in reorganizing, completing, and in 1883 leasing the system to the Grand Trunk. In 1880–81 he had been a member of the syndicate headed by Sir William Pearce Howland that lost in a bid to win the charter for the transcontinental railway.

In 1884 Cox invested substantial profits from his railway ventures in founding the Central Canada Loan and Savings Company and several subsidiary mortgage loan operations in Peterborough. Two years later he was invited to join the board of directors of the Toronto-based Canadian Bank of Commerce. He invested heavily in the stock of both the bank and Canada Life.

Cox moved to Toronto in 1888, probably because of the convenience of handling his business network from the province's main commercial centre, and possibly also because Scott Act supporters were distinctly unpopular in Peterborough. In 1890 he was elected president of the Bank of Commerce, which soon began a period of dynamic growth under the leadership of its brilliant general manager, Byron Edmund Walker. Cox's insurance agencies and mortgage loan companies were eventually managed by his three sons (Edward William, Frederick George, and Herbert Coplin) and his son-in-law Alfred Ernest Ames. In 1889 Ames founded a stockbrokerage firm in Toronto; most of its business must have been trading for Cox, who guaranteed Ames's credit at the Bank of Commerce.

A lifelong Liberal, Cox was one of the group that had bought the Toronto *Globe* in the 1880s, and also of the consortium that purchased and reorganized the *Toronto Evening Star* in 1899. He was presumably a major financial backer of the Liberal party, but records have not been found of what were probably large cash donations. In 1896 the newly elected government of Wilfrid Laurier appointed Cox to the Senate, where he was usually inactive. In 1903–4 his name was put forward by Laurier for a knighthood, but Governor General Gilbert John Murray-Kynynmound, 4th Earl of Minto, was cool to the proposal. "Cox I had always doubts about," he wrote, "it was purely a political recommendation as a wealthy Govt. supporter."

In Toronto Cox was a pillar of Sherbourne Street Methodist Church, which became known as the "Millionaires' Church" because of the prominence of wealthy businessmen such as Cox, Ames, Harris Henry Fudger, Albert Edward Kemp, and Joseph Wesley Flavelle, an occasional Cox protégé who had also emigrated from Peterborough. For many years Cox was president of the Ontario Ladies' College in Whitby, Ont., and bursar of Victoria College, the Methodist component of the University of Toronto. He continued to be an active temperance worker, and was a generous supporter of church organizations, the Toronto General Hospital, and other worthy causes.

During the early 1890s Cox moved to gain effective control of Canada Life. He accumulated all the shares he could and forced his way onto its board in 1892, at the cost of considerable resentment by other shareholders and directors. In 1899 Cox, who owned or controlled close to a 50 per cent interest, was instrumental in persuading the board to move Canada Life's head office to Toronto, another step in the centralization of commercial and financial power in Ontario's Queen City. Cox became president and general manager of Canada Life in 1900. As president of the Bank of Commerce and the Central Canada Savings and Loan in that year, he was the man at the centre of one of the country's most important financial networks, controlling the placement of more than $70 million in assets.

The Cox companies formed an identifiable financial family, with intimately interlocking boards, routine and significant inter-firm transactions, and heavy reliance on a managerial/directorial group related to Cox by ties of blood, marriage, religion, or old home town. The network included two fire-insurance companies of which Cox was president, British America Assurance and Western Assurance, and it continued to expand with the founding of Imperial Life Assurance in 1897, National Trust in 1898, and Dominion Securities, a bond-trading company, in 1901. A number of the young men who got their start in Cox companies, such as William Thomas White, Edward Rogers Wood, James Henry Gundy, and Edward Robert Peacock, went on to outstanding careers in politics and finance. In 1898 Cox also briefly held a controlling interest in Manufacturers' Life and the Temperance and General Life Assurance Company.

In the late 1890s and early 1900s the Cox companies seized a striking number of opportunities to invest the capital of their shareholders, policyholders, and depositors in new business ventures. In the early 1890s the Bank of Commerce and Cox had helped underwrite William Mackenzie's Toronto Railway Company, which electrified the city's street-railway system. The Mackenzie connection led the Cox group into financing railways and street railways elsewhere in Canada and in the United States, the most spectacular being the Canadian Northern, the transcontinental line of Mackenzie and Donald Mann.

The familiarity with electrical technology of Mackenzie and some of his associates, including Henry Mill Pellatt, Frederic Thomas Nicholls, and American engineer-promoter Frederick Stark Pearson, led to utility adventuring at home and abroad that was sometimes glitteringly successful. The Cox family's promotion in 1900 of the São Paulo Tramway, Light and Power Company in Brazil, for example, became the basis of the set of enterprises that evolved by 1912 into Brazilian Traction, Light and Power. It became South America's largest utility company and one of the most significant foreign investments by Canadians. The Cox group's equally promising venture to bring power to Toronto from Niagara Falls through the Electrical Development Company of Ontario Limited, founded in 1903, was soon short-circuited by the competing movement for publicly owned low-cost electrical distribution.

In 1899–1900 the Cox companies advanced several prominent mergers and industrial promotions, including the Carter-Crume Company Limited, a manufacturer of sales-books, which evolved into the Moore Corporation, and the Canada Cycle and Motor Company, a merger of bicycle firms that, after some teething troubles, entered automobile manufacturing as well. Cox and several of his associates were active too in mining in British Columbia through the Crow's Nest Pass Coal Company Limited, incorporated in 1897. From 1895 Cox had headed the syndicate that evolved into this company, of which he became president. His group's connection with the Laurier government helped facilitate the Crowsnest Pass agreement with the Canadian Pacific Railway in 1897. Cox also served as a director of the transcontinental Grand Trunk Pacific Railway – even while the Bank of Commerce was backing the Canadian Northern – and of the Dominion Iron and Steel Company Limited in Sydney, N.S. In the first decade of the 20th century his list of directorships expanded to encompass 46 firms, great and small. Literally the landlord of the Toronto Stock Exchange, Cox was one of the two or three most powerful financiers in Edwardian Canada, a mobilizer and investor of capital, hence a pure capitalist.

Because he left few personal or business records, Cox's character reveals itself dimly through a handful of terse letters and the recollections of some associates. Except for his church work, which seems to have involved more of his money than his time, he was single-mindedly devoted to his enterprises. He had no amusements or recreations, and read only newspapers and books about business. His associates marvelled at his grasp of business detail, his knack for figures, and his extraordinary self-possession. As a businessman he appears to have stressed the need to departmentalize large businesses to facilitate close accounting, and to have minimized risk by moving money into opportunities developed by members of proven capacity within his business family.

The public Cox was a close-mouthed man of affairs; the private Cox was said to be a simple, kindly man who supported many unlucky Peterboronians and others in need. Living in a handsome home in an older neighbourhood of Toronto, he chose not to participate in the burst of ostentatious mansion building that consumed the energies and fortunes of some of his younger associates.

Aside from occasional troubles brought on by dips in the business cycle, most of the Cox companies prospered handsomely during the Laurier years. Their business methods came under close scrutiny by the federal royal commission appointed in 1906 to investigate the Canadian life-insurance industry. Its proceedings revealed substantial cross-trading, subsidization, and other insider exchanges among Canada Life, Imperial Life, and other Cox family firms; some of these transactions were covert and/or technically illegal. The commissioners concluded, in their Report of 1907, that Cox's absolute control of Canada Life had "to a marked extent influenced the investments of the company, which have been made to serve not only the interests of the Canada Life Assurance Company, but also his own interests.... In many of these transactions the conflict of Mr. Cox's interest with his duty is so apparent that the care of the insurance funds could not always have been the sole consideration."

Cox found the implication that he had abused situations in which he had multiple interests puzzling, largely because no one could prove that any of his transactions had failed to maximize the interests of policyholders or other investors in his companies. His defence of his conduct in the Senate in April 1907 was a classic apologia for unregulated capitalism, in which he particularly stressed the obvious personal integrity of the men who served on the boards of his firms.

In fact, a number of Cox's associates were becoming increasingly anxious about the ageing financier's determination to use Canada Life as a vehicle for the advancement of his personal family. They privately complained about the quality of Edward Cox's work as general manager, about the covering up of Herbert's incompetence, and about Cox Sr's desire to increase his own salary. In 1911 Zebulon Aiton Lash, for many years the high-minded and brilliant lawyer to the Cox group, resigned from the board of Canada Life, along with Walker and two other directors, in protest against what Lash considered George Cox's "glaring and objectionable ... nepotism." Flavelle, whose intimate business and church associations with the Cox family had begun in Peterborough in the 1860s, had left the board a few years earlier; he had concluded that "Mr. Cox does not possess the moral qualities which enable him to understand trustee relationships."

Cox had relinquished the presidency of the Bank of Commerce in 1907, possibly as a result of concern about bad publicity from the life-insurance inquiry. After his death in 1914, the presidency of Canada Life subsequently passed to one son, then to another; eventually the firm was mutualized and the Cox influence disappeared. Although some of the interlocking relationships in the old Cox family of companies were maintained into the 1980s, many firms had grown, merged, failed, or otherwise drifted out of the system. There was never another godfather to knit a group together as tightly as George Cox had with the "Peterborough Methodist mafia."

G. A. Cox became a millionaire in an age when a million dollars was still a fabulous sum. He had undoubtedly settled large amounts of money on his heirs before his death, so that his final estate of $870,000 would not be a true indicator of the real wealth he had accumulated. He first flourished supplying financial services, dealing in real estate, and promoting railways in a portion of central Ontario where the bounty of resources was creating a measure of general prosperity. His move to Toronto was part of the late-19th-century concentration of sophisticated financial services in that city. By 1900 he had become the wizard of finance at the centre of its most important web of banks, insurance companies, and investment firms. Cox and his associates then became instrumental in the spectacular maturing of the Canadian capital market; they perceived opportunities and developed techniques for funnelling the savings of Canadians, which had hitherto been concentrated in mortgages and bank and railway stock, into new opportunities in utility companies and industrials, sometimes located thousands of miles from Ontario.

The methods Cox used in his career of creative financial intermediation were not unusual for the era. The creation of families or networks of closely interrelated companies was standard practice in 19th-century business, particularly finance. Cox lived into and became somewhat discredited in a time of increased doubt that capitalists could be trusted to finesse their way, on moral character alone, through the conflicts inherent in so many forms of self-dealing. Ironically, the most serious distortions of his judgement arose because George Cox wanted to help out sons who had not inherited his own business ability.

MICHAEL BLISS

Further reading

Christopher Armstrong and H. V. Nelles, *Southern exposure: Canadian promoters in Latin America and the Caribbean, 1896–1930* (Toronto, 1988).

Michael Bliss, "Better and purer: the Peterborough Methodist mafia and the renaissance of Toronto," in *Toronto remembered: a celebration of the city*, comp. William Kilbourn (Toronto, 1984), 194–205.

I. M. Drummond, "Canadian life insurance companies and the capital market, 1890–1914," *Canadian Journal of Economics and Political Science* (Toronto), 28 (1962): 204–24.

Duncan McDowall, *The Light: Brazilian Traction, Light and Power Company Limited, 1899–1945* (Toronto, 1988).

Sir JOHN MORISON GIBSON,

militia officer, lawyer, office holder, politician, and businessman; b. 1 Jan. 1842 in Toronto Township, Upper Canada, son of William Gibson and Mary Sinclair; m. first 26 Oct. 1869 Emily Annie Birrell (d. 1874) in London, Ont.; m. secondly 26 Sept. 1876 Caroline Hope (d. 1877) in Hamilton, Ont., and they had a daughter who died at birth; m. there thirdly 18 May 1881 Elizabeth Malloch, and they had four sons and two daughters; d. there 3 June 1929.

John Gibson's father immigrated from Scotland in 1826 and found work as a stonemason in the Hamilton area. Following his marriage to the daughter of a farmer in Nelson Township, he purchased a farm in Toronto Township to the east. Not long before he died of consumption in 1845, he wrote to his nephew David Gibson that this farm was not large enough to support his growing family and that adjacent property was too expensive to purchase. It was left to Mary Gibson to move her family in 1851 to a farm in Oneida Township.

After a year of school there, John was sent to Hamilton, where his sister Jane had located after her marriage, to attend the Hamilton grammar school. In 1854 he transferred to the recently opened Central School, where he flourished academically. In later years he would attribute his success to hard work and perseverance, which he credited principal John Herbert Sangster with teaching him. In June 1859, as the school's head boy, he was selected to test the jets of the Hamilton waterworks during their first public display, in Gore Park. As his career developed, he and his supporters would frequently cite this event as proof of his identification with progressive change in Hamilton.

Gibson wrote the matriculation examination for the University of Toronto in September 1859 and was awarded a scholarship. A member of the inaugural class of University College, he eventually amassed many honours, including the silver medal in classics and modern languages, a prize in oriental languages, and the Prince of Wales medal in his graduating year (BA 1863). In 1861, upon hearing news of the *Trent* affair, he had been one of the first to join the university company of the 2nd Battalion Volunteer Militia Rifles (later the Queen's Own Rifles). On his return to Hamilton in 1864, after he had completed his MA, he became an ensign in the 13th Battalion Volunteer Militia Light Infantry. Promoted lieutenant in early 1866, in June he was part of the Hamilton unit that, with other militiamen, confronted the Fenians at Ridgeway. Gibson worked his way through the ranks and from 1886 to 1895 he commanded the battalion, spearheading a major recruiting drive and overseeing construction of a new armoury. Following his resignation, on 9 Nov. 1895 he was named honorary lieutenant-colonel.

The focuses of the militia were drill and rifle-shooting. Mastering them required discipline and precision, what Gibson summarized as "faithful and persevering industry," a central tenet in his world-view. Recognized for his marksmanship, he competed as a member of the Canadian team at Wimbledon (London), England, in 1874, 1875, and

1879; he commanded the team in 1881 and the Bisley Cup team in 1907. From 1893 to 1907 he served as president of the Dominion Rifle Association and in 1891–92 and 1897 he was president of the Canadian Military Institute. In 1901 he was appointed honorary colonel of his old battalion and served on the committee that approved the infamous Ross rifle, and from 1904 to 1909 he commanded the 15th Infantry Brigade, with headquarters in Hamilton.

In 1866 Gibson had joined the Hamilton law firm of Burton and Bruce as a student. George William Burton, a business specialist, the city's solicitor, and a leading Reformer, became Gibson's mentor, and he provided the young man with an entrée to Hamilton's commercial and political elite. After his call to the bar in Michaelmas term 1867, Gibson continued his legal studies, gaining an LLB from the University of Toronto in 1869. The following year he formed a partnership in Hamilton with Francis Mackelcan, whom he had met through rifle-shooting. Responsibilities were divided, with Gibson concentrating on business law. The firm's reputation was enhanced in 1871 by his nomination as an examiner in law at the University of Toronto and in January 1873 by the appointment of the firm, now Mackelcan, Gibson, and Bell, as solicitor for Hamilton. Gibson would be named a QC in 1890 and elected a bencher of the Law Society of Upper Canada in 1899.

In the 1870s the stage was set for his move into public service. As he would later explain, he was eager "to do all he could for the benefit of those institutions which had helped him as a boy." From 1871 to 1884 he sat on Hamilton's Board of School Trustees, serving as chairman for two years. He championed the upgrading of educational facilities and the hiring of better-educated teachers, and urged the creation of an industrial school and a public library. In addition, he supported the establishment of the Hamilton Art School and was its president for many years. The remarkably active Gibson was, as well, a leading member of Central Presbyterian Church and a supporter of the Hamilton Health Association; he helped organize the Wentworth Historical Society in 1889 and was president of the St Andrew's Society in 1891–92. Beyond Hamilton, he sat in the senate of the University of Toronto from 1873 to 1888. A freemason since 1867, he rose to serve as grand master of the lodge in Canada in 1892–94. In 1896 he collaborated with George Ansel Sterling Ryerson and others in founding the Canadian

Red Cross Society, and he was its president until 1914; in recognition he was made a knight of grace of the Order of St John of Jerusalem in England in 1911. Honorary LLDS also came his way, from the University of Toronto (1903) and McMaster University (1909).

Gibson's political career stemmed from the mentorship of George Burton. Largely as a result of his university and Toronto contacts, he also had connections with such leading Reformers as Edward Blake and George Brown, and these links made him a valuable asset. He served his apprenticeship as secretary of the Hamilton Reform Association and as a local organizer during the federal election of 1878. He himself ran provincially in Hamilton the following year. During the campaign his allegiance to the city was called into question, with the Tory press portraying him as a "carpetbagger" with ties to Toronto, but he won by a narrow margin.

As a novice MLA, the former chair of the Hamilton board was naturally drawn to educational issues, favouring such causes as the admission of women to the University of Toronto, the "Canadianization" of its faculty, and the abolition of special funding for Upper Canada College. Faced by Knights of Labor opponents in February 1883 and December 1886, Gibson was victorious each time. In February 1886 Liberal provincial secretary Arthur Sturgis Hardy said that Gibson and a few other members had "sailed in under the flag of the workingman" by backing many of the demands of the Knights. Gibson, in fact, like his leader, Oliver Mowat, was a successful practitioner of co-option, supporting just enough labour-advocated reform to undermine the Knights' call for independent working-class action. During the 1887 federal campaign he used his reputation as a "friend of the workingman" to broker an agreement between labour and the Hamilton Liberals in an unsuccessful attempt to defeat the Tory incumbents.

Although some Reform colleagues grumbled about Gibson's "progressive" tendencies, Mowat and others were sympathetic. From 1884 to 1899 Gibson was chairman of the legislature's private bills committee. Fellow MLA Charles Clarke remembered him as a "deliberate, if not painfully slow" speaker, though in committee "he seemed intuitively to realize the dubious points of every measure brought before him." A year after Gibson's appointment as provincial secretary in 1889, he suffered an unexpected and disheartening defeat by Thomas Henry Stinson, a popular local businessman and Conservative. Stinson's election was overturned, however, and in the by-election that followed, in 1891, Gibson was again returned. After resuming office as provincial secretary, in 1893 he guided through the legislature the Act for the prevention of cruelty to and better protection of children (the Gibson Act), which, significantly, made child abuse an indictable offence, promoted foster care, strengthened the powers of children's aid societies, and established the office of superintendent of neglected children, to which Gibson appointed John Joseph Kelso. Elected for the new riding of Hamilton West in 1894, Gibson was made commissioner of crown lands in 1896, in the government of A. S. Hardy. During his tenure (until 1899), he encouraged reforestation in northern Ontario and oversaw new game legislation and the Forest Reserves Act of 1898. In March 1898 he again lost his seat, but in a by-election in Wellington East in October he was returned to Queen's Park.

In October 1899 Gibson was appointed attorney general in the government of George William Ross. A frequent spokesman for an administration that was losing public confidence, his own reputation tainted by scandals that suggested he had participated in or gone along with vote rigging, he found his political position increasingly tenuous. Lost in the bitter partisanship of the Ross years were some of his better pieces of work, including the new municipal assessment and taxation act of 1904. Ross's cabinet shuffle of November 1904, including Gibson's demotion to minister without portfolio, recognized his professions of ill health, and most likely his political liability. Never close to Wellington East, he was a prime candidate for defeat in James Pliny Whitney's Conservative sweep of January 1905.

The loss prompted Gibson to shift his full energy to the carefully structured realm of business that overlapped his politics. Capitalizing on his political and social connections, he had first made his mark in 1877, when, with his then father-in-law, Adam Hope, he helped organize and promote the Landed Banking and Loan Company, which invested in mortgages and municipal debentures and operated a savings bank. Gibson used his connections to attract investors, among them Edward Blake, and he found his own niche as the company's legal adviser. Among the ventures that followed were the Canada Clock Company Limited, chartered by Gibson, Francis Mackelcan, and others in 1881.

It was as a lawyer that Gibson began his profitable association with John Patterson, a Hamilton businessman who ran an integrated operation that included property management, real estate, mills, a lumber yard, and construction. Their first recorded contact occurred in the fall of 1883 when Gibson and Mackelcan represented the city in a lawsuit brought by Patterson and his brother. Soon, Gibson was their attorney and was offering them mortgage funds to finance their operations; by the late 1880s the Pattersons were Landed Banking's primary customers. From here Gibson took the short step to real-estate investment: by the early 1890s he had assembled a block of almost 200 building lots in eastern Hamilton, some of which he owned outright and in others of which he was a co-owner.

Gibson and Patterson, like other developers there, recognized that new industry could intensify the demand for land and thus boost values. In 1893 Gibson, while city solicitor, acted as legal adviser to the Pattersons in their negotiations to sell east-end land for a smelting works, and he advocated municipal bonuses for the enterprise. Clearly in conflict of interest, he brazenly denied the charge when it was aired in the press. The accusation was not pursued, but the Mackelcan–Gibson law firm was dissolved – Gibson would soon form another, with W. W. Osborne – and he resigned as city solicitor.

Financial interest most certainly underlay his enthusiasm for the establishment of a factory by the Westinghouse Manufacturing Company Limited in the mid 1890s. The proposed site was less than half a mile north of his holdings. When negotiations with the city for municipal bonuses for Westinghouse stalled, Gibson personally renewed the company's option on the site and lobbied council. At the time of the smelting-works controversy, he had argued that, though he opposed municipal bonusing to promote industrial development, there were always exceptions. Westinghouse was one. The *Hamilton Spectator*, never an admirer of Gibson, was forced to admit that credit for the agreement between the city and the company was due "in large measure" to him. For his part in assisting Westinghouse, Gibson was appointed to its board of directors; in 1903 he would transfer this directorship to the newly formed Canadian Westinghouse Company Limited.

Gibson and Patterson's move into transportation was envisaged as yet another way to increase the value of their real estate. In 1894 they began promoting the Hamilton Radial Electric Railway, the route of which was eventually changed to pass over Gibson's land. Together with Liberal businessmen John Dickenson, John Moodie Sr, and John William Sutherland, they also launched a scheme to generate hydroelectricity at DeCew Falls (near St Catharines) and transmit it to Hamilton. Their corporate means, the Cataract Power Company of Hamilton Limited, formed in 1896 with Gibson as president, soon absorbed its local competitors. By 1908, through the purchase of existing local radial and street railways and power companies, Cataract (reorganized in 1907 as Dominion Power and Transmission Company Limited) controlled the electrical supply and radial-railway network of an area stretching from Brantford to Oakville and from Hamilton to Vineland. The company's ambition was to extend its operations to Windsor and Toronto and to meet American transportation systems at Buffalo, N.Y.

The Five Johns, as Gibson's group became known, formed the core of the interlocking directorates that linked the Dominion Power holding company and its subsidiaries. Gibson moved effortlessly from the presidency of Cataract to that of Dominion when it was formally established in March 1907, and he sat on the boards of a number of associated companies, while his law firm provided legal counsel to the conglomerate. In the mid 1910s the Hamilton Hotel Company Limited, which Gibson headed, constructed the Royal Connaught Hotel adjacent to Dominion Power's Terminal Building, thus integrating transit with the potentially profitable service sector. Similarly, the establishment in 1914 of the plant of the National Steel Car Company Limited, of which Gibson was also president, was tied to negotiations between Dominion Power and the city over the Hamilton Street Railway franchise.

Gibson's grand industrial scheme began to founder when he attempted to enter the high-stakes field of nickel refining. As the demand for nickel had grown in the 1890s, Gibson, in concert with Patterson, Moodie, Andrew Trew Wood, Samuel J. Ritchie (a disgruntled former member of the Canadian Copper syndicate at Sudbury), and others, devised a plan to establish a electrolytic refining complex in Hamilton, where existing steel operations undoubtedly gave encouragement to the venture. Though Gibson did not directly invest in the nickel syndicate, members of his family, including his wife and brother-in-law, and many close associates did. That the proposed location of the works was near his tract demonstrated once again how industrial promotion and real-estate speculation went hand in hand.

There was another factor that contributed to Gibson's enthusiasm. Industrial demands for electricity offered Cataract the opportunity to expand generation and even out the periods of peak load. The proposed refining process required huge quantities of electricity. In early 1899 Gibson's law firm applied for letters patent for the Hoepfner Refining Company, to mine and refine zinc, lead, silver, and nickel and copper ore. Following his appointment as its president, work began on the plant and a contract was reached with Cataract. Not long after construction had been completed, it was discovered that the process did not work. But, too much had been invested for the project to be abandoned. A number of shareholders banded together to lease the Hoepfner premises and experiments were conducted to discover a new electrical refining process. Gibson believed that, once this process had been found, Hamilton would possess "the largest nickel and copper refining plant in the world." The experiments failed, however, and the refinery never opened.

So critical was the nickel-steel enterprise to Gibson's design that he had reversed his long-standing support for free trade to advocate protective tariffs. As commissioner of crown lands, he had opposed the call of lumbermen for a "manufacturing condition" (export duties on unprocessed material), arguing that it would constitute a breach of faith with timber licensees. The Hardy government, however, reluctantly instituted the condition. For nickel Gibson was willing to abandon free trade. First, he and his partners attempted to use their Liberal connections to persuade the federal government of Wilfrid Laurier of the need for export duties on nickel ore. When this tactic failed, Gibson pressed his provincial colleagues to extend the manufacturing condition to nickel. Ross initially appeared receptive and brought in an amendment to the Mines Act in 1900, but various factors, including the realization that Gibson's involvement constituted a dangerous conflict of interest, led the government to let the amendment die.

Cataract's electricity nonetheless remained a popular component of Hamilton's identity and Gibson's conglomeration. Public approval began to decline, however, in the early 1900s. As a result of a bitter street-railway strike in 1906, opinion swung to the side of labour. Moreover, clashes with civic authorities over the quality and cost of transportation and electrical services and the extension of rail lines engendered support for public ownership. In 1914 a municipally run hydroelectric system began operating in direct competition with Dominion Power.

Gibson was unswayed by these trends. He served as his company's principal spokesman during the strike and in the early stages of the battle over municipal ownership. He was still close to the peak of his corporate power – socially prominent and unencumbered by public office, but politically influential nevertheless, and quite prepared to redefine his principles. In 1907 he aggressively pushed for a federal chartering of the Hamilton Radial Electric Railway as a work of general advantage to Canada, which would free it from provincial interference. In so doing he hoped to avoid the justifiable hostility of the Whitney government and overstepped his prior provincialist objection to federal charters for purely local lines. Early in 1908 the Hamilton charter was reluctantly granted by the federal Liberals, with whom Gibson still managed to maintain friendly personal relations.

After his appointment as lieutenant governor of Ontario in September 1908, which brought him to Toronto, Gibson's move from corporate autocracy to viceregal discretion was a rough experience. Initially he planned to carry on as president of Dominion Power. He soon gave it up, but he remained disinclined to accept the notion that he could no longer express his opinions on controversial issues, particularly the ownership of utilities and relations between labour and business. His public criticism of international unions, for example, drew indignant protest from the Trades and Labor Congress of Canada at its gathering in Quebec City in September 1909; that same month, at the opening of a new waterworks system in Guelph, Ont., he blurted out that civic control was not always desirable. Such pronouncements led to calls for him to step down. Only belatedly did he limit himself to ceremonial functions, such as the official opening in June 1913 of the new Toronto General Hospital and of the Grange as the home of the Art Museum of Toronto. Still, he continued to chafe over the restrictions imposed by his office and the unwillingness of the Whitney government to consult him concerning policy. But there were some rewards: on 1 Jan. 1912 he had been made a KCMG.

Following the expiry of his term in September 1914, a month after the outbreak of war in Europe, Gibson returned to Hamilton, where he met great demand to attach his name to a host of charities and projects. He resumed many of his business and legal responsibilities – the descent of National Steel Car into near-bankruptcy proved particularly trying

– but mostly his time was spent on war work: colonel-in-chief of the Hamilton Home Guard; a reorganizer of the Hamilton branch of the Red Cross; president of the Soldiers' Aid Commission, set up to raise funds for the families of those serving overseas; vice-president of the Speakers' Patriotic League, which promoted recruitment and the funding of flag-waving associations; and chair of the national committee formed to find ways to get enough steel and nickel for artillery. He was joined in his efforts by Lady Gibson, who, for her part, received the Order of St John of Jerusalem in England in 1916.

Gibson's philosophy of public service had always been voluntar-ism, so it was with some reluctance that he accepted conscription. Once convinced, he became a leading spokesman for the Hamilton Recruit-ing League and embarked on a lengthy correspondence to persuade his old friend Laurier of the necessity of conscription. In the end Gibson's strong feelings caused him temporarily to abandon the Liberals and sup-port the Union government of Sir Robert Laird Borden. In 1917 he chaired the board of selection formed to establish exemption tribunals under the Military Service Act.

Having experienced great family loss in his early life, Gibson was again afflicted after the turn of the century by the death of three of his sons – John Gordon of tuberculosis in 1908, Francis Malloch in action in France in 1915, and Archibald Hope (a partner in his law firm) of influenza in 1920. Nonetheless, throughout the 1920s he continued to promote philanthropic causes in and outside Hamilton; he was president, for example, of the Canadian National Safety League. One of the oldest members of the active militia, he was promoted major-general in 1921, at the age of 79. His political involvement was largely restricted to offering guidance to such younger Liberals as William Lyon Mackenzie King. As well, his involvement in Dominion Power, in which he had continued as a director, declined, particularly after its sale to the Power Corporation of Canada in 1925. He then took on a role as the company's corporate memory, offering advice based on his long years of experience.

Sir John Morison Gibson died of a stroke at his home, Ravenscliffe, on 3 June 1929. Buried in Hamilton Cemetery, he left an estate val-ued at more than $763,000. In eulogies the press made much of his distinguished political, legal, and military careers and his philanthropic involvement. Less attention was paid to his business activities, but it was there that Gibson had truly left his mark by promoting development and providing the infrastructure that helped define Hamilton as a major industrial centre. At the same time his embracement of industrial capitalism had led to a sharp break from the reform tendencies of his early political career and contributed to the disintegration of the increasingly illusionary "community of interests" which, he had argued, he and his companies shared with the citizens of Hamilton.

CAROLYN E. GRAY

Further reading

Christopher Armstrong and H. V. Nelles, *Monopoly's moment: the organization and regulation of Canadian utilities, 1830–1930* (Philadelphia, 1986).

Christopher Armstrong, *The politics of federalism: Ontario's relations with the federal government, 1867–1942* (Toronto, 1981).

H. V. Nelles, *The politics of development: forests, mines & hydro-electric power in Ontario, 1849–1941* (Toronto, 1974).

G. S. Kealey and B. D. Palmer, *Dreaming of what might be: the Knights of Labor in Ontario, 1880–1900* (Cambridge, Eng., and New York, 1982).

J. C. Weaver, *Hamilton: an illustrated history* (Toronto, 1982).

Sir BYRON EDMUND WALKER,

banker, philanthropist, and patron of the arts; b. 14 Oct. 1848 near Caledonia, Upper Canada, son of Alfred Edmund Walker and Fanny Murton; m. 5 Nov. 1874 Mary Alexander (d. 1923) in Hamilton, Ont., and they had four sons and three daughters; d. 27 March 1924 in Toronto.

Byron Edmund Walker, born in "the back woods" a half-day's journey south of Hamilton, became a Canadian Medici and one of the most eminent personalities of his generation. He was the eldest son of an unremarkable family, the second of seven children. He claimed to owe his father "whatever qualities I may possess." Alfred Walker was the son of middle-class English immigrants who had settled in the Grand River region in the 1830s. Indifferent health made him unsuited to rural life, and in 1852 he, his wife, and their children moved to Hamilton. A clerk, he never distinguished himself in business but he became a noted amateur geologist and palaeontologist. To his son he transmitted his passion for natural history. "I was taught to appreciate that the truth regarding nature was the divine thing," Walker recalled in 1918, "and that we must learn it so far as it is possible." There was nothing unusual about their interest in fossils; collecting had become a popular pastime in Victorian Canada. What set young Byron apart was his desire to understand how his discoveries explained the world around him. A lack of formal education never impeded him. He was a dedicated autodidact and his inherited spirit of inquiry led him to master a broad array of subjects. Combined with his organizational acumen, ability to influence, and access to powerful individuals, Walker's talents served to develop more aspects of Canadian life than those of any of his contemporaries.

It is principally his contribution to commercial life, however, that remains known. One biographer claims that Walker derived his business skills from his mother. Fanny Murton's parents were also English immigrants of the 1830s, her father, according to Walker's sister Edith, "a gentleman farmer" who had studied law and her mother an educator who "spoke French and Italian fluently, and was the only woman west of Toronto who could play the harpsichord." Mrs Murton ran a private school in Hamilton, and it was there that four-year-old Byron began his schooling. He continued at the Central School, finished after grade 6, and at age 12 prepared to enter teachers' college in Toronto. But doctor's orders prevented him: "I had better run about, and get a little flesh on my bones" was how Walker remembered the directive. Instead, the boy went to work in August 1861 at the exchange office of his uncle John Walter Murton. The previous winter and spring 11 American states had seceded from the Union. Bonds and paper money issued by the United States government as war measures complicated the already complex North American currency situation. Walker's duties included the authentication of coins and notes. Pieces of eight, greenbacks, English silver, and the notes of dozens of failed banks: he handled them all. In 1868 he moved to Montreal to run an exchange firm there, but feeble health (which would plague him for another 20 years) forced him back to Hamilton a few months later to work in the local branch of the recently formed Canadian Bank of Commerce.

The bank had been established in 1867 by Irish-born merchant William McMaster and a consortium of Toronto businessmen in reaction to the growing dominance of the Bank of Montreal. Farmers and businessmen in the province needed greater access to credit, and branches of the Commerce were opened in a number of towns. Walker became a discount clerk in Hamilton. An evaluation from 1869 characterizes him as "an invaluable officer, competent in every respect." He rose through the ranks swiftly, becoming chief accountant in Toronto in 1872 and junior agent in New York in 1873. Business failures were commonplace during the depressed 1870s, and Walker appears to have been especially skilled at helping his bank minimize its losses. In 1875 he was sent to Windsor, Ont., to disentangle the Commerce from several sour lumber investments. Later he served as manager at the London (1878–79) and Hamilton (1880–81) branches. As inspector at the head office in Toronto from 1879 to 1880, he introduced the use of telegraphy in multiple-branch banking and implemented printed regulations and operating procedures. Subsequently he reorganized the bank into discrete departments, a measure which anticipated modern business practice.

Also during his Toronto stint Walker produced for McMaster (now a senator) and federal opposition leader Edward Blake a report on how Canadian banking differed from the American system. The government was in the process of reforming the Bank Act of 1871 after a spate of financial woes. A number of banks had failed during the 1870s and critics began to advocate the United States model of more numerous but smaller local banks (though these were frequently undercapitalized) and centralized control of note circulation. Drawing on his New York experience and his training in an exchange office, Walker compared the two systems and favoured Canadian practices. "We have a system which, while it can be improved in some of its details, is fundamentally sound: our bank issues, owing to the strength and peculiar organization of our Banks, pass at par everywhere in the Dominion ... and the notes are, from the small number of Banks, well known to the most ignorant of tradesmen, mechanics or agriculturists. No practical fault can be found with our Bank-issue as a circulating medium; ... if it lacks anything in uniform it possesses a much more important virtue in being elastic." Owing to the structure of Canadian finance, banks were less likely to fail and both borrowers and depositors could be served more securely and conveniently. Partly on the strength of Walker's report, finance minister Sir Samuel Leonard Tilley proposed a new general bank act in 1880 which effected only minor changes. The system that had evolved since before confederation remained intact, although decennial revisions of the act meant that the chartered banks regularly had, in Walker's words, "to fight for our existence."

His peregrinations continued. In 1881 he began a five-year sojourn in New York, conducting the Commerce's growing role as a foreign-exchange bank. Walker returned to Toronto in autumn 1886 to become general manager. The previous two years are described in the firm's official history as "possibly the most difficult" for the bank. It had suffered through customers' failures in land and timber operations. General manager Walter Nichol Anderson had resigned and Walker was appointed to turn around the company's fortunes. His first task was a thorough re-evaluation of the bank's assets and operations. Several changes were necessary, most significantly an adjustment to its deposits-to-capital ratio. The Commerce's dividends improved markedly as a result, and within ten years Walker had made it the most profitable financial institution in Ontario. Much of this success was due to the program of weekly reports that he implemented in 1889. All branches were required to file a "gossip sheet," which Walker and his staff used in devising the bank's plans and objectives. A distillation of these reports was delivered each year in Walker's address to shareholders. For 35 years financiers and economists in Canada and the United States would benefit from his annual review of the nation's financial and industrial "pulse." It was also during his tenure as general manager that the Commerce began to expand its operations westward with branches in Winnipeg, Vancouver, and Dawson, Y.T., for example, and to build up a presence in the Maritimes.

In January 1907 Walker became president of the bank, succeeding Senator George Albertus Cox. He would hold the office until his death in 1924, although after 1915 he was no longer chief executive officer. His years were ones of tremendous growth: the company's total assets were

$22,000,000 in 1886; by 1915, when John Aird took the helm, they had increased more than tenfold, as had the number of branches. Walker transformed the bank into a modern corporation with such innovations as a realty company to manage the Commerce's buildings, a pension fund for retired employees, and a bank archives. After 1915 he continued "to dispense optimism and sober reproof," guiding junior officers with wisdom earned in nearly a half-century in the bank's service.

Walker's high position brought him directly into the exclusive circles of Canadian capitalism. These were interconnected groups of entrepreneurs, bankers, and lawyers who to a great extent had succeeded in concentrating control of the nation's financial resources. One such group involved railway promoters William Mackenzie and Donald Mann. Their dream of a northern route to the burgeoning west took them several times to the brink of bankruptcy. Walker was their banker, and he continued to extend credit to them despite worries, widespread among politicians and journalists, that the Canadian Northern's recklessness would bring it and the Commerce crashing down. His fidelity to the Northern rested on three things: Mackenzie's friendship, optimism about the potential for profit in the west, and belief in the rightful role of private enterprise to develop Canada clear of government interference. Mackenzie and Mann typified the businessman as nation-builder, and Walker, sharing their vision, gave the bank's unswerving support, as he did with a variety of other development and utilities schemes at home and abroad.

His reputation in business owed as much to his activities apart from the Commerce. He led the bankers' section of the Toronto Board of Trade and was instrumental in founding the Canadian Bankers' Association in 1891 (he would be elected president in 1893 and 1894). His involvement was motivated by his belief that public discourse was too much influenced by journalists who had no expertise in economics. When bank charters were up for renewal in 1890, the newspapers had pressured finance minister George Eulas Foster to overhaul the current legislation by introducing American-style fixed reserves, a measure favoured as well by Foster's deputy minister, John Mortimer Courtney, and by imposing a higher degree of state control over inflation. But Canada's laissez-faire bankers were hesitant to relinquish any of their privileges. Acting in concert under the leadership of Walker, Edward

Seaborne Clouston (Bank of Montreal), Thomas Fyshe (Bank of Nova Scotia), and George Hague (Merchants' Bank of Canada), they were able to preserve their relative independence.

Walker tended to couch his rhetoric in terms of service and development. The branch system, with its handful of chartered banks present from coast to coast, promoted unity and nation-building. Rather than acting out "a compromise between the necessities of the government, arising from war or extravagance, and the commercial requirements of the nation," Canadian bank policy was the result of a "happier condition where the law-maker and the banker have been mainly concerned to give the people the best instrument in aid of commerce that they could devise." The Canadian model had served the country relatively well, and was constantly perfecting itself. For as long as Walker remained involved, the banks maintained most of their rights. Where reforms were introduced – for example, the creation of a bank circulation redemption fund, whereby each bank was obliged to deposit with the government an amount equal to five per cent of its average circulation – they were often prompted by his proposals. Only under the strain of war did the state stray from his advice. The Finance Act of 1914 moved Canadian banking away from its laissez-faire origins, a measure which in some ways prefigured the creation of a central bank in 1935.

Walker also enjoyed an international reputation as a banker. "No name is better known among the banking fraternity than yours," an American colleague told him. In 1913 he was asked to testify before the United States House of Representatives committee on banking, and he frequently addressed foreign audiences on such matters as "Why Canada is against bimetallism," "Banking as a public service," "The relations of banking to business enterprise," and "Abnormal features of American banking." His knowledge of bank history and his economic theories were promulgated in numerous pamphlets and books, among them *A history of banking in Canada*. Known as "the pope of the banking system," Walker often pontificated in defence of financial institutions. "It is the fashion of certain demagogues to speak of bankers and of insurance men as non-producers," he told the International Convention of Life Underwriters in 1918, "but not even the powers of steam and electricity have done more for industry than credit and insurance." Credit did more than pave the way to material prosperity; it was an engine of social uplift.

For his many services to Canada, in 1908 Walker had been made a CVO. Two years later King George V knighted him. Although he had been quiet about his politics – "the interests of the Bank are so extensive that I have found it expedient to keep out of politics," he explained – he had long been a Liberal. In 1911, however, his political aloofness came to an end. The issue was reciprocity, free trade in natural products between Canada and the United States. Canada had prospered under the National Policy of high tariffs on manufactured goods, a creature of Sir John A. Macdonald's Conservative government. The Liberal opposition favoured unrestricted reciprocity, but by the time its leader, Wilfrid Laurier, came to power in 1896, the political and economic usefulness of protectionism had been realized. The Liberal government nevertheless chose to gamble on a policy of free trade in agricultural products, and in January 1911 announced the terms of the Taft–Fielding agreement. Within a month Canadian businessmen had emerged squarely against the deal: free trade in some products now, they argued, meant unrestricted reciprocity later, a break with the British empire, and eventually annexation.

It was in fact the business community, not the ineffectual Conservative opposition, that led the campaign against Laurier. The most highly organized and nationally prominent anti-reciprocity force was the "Toronto Eighteen," headed by Walker. Described by one historian as "an inter-locking structure of banking, transportation, insurance, manufacturing and other related interests," they unleashed, in the words of another, "a firestorm of anti-American sentiment." They helped create such propaganda bodies as the Canadian National League and the Canadian Home Market Association, published anti-free trade tracts, cartoons, and advertisements, and blanketed the nation with pamphlets publicizing their position. In the general election of September 1911 voters defeated the Liberal government. Walker had been invited by Robert Laird Borden, leader of the opposition, to run as a Conservative but had declined. However, he advised the new prime minister on a variety of issues during his term. Laurier likely never forgave him. A Toronto newspaper was surprised to find the two seated side by side at a University of Toronto gathering in 1914. The banker quipped, "Well, if Sir Wilfrid does not object I see no reason why I should."

Walker's opposition to reciprocity stemmed from his views on how best to develop Canada's economic position. This small nation could either continue to prosper as a dominion within the empire, he believed, or disappear into the United States. He never liked the way the American economy had taken shape. For example, he denounced the overthrow of founding father Alexander Hamilton's financial system, which he considered sane and intelligent. He also disparaged America's "gross materialism" and tendency to waste. His anti-free trade protest was, therefore, based on "much more than a trade question.... The question is between British connection and what has been well called Continentalism." The extent of his anti-Americanism, however, is open to argument. He would tell Canadian audiences they should "save and increase such good qualities as tend to differentiate us from the United States," among them a disdain for "extreme democracy" and suspicion of industrial oligarchy and "machine politics." On the other hand, he told Americans that, while he disliked some features of their country, he greatly admired others. He simply valued Canada's ties to Britain much more and did not think they could be maintained if America's influence grew too strong. Walker was an imperialist, with James Mavor, Edward Joseph Kylie, and George MacKinnon Wrong a member of the Round Table movement, and a believer in the empire as "the greatest political and social enterprise in the history of the world."

It has been suggested that Walker's fight against reciprocity was in part motivated by anti-immigrant sentiment. He was not a hateful man, no more so than any of his contemporaries. He was "proud to feel that Canada was a place where every color and every kind could have an opportunity," but objected to immigrants' seeming hesitance to integrate with British Canadian society. He blamed agricultural settlers in the west for Laurier's departure from protectionism. Immigration itself was not a menace; in fact, Walker understood it to be the catalyst to the economic boom of the century's first decade. Yet he was concerned that Canada had taken in more foreigners than it could absorb. Without proper measures, they could threaten law and order, and indeed seemed to be weakening the imperial tie.

Walker frequently spoke of particular "Canadian ambitions" and felt that these should be inculcated in newcomers. The alternative was to become too much like the materialistic, polyglot, and potentially unstable United States. "No great nation," he remarked in 1907, "was ever built up solely on the basis of material prosperity," and he insisted that Canadians strive for something greater. This ideal could be attained by cultivating proper tastes and sensibilities and would be aided principally by two things: higher education and the fine arts. To these ends, Walker promoted a wide array of institutions, first among them schools "where the duties of citizenship and the ethical aspects of life are taught in the fullest manner." He was a Toronto Board of Education trustee in 1904, and in 1911 founded the Appleby School in Oakville, Ont.

The University of Toronto benefited most from his efforts. After his return from New York to stay, his family had acquired Long Garth, a large home literally in the university's backyard. In 1890 fire destroyed a good part of the main college building. In addition to witnessing the blaze, Walker was asked by President Sir Daniel Wilson to head the campaign to raise funds for restoration. His bank donated $1,000 and many local and national businesses followed the example. Subsequently Chancellor Edward Blake asked him to supervise the university's financial situation, and later he worked with Joseph Wesley Flavelle on the royal commission on the University of Toronto (1905–6), which suggested major changes to funding and management. Shortly before it federated with the university in 1904, Trinity College had made him an honorary DCL and in 1905 the university itself granted him an honorary LLD. He served the university as a trustee (1891–1906), senator (1893–1901), governor (1906–23), and chairman of the board of governors (1910–23), and assumed the office of chancellor upon Sir William Ralph Meredith's death in 1923. Walker considered the university to be "the most important institution in Canada apart from the Government itself." In 1918 the minister of education, Henry John Cody, elaborated on Walker's views: "He believed in the value and power of education in the whole life of the Province and Dominion. Education is at once the key to efficiency and the safeguard of democracy…. The universities … can render an incalculable service both to the higher life of our people and to the commercial and manufacturing interests of the country."

Among its many recommendations the Flavelle report had proposed a museum for the university. Walker had been advocating such an institution since 1888 when he approached the premier, Oliver Mowat. He believed that museums afforded the public an opportunity to appreciate the country and the world around them. They would be "shop windows" in which newcomers and Canadians of long standing could understand, at a single glance, the nation's potential. But only in 1909 did the government consent to funding, and not before Walker and Edmund Boyd Osler had independently raised some money to establish the Royal Ontario Museum. Five years before, Walker had donated his library and his collection of fossils to set the organization in motion.

During their New York years, Walker and his wife had had a rich social life, complete with visits to museums, concert halls, and libraries where they cultivated a love of literature. Their return to Toronto in 1886, therefore, came as a disappointment. The Queen City was growing but it had none of the cultural life of other centres. Nonetheless, its artists and business class aspired to such development. What mainly lacked was leadership. Walker was able to provide the missing element and was unmatched in the range of his accomplishments. For example, local artists had for many years sought an art museum. Painter George Agnew Reid, president of the Ontario Society of Artists, had been unable to establish a permanent one, but in 1900 Walker joined the cause, raised money privately, set up a board of trustees, and arranged with Harriet Elizabeth Mann Smith and Goldwin Smith to have their house, the Grange, bequeathed to the Art Museum of Toronto. The Toronto Guild of Civic Art, which adjudicated public art and urban planning schemes, also benefited from his participation.

Walker's involvement in art was more than organizational. He was also a collector, and though his holdings were not as extensive as some, he had extraordinary access to important private collections abroad and knew many artists personally. He advised his friends on building private galleries, and as a result many Canadian collections came to reflect his preference for Dutch interiors and the Barbizon School. He was fondest of Italian art and in 1894 lectured about it at the University of Toronto. In his later years he developed an exquisite collection of Japanese prints (now in the Royal Ontario Museum). His taste in art was cultivated by extensive reading and travelling. He journeyed throughout Europe, spent long periods in England, and visited South America and the Far East.

His cultural activities also took place at the national level. He felt his most important contribution to Canada was the founding in 1905, with historian George M. Wrong and librarian James Bain, of the Champlain Society, an organization which publishes historical documents. His interest in history also led him to serve the National Battlefields Commission, the Quebec tercentenary committee, and the Historical Manuscripts Commission. During the 1914–18 war William Maxwell Aitken, 1st Baron Beaverbrook, sought his advice on developing the Canadian War Memorials Fund, and Walker successfully suggested that Canadian artists be commissioned to paint war scenes.

Walker was embroiled in a number of controversies concerning art. One stemmed from his involvement with the National Gallery of Canada. The Royal Canadian Academy of Arts had helped found the gallery in 1880. However, after a quarter-century it was still little more than a repository of diploma works. Artists lobbied for a more complete institution, and in 1907 the government appointed the Advisory Arts Council. Walker became its head in 1910 and in 1913 chairman of the reincorporated National Gallery's board of trustees. Among other tasks he and his colleagues were instructed to build up the national collection. None was an artist, and all came in for criticism, especially Walker because of his very definite likes and dislikes. The most public conflict took place in 1923 when the RCA took strong exception to the National Gallery's selection of a jury which would choose works of art to represent Canada at the British Empire Exhibition. Critic Hector Willoughby Charlesworth agreed and argued that Walker and gallery director Eric Brown were wrong to show favouritism to Canadian painters whose work he considered "labored, dull, and unimaginative." Charlesworth called the gallery a "national reproach," echoing MP Charles Murphy who in 1921 had labelled it "a haven for the special pets of Sir Byron Walker." Despite the criticism, Walker had built a permanent foundation for the gallery, had seen that it survived the war years, and had helped secure relatively generous public funding. Indeed, his death was seen as a loss to the arts in Canada. Walker himself recognized the progress his generation of patrons facilitated: young Canadian painters had begun to "paint our country in moods, colours and atmosphere which cannot be mistaken for anything but Canada"; in a short period, he said in 1923, aesthetic standards had increased to the point that Canada had become much "nearer to the great centres of the world."

Music also benefited from Walker's dedication and acumen. He worked with the Toronto Conservatory of Music and its director, Augustus Stephen Vogt, and arranged the school's affiliation with the university.

Particular pleasure he derived from his involvement in the Toronto Mendelssohn Choir, founded by Vogt, which he helped reorganize in 1900. He secured funding for the group and was named its honorary president. He enjoyed travelling with the choir, and in early 1924 was on tour with them in the United States when he contracted pneumonia. Minnie, his wife of nearly 50 years, had just died and Walker coped with his grief by burying himself in his projects. He had begun to work long nights settling the estate of his friend Sir William Mackenzie, and was about to leave for England to attend the British Empire Exhibition when he expired.

Walker admonished students to avoid committing "the historical estimate." He said they should not hold a person in high regard simply "because he accomplished work important for his time"; however, someone whose deeds were "important for all time" was to be valued. Certain of his contemporaries considered Walker to be too powerful and overextended into areas they said he knew little about. He was sometimes seen as "arrogant, domineering, and pretentious." But Walker simply trusted his own judgement and ability. Furthermore, he "had an extraordinary power of creating enthusiasm." In retrospect, the worst his enemies could say about him was that he was "a strong man with a liking for his own way of doing things." "Remember each day," he told the Schoolmen's Club, "that we shall be judged by our children according to the use we have made of the really vast opportunity which fortune has placed in our hands." Clearly he accomplished much, in many fields, at several levels, and in lasting ways.

DAVID KIMMEL

Further reading

C. W. Colby, "Sir Edmund Walker," *Canadian Banker* (Toronto), 56 (1949): 93–101.

R. D. Cuff, "The Toronto Eighteen and the election of 1911," *Ontario History* (Toronto), 57 (1965): 169–80.

G. P. de T. Glazebrook, *Sir Edmund Walker* (London, 1933).

E. P. Neufeld, *The financial system of Canada: its growth and development* (Toronto, 1972).

Victor Ross and A. St L. Trigge, *A history of the Canadian Bank of Commerce, with an account of the other banks which now form part of its organization* (3v., Toronto, 1920–34).

WILMOT DELOUI MATTHEWS,

businessman; b. 22 June 1850 in Burford Township, Upper Canada, son of Wheeler Douglas Matthews and Maria Susanna Colton; m. 29 Aug. 1872 Annie Jane Love in Toronto, and they had two sons and two daughters; d. there 24 May 1919.

Wilmot D. Matthews's paternal grandfather, Abner Matthews, a native of New Hampshire, settled in Burford before 1801 and was ordained as a Methodist Episcopal minister in 1820. Wheeler Matthews built up a business there as a miller and grain and produce dealer. In 1856 he and his family moved to Toronto, where he specialized, under the name W. D. Matthews and Company, in supplying the malting industry. Eventually known as the "barley king" of southwestern Ontario, he recognized the preference of American breweries for Canadian barley and engaged in cross-border trade, setting up regional bases in Le Roy and Attica, N.Y.

Educated at the Normal School in Toronto, Wilmot entered his father's business as a clerk about 1867. In 1873, a year after marrying the daughter of a prominent Toronto druggist, he became a partner. In the early 1880s his reputation in the grain trade was substantial enough that he was made president of the Toronto Corn Exchange Association, which he represented in 1883 before a parliamentary standing committee on the bill to form a court of railway commissioners in Canada. By 1886 W. D. Matthews and Company was one of the more prosperous flour, grain, and malt businesses in the country, with two malt-houses in Ontario and four in the United States. The deaths of Wilmot's father in

1888 and his mother two years later left him wealthy and firmly in control of the company. In 1893 he formed a malt dealership with Lionel Herbert Clarke (L. H. Clarke and Company); seven years later the two would also set up the Canada Malting Company Limited. In addition, by 1898 Matthews was a director of the Empire Produce Company and chairman of the government's eastern board for grain standards.

The grain trade in Ontario, however, was in decline, largely because of the shift to the western prairies. Matthews recognized that Toronto would be marginalized in the trade, and he diversified by carefully reinvesting in sectors of the Ontario economy with brighter futures. His earliest interest was the Dominion Bank, of which he had become a director on 27 Sept. 1882. He also became a director of Canadian Lloyds (a cargo company) and, in 1888, of the Canadian Pacific Railway, the most prestigious enterprise in the country. His business stature grew rapidly. In 1888–89 he served as president of the Toronto Board of Trade, in which office he presided over the erection of the board's new building at Yonge and Front. By 1891 he had built an elegant stone house at Hoskin Avenue and St George Street, a permanent monument to his success.

As a result of his diversification, Matthews, over the next two decades, would be identified far more with finance and big business than with the grain trade. During the era of prosperity that coincidentally began with Wilfrid Laurier's election as prime minister in 1896 and ended with the merger boom of 1909–13, new industrial and financial enterprises with a pan-Canadian reach would absorb or marginalize many of the regional enterprises that had once dominated the economic landscape. The main poles of this change were Montreal and Toronto. Matthews's membership in the business élite of Toronto meant that he could pick and choose his associates and investments. As founding president of the Toronto Incandescent Electric Light Company Limited in 1889, for example, he became aligned with utilities syndicator Frederic Thomas Nicholls. By 1902 Matthews's capitalistic involvement was exceptionally broad-based: a promoter of navigation, mining trust, coal, and cement companies in Canada and of street-railways in Cuba, he was a director of the Canadian General Electric Company Limited (with Nicholls, George Albertus Cox, Robert Jaffray, Edmund Boyd Osler, and others) and of the Trusts Corporation of Ontario.

Cox was possibly the richest and best-connected Toronto businessman of the era, but Matthews's most important associate was undoubtedly Osler. After forming the Toronto brokerage firm of Osler and Hammond in 1882, he had flourished, part of a new generation of stockbrokers. Accepting shares in payment for his services, he became a director, among other concerns, of the CPR and the Dominion Bank. In 1901, at the same time that he was chosen the bank's president, Matthews joined him as vice-president. To their frequent business association was added a family connection when Matthews's son Wilmot Love, who had entered his grain business about 1899, married Osler's daughter Annabel Margaret in 1903.

A contemporary assessment that Matthews was "one of the shrewdest business men in Canada" merely hints at the skills and connections that had taken him to the inner circles of capitalism in Toronto. In particular, he showed sound vision in investing in the new manufacturing and financial operations at the core of Canada's growth. Many were CPR initiatives. In 1902 Matthews and Osler accompanied the railway's president, Sir Thomas George Shaughnessy, on his annual inspection tour of western Canada. That same year, during the CPR's reorganization of the Canada North-West Land Company (an Osler creation), Matthews and miller Robert Meighen were added to its board; in 1905 a syndicate headed by Matthews and Osler took over the western mining interests of George Gooderham and Thomas Gibbs Blackstock, a high-risk move that led to the incorporation in 1906 of the CPR-controlled, Toronto-based Consolidated Mining and Smelting Company of Canada Limited, with Matthews as president. In the enterprises with which he was affiliated, Matthews played three roles: well-connected director, figurehead president, and well-capitalized financier. In no case did he actually manage an enterprise.

Since Matthews's financial interests were so large and varied by the time of the merger wave of 1909–13, it was perhaps inevitable that he would be involved in two of the largest consolidations, the Canada Cement Company Limited and the Steel Company of Canada Limited. Along with Osler and Osler's son and partner, Francis Gordon, he had been instrumental in financing the merger of two cement mills in Marlbank, Ont., and plants in Deseronto and Napanee Mills (Strathcona). The new concern, the Canadian Portland Cement Company Limited, was incorporated in 1900 and its administrative head office was moved to Toronto. Overnight, an operation situated in small communities and controlled by the Rathbun family became an impersonal corporation dependent on money raised by powerful Toronto capitalists, despite the fact that Edward Wilkes Rathbun, owner of two of the plants and the pioneer who had successfully introduced the manufacture of Portland cement in Canada, continued as president and general manager.

The next few years would see the cement industry turned inside out. The upheaval was due to technological revolution, notably the use of metal reinforcement and the ability of Portland cement to support enormous loads and harden under water, and the construction of more plants by Canadian and American interests to supply the infrastructure boom of the early 1900s in Canada. Cement promoters came out of nowhere as money poured into expensive, ultramodern plants. Matthews and his partners responded by closing three of their mills, making improvements at the remaining one in Marlbank, and building a modern plant at Port Colborne, Ont., though by the time of completion it was already being outstripped by plants in Hull, Montreal, Calgary, and Exshaw, Alta. Then, disaster struck the industry. The financial panic of 1907 caused an industrial recession and a temporary halt in construction. Cement prices tumbled; by the end of 1908 Canadian production was exceeding consumption by some 25 per cent. Matthews's group desperately looked for a way out. When approached by a syndicate of owners represented by promoter William Maxwell Aitken who were trying to cartelize the industry, Matthews agreed to sell Canadian Portland on the condition that he receive cash for his assets as well as a large slice of the promotional stock in the new firm, which would be chartered as Canada Cement in August 1909. To the annoyance of the other owners when they discovered the truth, Matthews received $1.4 million for his two properties, the only owner not forced to accept securities alone as payment.

Of all the owners, Matthews had proved himself the shrewdest negotiator, surpassed in guile and acumen only by the young Aitken. Though both men viewed each other with suspicion, they were able to put their distrust aside to work together on a second immense consolidation. Matthews, again in partnership with E. B. Osler, owned a sizeable share of the Hamilton Steel and Iron Company Limited, and both were on its board of directors. With merger mania pushing up stock prices, they attempted to bring together a number of Ontario steel producers, but in the middle of negotiations, in 1910, they were approached by Aitken, who wanted to combine these companies with two Montreal producers. Matthews, who felt no compunction about folding the well-run Hamilton firm into a larger concern, wanted top dollar from Aitken for his share and a large part of the financial action in promoting and underwriting the shares of the new Steel Company consolidation.

Although Matthews received a good price for his interest in Hamilton Steel and Iron, as well as an inside track in financing the new company, he refused to give in on the price Aitken wanted for one of his Montreal companies. With negotiations seemingly deadlocked, Aitken put forward a compromise. He would accept what Matthews had originally argued was a reasonable price, subject to an independent appraisal. If it was lower than Matthews's price, Aitken and his Montreal associates would pay the difference; if the value was higher, Matthews and his Ontario friends would pay. When the appraisal came in, Matthews discovered that he had been outfoxed by Aitken to the tune of almost $1 million. What he lost, however, he gained back in the merger promotion itself. He had secured a substantial piece of the very profitable underwriting of the new issue, and was left with enough common stock to make him the fourth largest owner in the new entity and a director on its board. Moreover, his interest went beyond this initial organization. During the recession of 1913 he ensured that the Dominion Bank extended a $1.2 million loan to the Steel Company to help it through the year.

These complex mergers certainly did nothing to harm Matthews's sterling reputation, and few contemporaries ventured any critical examination of his solid corporate existence. In attempting to cut through to the sources of control within Canada's banks in 1913, former cabinet minister Henry Robert Emmerson identified Matthews, based on his presence in 18 companies, as one of the 23 "capitalist-directors" who "are the directive forces in practically all of Canada's economic life." Others went further. In 1909 Nathaniel Samuel Fineberg had calculated in *Moody's Magazine* (New York), from the sheer number of Matthews's directorships (17), that he was the second most influential business figure in the dominion.

Matthews had all the characteristics of a successful businessman. Photographs portray a slim, bearded, neatly attired gentleman in the Edwardian mould. In affiliations he was a freemason, an Oddfellow, and a member of the Toronto Club and the St James Club in Montreal; in religion he was a Methodist. His philanthropic interests appear to have been limited to local musical events: he was president in 1903 of the National Chorus, conducted by Albert Ham, and in 1910 he was on the Toronto executive of the dominion drama and music festival sponsored by Governor General Albert Henry George Grey, 4th Earl Grey. At his death he owned a summer place at Roaches (Roches) Point on Lake Simcoe.

In politics Matthews was a Liberal, unlike Osler, who was a Conservative and for several years an MP. With his many industrial and financial interests, all of which benefited handsomely from westward expansion, Matthews supported high tariff protection against the United States. This support posed no problem during most of the Laurier boom, but it did lead to a major rupture when the Liberal party began to move back to its old policy of free trade with a reciprocal, lower-tariff agreement with the United States, first proposed in January 1911. Laurier quickly discovered that the Ontario members of his cabinet were terrified of the reaction to reciprocity of industrialists and financiers such as Matthews. Labour minister William Lyon Mackenzie King, for example, concluded that he and others in Ontario would lose their seats in the next election. Rarely outspoken on public matters, Matthews was one of the 18 conspicuous Toronto Liberals who signed an anti-reciprocity manifesto in February and then proclaimed their opposition at a huge public meeting in Massey Music Hall in March. Unlike some of the "Toronto Eighteen," Matthews had unquestionably been a Liberal backer, so his decision actively to support Robert Laird Borden's Conservatives in the September election was a severe blow to the Liberals.

W. D. Matthews entered the war era comfortable at the head of numerous companies but, judging from his strong investment in Victory Loans, dedicated to Canada's war effort. His wife died in 1917 and two years later a stroke followed by pneumonia claimed his life, and he was buried in Mount Pleasant Cemetery. He had carried life insurance in excess of $130,000, an extraordinary amount for the time. His executors had the largest component of his estate, his stocks and bonds, appraised at $3,651,800 but they were revalued by the Surrogate Court to $1,880,800, a casualty of the recession that followed World War I.

GREGORY P. MARCHILDON

Further reading

G. P. Marchildon, *Profits and politics: Beaverbrook and the Gilded Age of Canadian finance* (Toronto, 1996).

J. A. Eagle, *The Canadian Pacific Railway and the development of western Canada, 1896–1914* (Kingston, Ont., 1989).

William Kilbourn, *The elements combined: a history of the Steel Company of Canada* (Toronto and Vancouver, 1960), 72–74.

R. D. Cuff, "The Toronto Eighteen and the election of 1911," *Ontario History* (Toronto) 57 (1965): 169–80.

R. L. Jones, *History of agriculture in Ontario, 1613–1880* (Toronto, 1946; repr. Toronto and Buffalo, N.Y., 1977), 239–41.

ANSON McKIM,

advertising executive, publisher, and businessman; b. 2 May 1855 in Ernestown Township, Upper Canada, son of John Nelson McKim and Jane Shibley; m. 1 Oct. 1884 Bessie True, daughter of George W. True of Portland, Maine, and they had one daughter; d. 26 Jan. 1917 in an accident at the railway station in Coteau Jonction (Coteau-Station), Que.

Anson McKim grew up on the family farm in Ernestown Township. He must have left school early, since he was on the staff of the Conservative Toronto newspaper, the *Mail*, when still a young man. His duties there are not known, but he may have had an opportunity to try his hand at journalism, as is sometimes suggested. Perhaps he was assigned various clerical tasks before he became involved in the sale of subscriptions and advertisements. He was employed in that area on 22 May 1879, the day the *Mail* announced he had just been transferred to its Montreal offices, which were located in the *Star* building on Rue Saint-Jacques. He was to head its bureau there as the person in charge of advertisements and subscriptions for the daily and weekly editions of the paper. Almost every day, the *Mail* carried a column entitled "Montreal News," and later "Montreal Affairs," which was a sort of society gossip column, with added items about political, commercial, and financial events. The paper also printed excerpts from the Montreal *Gazette*.

McKim gradually came to realize the commercial potential of newspaper advertising. If he could place the same advertisement in a large number of dailies across Canada, the economic impact would be exponential. And so it occurred to him to follow the American example and compile a collection of information about Canadian newspapers, their titles, place of publication, readership, and rates. It was difficult to accumulate this data, however, since McKim was identified with his own paper and was seen by many as a competitor. In 1884 the *Mail* published the *Canadian newspaper directory* in Toronto, but McKim's role in its compilation is not known. The venture must have proved a failure since the paper abandoned it. The standard reference again became the *American newspaper annual and directory*, which had been published in Philadelphia by N. W. Ayer and Son since 1868.

In January 1889, after ten years with the *Mail* in Montreal, McKim founded his own advertising agency, A. McKim and Company. He set out to develop the tools the agency needed for finding out about newspapers and also the markets connected with them. To that end, in 1892 he published the *Canadian newspaper directory*, which listed more than 1,000 periodicals by province and then by city, town, or village. It provided information about the population, commerce, and industries of these places, and about telephone and telegraph communication, railway transportation, mail service, and customs duties. The desired effect was slow in coming, however, and the second edition of the directory did not appear until seven years later, in 1899. There would be 32 editions before it ceased publication in 1941.

During the first decade of the 20th century, McKim's advertising agency was recognized as the foremost among the 19 such operations in Montreal. It was a model not only in its standards and working methods, but also in its precision and diligence. McKim now knew how to bring buyers and advertisers together. He had convinced both groups that the trade mark was more important than the product itself. An advertising campaign went through a series of stages which combined a thorough knowledge of the product's specifics with an understanding of the areas served by the newspapers, their readership, and the buying habits there. At the technical level, the services offered by the firm included graphics, typesetting, proofreading, quality control, and accounting.

In 1905 A. McKim and Company had 150 large corporate clients in Canada and the United States, including the Bank of Montreal, Henry Birks and Sons (Montreal), Chase and Sanborn (Boston), the T. Eaton Company Limited (Toronto), the International Stock Food Company (Minneapolis), Labatt and Company (London, Ottawa, and Montreal), and Henry Morgan and Company (Montreal). In 1907, aware of the competition that was growing year by year, McKim went into partnership with three investors – his brother John Nelson McKim, W. B. Somerset, and Henry Edward Stephenson – to form the A. McKim Advertising Agency Limited and thus increase the firm's capitalization and maintain its pre-eminent place in the market. In 1911 the agency had 65 employees in Montreal and about 10 in Toronto, as well as correspondents in New York, Boston, and London, England. Its capital shares increased from $200,000 in 1907 to $500,000 in 1912.

On the morning of 26 Jan. 1917, McKim left his home at 25 McGregor (Avenue du Docteur-Penfield) to get the train for Ottawa. Seating himself in a railway car at Bonaventure Station, he realized once it began rolling that he had taken the train for Toronto by mistake. At Coteau Jonction he rushed out to catch the Ottawa one, but was struck by another train en route for Chicago. Neither the engineer nor the brakeman had seen anyone on the tracks.

A courteous, meticulous, tactful, and hard-working man, Anson McKim belonged to the middle-class business world of Montreal. He was considered a model citizen, with his concerns about economic growth and social development, and was a member of many philanthropic and sports clubs, including the Mount Royal Club, the Montreal Racquet Club, and the Royal Montreal Golf Club. When the Canadian Association of Advertising Agencies was founded in 1915, McKim had been elected its president. In 1916 he had been second vice-president of the Montreal Board of Trade.

ANDRÉ BEAULIEU

Further reading

R. T. Johnston, *Selling themselves: the emergence of Canadian advertising* (Toronto, 2001).

P. W. Laird, *Advertising progress: American business and the rise of consumer marketing* (Baltimore, Md, 1998).

Mark Tungate, *Adland: a global history of advertising* (London, 2007).

PETER CHARLES LARKIN,

businessman and diplomat; b. 14 May 1855 in Montreal, son of Michael Larkin and Sarah McGill; m. 27 June 1883 Hannah Jean Ross in Cobourg, Ont., and they had one son and one daughter; d. 3 Feb. 1930 in London, England.

Peter Larkin always gave his date of birth incorrectly as 13 May 1856. Little is known about his early life and upbringing in what undoubtedly were modest circumstances. His father, a bricklayer, died when he was seven; his mother worked as a charwoman. He received his primary education in Montreal, and is said to have had some training in Toronto. Perhaps this occurred in the evenings after he moved there in his twenties. Young Peter's business career had begun when he went to work at age 13 for a retail grocer. By 1875–76 Montreal directories listed him as a bookkeeper for an unnamed employer. About 1877 he joined Tiffin Brothers, a grocery wholesaler in Montreal, as a commercial traveller calling on customers from Halifax to Winnipeg. At the time of his marriage he was based in Toronto.

In 1889 he left Tiffin Brothers to start his own business in Toronto as a tea broker and wholesaler of sugar, dried fruits, and nuts. An early indication of his commercial ability and shrewdness came two years later after he had fallen out with the city's Wholesale Grocers' Guild over his refusal to maintain the prices for granulated sugar its members had agreed upon. They were unable to match either the lower expenses he achieved by stocking a narrow line of high-volume items or the flexibility he gained by using public warehouses. Larkin's main interest, however, remained the tea trade, and soon it demanded almost his entire attention.

Beginning in the 1880s public taste in Britain, and in Canada, turned away markedly from the increasingly adulterated green teas of China and Japan toward the more robust black teas of India and Ceylon (Sri Lanka). Between 1882 and 1892 imports of China tea into Britain declined from 114 million pounds to 34, while imports from the Indian subcontinent rose from 31.5 million to 173. As well, the old way of selling tea, from open, lead-lined chests where it was prone to absorb strong odours in a grocer's shop, began to be superseded about 1890 by its sale in small, sealed, lead-foil packets.

Although Larkin was neither the first to introduce India and Ceylon teas to Canada nor the first to supply them in packets, he was in the vanguard of innovators and certainly the earliest importer to mix his own blends, which were marketed with a skill and drive unmatched by his competitors. As early as 1891 he advertised Ceylon tea in 50-pound chests to the grocery trade. A year later he refined his line by blending Ceylon teas and offering them to grocers in pound and half-pound packages as the Golden Teapot Blend from "The Salada Tea Co., L'td., Ceylon." No evidence has been found that this company, said to be named for a tea-growing district in India, was other than Larkin's invention. All mention of Golden Teapot Blend was soon dropped and Salada went on to become one of the strongest brand names in the Canadian and American markets.

Larkin's marketing strategy was to appoint agents to sell his product and to support them with extensive newspaper publicity. "In advertising," he said, "be sure you have the right article first, then don't spare the printer's ink." As of May 1893 more than 200 Toronto grocers stocked Salada. A year later, when sales in the city had grown to exceed those of all other packaged teas combined, Larkin turned his attention outside Toronto and rapidly signed up grocers throughout southern Ontario. Week after week the *Canadian Grocer* (Toronto) reported, like a railway conductor calling out stops, the towns where agents had been appointed. His next target was Montreal, where, within four months, some 225 accounts had been opened. By May 1895 Larkin boasted nearly 2,000 agents in eastern Canada; sales volumes were more than double those of the year before. With the opening of a wholesale depot in Vancouver in 1896, Salada gained national distribution. Backed by advertising in some 340 daily and weekly newspapers, it quickly captured about 75 per cent of the sales of packaged tea in the country.

As his brand's share of its market neared saturation, Larkin had a choice, either of slower growth as packaged tea made inroads on bulk sales, which still accounted for 85 per cent of Canada's black-tea market, or of expanding to the United States. He chose the latter, though per capita consumption of tea there was much lower than in Canada. His first American branch opened in Buffalo, N.Y., in mid 1896; others followed in quick succession in Pittsburgh, Boston, Rochester, and Detroit. The hub of his American business, however, was Boston. By early 1898 more than 500 grocers in that city and its suburbs were handling Salada.

Until 1900 Larkin's business – styled P. C. Larkin and Company, but usually known as the Salada Tea Company – was organized as a sole proprietorship. In that year the Salada Tea Company Limited was incorporated with 40,000 shares having a par value of $10 each. Larkin held all the shares except those needed by his wife and accountant to qualify as directors. Salada's offices and factory were then at 32 Yonge Street, Toronto, in a building acquired in 1898 after fire had damaged Larkin's previous quarters and stock. His income from tea was augmented by sales of his patented invention, the Ideal tea packer, which enabled three men to turn out 20,000 half-pound packages of tea per week. Even competitors such as Thomas J. Lipton Company acquired Ideal packers for their own use. By 1899, when Larkin was invited to join George Albertus Cox, William Mulock, Timothy Eaton and others in buying shares to support Joseph E. Atkinson's bid for control of the *Toronto Daily Star*, it was clear he had become a wealthy man. A few years later he was said to be the "heaviest insured man" in Canada.

Earlier, in the mid 1890s when Atkinson was the Toronto *Globe*'s Ottawa correspondent, he had interviewed Larkin about the Liberal party's policy of unrestricted reciprocity. Likely the tea merchant's opinion was sought not only because he was a leading businessman but also because he was a known supporter of the party and its charismatic leader, Wilfrid Laurier. While Larkin might doubt as late as 1899 that Laurier would remember him from their few previous contacts, this uncertainty was unwarranted by September 1905, when Larkin became treasurer of the General Reform Association of Ontario, a position he would hold for several years. In 1909 he helped found the Ontario Club, the party's chief social establishment in Toronto; he was its president in 1911–12. Following the Imperial Conference of 1911, which recommended a British royal commission on the natural resources, trade, and legislation of the dominions, he was appointed Canada's representative on the commission. Barely two months later, after the Liberals were soundly defeated in a general election by Robert Laird Borden's Conservatives, George Eulas Foster, the new minister of trade and commerce, lost no time in replacing Larkin.

Larkin's essentially benevolent view of life had been reflected in the other endeavours in which he was active during the century's first decade. In 1904, on the initiative of Joseph Wesley Flavelle, chairman of the Toronto General Hospital, Larkin was appointed to its board of trustees. For 17 years he would throw himself into the hospital's affairs as a member of several committees and as vice-chairman of the board, retiring with Flavelle only after the large new hospital built near Queen's Park had been finished and was free of debt. In 1909 Larkin became president of the Toronto League for the Prevention of Tuberculosis; he served in this capacity for 20 years and gave heavily of his time and funds to its work. In addition, he was credited in obituaries with being the first prominent person to advocate a system of old-age pensions, which took shape in parliament as the Government Annuities Act of 1908.

For all Larkin's involvement in politics, he was more comfortable as a power behind the throne rather than on it. Before the Liberals lost office in 1911, he was often spoken of as a possible senator. As Laurier went about rebuilding the party after the election, the two men became close friends. When Laurier visited Toronto he usually stayed at the Larkins' house on Elm Avenue in Rosedale. After the conscription issue split the country in 1917, Larkin was one of the few Ontario Liberals who backed their leader in opposing forced military service. He even resigned over the issue from the board of the *Globe*, where he had sat for almost ten years. Yet when it was suggested that he contest a seat in the election of December 1917, he declined on the grounds that his business could hardly do without him.

Larkin had a point. Though exact figures are not available, Salada Tea's volume had increased between five and ten times since 1900. He prided himself on being known as "The Tea King of America," in tribute to the company's domination of markets north and south of the border. Soon after World War I broke out, however, an embargo on tea exports from England made the company dependent on shipments direct from Ceylon and India, which took three months to arrive. To protect against any interruption in its supplies, Salada bought in unusually large quantities, borrowing heavily from its bankers to finance the purchases. Five or six years before the war Larkin had begun to turn over the day-to-day management of his company to his son, Gerald Ross, but when Gerald and more than two dozen key employees enlisted to fight in Europe, Larkin was forced to resume detailed charge. At one point his tea-taster in Boston joined up and he had to take the man's place for a while.

In the aftermath of the 1917 election, which was a disaster for the Liberals, Laurier again set about reviving his party, though illness began to hobble him the following summer. One of the last letters he received before his death in February 1919 came from Larkin asking if a seat in parliament could be found for William Lyon Mackenzie King, who had been defeated in the election (despite Larkin's financial backing), to avoid losing his talents to the United States. As events unfolded, King was chosen to succeed Laurier as leader in August, and he was returned to the House of Commons in a by-election two months later. He then led the opposition until the Liberals squeaked into office in December 1921.

One of King's first acts in power was to make Larkin Canada's high commissioner in London in place of Sir George Halsey Perley, who had retired after the election. The appointment, the highest within the gift of the government, was gazetted on 10 Feb. 1922, when Larkin was also sworn in as a privy councillor for Canada. In offering him the post, King had played down his influence by saying he was only carrying out Laurier's wish and expressed belief that "there is nothing too good for our friend Larkin." Although there were some grumblings – George MacKinnon Wrong of the University of Toronto had advised King not to pick someone with such limited formal education – on the whole bipartisan approval greeted the appointment. Larkin was thought by most to have the intelligence and urbanity to do Canada credit, as well as a business reputation the British would respect. He was tall and patrician, with coal-black eyes, a full, white moustache, and a well-formed head that had been bald since his thirties. Known for being particularly well-dressed, he usually wore formal attire with a black silk hat. Asked to describe himself, he said he was a "plain, blunt man," like Mark Antony, but drew attention to his literary tastes, the experience he had gained from travelling to Europe annually for many years, and his considerable knowledge of art and architecture. The prime minister had benefited from Larkin's interest in the decorative arts after Zoé, widow of Sir Wilfrid Laurier, left her house in Ottawa to the Liberal party as an official residence for its leader. Larkin contributed heavily to the costs of renovation and provided much of the furniture for the public rooms from a stock of Adam, Hepplewhite, and Sheraton pieces he had gathered in a Montreal warehouse. His involvement foreshadowed his role in creating Canada House in London.

When Larkin was appointed, it was made clear that the high commissioner would communicate directly with the prime minister on all matters of public policy, and avoid any gatherings of British officials and high commissioners that might pull Canada into a commitment to British foreign policy. Larkin was later quoted as saying, "The people of Canada think the high commissioner for Canada is a person of some importance in London. He is not." Since he shared King's sense of Canadian autonomy and his mistrust of the British government, Larkin was quite willing to conform to his prime minister's expectations. This understanding reflected not only the similarity of views and close ties between the two men, but also King's desire to exercise control over matters at a time when Canada's relationships with Britain and the other dominions were being redefined. To reinforce the chain of command, an order in council was passed concurrent with Larkin's appointment placing all agencies of the Canadian government in the United Kingdom under the high commissioner. On 23 April, barely two weeks after Larkin arrived in Britain, he wrote to King proposing that things be taken to their logical conclusion by concentrating all operations under one roof. The proposal soon became mixed up in the simmering issue of whether provincial agents-general in London would be recognized as equals to the high commissioner in matters where the British North America Act accorded powers to the provinces. After Frederick Coate Wade, British

Columbia's aggressive agent-general, was found to be using his influence against the sale of his province's well-located quarters to the Canadian government, which already leased part of it, King wrote Larkin on 22 June 1922 that he was not inclined "to go particularly out of my way towards seeking any added status for the representatives of the provinces in London." Finding an alternative site took Larkin another year, but the delay was well worth the wait when he secured from the Union Club its distinguished building on Trafalgar Square. Canada House was opened by King George V on 29 June 1925. The consolidation there of Canadian offices soon strained relations with the trade commissioners in Britain of the Department of Trade and Commerce, in part because the move facilitated Larkin's periodic interference in trade matters.

Meanwhile, there were other issues demanding the high commissioner's attention, including the lifting of a 30-year embargo on the importation of live cattle into Britain, settling Britain's war debt to Canada, and preparations for the British Empire exhibitions of 1924 and 1925. In addition, the high commissionship committed the Larkins to incessant socializing. Jean Larkin's contribution was the hosting of weekly receptions in their residence at Lancaster Gate, London. That King was grateful for such diligent work, not to mention Peter Larkin's financial support, is clear from the long and sentimental letter the prime minister, exhausted by constitutional tilting with Governor General Julian Hedworth George Byng, 1st Viscount Byng, wrote Larkin on New Year's Eve 1926. "I have no living friend for whom I have a greater or truer regard than for yourself," King told him. Although Larkin would continue to serve for another four years, until his death, King's words were a fitting tribute to his work as high commissioner.

Larkin died of a heart attack in 1930. After a memorial service at Christchurch, Lancaster Gate, his cremated remains were returned to Toronto for burial. Subsequently, uncashed cheques for his salary from the government were found in his desk. With an income said to have reached $650,000 annually from the Salada Tea Company, which during the 1920s had grown under Gerald Larkin's management to be the third-largest supplier of teas in the world, Peter Larkin had asked no more from his country than the honour of serving it.

STEPHEN A. OTTO

Further reading

Michael Bliss, *A living profit: studies in the social history of Canadian business, 1883–1911* (Toronto, 1974).

O. M. Hill, *Canada's salesman to the world: the Department of Trade and Commerce, 1892–1939* (Montreal and London, 1977).

Roy MacLaren, *Commissions high: Canada in London, 1870–1971* (Montreal and Kingston, Ont., 2006), 223–69.

GEORGES-ÉLIE AMYOT,

manufacturer, businessman, politician, and philanthropist;
b. 28 Jan. 1856 in Saint-Augustin-de-Desmaures, Lower Canada,
son of Dominique Amyot (Amyot, *dit* Larpinière), a farmer,
and Louise Nolin; m. 14 Nov. 1881 Joséphine Tanguay at Quebec,
and they had six children, five of whom survived;
d. 28 March 1930 in Palm Beach, Fla.

G eorges-Élie Amyot lived on a farm in Saint-Augustin-de-Desmaures until he was ten years old. He then moved with his family to Sainte-Catherine (Sainte-Catherine-de-la-Jacques-Cartier), where he attended school for a short time and was taught English by the Irish curé of the parish. At the age of 14 he went to Quebec; there he learned the trade of saddler from Louis Girard and entered into partnership with the saddler Louis Tanguay, his future father-in-law. In 1874 he joined his brother Bernard in New Haven, Conn., where the first manufacturer of corsets in the United States, the Strouse, Adler Company Corset Factory, had been founded in 1861; it had become the city's principal employer. Amyot subsequently lived for a time in Springfield, Mass., engaged in his trade. When he returned to his home province in 1877, he was employed in Montreal as a clerk in the wrought-iron business and the boot and shoe industry. In 1879 he began working as a clerk for his cousins Joseph and George-Élie Amyot, who were importers of novelty items in Quebec's Lower Town. He opened his own shop in the Upper Town in 1885, selling dry goods, fancy goods, and novelties. The following year, at the instigation of wholesaler Isidore Thibaudeau, Amyot's retail business was forced into bankruptcy. In 1894, when he was better off financially, he would reimburse his creditors, a gesture that his contemporaries said was unusual.

On 11 Oct. 1886 Amyot entered into a five-year partnership with Léon Dyonnet, who had been led to start manufacturing corsets by the success of the corset shop run since 1882 by his French wife, Hélène Goullioud, and her sister Clotilde. Each contributed $2,000 in capital, was entitled to half the profits, and could withdraw $800 a year for his personal expenses. Their agreement also stipulated that the two partners would be involved in every aspect of the business and that Dyonnet was to initiate Amyot "into all the manufacturing details and secrets and let him benefit from the experience he had gained in the said production process." The question arises where Amyot had obtained this money so soon after his bankruptcy. It had probably come from his in-laws or from a fellow merchant, perhaps Pierre-Joseph Côté, to whom he owed an advance of $1,500 in the fall of 1887. In any case, in December 1886 Amyot's wife renounced community of property, and thus put the family assets out of the creditors' reach. On 26 March 1889, reportedly following Dyonnet's departure for Brazil, the partnership was dissolved; in its stead the Dominion Corset Manufacturing Company was set up. Amyot's partners were his sister Odile until her marriage in July 1890 and afterwards his older sister Marie-Louise until 9 Oct. 1897. He then continued in the Dominion Corset Company on his own.

The enterprise soon met with promising success, and rented larger and larger premises in the industrial section of Saint-Roch ward. In 1898 Amyot would purchase the bankrupt shoe factory of G. Bresse and Company for $21,500. By November 1887 he was replacing the pedal-operated machines with steam-driven machinery, thereby substantially increasing his output and lowering the labour cost per unit. In his testimony to the royal commission on the relations of labour and capital in 1888, he said that he had about 60 employees, including 10 to 15 girls aged between 10 and 14. Most of the goods he produced went to markets outside Quebec City, in particular to the Montreal wholesale outlet, which opened in 1889, and then to the Toronto office, which was set up in 1892. Sales grew from $21,000 in 1887 to $58,000 in 1891 and $130,000 in 1895.

This expansion led Amyot to invest in related activities. From 1894, to ensure himself a steady and cheap supply of the cardboard boxes required for shipping his products, he manufactured them himself in a building adjacent to his corset factory. This operation was initially an integral part of Dominion Corset, but from 1906 it was carried on by a separate entity, the Quebec Paper Box Company. In 1916 Amyot would set up the Canada Corset Steel and Wire Corporation to manufacture the steel rods used in the corsets.

Amyot also went into the production of beer, opening a brewery in 1895. His partner, Pierre-Joseph Côté, contributed two-thirds of the capital and, in return for a basic salary, was to devote his full time to managing the enterprise. The partnership agreement had a clause allowing Amyot to buy back one-sixth of Côté's shares as well as to join him in working full-time in the business if its annual profits exceeded $10,000. This investment gave Amyot a contingency plan in the event that Dominion Corset failed. The brewery was located in Saint-Sauveur ward against the cliff where the spring water was drawn. On 12 Nov. 1896 beer merchant Michel Gauvin replaced Côté in the company, which became known as Amyot et Gauvin. It produced and distributed Fox Head beers, both ale and porter. In 1909, after buying Gauvin's share and engaging in a number of highly profitable financial transactions, Amyot sold the business to National Breweries Limited for $226,500 in shares and debentures of that company, which was in the process of amalgamating most of the province's breweries in Montreal and Quebec City.

From at least 1887, Amyot had been involved in politics. A member of the Liberal party, he focused mainly on finances and organization. He was particularly active in the debate on reciprocity with the United States, which by 1888 he supported. In 1897, a year after Wilfrid Laurier came to power, a tariff reform was introduced that granted special concessions to Great Britain. In his dealings with Laurier, as well as in the Canadian Manufacturers' Association (he was a member of the Quebec section) and the Quebec Chamber of Commerce (he served as president in 1906 and 1907), Amyot tried in vain to defend his business interests. He complained that the duty on imported corsets (which mainly came from Britain) had been lowered, while the duty on his raw materials – cotton and steel – were as high as ever.

When Charles Fitzpatrick was appointed chief justice of the Supreme Court of Canada in 1906, a by-election became necessary in the federal riding of Quebec. Seeking a businessman to represent the city's interests, Laurier offered the nomination to Amyot. His campaign, which was widely supported by the upper echelons of the Liberal party both federally and provincially, was organized by Cyrille-Fraser Delâge, the member of the Legislative Assembly for the same riding, and was financed by Amyot himself. Rebelling against the autocratic manner in which Laurier had chosen the candidate, a number of Liberals refused, however, to rally around Amyot. Lorenzo Robitaille, the 24-year-old son of a Beauport businessman, ran as an independent Liberal. He and his supporters attacked Amyot, calling him, among other things, a rich industrialist, an employer who treated his workers harshly, and Laurier's man. Robitaille won the backing of Armand La Vergne, and then of Henri Bourassa. The Nationalistes thus used the situation to enter the fray, in order to demonstrate their opposition to certain measures taken by the Laurier government and to embarrass the party leadership. Memorable mass meetings drew the protagonists of both camps, raising the level of the debate and transforming a by-election that should have been run off quietly into a popularity contest between Laurier and Liberals loyal to him and the Nationalistes clustered around Bourassa. Clearly overtaken by events, Amyot struggled on to the end, but on 23 October he had to concede defeat by 388 votes. In December 1911 the premier of Quebec, Sir Lomer Gouin, with whom he was closely associated, appointed him legislative councillor for the division of La Durantaye.

Because of his success in industry and his political connections, Amyot was picked in January 1922 to take up the formidable challenge of saving the Banque Nationale, which had opened at Quebec in 1860, from bankruptcy. After a period of strong growth during World War I, the bank found itself in a precarious position, mainly because of the financial problems of National Farming Machinery Limited, a company in Montmagny run by Charles-Abraham Paquet. The firm had prospered as a result of the war economy, but when it tried to switch to producing farm implements, it experienced serious difficulties. In 1922 it had to obtain loans from the Banque Nationale totalling $5 million. This growing financial burden, along with a marked decrease in deposits from which the *caisses populaires* had in particular gained, posed a threat to the bank's survival. Such was the situation in 1922, when four new directors were elected: Amyot, who also became president of the bank, Joseph-Herman Fortier, Sir Georges Garneau, and Charles-Edmond Taschereau, the brother of Premier Louis-Alexandre Taschereau. Scarcely had Amyot taken up office when he was obliged, with Gouin's support, to make an urgent request to the federal minister of finance for a loan of $2.5 million. Unable to offer sufficient security, he received only $1 million, and he also failed in his bid for increased federal government deposits.

At the end of March, Amyot turned to the leading figures in the economic and political life of the province and the city of Quebec, inviting them to subscribe to a $1 million issue of capital shares. Despite the risks of double liability, Amyot himself took a block of $200,000 and got commitments from Olivier-Napoléon Drouin and Fortier (for $100,000 each), as well as from a number of other businessmen and politicians, including Premier Taschereau (for amounts ranging from $10,000 to $50,000). The $1 million was officially subscribed within a few weeks and was in by the end of 1922. From 1922 to 1924, Amyot, whose face appeared on the newly printed bank notes, tried to recover as much of the assets of National Farming Machinery Limited as possible and obtained large deposits from the provincial government. Despite his efforts, by the end of 1923 the situation had deteriorated to such an extent that a solution had to be found at once, in the form of a merger with the Banque d'Hochelaga. The premier persuaded it to absorb the Banque Nationale by guaranteeing it a reserve of $15 million in government bonds to balance the liquidity of the two banks. The bill providing for this assistance was passed on 24 Jan. 1924 and was vigorously defended by Taschereau, whom the opposition accused of trying to rescue Liberal friends threatened with sizeable losses, including Amyot. Once the merger was confirmed, Amyot became vice-president of the new Banque Canadienne Nationale, in which he maintained interests that were particularly useful to him in promoting his real estate and industrial endeavours.

Throughout this period Amyot had continued his cautious management of Dominion Corset. In 1901 it had about 320 employees and was producing 175 dozen corsets a day (in 125 different models) and 8,000 to 10,000 cardboard boxes. By the end of the first decade of the

20th century, its output had a total value of $500,000, of which roughly a third was sold in Ontario, 15 per cent in Montreal, 45 per cent in the rest of Quebec, the Maritimes, and western Canada, and 6 to 7 per cent in Australia and New Zealand. Sales rose from $560,000 in 1909 to more than $1 million in 1913, reaching $1.6 million in 1918 and $2.6 million the following year. This remarkable growth made it necessary in 1909 to expand the plant, but on 27 May 1911 it was devastated by a fire that destroyed part of the neighbourhood. Despite losses of $250,000, Amyot immediately rebuilt the factory, making it larger than ever. In the absence of internal accounting data, the company's performance in some subsequent years is known only through company minutes. Between 1911 and 1915 revenues ranged from $100,000 to $200,000 per annum and rose noticeably afterwards. Information gathered by the Dominion Bureau of Statistics confirms that Dominion Corset increasingly dominated an industry that was tending to level off.

At the turn of the century Amyot already had sizeable financial resources, which he invested in real estate, among other things. In 1897, for example, he paid $6,000 cash for a fine property on Chemin Sainte-Foy in the suburbs of Quebec. Over the years he had bought and speculated in real estate in other parts of the city (especially on the Grande Allée), in Montreal, and even in Saskatchewan and British Columbia. In the course of various subscriptions to Victory Loans, he himself, with $200,000 in 1917 and $500,000 in 1918, managed to come close to the amount contributed by the Price empire. In the 1920s Amyot invested in and directed and promoted many projects, on his own, or through figureheads such as his son-in-law Henri Bray and his accountant Honoré-J. Pinsonneault, or as a member of some Canadian, British, or American politico-financial group. In addition to putting his money in real estate, he invested in numerous railway, shipping, and mining companies. During the winter he often spent time in resort areas in Europe (the French Riviera), the United States (Palm Beach, Fla), and Canada (Pointe-au-Pic, which would later become La Malbaie, in the Charlevoix region of Quebec), where he managed to make high-level personal and business connections. Direct and blunt, he did not skimp when it came to supporting causes dear to his heart, such as the church of Saint-Jean-Baptiste, the Asile du Bon-Pasteur, or the École Supérieure de Chimie at the Université Laval. In 1909 the minister of militia and defence, Sir

Frederick William Borden, appointed him honorary lieutenant-colonel of the 61st Regiment of Montmagny, a title he cherished.

Demanding but fair in his dealings with his employees, Amyot had brought his two sons into the business, beginning in 1906. Horatio, who had become deaf following surgery, was involved in the company's operations in Toronto, western Canada, and then Montreal. Adjutor, the elder, also worked at finding new markets, especially in Australia and New Zealand and later England. Georges-Élie's strong personality and thorough knowledge of the business world, however, left little room for Adjutor, who helped his father in the overall management but had little to do with day-to-day operations, which were entrusted instead to managers and accountants, including Pinsonneault. After putting in place an advantageous capital structure through various financial and legal transactions, Georges-Élie handed over control of Dominion Corset to Adjutor in 1924 through a private agreement. He transferred 11,499 of the 21,000 shares issued and subscribed, which were added to the 6,050 shares Adjutor already held, with the authority, however, to reduce the capital by selling them back to the company. In December of that year Adjutor conveyed all his shares except one to his father in trust, to be held until the latter's death, but this agreement was cancelled in 1929. These manoeuvres ensured that Adjutor would inherit the business.

In 1928, to guarantee the distribution and preservation of the capital investment, Amyot drew up a will reflecting his own image – all of a piece and absolutely solid – dividing among his heirs, with the exception of Adjutor, the usufruct from a capital that would amount to some $5.5 million, distributable on the death of the last of his grandchildren. Including Dominion Corset, the Amyot empire was worth, in 1930, at least $8 million in pre-Depression dollars and it constituted one of the great fortunes of Quebec City at that time.

Georges-Élie Amyot died suddenly in Palm Beach on 28 March 1930. In the ensuing days, the arrival of his body and the magnificent funeral attracted the political and commercial elite of Quebec City. Amyot was buried on 3 April in the cemetery of Notre-Dame de Belmont, in a marble mausoleum he had had prepared in 1908, as befitted the remarkable success of a French-speaking Quebec industrialist who had become a financier and entrepreneur on a continental scale.

MARC VALLIÈRES

Further reading

Marc Vallières *et al.*, *Histoire de Québec et de sa région* (Québec, 2008): 1161–62, 1166–67, 1175–77, 1637–38.

Marc Vallières, *Québec* (Québec, 2010).

Les ouvrières de la Dominion Corset à Québec, 1886–1988, sous la dir. de Jean Du Berger et Jacques Mathieu (Sainte-Foy [Québec], 1993).

Ronald Rudin, *Banking en français: the French banks of Quebec, 1835–1925* (Toronto, 1985).

Réal Bélanger, *Wilfrid Laurier: quand la politique devient passion* ([Québec], 2007).

Sir RODOLPHE FORGET
(baptized Joseph-David-Rodolphe),

businessman, politician, and philanthropist; b. 10 Dec. 1861 in Terrebonne, Lower Canada, son of David Forget and Angèle Limoges; m. first 12 Oct. 1885 Alexandra Tourville (d. 1891) in Montreal, and they had one daughter; m. secondly 3 April 1894 Blanche McDonald in Rivière-du-Loup, Que., and they had three sons and one daughter; d. 19 Feb. 1919 in Montreal.

One of the more controversial figures of the early 20th century in Canada, Rodolphe Forget was president and director of several of the country's most important commercial and industrial enterprises. With an extensive network of political and financial contacts, he pioneered major initiatives in transportation and banking and he played a key role in the evolution of the hydroelectric industry in Montreal and Quebec City. His financial and political activities were often intertwined and frequently the subject of considerable public attention.

The origins of the Forget family can be traced back to the middle of the 17th century when Nicolas Forget (Froget, *dit* Despatis) of Normandy arrived in the district of Montreal. For the most part the Forgets set-tled in Terrebonne, Repentigny, Lachenaie, and Saint-François-de-Sales (Laval). The parents of Rodolphe, David, a lawyer, and Angèle, half-sister to Louis-Olivier Taillon, later premier of Quebec, ultimately took up res-idence in Terrebonne, where they had four children. An only son, Forget commenced classical studies there at the Collège Masson. At age 15, he began an apprenticeship in the brokerage house of his uncle Louis-Joseph Forget. On completing his studies he was employed at L. J. Forget et Compagnie, which, during the 1880s, emerged as the most important brokerage firm in Montreal and gained recognition throughout Canada and abroad. The firm is said to have handled important investments for the Roman Catholic Church of Quebec. In 1890 he became a partner in the firm. It was his involvement in the Montreal Stock Exchange, how-ever, beginning at about the same time, which apparently accounted for his rapid rise in the business community.

The personalities and styles of Louis-Joseph and Rodolphe Forget were said to have complemented each other in their respective approach-es to business. Louis-Joseph was described as balanced and prudent in his dealings, whereas Rodolphe was spontaneous, daring, and self-assured. In 1910 *Saturday Night* stated that "what [Rodolphe] Forget will cheerfully undertake in the stock market would make the average broker stand aghast."

During the rapid expansion in industrial activity in Canada near the turn of the century the Forgets began investing in newly developing sec-tors of the economy. With his purchase of shares in the Royal Electric Company in 1890, Rodolphe entered the hydroelectric industry in ear-nest. Established in 1884, the company appeared to be in good standing as a result of important contracts for the lighting of streets in Montreal. An effort to widen its activities and increase its capital had invited the financial participation of new investors. Among them were the Forgets, who by 1898 controlled almost 50 per cent of the company's stock. The following year the Forgets and some associates acquired control of the company.

In 1900 the operations of the Royal Electric Company grew sub-stantially, in large part owing to contracts signed with the cities of Longueuil, Saint-Laurent, and Outremont, as well as to an agreement to furnish electricity to the Montreal Street Railway. The firm purchased the Chambly Manufacturing Company, which had a generating station on the Richelieu. In December 1900 Royal Electric sold the industrial side of its operations, its workshops, machines, patents, and manufacturing rights, to the Canadian General Electric Company in order to concentrate on the production and sale of electricity for domestic consumption. It was to receive shares in CGE worth $440,000 in exchange. Forget was in a strong position to obtain ratification of the deal since he possessed or had procurations on behalf of his clients for approximately 90 per cent of the shares in Royal Electric. Six months later the company sold its shares in CGE for over $605,000.

In a move to eliminate competition for the sale and distribution of electricity in Montreal, Forget entered into negotiations with Herbert Samuel Holt of the Montreal Gas Company. Holt welcomed a merger on the condition that he assume the presidency of the new corporation. With the capitalization of the proposed company estimated at about 17 million dollars, many members of the Montreal Stock Exchange were concerned about its feasibility. Louis-Joseph Forget urged his adventurous nephew to be cautious. On the successful completion of the merger, Rodolphe assumed the second vice-presidency of the new enterprise. (In addition, he was president of one of the merging companies, Royal Electric.) Although the merger had arisen in large measure from the actions of Rodolphe, Louis-Joseph played a critical role in the transaction, bringing together the diverse interests involved. During the first decade of the 20th century, the majority of shares of the Montreal Light, Heat and Power Company were controlled by the Forgets and L. J. Forget et Compagnie. From a financial standpoint, the merger proved to be a success. In an effort to gain control of the entire sector, the firm proceeded to absorb some of the remaining companies involved in the distribution of hydroelectricity in Montreal. By 1909 Rodolphe would begin to sell his shares in the Montreal Light, Heat and Power Company and in 1917 he would relinquish his position as second vice-president.

As early as 1907 Forget was rated a millionaire by the *Montreal Daily Star*. At a time when Canadian business was dominated almost entirely by Anglo-Saxon capital, he was one of the rare French Canadians to penetrate the élite. The *Courrier du Canada* (Québec) described him as one of the most powerful men in financial circles, a man who could make and unmake and was seldom beaten in a financial battle. Labelled "the young Napoleon of St. François Xavier Street" for his work on the Montreal Stock Exchange, he served as its chairman from 1907 to 1909.

Following the near-consolidation of the Montreal market in hydro-electricity, Forget had shifted his attention to railways and hydroelectric-ity in the region of Quebec City. At the turn of the century he already had significant railway holdings there. In 1904, during his successful campaign to represent Charlevoix in the House of Commons, he prom-ised to build a railway between Quebec City and La Malbaie. For his constituents, access to Quebec City was difficult. As the shipping sea-son came to an end each winter, economic activity abruptly halted. For-get looked to remedy this situation by extending an existing line from Quebec City to Saint-Joachim as far as La Malbaie. He considered the Quebec and Saguenay Railway, incorporated in 1905, only the begin-ning of a line that would eventually run along the north shore of the St Lawrence through Labrador and would facilitate transatlantic travel. In describing the project to potential investors he claimed that the regions to be serviced by the railway were among the richest in the province and offered significant possibilities in the development of forest products.

Despite this favourable description, the Quebec and Saguenay line was a difficult project which required considerable amounts of capital; it ultimately experienced major financial problems. As its troubles grew, Forget moved to merge it with his hydroelectric interests in Quebec City. In effect, he attempted to adopt a model similar to that established by the Montreal Light, Heat and Power Company.

Forget had begun the expansion of his operations in Quebec City with the purchase of the Quebec Gas Company from a group of Toron-to financiers in 1909. Along with James Naismith Greenshields, who owned the Frontenac Gas Company, Forget created in November of the same year the Quebec Railway, Light, Heat and Power Company. Often referred to as the Quebec merger or *Le Merger*, it involved a number of enterprises in which the Forgets had important investments, including the Quebec and Saguenay Railway Company, the Quebec Eastern Rail-way Company, the Canadian Electric Light Company Limited, and the Quebec Jacques-Cartier Electric Company. Among the other companies in the merger were the Quebec Railway, Light and Power Company and the Quebec County Railway Company. At the inaugural meeting of the board of directors in March 1910 the number of shares held by Forget placed him in the dominant position, permitting him to assume the presidency. Some of the firm's administrators came from the gas and electric industries; others were interested in the company's small railway lines, many of which were financially supported by the federal and provincial governments. Domestic consumption of electricity in Quebec City was far less significant than in Montreal and the profitability of this sector was limited. Moreover, by 1912 the Quebec merger faced competition from the Dorchester Electric Company. Supported by the mayor of Quebec City and several members of the city council, this company had as one of its main objectives the elimination of the monopoly held by Forget. Much of the capital for Dorchester Electric came from one of Forget's principal rivals, the Montreal brokerage firm of Louis de Gaspé Beaubien. In 1915 Dorchester Electric, almost bankrupt, was taken over by the Shawinigan Water and Power Company, which created the Public Service Corporation of Quebec to replace the ailing firm. Forget's merger found a formidable rival in this new company, and would eventually be absorbed by it in 1923. But perhaps the main threat directed at both the merger and the overall business operations of Forget stemmed from the efforts of his political opponents to obstruct his access to overseas capital.

Before World War I, London was the principal source of investment capital for Canadian businessmen. Indeed, some argued that this situation was an impediment for French Canadian enterprises. Forget believed that it was useful to diversify sources of capital and he looked to the French financial market for help. He had established an important network of French investors to support his projects in Quebec City. While doing so, he maintained contact with the British market, cognizant of its continued influence on the Canadian economy.

In 1904 Forget had seriously considered the idea of breaking with L. J. Forget et Compagnie and pursuing his own brokerage operations. A few years later, when Jack Ross, the only son of James Ross, attempted unsuccessfully to compete with the Forgets for brokerage business in Montreal, Rodolphe acutely embarrassed the younger Ross. His actions contributed to the outbreak of a major conflict between James Ross and Louis-Joseph Forget and resulted in some deterioration in the relationship between the two Forgets. Rodolphe left L. J. Forget et Compagnie in August 1907.

After separating from the firm, Forget oversaw the establishment of a brokerage house in Paris which was successful in attracting investment for Canadian firms. For many years he had wanted to create a banking institution in Canada drawing on investment from France. Under the Liberal administration of Prime Minister Sir Wilfrid Laurier, Forget, a Conservative MP, attempted unsuccessfully to obtain a licence for the initiative, but with the election of the Conservatives under Robert Laird Borden in 1911, he was able to obtain it. That year the Banque Internationale du Canada was created and a potentially important step was taken in enhancing the financial relationship between France and Canada. The BIC appeared to do a flourishing business until August 1912 (a period of 10 months). By then, a power struggle had broken out between its French and Canadian investors and when news of the dispute began to circulate depositors became anxious about the security of their investments. As the situation deteriorated, the group around Forget, which included Conservative MP Robert Bickerdike and financier Greenshields, looked to protect their own interests.

Forget's political and business rivals converged on him at a particularly difficult period. Growing increasingly concerned about rumours emphasizing the highly speculative character of the Quebec merger, French investors sent a representative to the province to examine the state of their holdings. A number of newspapers in France began to reproduce local articles about Forget's business dealings. By far the most damaging of them had appeared in *Le Soleil* (Québec), a Liberal newspaper whose editor was Henri-Victor Lefebvre d'Hellencourt. Originally from France, d'Hellencourt was concerned about the image French Canadians would have in the French financial market once investors understood the speculative nature of Forget's activities. Beginning on 30 Oct. 1912 he systematically attacked both the Quebec merger and the BIC and called for the creation of a royal commission of inquiry to look into Forget's business practices. He accused Forget of reaping exorbitant profits from the sale of the bank's stock and questioned the legality of some of his actions. In the case of the Quebec merger, he described the strategy adopted by Forget as "the merciless exploitation of the citizens of Quebec, [who,] without recourse, are condemned to be bled to death to furnish the necessary funds for this merger." Much of the response to d'Hellencourt's charges was published in the Conservative newspaper *La Patrie* (Montreal), of which Forget was a principal financial supporter.

One of his main defenders, Conservative MP David-Ovide L'Espérance, emphasized Forget's "good reputation and honesty," which were universally established and recognized.

Notwithstanding efforts to protect Forget's reputation, several of his projects were in serious financial difficulty. His East Canada Power and Pulp Company, which was to furnish most of the freight for the Quebec and Saguenay, was declared bankrupt in mid December 1912. The BIC was taken over late in the same year by the Home Bank of Canada, which purchased the shares of French investors. The demise of the BIC proved to have important financial and political repercussions for Forget, since French investors were badly shaken by the experience. In the House of Commons Liberal MP Rodolphe Lemieux went so far as to conclude that because of Forget's activities "the name of Canada has been besmirched in France and it will take years and years before the good name and reputation of the Dominion stands as high among the financial men of France as it should stand in the eyes of the financiers of all countries." The failure of the BIC was in no small part due to d'Hellencourt's campaign, said to be inspired by a number of federal Liberals. The Quebec and Saguenay Railway, not yet completed, was in trouble and Forget appealed to the federal government for help. A bill passed in 1916 authorized the sale of the railway to the government, although the transaction was not finalized until three years later.

Another major transportation project in which Forget was involved was the Richelieu and Ontario Navigation Company. A group of businessmen under the presidency of his uncle had obtained control of this important company in 1894 and in 1904, after ten years as a director, Forget became president. Under him, the company sought to expand its operations by establishing a terminal in Toronto and a larger steamer for the Montreal–Quebec line. To finance the expansion Forget went to the Conservative government for permission to issue additional stock. The Liberal opposition expressed concern about the mergers taking place in the transportation industry and the possibility of increased rates as a result of the monopolistic conditions created. Suspicious of Forget, the Liberals attacked the request, but their attempt to prevent the issue of additional stock failed. Because of their involvement in the Richelieu and Ontario, both Rodolphe and his uncle had promoted the development of tourist destinations. The firm constructed a hotel at Tadoussac and in 1899 at Pointe-au-Pic it built the famous Manoir Richelieu. The first luxury hotel of that name, the Manoir Richelieu was destroyed by fire in 1928; reconstruction of the facility that still dominates the Charlevoix region started the following year.

Forget was involved in numerous other enterprises. He served as president of the Eastern Canada Steel and Iron Works and the Mount Royal Assurance Company and as vice-president of the Canadian Securities Corporation and the Société d'Administration Générale. He participated in the formation of the Canada Cement Company and in the syndicate which brought together the feuding Dominion Iron and Steel Company Limited and the Dominion Coal Company Limited in 1910.

Forget identified himself as an independent Conservative who supported the party's philosophy but allowed for the possibility of deciding an issue on its merits. First elected to the House of Commons for Charlevoix in 1904, he continued to serve the riding until 1917. Following his re-election in 1908, he divided his time between the house, his business interests in Montreal, and his political activities in Charlevoix. He was elected for both Charlevoix and Montmorency in 1911 – said to be the first time a member previously in opposition was elected for two constituencies. That year, with the election of the Conservatives under Borden, his inclusion in the federal cabinet was given serious consideration, but a controversy arose regarding his appointment as minister without portfolio. The nationalist faction of the Borden administration, in particular Frederick Debartzch Monk, was fiercely opposed to the idea, as was nationalist MLA Armand La Vergne, who had campaigned vigorously for the federal Conservatives during the election. Whether their opposition was decisive is not known. One story suggests that Forget refused the post so as to permit the appointment of a representative of the English Protestants of Quebec, George Halsey Perley. It has also been suggested that Forget was refused admission to cabinet in order to avoid any conflict of interest arising out of his request for a licence for the BIC. Whatever the case, Borden recalled that "there was a movement in favour of Rodolphe Forget but for certain reasons, I thought it undesirable that he should enter the Government." Shortly thereafter, on 1 Jan. 1912, Forget was made a knight bachelor.

Most of Forget's speeches in the House of Commons were related to his controversial business dealings, but he did participate in some debates on questions of national interest. He was in favour of the creation of more than one province in the North-West Territories. He viewed positively the extension of railways into the west and agreed that the federal government, rather than the provinces, should maintain control of lands there, since the dominion treasury had already spent millions of dollars on immigration. Why, he asked, "should we leave [ownership of the lands] to these provinces which have been developed with the money of the whole country?"

Although Forget proposed to limit provincial control over public lands, he supported provincial autonomy in educational matters. The Conservative leadership had taken up the cause of provincial rights and demanded that the new provinces be given full control over education. Forget would have preferred guarantees for separate Roman Catholic schools in the western provinces as in Ontario and Quebec. The Catholic minority of the former territories, he believed, could not expect to procure such guarantees from the generosity of the majority and in consequence, "they must take what they could get." Forget expressed the hope that in future one of the western provinces would have a Catholic majority so as to prove which of the religious groups was more respectful of minority rights. He regretted the tendency among certain politicians to excite French against English, Catholics against Protestants, and province against province. "We are all Canadians in spirit as well as in fact," he stated. He described relations among Quebec's Catholics and Protestants as harmonious and suggested that religious differences did not interfere with the understanding between the two groups, which interacted frequently in both politics and business.

Forget was described as being at once a Conservative and a Quebec nationalist whose patriotism was none the less sincere. He understood well the importance of the imperial connection. In the years leading up to World War I, with the growing threat from Germany of military aggression against France and Britain, he used his influence in an attempt to persuade Canadians, and particularly French Canadians, to assist the two countries. He supported a direct contribution to the imperial navy, a position which attracted much attention because of the widespread anti-imperialist sentiment in Quebec. Seeking to strengthen Quebec's connection with France, he published a series of articles in *La Patrie* in which he stressed the need to act against the common enemy confronted by Britain and France. He reaffirmed that by helping Britain, French Canadians would also be helping France. When war was declared, he paraded with the 65th Regiment, of which he was honorary colonel. As the war continued, Borden believed that the best way to obtain sufficient recruits for the Canadian forces was to impose compulsory military service. Forget was opposed to the measure and his retirement from politics coincided with Borden's formation of a coalition government favourable to conscription.

A member of numerous social and sporting clubs, as well as of the Montreal Military Institute, Forget occupied official positions in many of these organizations. He was also active in a number of charitable projects. One newspaper described him as "the friend of the poor and the afflicted, the aged and the infirm. For their welfare and relief, he gives unsparingly. In Charlevoix as in Montreal, he has encouraged and supported innumerable good works." Since he was said to be discreet about his charitable contributions, the full extent of his generosity is difficult to ascertain. Others noted that he had a habit of withdrawing from a charity as quickly as he became involved. Perhaps his most important philanthropic contribution went towards the construction of a new building for the Notre-Dame Hospital in Montreal. A life governor of the institution and long-time member of its board of directors, Forget went to the archbishop of Montreal to seek assistance for the project. Informed that Notre-Dame was not considered a priority for the archdiocese at that time, Forget decided to promote the project and in 1904 he gave the hospital's corporation property worth $28,000. His contributions from 1906 to 1918 would total about $250,000.

Forget's involvement in the region of Charlevoix went beyond his business interests and his political activities. In 1901 he had a sumptuous villa, Gil'Mont, constructed at Saint-Irénée (Saint-Irénée-les-Bains). Its 16 bedrooms often accommodated visiting dignitaries and its dining hall comfortably sat 25. The estate included a prosperous farm, greenhouses, and a pavilion containing an indoor swimming-pool, a billiard-room, and a bowling-alley. In his will, Forget left substantial sums for the upkeep of the estate so that his family could continue to spend its summers there. The villa was destroyed by fire in 1965.

With his family Forget worshipped in the Roman Catholic faith. He founded a school at Saint-Irénée and had the Sisters of Charity of St

Louis, a French teaching order, staff it. This convent, maintained entirely at Forget's expense, existed for almost a decade and taught several hundred pupils. The ecclesiastical authorities and the local priest were especially displeased with Forget's initiative. Because of their opposition, the school was eventually forced to close and the nuns left.

Of his first marriage Forget had one child, Marguerite. After the death of his first wife, he married Blanche McDonald, the daughter of Alexander Roderick McDonald, district superintendent of the Intercolonial Railway. They had three sons, Gilles, Maurice, and Jacques, and one daughter, Thérèse, a well-known feminist and politician. Like her husband, Lady Forget was involved in philanthropic activities. She was a director of the Montreal Day Nursery and the Notre-Dame Hospital and was president of the Institution des Sourdes-Muettes of Montreal.

Sir Rodolphe Forget's influence on the Canadian political and business scene of the period remains inestimable. He died on 19 Feb. 1919, leaving behind him, at the age of 57, an extraordinary legacy.

JACK JEDWAB

Further reading

J. A. Dickinson and B. [J.] Young, *A short history of Quebec* (4th ed., Montreal and Kingston, Ont., 2008).

Roger Graham, "The cabinet of 1911," in *Cabinet formation and bicultural relations: seven case studies*, ed. F. W. Gibson (Ottawa, 1970), 47–62.

GORDON MORTON McGREGOR,

manufacturer and civic officer; b. 18 Jan. 1873 near Windsor, Ont.,
second son of William McGregor and Jessie Lathrup Peden;
m. 2 Nov. 1898 Harriet (Hattie) Dodds in Detroit, and they had
three daughters and two sons; d. 11 March 1922 in Montreal
and was buried in Windsor.

Gordon M. McGregor was born at his family's home south of Windsor, on the Detroit River. His father had a chequered career in business and as mayor of Windsor and Liberal MP for Essex. Reared in a Scottish Presbyterian family, Gordon was educated in Windsor and Winnipeg, where the McGregors lived for a time. He worked for a men's clothing store in Detroit and then with his father in a real estate and insurance agency in Windsor. By 1897 he was becoming active in Liberal politics. Known for his singing voice and socializing, he married the daughter of a wholesale druggist in Detroit, where he also kept the books for the Photokrome Company. In 1902, when McGregor Sr became collector of customs, he was installed with no experience as manager of the wagon works in Walkerville (Windsor) that his father and banker John Curry had acquired.

There McGregor witnessed four converging trends: the proliferation of American branch plants to bypass Canadian tariffs; the growth of machine trades related to the bicycle craze; the birth of an automotive industry in Michigan; and the decline of the wagon works following William McGregor's death in 1903. Unable as president to sustain production, Gordon watched its debt climb and work stop in July 1904. As early as January apparently, under pressure from Curry to reduce obligations, he had been thinking of reusing the factory as a branch of an automotive firm. He gambled on Henry Ford of Detroit, who faced a patent lawsuit but had achieved startling success with gasoline-powered runabouts. Initially uninterested, Ford, who likely came to admire McGregor's underlying hardness, soon saw his overture as an opportunity to expand and exploit Canada's access to imperial markets. He had already tested the waters. In 1903 Canada Cycle and Motor in Toronto began selling his first model and in the spring of 1904 he made a promotional trip into Ontario. Though McGregor was confident that a branch would enjoy support from the federal Liberal government, which raised the tariff on automobiles, his plan was risky: the market was unformed and finding capital was a huge challenge. Still, bolstered with promises of extra stock he had shrewdly demanded as compensation, McGregor raised $125,000. On 10 August, an agreement was concluded; in a key exchange, Ford would share his patents and plans. At the inaugural meeting of the Ford Motor Company of Canada Limited on the 29th, McGregor was made managing secretary.

By year's end 25 Model Cs had been assembled in Walkerville from chassis made in Michigan and advertising was appearing in Canadian sources. At the Madison Square Garden car show in New York in January 1905, McGregor witnessed the power of bold displays; he would have recognized too the modesty of his own operation. He exhibited at CCM's little show in February, he held a second job, and finding sales agents and producers for parts in Ontario was a slow process. At the same time, the Windsor *Evening Record* started to champion both the fledgling industry and McGregor.

In 1906 he dutifully backed Ford's venture into the luxury car field, but it was with the overlapping production of the Model N that the organization returned to its originator's quest for a "light, low-priced car." There were sales from Vancouver to Fredericton. Sent to Walkerville that year to manage production, George Dickert would remember McGregor as a pleasant, persuasive man bent on "peddling." The atmosphere at Walkerville struck visitors as casual, but groundwork was being laid. Production climbed to 327 vehicles in 1907. That year, at the Toronto Industrial Exhibition (later the Canadian National Exhibition), McGregor showed for the first time apart from CCM, which Thomas Alexander Russell had taken over to make a purely Canadian automobile. McGregor understood that his firm had a dual identity: it was promoted as Canadian within the dominion, while in the United States and some British territories, where American consuls were big boosters, the Detroit affiliation was highlighted. When he began exporting in 1906, to Australia, New Zealand, and Natal (South Africa), he utilized Ford Detroit's shippers.

By 1907–8 his gamble was succeeding. His salary was increased, he bought in stock from nervous investors, payments to the old wagon company were met, and he ventured further into public life. With others he tried in 1906 to revive Windsor's defunct board of trade; in 1908 he chaired the board formed to build First Presbyterian Church in Walkerville. Most satisfying was the maturation of the automobile industry, including the emergence of a trade press and show entrepreneurs, notably Robert Miller Jaffray. McGregor, who saw Canada's regions taking to the automobile in different ways, was most troubled by the trend among provinces and municipalities to regulate its use. Like his testers, with their upsetting noise and fumes, he liked to drive fast. In 1908 he joined other automakers and officials of the newly formed Ontario Motor League – possibly the earliest such lobby in Canada – to ask a committee of the legislature to curtail regulatory amendments. Their worries were unfounded: controls were routinely violated as the public came to terms with the "devil wagon." Moreover, regulation tended to lead to calls for better roads, a movement supported by McGregor. At the end of September he reported annual profits of more than $18,500.

Announced by Ford Canada that fall, the utterly utilitarian Model T would make McGregor, and revolutionize transportation in Canada by breaking down time and distance. Specifications began arriving in February 1909 and chassis in March; Canadian-made bodies and other components were used from the start. Between August and January 1910, in concert with Ford Detroit's development of its own foreign markets, McGregor went to Australia, New Zealand, India, and Ceylon (Sri Lanka) to consolidate his networks. At home the Border Cities (Windsor, Walkerville, Sandwich, and Ojibway) began blossoming as Canada's centre of automotive and parts manufacture. In 1910 and 1911–12 McGregor undertook expansions in cutting-edge reinforced concrete; the large machine tools essential to mass production followed; the first "power conveyor" appeared about 1911. For the rest of his career he would be engaged in rounds of structural and mechanical change. During the surge in production from 1,280 in 1910 to 6,388 in 1912, his company was reincorporated in 1911 under a federal charter.

A photograph of a bespectacled McGregor taken about this time in Detroit exudes affluence. In 1910 he bought a cottage lot near Kingsville, a summer retreat on Lake Erie. The next year, he and some neighbours leaned on the town to annex their area and give it water and fire protection. Socially ambitious, he belonged to the Oak Ridge Golf Club, which was incorporated as the Essex Golf and Country Club in 1910. The reciprocity debate and election of 1911 tested his politics. Conscious of the tariff's role in fostering industry, the Walkerville Board of Trade opposed reciprocity; so too did such Liberal automakers as Russell and Robert McLaughlin of Oshawa. McGregor, however, thought it the "best proposition" Canada ever faced, a partisan position he could afford to adopt: the tariff on cars would be reduced minimally and his markets would not be threatened. When Prime Minister Sir Wilfrid Laurier visited in September, McGregor proudly chauffeured him in a parade and went on stage for the ensuing speeches. Even with the Liberals' defeat, he came to master back-room politicking (with a reach that extended to the House of Commons) and he gained status. He purchased a stately house in Windsor in 1912, some commercial blocks, and a property for a showcase Ford dealership.

The real challenge facing McGregor's company was the need for a national distribution network to absorb the ever-increasing numbers of new Ford automobiles (11,584 in 1912–13). He assigned the task to Augustin Neil Lawrence, the bright young sales manager who, in consultation with McGregor and assistant manager Wallace Ronald Campbell, devised a "formula for organized selling." Representatives drove through every rural and urban section of the country, methodically charting their economic and physical condition and then calculating targets for sales and dealer recruitment. As part of this marketing tour de force, advertising was revamped (some of it quite unlike Ford Detroit's) and in 1913 the assertive *Ford Sales Bulletin* (for dealers) and the Canadian *Ford Times* were launched.

Ever-faster assembly line production, which was at the core of Ford Canada's drive to meet its targets and backlogs of orders, led to high turnover and new demands in labour relations. In a traditional manner, McGregor supported employee clubs and sports teams. Faced with a housing shortage, he applied to town council in 1912 for permission to house his workers in tents. A different test of his corporate sympathies came in April 1913 when, despite his opposition, Arsas Drouillard successfully applied for a licence to open a tavern near Ford's gates. Unwilling to bend, McGregor had the licence vetoed by provincial secretary William John Hanna, who was also a director of Imperial Oil, which supplied Ford Canada. He then proceeded confidently in May into litigation over the stock promised him in 1904, a case that would go to the Judicial Committee of the Privy Council in England. The *Evening Record*'s report of his initial testimony stressed his early struggle and manly "perseverance" – the start of fabricated legend.

McGregor was beginning to become known on the national scene. In September 1913 he attended the annual meeting of the Canadian Manufacturers' Association in Halifax. Foundry and machine journals noted his achievements, but until after the war he received little personal attention in the daily press. The American *Ford Times* gave coverage to his markets – they held an exotic appeal – but in a "Ford family" way it grouped his operation with the American organization. He was highlighted in the *Times*' poems and cartoons, wonderfully so, but never in the Canadian *Ford Times*, where deference to Henry Ford and his homespun philosophies was de rigueur. Locally he continued to make a name for himself. He backed the short-lived Ontario Border Development Bureau in 1913 and led the successful drive to bring Ontario Hydro to Walkerville.

In a manner that would become standard, McGregor carefully orchestrated the shareholders' meeting of October 1913. The disappointing decision to withhold a dividend, he explained with mock gravity, was due to the company's "financial situation." The *Evening Record* was led to suggest that, as in 1904, he was hard-pressed. In fact, he needed to conserve funds to institute the shorter nine-hour day and pay raises and bonuses already implemented at Ford Detroit to curb turnover and early signs of labour militancy. Nonetheless, business boomed and, following the "American policy," final assembly and costs were shifted to the branches, relieving pressure on the main plant at Ford City, which had been carved out of Walkerville. Dealers were forced to take early deliveries. Similar pressure was exerted overseas; in the instance of British Honduras (Belize), Lawrence lambasted the federal Department of Trade and Commerce in 1914 (even after the outbreak of war) for failing to provide adequate information on roads and market potential. Against this backdrop of growth – 38 per cent of the cars registered in Canada in 1914 were Fords – McGregor and his wife enjoyed social and golfing engagements, corporate gatherings, and vacations at American resorts; the loss of a young son in January 1914 was stoically endured.

In the opening months of World War I, he was positioned to become the most important cog in the Border Cities' civilian war effort. Adhering to America's neutrality (until 1917) and Henry Ford's personal anti-war stance, Ford Detroit initially made no war materials. McGregor followed suit. Instead, he built the "Made in Canada" theme, which had been in play in industry for years, into a brilliant marketing tool that linked greater production, the T's growing Canadian content, and patriotic conviction. Between October 1914 and March 1915 his plant was "practically at a shut down" but only because another addition was being built. The ethos of "efficiency" in production and sales had moral as well as patriotic implications. In April, after talks with Ford and Ford's secretary-manager, James Joseph Couzens (a native of Chatham, Ont.), McGregor introduced a $4/eight-hour day. This "profit-sharing" plan came laden not with formulations for future profits but with qualifying conditions for upright lifestyles supervised by new "sociological" and centralized employment departments. A range of authorities, especially the National Civic Federation in New York, categorized the plan as a blatant wage hike.

In June 1915 the Border Cities were rocked by a detonation of planted explosives at a garment shop that was making uniforms. Fearful of similar sabotage, McGregor said nothing of the Pinkerton detectives he privately hired between July and January to investigate "suspected depredations" at his factory. Just as problematic was Henry Ford's cavalier treatment of his Canadian company. His unfulfilled promise to build a tractor plant locally left McGregor vulnerable to poaching of the Ford name for tractors and forced him to solicit legal opinion on whether his 1904 agreement allowed him to manufacture them – it did not. It was over the war, however, that Ford emerged as a publicist's nightmare. His half-baked pronouncements struck raw nerves in Ontario. Embarrassed and threatened with boycotts by municipal buyers, McGregor, who would never adapt easily to negative publicity, replied that his 78-per-cent-Canadian-owned company was "absolutely with the allies." He persuaded Ford to make conciliatory noises and donate to the Red Cross, though Ford was not one to be coerced. "All the boycotts that Canadian politicians are threatening will have nothing to do with the public demand for Ford cars," he told the Toronto *Globe*. Fortunately for McGregor, reaction to Ford's "peace ship" and dream of a peace conference did not focus on Ford Canada. Moreover, dominated by Ford personnel, the Ford City branch of the Canadian Patriotic Fund that McGregor had helped organize was one of several successes for him. He had an alderman lobby Toronto's board of control, he generously funded the enlargement of the Essex golf club, a stunning 100-per-cent dividend was declared, and the JCPC confirmed his claim to the Ford shares, now worth some $200,000. In December he felt able to shake off his parent company's disinclination for philanthropy and ask Couzens, who had parted ways with Ford in an ugly separation in October, to help the Essex Health Association, which needed money for its sanatorium. Couzens turned him down, bluntly.

In February 1916 McGregor went to Ottawa to talk to officials about the federal budget, specifically the proposed tax on excess business profits. Initially supportive (compliance looked good), he came to dislike this tax intensely and greedily. More troublesome, as his firm struggled to move 18,771 autos in 1915 and 32,646 in 1916, was the wartime congestion on Canada's railways. Amazingly, McGregor did not back off. Production was boosted; in 1917 Ford was Canada's only exporter of cars. Company-sponsored newsreels and travelogues (many with Model Ts in imperial settings) took Ford into the culture of popular film across Canada and heralded Windsor as its automotive hub. An unusual puff in the *Canadian Motorist* (Toronto) in 1916 focused on "McGregor of Ford." In 1917 his office would take over all newspaper advertising from the dealers.

McGregor's industrial activities precluded military involvement, but he fully supported the martial efforts of his brother Walter Leishman, who in 1916 became lieutenant-colonel of the 241st Infantry Battalion (the Canadian Scottish Borderers), a unit the family wanted to attire in McGregor tartan. He was also restrained by increasing civic involvement. In 1916 he became the elected member for Ford City in the new Essex Border Utilities Commission, which was authorized by provincial statute to create a regional water and sewage system. The following year he became its chair. Almost immediately, common cause fell victim to opposing interests among the existing municipal commissions and councillors resentful of regional oversight, cost apportionments, and McGregor's corporate manner. Support came from the like-minded Border Chamber of Commerce, formed in January from the Windsor Board of Trade. McGregor was made a director in March and named to the labour committee.

These civic initiatives and squabbles faded in importance before gloomy war news and the unrestrained spread locally of manufacturers, including such new branches as Champion Spark Plug. Reports of revolutionary Russia sowed fears of Bolshevism and intensified antagonisms toward European workers, concerns shared by Ford Canada. In the fall of 1917 another phase of national fund-raising for the war, the Victory Loans, took McGregor to a new level of engagement. He was the natural choice to head the campaign in Essex: he had the connections, the organizational skills, and corporate resources. Ford accountants handled the finances, McGregor's film crews were everywhere, and employees were expected to subscribe. The drive included mass meetings, fireworks, John Philip Sousa's Marine Band from the United States, vaudevillian entertainments, and constantly elevated targets. McGregor raised $4,915,000, a figure exceeded only by the amounts raised in Toronto, Hamilton, Ottawa, and London.

The much-lauded campaign added to his civic weight. Within the EBUC, in early 1918 he moved debate forward slowly, in part by underlining the pollution found by the International Joint Commission. His private assets were bolstered by his purchase and reorganization, with others, of National Spring and Wire, which made fencing and seats for Fords. In April, on the question of adopting the federally initiated daylight saving, many factories, labour groups, and municipal councils followed Ford Canada's resistance, but when the tone-setting McGregor inexplicably reversed its position, all fell into line. In July the governor general, Victor Christian William Cavendish, 9th Duke of Devonshire, marvelled at his plant, as all visitors did.

Watching for spillover into Canada, McGregor monitored the war's impact on the American automotive industry. In 1917 the powerful National Automobile Chamber of Commerce had resisted attempts to reduce the production of passenger cars and supplies of steel. Worried that the Canadian government would impose restrictions, in January 1918 McGregor brought together, for "co-operative action," 34 automotive, parts, and tire producers to form the Automotive Industries of Canada, of which he became first president. It weakly emulated the NACC model; some effort went into cancelling automobile shows (except for the CNE) as a gesture of restraint. McGregor could be more effective on his own. In February he successfully lobbied the new War Trade Board in Ottawa to forgo a tax on all motor cars and adopt instead, in June, a tax on imports alone and the stoppage of luxury imports. On steel, it was the Canadian Ford, Chalmers, and Studebaker firms in the Border Cities and branches of other heavy industries that persuaded the American War Industries Board to lift its embargo on exports. Supplies of steel nevertheless remained restricted and production at Ford Canada dropped, though its revenues were boosted by the start of manufacture of trucks, the sale of parts and Fordson tractors, and, in step with Ford Detroit in February, a price increase on Model Ts, which sparked consumer angst.

What McGregor could not control fully was the fundamental shifts among the autoworkers. The chamber of commerce, where he became vice-president and other Ford officers held sway, could address such recurring concerns as the cross-border taxation of commuting workers and gain popularity by jabbing immigrants. In the auto plants, declining work because of material shortages bred trouble; at the same time, governments in both countries relaxed limits on union activity. In the Border Cities before the era of lasting auto unions, it was the International Association of Machinists that had the strongest presence. On 28 June 1918 a delegation filed into McGregor's office and, emboldened by a membership drive, strikes in Toronto and Detroit, and wage increases in Detroit, tabled a petition for a $5/eight-hour day. Dissatisfaction was voiced too, backed by employees returning from the war, over Ford's use of Europeans, though few would do the work they did in the barely tolerable heat-treating shops. When McGregor locked out his workers on 6 July, both sides rushed to secure the support of federal labour minister Thomas Wilson Crothers. The IAM claimed, correctly, that the lockout was illegal and that McGregor, contrary to his professions and even as he rejected war production for Canada, had been turning out parts for the tanks and warships being made by Ford Detroit. Ottawa, however, refused to recognize the disruption as anything more than a lay-off. On 12 August – most suspected McGregor had been holding the Detroit-set wage increase in reserve – he calculatingly conceded.

McGregor's public profile could not have been greater – in his golf club (where he was president in 1917–18), in the debate on water and sewers, as chair for the organization of a manufacturers' section in the chamber of commerce, and in September 1918 in Toronto at the annual meeting of the AIC. Scant attention was paid to the *Canadian Motorist's* complaints about his attempts to shut down shows for the duration of the war, which was winding down in any case, or to criticism in the press of Ford's reversal on pricing. After the lockout, McGregor moved to restore Ford's place in the war effort. Of the Ford-made films circulated by the Department of Trade and Commerce, one, dedicated to the Canada Food Board, merged footage on the greater production movement, the Border Manufacturers' Farmers Association, Fordson tractors, and good roads.

In the Victory Loan drive of October–November, McGregor once again devised a campaign brimming with theatricality. Reports of him announcing the armistice at campaign headquarters, and then jumping on a chair to lead the crowd in singing "Praise God from whom all blessings flow," present a stirring image. An outbreak of influenza produced only a temporary obstacle to the drive, and it would be some time before evidence of payment defaults and of embezzlement by a Ford accountant would surface. During the post-war years, McGregor had more serious problems. Both the EBUC and the chamber of commerce faced continued opposition. In January 1919 Windsor gained four labour councillors, including Archibald Hooper, a railway machinist and scrappy IAM mouthpiece who attacked the chamber over promotions that ensured neither housing nor jobs. McGregor and the EBUC attracted his particular ire. Bickering intensified as opposing technical plans were exchanged, though voter turnouts on related by-laws suggest low public concern. The commission, however, had the backing of the Ontario Railway and Municipal Board, and in July the province gave the EBUC additional power as a regional board of health.

As Ford Canada headed into an industry-wide post-war slump, McGregor, a master of corporate spin, remained optimistic. A wage increase in May and his initiation of an employees' welfare and housing fund in September may have forestalled IAM action. He had been re-elected president of the AIC, where he got on well with vice-president Robert Samuel McLaughlin of General Motors of Canada, which gained ground on Ford through its heavy manufacturing plant in Walkerville. In October, Ford Canada responded by taking over Dominion Forge and Stamping, an important supplier. The previous month McGregor had gone to Ottawa as an employers' delegate to the National Industrial Conference, but he did not deem it important. Praise for Henry Ford, not criticism, came from labour. McGregor ran off statements about profit-sharing, said industry had done enough to improve living conditions, and complained about his troubles with labour in Australia.

The call for him to head the final Victory campaign in October–November 1919 was predictable, but he begged off. Though he claimed to be busy with private business, which now included a hotel company, he knew that patriotic enthusiasms had been superseded by cost-of-living concerns and a collapse of charitable giving – he had tried unsuccessfully to mount a drive to fund a hospital for the Salvation Army. Always thrilled at the prospect of hosting aristocracy, however, he took on the social arrangements for the visit of the Prince of Wales in October, a task that included the contentious paring of guest lists. Back-to-back elections, provincial in October and municipal in January 1920, involved him in a political role, aggressively prominent but never a candidate save for the EBUC. Supported by his coterie, Windsor's Liberal candidate (and McGregor's former pastor) survived the sweep of the United Farmers of Ontario. McGregor declined to run for mayor of Windsor but readily agreed to serve as president of the new Municipal Electors' Association, which briefly crystallized the progressive urge of businessmen to reform municipal politics based on experiments in the United States. Windsor's labour councillors resented this heady, undemocratic challenge, which seemed like Ford on the hustings. McGregor took the lead in nominating aldermanic candidates; for the water boards he wanted sympathetic nominees. Sewage politics could be gritty. At a meeting he chaired on 30 December in a Jewish school, candidate Charles Robert Tuson (a former mayor and an adversary on the sewage issue) was sideswiped by the accusation that he had registered restrictions prohibiting the sale of properties to Jews. In 1920 McGregor was reappointed chair of the EBUC. In March he threw a "bombshell" into its proceedings when he took its secretary away to become advertising manager of Ford Canada. He expended more charitable effort on his wife's campaign to rebuild the sanatorium of the Essex Health Association.

That fall, McGregor's gang appeared in strength at the CNE along with Henry Ford and his secretary, Ernest Gustav Liebold. Ford Canada did not suffer as acutely as its parent in the slump of the early 1920s, but

McGregor still had to be careful, if not manipulative. In 1919 and again the next year he had delayed expansion; publicly he blamed the burden of federal taxes. At the same time he took accounting steps to shield his firm's true cash balances from the prying eyes of government and labour; he had his traffic manager challenge railway rates; and at a later point he probably took part in an arrangement between Canadian and American car makers to block the export of Canadian-made automobiles except for Fords. In 1920 he endured a number of personal difficulties. His mother and a sister died, and in November, after attending a directors' meeting of the Merchants' Bank of Canada in Montreal, he underwent surgery, reportedly for appendicitis.

While McGregor was recuperating, the hearings of the federal commission on tariffs re-opened debate on Ford Canada's prices. With his imprimatur, on 30 November assistant manager W. R. Campbell stepped up to refute claims that Ford was taking advantage of protection to maintain prices that exceeded the cost of Fords in the United States. Smaller scales of manufacture dictated different costs, he contended, but this argument was offset by testimony from other automobile executives and representatives from farmers' groups. Politically the Ford position changed no minds, and in perceptions of Ford there may have been other biases at work. Beyond the commission the Border Cities had a hard time explaining their affinity with Detroit: "It would almost seem that we are here in a little kingdom of our own and to some extent apart and away from the outer world," industrial commissioner F. Maclure Sclanders speculated in *Canadian Machinery and Manufacturing News* (Toronto).

A weakened McGregor returned to Windsor in January 1921, only to witness a flare-up of utility politics and more attacks on the chamber of commerce and his own "dictatorial" interventions. His response is obscure, but Archibald Hooper, who headed Windsor's campaign to withdraw from the EBUC, mysteriously lost his railway job and Queen's Park rejected Windsor's application. After offering some conciliation, McGregor, on his doctors' advice, resigned from the EBUC in March. For almost five years he had pushed an agenda, unique in Ontario, on the important if lacklustre issues of regional planning. Business concerns were just as taxing. When he was not occupied with petty requests from Henry Ford – his information on the banking of Ford's personal funds in Canada also shed light on Ford Canada's own strategic use of banks

– there were corporate problems to face. He authorized advertising in response to competition from GM and company resistance to actions by dealers over excise tax refunds and over price cuts on tires as a result of Ford's pressure on suppliers. In April he began losing key personnel in reaction to the economy, Henry Ford's purges, and a possible shift in the balance of control between McGregor and Campbell, whom Ford had tried to lure to Detroit.

McGregor spent time that spring at a West Virginian resort and then at his cottage. A photograph shows him with a cane, overweight but nattily attired as always. Back at home, he worked on committees for a public golf course and the health association's sanatorium. That fall he did more jobs for Henry Ford, catering to his interests in water-power in Ontario and railways, and, with threats of court action, protecting Ford's Canadian dividends and salary from local assessment. In addition, he went along with the anti-Semitism espoused by Ford's *Dearborn Independent*, had his staff distribute copies of extracts published as *The international Jew: the world's foremost problem* (1920–21), and reported to Liebold on Jewish activity in Windsor. He was not alone in such condonation: the Woman's Christian Temperance Union, for one, reprinted anti-Jewish material from the *Independent* in its newspaper.

In late 1921 McGregor's attention was again sidetracked by the price issue. Despite his company's slashing of prices in September and a revival in demand, the question was taken up by William Edgar Raney, Ontario's pugnacious attorney general. In the campaign leading up to the federal election of December, Raney threw his weight behind the Progressives and their agrarian, anti-protection platform. In a speech on 18 November he lashed out at the tariff on automobiles, higher prices, and the presumed complicity of Ford Canada. The address spread rapidly among Canadian newspapers. Unable to resist, and in a strong performance for an ailing man, McGregor thrust himself into the campaigns in Essex North and South. Audiences were amused by his characteristic gibes and numbed by his convoluted economics. The Liberals won overwhelming majorities.

McGregor could still handle an appreciable workload, including complex planning for a major plant expansion. In January 1922 Ford Canada announced its return to full-time production and the launch of its "greatest sales campaign ever," for its enclosed coupes and sedans –

the company never treated the T as an unchanging model. After meetings in Montreal on a takeover of the Merchants' Bank, McGregor fielded more menial requests from Ford and Liebold. The *Border Cities Star*, as the *Evening Record* had become, had long granted McGregor a revered place in "Motoropolis," though this reputation could be at odds with the opinions of consumers, agrarian radicals, labour journals, and lesser auto executives with independent views. In January 1922, for example, the wife of a Walkerville plumber told Henry Ford in a blistering letter that she desperately wanted a used Ford, but resented their exorbitant price and the profiteering of such "millionars" as McGregor. On 4 March McGregor visited his oak-lined office for the last time. Feeling unwell, he was X-rayed and sent to Montreal's Royal Victoria Hospital, where he died.

The *Star* announced his passing in headlines of a size rarely seen, even during the war. The cause of death was reported as intestinal trouble arising from an old injury suffered in a railway accident; the family believed it was cancer; pathological study points to a rare blood-vessel disorder. McGregor's mammoth funeral was attended by the automotive elite; his canonization in the *Star* reached full definition. The bulk of his estate, which was valued at more than $1,235,500, went to his widow, whose social withdrawal ended when she returned to renovating St Andrew's Church in Windsor, a project she and Gordon had planned. Not surprisingly, Ford Canada was identified as his "greatest work." Campbell assumed direction there to complete the expansion planned to meet the hurtful "competition" of the parent company. Between April and June 1922 the *Star* published a series on the regional and national impact of Ford Canada, a summary, the timing suggests, of McGregor's legacy. In the midst of this series, a blustery portrayal elevated him to an iconic level. In the search for a speedy form of road transportation to open up the country, "Henry Ford solved the problem for the world. The late Gordon McGregor solved it for Canada." Even allowing for his company's minimal technological contribution and the vital work of his department heads, there is some merit in this claim when one equates him with his cars.

DAVID ROBERTS

Further reading

David Roberts, *In the shadow of Detroit: Gordon M. McGregor, Ford of Canada, and Motoropolis* (Detroit, 2006).

Canada Science and Technology Museum, *Transformation Series* (18v. to date, Ottawa, 1992–   ), 15 (Richard White, *Making cars in Canada: a brief history of the Canadian automobile industry, 1900–1980*, 2007).

Section 7

The West Booms

FANNY BENDIXEN,

saloon-keeper; b. *c.* 1820 in France; d. 2 May 1899 in Barkerville, B.C.

Almost nothing is known of Fanny Bendixen's early life. Of French origin, she was apparently drawn to the gold-rush in California, where she married Louis A. Bendixen. Like many Californians, the couple were attracted by the Fraser River gold-rush in British Columbia, and in October of 1862 they opened the St George Hotel on View Street in Victoria, Vancouver Island. Both this venture and the marriage seem to have faltered, however, and Mme Bendixen travelled on her own to the booming gold-mining town of Barkerville in the summer of 1865. She did return to Victoria to winter at the St George, for the *Daily British Colonist* of 4 Dec. 1865 mentions that both she and her husband were involved in a violent dispute there with another French woman.

In 1866 Mme Bendixen took up permanent residence in the Cariboo and proudly announced the opening of the Parlour, her first saloon in Barkerville. Yet it was short-lived, perhaps because of the bankruptcy proceedings initiated against her husband in Victoria that fall. Louis Bendixen appears to have spent the next few years in Barkerville, but his wife had already established herself as an independent businesswoman. In June 1867 Mme Bendixen opened a second saloon, the Bella Union, which was advertised as being "fitted up in the most elegant style" and serving only the "best brands of liquors and cigars." Unfortunately, it was completely destroyed in the fire that swept through Barkerville in September 1868, and Mme Bendixen sustained losses estimated at $5,000.

She appears to have had difficulty re-establishing herself in Barkerville after the fire, although she went into partnership with James Burdick in 1869 and is listed as the proprietor of the St George Saloon in Barkerville in 1871. By this time, however, she was already moving her operations to Lightning Creek, where gold had recently been found. Her saloon at Van Winkle was declared to have "one of the finest reading rooms and picture galleries on the creek," and Mme Bendixen was a popular hostess even though she was not fluent in English. In 1874 she sold this saloon and opened another called the Exchange in the town of Stanley. By the late 1870s the heyday of the Cariboo gold-rush had passed, and Mme Bendixen returned to Barkerville, the one viable town left in the region. There she continued to run a saloon well into the 1890s and was the only woman to be regularly listed in the business directory for that community. On his last visit to the Cariboo in 1889, judge Sir Matthew Baillie Begbie found Mme Bendixen "in great form; indeed enormous, … though she was always of goodly diameter."

Mme Bendixen had been widowed by 1881. Before her death in 1899 she bequeathed her business interests, namely her saloon and two lots in Barkerville, to Hugh Cochrane, the town's notary public, who had married her grandniece Leonie Fanny. A codicil which Cochrane persuaded Mme Bendixen to attach to the will was, however, disputed after her death. In her original will she had specifically left her ear-rings to Mrs Andrew Kelly, the wife of a well-known hotel-keeper in Barkerville, but a few months before her death, when almost comatose, the dying woman had been assisted in signing the codicil which left them to her grandniece. Mrs Kelly prevented the will from being probated until a court decided that the codicil violated Mme Bendixen's true intent and that she had not been competent to sign it. Mrs Kelly thus inherited the prized ear-rings, a symbol of her friend Fanny Bendixen's success as a saloon-keeper during the gold-rush era in British Columbia.

SYLVIA VAN KIRK

Further reading

Craig Heron, *Booze: a distilled history* (Toronto, 2003).

Angel Kwolek-Folland, *Incorporating women: a history of women and business in the United States* (New York, 1998).

T. W. Paterson, "British Columbia characters," *Canada West Magazine* (Langley, B.C.), 7 (1977), no. 1: 37.

ROBERT DUNSMUIR,

coal-miner, entrepreneur, and politician; b. 31 Aug. 1825 near Kilmarnock (Strathclyde), Scotland, the son of James Dunsmuir; m. in 1847 Joanna (Joan) Olive White, and they had ten children; d. 12 April 1889 at Victoria, B.C.

Robert Dunsmuir was the son and grandson of Ayrshire coal-masters. He received his early education at the Kilmarnock Academy and at about age 16 entered the mines as an apprentice to his uncle and guardian, Boyd Gilmour. By 1850 Gilmour was overman at the Hudson's Bay Company coal-mine near Fort Rupert (near present-day Port Hardy) on northern Vancouver Island. On Gilmour's urging, Dunsmuir indentured himself to the company, arriving at Fort Rupert with his wife and three children in September 1851.

Dunsmuir entered a difficult situation, for despite dedicated efforts by men such as Gilmour and John Muir the mines were failing. The coal was limited in extent and quality, poor management by the HBC officers in charge had caused much unrest among the miners, machinery and skilled labour were in short supply, and hostile natives were a continual threat. During 1851–53 the HBC transferred its mining apparatus to the newly discovered coalfields at Nanaimo. The Dunsmuirs joined in the move to Nanaimo, though several miners, including Gilmour, soon returned to Scotland.

In 1855 Dunsmuir refused to join a strike of dissident miners, earning for his apparent loyalty to the HBC a free-miner's licence to work an abandoned HBC shaft. In 1862, when the HBC sold its coal mining operation to the Vancouver Coal Mining and Land Company, he contracted to work as a mines' supervisor for the new firm. Two years later, his record of independence, initiative, skill, and productivity brought him to the attention of Horace Douglas Lascelles and three other naval officers at Esquimalt who persuaded Dunsmuir to become resident manager of their newly formed Harewood Coal Mining Company. The company encountered difficulty in starting production, chiefly because of lack of capital, and was absorbed by the VCMLC; Dunsmuir, recognized as the most knowledgeable miner on the island, was hired once again by this company as mines' supervisor.

After joining the VCMLC Dunsmuir conducted clandestine explorations for coal on surrounding lands. He continued his secret surveys until 1869 when he discovered the Wellington seam, five miles northwest of Nanaimo harbour, the thickest and most extensive of the coal measures found until then in the Nanaimo basin. After laying claim, he was able to arrange short-term financing from San Francisco but was soon forced to seek more capital. He obtained £32,000 to develop the colliery from another group of naval officers, which included Lieutenant Wadham Neston Diggle. In addition to the claim Dunsmuir's contributions to the enterprise would be his expertise and his willingness to build and operate the colliery. He insisted upon and received half the shares plus full control over all operations. In 1873 the mine was incorporated under the name Dunsmuir, Diggle Limited, a ten-man partnership that included the naval officers, Dunsmuir, and his sons James and Alexander.

Dunsmuir's first years as a colliery owner were devoted to establishing a basic mining operation – a high risk venture given the economic recession of the time. He had to take into account the VCMLC's large plant, and to create the vital elements of several shafts for mining, a skilled work-force, and an efficient three-mile transport link from pit-head to wharves, which after 1870 meant a steam railway. Newspapers reported each step in the colliery's advance, and editorials were soon stressing the significance of Dunsmuir's efforts to the region's economy. By the end of 1874 the British Columbia minister of mines, John Ash, reported that "The Departure Bay [Dunsmuir] Mines are now in full operation," the returns from which "illustrate the value of the seams." That year Dunsmuir's coal output totalled 29,818 tons, of which only 2,384 tons were unsold. This production figure was more than half the VCMLC's output, and in the following year Dunsmuir's operation came within 10,000 tons of its chief competitor. By 1878 Dunsmuir had overtaken the other colliery's production, raising 88,361 tons of coal compared to 82,135.

Although the company had had sufficient financial backing from its partners to begin mining, it was mainly Dunsmuir who had taken the risks, and who had provided the management necessary to create, maintain, and expand the operation from a mere claim to British Columbia's foremost colliery. Until 1878 it appears that Dunsmuir ploughed most of the profits back into the firm; no additional shares were issued and there is no evidence indicating other sources of financing were necessary. His business success is even more impressive when it is realized that he kept pace with technical developments. Dunsmuir described his works in 1879 as having "4¾ miles of railway; 4 locomotives; over 400 waggons; 4 [hauling] engines and 2 steam pumps; 3 wharves for loading vessels, with bunkers, etc." In 1879 Dunsmuir, Diggle Limited purchased another colliery in the same seam, the South Wellington, to the south of Nanaimo. Together, the two operations provided underground access through one pit (160' deep) and two main shafts (one reaching 310'). The purchase gave the firm a further "4½ miles of railway; 1 locomotive; over 50 waggons; 1 steam pump; 2 large winding engines; 1 small engine"; the combined labour force was now 418.

The purchase of the South Wellington proved both a logical and a profitable move, as the output, workforce, and plant value of Dunsmuir, Diggle, all rose sharply. In 1881 Dunsmuir claimed that his coal operations were worth $245,000. Equally significant, he was by then employing 547 men (more than half of whom were Chinese) and his annual output had reached 181,048 tons of coal, fully 84.4 per cent of which was exported. Further expansion occurred in 1882 when Dunsmuir sank two additional main shafts; eventually a total of five mines were in production on the Wellington deposit. What probably gave Dunsmuir his greatest satisfaction, however, was his step-by-step purchase of the holdings of the non-family partners. Before the 1870s had ended, he had bought all but Diggle's interests. Then on 14 Sept. 1883 Victoria's *Daily British Colonist* reported that Diggle had sold his holdings to Dunsmuir for $600,000, and that henceforth the firm would conduct business "under the name and style of R. Dunsmuir & Sons."

Dunsmuir was a shrewd and opportunistic coal proprietor. Compared with other coal entrepreneurs of the 1870s and 1880s, he was not particularly lucky or especially ruthless, but he made the most of the important advantages he had over his competitors. He had been a thoroughly knowledgeable coal-miner and a highly experienced mines' supervisor before starting his own colliery, and by being the sole claimant of the island's richest coal seam when he began his first venture as a coal-mine proprietor, Dunsmuir's potential as a producer was the greatest on the island. Furthermore, although he was a latecomer to the province's coal trade, his entry occurred at a time when speculative coal enterprises were most profitable. What distinguished him above all from other promoters, the majority of whom failed to secure sufficient start-up capital, was his astute move in turning for support to the naval officers who had both an awareness of the value of the coalfields in the region and the financial means to make substantial investments. Also important was Dunsmuir's proximity to the colliery: as his usual residence was Nanaimo, nothing to do with the operation escaped his attention and day-to-day management decisions were made with ease. Finally, he was able to recruit and train as his chief subordinates his two sons, who were also in the original partnership, and a son-in-law, John Bryden; not only did he fix the colliery's management in the family's grip, he also ensured that as the company prospered the financial position of the family was correspondingly strengthened. Thus it was that most of Dunsmuir, Diggle's power and wealth came to be concentrated in the Dunsmuir family's hands. He was dedicated to the new coal industry and determined to dominate if not monopolize it.

Within ten years of starting operations Dunsmuir had generated sufficient capital from sales to build a colliery operation that surpassed in size and output the combined value of all other British Columbia coal mines, to purchase extensive holdings of coal-bearing lands in the Comox district, and to construct and operate a fleet of colliers; he also invested heavily in real estate on Vancouver Island and in an iron foundry, a theatre in Victoria, agricultural lands, and a mainland diking scheme. Most of Dunsmuir's wealth was in the form of equity capital, but it none the less gave him all the security he needed to continue making acquisitions whenever and wherever he chose. This was, after all, a time in Canadian history when neither corporate nor income taxes existed, and what coal royalties there were had little impact on profits. Indeed, it was a period in which governments appeared more eager to give money to men like Dunsmuir than to take it from them. A case in point is his involvement in the building of a railway on Vancouver Island.

A rail link between Nanaimo and Victoria had been planned as early as 1873, but no serious effort to start construction was made until December 1883 when the province transferred to the federal government sufficient crown lands for the project. To safeguard control of the island's economic future, and prevent the possibility of the Northern

Pacific Railroad gaining the contract, many businessmen and politicians urged Dunsmuir to build the line. Dunsmuir was reluctant to accept the task, thinking it of little benefit to his colliery operations. He submitted a proposal to the Canadian government, however, and despite the severity of his terms he emerged as the sole acceptable alternative to foreign builders. After much shrewd bargaining in Ottawa Dunsmuir agreed to construct the railway in return for a subsidy of $750,000 in cash and a parcel of land comprising some two million acres – fully one-fifth of Vancouver Island. Significantly, the land grant came with "all coal, coal oil, ores, stones, clay, marble, slates, mines, minerals, and substances whatsoever in, on or under the lands so to be granted." He received also all foreshore rights for the lands, all mining privileges (including the right to mine under adjacent seabeds), and the retention of all coal and other minerals taken from the land. Additionally, as contractor he was permitted to cut whatever timber and erect whatever structures he saw fit to build the line. To promote settlement, provision was made for the sale of farmlands to homesteaders at one dollar per acre. Squatters of at least one year's residence were allowed to buy up to 160 acres, and those settlers with title were allowed to retain their holdings, but virtually all else would go to the contractor in right of performance. It was, in short, a major give-away of British Columbia's natural resources.

Although Dunsmuir had been chosen to prevent the Americans from gaining control of the railway, the lands, and the area's mineral rights, he was not averse to exploiting American talent and experience in constructing the railway. The contract which Dunsmuir drew up for the Esquimalt and Nanaimo Railway named himself, his son James, and his son-in-law John Bryden as contractors, and Charles Crocker, Mark Hopkins, Leland Stanford, and Collis Potter Huntington, all officials of the Southern Pacific Railroad, as subcontractors. Construction began at Esquimalt on 26 Feb. 1884 and proceeded on schedule. Sir John A. Macdonald, prime minister of Canada, drove the "last spike" at Shawnigan Lake on 13 Aug. 1886, and by September trains were running into Victoria along lines laid from Esquimalt across Indian lands Dunsmuir had managed to have expropriated for his use.

Building the railway was Robert Dunsmuir's last major entrepreneurial effort. James Dunsmuir and John Bryden were now the driving forces behind further expansion of the family's business, and their time was filled with consolidating and operating the huge industrial, transportation, and commercial activities created chiefly by the elder Dunsmuir. Robert was content to leave such matters to his successors, busying himself more with his other investments, particularly those in Victoria where he then resided. He had already built a mansion in Nanaimo; he now busied himself with plans to build a sandstone castle (Craigdarroch), a task that both challenged his remaining energies and suited his image as British Columbia's leading 19th-century industrialist.

Part of Robert Dunsmuir's notoriety stemmed from his business acumen, but a greater part resulted from his approach to labour relations. He believed the mines he owned were his to do with as he chose. In his mind, he alone had been responsible for raising the capital, building the collieries, opening the markets, and maintaining the plant. He had tended always to pay lower wages than his competitors, and he had preferred to employ Chinese who were willing to work for half the pay other miners would accept. His coal operations were generally safer than those of his main competitor, the VCMLC, though like all colliery owners of the time the Dunsmuirs resisted many of the demands for safety improvements made by provincial inspectors of mines, thereby perpetuating the hazardous conditions that led to accidents, including the 1876 disaster at Wellington. In 1877 when all the island colliers were threatening to strike over wages, Dunsmuir was to be struck first, but before the threatened work-stoppage could spread to Nanaimo, Robert locked out his employees, claiming he alone would break the resistance. Four months were lost before the miners, harassed by both police and militia sent north from Victoria at Robert's demand, and plainly destitute, agreed to return to work. Yet Dunsmuir, clearly victorious, chose also to be vindictive, and offered the men a maximum daily wage of $2.50 — a rate one-third lower than his best-paid employees were earning before the strike. He effectively had broken the most significant attempt up to that time to organize mine workers in British Columbia, and he never faced another major rebellion by labour. For this action especially, Robert Dunsmuir gained a reputation as the province's most ruthless, avaricious employer.

Yet, to the middle and upper levels of island society, Dunsmuir symbolized wealth, success, and moral authority, a circumstance which encouraged him when he was extricating himself from direct management of the collieries to pursue new interests. He entered politics in the provincial election of 1882 as a candidate for Nanaimo. He was elected and returned again in July 1886, but, apart from becoming president of the Executive Council in the administration of Alexander Edmund Batson Davie in 1887, Dunsmuir left no appreciable mark as a politician.

For much of his later life, Robert was alienated from his wife, though she inherited his entire estate. The Dunsmuir children were educated and treated in a fashion befitting their father's wealth. He made the collieries a family business, drawing the menfolk in first as workers and then as managers. They, in turn, retained control until 1910, when the main Dunsmuir interests were sold to William Mackenzie and Donald Mann. James Dunsmuir was premier of British Columbia from 1900 to 1902 and lieutenant governor from 1906 to 1909.

Robert Dunsmuir was and has remained the most controversial person in the province's history. He has been recognized by most historians as a great builder, a pioneer industrialist intent upon shaping his province as much as increasing his personal fortune. He has, on the other hand, been more recently presented, by writers probing the province's early industrial activities, as British Columbia's chief symbol of unbridled capitalism, and a ruthless exploiter of men and material. The most recent research reveals that neither view is fully accurate, and suggests strongly that a full-scale study of his personal and business career and the social context in which he lived is needed.

DANIEL T. GALLACHER

Further reading

Lynne Bowen, *Robert Dunsmuir: laird of the mines* (Montreal, 1999).

Terry Reksten, *The Dunsmuir saga* (Vancouver, 1991).

J. R. Hinde, *When coal was king: Ladysmith and the coal-mining industry on Vancouver Island* (Vancouver, 2003).

Jan Peterson, *Black Diamond City: Nanaimo, the Victorian era* (Surrey, B.C., 2002).

FRANCIS JONES BARNARD,

businessman and politician; b. 18 Feb. 1829 at Quebec City, Lower
Canada, son of Isaac Jones Barnard, harness maker, and Catherine
Telfer; m. 6 July 1853 Ellen Stillman, and they had two sons, Sir
Frank Stillman and George Henry, and a daughter, Alice, who
married John Andrew Mara; d. 10 July 1889 at Victoria, B.C.

Francis Jones Barnard, who came from a loyalist background, attended school in Quebec City until the age of 12 when he went to work
to support his recently widowed mother. In 1855 he moved from Quebec City to Toronto, but three years later Barnard set out for the Fraser
River gold-fields, travelling via New York and Panama. He reached Fort
Yale (Yale, B.C.) in 1859. There he mined for gold without success, sold
his claim, found work splitting cordwood, and then became a constable.
In 1860 he was purser on the Fraser River steamer, *Fort Yale*; on 14 April
1861 the engines blew up near Hope. He then helped to build the trail
from Yale to Boston Bar, and on its completion obtained a contract to
clear and grade Douglas Street in Yale. Barnard and his family made
their home in this town from 1861 until 1868.

In December 1861 Barnard acquired the business of Jeffray and
Company, which carried the official mail from Victoria to Yale without
charge; that winter he took the mail on foot from Yale to New Westminster and back, a distance of 200 miles. The next spring, charging two
dollars a letter, he carried mail between Yale and the Cariboo, a round
trip of 760 miles. In May 1862 Governor James Douglas called for tenders for delivering the official mail from Yale to Williams Creek in the
Cariboo. Barnard and his partner Robert Thompson Smith organized
the British Columbia and Victoria Express Company, submitted a bid
of £1,555 for one year, and on 25 June were awarded the contract for
monthly delivery during the winter and bi-weekly at other times. On 1
July the establishment of regular service was announced, and on 7 July
Barnard started out from Victoria with her majesty's mail.

During his first year Barnard had only a pony which he led on foot
from Yale to Williams Creek. In 1863 he acquired two-horse wagons to

use between Lillooet and Alexandria and entered into an arrangement with George Dietz and Hugh Nelson to convey the government mail from Victoria and New Westminster to Yale, the start of the Cariboo Road, and to Douglas, the start of the Harrison–Lillooet Road. Commencing on 1 May 1864 Barnard's Cariboo Express left both Yale and Douglas every ten days, converged at Williams Lake, and then ran to Soda Creek; from there the mail was shipped by river steamer and saddle-train to Williams Creek. On 22 June, in conjunction with Dietz and Nelson, he obtained the government contract of £5,000 a year to make three deliveries of mail a month to Barkerville. In December he received another £2,000 for providing weekly service.

In addition to his mail and express business Barnard had established a stage-coach line earlier that year, using four-horse thorough-brace Concord stagecoaches from California. These vehicles proved so popular with the passengers transported by Dietz and Nelson from Victoria and New Westminster to Yale and Douglas that Barnard purchased larger, 14-passenger, 6-horse Concord coaches. By employing "crack whips" and having relays of fresh horses every 13 miles along the Cariboo Road, he was able to travel the 240 miles from Yale to Soda Creek in 48 hours. During the 1864 mining season Barnard's stagecoaches travelled some 110,000 miles, carried all the mail to the interior, transported 1,500 passengers to and from Soda Creek at the one-way fare of $130, and conveyed $4,619,000 worth of gold from the Cariboo to Yale. He employed 38 men, owned 400 horses, and had a way-station and stock ranch at 134 Mile House. When the full length of the Cariboo Road was completed to Barkerville in 1865, he had more property and way-stations, and in 1870 he acquired still more land in Lillooet and Lytton.

Late in 1865 the mining boom faltered, passengers grew fewer, and the volume of express freight declined, but by that time Barnard had established a monopoly over gold-carrying after the government in 1864 suspended its armed gold escort. Confident of Barnard's reliability and honesty, bankers and miners entrusted conveyance to him, sometimes in amounts of $10,000 and $20,000. He reduced his service to Williams Creek to once a week in 1866. There was a boom on the Big Bend of the Columbia River that year, but it, and Barnard's Kootenay express service, were short-lived.

In 1867, with a contract to deliver mail throughout the colony

from January 1868 to October 1870 for $16,000 annually, he absorbed
the express company of Dietz and Nelson and controlled all business
between Victoria and Barkerville. He began to dream of a transcontinental transportation enterprise and in December wrote a friend that
he planned to bring mustangs from California to breed stock in British
Columbia "preparatory to running a coach from Yale to Lake Superior.
Don't put me down for crazy." He sent his driver Stephen Tingley to
purchase the horses. Near the northern end of Okanagan Lake he founded the B X Ranch, which his son Frank expanded in the 1880s until it
had 2,000 head on 7,000 acres.

In 1867 he had been elected to the Legislative Council of British
Columbia. In September of the following year, as the delegate from Williams Lake, he played a prominent part in the Yale Convention, which
passed resolutions favouring immediate union with Canada. Later he
urged the Legislative Council to include, as a term of union with Canada, the demand for a wagon road from Upper Fort Garry (Winnipeg) to
British Columbia. When in 1870 the Canadian government promised
instead a railway to the Pacific, Barnard realistically decided not to compete with the railway but to confine his business to the Pacific slope.

In 1870 Barnard resigned from the Legislative Council to avoid a
charge of conflict of interest and organized the British Columbia General Transportation Company with Josiah Crosby Beedy. In October,
after he was unsuccessful in a request for a $32,000 government subsidy
to import from Scotland specially constructed steam carriages for the
Cariboo Road, he lost the mail contract, but two years later the federal
government awarded him the provincial mail contract and the traffic on
the road increased as surveying for the railway began. In 1874 Barnard
himself won the federal contract to build the 700-mile section of the
Canadian Pacific Railway telegraph line from Fort Edmonton (Alta) to
Cache Creek (B.C.) passing through the Yellowhead Pass. He invested
so much of his money in this project that it became necessary to reduce
his financial interest in his express company. In 1872 two of his drivers,
Tingley and James Hamilton, had been made partners in F. J. Barnard
and Company, and six years later, when the British Columbia Express
Company was incorporated with a capital of $200,000, it included as
additional partners Barnard's son, Frank, and his brother-in-law, George

Andrew Sargison. Frank became the general manager in 1880 and the president in 1883.

Barnard suffered a grave financial reverse when the government of Sir John A. Macdonald abandoned the Yellowhead Pass railway route and in 1879 cancelled his contract for the telegraph line. He brought suit against the crown for $225,000 in damages. His success in the federal by-election in Yale in July 1879 did not go unnoticed in the east. The Toronto *Globe* charged that his only interest was in a financial settlement, and that his claim was of "the most fraudulent character." During the inquiry into his claim, held in British Columbia early in 1880, George Anthony Walkem, the premier and attorney general of the province, acted as counsel for the federal government against Barnard. Later, when his own political quarrel with the dominion was at its height, Premier Walkem conducted Barnard's case against the crown but failed to get compensation.

Worry over the matter affected Barnard's health and in 1880 he suffered a severe stroke. He was re-elected to the House of Commons in 1882 but was soon an invalid, and did not run in 1887. The following year he declined a seat in the Senate. On 10 July 1889 he died at Duval Cottage, his home in Victoria after 1868, leaving an estate of less than $30,000.

During the gold-rush period Barnard had successfully eliminated on mainland British Columbia the competition of the small American transport companies as well as the powerful Wells, Fargo and Company, and had established a virtual Canadian monopoly in the essential carriage of mail, express freight, passengers, and gold. His famous "B X" Company, which in 1874 delivered mail through Wrangell, Alaska, to the Cassiar mines (B.C.), was said to be the longest stage line in North America; it certainly was unrivalled for efficiency and dependability. Tingley took over the company in 1886 and it lasted, under various owners, until 1913 when automobiles replaced coaches on the upper Cariboo Road. An entrepreneur who envisioned further Canadian participation in the economic development of the Pacific seaboard, Barnard was one of the prime movers in obtaining British Columbia's union with Canada.

MARGARET A. ORMSBY

Further reading

Jean Barman, *The west beyond the west: a history of British Columbia* (Toronto, 1996), 75–103.

R. E. Ficken, *Unsettled boundaries: Fraser gold and the British-American northwest* (Pullman, Wash., 2003).

P. E. Roy and J. H. Thompson, *British Columbia: land of promises* (Toronto, 2005), 32–64.

FRANÇOIS-XAVIER LETENDRE, *dit* Batoche,

merchant, rancher, and farmer; b. *c.* 1841 in St Boniface (Man.), son of Louis (Louison) Letendre, *dit* Batoche, and Marie Hallet; m. 19 May 1863 Marguerite Parenteau in St Norbert (Man.), and they had 13 children; d. 25 April 1901 in Batoche (Sask.).

Xavier Letendre, also known as Monsieur Batoche, was the grandson of a French Canadian voyageur, Jean-Baptiste Letendre, *dit* Batoche, and a Cree woman named Josephte. During the 1860s he and his family wintered near the Fourche des Gros-Ventres (as the South Saskatchewan River was known). In 1872, following the political upheaval in Manitoba, he decided to move permanently to the northwest. William Francis Butler, who met him during the winter of 1872–73, described him as "a genial, good-humoured, handsome fellow." Letendre founded a village he called Batoche, built a store there, and set up a ferry service which became known as Batoche's Ferry. He filed claims for a number of river lots to enable his sisters, brothers, and other relatives to join him. In 1882, eager to draw settlers, he dictated a report to missionary Valentin Végréville in which he praised the village's attractions, pointing out "the advantages of the place and of its future ... at the centre of the great thoroughfares of communication ... where the settler will find good land, hay, water, and wood." By 1883 the population of Batoche and the surrounding area had increased to more than 800.

Letendre's commercial network extended northeast to Fort-à-la-Corne and northwest to Frog Lake (Alta), where he had trading-posts. There the Cree exchanged their furs for manufactured articles brought in by Letendre's freighters – the drivers of the Red River carts that travelled back and forth between Winnipeg, Batoche, and his northern posts. By 1878 he was a rich man. He had a luxurious house built for himself, "the finest west of Winnipeg," as he would later say. It was appraised in 1886 at $5,500. He played host to many visitors, including Governor General John George Edward Henry Douglas Sutherland Campbell, Marquess of Lorne, and Lieutenant Governor Joseph Royal.

Active at all levels of community life, Letendre conducted negotiations to get a resident priest and oversaw the construction of the church and rectory of Saint-Antoine-de-Padoue parish. He was a generous benefactor, but above all a shrewd businessman. For instance, he promised to donate $100 for every $500 raised by Bishop Vital-Justin Grandin of St Albert for the building fund. In recognition of his financial assistance, Letendre was named godfather of the church bell, which was christened Marie-Antoinette.

Letendre was deeply involved in the political and social debates that rocked the Métis community in 1884–85. He sat on committees that met to put the Métis claims to land and political rights before an insensitive government in Ottawa. But when the resistance became militant in the spring of 1885, Letendre and the middle class dissociated themselves from the "revolutionaries." He did not openly criticize the leaders, Louis Riel and Gabriel Dumont, but he took a more pragmatic view of the issue. However, his brothers were involved in the "national war" and several members of his family took up arms. His elderly mother and his daughters nursed the battle casualties in his house, which had been requisitioned by the insurgents. Always a discreet man and a skilful diplomat, Letendre, who was then at Fort-à-la-Corne, informed Riel's emissaries that he could not let them have his large supply of provisions, but he did give them rifles and ammunition.

The battle of Batoche, fought from 9 to 12 May against troops under Frederick Dobson Middleton, was devastating. In his claim to the Rebellion Losses Commission established in 1886, Letendre reported that his house had been looted by the Canadian militia, his stores emptied, his livestock wiped out, and his family forced to eat dog meat in order to stay alive. He received $19,000 in compensation for losses estimated at nearly $40,000. He fared far better than the poor and uninfluential Métis combatants, who were denied compensation on the pretext that "they had contributed to their own losses." Letendre had powerful friends among the clergy and in the Conservative party. Archbishop Alexandre-Antonin Taché of St Boniface, Bishop Grandin, and Joseph Royal testified on his behalf.

For Letendre the period after 1885 was a time of reconstruction and new directions. He repaired his buildings and re-established his business. He secured letters patent in 1888 for the 686 acres to which he claimed title. In 1891 he set up a ranch near Alvena, southeast of Batoche, where he kept more than 200 head of cattle and 30 horses. He moved there with his family the following year. In 1895 he sold his house and a parcel of land in Batoche to the North-West Mounted Police, who set up a barracks there.

Letendre continued to play a role on the political and cultural scene. Between 1886 and 1890 he put his mark (in Cree syllabics) to many petitions to the federal and territorial governments demanding free lands for the Métis by virtue of their rights as the first inhabitants, economic aid to facilitate the transition to agriculture, and more equitable political representation. In December 1888 Letendre went to Ottawa to deliver a petition from the Conservatives in the Batoche area to Prime Minister Sir John A. Macdonald. He became more important politically when his son-in-law, Charles-Eugène Boucher, was elected to the Legislative Assembly of the North-West Territories in 1891. Letendre also served as a school trustee and for several years was in charge of the committee organizing the annual Fête des Métifs, the national celebration held in Batoche on 24 July. In 1900 he sat on a committee to erect a monument to the victims of the fighting in 1885; the memorial, bearing the names of the Métis and Indians who had died in combat, was put up in the local cemetery the following year.

"Monsieur Batoche" was still a person of considerable influence in the region at the turn of the century, although it was clear by about 1895 that his economic situation was deteriorating. His personal and family life was also marked by severe trials and tensions. His sons suffered from the growing prejudice towards the Métis community and found it difficult to make their way in life. Influenza and tuberculosis ravaged the Métis population and Letendre and three of his daughters fell victim to illness.

Xavier Letendre belonged to the last generation of Métis termed the free people in the Canadian west. Colonization by Canadians of European origin isolated and dispossessed the Métis, but they continued to maintain their economic and social traditions. Letendre adopted some of the values and institutions of the newcomers but still respected his native and "métchif" heritage. The following generations subsisted on the fringes of Euro-Canadian society until the economic and social renaissance dating from the 1970s.

DIANE PAULETTE PAYMENT

Further reading

D. [P.] Payment, *The free people – Li gens libres: a history of the Métis community of Batoche, Saskatchewan* (Calgary, 2009).

G. J. Ens, *Homeland to hinterland: the changing worlds of the Red River Metis in the nineteenth century* (Toronto, 1996).

Gerald Friesen, "The metis and the Red River settlement, 1844–70," in his *The Canadian prairies: a history* (Toronto, 1987), 91–128.

ROSETTA ERNESTINE WATSON (Carr),

photographer and businesswoman; b. 1845 in Drummond Township, Upper Canada, daughter of Henry Watson, a farmer, and Rosetta Goodall; m. ——— Carr; they had no children; d. 6 July 1907 in Ottawa.

Rosetta Ernestine Watson's paternal grandfather was a British soldier who had moved to Drummond Township after the War of 1812. At the time of the 1871 census she was still unmarried and living with her family. She trained as a photographer in New York City, in New Haven, Conn., and at the Ottawa studio of William Notman. In 1884, a year after moving to Winnipeg, Rosetta Carr purchased Searl and Company, the photographic business of George Searl. In the local press the buyer was not identified and the company was renamed the American Art Gallery rather than after its new owner, probably because it was unusual for businesses to be owned by women. She was later referred to as a widow, but the date of her marriage and information on her husband remain elusive. She advertised "the services of a first-class artist from Cleveland, Ohio" (it is not known if this reference was to herself or another employee), and the most complete studio in Winnipeg. Searl continued on staff for several years and there were other employees. Carr acted as "photographic artist" with skills in different techniques and poses, and in the finishing of pictures with watercolours and oils.

During the boom years of the early 1880s the number of photography firms in Winnipeg more than doubled, and competition was keen. Carr therefore had to maintain high standards. She demonstrated familiarity with dry-plate printing, which was new in Winnipeg, and later adopted improved methods such as the photo-crayon process and platinotypes. Trips east involved visits to galleries in the United States and central Canada for information and occasionally the recruitment of personnel. To maintain a thriving business she used various marketing devices: special prices for babies and children, gifts, coupons, trading-stamps, reduced rates on holidays, and special programs which included free exhibitions and music. The amenities of the gallery also attracted patrons. It had handsomely furnished parlours, large, excellently lit studios, and dressing-rooms and work-rooms equipped with "every convenience and the latest apparatus." In 1891 the "homelike" parlours were refurnished.

Carr's strength, however, lay in the quality of her work, especially her portraits. Admired for their easy poses, natural expressions, and skilful shading, these portraits ranged from pictures of children to photographs of such public figures as Premier John Norquay and Roman Catholic archbishop Alexandre-Antonin Taché of St Boniface. Among the many groups were hospital nurses and college students, tobogganists and hockey players, and societies of all types. She also photographed landscapes of the country between Port Arthur (Thunder Bay), Ont., and the Rockies. Often she entered exhibitions. She took pride in a diploma and medal won at the Colonial and Indian Exhibition in London, England, in 1886 and frequently received prizes in the art section of the Winnipeg Industrial Exhibition. In 1893, because she had been granted the exclusive right to photograph the exhibition grounds, her colleagues boycotted the show. The sole entrant in the professional class, she displayed several hundred works and won all the prizes.

Carr's last years in business were dogged by ill health. She sold the American Art Gallery in 1899 and later moved to Ottawa. At her death she was remembered for her reputation as a fine photographer, her business acumen, and her ability to prosper during 16 years of fluctuating economic conditions in Winnipeg.

VIRGINIA G. BERRY

Further reading

Ralph Greenhill, *Early photography in Canada* ([Toronto, 1965]).

Susan Close, *Framing identity: social practices of photography in Canada, 1880–1920* (Winnipeg, 2007).

Laura Jones, *Rediscovery: Canadian women photographers, 1841–1941* (exhibition catalogue, London Regional Art Gallery, Ont., 1983).

ELLEN CASHMAN
(also known as Nellie Pioche and Irish Nellie),

miner, prospector, philanthropist, and businesswoman; b. *c.* 1845 near Queenstown (Cobh, Republic of Ireland), daughter of Fanny Cashman; d. unmarried 4 Jan. 1925 in Victoria.

With thousands of other desperate Irish Catholic immigrants, Nellie Cashman came to Boston with her mother and sister about

1860. They then moved west, making their home in San Francisco in 1869. It was there that Nellie and her mother contracted mining fever and they soon left for the silver camps of Nevada, stopping in Virginia City, the Comstock, and Pioche. In 1872 the Cashmans opened the Miner's Boarding House in Pioche, a venture that marked the beginning of Nellie's lifelong pattern of operating a small business to support her mining ventures. After only a year in Pioche, Nellie, with an otherwise all-male party of 200 Nevada prospectors, headed for the remote Cassiar gold-mining district of northern British Columbia. There, she later told reporters, she "alternately mined and kept a boarding house for miners," which she ran through the summer of 1873. In the fall she relocated in Victoria, where she intended to winter in the milder climate of the coast.

While Cashman was sitting out the winter, news of a shortage of supplies and an outbreak of scurvy at a camp in the Cassiar incited her to action. After persuading six men to accompany her, she set out on a relief run against all odds. For 77 days they trudged through deep snow, surviving avalanches, extreme temperatures, and all manner of storms. Upon her arrival, Cashman nursed the scurvy victims and distributed food and supplies. She spent two years in the Cassiar, during which time she helped the Sisters of St Ann raise funds to build St Joseph's Hospital in Victoria. Her heroic winter journey and her philanthropic commitment earned her the nicknames Miner's Angel and Angel of the Cassiar. Moreover, her colourful personality and quick wit established her as a favourite with journalists, who would follow her activities for many years. (Much of the information about her is difficult to verify because various newspapers reported wildly different stories.)

Cashman left the Cassiar in 1876 and toured the mining camps of the American west before arriving in 1879 in Tucson, in the Arizona Territory, to prospect and establish the Delmonico Restaurant. Tucson's boom was waning, however, and within a few months she pushed on to the new silver camp of Tombstone. Here Irish Nellie funded her mining ventures with a series of businesses that included a boot and shoe store, a grocery, a restaurant, a boarding house, and a hotel.

As she had done in British Columbia, she balanced her businesses and prospecting with charitable work. She raised money to establish St Mary's Hospital in Tucson in 1880 and a Roman Catholic church, a hospital, and the first public school in Tombstone between 1880 and

1885. In Tombstone she was also an active member of the Irish National Land League, which supported the needy families of Irish miners. After the death in 1884 of her sister, Frances, she acted briefly as foster mother to her five nieces and nephews. Her reputation for warm-heartedness would follow her for the rest of her life. Unlucky miners could almost always find a room and a meal at her establishments even if they could not pay, and miners without money for a new prospect could often negotiate a grubstake with her. She might have lived out her life in ease, but Tombstone's boom went bust in 1886 and her businesses collapsed. The following year she headed out for new eldorados, a prospecting tour that included New Mexico, Idaho, Wyoming, Mexico, South Africa, and new camps in Arizona.

In 1897, at her hotel in Yuma (Ariz.), Cashman heard of the great gold discoveries in Canada's Yukon territory. She could not resist the call of the Klondike. As she told the *Arizona Daily Citizen* (Tucson) in September, she intended to leave as soon as she could organize a party of prospectors and raise $5,000. By February 1898 she and two male companions were in Victoria assembling supplies and planning their route northward. When asked by the Victoria *Daily Colonist* what a lady prospector might wear for such a journey, she shocked the journalist by replying, "I dress ... in many respects as a man does, with long heavy trousers and rubber boots. Of course, when associating with strangers, I wear a long rubber coat. Skirts are out of the question up north as many women will find out before they reach the gold fields." Interestingly, all of the surviving pictures of Cashman show her wearing respectable full-length skirts and shirtwaists, characteristic of female attire of the period.

Cashman was among the 30,000 or more stampeders who descended on Dawson in the early summer of 1898. Like many others, she had arrived too late to stake a claim on the richest ground, though the one she purchased on Bonanza Creek yielded over $100,000. But wealth was fleeting for Nellie Cashman: "I spent every red cent of it buying other claims and prospecting the country. I went out with my dog team or on snow shoes all over that district looking for rich claims." As a female miner, Cashman was exceptional – in 1901 only one per cent of the miners in the Yukon were women. The largest group of mining women appear to have established claims only to increase family holdings. To support her mining habit during her residence in Dawson, Cashman operated a restaurant and later a grocery store in the Donovan Hotel, one of two run by female proprietors in Dawson in 1901 (the other 27 shops were owned by men, often as family enterprises).

From Dawson, Cashman followed the lure of gold to Alaska, first to Fairbanks in 1905 and then in 1907 to the Koyukuk region, where she mined and prospected into her late seventies. In the spring of 1924 she contracted double pneumonia and was hospitalized in Fairbanks; determined to come "home to die," she moved to St Joseph's Hospital in Victoria in October. She passed away there in January 1925 and was buried in Ross Bay Cemetery.

CHARLENE PORSILD

Further reading

Don Chaput, *Nellie Cashman and the North American mining frontier* (Tucson, Ariz., 1995).

Suzann Ledbetter, *Nellie Cashman: prospector and trailblazer* (El Paso, Tex., 1993).

C. [L.] Porsild, *Gamblers and dreamers: women, men, and community in the Klondike* (Vancouver, 1998).

Sally Zanjani, *A mine of her own: women prospectors in the American west, 1850–1950* (Lincoln, Nebr., 1997).

CHANG TOY
(Chen Cai in Mandarin), known also as Chan Doe Gee (Chen Daozhi) and Chan Chang-Jin, but generally as Sam Kee (San Ji),

labourer and businessman; b. 16 May 1857 in Cheong Pan village, Panyu county, Guangdong province (People's Republic of China); m. twice, and had at least six sons and two daughters; d. 1921.

Chang Toy was of Hakka origin, a member of an ethnic and linguistic minority in Guangdong province. Although family tradition claims that his parents were farmers, several factors suggest that they were members of the local elite, even if they did not have gentry status. When Chang was three years old, his father died. Normally such a death would be a severe economic setback for a peasant family, but the fact that Chang was still able to receive three years of schooling indicates that his family did not need his labour to survive and hence was relatively well off. The circumstances of his first marriage, arranged when he was a child so that his mother could keep his child bride as a servant, also imply a certain prosperity. High status is further suggested by an incident involving his elder brother Boon Bak. Accused of counterfeiting, Boon Bak successfully intervened with a district magistrate to have the officials who had come to arrest him reprimanded, and apparently the charges were dropped as well. Boon Bak, whatever his activities, must have been sufficiently wealthy or well connected to gain the favour of the magistrate. Along with Yee Bak, Chang's second eldest brother and eventual business associate, Boon Bak played an important role in Chang's upbringing, teaching him martial arts. This training appears to have instilled in him considerable self-confidence, which stood him in good stead, both in China and in Canada.

Leaving his wife in China, Chang came to British Columbia in 1874 as a contract labourer. Like many other migrants from Guangdong, he had agreed to work in a fish cannery for a season in exchange for his passage money. Unfavourable winds delayed his ship's arrival, so he had to work only for a month and a half to fulfil his contract. He then moved to

Victoria, where he stayed for a short time at the Wing Chong Company. There he came to the attention of the proprietor, Chu Lai, a Hakka from the same village. Chang declined an offer to join Chu's business, but the two became close friends. Chu would even arrange Chang's second marriage in 1892. Around 1876 he worked at a sawmill in New Westminster. While there, at the urging of the foreman, he used his martial arts training to knock down a white co-worker who had been harassing him and he thus earned the respect of his fellow workers. After a year at the sawmill Chang moved to Granville (Vancouver), where he bought an interest in a Chinese laundry, probably the Wah Chong laundry, which also sold a few Chinese groceries. Shortly after his arrival, Chang's partner sold him his interest in the store. Chang then arranged for the Wing Chong Company to be his wholesale supplier. His store quickly became a contact point for other Hakka and natives of Panyu in search of work. He started contracting their labour for land clearing, salmon canning, and sugar refining. Within a few years he was also carrying on a trade in charcoal, operating three charcoal burners. The charcoal was a by-product of the land-clearing operations and was readily marketed to the Canadian Pacific Railway as well as to local consumers. After the great fire of 1886 in Vancouver, Chang moved to Steveston, where he opened a store and continued labour contracting.

The Sam Kee Company, for which Chang is best known, was operating in Vancouver by the early 1890s. Chang was the principal partner in the firm, which became an extensive import and export business. It acted as a wholesaler of rice and of merchandise from China for businesses owned by natives of Guangdong and Anglo-Europeans alike, while at the same time exporting commodities such as salmon and salt herring from British Columbia to China and Japan. Chang was the main supplier of capital for some of the fish packers with whom he dealt. For others he acted as a purchaser of supplies. Still others rented land, buildings, or equipment from him. In 1907 the company's annual revenues were between $150,000 and $180,000 and it was one of the four most important firms in Vancouver's Chinatown. The firm's real estate holdings were also extensive. They included ten lots in Chinatown itself as well as lots in other parts of Vancouver and waterfront property and buildings in Nanaimo. In Vancouver it also owned five residential hotels in 1910 and operated another two for a German investor. These businesses were often fronted by Anglo-European factotums.

Chang's business activities brought him into considerable contact with whites, even though he spoke little or no English. The closeness of these relations was demonstrated after the anti-Asian riot of 1907 in Vancouver. During the night of 6–7 September, following a rally organized by the Asiatic Exclusion League, a mob rampaged through Chinatown. Chang responded by sending his two younger sons to stay in the homes of prominent Vancouver citizens Ewan Wainwright McLean and John Joseph Banfield. In another instance, after the Chinese revolution of 1911, Chang was able to pressure the British authorities in Hong Kong to intercede with the Chinese government in Canton to get a shipment of lumber which had been waylaid delivered to its proper destination. His close connections to the Anglo-European business establishment did not delude Chang as to the extent of anti-Chinese racism. He had also responded to the riot of 1907 by proceeding with his partner, Shum Moon, who was president of the Vancouver Chinese Benevolent Association, to local hardware merchants McLennan and McFeely, where they purchased the firm's stock of revolvers to distribute to their fellow merchants. This activity occasioned considerable apprehension in the English-language community. At the same time Chang was not above profiting from the system of racial discrimination. By 1905 his company had become the Chinese agents for the Blue Funnel Line, which rivalled the CPR's ships on the trans-Pacific route. Chang's advertisements in Chinese specified that since the line had only one class of accommodation (unlike the Canadian Pacific) Chinese would face no discrimination on board.

Chang was also active within the Chinese community. He was one of a group of Chinese merchants who petitioned Vancouver's city hall in 1899 protesting against indiscriminate police raids in Chinatown. A founder of the Chinese Empire Reform Association in 1900, he served as president of its Vancouver chapter. In 1905 he established the association's school and a suite for travelling scholars on the third floor of the Sam Kee Company building, sending his own children there. He was invited to be the first Chinese consul in 1908, but he refused on the grounds that his English was not good enough. Chang carried on business until 1920. He passed away the following year at an undetermined location.

Chang Toy was among the handful of migrants from China to Canada during the 19th century who were able to parlay business acumen, hard work, and family and ethnic connections into a sizeable fortune. By the early 20th century he was one of the leading merchants of British Columbia. His business interests spanned both sides of the Pacific and extended beyond the Guangdong ethnic sector into the mainstream of the British Columbian economy.

TIMOTHY J. STANLEY

Further reading

Paul Yee, "Sam Kee: a Chinese business in early Vancouver," *BC Studies* (Vancouver), nos.69/70 (spring–summer 1986): 70–96; *Saltwater city: an illustrated history of the Chinese in Vancouver* (Vancouver, 1988); "Chinese business in Vancouver, 1886–1914" (MA thesis, Univ. of B.C., Vancouver, 1983).

Harry Con *et al.*, *From China to Canada: a history of the Chinese communities in Canada*, ed. Edgar Wickberg (Toronto, 1982; repr. 1988).

WILLIAM FORBES ALLOWAY,

businessman, politician, banker, and philanthropist; b. 20 Aug. 1852 in The Derries (Republic of Ireland), son of Arthur William Alloway, a veterinary surgeon, and Mary Frances Johnson; m. 3 Sept. 1878 Elizabeth MacLaren (d. 1926), daughter of James Maclaren, in Buckingham, Que., and they had one son who died in infancy; d. 2 Feb. 1930 in Winnipeg.

In 1855, at age three, William Forbes Alloway immigrated to Hamilton, Upper Canada, with his family. There his father opened a veterinary surgery, a horseshoeing establishment, and a riding school. Less than two years later his father moved the family and business to Montreal, where William attended the High School of Montreal.

Four days after his 18th birthday, Alloway arrived in Winnipeg as a private in the expeditionary force under Colonel Garnet Joseph Wolseley sent to quell the Métis uprising led by Louis Riel. Subsequently he was among the 19 persons selected to form the nucleus of a mounted constabulary force for Manitoba. Discharged from the militia in April 1871, he settled in Winnipeg, where he was, like his father, a veterinarian, as well as a tobacconist and an auctioneer of horses. In 1874 he went to work as foreman for the well-known freighter and politician James McKay and the following year became his partner in the transportation business.

In 1876 Alloway struck out on his own. For the next four years forwarding and trading occupied his attention. He speculated in land and scrip on the side. Alloway obtained most of his work from Thomas Nixon, purveyor for the Department of the Interior at Winnipeg, with whom he developed a rather cosy relationship as Nixon's landlord. Later Nixon would be severely censured by a royal commission for his lack of diligence in business. On behalf of the dominion government, Alloway purchased horses for the surveying parties of the Canadian Pacific Railway. Buying principally from the Métis at the prevailing price of $50 for a good carthorse, he "reaped considerable advantage" by reselling them to the government at prices ranging on average from about $90 to $157. His enemies referred to him contemptuously as a "horse jockey."

Alloway also provided the surveyors with the common "bushed and banded" native carts (so called because of the iron boxing around the axles and the bands on the hubs) and shamelessly lined his pockets further by engaging with Nixon in the resale of abandoned government carts and harnesses. At one time he used Nixon to help him raise money on their joint liability. Alloway's questionable dealings with Nixon led to lucrative transportation contracts with the government, some of which were never advertised. He always subcontracted the work, which involved freighting supplies and carrying the mails to the construction crews of the CPR via the Dawson Road and Lake of the Woods, as well as supplying the various outposts of the North-West Mounted Police. Over the years his transactions with the government amounted to $40,000 or more.

Alloway's business ambitions led him into local politics. He served four year-long terms on the municipal council in 1876–77 and 1879–80. He also sat on the first two councils of the reinvigorated Winnipeg Board of Trade, which finally became fully functional in 1879. Alloway

had an unshakeable faith that the west must "fill up with people" and that
Winnipeg must grow in "importance, size, wealth and prestige." Photographs of him reveal a frank look and a fearless demeanour, characteristics which would earn him the respect and admiration of the business
community in his efforts to help quicken the city's commercial pulse.

On 28 Nov. 1879 Alloway formed a partnership in Winnipeg with
Henry Thompson Champion, an accountant with the Merchants' Bank
of Canada, who had also come west with Wolseley's expedition. They
formalized their partnership in March 1880 as Alloway and Champion,
"bankers, brokers, commission merchants, freighters, traders, and real
estate agents." The capital of the new firm was $7,000, of which Allo-
way contributed $5,000.

Starting in the unstable conditions incident to the building of the
CPR, Alloway and Champion eschewed the real estate mania of 1881–
82. As a private bank, the firm was free to deal in land and to lend money
on its security, but the partners competed only for "legitimate business"
rather than business connected with land speculation. Through Alloway's foresight, the firm acquired a large inventory of "well selected farm
lands" in every township in the province as well as in the North-West
Territories which were sold "at reasonable prices and on easy terms." The
firm would also lend up to $25,000 on first mortgages.

By 1882 Alloway and Champion had increased its capital to some
$175,000. About the same time, the firm became an agent for the CPR's
lands. To its work as a real estate agency, it later added payments for
pre-emptions of federal lands and transactions for the Canada North-
West Land Company. Most of its dealings in land, however, were done
indirectly through the purchase and resale of land- and money-scrip,
military bounty warrants, and tax sale certificates. The acquisition of
scrip was greatly facilitated by William's brother Charles Valentine, who
would become a junior partner in the firm in 1885.

Alloway and Champion had opened in 1881 a branch in Portage
la Prairie. That same year Alloway had become one of the founding
directors of the Ogilvie Milling Company, the western subsidiary of
A. W. Ogilvie and Company. In 1882 he helped establish the Manitoba
Cartage and Warehousing Company and together with Champion and
others he tried to organize a stock exchange. Although the exchange
was not set up immediately because of the business collapse that spring,
the firm soon turned its attention to the buying and selling of stocks on

the Toronto, Montreal, New York, and Chicago exchanges. It also traded produce in the New York and Chicago markets.

In the early 1890s Alloway and Champion expanded its foreign exchange department to keep up with the demand of Manitoba's rapidly growing immigrant population, mainly from eastern Europe, to convert its gold, silver, and national currencies into Canadian dollars and to remit funds abroad. By 1904 the exchange business had reached such a volume that the partners decided to establish a branch in Winnipeg's north end. It opened the following year with five interpreters (later increased to ten). Acting generally as steamship and railway agents, Alloway and Champion helped to bring over many family members of those already established in the city. Alloway himself was extremely proud of the personal relationship which in large measure governed the branch's business dealings with these new Canadians. This intimacy was expressed by one of its first employees, a Romanian Jew, who – commenting on the branch's close connection with the Jewish community – fondly referred to it as the "Jewish Bank."

During the boom years following the turn of the century, the firm became involved with the promotion of local industrial capital through Champion's membership on the Winnipeg Stock Exchange, which opened in February 1909. Alloway and Champion's astonishing success is evident in its financial strength: it rose to over $1,000,000 by 1912. That September the firm was incorporated as Alloway and Champion Limited with an authorized capital stock of $3,000,000 and a reserve of $125,000. The paid-up capital of $1,025,000 was mostly held by the original partners. Alloway and Champion had now become the largest and strongest private bank in the dominion. In 1919, three years after Champion's death, Alloway sold the company to the Canadian Bank of Commerce, but he carried on as president until 1923. The business continued under the name Alloway and Champion Limited until his death in 1930.

The bank founded by William Forbes Alloway played an important role in the settlement and economic development of Manitoba and Winnipeg. Mindful, however, of the poverty and disadvantage wrought by unbridled growth, Alloway, a millionaire by 1910, was a generous supporter of many benevolent institutions through his annual contribution of $5,000 to the Federated Budget Board. He became a life governor of the Winnipeg General Hospital in 1884 and a member of its board of trustees from 1912 until his death. He was also a member for 25 years of the advisory board of the Margaret Scott Nursing Mission. His proudest achievement, however, was the incorporation in 1921 of Canada's first community trust, the Winnipeg Foundation, which he endowed with an initial gift of $100,000. His wife, Elizabeth, took a deep interest in the foundation as well, and together their donations amounted to $2,654,764. The trust has been mentioned in the wills of numerous Manitobans and its impressive record of service in advancing human welfare and knowledge stands as Alloway's abiding social testament.

PETER HANLON

Further reading

W. L. Morton, *Manitoba: a history* (Toronto, 1957).

Peter Lowe, "All western dollars," Man., Historical and Scientific Society, *Papers* (Winnipeg), 3rd ser., no.2 (1945–46): 10–25.

Victor Ross and A. St L. Trigge, *A history of the Canadian Bank of Commerce, with an account of the other banks which now form part of its organization* (3v., Toronto, 1920–34).

WILLIAM EDWARD COCHRANE,

rancher; b. 8 Sept. 1858 in Packington, near Lichfield, England,
son of Basil Edward Arthur Cochrane and Sally Caroline Fitzgerald;
m. 19 Feb. 1887 Evelyn Constance Clementina Lamb
(d. 28 May 1908) in London, and they had one son; d. 7 March 1929
in Ballycarney (Republic of Ireland).

William E. Cochrane, known as Billy, was a grand-nephew of the famous seaman Thomas Cochrane, 10th Earl of Dundonald. Among his other relatives were Sir Thomas John Cochrane, an early gov-

ernor of Newfoundland, and Douglas Mackinnon Baillie Hamilton Cochrane, who as the 12th Earl of Dundonald would become commander
of the Canadian militia. Billy was one of a number of well-to-do young
Britons who came to the Alberta foothills in the 1880s in search of adventure. He stayed to play an important part in the economic and social
development of the region. Although the historiography of the Canadian
range has tended to emphasize the role of four or five large corporate
ranch companies, more recently it has been argued that numerous smaller
family ranches buttressed the cattle industry with capital and contributed
enormously to innovation and adaptation in ranching. Cochrane's life in
Alberta epitomized the achievements of this group.

The Little Bow Cattle Company, known as the CC Ranch because
of its brand, was organized in 1884 by Cochrane, his cousin Thomas
Belhaven Henry Cochrane, Hugh Graham, and brothers Ted and Frank
Jenkins. A foundation herd of 359 head of cattle and 12 saddle-horses
was imported from Montana in September 1884. A snugly sited ranch
house was built on Mosquito Creek, a few miles west of Cayley. Early set-
backs encouraged Billy's partners to pursue other options and Cochrane
was left the sole boss of the CC. His pride and joy was a small herd of
purebred Galloway cattle. From it he raised young bulls to sell to neigh-
bouring ranchers. They were prized for their hardihood and foraging
abilities. In addition, Cochrane ran a regular range herd of about 400
cows, which yielded 220–75 calves each year. The ranch reported a total
of 800 head of cattle and 40 horses in 1890.

Cochrane matured to become a conscientious and responsible rancher, always looking for ways to improve his stock and streamline production. Not only did he nurture a purebred herd on enclosed pastures, but
he put up hay for calves and weak cattle from an early date. Later he
pushed the stock association to keep the bulls separate from the cows
until midway through the summer so that winter calving would be eliminated. Cochrane had thus brought with him attitudes towards stock rear-
ing drawn from the British pastoral tradition. The geographer Terry G.
Jordan has shown how these ideas fused with methods from the mid-
western United States to ensure that ranching in the Canadian foothills
differed markedly from the extensive open range methods of "the Anglo-
Texan ranching complex." Cochrane's leadership was felt far beyond the
boundaries of his ranch. For several years he organized the cowboys who

rode for the Mosquito Creek Wagon at the roundup, and when his neighbour Alfred Ernest Cross was laid up after an accident Cochrane managed
the A7 Ranche for him. He was a leading figure in the fight against pred-
ators, and, in 1904, it was he who built the huge dipping vat in which all
the district's cattle were treated for mange.

Cochrane was one of a group of friends who provided capital for
Cross's Calgary Brewing and Malting Company; he purchased $1,000
of stock in 1892 and later added another $500. Perhaps more important
than his financial backing was his wholehearted personal support for his
friend. When Cross was sick and beset with problems in the late 1890s,
Billy wrote: "It seems hard that you should chuck up now, after bearing all the expense and trouble and considerable wear and tear.... I am
quite willing to stay with the brewery as long as you do and as long as
you control the management." The company would continue to provide
Cochrane with a modest income until his death.

There was, however, another side to Billy Cochrane. One of his
friends described him as having "a kiss from the devil on his cheek." He
enjoyed the physical demands of working an isolated ranch and earned
the respect of his men by his willingness to turn his hand to any chore, but
he expected to play as hard as he worked. During his first years in Alberta
he was a leading member of the Wolves' Den, an extremely ungentleman-
ly "gentlemen's club," which met in an old boxcar by the rail tracks in Calgary. Cochrane knew the Grant family, who produced Glen Grant Scotch
whisky, and was able to ensure that there was always a barrel of ten-year-
old whisky on hand to nourish their storytelling and poker games. While
at their ranch, Billy and his wife, Evelyn, hunted coyotes on horseback,
played and supported polo, shot and fished, and entertained frequently.
Once Cochrane could rely on a trusted foreman, he adopted the habit of
spending the winter in Britain, where he enjoyed fox-hunting from his
family home in Leicestershire and shooting grouse in Scotland and pheas-
ants in Dorset. The couple would also spend time in London, staying at
the British Hotel, dining at the Café Royal, and catching up with the latest
plays. In 1909, after Evelyn's death, Cochrane sold his ranch and retired
to Scotland. He continued to hunt and fish, and travelled widely, making frequent visits to Alberta. During World War I he falsified his age to
join the 1st Sportsman's Battalion of the Royal Fusiliers (City of London
Regiment), but he did not see action. At his death his principal residence

was Ravenstone Castle, near Whithorn, Scotland. He left an estate worth $1,250,000, which took some years to wind up.

Billy Cochrane displayed many of the characteristics of the reviled "remittance man." He had a wild streak which he made no attempt to control even when he was a middle-aged family man. He expressed his support for Calgary Brewing and Malting by sampling beer copiously wherever he happened to be and then sending reports to Cross. He also made every effort to lure the overly conscientious Cross into a night or two on the town. Cochrane was a creature of his times during which money insulated the landowning class from many of the realities of life. His story is important because it demonstrates that the cultural baggage that well-off Britons brought to Alberta – customs which seemed bizarre and risible to others – in no way precluded these privileged immigrants from making substantial contributions to the settlement of what Billy often referred to as "the bald headed" prairie.

SIMON M. EVANS

Further reading

D. H. Breen, *The Canadian prairie west and the ranching frontier, 1874–1924* (Toronto, 1983).

Edward Brado, *Cattle kingdom: early ranching in Alberta* (Vancouver, 1984).

S. M. Evans, *The Bar U & Canadian ranching history* (Calgary, 2004).

High River Pioneers' and Old Timers' Association, *Leaves from the Medicine Tree* ... ([Lethbridge, Alta], 1960).

L. G. Thomas, *Ranchers' legacy: Alberta essays*, ed. P. A. Dunae (Edmonton, 1986).

Contributors

Armstrong, Frederick H. Professor emeritus of history, University of Western Ontario, London, Ontario.
John Kinder Labatt.

Baker, Melvin. Archivist and historian, Memorial University of Newfoundland, St John's, Newfoundland.
Benjamin Bowring.

Ball, Norman R. Formerly director, Centre for Society, Technology and Values, University of Waterloo, Ontario.
James Miller Williams [in collaboration with E. Phelps].

Barker, Diane Murray. Formerly educational administrator, Halifax, Nova Scotia.
Enos Collins [in collaboration with D. A. Sutherland].

Beaulieu, André. Archiviste à la retraite, Archives nationales du Québec, Québec.
Anson McKim.

Bélanger, Guy. Historien, Société historique Alphonse-Desjardins, Lévis, Québec.
Alphonse Desjardins [in collaboration with P. Poulin].

Benidickson, Jamie. Professor of law, University of Ottawa, Ontario.
John Rudolphus Booth.

†Berry, Virginia G. Researcher, Winnipeg, Manitoba.
Rosetta Ernestine Watson (Carr).

†Blakeley, Phyllis R. Formerly provincial archivist, Public Archives of Nova Scotia, Halifax, Nova Scotia.
Sir Samuel Cunard.

Bliss, Michael. University professor emeritus of history, University of Toronto, Ontario.
George Albertus Cox.

Bosher, J. F. Professor emeritus of history, York University, Toronto, Ontario, and adjunct professor, Carleton University, Ottawa, Ontario.
Joseph-Michel Cadet.

Burgess, Joanne. Professeure d'histoire, Université du Québec à Montréal, Québec.
Pierre Foretier.

Cahill, Barry. Information access and privacy professional, Halifax, Nova Scotia.
John Fitzwilliam Stairs.

Cell, Gillian T. Professor emeritus of history, University of North Carolina, Chapel Hill, North Carolina, and professor of history emerita, College of William & Mary, Williamsburg, Virginia.
John Guy.

Chard, Donald F. Formerly historic park planner, Parks Canada, Halifax, Nova Scotia.
Joshua Mauger.

Clarke, John. Distinguished research professor of geography, Carleton University, Ottawa.
François Baby.

Comeau, Gayle M. Contract faculty, Department of History, Glendon College, York University, Toronto, Ontario.
Theodor August Heintzman.

†Cooper, John Irwin. Formerly professor emeritus of history, McGill University, Montreal, Quebec.
James McGill.

Cuff, Robert H. Historian and writer, Gerald Penney Associates Limited, St John's, Newfoundland.
Sir Robert Gillespie Reid.

†Dechêne, Louise. Professor emerita of history, McGill University, Montréal, Québec.
William Price.

†Drolet, Antonio. Bibliothécaire en chef, Archives du Québec, Québec.
Charlotte-Françoise Juchereau de Saint-Denis, known as Comtesse de Saint-Laurent (Viennay-Pachot; Dauphin de La Forest).

Dubuc, Alfred. Professeur d'histoire à la retraite, Université du Québec à Montréal, Québec.
John Molson.

Evans, Simon M. Adjunct professor of geography, University of Calgary, Alberta.
William Edward Cochrane.

Filteau, Hélène. Travailleuse sociale, Centre de santé et de services sociaux du Grand-Littoral, Lévis, Québec.
Louis-Adélard Senécal [in collaboration with J. Hamelin and J. Keyes].

Fisher, Robin. Provost and vice president academic, Mount Royal University, Calgary, Alberta.
Muquinna.

Gallacher, Daniel T. Curator emeritus, Canadian Museum of Civilization, Gatineau, Quebec.
Robert Dunsmuir.

Gray, Carolyn E. Hamilton, Ontario.
Sir John Morison Gibson.

†Hamelin, Jean. Directeur général adjoint, Dictionnaire biographique du Canada/Dictionary of Canadian Biography, Université Laval, Québec, Québec.
Louis-Adélard Senécal [in collaboration with H. Filteau and J. Keyes].

Hanlon, Peter. Historian, Winnipeg, Manitoba.
William Forbes Alloway.

Holman, Harry Tinson. Director, Culture, Heritage and Libraries Division, Department of Tourism and Culture, Charlottetown, Prince Edward Island.
Robert Tinson Holman.

Jedwab, Jack. Executive director, Association for Canadian Studies, Montreal, Quebec.
Sir Rodolphe Forget.

Keyes, John. Commissaire, Commission d'évaluation de l'enseignement collégial, Québec, Québec.
Louis-Adélard Senécal [in collaboration with H. Filteau and J. Hamelin].

Kimmel, David. Lead information developer, BMC Software, Montreal, Quebec.
Sir Byron Edmund Walker.

†Lamb, W. Kaye. Formerly dominion archivist, Public Archives of Canada, and national librarian, National Library of Canada, Ottawa, Ontario.
John McLoughlin.

Lee, David. Formerly historian, Parks Canada, Ottawa, Ontario.
Charles Robin.

McCalla, Douglas. University professor emeritus of history, University of Guelph, Ontario, and professor emeritus of history, Trent University, Peterborough, Ontario.
Isaac Buchanan.

McCallum, Margaret E. Professor of law, University of New Brunswick, Fredericton, New Brunswick.
Gilbert White Ganong.

Marchildon, Gregory P. Professor and Canada Research Chair in Public Policy and Economic History, Johnson-Shoyama Graduate School of Public Policy, University of Regina, Saskatchewan.
Wilmot Deloui Matthews.

Miller, Carman. Professor emeritus of history, McGill University, Montreal, Quebec.
Sir Edward Seaborne Clouston.

Miquelon, Dale. Professor emeritus of history, University of Saskatchewan, Saskatoon, Saskatchewan.
Marie-Anne Barbel (Fornel). François Havy.

Nelles, H.V. L.R. Wilson professor of history, McMaster University, Hamilton, Ontario, and distinguished research professor of history emeritus, York University, Toronto, Ontario.
Sir Adam Beck.

†Ormsby, Margaret A. Formerly professor emerita of history, University of British Columbia, Vancouver, British Columbia.
Francis Jones Barnard.

Otto, Stephen A. Historian, Toronto, Ontario.
Peter Charles Larkin.

Paré, Hélène. Traductrice et rédactrice, Montréal, Québec.
Louise de Ramezay.

Payment, Diane Paulette. Historienne, Winnipeg, Manitoba.
  François-Xavier Letendre, dit Batoche.

†Phelps, Edward. Formerly regional history librarian and archivist,
D. B. Weldon Library, University of Western Ontario, London, Ontario.
  James Miller Williams [in collaboration with N. R. Ball].

Porsild, Charlene. Associate research professor, School of Public
Administration, and assistant director, R. W. J. F. Center for Health
Policy, University of New Mexico, Albuquerque, New Mexico.
  Ellen Cashman.

Poulin, Pierre. Responsable du Projet d'histoire du mouvement
Desjardins, Société historique Alphonse-Desjardins, Lévis, Québec.
  Alphonse Desjardins [in collaboration with G. Bélanger].

Regehr, Theodore D. Professor emeritus of history, University of
Saskatchewan, Saskatoon, Saskatchewan, and adjunct professor of
history, University of Calgary, Alberta.
  Sir William Cornelius Van Horne.

Roberts, David. Scarborough, Ontario.
  George Allsopp. Hart Almerrin Massey. Gordon Morton McGregor.

Sandberg, L. Anders. Professor of environmental studies, York University, Toronto, Ontario.
  James William Carmichael.

Santink, Joy L. Don Mills, Ontario.
  Timothy Eaton.

Stanley, Timothy J. Professor of education, University of Ottawa,
Ontario.
  Chang Toy.

Sutherland, David A. Adjunct professor, Dalhousie University, Halifax,
Nova Scotia.
  Enos Collins [in collaboration with D. M. Barker].

Triggs, Stanley G. Formerly curator, Notman Photographic Archives, McCord Museum, Montreal, Quebec.
William Notman.

Tulchinsky, Gerald J. J. Professor emeritus of history, Queen's University, Kingston, Ontario.
John Redpath. Sir Hugh Allan [in collaboration with B. Young].

Vallières, Marc. Professeur associé d'histoire, Université Laval, Québec, Québec.
Georges-Élie Amyot.

Van Kirk, Sylvia M. Professor emeritus of history, University of Toronto, Ontario.
Fanny Bendixen.

Vaugeois, Denis. Historien et éditeur, Québec, Québec.
Aaron Hart.

†Wilson, Bruce Gordon. Formerly chief, London Office, Public Archives of Canada, London, England.
Robert Hamilton.

Young, Brian. Professor emeritus of history, McGill University, Montreal, Quebec.
Sir Hugh Allan [in collaboration with G. J. J. Tulchinsky].

Zoltvany, Yves F. Professeur d'histoire à la retraite, Université Laval, Québec, Québec.
Charles Aubert de La Chesnaye. François Hazeur.

Illustration Credits

Library and Archives Canada (Ottawa): Gaspé, Que., about 1871 (Peter Winkworth Collection of Canadiana, R9266-13-X-E); Norway House – inside the fort, Man., 1878 (Robert Bell, C-000652); Part of sealing fleet laid up in Victoria harbour, Oct. 1891 (C-086451); Specimen of mining scenery, B.C., 1865 (Charles Gentile, C-088926); Public auction at old town hall, Regina, 1906 (Dept. of Interior fonds, PA-044507).

Greater Sudbury Public Library (Sudbury, Ont.): Charles Labelle's store, 1894 – house and sign painter and decorator, Sudbury (Greater Sudbury Historical Database, MK1553EN, donation of Edwin George Higgins and Sam Rothschild).

City of Toronto Archives: Jewish butcher sign, the Ward, Toronto, about 1910 (1244 (William James family fonds), 2548); Inauguration of hydro-electric power in Toronto, City Hall, May 2, 1911 (1244, 323L); Toronto Stock Exchange board, 1910 or 1912 (1244, 144); His Majesty's Airship R-100, over the Canadian Bank of Commerce, the tallest building in the British empire, Toronto, August 1930 (16 (Toronto Transit Commission fonds), 71 (Central photography series), 7921).

McCord Museum of Canadian History (Montreal): Wm. Notman and Son, Market day, Jacques Cartier Square, Montreal, Que., about 1900 (VIEW-3213); Alexander Henderson, Montreal harbour from Custom House, about 1872 (MP-0000.1452.53); Eugene Haberer, A young Canadian worker, 1877 (M984.306.512); William Notman, Assorting the ore, Huntington Copper Mining Company's works, Bolton, Que., 1867 (N-0000.94.56); Anonymous, Finished roll of newsprint, Spanish River Pulp & Paper Co., Sault Ste Marie, Ont., about 1925 (MP-0000.25.872); Notman and Sandham, Grand Trunk Railway Engineering Department group, composite 1877 (N-0000.73.19); Henri Julien, Line 45; or our Wall of China (12 Feb. 1876) (M982.530.5307); Notman and Sandham, William Notman Studio, 17 Bleury Street, Montreal, Que., about 1875 (N-0000.157); Wm. Notman and Son, Anson McKim's office, Montreal, Que., 1903 (II-145305); Anonymous, American tourists in an automobile, Ottawa, Ont., 1925 (MP-0000.25.1036).

Index

Numbers in **boldface** indicate pages with a subject's biography.
Numbers in *italic* indicate pages with photo captions.